Business Premises: Possession and Lease Renewal

Fifth Edition

Gary Webber
Barrister and Mediator

and

Daniel Dovar
Barrister

SWEET & MAXWELL   THOMSON REUTERS

Published in 2015 by Thomson Reuters (Professional) UK Limited trading as Sweet & Maxwell, Friars House, 160 Blackfriars Road, London, SE1 8EZ (Registered in England & Wales, Company No 1679046.

Registered Office and address for service: 2nd floor, Aldgate House, 33 Aldgate High Street, London EC3N 1DL)

For further information on our products and services, visit
www.sweetandmaxwell.co.uk

Typeset by Wright & Round Ltd, Gloucester.

Printed and Bound by CPI Group (UK) Ltd, Croydon, CR0 4YY

No natural forests were destroyed to make this product; only farmed timber was used and re-planted.

A CIP catalogue record of this book is available for the British Library.

ISBN: 978-0-414-03435-8

Thomson Reuters and the Thomson Reuters logo are trademarks of Thomson Reuters.

Sweet & Maxwell ® is a registered trademark of Thomson Reuters (Professional) UK Limited.

Crown copyright material is reproduced with the permission of the Controller of HMSO and the Queen's Printer for Scotland.

Preface

This new edition incorporates changes to the law of business premises brought about by nearly fifty new cases. Whilst there have been no major changes in this area, it was time to bring the book up to date to take into account the refinement of the law. There has also been some re-organisation, with the chapter dealing with grounds for opposing lease renewal moved forward to a more appropriate place in the text.

Mediation now plays an enormous part in the resolution of legal disputes generally but particularly in commercial landlord and tenant cases. We have therefore expanded the section dealing with mediation, so as to give much greater guidance on how to prepare, the documents that are required and what actually happens during the process.

Finally, we have a new chapter on the Telecommunications Code written by guest contributor Thekla Fellas, who is a specialist in this area at Fladgate LLP. Thekla has provided a helpful new chapter that explains clearly the core elements of the Code.

The law is stated as at November 2014. Updates can be found at www.propertylawuk.net.

Gary Webber
www.propertylawuk.net

Daniel Dovar
Tanfield Chambers

Contents

Part 2
Termination on Default by the Tenant

7 Forfeiture: General Rules

8 Non-payment of Rent

9 Forfeiture: Other Covenants (General)

10 Assignment, Subletting and Parting with Possession

11 Forfeiture: Repairs

12 Relief from Forfeiture

13 Claims against Third Parties

Part 3
Termination by Notice

14 Landlord's Notices to Terminate

15 Tenant's Notices to Terminate or Renew

16 Obtaining Information

17 Landlord's Grounds

Part 4
Other Cases of Termination

18 Expiry of Fixed Term

19 Surrender, Merger, Frustration and Repudiation

20 Disclaimer

21 Dissolved and Struck-off Companies and Death

Part 5
Proceedings for Possession

22 Landlord's Application to Terminate Continuation Tenancy

25 Interim Rent

26 New Tenancy Ordered

27 Refusal to Order a New Tenancy

28 Telecommunications Apparatus

Part 7
Appendices

Appendix 1

Appendix 2

Appendix 3

Appendix 4

List of Forms

Table of Cases

Table of Statutes

Table of Statutory Instruments

Part 1

Introduction

CHAPTER 1

THE BUSINESS TENANCY CODE

· ·

Whether or not a tenant of business premises is entitled to security of tenure depends upon the provisions of Pt II of the Landlord and Tenant Act 1954 (ss.24 to 46, plus some supplementary sections) as amended. This chapter explains how the Act operates. Chapter 2 explains the precise circumstances in which the Act applies but, to put it briefly, the Act will apply where the tenant occupies the premises for the purposes of his business.

1–01

Where the Act does apply there are two components to the security provided:

- automatic continuation of the existing tenancy; and
- the ability in certain circumstances to apply for a new tenancy.

Automatic continuation of the tenancy

Landlord and Tenant Act 1954 s.24(1), (2)

24.–(1) A tenancy to which this Part of this Act applies shall not come to an end unless terminated in accordance with the provisions of this Part of this Act; and, subject to the following provisions of this Act either the tenant or the landlord under such a tenancy may apply to the court for an order for the grant of a new tenancy—

1–02

    (a)   if the landlord has given notice under section 25 of this Act to terminate the tenancy; or

    (b)   if the tenant has made a request for a new tenancy in accordance with section 26 of this Act.

(2) The last foregoing subsection shall not prevent the coming to an end of a tenancy by notice to quit given by the tenant, by surrender or forfeiture, or by the forfeiture of a superior tenancy unless—

    (a)   in the case of a notice to quit, the notice was given before the tenant had been in occupation in right of the tenancy for one month;

3

If the 1954 Act applies, the tenancy (whether it is for a fixed or periodic term) automatically continues at the expiry of the fixed term if the tenant remains in occupation. However, if he is not in occupation at that date, the tenancy will come to an end at that point and the tenant will be obliged to pay no more rent (s.27(1A)). This is the situation even if the tenant has applied for a new tenancy. So long as he leaves prior to the expiry date in the lease the tenancy will come to an end on that date—although the circumstances may be such that an estoppel may arise requiring further rent from the tenant (*Single Horse Properties Ltd v Surrey CC* [2002] EWCA Civ 367).

The methods of termination provided for by the 1954 Act are as follows (s.24(2)):

(1) Termination notice served by the landlord pursuant to s.25 (see Ch.14), followed by an application by the landlord to apply to the court for termination of the continuation tenancy (see Ch.22).
(2) Request for a new tenancy served by the tenant pursuant to s.26 (see Ch.15), followed by an application by the landlord to apply to the court for termination of the continuation tenancy (see Ch.22).
(3) Notice by tenant terminating the tenancy pursuant to s.27 (see Ch.15).
(4) Where the tenancy is a periodic tenancy, notice to quit served by the tenant (see Ch.15).
(5) Forfeiture (see Chs 7–12).
(6) Surrender or merger (see Ch.19).

Except in the one circumstance stated above in (4), service of a common law notice to quit is ineffective to terminate a tenancy to which the 1954 Act applies.

The right to apply for a new tenancy and landlord's application to terminate

1-03 Where the Act applies and a termination notice has been served by the landlord pursuant to s.25 of the Act ("s.25 notice") or a request for a new tenancy has been served by the tenant pursuant to s.26 of the Act ("s.26 request"), the tenant may apply to the court for a new tenancy (see Ch.24). The landlord may agree to the grant of a new tenancy or he may seek to oppose the grant on one of a number of grounds set out in s.30 of the 1954 Act (see Ch.17). In common parlance landlords, tenants and their lawyers usually refer to the tenant's application for a new "lease". More accurately, the interest granted to the tenant is a new "tenancy". The lease is the document which embodies the terms of the tenancy and which serves to convey that interest to the tenant (cf. s.205(1)(ii) of the Law of Property Act 1925).

The landlord may also apply to the court for a new tenancy to be granted to the tenant; i.e. the landlord can do so without waiting for the tenant to set the process in motion (see Ch.24).

On the other hand, if the landlord does not want a new lease to be granted he can oppose the tenant's application or the landlord can apply for the tenancy to be terminated on one of a number of specified grounds (see Ch.17).

Sub-tenants

It will be seen in later chapters that "the landlord" in proceedings under the 1954 Act is not necessarily the tenant's immediate landlord but may be a superior landlord. This is a consequence of s.69 of the Act which states that the term "tenancy" includes a tenancy "created . . . derivatively out of the freehold . . . by underlease . . . ". Furthermore, the fact that the tenancy may not be protected by the Act does not mean that the sub-tenancy is not protected. These are important points that should always be borne in mind when one is dealing with tenancies of business premises (see in particular para.14–16 and para.15–07). See also para.18–04 for the position of the sub-tenant where the tenant's tenancy comes to an end at the conclusion of the tenant's fixed term; para.14–42 where the tenant's tenancy comes to an end by notice to quit and para.27–06 after a tenant's unsuccessful application for a new tenancy.

1–04

It is not possible for a tenant and a sub-tenant both to occupy premises for the purpose of a business at the same time. If the property has been sublet and the sub-tenant is in occupation it will be the sub-tenant who has the rights under the Act (see further para.2–06; *Graysim Holdings Ltd v P&O Property Holdings Ltd* [1994] 3 All E.R. 897).

Unlawful sub-tenants (i.e. sub-tenants who have been granted tenancies in breach of covenant) have rights under Pt II of the 1954 Act as against superior landlords as well as against their own immediate landlords (*D'Silva v Lister House Development* [1970] 1 All E.R. 858). This is a point that is not frequently understood by practitioners. However, the landlord may possibly be able to forfeit the headlease (if it is not too late) and if he has not waived the right to do so (see generally para.7-14).

Divided reversions

1-05   Where the tenant holds one lease but the different parts of the property that he occupies is each owned by a different landlord particular problems arise. Should all the landlords join together to serve one s.25 notice or do they serve separate notices (para.14-22)? Does the tenant serve one s.26 request and if so upon whom (para.15-09)? If the tenant is successful on an application to renew does he get one new tenancy or a different tenancy for each part (para.26-16)? All these points are dealt with in the appropriate sections at the paragraph numbers indicated.

Examples of how Pt II of the 1954 Act works

1-06   The structure of the Act and the way it works is best explained by looking at a number of common situations that arise.

Landlord wants to recover possession

1-07   As stated above, if the tenant is in occupation at the expiry of the fixed term the contractual tenancy continues unless determined in accordance with the provisions of Pt II of the Act. If the tenant has failed to pay his rent or is in breach of some other covenant the landlord may, if the tenancy contains a forfeiture clause, forfeit the lease. Assuming, however, that the tenant is not in breach the method by which the landlord terminates the tenancy is by service of a s.25 notice, whether the tenancy is for a fixed or periodic term. The notice will contain a termination date that must be not more than 12 nor less than six months after service. It may not be served so as to expire prior to the end of the fixed term (para.14-12). (Note that even if there is a breach of the lease the landlord may prefer to use the 1954 Act procedures because of the uncertainties of relief from forfeiture—see further Ch.12.)

If, in response to the s.25 notice, the tenant applies to the court for a new tenancy within the time limits specified in the 1954 Act—see para.24–08, the original tenancy continues until the case has been finally disposed of and for a further period of three months thereafter (s.64; see further para.27–02). Either the landlord or the tenant may apply for an interim rent pending the outcome of the proceedings (see Ch.25).

The landlord may oppose the granting of a new lease on one or more of a number of specified grounds, so long as he has previously stated those grounds in his s.25 notice (Ch.17). If he establishes a ground, the court will refuse to grant a new tenancy, the continuation tenancy will generally come to an end three months after the final disposal of the case (s.64; para.27–02) and the tenant will have to leave.

The landlord is also entitled to apply for the tenancy to be terminated on one of these grounds, i.e. he does not have to wait for the tenant to apply for a new tenancy and then oppose. As will be seen, he is able to apply for an order for termination as soon as he has served a s.25 notice (Ch.22).

If the landlord fails to establish a ground of opposition a new lease will be ordered (see para.22–15 for termination claims and Ch.26 generally). The duration, rent and terms of the new lease are those agreed between the landlord and the tenant or in default of agreement as determined by the court. If the tenant is not happy with the tenancy as ordered, he has the option not to take it (see para.26–33).

Tenant wants a new tenancy

If the landlord fails to serve a s.25 notice the tenant remains in occupation under the terms of the original tenancy, pursuant to s.24 of the Act. However, there is no certainty in this situation. The tenant does not know when or if the landlord will serve a s.25 notice. Furthermore, in some periods the last thing the tenant wants to do is to continue to pay the current rent which may well be a great deal higher than the market rent. The Act therefore provides a method whereby the tenant may bring matters to a head, namely the s.26 request (para.15–02). After service of the request he may apply to the court for a new

1–08

tenancy. As with the position where the landlord serves a s.25 notice the current tenancy remains in existence until three months after the final disposal of the claim. Both the landlord and the tenant may apply for an interim rent. This can be of great benefit to tenants in a falling market (see further Ch.25).

Action by landlord who is content to grant a new tenancy

1-09 If the landlord is content to grant the tenant a new tenancy he has the following options:

- He can wait for the tenant to apply for a new tenancy and then put forward his proposals in the proceedings (see para.24–44).
- Instead of waiting for the tenant to apply the landlord can apply himself for the tenant to be granted a new tenancy. If the parties cannot agree the terms, these will be determined by the court in the proceedings (see para.24–04).
- The landlord and tenant can agree to a new tenancy under s.28 of the Act (see para.A1–11).

Action by tenant who does not want a new tenancy

1-10 Where the tenant wishes to give up his tenancy he may:

- simply leave prior to the expiry date in the lease (s.27(1A)–see para.15–15); or
- serve a notice under s.27(1) of the 1954 Act terminating the tenancy at the expiry date in the lease by giving not less than three months' notice (see para.15–15); or
- serve a notice under s.27(2) terminating the tenancy at any time thereafter by giving not less than three months' notice (see para.15–17).

For periodic tenancies and the exercise of break clauses by tenants see para.15–18.

Landlord wants an increase in rent

1-11 If the landlord fails to serve a s.25 notice and the tenant fails to serve a s.26 request (or a s.27 notice or notice to quit), the tenancy will simply continue on the same terms and at the same rent as set out in the lease. The court has no power to award an increase in rent unless the procedures under Pt II of the 1954 Act have been invoked. If the landlord requires an increase in rent he will have to terminate the tenancy by service of a s.25 notice so that a new lease at an increased rent may be granted. Where a s.25 notice (or s.26 request) has been served an application for an interim rent may be made (Ch.25).

Where the parties are in agreement, an increased rent can be achieved by a variation of the terms without the need for a surrender of the old tenancy and the grant of a new tenancy (see para.19–07).

The 1954 Act has never applied

If Pt II of the 1954 Act has never applied (perhaps because the tenant has never occupied the premises for the purposes of his business) and assuming of course that no legislation applicable to residential premises applies or if the tenancy is "contracted out" (see Ch.3), the tenancy will come to an end at the expiry date provided for in the lease and the landlord will be entitled to possession (see para.18–03). If the tenancy is a periodic one the landlord will be able to bring the lease to an end by service of a notice to quit (see para.14–28). **1–12**

Termination where the 1954 Act ceases to apply

Where the tenancy ceases to be a tenancy to which the Act applies during the fixed term, it will automatically come to an end by effluxion of time on the date specified in the lease (see para.1–02). Where the tenancy was originally for a fixed term and continued thereafter as a continuation tenancy under the Act, but the Act has now ceased to apply, it may be determined by the landlord giving the tenant not less than three nor more than six months' notice in writing (see s.24(3)(a); para.14–27). The tenant may determine it by giving three months' notice under s.27 (see para.15–17). **1–13**

CHAPTER 2

DOES PART II OF THE 1954 ACT APPLY?

. . . .

Introduction

2-01 In deciding whether Part II of the 1954 Act applies there are four issues to be considered:

(1) *Tenancy or licence?* Does the person in occupation occupy the property pursuant to a tenancy or a licence? The Act applies only to tenancies (s.23(1); see below). The term "tenancy" is defined by s.69(1) of the 1954 Act. (The distinction between a tenancy and a licence is dealt with in Ch.6.)

Landlord and Tenant Act 1954 s.69(1)

Definition of "tenancy"

2-02 69.–(1) ... "tenancy" means a tenancy created either immediately or derivatively out of the freehold, whether by a lease or underlease, by an agreement for a lease or underlease or by a tenancy agreement or in pursuance of any enactment (including this Act), but does not include a mortgage term or any interest arising in favour of a mortgagor by his attorning tenant to his mortgagee, and references to the granting of a tenancy and to demised property shall be construed accordingly;

(2) *Occupation of premises for purposes of a business.* Part II applies only where the tenant occupies the property for the purposes of a business. There are really three issues here:

    (a) Is the person concerned in "occupation" of "premises"? (para.2–04)

    (b) Is the user a business user? (paras 2–10 to 2–19)

    (c) Is the user that of the tenant or some other person such as the tenant's company? (paras 2–20 to 2–27)

(3) *Excluded tenancies.* The Act does not apply to tenancies at will (see para.2-29). There is also a list of excluded tenancies set out in s.43 of the 1954 Act. The most important exception relates to short lets (see below, para.2-35). (The Act does apply to a tenancy by estoppel: *Bell v General Accident Fire & Life Assurance Corp Ltd* [1998] 1 E.G.L.R. 69 CA—landlord had no actual interest in the property, which belonged to a different company in the group.)

(4) *Contracting out of the Act.* Have the provisions of Part II of the 1954 Act been excluded by a valid agreement between the parties? Strictly speaking in this case the Act applies to the tenancy but the tenancy is excluded from the benefits of the security offered by the Act. (see Ch.3).

Occupation of premises for the purposes of a business

Landlord and Tenant Act 1954 s.23(1), (2)

23.—(1) Subject to the provisions of this Act, this Part of this Act applies to any tenancy where the property comprised in the tenancy is or includes premises which are occupied by the tenant and are so occupied for the purposes of a business carried on by him or for those and other purposes.

(2) In this Part of this Act the expression "business" includes a trade, profession or employment and includes any activity carried on by a body of persons, whether corporate or unincorporate.

2-03

The 1954 Act will apply only where the property is, or includes premises, occupied by the tenant for the purposes of a business carried on by him or for those and other purposes (s.23). Section 23 gives rise to the following issues.

"Occupation" of "premises"

In most cases there will be little difficulty in determining whether or not the tenant is in occupation of premises. This will be a straightforward question of fact. However, some cases are not always so obvious. In *Bracey v Read* [1962] 3 All E.R. 472 the landlord "let on lease to the tenant the right to train and exercise racehorses on the gallops". The court held that the term "premises" in s.23 of the 1954 Act is not confined to buildings. It is not the narrow popular meaning of the word that

2-04

applies but the wider legal meaning. It covers any sort of property of which a lease can be granted. The gallops were "premises" within the meaning of the section.

Whether or not an incorporeal right such as an easement of way was capable of being "occupied" was considered in *Land Reclamation Co Ltd v Basildon DC* [1979] 2 All E.R. 993. The court held that the word "occupied" in s.23 of the 1954 Act is not interchangeable with the word "used". In coming to its conclusion the court had regard to the law of rating. It considered that the word "occupied" in s.23 had the same meaning as it would have in rating cases. As a right of way is an incorporeal hereditament that per se is not rateable, it is not capable of being occupied for the purposes of s.23 of the 1954 Act either. Compare parking spaces, below. In *Wandsworth LBC v Singh* [1991] 2 E.G.L.R. 75, it was held that a small open space improved and maintained by a local authority for the pleasure of the local residents was property "occupied" by the local authority within s.23 of the Act.

Parking spaces/Moorings

2-05   Parking spaces are "premises" that can be "occupied" for the purposes of s.23 (*Pointon York Group plc v Poulton* [2006] EWCA Civ 1001). See in particular paras 16 and 29 of the judgment of Arden LJ; and paras 24 and 25:

> "I reject the submission that an incorporeal hereditament cannot constitute premises for the purposes of section 23. That conclusion may in some cases lead to the conclusion that a tenancy may qualify under section 23 even though only the incorporeal hereditament is occupied for business purposes. But I do not see why in such a case that should not be possible *if the incorporeal hereditament is capable of being occupied.* It is possible to have a business use of the incorporeal hereditament alone, such as where a house is let with right to use garages or stables which are occupied used for business purposes. It is difficult to see why this business use should not be protected even though the house is not used as part of the business. Section 23 expressly applies where only part of the premises is occupied for business use." (*Emphasis added*).

On the facts of this case, the judge found that the tenant had occupied the parking spaces during business hours; and that was sufficient.

Are moorings "premises" capable of being occupied for the purposes of a business? For example, what would be the position of a restaurant on a barge moored against a riverbank? It has been held that where a mooring is fixed to the bed of a river or to the river bank a person can be said to be in occupation for rating purposes (*Bradshaw v Davey* [1952] 1 All E.R. 350). It may therefore also be that such a person may be held to be in occupation for the purposes of Pt II of the 1954 Act. However, compare *Chelsea Yacht & Boat Co Ltd v Pope* [2000] L&TR 401 CA where it was held that a houseboat cannot be a tenancy of a dwelling-house unless the boat is sufficiently annexed to the land so as to become part of the land.

In *Port of London Authority v Ashmore* [2009] EWHC 954 Ch, it was held that an owner of a barge that had been moored to mooring rings on the tidal part of the River Thames acquired title by way of adverse possession to the river bed for the footprint of the barge. The vessel only rested on the bed at low tide but it was held that adverse possession does not require physical contact with the river bed at all times. So perhaps an agreement by the owner of a river bed permitting such possession might also give rise to a tenancy and occupation of the river bed for the purposes of Pt II of the Act.

Ceasing occupation

The 1954 Act ceases to apply if the tenant vacates before the expiry date specified in the lease (s.27(1A); para.15–15). In these circumstances, the tenant will not be required to serve any further termination notice, even if he has applied for a new tenancy (*Single Horse Properties Ltd v Surrey CC* [2002] EWCA Civ 367; see further para.15–15). **2–06**

If the tenant remains in occupation beyond the date of the fixed term, the tenancy will continue until determined by a notice under s.27(2) (see further para.15–17). However, the tenant will not be able to continue with any application for a new tenancy unless the Act continues to apply see (para.24–02) i.e. in this context, unless the tenant continues to occupy the premises for the purposes of his business. Ceasing to occupy can also have important consequences in respect of compensation payable under the Act (see para.27–20). Determining whether or not the tenant has continued to do so will usually be straightforward but there are uncertain cases.

In *Bacciocchi v Academic Agency Ltd* [1998] 3 E.G.L.R. 157 the tenancy came to an end on August 11, 1994. T physically vacated and handed over the keys to his solicitors 12 days beforehand. It was held that he was still to be regarded as in occupation for the last 12 days for the purposes of s.38(2) of the Act (see para.27–24—Restrictions on agreements excluding or reducing compensation).

> "Whenever business premises are empty for only a short period, whether mid-term or before or after trading at either end of the lease, I would be disinclined to find that the business occupancy ceased (or not started) for that period provided always that during it there exists no rival for the role of business occupant and that the premises are not being used for some other, non-business purpose . . . the tenant's physical possession will not invariably require permanent physical possession throughout the whole term of the lease and he ought not to have to resort to devices like storage of goods or token visits to satisfy the statutory requirements of continuing occupation. If of course the premises are left vacant for a matter of months, the court would be readier to conclude that the thread of continuity has been broken". (Simon Brown LJ).

In *Sight & Sound Education Ltd v Books etc Ltd* [1999] 3 E.G.L.R. 45, T left five months before the date specified in the s.25 notice. This meant he did not have 14 years occupation prior to that date and was not entitled to double compensation under s.37. (See further para.27–20).

In *Pointon York Group plc v Poulton* [2006] EWCA Civ 1001 the Court of Appeal confirmed that the principles in *Bacciocchi* apply to occupation under s.23 so that:

> " . . . a tenant need not be physically present in the premises if he is using them in some other way as an incident in the ordinary course or conduct of business life, provided that the premises are occupied by no other business occupier and are not used for any non-business purpose" (para.31).

Short gap at end of term after subletting

Pointon was concerned with a short gap at the end of a term **2–07** after a subletting. Prior to the end of the sublease, the subtenants employed contractors to decorate the offices and put in new carpets. While this work was being carried out the tenant's staff went to the premises to check on the progress of the work. The tenant intended to use the premises for its own business after expiry of the sublease and wanted to plan how the offices could be used in the future. The decorating and re-carpeting were finished the day after the sublease expired. On that day a director of the tenant went to the premises and spoke to the carpet layers. He confirmed that the works were suitable for the company's business occupation. It was also necessary to put in new wiring and computer systems but this could not be done in the few days between the end of the sublease and the end of the lease and were left to be carried out shortly afterwards. These facts were sufficient to constitute occupation and the landlord's action in evicting the tenant the day after the expiry date in the headlease was unlawful. The lease had continued under Pt II of the 1954 Act.

Occupier: tenant or sub-tenant?

It is not possible for a tenant and a sub-tenant to occupy the **2–08** same property for the purposes of the 1954 Act at the same time (*Graysim Ltd v P&O Property Holdings Ltd* [1995] 4 All E.R. 831 HL, at 836j). Thus, where the premises consist of a hostel, a market hall, serviced offices or some other similar multi-occupied building, whether or not the tenant of the whole is in occupation for the purposes of the Act will depend on whether or not the tenant has sublet parts to the occupiers. In *Graysim Holdings Ltd v P&O Property Holdings Ltd* the tenant of a market hall was held not to be in occupation of the hall where the individual traders had exclusive possession and thus tenancies of their individual stalls:

> "the very nature of some businesses involves the owner parting with the occupation of his land. Graysim's business was such a business. It sublet parts of the market hall. The use of the parts retained by Graysim was ancillary to the traders' use of the sublet units, providing access and other facilities for the traders and their potential customers. Part II of the 1954 Act is concerned to protect tenants in their occupation of property for the purposes of their business.

But Graysim itself did nothing on the units. Graysim did not itself carry on business in the units. It let the units for others to do business there. Its income from Wallasey Market consisted solely of rentals from these lettings. The Act is not concerned to give protection to tenants in respect of such income. The Act looks through to the occupying tenants, here the traders, and affords them statutory protection, not their landlord. Intermediate landlords, not themselves in occupation, are not within the class of persons the Act was seeking to protect." (Lord Nicholas of Birkenhead at 842e.)

Earlier cases, in particular *Lee-Verhuist (Investments) Ltd v Harwood Trust* [1972] 3 All E.R. 619 need to be read in the light of *Graysim v P&O Property Holdings Ltd*. In *Lee-Velhurst*, the property was a house divided into 20 flats. The tenant company serviced the rooms daily and exercised control over the way the occupancies were conducted to a degree much beyond that which is usual when a flat is let to a tenant on a normal lease. The Court of Appeal upheld the decision of the judge in the county court that the company occupied the whole building for the purposes of s.23. It would seem that so far as the decision is based on the occupiers of the individual rooms being licensees it is correct, but insofar as they may have been tenants the decision was incorrect (see Lord Nicholls in *Graysim v P&O Property Holdings Ltd* at 837j). Compare *Bagettes Ltd v GP Estates Co Ltd* [1956] 1 All E.R. 729 where there were sublettings of unfurnished residential flats. The Court of Appeal held that the tenancy of the whole building was not a business tenancy (approved in *Graysim v P&O Property Holdings Ltd* at 838j).

In a later county court case, *Smith v Titanate* [2005] 20 E.G. 262, the judge set out what he considered to be the principles in the light of *Graysim*. The property was divided into six flats. The tenant ran a business of letting out the flats. The longer term lettings were on standard assured shorthold tenancies. Other lettings were on terms that included the provision of services but the judge held that these were tenancies. The question for the court was whether the tenant was in occupation of the individual flats for the purpose of a business. *Held*: No. The 1954 Act did not therefore apply (*Graysim* applied). The judge analysed three different types of situation that might arise:

- Cases where flats are let on conventional terms, with the landlord doing no more than receiving the rents and performing the landlord's covenants. In those cases there is no business occupation of the flats.
- At the other end of the spectrum cases such as common lodging houses, or hostel / student halls of residence, where there is a high degree of control and the services are performed in circumstances in which the landlord has an unfettered access to the rooms for that purpose.
- Cases in the middle where there is some degree of control and/or less restricted access and/or a greater degree of intrusive service provision. Depending on the facts these may fall on either side of the line.

Tenant temporarily out of occupation

2–09 There are circumstances in which the tenant may be temporarily forced out of occupation, for example, if the property has been severely damaged by fire. In such a case the tenant will remain entitled to the protection of the Act if "he continues to exert and claim his right to occupancy" (*Morrison Holdings Ltd v Manders Property (Wolverhampton) Ltd* [1976] 1 W.L.R. 533, per Scarman LJ at 540B). For an example see *Flairline Properties v Hassan* [1999] 1 E.G.L.R. 138—tenant absent from restaurant premises as a result of a fire continued to be in occupation even though he had opened other premises round the corner.

In other cases the tenant may be voluntarily out of occupation for a period of time and as a result may lose his rights under the 1954 Act. When deciding whether the tenant has retained sufficient occupation for the Act to apply the court must look at all the facts (*Aspinall Finance Ltd v Viscount Chelsea* [1989] 1 E.G.L.R. 103). In that case the tenant had ceased to use the property for business purposes both prior to the commencement of the proceedings and the expiry date in the lease but it was the intention of the tenant to so use the property once again in the event of the court ordering the grant of a new tenancy. The court held that "the thread of continuity" had been broken and that the Act did not apply.

> "The mere fact that the tenant is not occupying at the relevant date is not conclusive. Tenants do not have to occupy and carry on business for every hour of every day. Some breaks are inevitable. At the smallest level, the

17

premises may be closed for the night for business. They may be closed for a longer period while repairs can be carried out. They may be closed in order that the tenant and his staff can have a holiday. They may be closed because the business is a seasonal one. So one gets businesses that are only open in the summer months and are closed throughout all the winter months.

In all those types of case it can be said that the tenants are occupying for business purposes, even though when the application is made or when the lease ends, or both, falls within a period of closure.

The test which has been adopted is whether the thread of continuity of business user continues or whether it has been broken, to take a metaphorical expression, which I think was coined by Cross J . . . in the case of *I & H Caplan Ltd v Caplan (No.2)* [1963] 1 W.L.R. 1247 . . . .

What I get out of [that case], I think, is that one has obviously to look at all the facts, the time that the business has not been carried on, the intention to resume and the reason why the business is not being carried on, whether the reasons were forced on the tenant or whether the tenant voluntarily went out. All those are factors, none of which is conclusive, to enable the judge to decide whether the premises are occupied for the purpose of a business." (*Aspinall Finance Ltd v Viscount Chelsea* [1989] 1 E.G.L.R. 103 per H.H. Judge Paul Baker Q.C. (sitting as a judge of the High Court) at 104J and 105C.)

Business: trade, profession or employment

2-10 The term "business" includes a trade, profession or employment and includes *any* activity carried on by a body of persons whether corporate or unincorporate (s.23(2); para.2-03). A distinction therefore has to be made between individuals and bodies of persons. In the later case "any activity" will constitute a business. For an example see *Addiscombe Garden Estates Ltd v Crabbe* [1957] 3 All E.R. 563 at 572—a tennis club.

Whether any particular activity is a business is a question of fact to be decided in the light of all the circumstances (*Lewis v*

Weldcrest [1978] 1 W.L.R. 1107—a tenant who took in five lodgers at very low rents that provided very little profit was held not to be carrying on a trade).

Prohibition of business user

Landlord and Tenant Act 1954 s.23(4)

23.—(4) Where the tenant is carrying on a business, in all or any part of the property comprised in a tenancy, in breach of a prohibition (however expressed) of use for business purposes which subsists under the terms of the tenancy and extends to the whole of that property, this Part of this Act shall not apply to the tenancy unless the immediate landlord or his predecessor in title has consented to the breach or the immediate landlord has acquiesced therein.

In this subsection the reference to a prohibition of use for business purposes does not include a prohibition of use for the purposes of a specified business, or of use for purposes of any but a specified business, but save as aforesaid includes a prohibition of use for the purposes of some one or more only of the classes of business specified in the definition of that expression in subsection (2) of this section.

2–11

Where the tenancy contains a general prohibition against the use of the whole of the property for business purposes the Act cannot apply unless the immediate landlord or his predecessor has *consented* to the breach or the immediate landlord has *acquiesced* in the breach.

"Acquiescence" involves no more than a passive standing by without objecting to a breach of covenant of which the person acquiescing has knowledge. If a landlord has no knowledge of the fact that gives rise to the breach he cannot be said to have acquiesced in its continuance. "Knowledge is a prerequisite of acquiescence". (*Methodist Secondary Schools Trust Deed Trustees v O'Leary* [1993] 1 E.G.L.R. 105 CA at 108B—occupation by a school caretaker required to live at residential premises amounted to occupation by the employer for business purposes but was in breach of the user covenant so that the Act did not apply.) "Consent" requires a positive, affirmative act accepting the breach, such as a written or oral acceptance or an implied acceptance by positive conduct. The purpose of the distinction is to ensure that the immediate landlord is not bound by mere acquiescence on the part of the immediate predecessor in title (*Bell v Alfred Franks & Bartlett Co Ltd* [1980] 1 All E.R. 356 CA, per Shaw LJ at 360b-f).

Mixed user: business and residential

2–12   The Rent Act 1977 (s.24), the Housing Act 1988 (para.4 of Sch.1) and the Housing Act 1985 (Sch.1 para.11) each provide that a tenancy will not be respectively regulated, assured or secure where Pt II of the 1954 Act applies. Thus, even where a house was originally let to the tenant "as a dwelling" (a phrase used in each of those Acts) the security of tenure provisions of the Housing and Rent Acts will not apply where "the property comprised in the tenancy is or includes premises which are occupied by the tenant and are so occupied for the purposes of a business carried on by him or for those and other purposes" (s.23(1)).

It is not uncommon for the tenant to use the property for mixed purposes. If this is the position the tenancy will be governed by the 1954 Act only if the business purpose is *significant*; if the business purpose is merely *incidental* to the residential purpose the 1954 Act will not apply (*Cheryl Investments Ltd v Saldanha* [1979] 1 All E.R. 5). To put it another way, "[it] is only if the [business] activity is part of the reason for, part of his aim and object in occupying the house that [the 1954 Act] will apply" (*Cheryl Investments*, per Lane LJ at p.13).

Thus, if the property comprised in the tenancy is a shop with a flat above the business purpose is significant and the 1954 Act will apply (e.g. see *Kent Coast Property Investments Ltd v Ward* [1990] 2 E.G.L.R. 86). But if a person has an office at home in which he works in the evenings, the business purpose will be incidental and the 1954 Act will not apply (see *Cheryl Investments Ltd v Saldanha*, Lord Denning's first example at p.9). For a case in which the principle was applied see *Gurton v Parrott* [1991] 1 E.G.L.R. 98. The tenancy of a dwelling-house and outbuildings in which the latter were used as kennels for a number of years was held not to be a tenancy within the 1954 Act.

A "statutory tenancy" under the Rent (Agriculture) Act 1976 (and presumably under the Rent Act 1977), as opposed to the original contractual tenancy, does not become a tenancy to which Pt II of the 1954 Act applies if the tenant uses the premises for business purposes (*Durman v Bell* [1988] 2 E.G.L.R. 117).

The fact that the 1954 Act does not apply does not automatically mean that the Housing and Rent Acts do apply. It is necessary to apply the provisions of the appropriate Act to the particular facts of the case. However, premises that were originally governed by one of these Acts and then became governed by the 1954 Act (because a significant business purpose was adopted) may once again become subject to the Rent Acts when the business user ceases. In *Tomkins v Basildon DC* [2002] EWCA Civ 876 a property initially let under a business tenancy and later used for residential purposes were not protected by the Housing Act 1985. There was no surrender of the original business tenancy and re-grant of a residential tenancy. The landlord had simply not enforced the user covenant in the lease. For a fuller discussion of these aspects see *Residential Possession Proceedings,* 9th edn (Sweet & Maxwell) para.17.012 by Webber and Dovar.

See s.64(2) of the Housing Act 1980 for any tenancy that was a controlled tenancy on November 22, 1980; any such tenancy is deemed to be a s.24 continuation tenancy if it is occupied for the purposes of a business etc. and none of the exceptions applies.

Peaceable re-entry cannot be used for mixed use premises, i.e. residential and commercial (*Pirabakaran v Patel* [2006] EWCA Civ 685; see para.23–01).

Mixed user: business and agricultural

Landlord and Tenant Act 1954 s.43(1)(a)

43.–(1) This Part of this Act does not apply–   **2–13**

    (a)   to a tenancy of an agricultural holding which is a tenancy in relation to which the Agricultural Holdings Act 1986 applies or a tenancy which would be a tenancy of an agricultural holding in relation to which that Act applied if subsection (3) of section 2 of that Act did not have effect or, in a case where approval was given under subsection (1) of that section, if that approval had not been given;

    (aa) to a farm business tenancy;

    (b)   to a tenancy created by a mining lease . . .

Farm business tenancy

These tenancies were introduced by the Agricultural Tenancies   **2–14**
Act 1995.

Agricultural Tenancies Act 1995 s.1

1.–Meaning of "farm business tenancy".

(1) A tenancy is a "farm business tenancy" for the purposes of this Act if–

    (a)   it meets the business conditions together with either the agriculture condition or the notice conditions, and

    (b)   it is not a tenancy which, by virtue of section 2 of this Act cannot be a farm business tenancy.

(2) The business conditions are–

    (a)   that all or part of the land comprised in the tenancy is farmed for the purposes of a trade or business, and

    (b)   that, since the beginning of the tenancy, all or part of the land so comprised has been so farmed.

(3) The agriculture condition is that, having regard to–

    (a)   the terms of the tenancy,

    (b)   the use of the land comprised in the tenancy,

    (c)   the nature of any commercial activities carried on on that land, and

    (d)   any other relevant circumstances,

the character of the tenancy is primarily or wholly agricultural.

(4) The notice conditions are–

    (a)   that, on or before the relevant day, the landlord and the tenant each gave the other a written notice–

        (i) identifying (by name or otherwise) the land to be comprised in the tenancy or proposed tenancy, and

      (ii) containing a statement to the effect that the person giving the notice intends that the tenancy or proposed tenancy is to be, and remain, a farm business tenancy, and

    (b)   that, at the beginning of the tenancy, having regard to the terms of the tenancy and any other relevant circumstances, the character of the tenancy was primarily or wholly agricultural.

(5) In subsection (4) above "the relevant day" means whichever is the earlier of the following–

(a) the day on which the parties enter into any instrument creating the tenancy, other than an agreement to enter into a tenancy on a future date, or

(b) the beginning of the tenancy.

    (6)   The written notice referred to in subsection (4) above must not be included in any instrument creating the tenancy

2.–Tenancies which cannot be farm business tenancies.

(1) A tenancy cannot be a farm business tenancy for the purposes of this Act if–

    (a)   the tenancy begins before 1st September 1995, or

(b)   it is a tenancy of an agricultural holding beginning on or after that date with respect to which, by virtue of section 4 of this Act, the Agricultural Holdings Act 1986 applies.

(2) In this section "agricultural holding" has the same meaning as in the Agricultural Holdings Act 1986.

Generally speaking, the Agricultural Tenancies Act 1995 does not apply in relation to any tenancy beginning before September 1, 1995 (s.4(1) of the 1995 Act). Before that date the regime relating to Agricultural Holdings applies.

Exclusion of agricultural holdings

The term "agricultural holding" is defined by s.1 of the Agricultural Holdings Act 1986. The terms "agriculture", "livestock" and "tenant", which are particularly relevant to the definition of "agricultural holding", are themselves defined in s.96(1) of the 1986 Act.

2-15

Agricultural Holdings Act 1986 ss.1, 96

1.–(1) In this Act "agricultural holding" means the aggregate of the land (whether agricultural or not) comprised in a contract of tenancy which is a contract for an *agricultural tenancy*, not being a contract under which the land is let to the tenant during his continuance in any office, appointment or employment held under the landlord.

2-16

(2) For the purposes of this section, a contract of tenancy relating to land is a contract for an *agricultural tenancy* if, having regard to—

(a)   the terms of the tenancy,
(b)   the actual or contemplated use of the land at the time of the conclusions of the contract and subsequently, and
(c)   any other relevant circumstances,

the whole of the land comprised in the contract, subject to such exceptions only as do not substantially affect the character of the tenancy, is let for use as *agricultural land*.

(3) A change in user of the land concerned subsequent to the conclusion of a contract of tenancy which involves any breach of the terms of the tenancy shall be disregarded for the purpose of determining whether a contract which was not originally a contract for an agricultural tenancy has subsequently become one unless it is effected with the landlord's permission, consent or acquiescence.

(4) In this Act "*agricultural land*" means—

(a)   land used for agriculture which is so used for the purposes of a trade or business, and
(b)   any other land which, by virtue of a designation under section 109(1) of the Agriculture Act 1947, is agricultural land within the meaning of the Act.

(5) In this Act "*contract of tenancy*" means a letting of land, or agreement for letting land, for a term of years or from year to year; and for the purposes of this definition a letting of land, or an agreement for letting land, which, by virtue of subsection (6) of section 149 of the Law of Property Act 1925, takes effect as such a letting of land or agreement for letting land as is mentioned in that subsection shall be deemed to be a letting of land or, as the case may be, an agreement for letting and, for a term of years.

2–17   **96.–**(1) . . . "agriculture" includes horticulture, fruit growing, seed growing, dairy farming and livestock breeding and keeping, the use of land as grazing land, meadow land, osier land, market gardens and nursery grounds, and the use of land for woodlands where that use is ancillary to the farming of land for other agricultural purposes and "agricultural" shall be construed accordingly;

. . .

"livestock" includes any creature kept for the production of food, wool, skins, or fur or for the purpose of its use in the farming of land or the carrying on in relation to land of any agricultural activity;

. . .

"tenant" means the holder of land under a contract of tenancy, and includes the executors, administrators, assigns, or trustee in bankruptcy of a tenant, or other person deriving title from a tenant;

Some examples

2–18   The keeping and breeding of pheasants for sport is not an agricultural activity within the meaning of s.96(1) because the pheasants are not "kept for the production of food". They are not therefore "livestock" within the meaning of s.96(1) (*Earl of Normanton v Giles* [1980] 1 All E.R. 106).

The use of land as a stables or a riding school is not an agricultural activity (*Rutherford v Maurer* [1961] 2 All E.R. 775 CA). Nor is the running of a stud farm (*McClinton v McFall* (1974) 232 E.G. 707 CA).

Mixed user

2–19   Where the land is partly used for agricultural purposes and partly used for other purposes:

"one must look at the substance of the matter and see whether, as a matter of substance, the land comprised in the tenancy, taken as a whole, is an agricultural holding. If it is, then the whole of it is entitled to the protection of the Act. If it is not, then none of it is so entitled" (*Howkins v Jardine* [1951] 1 K.B. 614, per Jenkins LJ at p.628).

The land can cease to be an agricultural holding if the agricultural use is abandoned but:

"the tenancy is not to be regarded as alternating between being within and outside the [1986] Act as minor changes of user take place, and that, when the tenancy is clearly an agricultural one to start with, strong evidence is needed to show that agricultural use has been abandoned." (*Wetherall v Smith* [1980] 2 All E.R. 530, per Sir David Cairns at p.537G.)

In *Short v Greeves* [1988] 1 E.G.L.R. 1 the tenancy began as a horticultural enterprise with retail sales in a greenhouse at the front and was an agricultural holding. As time passed an increasing number of items were brought on to the land from elsewhere for sale so that the judge thought that approximately 60 per cent of the items were brought in and 40 per cent were home produced. He nevertheless held that the tenancy was still that of an agricultural holding. The Court of Appeal refused to interfere with his decision.

"The court is not lightly to treat a tenancy as having ceased to be within the protection of the Agricultural Holdings Act." (per Dillon LJ at p.3D.)

Is the occupation and business that of the tenant?

Landlord and Tenant Act 1954 s.23(1)

23.—(1) Subject to the provisions of this Act, this Part of this Act applies to any tenancy where the property comprised in the tenancy is or includes premises which are occupied by the tenant and are so occupied for the purposes of a business carried on by him or for those and other purposes.

2-20

Section 23 of the 1954 Act provides that the business tenancy code contained in Pt II applies if the premises are "occupied by *the tenant* and are so occupied for the purposes of a business carried on by *him* or for those and other purposes". However, the business carried on at the property is not always that of the tenant. Sometimes the business is carried on by a company of which the tenant is a director or major shareholder. On other occasions the business is run by beneficiaries under a trust, by some of the original partners who took the lease (others having ceased to be partners) or by an associated company. All these situations require consideration.

Companies

2-21 A limited liability company occupies a property through its officers or employees (*Parkes v Westminster Roman Catholic Diocese Trustee* [1978] 36 P. & C.R. 22 CA).

It is common for the lease to be in the name of an individual but for the entity occupying the premises for the purposes of a business to be that of a company of which the tenant is a director and major shareholder. Prior to the Regulatory Reform (Business Tenancies) (England and Wales) Order 2003 SI 2003/3096, in these circumstances, the Act did not apply. However this situation was reversed by the introduction of subss.(1A) and (1B) to s.23 which provide that:

- an individual tenant is deemed to satisfy the requirement to occupy the premises if the company occupying the premises for the purposes of the business is a company under his control; and
- a company tenant is deemed to satisfy the requirement to occupy if the individual who controls the company occupies the premises for the purposes of a business carried on there.

Associated companies

2-22 Where the tenant is a company that is part of a group of companies, occupation of the property by another company in the group, it is treated as equivalent to occupation by the tenant (s.42; see below). Companies are treated as being in the same group if one is a subsidiary of the other or if both are subsidiaries of a third company. A company will also be able to exercise rights under the Act where the same person has a controlling interest, whether or not the companies themselves have a formal relationship with each other.

Landlord and Tenant Act 1954 ss.23(1A), (1B), 42 and 46(2)

2-23   23.–(1A) Occupation or the carrying on of a business—

　　　(a)　by a company in which the tenant has a controlling interest; or

(b) where the tenant is a company, by a person with a controlling interest in the company,

shall be treated for the purposes of this section as equivalent to occupation or, as the case may be, the carrying on of a business by the tenant.

(1B) Accordingly references (however expressed) in this Part of this Act to the business of, or to use, occupation or enjoyment by, the tenant shall be construed as including references to the business of, or to use, occupation or enjoyment by, a company falling within subsection (1A)(a) above or a person falling within subsection (1A)(b) above.

42.–(1) For the purposes of this section two bodies corporate shall be taken to be members of a group if and only if one is a subsidiary of the other or both are subsidiaries of the third body corporate or the same person has a controlling interest in both.

(2) Where a tenancy is held by a member of a group, occupation by another member of the group, and the carrying on of a business by another member of the group, shall be treated for the purposes of section 23 of this Act as equivalent to occupation or the carrying on of a business by the member of the group holding the tenancy; and in relation to a tenancy to which this Part of this Act applies by virtue of the foregoing provisions of this subsection–

(a) references (however expressed) in this Part of this Act and in the Ninth Schedule to this Act to the business of or to use occupation or enjoyment by the tenant shall be construed as including references to the business of or to use occupation or enjoyment by the said other member;

(b) the reference in paragraph (d) of subsection (1) of section 34 of this Act to the tenant shall be construed as including the said other member; and

(c) an assignment of the tenancy from one member of the group to another shall not be treated as a change in the person of the tenant.

(3) Where the landlord's interest is held by a member of a group–

(a) the reference in paragraph (g) of subsection (1) of section 30 of this Act to intended occupation by the landlord for the purposes of a business to be carried on by him shall be construed as including intended occupation by any member of the group for the purposes of a business to be carried on by that member; and

(b) the reference in subsection (2) of that section to the purchase or creation of any interest shall be construed as a reference to a purchaser from or creation by a person other than a member of the group.

46.–(2) For the purposes of this Part of this Act, a person has a controlling interest in a company if, had he been a company, the other company would have been its subsidiary; and in this Part–

"company" has the meaning given by section 735 of the Companies Act 1985; and

"subsidiary" has the meaning given by section 736 of that Act.

Trusts

2-24   Special provision is made for the situation where the tenants are trustees (s.41; see below). If the property is occupied by some or all of the beneficiaries the property is treated as being occupied by the tenant and the 1954 Act will apply. However, it should be noted that the trustees remain the ones to whom the Act applies and who may apply for a new tenancy. It would appear that the court has the power to require unwilling trustees to apply for a new lease at the behest of willing trustees but that it is unlikely to do so (*Harris v Black* (1983) 127 Sol. Jo. 224 CA).

Landlord and Tenant Act 1954 s.41

2-25   **41.**–(1) Where a tenancy is held on trust, occupation by all or any of the beneficiaries under the trust, and the carrying on of a business by all or any of the beneficiaries, shall be treated for the purposes of section 23 of this Act as equivalent to occupation or the carrying on of a business by the tenant; and in relation to a tenancy to which this Part of this Act applies by virtue of the foregoing provisions of this subsection–

(a)   references (however expressed) in this Part of this Act and in the Ninth Schedule to this Act to the business of, or to carrying on of business, use, occupation or enjoyment by, the tenant shall be construed as including references to the business of, or to carrying on of business, use, occupation or enjoyment by, the beneficiaries or beneficiary;

(b)   the reference in paragraph (d) of subsection (1) of section 34 of this Act to the tenant shall be construed as including the beneficiaries or beneficiary; and

(c)   a change in the persons of the trustees shall not be treated as a change in the person of the tenant.

(2) Where the landlord's interest is held on trust the references in paragraph (g) of subsection (1) of section 30 of this Act to the landlord shall be construed as including references to the beneficiaries under the trust or any of them; but, except in the case of a trust arising under a will or on the intestacy of any person, the reference in subsection (2) of that section to the creation of the interest therein mentioned shall be construed as including the creation of the trust.

Joint tenants and partnerships

2-26   Where there are joint tenants, it sometimes occurs that by the expiry date of the lease only some of the tenants remain in occupation. For example, the lease may originally have been taken in the name of three partners. Subsequently, one of the partners left the partnership leaving the remaining two in occupation and carrying on the original business.

In *Jacobs v Chaudhuri* [1968] 2 All E.R. 124 the Court of Appeal held that the court had no jurisdiction to entertain an application by only some of the joint tenants because the words "the tenant under such a tenancy" in s.24(1) of the Landlord and Tenant Act 1954 referred to all the persons who were granted the tenancy or their successors in title.

That decision was reversed by the introduction of s.41A of the 1954 Act in so far as it relates to business partners (see below) but continues to have effect in relation to joint tenants who are not partners. For example, two persons carrying on separate businesses (such as barristers in a set of chambers) may have taken a lease jointly and shared the accommodation. At the expiry of the lease one of the tenants may have gone out of business and left. By virtue of the decision in *Jacobs v Chaudhuri*, the other cannot apply for a new tenancy on his own.

However, it may be possible for all the joint tenants to apply on behalf of those who remain in occupation. The application would be made pursuant to s.41 of the 1954 Act (the trustee provision—see above). The argument would be that all the joint tenants hold the lease on trust for those tenants who remain in occupation and that by virtue of s.41 the carrying on of the business by the beneficiary (the tenant who is still in occupation) is equivalent to a carrying on by the trustees (all the joint tenants) who may therefore exercise the statutory right to apply for a new tenancy (*Jacobs v Chaudhuri*, per Harman J at p.129).

Landlord and Tenant Act 1954 s.41A

41A.—(1) The following provisions of this section shall apply where— **2–27**

    (a)   a tenancy is held jointly by two or more persons (in this section referred to as the joint tenants); and

    (b)   the property comprised in the tenancy is or includes premises occupied for the purposes of a business; and

    (c)   the business (or some other business) was at some time during the existence of the tenancy carried on in partnership by all the persons who were then the joint tenants or by those and other persons and the joint tenants' interest in the premises was then partnership property; and

    (d)   the business is carried on (whether alone or in partnership with other persons) by one or some only of the joint tenants and no part of the property comprised in the tenancy is occupied, in right of the tenancy, for the purposes of a business carried on (whether alone or in partnership with other persons) by the other or others.

(2) In the following provisions of this section those of the joint tenants who for the time being carry on the business are referred to as the business tenants and the others as the other joint tenants.

(3) Any notice given by the business tenants which, had it been given by all the joint tenants, would have been—

(a) a tenant's request for anew tenancy made in accordance with section 26 of this Act; or

(b) a notice under subsection (1) or subsection (2) of section 27 of this Act; shall be treated as such if it states that it is given by virtue of this section and sets out the facts by virtue of which the persons giving it are the business tenants;

and references in those sections and in section 24A of this Act to the tenant shall be construed accordingly.

(4) A notice given by the landlord to the business tenants which, had it been given to all the joint tenants, would have been a notice under section 25 of this Act shall be treated as such a notice, and references in that section to the tenant shall be construed accordingly.

(5) An application under section 24(1) of this Act for a new tenancy may, instead of being made by all the joint tenants, be made by the business tenants alone; and where it is so made—

(a) this Part of this Act shall have effect, in relation to it, as if the references therein to the tenant included references to the business tenants alone; and

(b) the business tenants shall be liable, to the exclusion of the other joint tenants, for the payment of rent and the discharge of any other obligation under the current tenancy for any rental period beginning after the date specified in the landlord's notice under section 25 of this Act or, as the case my be, beginning on or after the date specified in their request for a new tenancy.

(6) Where the court makes an order under section 29 of this Act for the grant of a new tenancy it may order the grant to be made to the business tenants or to them jointly with the persons carrying on the business in partnership with them, and may order the grant to be made subject to the satisfaction, within a time specified by the order, of such conditions as to guarantors, sureties or otherwise as appear to the court equitable, having regard to the omission of the other joint tenants from the persons who will be the tenants under the new tenancy.

(7) The business tenants shall be entitled to recover any amount payable by way of compensation under section 37 or section 59 of this Act.

Excluded tenancies

2-28   There are a number of circumstances in which a tenancy will not be protected by the provisions of Pt II of the 1954 Act. The

Act of course applies only to tenancies (para.2–01) and so a licence of business premises will not be protected (see Ch.6).

Note that the mere fact that a tenancy is excluded from the rights afforded by the 1954 Act does not mean that the Act does not apply to any sub-tenancy (para.1–04). Thus, a landlord may be bound by the interest of a sub-tenant even though the 1954 Act does not apply to his immediate tenant (see further in relation to service of notices; para.14–16 by landlord and para.15–07 by tenant).

Tenancies at will

The business tenancy code does not apply to a tenancy at will **2–29** as such a "tenancy" does not fall within the definition of "tenancy" in s.69(1) of the 1954 Act (*Hagee (London) Ltd v Erikson (AB) and Larson* [1975] 3 All E.R. 234; para.2–02). It is not therefore necessary for a landlord to serve a s.25 notice to bring a tenancy at will to an end. A tenancy at will exists where a tenancy is created on terms that either party may determine at any time (e.g. see para.4–11).

Farm Business Tenancies and Agricultural holdings

Farm business tenancies and Agricultural holdings are excluded **2–30** from the provisions of the Act by s.43(1)(a) and s.43(1)(aa): see above para.2–13.

Mining leases

By virtue of s.43(1)(b) of the 1954 Act mining leases are **2–31** excluded from the provisions of the Act.

Licensed premises

Prior to the Landlord and Tenant (Licensed Premises) Act 1990, **2–32** public houses were not subject to the 1954 Act. Some other licensed premises such as hotels and restaurants were subject to the Act (s.43(1)(d)). The 1990 Act changed the position so that any tenancy of licensed premises granted on or after July 11, 1989 (otherwise than in pursuance of a contract made before that date) is protected by the 1954 Act.

Further, s.43(1)(d) ceased to have effect from July 11, 1992 in relation to any old unprotected tenancy, which was still in existence at that date (s.1(2) of the 1990 Act).

Office holders and employees

2-33 By virtue of s.43(2) of the 1954 Act, the Act does not apply where the tenancy was granted because the tenant was the holder of an office, appointment or employment and where the tenancy continues only so long as that office, appointment or employment continues. If the tenancy was granted after the 1954 Act came into force, the exclusion applies only if the tenancy was created by a written instrument which expressed the purpose for which the tenancy was granted.

Landlord and Tenant Act 1954 s.43(2)

2-34 **43.**–(2) This Part of this Act does not apply to a tenancy granted by reason that the tenant was the holder of an office, appointment or employment from the grantor thereof and continuing only so long as the tenant holds the office, appointment or employment, or terminable by the grantor on the tenant's ceasing to hold it, or coming to an end at a time fixed by reference to the time at which the tenant ceases to hold it:

Provided that this subsection shall not have effect in relation to a tenancy granted after the commencement of this Act unless the tenancy was granted by an instrument in writing which expressed the purpose for which the tenancy was granted.

Tenancies of six months or less

Landlord and Tenant Act 1954 s.43(3)

2-35 **43.**–(3) This Part of this Act does not apply to a tenancy granted for a term certain not exceeding six months unless—

(a) the tenancy contains provision for renewing the term or for extending it beyond six months from its beginning; or
(b) the tenant has been in occupation for a period which, together with any period during which any predecessor in the carrying on of the business carried on by the tenant was in occupation, exceeds twelve months.

The Act does not apply to a tenancy of six months or less unless the tenancy contains an option for renewing the term or extending it beyond the period of six months or the tenant has been in occupation for more than 12 months (or the period of the tenant's occupation plus that of any predecessor carrying on the same business is more than 12 months). The continuation of the occupation must be as a tenant, properly so called. Extension by a tenancy at will not suffice.

> "Thereafter the plaintiff remained in occupation of the premises but not as a tenant. It was a tenant at will. It seems to me that whether it was a tenant at will, a licensee or a trespasser, it cannot be right that a period of occupation in any of those capacities could retrospectively resurrect a tenancy that had expired by effluxion of time and bring it within the 1954 Act." (*Cricket Ltd v Shaftesbury plc* [1999] 2 E.G.L.R. 57, Neuberger J)

Query whether a tenant who has taken over a business of a person who was not a tenant (e.g. a freeholder or licensee) can one take into account the previous period of occupation by the predecessor?

Periodic tenancies are not covered by the exception. Thus, a periodic tenancy even if it has continued for less than six months is a tenancy to which the Act applies.

Leasehold enfranchisement

Where a tenant has acquired an extended tenancy of a house **2–36** and premises pursuant to s.14 of the Leasehold Reform Act 1967, the 1954 Act does not apply to the property in the extended tenancy (s.16(1)(c) of the 1967 Act). Nor does it apply after the extended term date to any sub-tenancy derived out of that tenancy (s.16(1)(d)). The position is the same in respect of a new lease acquired under s.56 of the Leasehold Reform, Housing and Urban Development Act 1993 (s.59(2)(b)(ii) of the 1993 Act).

Public bodies, national security, development areas and the Church

Section 56 of and Sch.8 to the 1954 Act deals with the **2–37** application of the Act to the Crown. Section 57 modifies the Act in respect of a number of public bodies so as to exclude the right to apply for a new tenancy where the public interest requires it. Section 58 excludes rights under the Act in cases of national security. Section 59 makes provision for compensation to be paid where ss.57–58 are relied upon to deprive a tenant of his right to a new tenancy under the Act. Section 60 makes special provision requiring the court to include a term in the tenancy excluding rights to assign or sub-let in certain cases where the property is in a "development" or "intermediate" area (terms which are defined in the section).

There are also miscellaneous exclusions in other Acts not covered in this book.

CHAPTER 3

CONTRACTING OUT OF THE 1954 ACT

- -

Contracting out prima facie void

Landlord and Tenant Act 1954 s.38

38.–(1) Any agreement relating to a tenancy to which this Part of this Act applies (whether contained in the instrument creating the tenancy or not) shall be void (except as provided by section 38A of this Act) in so far as *it purports to preclude* the tenant from making an application or request under this Part of this Act or provides for the termination or the surrender of the tenancy in the event of his making such an application or request or for the imposition of any penalty or disability on the tenant in that event.

3–01

The normal rule is that parties to a tenancy to which Pt II of the Act applies may not contract out of the security provisions of the Act. Any such agreement is void in so far as it:

- purports to preclude the tenant from making an application or request under Pt II of the Act; or
- provides for the termination or surrender of the tenancy in the event of such an application or request (s.38(1)).

Note that the reference to surrender in s.38 is a reference to the agreement providing for surrender *in the event of an application or request*. It does not explicitly refer to surrender in any other set of circumstances. However, a straightforward agreement to surrender a tenancy at some future date is also void because *"it purports to preclude"*, that is it has the effect of precluding, the tenant from making such an application, and so is caught under the first limb; see further para.18–10.

Permissible contracting out

Landlord and Tenant Act 1954 s.38A

3-02   **38A.**—(1) The persons who will be the landlord and the tenant in relation to a tenancy to be granted for a term of years certain *which will be a tenancy to which this Part of this Act applies* may agree that the provisions of sections 24 to 28 of this Act shall be excluded in relation to that tenancy.

(3) An agreement under subsection (1) above shall be void unless—

(a)   the landlord has served on the tenant a notice in the form, or substantially in the form, set out in Schedule 1 to the Regulatory Reform (Business Tenancies) (England and Wales) Order 2003 ("the 2003 Order"); and

(b)   the requirements specified in Schedule 2 to that Order are met.

It is possible to enter into an agreement excluding the provisions of ss.24–28 of the 1954 Act (which include the provisions providing for renewal of the tenancy) so long as certain prescribed procedures are complied with.

Under the old law (i.e. prior to June 1, 2004) it was necessary to make an application to the court for approval of the agreement. The 2003 Reform Order provided a completely new system based on notice to the tenant warning him that he will be losing certain rights under the Act. There are some preliminary points to appreciate which are common with the previous regime:

● The proposed transaction must be *a tenancy to which Pt II of the Act applies* (see the wording of s.38(A)(1)). Although the phrase "contracted out lease" is frequently used, the contracting out is merely out of the security provisions in ss.24 to 28. The tenancy must still be a tenancy within s.23, i.e. a "tenancy where the property comprised in the tenancy is or includes premises which are occupied by the tenant . . . for the purposes of a business carried on by him or for those and other purposes". It cannot be a tenancy at will, nor a licence. Indeed if it is either of those, it is not necessary to use the contracting out system because the tenant is not afforded the protection of the Act in the first place (para.2–01).

● The tenancy must be for a term *exceeding six months* or subs.(a) or (b) of s.43(3) must apply (i.e. option to renew or tenant in occupation for a period exceeding 12 months). If not, the Act does not apply to the tenancy (see s.43(3); see para.2–35).

- The tenancy must be "for a *term of years certain*" (s.38(A)(1)), not a periodic tenancy (*Nicholas v Kinsey* [1994] 2 W.L.R. 622–tenancy for a fixed term and thereafter year to year not validly authorised by the court under the old procedures). A fixed term of nine months is "for a term of years certain" for these purposes (*Land and Premises at Liss Hants, Re* [1971] 3 All E.R. 380). The existence of a break clause does not prevent the lease from being for a term of years certain (*Receiver for Metropolitan Police v Palacegate* [2000] 13 E.G. 187). In *London Borough of Newham v Thomas-Van Staden* [2008] EWCA Civ 1414 the lease was granted for a term "from and including [January 1, 2003] to [September 28, 2004] (hereinafter called 'the term' which expression shall *include any period of holding over or extension* of it whether by statute of at common law or by agreement". A court order (under the old system) was obtained, authorising the contracting out of the tenancy. After the initial fixed period had passed the tenant remained in possession. The landlord subsequently wanted possession in order to carry out a redevelopment and served a notice terminating the continuing tenancy (pursuant to a term in the lease). The tenant refused to leave. *Held*: On a true construction of the lease, the term was not for "a term of years certain". It could not therefore be excluded from the provisions of ss.24 to 28; the court order was a nullity and the landlord was not entitled to possession.

Procedure for contracting out

The procedure for contracting out is contained in Schs 1 and 2 to the 2003 Reform Order. The relevant notice is in Sch.1 (para.3–21) and the procedural requirements are in Sch.2 (para.3–22). The procedure contains three elements: **3–03**

- Service of a *notice on the tenant* warning him of the consequences of entering into the agreement excluding the protection afforded by ss.24 to 28 and advising him to obtain professional advice.
- Confirmation from the tenant in the form of a *written declaration* that he has received the notice, read it and accepts the consequences of entering into the agreement to contract out.

• *Reference* to the notice, the declaration and the agreement to contract out in the tenancy agreement.

The basic ideal envisaged by Schs 1 and 2 is that the notice should be served not less than 14 days prior to the tenant entering into the tenancy, or if earlier becoming contractually bound to do so (i.e. under an agreement for a lease). However, the scheme does recognise that it is not always possible to comply with such a deadline. Hence, there are slightly different procedures depending upon whether the 14-day deadline can be met or not. The precise details are as follows.

The usual case—14 days' notice

3-04   *Notice:* a notice must be served on the tenant not less than 14 days before the tenant enters into the tenancy to which it applies or, if earlier, becomes contractually bound to do so. The notice served must be *in the form, or substantially in the form,* set out in Sch.1 to the 2003 Reform Order. The form contains what has been described as a "health warning", telling the tenant in no uncertain terms that the security provisions of the Act will not apply.

Simple declaration: if 14 days' notice is given the tenant (or a person duly authorised by him to do so) must, before the tenant enters into the tenancy to which the notice applies, or (if earlier) becomes contractually bound to do so, make a declaration (in the notice called a *"simple declaration"*) stating that the notice has been served not less than 14 days before hand, that he has read the notice and accepts the consequences of entering into the agreement. The precise form of this declaration is set out in para.7 of Sch.2. The declaration must be in that form or substantially in that form (para.7 of Sch.2).

Although the rules say that the tenant must make a simple declaration, if in fact the tenant makes a statutory declaration (see below) that will still be effective (*The Chiltern Railway Co Ltd v Patel* [2008] EWCA Civ 178). Lord Neuberger at para.11:

"It would . . . be 'bordering on the absurd' if a statutory declaration was held to be ineffective on the grounds that it differed from the prescribed form because a) it was both expressly and in law in a more solemn form than that form; and b) although it stated that notice was served before the lease was entered into, it did not state that it was served more than fourteen days before the lease was entered into."

14-day requirement not met

Notice: if it is not possible to meet the 14-day requirement for service of the notice, it must still be served on the tenant before the tenant enters into the tenancy to which it applies, or (if earlier) becomes contractually bound to do so.

3–05

Statutory declaration: if it has not been possible to meet the 14-day requirement the tenant, or a person duly authorised by him to do so, must make a statutory declaration before the tenancy is entered into or (if earlier) the tenant becomes contractually bound stating that the notice has been served, that he has read the notice and accepts the consequences of entering into the agreement. The *statutory declaration* must be in the form, or substantially in the form, set out in para.8 of Sch.2 to the 2003 Reform Order (para.4 of Sch.2). See para.3–22.

Comment: there is no requirement for the solicitor or commissioner for oaths before whom the declaration is made to give the tenant any advice.

Explanation: it will be difficult for the reader who did not follow the process leading up to the making of these provisions to understand why there should be a statutory declaration if less than 14 days' notice is given, with the extra costs required, and only a "simple declaration" if the full 14 days' notice is given. Originally, only the statutory declaration was proposed, in relation to cases where it was not possible to give 14 days' notice. It was thought that this extra burden might give the tenant some extra protection:

"This alternative procedure is less administratively convenient than the advance warning procedure, and it is hoped that this will deter abuse." (ODPM).

However, when the proposals went to Parliament for approval, the House of Commons committee considering the changes wanted each tenant to sign a declaration of some sort that he had read the notice and understood its implications. This led to the "simple declaration".

Reference to the notice, declaration and the agreement in the tenancy

3–06   *Notice and declaration*: whether or not the 14-day requirement was met, a reference to the notice and to the declaration (simple or statutory) must be contained in, or endorsed on, the instrument creating the tenancy (para.5 of Sch.2).

Agreement: the agreement to exclude the provisions of ss.24 to 28 of the Act or a reference to it must be contained in or endorsed upon the instrument creating the tenancy (para.6 of Sch.2).

Comment: if the tenant has signed a declaration that he has received the notice and that declaration is referred to in the tenancy (as required by the provisions) it is difficult to see how the tenant will ever be able to deny that the notice was given and to deny that the notice given related to the tenancy that was eventually signed. However, in order to ensure that problems relating to proof are avoided, the author suggests that the original declaration (which contains a copy of the form of the notice) be attached to the counterpart lease and that a copy be attached to the original tenancy. It is also suggested that the agreement contracting out and the reference to the notice and to the declaration be placed immediately above the place where the tenant signs the tenancy.

Suggested wording for the agreement and the reference to the notice and declaration (with appropriate variations depending upon the circumstances) is as follows:

> "It is hereby agreed that the provisions of ss.24–28 of the Landlord and Tenant Act 1954 do not apply to the tenancy created by this lease.
>
> A notice in the form set out in Schedule 1 of The Regulatory Reform (Business Tenancies) (England and Wales) Order 2003 ("the 2003 Reform Order") was served on the Tenant by the Landlord [not less than 14 days]

before the Tenant entered into the tenancy created by this lease.

Before entering into the tenancy created by this lease the [Tenant /.................. ......being a person duly authorised by the Tenant] made a declaration in the form set out in paragraph [7/8] of Schedule 2 of the 2003 Reform Order. A copy of the declaration is attached to this lease. [The original declaration is attached to this counterpart lease]."

Issues arising out of the service and contents of the notice and declaration

Does the notice need to be served on "the tenant"? Or can it be served on an agent?

The authors' view is that the notice can be served on a person who has actual or ostensible authority to receive it. If so, requiring confirmation from the tenant's agent (usually a solicitor) that he has authority is an obvious cautionary step to take; confirmation from the tenant would be even safer. Others have argued that the notice should be served on the actual tenant because it is so clearly addressed to him. It has also been suggested that the fact that Sch.2 expressly states that a "person duly authorised" may sign the simple or statutory declaration (see Sch.2 paras 3 and 4) implies that such a person may not receive the notice. The view of the author is that this is incorrect. The express reference to the signature of a duly authorised person in that context is surely only intended to make it clear that where there is a corporate tenant the declaration should be signed by an authorised person. However, if a landlord is in any doubt the safest course is to serve the notice directly on the tenant.

3-07

Is it necessary to attach the proposed tenancy agreement to the notice?

The answer is "no". Although paras 2 and 4 of Sch.2 link the tenancy to service of the notice by the words "the tenancy to which it applies", the details of the tenancy are not actually referred to in the notice and there is no express requirement to attach the tenancy agreement to the notice.

3-08

It has been suggested that in some cases it might be wise to attach the proposed tenancy to the notice in order to establish that the notice does indeed relate to the tenancy. For example, a number of different properties might have been the subject of negotiations. There could be some confusion as to precisely which property the tenancy relates. However, taking this step might lead to problems if the tenancy agreement as completed is not exactly the same as the draft attached to the notice. (Compare the position under the old law—see *Palacegate Properties Ltd* referred to below: para.3-15.) Surely it is better to attach the declaration (confirming that the notice was served) to the counterpart lease (as suggested above; para.3-06).

How long before the tenancy can the notice be served? Can it be served before the heads of terms? Can it be served before the tenancy agreement is drafted?

3-09   It is quite clear that there is no link between the notice and the heads of terms or a draft tenancy agreement etc. The notice itself does not give *any* details of the specific tenancy. It should be borne in mind that the purpose of the changes brought about by the 2003 Reform Order was to make life easier for landlords and tenants. They are not designed to create new traps. There is a clear intention to protect the tenant but the protection is simply to ensure that he realises that he is entering into a tenancy that will not have the protection afforded by ss.24 to 28. The precise terms of the tenancy are surely irrelevant.

What happens if the notice is served but for some reason the tenant does not enter into the tenancy agreement for a considerable period of time?

3-10   The declaration (simple or statutory) does require the tenant to identify the premises and the commencement date, thereby creating a link between the notice and the tenancy. If there is a long period of delay it may be that the link between the notice and the tenancy will be considered to have been broken requiring a fresh notice. However, once again it is difficult to see how any of this can cause a problem given that the declaration confirms that a notice has been served before entry into "the tenancy", particularly if the declaration is attached to the counterpart lease (see para.3-06). Surely, there can then be no doubt that a notice relating to that tenancy has been served?

How can I be sure that the tenant is signing the correct declaration?

Where the notice was served round about the period of 14 days **3-11** before the tenancy or agreement for a lease is due to be signed, the landlord may be unsure as to whether or not the correct declaration is being signed. The answer is to use a "statutory declaration". Use of such a declaration will not be held to be invalid if in fact all that was required was a simple declaration (see *The Chiltern Railway Co Ltd v Patel*, para.3-04 above).

What is the commencement date that should be stated in the declaration?

The declaration uses the phrase "for a term commencing on". **3-12** Does this mean the date of the grant or the commencement date as defined in the lease from which the period of the term is calculated? What if neither date is known at the date of the declaration? Presumably, if the date of the grant is the commencement date for the term and the tenancy is granted later than the commencement date stated in the declaration the agreement to contract out will still be valid so long as the notice still relates to the same tenancy. Once again that link can be established by attaching the declaration to the lease (see para.3-06).

If the declaration is signed by one person in relation to an agreement to enter into a tenancy and a subsequent person actually takes the tenancy (perhaps another company in a group) is it necessary to serve a further notice and require a further declaration?

In the view of the authors para.4 of Sch.2 makes it clear that **3-13** only one notice is required. Note the use of the word "or". Further, it is difficult to see that there can be any justification for requiring the landlord to serve another notice. The agreement is binding and the lease must be taken. If the benefit of the agreement has been assigned, it is the benefit of a contracted out lease that has been taken. The party to the agreement to the lease will already have signed a declaration that he has received the notice.

> *Is it necessary to serve a fresh notice before a tenant enters into a new lease pursuant to an option clause in a contracted out lease giving him the right to renew?*

3–14   Section 38A(1) states that the persons "who will be the landlord and the tenant in relation to *a tenancy to be granted*" may agree to contract out. This is a fresh tenancy and so a new notice needs to be served. Further, para.2 of Sch.2 states that the notice must be served not less than 14 days before the tenant enters into the tenancy to which it applies "or (if earlier) becomes contractually bound to do so" (see also para.4). Here there is a potential trap for landlords. The parties become contractually bound when the tenant serves the notice exercising the option. How is the landlord to know whether or not the tenant is going to exercise the option? There is often a limited time period during which options can be exercised and so it may be that service of the notice some time just before that period might be sufficient. It is necessary to consider carefully the drafting of option clauses. Perhaps the tenant should be required to give the landlord sufficient notice of his intention to exercise the option so as to give the landlord the opportunity to serve the Sch.1 notice on the tenant.

Transitional provisions

Existing contracted out tenancies

3–15   There are still leases in existence that were excluded under the previous s.38 provisions of the 1954 Act. Nothing in the 2003 Reform Order "has effect in relation to an agreement . . . which was authorised by the court under section 38(4) before this Order came into force" on June 1, 2004 (Art.29(2)(a)(ii)). Note that it was the date of authorisation that was relevant. If an order authorising contracting out was made before June 1, 2004 the lease will (in the author's view) be validly contracted out even if entered into after that date. (Note also that there is a further transitional provision that allows the court to make orders under the old s.38(4) on or after June 1, 2004 where there was an agreement to take a tenancy made before that date; see below, para.3–21.)

In the case of some old leases it will be necessary to consider whether or not the lease was validly excluded under the old s.38(4). Key points to note in relation to the old s.38 are as follows:

- The terms of the final lease must be substantially similar to those that were before the court but need not necessarily be identical. "In particular, changes material to the need for protection may nullify the authority granted. For example, the length of the term would be a material consideration in the case of a lease that contemplated substantial capital expenditure by the tenant." (*Receiver for Metropolitan Police v Palacegate Properties Ltd* [2000] 1 E.G.L.R. 63 CA, Pill LJ—rent under the draft lease payable annually in arrears. Under the lease as actually agreed it was payable quarterly in advance. However, this difference was held to be irrelevant. It had no bearing on security.)
- An exclusion agreement that was binding upon the parties pursuant to the principle in *Walsh v Lonsdale* (1882) 21 Ch. D. 9 (see para.4–18) is effective under the old s.38(4) even though no lease was ever formally executed (*Tottenham Hotspur Football & Athletic Co Ltd v Princegrove Publishers Ltd* [1974] 1 W.L.R. 113 QBD). In *Tottenham Hotspur*, an existing landlord and tenant settled an application for a new tenancy at court by providing for a new lease to be granted for one year. It was agreed that ss.24–28 of the Act would not apply to the new tenancy. The judge made a consent order in the precise terms of the compromise agreement and thus gave his approval to the exclusion agreement. No formal lease was ever executed and at the end of the year the tenant refused to leave. The court held that the exclusion agreement was effective and made an order for possession.
- In *Brighton and Hove City Council v Collinson* [2004] 21 E.G. 150, the lease was to be granted to a company controlled by two brothers who were directors. The application named *the company and the brothers as respondents*. The draft lease that was attached named the *company as tenant and the brothers as guarantors*. After the contracting out order was made the brothers requested that the lease be granted *to them personally*, and not to the company. The landlord agreed and the lease was so granted. Subsequently the issue arose as to whether or not the lease was validly contracted out. *Held*: The brothers were party to the application and the lease was granted to them. The fact that they were not named as parties to the lease on the draft attached to the

application did not matter. The important thing was that the prospective tenant should understand that he was foregoing the security protection afforded by the Act. The court order was the governing document, not the draft lease. An overly technical view should not be taken of the rules; and one should look at the purpose of the system when deciding whether or not it has been carried out defectively.

The consequences of failure to obtain approval *prior* to the grant of the original lease is illustrated by *Essexcrest Ltd v Evenlex Ltd* [1988] 1 E.G.L.R. 69. The parties obtained the court's approval *after* the lease was executed. At the end of the term the tenant applied for a new tenancy. The landlord's contention that the tenant's rights had been validly excluded was rejected.

Another potential pitfall was demonstrated by the case of *Nicholas v Kinsey* [1994] 1 E.G.L.R. 131; [1994] 2 W.L.R. 622 CA). As with the present s.38 the old s.38(4)(a) provided that the court could authorise an agreement excluding ss.24–28 of the Act if the tenancy was "for a term of years certain". In that case, the tenancy was expressed to be for a fixed term and thereafter from year to year. The court therefore had no power to authorise an agreement excluding the Act but in error had done so. The Court of Appeal held that the order was invalid and that the tenant was able to apply for a new tenancy. A fixed term of nine months is for a "term of years certain" (*Land and Premises at Liss Hants, Re* [1971] 3 All E.R. 380).

See also *London Borough of Newham v Thomas-Van Staden* (para.3–02 above) where lease was granted for a term "from and including [January 1, 2003] to [September 28, 2004] (hereinafter called 'the term' which expression shall include any period of holding over or extension of it whether by statute of at common law or by agreement". This was held not to be "for a term of years certain" so that the contracting out was not valid. A fixed term of nine months is "for a term of years certain" (*Land and Premises at Liss Hants, Re* [1971] 3 All E.R. 380).

Landlord and Tenant Act 1954 s.38 (as it existed prior to June 1, 2004)

3–16 **38.**–(1) Any agreement relating to a tenancy to which this Part of this Act applies (whether contained in the instrument creating the tenancy or not) shall be void (except as provided by subsection (4) of this section) in so far as it purports to preclude the tenant from making an application or request under this Part of this Act or provides for the termination or the surrender of the tenancy in the event of his making such an application or request or for the imposition of any penalty or disability on the tenant in that event.

. . .

(4) The court may:

(a) on the joint application of the persons who will be the landlord and the tenant in relation to a tenancy to be granted for a term of years certain which will be a tenancy to which this part of this Act applies, authorise an agreement excluding in relation to that tenancy the provisions of sections 24 to 28 of this Act; and

(b) on the joint application of the persons who are the landlord and the tenant in relation to a tenancy to which this Part of this Act applies, authorise an agreement for the surrender of the tenancy on such date or in such circumstances as may be specified in the agreement and on such terms (if any) as may be so specified;

if the agreement is contained in or endorsed on the instrument creating the tenancy or such other instrument as the court may specify; and an agreement contained in or endorsed on an instrument in pursuance of an authorisation given under this subsection shall be valid notwithstanding anything in the preceding provisions of this section.

Covenants for subletting

Certain covenants in existing leases, which make provision for subletting, are incompatible with the new law as they refer specifically to the old s.38 procedures. Such a covenant will usually require a tenant wishing to sublet first to obtain an order from the court under the old s.38 approving an agreement for the exclusion of security of tenure from the prospective subletting. Following the abolition of s.38 court orders, it is impossible to comply with such covenants. The 2003 Reform Order (Art 29(3)) therefore provides that any references to the procedures under s.38, in leases taken out before the reforms came into effect on June 1, 2004, are to be construed as references to use of the modified s.38 procedures.

3-17

Article 29 of the 2003 Order

29.–(3) Any provision in a tenancy which requires an order under s.38(4) of the Act to be obtained in respect of any subtenancy shall, so far as is necessary after the coming into force of this Order, be construed as if it

3-18

required the procedure mentioned in s.38A of the Act to be followed, and any related requirement shall be construed accordingly.

Agreements for lease

3-19   In the case of agreements for lease entered into before June 1, 2004 (if there are any left in existence), the old arrangements for joint applications to the court before entering into an agreement to exclude security of tenure have been preserved (art.29(4)).

Art.29(4) of the 2003 Order

3-20   **29.**–(4) If a person has, before the coming into force of this Order, entered into an agreement to take a tenancy, any provision in that agreement which requires an order under s.38(4) of the Act to be obtained in respect of the tenancy shall continue to be effective, notwithstanding the repeal of that provision by Article 21(2) of this Order, and the court shall retain jurisdiction to make such an order.

3-21

Form 1

SCHEDULE 1

FORM OF NOTICE THAT SECTIONS 24 TO 28 OF THE LANDLORD AND TENANT ACT 1954 ARE NOT TO APPLY TO A BUSINESS TENANCY

To:

....

....

....

[Name and address of tenant]

From:

....

....

....

[Name and address of landlord]

cont

---

cont

IMPORTANT NOTICE

You are being offered a lease without security of tenure. Do not commit yourself to the lease unless you have read this message carefully and have discussed it with a professional adviser.

Business tenants normally have security of tenure—the right to stay in their business premises when the lease ends.

If you commit yourself to the lease you will be giving up these important legal rights.

- You will have **no right** to stay in the premises when the lease ends.

- Unless the landlord chooses to offer you another lease, you will need to leave the premises.

- You will be unable to claim compensation for the loss of your business premises, unless the lease specifically gives you this right.

- If the landlord offers you another lease, you will have no right to ask the court to fix the rent.

It is therefore important to get professional advice—from a qualified surveyor, lawyer or accountant—before agreeing to give up these rights.

If you want to ensure that you can stay in the same business premises when the lease ends, you should consult your adviser about another form of lease that does not exclude the protection of the Landlord and Tenant Act 1954.

If you receive this notice at least 14 days before committing yourself to the lease, you will need to sign a simple declaration that you have received this notice and have accepted its consequences, before signing the lease.

But if you do not receive at least 14 days notice, you will need to sign a "statutory" declaration. To do so, you will need to visit an independent solicitor (or someone else empowered to administer oaths).

Unless there is a special reason for committing yourself to the lease sooner, you may want to ask the landlord to let you have at least 14 days to consider whether you wish to give up your statutory rights. If you then decided to go ahead with the agreement to exclude the protection of the Landlord and Tenant Act 1954, you would only need to make a simple declaration, and so you would not need to make a separate visit to an independent solicitor.

cont

3-22

cont

SCHEDULE 2

REQUIREMENTS FOR A VALID AGREEMENT THAT SECTIONS 24 TO 28 OF THE LANDLORD AND TENANT ACT 1954 ARE NOT TO APPLY TO A BUSINESS TENANCY

1. The following are the requirements referred to in section 38A(3)(b) of the Act.

2. Subject to paragraph 4, the notice referred to in section 38A(3)(a) of the Act must be served on the tenant not less than 14 days before the tenant enters into the tenancy to which it applies, or (if earlier) becomes contractually bound to do so.

3. If the requirement in paragraph 2 is met, the tenant, or a person duly authorised by him to do so, must, before the tenant enters into the tenancy to which the notice applies, or (if earlier) becomes contractually bound to do so, make a declaration in the form, or substantially in the form, set out in paragraph 7.

4. If the requirement in paragraph 2 is not met, the notice referred to in section 38A(3)(a) of the Act must be served on the tenant before the tenant enters into the tenancy to which it applies, or (if earlier) becomes contractually bound to do so, and the tenant, or a person duly authorised by him to do so, must before that time make a statutory declaration in the form, or substantially in the form, set out in paragraph 8.

5. A reference to the notice and, where paragraph 3 applies, the declaration or, where paragraph 4 applies, the statutory declaration must be contained in or endorsed on the instrument creating the tenancy.

6. The agreement under section 38A(1) of the Act, or a reference to the agreement, must be contained in or endorsed upon the instrument creating the tenancy.

7. The form of declaration referred to in paragraph 3 is as follows:–

I

....

(*name of declarant*) of

....

(*address*) declare that—

1. I

....

(*name of tenant*) propose(s) to enter into a tenancy of premises at

cont

cont

....

(*address of premises*) for a term commencing on

....

2. I/The tenant propose(s) to enter into an agreement with

....

(*name of landlord*) that the provisions of sections 24 to 28 of the Landlord and Tenant Act 1954 (security of tenure) shall be excluded in relation to the tenancy.

3. The landlord has, not less than 14 days before I/the tenant enter(s) into the tenancy, or (if earlier) become(s) contractually bound to do so served on me/the tenant a notice in the form, or substantially in the form, set out in Schedule 1 to the Regulatory Reform (Business Tenancies) (England and Wales) Order 2003. The form of notice set out in that Schedule is reproduced below.

4. I have/The tenant has read the notice referred to in paragraph 3 above and accept(s) the consequences of entering into the agreement referred to in paragraph 2 above.

5. (*as appropriate*) I am duly authorised by the tenant to make this declaration.

DECLARED this

....

day of

....

FORM OF NOTICE THAT SECTIONS 24 TO 28 OF THE LANDLORD AND TENANT ACT 1954 ARE NOT TO APPLY TO A BUSINESS TENANCY

To:

....

....

....

[*Name and address of tenant*]

From:

....

....

....

[*Name and address of landlord*]

cont

cont

IMPORTANT NOTICE

You are being offered a lease without security of tenure. Do not commit yourself to the lease unless you have read this message carefully and have discussed it with a professional adviser.

Business tenants normally have security of tenure—the right to stay in their business premises when the lease ends.

If you commit yourself to the lease you will be giving up these important legal rights.

- You will have **no right** to stay in the premises when the lease ends.

- Unless the landlord chooses to offer you another lease, you will need to leave the premises.

- You will be unable to claim compensation for the loss of your business premises, unless the lease specifically gives you this right.

- If the landlord offers you another lease, you will have no right to ask the court to fix the rent.

It is therefore important to get professional advice—from a qualified surveyor, lawyer or accountant—before agreeing to give up these rights.

If you want to ensure that you can stay in the same business premises when the lease ends, you should consult your adviser about another form of lease that does not exclude the protection of the Landlord and Tenant Act 1954.

If you receive this notice at least 14 days before committing yourself to the lease, you will need to sign a simple declaration that you have received this notice and have accepted its consequences, before signing the lease.

But if you do not receive at least 14 days notice, you will need to sign a "statutory" declaration. To do so, you will need to visit an independent solicitor (or someone else empowered to administer oaths).

Unless there is a special reason for committing yourself to the lease sooner, you may want to ask the landlord to let you have at least 14 days to consider whether you wish to give up your statutory rights. If you then decided to go ahead with the agreement to exclude the protection of the Landlord and Tenant Act 1954, you would only need to make a simple declaration, and so you would not need to make a separate visit to an independent solicitor.

cont

cont

8. The form of statutory declaration referred to in paragraph 4 is as follows:–

I

....

(*name of declarant*) of

....

(*address*) do solemnly and sincerely declare that—

1. I

....

(*name of tenant*) propose(s) to enter into a tenancy of premises at

....

(*address of premises*) for a term commencing on

....

2. I/The tenant propose(s) to enter into an agreement with (name of landlord) that the provisions of sections 24 to 28 of the Landlord and Tenant Act 1954 (security of tenure) shall be excluded in relation to the tenancy.

3. The landlord has served on me/the tenant a notice in the form, or substantially in the form, set out in Schedule 1 to the Regulatory Reform (Business Tenancies) (England and Wales) Order 2003. The form of notice set out in that Schedule is reproduced below.

4. I have/The tenant has read the notice referred to in paragraph 3 above and accept(s) the consequences of entering into the agreement referred to in paragraph 2 above.

5. (*as appropriate*) I am duly authorised by the tenant to make this declaration.

FORM OF NOTICE THAT SECTIONS 24 TO 28 OF THE LANDLORD AND TENANT ACT 1954 ARE NOT TO APPLY TO A BUSINESS TENANCY

To:

....

....

....

[*Name and address of tenant*]

cont

---

cont

From:

....

....

....

[*Name and address of landlord*]

IMPORTANT NOTICE

You are being offered a lease without security of tenure. Do not commit yourself to the lease unless you have read this message carefully and have discussed it with a professional adviser.

Business tenants normally have security of tenure—the right to stay in their business premises when the lease ends.

If you commit yourself to the lease you will be giving up these important legal rights.

- You will have **no right** to stay in the premises when the lease ends.

- Unless the landlord chooses to offer you another lease, you will need to leave the premises.

- You will be unable to claim compensation for the loss of your business premises, unless the lease specifically gives you this right.

- If the landlord offers you another lease, you will have no right to ask the court to fix the rent.

It is therefore important to get professional advice—from a qualified surveyor, lawyer or accountant—before agreeing to give up these rights.

If you want to ensure that you can stay in the same business premises when the lease ends, you should consult your adviser about another form of lease that does not exclude the protection of the Landlord and Tenant Act 1954.

If you receive this notice at least 14 days before committing yourself to the lease, you will need to sign a simple declaration that you have received this notice and have accepted its consequences, before signing the lease.

cont

---

cont

But if you do not receive at least 14 days notice, you will need to sign a "statutory" declaration. To do so, you will need to visit an independent solicitor (or someone else empowered to administer oaths).

Unless there is a special reason for committing yourself to the lease sooner, you may want to ask the landlord to let you have at least 14 days to consider whether you wish to give up your statutory rights. If you then decided to go ahead with the agreement to exclude the protection of the Landlord and Tenant Act 1954, you would only need to make a simple declaration, and so you would not need to make a separate visit to an independent solicitor.

AND I make this solemn declaration conscientiously believing the same to be true and by virtue of the Statutory Declaration Act 1835.

DECLARED at

....

this

....

day of

....

Before me

(*signature of person before whom declaration is made*)

A commissioner for oaths or A solicitor empowered to administer oaths or (*as appropriate*)

cont

CHAPTER 4

POSSESSION WITHOUT A LEASE

. . . .

4-01 The businessman with a new idea is often impatient to get into the property he wants to occupy and to start running his business. The formalities of the law run too slowly. Sometimes he does not bother with the formalities at all. When things go wrong and the owner of the property wishes to remove the occupier the rights of the parties are not always straightforward. This chapter deals with the various types of occupancy and problems that arise when a person enters into occupation of a property otherwise than pursuant to the formal grant of a lease, including the position where the occupier is intending to purchase the freehold or an existing lease. First, it is necessary to consider whether or not a valid tenancy has been created. (Licences are specifically dealt with in Ch.6.)

Has a tenancy been created?

The requirement of certainty

4-02 A fundamental requirement of all leases and tenancy agreements is that the commencement date and the duration of the term must be certain. The parties must be able to ascertain the maximum duration of the term at the outset of the tenancy. If it is not possible to do so the lease is void. However, if the tenant takes possession and pays rent on a periodic basis in accordance with the terms of the agreement so far as they are consistent with a periodic tenancy, such a tenancy is certain because each party has the power to determine it by service of an appropriate notice to quit (*Prudential Assurance Co Ltd v London Residuary Body* [1992] 2 A.C. 386).

The requirement of certainty was raised in *Mexfield Housing Co-operative v Berrisford* [2012] 1 AC 995 where the agreement was stated to run "from month to month until determined as provided by this agreement." The only term in relation to termination by the landlord was for re-entry in the event of default by the tenant. As there was no ability for the landlord to determine the tenancy by a notice to quit, it was for an uncertain term. However, it took effect as a 90 year lease determinable on death (by virtue of s.149 of the Law of Property Act 1925), which could otherwise only be determined in accordance with the right of re-entry clause in the agreement. It could not be determined, as was argued by the landlord, by a one-month notice to quit.

Granting a tenancy to oneself

A contract granting a tenancy involves the creation of mutual rights and obligations that can be given any meaning only if the contract is between two independent parties. No person can contract with himself. A nominee cannot therefore grant a lease to his principal—see *Ingram v Inland Revenue Commissioners* [1995] 4 All E.R. 334 Ch D. In this case, a lease purportedly granted by a solicitor, who held the freehold of a property as nominee for a client, to that client, pursuant to a tax avoidance scheme, was a nullity (see further "Merger", para.19–16).

4–03

Fixed terms

Where the tenancy is for a fixed term of more than three years it must be created by deed. If it is not created by deed it will be void (unless a periodic tenancy can be implied or it operates as an equitable lease; see below, para.4–18). A fixed term of three years or less, may be granted either orally or in writing if it takes effect in possession (i.e. if it takes effect from the time it is created) at the best rent which can be reasonably obtained without taking a fine (see ss.52 and 54(2) of the Law of Property Act 1925). A lease is regarded as being for a term of more than three years even if it contains a term permitting termination within that period (*Kushner v Law Society* [1952] 1 All E.R. 404).

4–04

Law of Property Act 1925

52.–(1) All conveyances of land or of any interest therein are void for the purpose of conveying or creating a legal estate unless made by deed.
(2) This section does not apply to—
...

    (d)   leases or tenancies ... not required by law to be made in writing

4–05

. . .

. . .

    (g)   conveyances taking effect by operation of law.

53.–(1) Subject to the provisions hereinafter contained with respect to the creation of interests in land by parol–

    (a)   no interest in land can be created or disposed of except by writing signed by the person creating or conveying the same or by his agent thereunto lawfully authorised in writing, or by will, or by operation in law; . . .

54.–(1) All interests in land created by parol and not put in writing and signed by the persons so creating the same, or by their agents thereunto lawfully authorised in writing, have, notwithstanding any consideration having been given for the same, the force and effect of interest at will only.

(2) Nothing in the foregoing provisions of this Part of this Act shall affect the creation by parol of leases taking effect in possession for a term not exceeding three years (whether or not the lessee is given power to extend the term) at the best rent which can be reasonably obtained without taking a fine.

55.–Nothing in the last two foregoing sections shall–

  . . .

    (c)   affect the right to acquire an interest in land by virtue of taking possession;

Creation by deed

4–06   Since July 31, 1990 it has no longer been necessary for an individual to seal a deed. The deed is validly executed if it is duly signed and delivered. The procedure is governed by s.1 of the Law of Property (Miscellaneous Provisions) Act 1989 (as amended). The key provisions of which are set out below:

Law of Property (Miscellaneous Provisions) Act 1989 s.1

4–07   **1.**–(1) Any rule of law which–

    (a)   restricts the substances on which a deed may be written;

    (b)   requires a seal for the valid execution of an instrument as a deed by an individual; or

    (c)   requires authority by one person to another to deliver an instrument as a deed on his behalf to be given by deed, is abolished.

    (2) An instrument shall not be a deed unless–

    (a)   it makes it clear on its face that it is intended to be a deed by the person making it or, as the case may be, by the parties to it (whether by describing itself as a deed or expressing itself to be executed or signed as a deed or otherwise); and

(b)   it is validly executed as a deed—
  (i)   by that person or a person authorised to execute it in the name or on behalf of that person, or
  (ii) by one or more of those parties or a person authorised to execute it in the name or on behalf of one or more of those parties.

(2A) For the purposes of subsection (2)(a) above, an instrument shall not be taken to make it clear on its face that it is intended to be a deed merely because it is executed under seal.

(3) An instrument is validly executed as a deed by an individual if, and only if—

(a)   it is signed—
  (i)   by him in the presence of a witness who attests the signature; or
  (ii) at his direction and in his presence and the presence of two witnesses who each attest the signature; and

(b)   it is delivered as a deed. . . .

(4) In subsections (2) and (3) above "sign", in relation to an instrument, includes—

(a)   an individual signing the name of the person or party on whose behalf he executes the instrument; and
(b)   making one's mark on the instrument, and "signature" is to be construed accordingly.

(4A) Subsection (3) above applies in the case of an instrument executed by an individual in the name or on behalf of another person whether or not that person is also an individual.

(5) Where a solicitor, duly certificated notary public or licensed conveyancer, or an agent or employee of a solicitor, duly certificated notary public or licensed conveyancer, in the course of or in connection with a transaction . . . , purports to deliver an instrument as a deed on behalf of a party to the instrument, it shall be conclusively presumed in favour of a purchaser that he is authorised so to deliver the instrument.

In *Longman v Viscount Chelsea* [1989] 2 E.G.L.R. 242 Nourse LJ explained that there are three ways in which a deed may be "delivered":

"First, it may be delivered as an unconditional deed, being irrevocable and taking immediate effect. Second, it may be delivered as an escrow, being irrevocable but not taking effect unless and until the condition or conditions of the escrow are fulfilled. Third, it may be handed to an agent of the maker with instructions to deal with it in a certain way in a certain event, being revocable and of no effect unless and until it is so dealt with, whereupon it is delivered and takes effect." (*Longman v Viscount Chelsea* [1989] 2 E.G.L.R. 242 per Nourse LJ at 245E.)

For an excellent guide to the execution of deeds by individuals and companies see the Land Registry Practice Guide No.8 on the Land Registry website (*http://www.landregistry.gov.uk/professional/guides/practice-guide-8* [accessed November 13, 2014]).

For a case which gives rise to some doubt as to whether or not it is permissible to change the terms of a deed between signing by the client and delivery to the other side see *R. (on the application of Mercury Tax Group Ltd) v HMRC* [2008] EWHC 2721 Admin.

Periodic tenancies

4-08   Periodic tenancies are those that are granted on a yearly, monthly, weekly or indeed any other periodic basis. They are not tenancies just for the period but are tenancies that continue from period to period indefinitely until determined by notice to quit (*Leek and Moorlands Building Society v Clark* [1952] 2 Q.B. 788 at 793). A periodic tenancy may be created by oral agreement (*Hammond v Farrow* [1904] 2 K.B. 332, 335).

A periodic tenancy may come about after the end of a fixed term. In *Macattram v London Borough of Camden* [2012] EWHC 1033 (Admin), Judge at para.17 (and following *Clarke v Grant* [1950] 1 KB 105 CA) set out a useful reminder of how it works:

> "The whole premise of the inference of a periodic tenancy which arises after expiry of a fixed term by virtue of the payment and acceptance of rent is that by their conduct the parties are taken to have agreed to enter into a tenancy. Although the relationship of landlord and tenant continues, the agreement between them is not one of continuation of a previous fixed term that has expired, rather it is the commencement of a new and different term of years, a monthly periodic tenancy. Although that

tenancy is on the same terms and conditions as the previous lease, that again is based on an inference from the party's conduct. Those previous terms only apply insofar as they are not inconsistent with the terms of the new and different tenancy, namely the monthly periodic tenancy."

See further 18–03, where there is a discussion as to whether or not a tenant who holds over is a tenant at sufferance, a tenant at will or a periodic tenant.

The business tenancy code contained in Pt II of the Landlord and Tenant Act 1954 will apply to a periodic tenancy even if it has been in existence for less than six months (see para.2–35). The Act will be excluded only if one of the exceptions applies (see para.2–28).

Estoppel between landlord and tenant

Once the parties have executed a valid lease, or have agreed to become landlord and tenant and the tenant has entered into possession and paid the rent both parties are estopped from denying the tenancy. The landlord cannot derogate from the tenant's grant and the tenant cannot dispute the landlord's title, even if the landlord does not actually have an interest in the land. Thus, if the landlord sues the tenant for possession the tenant cannot defend himself by saying "the property does not belong to you but to another" (*Industrial Properties (Barton Hill) Ltd v Associated Electrical Industries Ltd* [1977] Q.B. 580 at 596; *Stratford v Syrett* [1958] 1 Q.B. 107). The doctrine does not depend upon the grantor having purported to grant a tenancy. Even if he is purporting to grant a licence, if in fact it is a tenancy the grantor will be estopped from denying that there is a tenancy (*Bruton v London Housing Trust* [1999] 3 All E.R. 481 HL at 487 and 488C). The principle applies whether the tenancy was created by deed, other writing or orally and whatever the length or period of the term. The estoppel applies to successors in title (*Mackley v Nutting* [1949] 2 K.B. 55).

An estoppel between a landlord and a tenant does not prevent the true owner of the property with a better claim to possession from denying the tenancy. Where a tenant has been removed by such a person the tenant will be able to sue his landlord for

4–09

breach of the covenant for quiet enjoyment only if the covenant is an unqualified one.

See also *Asher v Whitlock* (1865) L.R. 1 Q.B. 1, referred to in *Wibberley Ltd v Insley* [1999] 2 All E.R. 897 HL at 901a, for the general principle that "possession is good against all the world except the person who can show a good title" which applies to all persons in possession including trespassers who can therefore evict subsequent trespassers.

Registration of leases

4-10   Since the coming into force of the Land Registration Act 2002 on October 13, 2003 it has been necessary to register all leases granted for more than seven years from the date of the grant (s.4(1)(c) of the 2002 Act). It has also been necessary to register the grant of a lease "to take effect in possession after the end of the period of three months beginning with the date of the grant (s.4(1)(d)), the grant of any right to buy lease (s.4(1)(e)), the grant of any preserved right to buy lease, i.e. a person previously a secure tenant (s.4(1)(f)); and also the assignment of a lease with more than seven years to run at the date of the assignment (s.4(1)(a)). These provisions do not apply where the transfer takes effect by operation of law or to any assignment or surrender of a lease to the owner of the immediate reversion where the term is to merge in that reversion (s.4(3)(4)). If the registration requirement is not carried out the transfer, grant or creation becomes void (see further ss.7 and 8 of the 2002 Act). However, in situations where the tenant is in occupation under the void lease, the parties will generally be regarded in equity as being landlord and tenant and the landlord will be unable to recover possession. The issue of registration or lack of it takes on more importance where the landlord has assigned the reversion (see para.5–03).

Prior to the coming into force of the 2002 Act the general position was that a lease granted for a term of more than 21 years was required to be registered. See further ss.8, 22, 123 and 123A of the Land Registration Act 1925, as amended by the Land Registration Act 1997, in respect of leases granted on or after April 1, 1998. For leases granted before that date see ss.8, 22 and 123 prior to amendment by the 1997 Act.

Entry into possession during negotiations

Negotiations for grant of tenancy

Where a person enters into occupation during negotiations for **4–11** the grant of tenancy he may be held to be in occupation under:

- a licence or a tenancy at will, to which the 1954 Act will not apply; or
- a periodic tenancy, to which the 1954 Act will apply.

In *Javad v Aqil* [1991] 1 All E.R. 243 CA the defendant went into occupation of business premises while negotiations proceeded for the grant to him of a 10-year lease. He was there for some months with consent. On three occasions he paid rent on a quarterly basis before negotiations broke down and the owner asked him to leave. The court came to the conclusion that the defendant was a tenant at will.

> "Where parties are negotiating the terms of a proposed lease, and the prospective tenant is let into possession or permitted to remain in possession in advance of, and in anticipation of, terms being agreed, the fact that the parties have not yet agreed terms will be a factor to be taken into account in ascertaining their intention. It will often be a weighty factor. Frequently in such cases a sum called 'rent' is paid at once in accordance with the terms of the proposed lease: for example, quarterly in advance. But depending on all the circumstances, parties are not to be supposed thereby to have agreed that the prospective tenant shall be a quarterly tenant. They cannot sensibly be taken to have agreed that he shall have a periodic tenancy, with all the consequences flowing from that, at a time when they are still not agreed about the terms on which the prospective tenant shall have possession under the proposed lease, and when he has been permitted to go into possession under the proposed lease or remain in possession merely as an interim measure in the expectation that all will be regulated and regularised in due course when terms are agreed and a formal lease granted . . .
> Entry into possession while negotiations proceed is one of the classic circumstances in which a tenancy at will may exist." (*Javad v Aqil* [1991] 1 All E.R. 244 CA, per Nicholls

L.J. at pp.248 and 254; see also *Barclays Wealth Trustees (Jersey) Ltd v Erimus Housing Ltd* [2014] EWCA Civ 303.)

As can be seen from the passage of the judgment of Nicholls LJ, quoted above, whether or not a person has been granted a tenancy at will or a periodic tenancy is a matter of intention of the parties but it is likely that where a person is in occupation during negotiations for a lease that he will be held not to have been granted a periodic tenancy. The position is even clearer where the:

"parties intend to enter into the relationship of landlord and tenant without a preliminary contract for the grant and acceptance of a lease, and their negotiations are expressed to be 'subject to the completion of a lease', 'subject to lease', 'subject to contract' or the like, then, so long as the qualification remains in force, the relationship does not become binding on them unless and until there is an exchange of lease and counterpart, before which either party can withdraw." (*Longman v Viscount Chelsea* [1989] 2 E.G.L.R. 242, per Nourse LJ at 244M—a case in which the tenant was already in occupation under a tenancy and in which the parties were negotiating a new lease.)

A "tenancy at will exists where the tenancy is on terms that either party may determine it at any time" as opposed to a periodic tenancy, which is one that "continues from period to period indefinitely until determined by proper notice" (*Javad v Aqil* [1991] 1 All E.R. 243 CA, per Nicholls LJ at 244). A tenancy at will may therefore be determined by simply asking the tenant to leave, or by the service of proceedings for possession (*Martinali v Ramuz* [1953] 2 All E.R. 892). No special form of notice is required.

The business tenancy code contained in Pt II of the Landlord and Tenant Act 1954 does not apply to tenancies at will (*Hagee (London) Ltd v Erikson (AB) and Larson* [1975] 3 All E.R. 234; see para.2–29). Thus, the defendant in *Javad v Aqil* was not entitled to the protection of that Act and was required to leave after the plaintiff had told him to go.

In *Javad v Aqil*, the court did not consider whether the defendant might have been a licensee (see Nicholls LJ at 247d). For a case in which a person in occupation negotiating "subject to contract" was held to be a licensee see *Isaac v Hotel de Paris* [1960] 1 All E.R. 348 (approved in *Street v Mountford* [1985] 2 All E.R. 289 at 297). However, as both tenants at will and licensees are unable to claim the benefits of Pt II of the Landlord and Tenant Act 1954 it is unlikely that it will matter whether the occupier is a licensee rather than a tenant at will.

Negotiations for sale of freehold or existing leasehold

The position is rather different where a person enters into occupation during negotiations for a sale of the freehold or an existing leasehold. In *Bretherton v Paton* [1986] 1 E.G.L.R. 172 the potential purchaser was let into occupation of the premises during the negotiations and made periodic payments to the owner that were described by the parties as a contribution towards insurance. The Court of Appeal held that she had been granted exclusive possession for a term at a rent and that she was therefore a periodic tenant (as opposed to a licensee) even though she entered into possession with the intention of purchasing the property and even though neither party intended that a tenancy should be created.

4–12

Possession after contract for "sale" of land: the Standard Conditions

Parties may enter into an agreement for the "sale" of land either by selling the freehold or an existing lease or by the grant of a new lease.

4–13

Sale of freehold or existing lease

Where the vendor of land permits the purchaser to go into occupation prior to completion of the contract, he normally permits him to do so as licensee, notwithstanding that the purchaser enjoys exclusive possession. The circumstances are such that the prima facie intention, normally construed from the granting of the right to exclusive possession, is negated (*Street v Mountford* [1985] 2 All E.R. 289 at 295j). The situation is dealt with in Condition 5 of the Standard Conditions of Sale 5th edn, *Law Society Publications*.

4–14

Standard Conditions of Sale

Condition 5

4-15

5.2.1 If the buyer is not already lawfully in the property, and the seller agrees to let him into occupation, the buyer occupies on the following terms.

5.2.2 The buyer is a licensee and not a tenant. The terms of the licence are that the buyer:

(a) cannot transfer it

(b) may permit members of his household to occupy the property

(c) is to pay or indemnify the seller against outgoings and other expenses in respect of the property

(d) is to pay the seller a fee calculated at the contract rate on the purchase price (less any deposit paid) for the period of the licence

(e) is entitled to any rents and profits from any part of the property which he does not occupy

(f) is to keep the property in as good a state of repair as it was in when he went into occupation (except for fair wear and tear) and is not to alter it

(g) if the property is leasehold, is not to do anything which puts the seller in breach of his obligations in the lease, and

(h) is to quit the property when the licence ends.

5.2.4 The buyer's licence ends on the earliest of: completion date, rescission of the contract or when five working days' notice given by one party to the other takes effect.

Grant of new lease

4-16

Where parties enter into an agreement for the grant of a lease the Standard Conditions of Sale may well be incorporated into the contract. However, the agreement is likely to provide that the Conditions are incorporated into the agreement "so far as the same are not inconsistent herewith". This was the situation in *Joel v Montgomery and Taylor Ltd* [1966] 3 All E.R. 763 where the plaintiff agreed to grant an underlease to the defendant at a premium. The defendant paid the deposit and went into possession prior to completion, paying rent in accordance with the terms of the agreement and the underlease. It was held that the relationship between the parties was not that of vendor and purchaser but of landlord and tenant. The relevant condition was inconsistent with the agreement and thus did not make the defendant a licensee. The status of a person who has entered into occupation pursuant to an agreement for a lease is dealt with immediately below.

Possession pursuant to a contract for a lease or void lease

Introduction

Where a finally concluded agreement for a lease has been entered into (see para.4-19) but no lease has actually been granted, or where a lease is void because it was granted for a term of more than three years and was not made by deed (see para.4-04), the parties will nevertheless be regarded as landlord and tenant if the latter has actually entered into possession. However, the precise status of the occupant is different depending upon whether the common law applies or the rules of equity apply.

4-17

Difference between common law and equity

If the agreement provides for rent to be calculated on a yearly basis the tenant is regarded by the common law as being a tenant from year to year upon the terms of the intended lease but only so far as they are consistent with a yearly tenancy. Thus, whatever the terms of the proposed lease the tenancy is determinable by six months' notice to quit, (see para.14-30), although note that at the end of the intended term the tenancy comes to an end without the necessity of a notice. If the rent is calculated on a monthly or weekly basis the tenant has only a monthly or weekly tenancy (*Alder v Blackman* [1953] 1 Q.B. 146).

4-18

The rules of equity take the matter further. If the agreement is such that it is capable of being specifically enforced, the tenant will be treated in equity as holding the property under the same terms as if the lease had been granted (*Walsh v Lonsdale* (1882) 21 Ch. D. 9; *Amec Properties Ltd v Planning Research & Systems plc* [1992] 1 E.G.L.R. 70 CA). A void lease (i.e. a lease in respect of which the formal requirements have not been complied with) is treated for this purpose as being an agreement for a lease on the terms contained therein (*Parker v Taswell* (1858) 2 De G&J 559).

Where the *Walsh v Lonsdale* doctrine applies the tenant may rely upon it as a defence to a claim for possession whether the landlord brings the claim in the High Court or the county court (*Kingswood Estate Co Ltd v Anderson* [1963] 2 Q.B. 169). However, an action for specific performance of the agreement may be commenced in the county court only if the value of the property (i.e. of the freehold interest) does not exceed the county court limit, currently £30,000 (County Courts Act 1984, s.23(d); *Foster v Reeves* [1892] 2 Q.B. 255; *Angel v Jay* [1911] 1 K.B. 666; *Amec Properties Ltd v Planning Research & Systems* [1992] 2 E.G.L.R. 70); unless the parties confer jurisdiction by agreement under s.24 of the 1984 Act.

Finally concluded agreement

4–19   It cannot be stressed too highly that there must be a finally concluded agreement. The court will not order specific performance if there are any terms still to be negotiated. For a case in which there was no finally concluded agreement see *Brent LBC v O'Bryan* [1993] 1 E.G.L.R. 59 CA–agreement to let out a scout hut on a monthly basis on terms to be laid down by valuers.

However, for the *Walsh v Lonsdale* doctrine to apply it is not necessary that all the terms should have been agreed. What is required is agreement as to the "essential terms", that is agreement as to the parties to the lease, the property to be let, the commencement and duration of the term or other consideration to be paid. If those terms have been agreed and no other terms have been offered but left unaccepted the court will, subject to any equitable reasons for not doing so, make an order for specific performance of a lease, such lease to contain "usual covenants" (see further note (9) below, para.4–21).

Agreement to be in writing

4–20   By virtue of s.2 of the Law of Property (Miscellaneous Provisions) Act 1989 a contract for the grant of a lease of more than three years (s.2(5)(a)), entered into on or after September 27, 1989 (the date upon which the Act came into force), can be made only in writing and all the terms *which the parties have expressly agreed* must be contained in one document, which must be signed by or on behalf of each party to the contract.

Where contracts are exchanged, all the express terms must be contained in each contract and one of the documents, but not necessarily the same one, must be signed by or on behalf of each party.

Law of Property (Miscellaneous Provisions) Act 1989 s.2

2.–(1) A contract for the sale or other disposition of an interest in land can only be made in writing and only by incorporating all the terms which the parties have expressly agreed in one document or, where contracts are exchanged, in each.

4–21

(2) The terms may be incorporated in a document either by being set out in it or by reference to some other document.

(3) The document incorporating the terms or, where contracts are exchanged, one of the documents incorporating them (but not necessarily the same one) must be signed by or on behalf of each party to the contract.

(4) Where a contract for the sale or other disposition of an interest in land satisfies the conditions of this section by reason only of the rectification of one or more documents in pursuance of an order of a court, the contract shall come into being, or be deemed to have come into being, at such time as may be specified in the order.

(5) This section does not apply in relation to—

(a)   a contract to grant such a lease as is mentioned in section 54(2) of the law of Property Act 1925 (short leases);

(b)   a contract made in the course of a public auction; or

(c)   a contract regulated under the Financial Services and Markets Act 2000, other than a regulated mortgage contract;

and nothing in this section affects the creation or operation of resulting, implied or constructive trusts.

(6) In this section—

"disposition" has the same meaning as in the law of Property Act 1925;

"interest in land" means any estate, interest or charge in or over land.

(7) Nothing in this section shall apply in relation to contracts made before this section came into force.

(8) Section 40 of the Law of Property Act 1925 (which is superseded by this section) shall cease to have effect.

Note:

(1) Section 2 is relevant only to executory contracts. It has no relevance to contracts that have been completed. If parties choose to complete a contract that does not

comply with the section they are free to do so (*Tootal Clothing Ltd v Guinea Properties Management Ltd* [1992] 2 E.G.L.R. 80).

(2) As to the meaning of "where contracts are exchanged" see *Commissioner for New Towns v Cooper (Great Britain) Ltd* [1995] 2 E.G.L.R. 113—exchange of letters not good enough).

(3) Any variation of the contract which is material to the disposition of the land must also comply with the provisions of the Act (*McCausland v Duncan Lawrie* [1996] 4 All E.R. 995 CA).

(4) Where the agreement is signed by an agent s.2 does not require the agent's authority to sign the contract to be in writing (*McLaughlin v Duffill* [2009] EWCA Civ 1627—estate agent had oral authority to sign a sale contract on behalf of his seller client—seller bound by the contract). However, it is obviously advisable to require that person to provide evidence that he does indeed have authority to sign.

(5) Nothing in the section affects the creation or operation of resulting, implied or constructive trusts. There is also such a close relationship between constructive trusts and estoppel—particularly in the area of joint enterprises for the acquisition of land—that the doctrine can operate to give effect to an agreement rendered void by the section (*Yaxley v Gotts* [2000] 1 All E.R. 711 CA). In *Kinane v Mackie-Conteh* [2005] EWCA 45 an agreement, contained in a letter from D to C, whereby D purported to grant C a charge over a property to secure a loan did not comply with s.2(1). Nor was it a valid equitable agreement within s.53(1)(c) of the Law of Property Act 1925 (which provides for disposition of equitable interests to be in writing and signed) because that provision only applies to subsisting equitable interests. However, the judge found that C was not prepared to advance the money until the security was in place. In the circumstances a constructive trust arose and the agreement was valid by virtue of s.2(5) of the 1989 Act. Thus, when the loan was not repaid C was able to obtain an order for sale over the property. *Yaxley v Gotts* [2000] Ch. 162 applied. (In *Yeomans Row Management Ltd v Cobbe* [2008] UKHL 55 Lord Scott suggested (obiter), at para.29, that a complete agreement that did not comply with s.2 of the 1989 Act could not be made enforceable

via the route of proprietary estoppel. However, he did not refer to *Yaxley v Gotts* or *Kinane*).

(6) An oral compromise of a dispute, whereby the property was to be put on the market, containing a term which stated that "the property be sold with vacant possession at the best price available" was not a contract for the sale or other disposition of an interest in land. It amounted only to an agreement to enter into a contract and could not, therefore, amount to contract to sell or dispose of an interest in land (*Nweze v Nwoko* [2004] EWCA Civ 379). The compromise was therefore enforceable by specific performance.

(7) An agreement for the *grant* of an option falls within s.2 and must therefore be signed by, or on behalf of, all parties to the contract, but a letter *exercising* the option is not a "sale or other disposition of an interest in land" and so need be signed only by the purchaser (*Spiro v Glencrown Properties Ltd* [1991] 1 All E.R. 600).

(8) The section does not apply where the lease is to be for a term of three years or less. Nor does it apply to auction sales or contracts regulated by the Financial Services Act 1986.

(9) Section 2(1) does not prevent parties from structuring a transaction, for example, for the sale of the whole of a company's assets, in such a way that the land sale is dealt with in a different document from the sale of stock, work or progress, unless the sale of the land is conditional upon the sale of the other assets (*North Eastern Properties Ltd v Coleman* [2010] EWCA Civ 277.)

(10) Section 2(1) of the 1989 Act requires all terms "which the parties have expressly agreed" to be in one document or, where contracts are exchanged, in each. The authors' understanding of this section is that it does not affect the old rule that it is necessary expressly to agree only the essential terms (see above, para.4–19) and that the court will still make an order for specific performance so long as the requirements of the section have been complied with in relation to those terms.

(11) The printing or the typing of a name is not a signature within the meaning of s.2(3). Under the 1989 Act the term "signed" has the meaning which an ordinary person would understand it to have (*Firstpost Homes Ltd v Johnson* [1996] 13 E.G. 125 CA).

(12) Where the agreement was entered into before September 27, 1989 the provisions of s.40 of the Law of Property Act 1925 apply to the contract.

Effect of the 1954 Act

4-22 The term "tenancy" in Pt II of the 1954 Act includes "an agreement for a lease or underlease" (s.69(1); see para.2-02). The Act will therefore apply to the agreement unless one of the exceptions applies (para.2-28). If the Act does apply, the difference between the position at law and in equity is unlikely to be of importance. Where the 1954 Act does not apply, the difference could be crucial. If for example the landlord serves a six-month notice to quit so as to determine the tenancy at the end of the first year, he will not be entitled to possession at its expiry if the tenant can show that he has an equitable lease for a term greater than one year.

CHAPTER 5

ASSIGNMENT OF THE LANDLORD'S INTEREST

In this chapter we are concerned with the effect of the sale of the landlord's interest in the property, i.e. the assignment of the reversion, and with the following questions. Will the tenancy bind the new landlord? What are the rights and liabilities of the new landlord against the tenant? Can the new landlord sue existing sureties or previous assignee of the lease? When does the assignment take effect?

5–01

(For a fuller discussion of many of the problems that can arise, particularly in relation to "new" tenancies, than is possible in this chapter see T.M. Fancourt Q.C., *Enforceability of Landlord and Tenant Covenants* (Sweet & Maxwell)).

Introduction: Landlord and Tenant (Covenants) Act 1995

The law is now governed by two sets of rules: those applying to old tenancies (i.e. generally those granted before January 1, 1996, when the Act came into force) and those applying to new tenancies (i.e. generally those granted on or after January 1, 1996). For a more precise definition of new tenancies (in particular where the lease was granted on or after January 1, 1996 pursuant to an agreement made before that date) see para.13–02. The law applying to old tenancies is to be found substantially in ss.141 and 142 of the Law of Property Act 1925 together with an old common law rule. The law applying to new tenancies is to be found in the 1995 Act.

5–02

Binding nature of tenancy on new landlord

Where a lease was registered under the Land Registration Act 1925 or the Land Registration Act 2002 the interest is deemed

5–03

to be vested in the lessee (ss.9, 12 and 23 of the 1925 Act and s.12 of the 2002 Act; Sch.12 para.1 of the 2002 Act) and any purchaser of the landlord's interest will take subject to the lease. (See also para.4–10).

Where a lease was "granted for a term" of 21 years or less prior to October 13, 2003 (when the 2002 Act came into force) it will constitute an overriding interest under s.70(1)(k) of the 1925 Act and will continue to bind purchasers of the landlord's estate (2002 Act, Sch.12 para.12) whether or not the tenant is in occupation (*City Permanent Building Society v Miller* [1952] Ch. 840 at 848).

The position in respect of overriding interests is different where the lease was granted on or after October 13, 2003. The general position is that the tenancy will constitute an overriding interest if it was granted for a term seven years or less (see further para.1 of Sch.1 and Sch.3 of the 2002 Act). For other interests that might be binding as overriding interests (such as an agreement for a lease held by a person in occupation) see para.2 of each of those Schedules.

Where the tenant's interest was not an overriding one it may, under the 1925 Act, have been protected by an entry on the register of a notice or caution and remains protected (1925 Act, s.59(2); 2002 Act, Sch. 12 paras 1 and 2). Under the 2002 Act a lease may not be protected by a notice if it was granted for a term of three years or less from the date of the grant and is not required to be registered (s.33(b)). It will have to rely upon its overriding status. If a lease is protected by notice under the 2002 Act it ceases to have priority as an overriding interest (s.29(3)).

If the land is unregistered the purchaser takes subject to any tenant with a legal estate. If the tenant only has an equitable interest (i.e. an agreement for a lease operating in equity as a lease) the purchaser is bound by it if it is registered under the Land Charges Act 1972.

If the new landlord is bound by the tenant's interest he will not be able to obtain possession unless the old landlord would have been able to.

Rights of new landlord against tenant

Old tenancies

Law of Property Act 1925 s.141

141.–(1) Rent reserved by a lease, and the benefit of every covenant or provision therein contained, having reference to the subject-matter thereof, and on the lessee's part to be observed or performed, and every condition of re-entry and other condition therein contained, shall be annexed and incident to and shall go with the reversionary estate in the land, or in any part thereof, immediately expectant on the term granted by the lease, notwithstanding severance of that reversionary estate, and without prejudice to any liability affecting a covenantor or his estate.

   (2) Any such rent, covenant or provision shall be capable of being recovered, received, enforced, and taken advantage of, by the person from time to time entitled, subject to the term, to the income of the whole or any part, as the case may require, of the land leased.

   (3) Where the person becomes entitled by conveyance or otherwise, such rent, covenant or provision may be recovered, received, enforced or taken advantage of by him notwithstanding that he becomes so entitled after the condition of re-entry or forfeiture has become enforceable, but this subsection does not render enforceable any condition of re-entry or other condition waived or released before such person becomes entitled as aforesaid.

5–04

On assignment of the reversion of an old tenancy (i.e. generally a tenancy granted before January 1, 1996: see introduction para.5–02), the right to sue the tenant in respect of all future *and* any outstanding breaches committed prior to the date of the assignment passes to the *new landlord* (s.141 of the Law of Property Act 1925). The provision applies to all tenancies including oral ones (see definition of lease in s.205(xxii) of the Law of Property Act 1925; *King, Re, Robinson v Gray* [1963] 1 All E.R. 781, per Upjohn L.J. CA) and to a specifically enforceable agreement for lease *Rickett v Green* [1910] 1 K.B. 253). Thus, the new landlord (and only the new landlord) is entitled to recover any arrears of rent that accrued before the assignment, whether from the tenant (*London and County (A&D) v Wilfred Sportsman Ltd* [1971] Ch. 764) or where the lease has been assigned from the original tenant (*Arlesford Trading Co Ltd v Servansingh* [1971] 1 W.L.R. 1080).

In *Scribes West Ltd v Relsa Anstalt* [2004] EWCA Civ 1744 the question related to the right to forfeit a lease of registered land (under the Land Registration Act 1925) in the period between execution of a transfer of the reversion and its registration. It was held that for the purposes of a valid forfeiture by the purchaser of the reversion, it was sufficient that the transfer of the reversion had been executed and notice given to the lessee, *notwithstanding that the transfer had not been registered.* The purchaser could forfeit because it was the "person entitled to income" for the purposes of s.141(2) of the Law of Property Act 1925. The word "entitled" does not of itself import a distinction between legal and equitable interests. It simply connotes an enforceable right to the relevant income.

The tenant is not to be considered to be in breach of covenant by failure to pay rent to the new landlord before notice of the assignment has been given to him; and payment to the old landlord before that time is a sufficient discharge of the obligation to pay rent (s.151 of the Law of Property Act 1925).

Law of Property Act 1925 s.151

5-05   151.–(1) Where land is subject to a lease—

    (a)   the conveyance of a reversion in the land expectant on the determination of the lease; . . .

    (b)   . . . shall be valid without any attornment of the lessee:
Nothing in this subsection—

       (i) affects the validity of any payment of rent by the lessee to the person making the conveyance or grant before notice of the conveyance or grant is given to him by the person entitled thereunder; or

     (ii) renders the lessee liable for any breach of covenant to pay rent, on account of his failure to pay rent to the person entitled under the conveyance or grant before such notice is given to the lessee.

If the tenant pays the rent before it is due and before that date the landlord assigns his interest, the tenant remains liable to the new landlord for the rent (*De Nicholls v Saunders* (1870) L.R. 5 C.P. 589 at 594).

New tenancies

5-06   Where the tenancy is a new tenancy (i.e. generally a tenancy granted on or after January 1, 1996; see para.5-02), the effect of s.23 of the 1995 Act (para.5-08) is that the right to sue for the pre-assignment arrears remains with *the assignor* of the reversion (*Edlington Properties Ltd v JH Fenner & Co Ltd* [2006] EWCA Civ 403 para.48) unless there is an express assignment of the chose in action under s.136 of the Law of Property Act 1925. Further:

"[the] tenant cannot set off, against rent falling due after the transfer, a claim for the agreement pursuant to which the lease was granted, unless of course the lease specifically provides that he should have that right." (*Edlington Properties Ltd*, Neuberger L.J. at para.64).

It would seem that the provisions of s.151 of the 1925 Act (see para.5–05 above) apply as much to new tenancies as to old.

Forfeiture clauses

Whether the tenancy is an old tenancy or a new tenancy, the new landlord is entitled to the benefit of the right of re-entry in the lease. This is usually taken for granted but is a consequence of s.141 of the Law of Property Act 1925 in relation to old tenancies (see para.5–04) and s.4 of the 1995 Act in relation to new tenancies. In each case the new landlord is entitled to exercise the right of re-entry in relation to all breaches of covenant including those that occurred before the assignment unless there has been a waiver or release (s.141(3) of the 1925 Act; s.23 of the 1995 Act).

5–07

Landlord and Tenant (Covenants) Act 1995 ss.4 and 23

4. The benefit of a landlord's right of re-entry under a tenancy—

5–08

(a) shall be annexed and incident to the whole, and to each and every part, of the reversion in the premises demised by the tenancy, and

(b) shall pass on an assignment of the whole or any part of the reversion in those premises.

. . .

23.–(1) Where as a result of an assignment a person becomes, by virtue of this Act, bound by or entitled to the benefit of any covenant, he shall not by virtue of this Act have any liability or rights under the covenant in relation to any time falling before the assignment.

(2) Subsection (1) does not preclude any such rights being expressly assigned to the person in question.

(3) Where as a result of an assignment a person becomes, by virtue of this Act, entitled to a right of re-entry contained in a tenancy, that right shall be exercisable in relation to any breach of a covenant of the tenancy occurring before the assignment as in relation to one occurring thereafter, unless by reason of any waiver or release it was not so exercisable immediately before the assignment.

Surety covenant after assignment of reversion

Old tenancies

5-09 There is no privity of contract (para.13-05) between the assignee of a reversion and a surety of a tenant. Nor does s.141 of the Law of Property Act 1925 apply. That section applies only to covenants in a lease to be observed by the tenant. However, at common law a covenant by a surety guaranteeing the performance of the tenant's covenants "touches and concerns the land" and is therefore enforceable by an assignee of the reversion against the surety without the need for express assignment of that right (*P&A Swift Investments v Combined English Stores Group plc* [1988] 2 All E.R. 885 HL). It does not matter whether the surety is a guarantor of the original tenant's obligations or of the obligations of an assignee of the lease (see the facts of *Kumar v Dunning* [1987] 2 All E.R. 801 CA, which decision was approved by the House of Lords in *P&A Swift Investments*, in particular at p.889f).

> "The relationship between the landlord and a surety in a case such as the present is, of course, contractual only. The surety has no interest in the land the subject matter of the demise and there is thus no privity of estate. In seeking, therefore to enforce the surety's covenant, an assignee of the reversion cannot rely on . . . s.141 of the Law of Property Act 1925 . . . which [applies] only to covenants between landlord and tenant. His claim to enforce rests on the common law rule under which the benefit of the covenant would run with the land if, but only if, the assignee had the legal estate in the land and the covenant was one which 'touched and concerned' the land." (*P&A Swift Investments v Combined English Stores Group plc*, per Lord Oliver of Aylmerton at p.888h.)

> "The surety covenant is given as a support or buttress to covenants given by a tenant to a landlord. The covenants by the tenant relate not only to the payment of rent, but also to repair, insurance and use of the premises. All such covenants by a tenant in favour of the landlord touch and concern the land, i.e. the reversion of the landlord" (per Sir Nicholas Browne-Wilkinson V.C. in *Kumar v Dunning* [1987] 2 All E.R. 801 CA, cited with approval in *P&A Swift* at p.890c).

A covenant by a surety to accept a lease in place of a lease that has been disclaimed on behalf of an insolvent tenant either by a trustee in bankruptcy or a liquidator in the case of a company is a covenant that touches and concerns the land so that the benefit of the covenant runs with the reversion without the need for any express agreement; and which may therefore be enforced by an assignee of the reversion (*Coronation Street Industrial Properties Ltd v Ingall Industries plc* [1989] 1 All E.R. 979 HL).

New tenancies

There is no express provision in the 1995 Act relating to the passing of the benefit of surety covenants. The position in relation to new tenancies will presumably therefore be governed by the rules relating to old tenancies. If so, the new landlord will be able to recover from the surety on the basis that the covenant touches and concerns the land. (See further below in relation to assignees.)   **5–10**

Rights against former assignees of the lease

The situation envisaged in this section of the book is one where a new landlord is seeking to enforce an agreement by a former assignee of the lease (who was not an original tenant), contained in a licence to assign, entered into between that assignee and a former landlord. The obligations of the former assignee are dealt with in para.13–23.   **5–11**

Old tenancies

Section 141 of the Law of Property Act 1925 does not apply to covenants in a licence to assign. That section applies only to covenants in a lease (see para.5-04). However, at common law the current landlord may rely upon the benefit of a covenant in a licence to assign that runs with the land if the covenant is one that "touches and concerns the land". Covenants as to payment of rent, repair, insurance and user "touch and concern" the land (*P&A Swift Investments v Combined English Stores Group plc* [1988] 2 All E.R. 885 HL—a case relating to a surety covenant (see above) but the same principle applies).   **5–12**

New tenancies

5-13 Where the tenancy is a new tenancy former tenants are released from liability on assignment (s.5 of the 1995 Act; para.13–20) unless they have entered into an authorised guarantee agreement under s.16 of the Act. It is not clear whether the new landlord can recover against the former tenant under the terms of the authorised guarantee agreement. A covenant in an authorised guarantee agreement is not a "tenant covenant" (s.28(1)) and so the benefit of the agreement will not pass automatically under s.3. However, s.16(8) does state that "the rules of law relating to guarantees . . . are, subject to its terms, applicable in relation to any authorised guarantee agreement as in relation to any other guarantee agreement" (see para.13–22). Perhaps the rule in *P&A Swift* referred to above applies by virtue of this subsection.

Liabilities of old and new landlord after assignment

Old tenancies

Law of Property Act 1925 s.142

5-14 **142.**–(1) The obligation under a condition or of a covenant entered into by a lessor with reference to the subject matter of the lease shall, if and as far as the lessor has power to bind the reversionary estate immediately expectant on the term granted by the lease, be annexed and incident to and shall go with that reversionary estate, or the several parts thereof, notwithstanding severance of that reversionary estate, and may be taken advantage of and enforced by the person in whom the term is from time to time vested by conveyance, devolution in law, or otherwise; and, if and as far as the lessor has power to bind the person from time to time entitled to that reversionary estate, the obligation aforesaid may be taken advantage of and entered against any person so entitled.

(2) This section applies to leases made before or after the commencement of this Act, whether the severance of the reversionary estate was effected before or after such commencement:

Provided where the lease was made before 1 January 1882, nothing in this section shall affect the operation of any severance of the reversionary estate effected before such commencement.

This section takes effect without prejudice to any liability affecting a covenantor or his estate.

By virtue of s.142 of the Law of Property Act 1925, the new landlord becomes liable to comply with the obligations under the lease on the assignment of the reversion but he is not liable in damages for breaches that occurred prior to the date of the assignment of the landlord's interest (*Duncliffe v Caerfelin Properties Ltd* [1989] 2 E.G.L.R. 38 QBD). The tenant will therefore have to sue the old landlord in respect of any such breaches. However, the tenant may set-off against a rent debt, which has passed to the new landlord under s.141 (see para.5-04), any damages due to him as a result of the assignor's breach of his repairing obligations because the debt vests in the new landlord as assignee subject to all equities that are available to the tenant against the assignor (*Smith v Muscat* [2003] EWCA Civ 962, Sedley L.J. at paras 28 and 33).

Section 142 applies to obligations in a side letter and will therefore bind the new landlord after an assignment if on the letter's true construction the parties intended that the obligation should run with the land (*System Floors Ltd v Ruralpride Ltd* [1995] 1 E.G.L.R. 48 CA—agreement in a letter given to the tenant at the same time as the grant of a lease, whereby the tenant was given the right to surrender the lease after each rent review, was binding on purchaser of the landlord's interest. The letter contained no reference to successor's in title but commercial reality required the concession to be construed as binding on successors otherwise the concession could have been easily circumvented by assigning the reversion). See also *Lotteryking Ltd v AMEC Properties Ltd* [1995] 2 E.G.L.R. 13 Ch D where it was held that the obligations assumed by the landlord under two collateral agreements, to carry out repairs, were assumed by reference to the demised premises and accordingly ran with the reversion.

By virtue of the contract between them, an original landlord continues to be liable to an original tenant on his covenant after assignment of the reversion (see final sentence of s.142). In all other circumstances the landlord, in principle, ceases to be liable after an assignment of the reversion because there is no longer any privity of estate between landlord and tenant. However, where the premises include a dwelling the liability does not actually cease until the tenant has been notified of the new landlord's name and address in accordance with s.3(1) of the Landlord and Tenant Act 1985 (see s.3(3A)).

New tenancies

The rights and liabilities of the new landlord are set out in ss.2, 3 (see below) and s.23 of the 1995 Act (see para.5-08). After

5-15

the assignment he becomes liable on the landlord covenants in the lease whether or not they have reference to the subject matter of the tenancy (i.e. whether or not they "touch and concern the land"): s.2(1).

The old landlord is not automatically released from his covenants when he assigns the reversion. If he wishes to be released from those covenants, he needs to serve an appropriate notice on the tenant. If he objects within the specified time limit, an application can be made to the court (ss.6 and 8 of the 1995 Act; which are not set out in this book). A former landlord may also apply to be released from covenants to which he is still bound on a subsequent assignment of the reversion (ss.7 and 8; not set out in this book). The relevant notices are in prescribed form (see Forms 3 to 6) of the Landlord and Tenant (Covenants) Act 1995 (Notices) Regulations 1995 (SI 1995/2964). See also *BHP Great Britain Petroleum Ltd v Chesterfield Properties Ltd* [2001] EWCA Civ 1797.

Where the landlord has transferred part of his interest to a new landlord see s.9(2) of the 1995 Act and Form 8 of the 1995 Regulations.

Landlord and Tenant (Covenants) Act 1995 ss.2, 3 and 30

5-16   **2.**–(1) This Act applies to a landlord covenant or a tenant covenant of a tenancy–

> (a)   whether or not the covenant has reference to the subject matter of the tenancy, and
> (b)   whether the covenant is express, implied or imposed by law,

but does not apply to a covenant falling with subsection (2).

[Subsection (2) is not relevant to commercial premises]

3.–(1) The benefit and burden of all landlord and tenant covenants of a tenancy–

> (a)   shall be annexed and incident to the whole, and to each and every part, of the premises demised by the tenancy and of the reversion in them, and
> (b)   shall in accordance with this section pass on an assignment of the whole or any part of those premises or of the reversion in them.

(2) . . .

(3) Where the assignment is by the landlord under the tenancy, then as from the assignment the assignee–

(a)   becomes bound by the landlord covenants of the tenancy
except to the extent that—
  (i) immediately before the assignment they did not bind the
      assignor, or
  (ii) they fall to be complied with in relation to any demised
       premises not comprised in the assignment; and

(b)   becomes entitled to the benefit of the tenant covenants of the
tenancy except to the extent that they fall to be complied with
in relation to any such premises.

(5) . . .
(6) Nothing in this section shall operate—

(a)   in the case of a covenant which (in whatever terms) is
expressed to be personal to any person, to make the covenant
enforceable by or (as the case may be) against any other
person; or
(b)   to make a covenant enforceable against any person if, apart
from this section, it would not be enforceable against him by
reason of its not having been registered under the Land
Registration Act 2002 or the Land Charges Act 1972.

(7) . . .

*****

30.— . . . (4) In consequence of this Act nothing in the following
provisions, namely—

(a)   sections 78 and 79 of the Law of Property Act 1925 (benefit
and burden of covenants relating to land), and
(b)   sections 141 and 142 of that Act (running of benefit and
burden of covenants with reversion),

shall apply in relation to new tenancies.

Other routes to avoiding continuing liability

The fact that a release can be obtained by ss.6 to 8 of the Act   **5–17**
does not prevent the landlord and tenant from agreeing any
other mechanism for release. Any such mechanism does not
"frustrate the operation" of ss.6 to 8 of the Act so as to fall foul
of the anti-avoidance provisions in s.25 of the Act. Thus, in
London Diocesan Fund v Avonridge Property Co Ltd [2005]
UKHL 70 it was held that a term in a sub-lease stating that the
tenant would not be liable to the sub-tenant under the covenant
for quiet enjoyment in the sub-lease after it had disposed of the
property was not to be regarded as void under the
anti-avoidance provisions of s.25. Lord Nicholls at paras 16 and
17:

"16. . . . Sections 5 to 8 are relieving provisions. They are intended to benefit tenants, or landlords, as the case may be. That is their purpose. That is how they are meant to operate. These sections introduced a means, which cannot be ousted, whereby in certain circumstances, without the agreement of the other party, a tenant or landlord can be released from a liability he has assumed. The object of the legislation was that on lawful assignment of a tenancy or reversion, and irrespective of the terms of the tenancy, the tenant or the landlord should have an exit route from his future liabilities. This route should be available in accordance with the statutory provisions.

17. Thus the mischief at which the statute was aimed was the absence in practice of any such exit route. Consistently with this the legislation was not intended to close any other exit route already open to the parties: in particular, that by agreement their liability could be curtailed from the outset or later released or waived. . . . "

Date upon which assignment takes effect

5–18 Where the landlord's interest is a freehold or a lease of more than three years, the assignment of the interest must be made by deed (ss.52 and 54 of the Law of Property Act 1925). Section 141 of the Law of Property Act (in relation to old tenancies) and s.3 of the Landlord and Tenant (Covenants) Act 1995 (in relation to new tenancies) does not therefore come into operation, and the new landlord may not enforce the covenants or forfeit, until the legal estate is conveyed to him by the deed.

Further, where the land is registered, the new landlord may not take steps to enforce the covenants or forfeit until the disposition of the estate has been registered (see s27 of the Land Registration Act 2002, which states that: "If a disposition of a registered estate . . . is required to be completed by registration, it does not operate at law until the relevant registration requirements are met.")

If proceedings are commenced by the old landlord the new landlord can be substituted as claimant once the legal interest has been vested in the new landlord (see para.23–11).

CHAPTER 6

LICENCES OF BUSINESS PREMISES

. . . .

Whether an agreement for the occupation of business premises **6-01** is a licence or tenancy is a matter of great importance. Unless the agreement is a tenancy the provisions of Pt II of the Landlord and Tenant Act 1954, which provide business tenants with security of tenure, do not apply (see para.2-01). There have been a number of cases dealing with this issue in relation to residential accommodation, the most important of which is undoubtedly the House of Lords decision in *Street v Mountford* [1985] 2 All E.R. 289. Unfortunately, there have been fewer cases concerned with premises occupied for the purpose of a business. Some of those that have been reported have tended to confuse rather than clarify the position. It is submitted that, although *Street v Mountford* is a case concerned with residential accommodation, its general principles apply to business premises (notwithstanding some views to the contrary).

General principles: *Street v Mountford*

"The traditional view that the grant of exclusive **6-02** possession for a term creates a tenancy is consistent with the elevation of a tenancy into an estate in land. The tenant possessing exclusive possession is able to exercise the rights of an owner of land, which is in the real sense his land albeit temporarily and subject to certain restrictions. A tenant armed with exclusive possession can keep out strangers and keep out the landlord unless the landlord is exercising limited rights reserved to him by the tenancy agreement to enter and view and repair. A licensee lacking exclusive possession can in no sense call the land his own and cannot be said to own any estate in the land. The licence does not create an estate in the land to which it relates but only makes an act lawful which would otherwise be unlawful . . . the traditional distinction between a tenancy and a licence lay in the grant of land for a term at a rent with exclusive possession.

The consequences in law of the agreement, once concluded, can only be determined by consideration of the effect of the agreement. If the agreement satisfied all the requirements of a tenancy, then the agreement produced a tenancy and the parties cannot alter the effect of the agreement by insisting that they only created a licence. The manufacture of a five-pronged implement for manual digging results in a fork even though the manufacturer, unfamiliar with the English language, insists that he intended to make and has made a spade . . . the only intention which is relevant is the intention demonstrated by the agreement to grant exclusive possession for a term at a rent" (*Street v Mountford* [1985] 2 All E.R. 289, per Lord Templeman at 292d, 292g, 294j and 300b). (See below "Shams and Pretences" para.6–06).

In *Street v Mountford*, the House of Lords reaffirmed the traditional link between exclusive possession and the creation of a tenancy. If the occupier of the premises has not been granted exclusive possession he cannot be a tenant. More specifically Lord Templeman, who gave the judgment, stated that the traditional distinction between a tenancy and a licence lay in the grant of land "for a term at a rent with exclusive possession". It is only in exceptional circumstances that a person with exclusive possession will not be a tenant (see further para.6–07 in relation to those exceptional circumstances).

Lord Templeman also made it clear that in determining whether or not a person is a tenant or a licensee it is not permissible to trawl through the agreement between the parties to see whether some of the terms are more appropriate to a tenancy and whether some are more appropriate to a licence. For example, it is often said that a covenant against assigning is more appropriate to a lease and that such a term will therefore indicate that the agreement is a tenancy. This is the incorrect approach. When construing the terms of the agreement one must simply look at the whole document *to see whether or not it grants exclusive possession*. Furthermore, the label that the parties attach to the agreement is not conclusive.

Although the grant of exclusive possession for a term at a rent will (save for exceptional circumstances; see para.6-07) create a tenancy the important ingredients are exclusive possession and a certain term. A tenancy may exist even where no rent is payable. The term may be either a fixed term, a periodic term or some other period that, although not fixed, can be brought to an end by either party in circumstances that are known to the parties at the commencement and which are free from uncertainty (*Ashburn Anstalt v Arnold* [1988] 2 All E.R. 147).

Application of *Street v Mountford* to business premises

In *Street v Mountford*, Lord Templeman applied the general principles to residential premises by stating that:

6-03

> "[i]n the case of residential accommodation there is no difficulty in deciding whether the grant confers exclusive possession. An occupier of residential accommodation at a rent for a term is either a lodger or a tenant. The occupier is a lodger if the landlord provides attendance or services which require the landlord or his servants to exercise unrestricted access to and use of the premises."

Do the general principles also apply to business premises? In coming to his conclusions Lord Templeman considered all the earlier authorities including those concerned with business premises and so it would seem that the passages quoted above do have general application. However, the cases that have been decided since *Street v Mountford* are not unanimous in their view as to its applicability to business premises.

In *University of Reading v Johnson-Houghton* [1985] 2 E.G.L.R. 113 QBD the plaintiff granted the defendant the right to use gallops, that is the right to exercise race horses over land belonging to the plaintiff. The judge held that the defendant had exclusive possession of the gallops and applied *Street v Mountford* in holding that the defendant was a tenant. (See para.2-04 in relation to the right to apply for a new tenancy of gallops.) In *London & Associated Investment Trust v Calow* [1986] 2 E.G.L.R. 80, His Honour Judge Paul Barker rejected an argument that the doctrine stated by Lord Templeman in *Street v Mountford* did not apply to business premises. The judge thought it possible that there might be "special cases of some sort of trading properties, areas in shops and so forth, or stalls in markets" but he could not see any difference between a residence and self-contained business offices (at 84D). In *Dellneed Ltd v Chin* [1987] 1 E.G.L.R. 75 Millett J. applied the principle stated in *Street v Mountford* in deciding that an occupier of a restaurant was a tenant.

In *Dresden Estates v Collinson* [1987] 1 E.G.L.R. 45 CA there was some suggestion that there is a distinction to be drawn between residential and business premises and that the principle set out in *Street v Mountford* does not necessarily directly apply to business premises (per Glidewell L.J. at 47A—see further para.6–04). In *Smith v Northside Developments Ltd* [1987] 2 E.G.L.R. 151 CA the appellants initially shared occupation of a unit in Camden Lock Market with another trader. The other trader later departed leaving the appellant in sole occupation. In coming to its conclusion that the appellant was not a tenant the Court of Appeal sought to distinguish *Street v Mountford* on the basis that Lord Templeman was dealing with a written agreement whereas the appellants in *Smith v Northside Developments Ltd* were in occupation under an oral agreement. However, there would appear to be no good reason why the doctrine enunciated by Lord Templeman should not apply to oral agreements and the decision in *Smith v Northside Developments Ltd* is perhaps best explained on the basis that the court found on the facts of the case that the appellant was not entitled to exclusive possession.

In *Esso Petroleum Co Ltd v Fumegage Ltd* [1994] E.G.L.R. 91 CA at 93 the Court of Appeal applied the decision in *Street v Mountford* in coming to the conclusion that three agreements that provided for occupation of two service stations did not grant exclusive possession to the occupiers.

In *Nation Car Parks Ltd v Trinity Development Co (Banbury) Ltd* [2001] EWCA Civ 1686 the Court of Appeal confirmed that the principles of *Street v Mountford* do apply to business premises. The essential ingredient is whether or not the occupier has been granted exclusive possession. However, the court did also hold that the fact that the parties called the document a "licence" is a factor that can be taken into account when deciding whether or not exclusive possession has been granted.

It is difficult to see what the differences in principle can be between residential and business premises and it is submitted that the doctrine stated by Lord Templeman in the passages cited on para.6–02 apply to business premises, even in special cases such as areas in shops and market stalls. If the stall holder etc. does not have exclusive possession he does not have a tenancy.

Advertising hoardings

In *Clear Channel UK Ltd v Manchester City Council* [2005]　**6–04**
EWCA Civ 1304 the agreement was to allow Clear Channel to erect and maintain 13 large advertising hoardings at various prominent sites in Manchester owned by the Council. Each advertising display consisted of a substantial superstructure in the shape of a large "M". The superstructure was fixed to a rectangular concrete base, which was embedded in the ground. The position where the base of each hoarding should go was marked out by agreement on the ground. Clear Channel conceded that:

> "it is of the essence of a right of exclusive possession, and hence of a tenancy, that the area or areas of land over which the right is said to exist should be capable of precise identification at the date when the right is said to be created. . . . Accordingly if the Agreement, on its true construction, does not sufficiently identify the land in respect of which a tenancy is said to have been created, the case for a tenancy must fail."

Clear Channel therefore argued that on its true construction the agreement created a tenancy of the land occupied by the concrete bases. However, on a true construction of the agreement it was held that "the Sites" mentioned in the agreement were not the areas of the concrete bases of the M's, but larger undefined areas of land owned by the council. This prevented the agreement from being a tenancy. (See further para.6–05).

Preventing the occupier from acquiring exclusive possession

"Landlords" frequently attempt to draft agreements that will　**6–05**
deprive occupiers of exclusive possession of any part of the

space used by them. This is particularly common in buildings containing a number of "office suites" in which certain facilities are shared. If the owner of the property genuinely manages to give a person the right to occupy while at the same time not granting exclusive possession, the occupier will not be a tenant.

In *Dresden Estates Ltd v Collinson* [1987] E.G.L.R. the defendant was a scaffolder and builder who required accommodation in which to store his plant and equipment. He entered into a written agreement called a "Licence". The premises were described as the "Ground Floor Unit at Sneyd Hall Works . . . as shown on attached Plan and subject to a right of way to First Floor". A "licence fee" of £200 per month was payable. At first sight, therefore, it seems that the defendant was granted exclusive possession of a defined part of the premises for a term at a "rent" albeit that it was called a "licence fee". However, the clauses of the agreement contained the following provisions:

(b)   this Licence confers no exclusive right for the Licensee to use and occupy the Premises and the Licensors shall be entitled from time to time on giving the Required Notice to require the Licensees to transfer this occupation to other premises with the Licensor's adjoining property.
(f)   the Licensors may by giving the Required Notice to the Licensees increase the Licence fee to such amount as may be specified in such notice.

The Court of Appeal held that these provisions, in particular clause (b), were inconsistent with the grant of exclusive possession. Whether or not clause (f) is inconsistent with a tenancy may be doubted.

Those acting for "licencees" in these cases should also consider whether the presence of a clause such as clause (b) in *Dresden Estates Ltd v Collinson* is a "pretence" (see below).

For a case in which the occupiers of a service station were under agreements which withheld exclusive possesson, see *Esso Petroleum Co Ltd v Fumegage Ltd* [1994] E.G.L.R. 91 CA, at 93). (For cases concerned with residential premises in which agreements withholding exclusive possession have been considered and the occupiers held to be licensees see *AG Securities v Vaughan* [1988] 3 All E.R. 1058 HL, *Stribling v*

Wickham [1989] 2 E.G.L.R. 35 CA and *Mikover Ltd v Brady* [1989] 3 All E.R. 618.)

In *Clear Channel UK Ltd v Manchester City Council* [2005] EWCA Civ 1304 (advertising hoardings—see para.6-04 above) the agreement contained a term that stated:

> "This Agreement shall constitute a licence in respect of each Site and confers no tenancy on [the company] and possession of each Site is retained by [the Council] subject however to the rights and obligations created by this Agreement".

In relation to that clause Parker, LJ, at the end of his judgment said this:

> "I venture to make one additional comment, however. I find it surprising and (if I may say so) unedifying that a substantial and reputable commercial organisation like Clear Channel, having (no doubt with full legal assistance) negotiated a contract with the intention *expressed in the contract* . . . that the contract should *not* create a tenancy, should then invite the Court to conclude that it did. In making that comment I intend no criticism whatever of [counsel for Clear Channel], who sought valiantly to make bricks without straw. Nor, of course, do I intend to cast any doubt whatever on the principles established in *Street v Mountford*. On the other hand the fact remains that this was a contract negotiated between two substantial parties of equal bargaining power and with the benefit of full legal advice. Where the contract so negotiated contains not merely a label but a clause which sets out in unequivocal terms the parties' intention as to its legal effect, I would in any event have taken some persuading that its true effect was directly contrary to that expressed intention. In the event, however, as the judge so clearly demonstrated, the case admits of only one result."

It is important not to read too much into these final comments in the judgement. They do not mean that inserting a clause stating that the agreement constitutes a licence will be conclusive. That was not the basis of the decision (see para.6-04) and as Parker L.J. makes clear the court was not seeking to undermine the principles set out in *Street v Mountford*.

"Shams" and "pretences"

6-06   It is clear that parties cannot convert a tenancy into a licence merely by labelling the agreement with the heading "Licence" (*Street v Mountford*, per Lord Templeman at 294j; see above at para.6-02). However, parties do not confine their attempts at disguising tenancies to the label that is attached to the document. As seen above, they also include terms that are designed to show that the "tenant" has not been granted exclusive possession. The purpose in the context of residential accommodation has been to avoid the Housing and Rent Acts.

As parties to an agreement for the provision of residential accommodation are not permitted to contract out of the Rent Acts the courts are astute enough to detect and frustrate pretences designed to evade those Acts (*Antoniades v Villiers* per Lord Templeman at 1064f and 1067h). If, in the light of all the circumstances, the relevant provisions of a document do not truly represent the bargain between the parties they will be regarded as a pretence and ignored (*Aslan v Murphy (Nos 1 and 2)* [1989] 3 All E.R. 130). Thus, the terms of a document which purport to withhold exclusive possession from a tenant will be ignored if the reality is that such a right has in fact been agreed between the parties.

> "Quite apart from labelling, parties may succumb to the temptation to agree to pretend to have particular rights and duties which are not in fact any part of the true bargain. *Prima facie* the parties must be taken to mean what they say, but given the pressures on both parties to pretend, albeit for different reasons, the courts would be acting unrealistically if they did not keep a weather eye open for pretences, taking due account of how the parties have acted in performance of their apparent bargain. This identification and exposure of such pretences does not necessarily lead to the conclusion that their agreement is a sham, but only to the conclusion that the terms of the true bargain are not wholly the same as that of the bargain appearing on the face of the agreement. It is the true rather than the apparent bargain which determines the question: tenant or lodger?" (*Aslan v Murphy (Nos 1 and 2)* [1989] 3 All E.R. 130, per Lord Donaldson at 113g).

As with the Housing and Rent Acts, parties to an agreement are not permitted to contract out of Pt II of the 1954 Act (except where the exclusion of the Act is approved by the court; see Ch.3). Presumably, therefore the courts would adopt the same reasoning in relation to business premises as they apply in relation to residential accommodation when considering whether or not a document purporting to create a licence is in fact a tenancy.

Exceptions: occupiers with exclusive possession who are not tenants

There can be no tenancy unless the occupier enjoys exclusive possession but there are exceptional cases where an occupier with exclusive possession is not a tenant.

6–07

> "In *Errington v Errington* and in the cases cited by Denning L.J. there were exceptional circumstances which negatived the *prima facie* intention to create a tenancy notwithstanding that the occupier enjoyed exclusive occupation. The intention to create a tenancy was negatived if the parties did not intend to enter into legal relationships at all, or where the relationship between the parties was that of vendor and purchaser, master and service occupier, or where the owner, a requisitioning authority, had no power to grant a tenancy (*Street* 295j to 296a). These exceptional circumstances are not to be found in the present case, where there has been the lawful, independent and voluntary grant of exclusive possession for a term at a rent." (*Street v Mountford* [1985] 2 All E.R. 289, per Lord Templeman at 299j.)

One can see from the judgment of Lord Templeman in *Street v Mountford* (above) that in the following cases an agreement granting the occupier the right to exclusive possession of business premises for a term at a rent will not be a tenancy:

(1) Where there has been no intention to create legal relations, for example where there has been in the circumstances such as a family arrangement, an act of friendship or generosity (see Lord Templeman at pp.294e; 295b, j; 298f). Where one is concerned with commercial premises it is perhaps less likely that the

court will find that there was no intention to create legal relations but it is presumably possible. Note that the mere fact of family relationship or act of friendship etc. will not necessarily prevent the creation of legal relations. There are of course many cases where one member of a family grants to another a tenancy of premises.

(2) Occupancy by reference to the holding of an office (Lord Templeman at 300d; see further s.43(2) of the 1954 Act para.2-33).

(3) Body conferring right to exclusive possession having no power to grant a tenancy (Lord Templeman at 295j).

(4) Contract between vendor and purchaser for the sale of land (see para.4-14).

Termination of revocable licences

Notice period required

6-08 A licensor wishing to revoke a contractual licence should give such notice as is required by the terms of the agreement. Where there are no such terms the licensor should give the licensee a reasonable amount of time to leave (*Minister of Health v Bellotti* [1944] K.B. 298; *Vaughan v Vaughan* [1953] 1 Q.B. 762). Whether or not the amount of time that has been given is reasonable is a question of fact in each case. The periods in respect of which licence fees are paid will be relevant as will the length of time that the licensee has been in occupation.

In *Governing Body of Henrietta Barnet School v Hampstead Garden Suburb Institute* [1995] E.G.C.S. 55; *The Times*, April 13, 1995 Ch D it was held that a notice requiring a school to vacate premises within nine months was too short. It did not give sufficient time for practical arrangements to be made to safeguard the public service that the school provided. The school governors were required under statute to give the secretary of state not less than two years' notice of their intention to discontinue the school. The notice given should not be less than that period of two years.

The licence is revoked immediately the notice is given even if the amount of time given to leave is unreasonably short. Thus, the court will make an order for possession if a reasonable period has passed before proceedings have been commenced (*Minister of Health v Bellotti*). It is submitted that, as the licence has been revoked, the court has power to make an order for possession if a reasonable amount of time has elapsed at the date of the hearing even if it had not done so at the date proceedings were commenced.

The general rule is that one of two joint licensors (as with landlords) may revoke an oral licence without the consent of the other (see eg *Annen v Rattee* [1986] 1 EGLR 136). However, where the agreement is in writing whether or not one of the licensors can terminate will depend upon a construction of the agreement. In this case the notice terminating the licence had to be served by, or on behalf of, all joint licensors. Service by only one of joint licensors was therefore invalid (*Fitzhugh v Fitzhugh* [2012] EWCA Civ 694).

A notice to terminate a licence of business premises does not need to be in any particular form. Section 5 of the Protection from Eviction Act 1977 requires such a notice to be in prescribed form only where premises are "let as a dwelling".

Termination on assignment, insolvency or death

A revocable licence is automatically terminated by the bankruptcy or the death of the licensor or by the licensor voluntarily assigning the land over which the licence is exercised (see *Terunnanse v Terunnanse* [1968] A.C. 1086, per Lord Devlin at 1095G). Where the licensee goes bankrupt or dies the licence automatically terminates (*Coleman v Foster* (1856) 1 H&N 37). A licensee may not assign the benefit of the agreement unless there is a term in the agreement, express or implied, permitting him to assign (*Dorling v Honnor Marine Ltd* [1964] Ch. 560; and see s.136 of the Law of Property Act 1925). Any purported but impermissible assignment would therefore probably have the effect of terminating the licence.

6–09

Irrevocable licences

Determining whether or not the licence is irrevocable

There will be few circumstances in which a licence of business premises will be irrevocable. Whether or not a licence is

6–10

revocable depends upon the terms of the agreement (*Millennium Productions Ltd v Winter Garden Theatre (London) Ltd* [1946] 1 All E.R. 680, per Lord Greene M.R.; *Hounslow LBC v Twickenham Garden Developments Ltd* [1971] Ch. 233. A contractual licence under which a person is given the right to occupy premises indefinitely "gives rise to a constructive trust under which the legal owner is not allowed to turn out the licensee" (*DHN Food Distributors v London Borough of Tower Hamlets* [1976] 3 All E.R. 462, per Lord Denning at 467a).

A licensee does not necessarily have to show that there is a contract before he can argue that he has an irrevocable licence. He may instead be able to rely upon the equitable doctrine of estoppel. There are three elements to consider where a party raises the issue of estoppel:

(a)   a representation of fact;
(b)   reliance upon the representation; and
(c)   detriment resulting from the reliance.

The licensee must show that the licensor has made a representation intending that the licensee should act upon it. A presumption then arises that the licensee relied upon the representation, which it is up to the licensor to rebut (*Greasley v Cooke* [1980] 3 All E.R. 710). Finally, the licensee must establish that he has suffered a detriment as a result of that reliance (*Stevens & Cutting v Anderson* [1990] 1 E.G.L.R. 95). The licensor may be able to resist the licensee's assertion by showing that the licensee has not come to court with "clean hands" (*Williams v Staite* [1979] Ch. 291; *Willis & Son v Willis* (1985) 277 E.G. 1133).

Effect of irrevocable licences on third parties

6-11   Irrevocable licences have been held to bind a purchaser of the licensor's interest in the land who had notice of the licence (*Binions v Evans* [1972] Ch. 359), a licensor's trustee in bankruptcy (*Sharpe (a bankrupt, Re)* [1980] 1 W.L.R. 219), and the personal representatives and beneficiaries of a licensor's estate (*Errington v Errington and Woods* [1952] 1 K.B. 290; *Inwards v Baker* [1965] 2 Q.B. 29). But all these cases should now be read in the light of *Ashburn Anstalt v Arnold* [1988] 2 All E.R. 147 CA (overruled on another point in *Prudential Assurance Co v London Residuary Body* [1992] 3 All E.R. 504 HL) where it was held that a contractual licence was not an interest in land capable of binding a purchaser even where that purchaser had notice of the licence. The only circumstances in which the licence may be binding upon third parties is where a constructive trust is imposed and the court will not impose such a trust unless it is satisfied that the conscience of the purchaser is affected. See also *Yaxley v Gotts* [2000] 1 All ER 711 CA.

Proceedings for possession

Licensees (like tenants; see para.4–09) may not dispute their   **6–12**
"landlords' " title (*Government of State of Penang v Oon* [1972] A.C. 425 at 433E). Thus, a licensee may not seek to avoid an order for possession by arguing that the licensor has no interest in the property.

Where the proceedings have been commenced in the County Court the court may not postpone its order for possession:

> "(whether by the order or any variation, suspension or stay of execution) to a date later than 14 days after the making of the order, unless it appears to the court that exceptional hardship would be caused by requiring possession to be given by that date"

in which case the court has power to postpone the order for up to six weeks (s.89 Housing Act 1980—which applies to all orders for possession whether of residential or business premises, see para.23–48).

The limitations imposed on the court's discretion by s.89 apply when proceedings are in the High Court as well as the County Court (*Boyland and Son Ltd v Rand* [2006] EWCA Civ 1860 but do not apply to a court exercising appellate jurisdiction during the appeal process, so that a warrant can be stayed pending appeal (*Admiral Taverns (Cygnet) Ltd v Daniel* [2008] EWHC 1688).

Part 2

Termination on Default by the Tenant

CHAPTER 7

FORFEITURE: GENERAL RULES

. . . .

This chapter deals with a number of matters that may be relevant in all cases where a landlord is seeking to forfeit a lease, whether by proceedings or otherwise. It includes certain procedural points that are particularly relevant to proceedings for possession based upon forfeiture of the lease.

7–01

Matters specifically relevant to rent claims are dealt with in Ch.8. Particular points of relevance in cases where the tenant is in breach of covenants other than those relating to rent are dealt with in Ch.9. Certain special cases are dealt with in Chs 10 and 11. Relief from forfeiture is dealt with in Ch.12.

The landlord's right to re-enter the property and forfeit the lease

The proviso for re-entry/forfeiture clause

The usual name for the term in a lease entitling the landlord to bring the tenancy to an end prior to its originally intended expiry date is the "Proviso for re-entry". The proviso operates by entitling the landlord to re-enter the property if one of a number of stated events occurs and goes on to declare that upon re-entry the lease comes to an end. Hence the other title used: "Forfeiture clause". By re-entry the landlord forfeits the term. Many forfeiture clauses are unnecessarily lengthy and difficult to read. The Law Society's business lease is a model of clarity:

7–02

The Law Society Business Lease

Forfeiture

7–03   **12.** This lease comes to an end if the Landlord forfeits it by entering any part of the property, which the Landlord is entitled to do whenever:

(a)   payment of any rent is fourteen days overdue, even if it was not formally demanded;

(b)   the Tenant has not complied with any of the terms in this lease;

(c)   the tenant if an individual (and if more than one, any of them) is adjudicated bankrupt or an interim receiver of his property is appointed;

(d)   the Tenant if a company (and if more than one, any of them) goes into liquidation (unless solely for the purpose of amalgamation or reconstruction when solvent), or has an administrative receiver appointed or has an administration order made in respect of it.

The forfeiture of this lease does not cancel any outstanding obligation of the Tenant or Guarantor.

Note:

(1) That the landlord may forfeit by entering any part of the property. This is a common formula in forfeiture clauses.

(2) That in addition to actual physical re-entry a lease may be forfeited by serving proceedings for possession or by coming to an arrangement with occupiers in the property other than the tenants such as sub-tenants and trespassers (see para.7–13).

No implied forfeiture clause

7–04   Where there is no express forfeiture clause in a lease no such clause will be implied. The landlord may however be able to forfeit without a forfeiture clause if an event occurs which is specified as being a condition of the term (see s.146(7) of the Law of Property Act 1925, and see generally *Woodfall: Landlord and Tenant* para.17.058. Impugning the landlord's title amounts to breach of an implied condition entitling the landlord to forfeit: *WG Clarke (Properties) Ltd v Dupre Properties Ltd* [1992] 1 All E.R. 596, Ch D).

However, the following comments of May LJ in *Crisp v Eastaugh* [2007] EWCA Civ 638 should be noted (at [44]–[47]):

"Forfeiture of a lease for denial of title is a largely outdated medieval procedure . . . Insofar as it survives at all, as it may, it does so if the denial of title may properly be seen as in the nature of a repudiation of the lease and if there has been an acceptance of that repudiation; see *Abidogun v Frolam Healthcare Ltd* . . . A contention that a Landlord is entitled to forfeit a lease because of the form or content of a pleading in proceedings between the landlord and the tenant has now to be seen in the context of modern practice and the recently introduced Civil Procedure Rules whose central philosophy is to facilitate proper access to justice. In my judgment, there are two clear general reasons why the form or content of a pleading will normally now not be a proper basis for a landlord to be entitled to forfeit a lease for denial of title. First, the tenant may have one or more properly pleadable reasons for promoting or defending court proceedings against a landlord which may or may risk being seen as questioning or denying the landlord's title. Proper access to justice, in my view, must mean that the tenant must be able to advance those reasons in a pleading without for that reason alone risking forfeiture of the lease. If that were not so, the tenant would not be properly able to bring before the court what may in truth, at least until the court has decided the matter, be a perfectly arguable case and which may in some cases in fact be correct. Second, I cannot see, and certainly it does not arise in this case in my judgment, that a pleading containing material of this kind would normally be seen as a repudiation of the lease, unless possibly and exceptionally the landlord was able to establish that the relevant part of the pleading was advanced in bad faith. Parties are constitutionally entitled to bring their disputes before a court for determination. By doing so, they are inviting the court to determine the disputes but are normally to be regarded as content to abide by the court's decision. That, in my judgment, is a process which can scarcely result in an upholdable plea of repudiation."

Disguising the forfeiture clause: attempts to avoid relief provisions

The purpose of the forfeiture clause is to provide security for performance of the terms of the lease. The courts "lean against   **7–05** forfeiture" and if the tenant remedies the breach he will invariably be able to obtain relief from forfeiture (Ch.12). However, the fact that the law leans against forfeiture has not prevented landlords from attempting to take advantage of breaches to recover possession so that they can re-let the property at an increased rent and possibly obtain a further premium. They have attempted to exclude the court's equitable and statutory jurisdiction to grant relief by dressing up forfeiture clauses as something else, for example, by introducing a notice provision in the clause. These attempts have been unsuccessful. Thus, where a clause provided for termination of the lease on non-payment of rent, insertion of a notice provision requiring the landlord to serve a termination notice in that event did not deprive the clause of its status as a forfeiture clause and the tenant did not lose his right to claim relief (*Richard Clarke & Co Ltd v Widnall* [1976] 1 W.L.R. 845 CA). But a clause requiring notice of termination upon default will operate as a forfeiture clause only if it brings the lease to an end before its natural termination date (*Clays Lane Housing Cooperative v Patrick* (1984) 49 P.&C.R. 72).

Furthermore s.146(12) of the Law of Property Act 1925 expressly provides that the relief provisions of that section will have effect notwithstanding any stipulation to the contrary (para.9–01). A forfeiture in the guise of a surrender remains a forfeiture for the purposes of the section (*Plymouth Corp v Harvey* [1971] 1 All E.R. 623).

Relevance of Part II of the Landlord and Tenant Act 1954: holding over

7–06   As has been seen in Ch.1 a lease of business premises to which Pt II of the Landlord and Tenant Act 1954 applies may not, in the ordinary course of events, be brought to an end by the landlord otherwise than by service of a notice under s.25 of the 1954 Act (s.24(1) of the 1954 Act). However, s.24(1) does:

> "not prevent the coming to an end of a tenancy by . . . forfeiture, or by forfeiture of a superior tenancy . . . " (s.24(2); see para.1–02).

If the original lease contained a forfeiture clause the continuation tenancy under Pt II of the 1954 Act will be subject to that right of re-entry and if the tenant fails to pay the rent or otherwise breaches the terms of the lease the landlord will be able to rely upon the remedy of forfeiture.

Where the tenant holds over in circumstances in which Pt II of the 1954 Act does not apply to the tenancy so that he becomes a periodic tenant the forfeiture clause in the fixed term is carried over into the periodic term (*Thomas v Packer* (1857) 1 H.&N. 699).

Deciding whether or not to forfeit

Effect of forfeiture

Where a tenant has failed to pay his rent, or is in breach of covenant in some other respect, or has become insolvent the landlord will usually wish to rely upon the remedy of forfeiture but before taking that step he should be aware of the effects of forfeiture.

7–07

Forfeiture brings the tenancy, and all interests derived from the tenancy (i.e. sub-tenancies, mortgages and other charges), to an end so that the landlord is immediately entitled to possession (*Official Custodian for Charities v Mackey* [1984] 3 All E.R. 689) except as against lawful assured tenants of any part of the property that is a dwelling (see para.23–01). If the tenant wishes to retain possession he will have to apply for relief from forfeiture which will invariably require payment of any arrears and the remedying of any breach of covenant. Normally the tenant will wish to apply for relief so that he can carry on his business or, perhaps, so that he can sell the lease at a premium. However, in times of severe recession forfeiture of the lease may be the perfect solution to the tenant's problems. As forfeiture brings the tenancy to an end the landlord ceases to be entitled to rent that would otherwise become payable and may no longer rely upon the tenant's covenants in the lease—although he may sue in respect of past arrears and breaches. The tenant will therefore escape his future obligations by reason of the forfeiture. In a depressed letting market the landlord may prefer to retain the tenant and to pursue another remedy.

If the landlord elects to pursue an alternative remedy and to waive the right to forfeit in respect of a particular breach he will not subsequently be allowed to forfeit in respect of that breach. "Waiver" is dealt with in detail below, para.7–14.

Other remedies

7-08   There are a number of options that the landlord may wish to pursue other than forfeiture. For example, where there are arrears of rent he may sue for those arrears or where applicable, rely on the Commercial Rent Arrears Recovery procedure in order to take goods. If there has been a breach of covenant he may sue for damages or may seek an injunction to prevent further breaches. In some cases he may be able to obtain a mandatory injunction requiring the tenant, and possibly others, to put matters right, e.g. to accept a reassignment after an unlawful assignment or a surrender of an unlawful sublease (see para.10-06). Where the performance of the lease has been guaranteed the landlord may wish to bring a claim for rent or for damages against the surety. Where the lease is held by an assignee he may wish to sue the original tenant. On the other hand, if the landlord does forfeit the lease, and the option is open to him, he may require the surety to take the lease for the remainder of the term. See further Ch.13 where claims against persons other than the tenant are discussed.

Methods of re-entry

7-09   Where an event has occurred permitting the landlord to forfeit he must do something evidencing his intention to re-enter. There are three possibilities:

(1) The landlord may peaceably re-enter the property.
(2) Service of proceedings for possession is equivalent to re-entry.
(3) In certain circumstances, an arrangement made between the landlord and third persons in occupation may constitute a re-entry.

Peaceable re-entry

7-10   There are no statutory restrictions preventing the landlord of business premises from forfeiting the lease by peaceably re-entering the property. Self-help in this manner is prohibited only where the property was "let as a dwelling" which is taken to include a situation where the property consists of a shop with a flat above (s.2 of the Protection from Eviction Act 1977; see further discussion at para.23-01).

Protection from Eviction Act 1977 s.2

2. Where any premises are *let as a dwelling* on a lease which is subject **7–11**
to a right of re-entry or forfeiture it shall not be lawful to enforce that right
otherwise than by proceedings in the court while any person is lawfully
residing in the premises or part of them.

However, even where the premises are purely commercial the
re-entry must be peaceful. The landlord may not use force to
enter the property where there is someone in occupation. If he
does so, he commits a criminal offence (Criminal Law Act 1977
s.6; para.23–05) and it would seem that the re-entry is
ineffective (*Billson v Residential Apartments Ltd* [1992] 1 All
E.R. 141 at 146e). Self-help is, therefore, usually a practical
proposition only where the premises are empty.

For a re-entry to be effective the landlord must actually re-enter
the property with the intention of terminating the tenancy but
he does not need to be in possession for any substantial period
of time (*Billson v Residential Apartments Ltd* [1992] 1 All E.R.
141 HL). In that case the tenant was carrying out extensive
building works to the property. At 6am one morning the
landlord's agents peaceably re-entered the property, which was
vacant, and changed the locks. They left the property shortly
thereafter. By 10am the same day the tenant's workmen were
back in occupation and were carrying on with the building
works. It was held that the landlord's action was sufficient to
bring the lease to an end.

It is the intention to re-enter which is important. So long as the
landlord intends to bring the lease to an end, it does not matter
that he has made a mistake as to the identity of the tenant
(*Eaton Square Properties Ltd v Beveridge* [1993] E.G.C.S.
91).

Where a landlord with a right to forfeit does an act that is
inconsistent with the continued existence of the lease, such as
taking possession, it is not open to him later to argue that he
did not intend to forfeit the lease (*AGB Research plc, Re* [1994]
E.G.C.S. 73 Ch D). However, not every act that initially looks
like a re-entry is so. For example, if the circumstances are such
that the tenant appears to have disappeared from the property
and the landlord has merely re-entered for the purpose of
securing the premises the lease will not have been brought to
an end (*Relvock Properties Ltd v Dixon* (1972) 25 P. & C.R. 1
CA; see further in relation to surrender para.19–05).

Proceedings for possession

7-12   The landlord may determine a lease by the issue *and* service of a claim for possession. The service of the claim form operates as the decisive election to forfeit and is equivalent to re-entry (*Canas Property Co Ltd v K.L. Television Services Ltd* [1970] 2 All E.R. 795). Thereafter the former tenant remains in occupation as a trespasser and the landlord's claim is for possession. Forfeiture as such is not claimed. Rather, it is the basis upon which the claim for possession is made. For the consequences that follow from the rule that it is the service of the proceedings that brings the lease to an end and for the procedure to be adopted where the landlord elects to forfeit by proceedings see para.7-33.

Dealing with third parties

7-13   Where a person is in occupation of a property as a trespasser as against the tenant, the landlord may forfeit the lease by coming to an arrangement with the trespasser whereby the latter remains in occupation as the immediate tenant of the landlord. It is not necessary for the landlord to go through the "idle ceremony" of evicting the trespasser and then re-letting the property to him (*London & County (A&D) Ltd v Wilfred Sportsman Ltd* [1970] 2 All E.R. 600 at 607d).

A landlord may also effect a re-entry against his immediate tenant by an arrangement with an existing sub-tenant whereby the sub-tenant is to remain in occupation as the immediate tenant of the landlord on the terms of a *new tenancy.* However, the mere receipt of rents payable under an underlease is insufficient as it is not an assertion of the right of re-entry as against the sub-tenant; and so the coming to an arrangement with an existing sub-tenant under which he is to remain in occupation as a tenant of the landlord "for the residue and otherwise on the terms of his *existing sub-lease*" does not operate as a re-entry. (See *Ashton v Sobleman* [1987] 1 All E.R. 755 at 763f and 764h; *Hammersmith and Fulham LBC v Top Shop* [1989] 2 All E.R. 655 at 669e.) See also *Redleaf Investments Ltd v Talbot* (1994) *The Times,* May 5, Ch D. In that case the tenant was a company in administration. It was in arrears of rent and was no longer in occupation. The landlord granted an immediate lease to a third party. This grant was held to operate as a forfeiture of an existing lease and not the grant of a reversionary lease.

Waiver

Exercise of the landlord's election

"... The basic principle is that the court leans against **7–14** forfeiture. Therefore, if a landlord, after he knows of a breach of covenant entitling him to forfeit a lease, either communicates to the tenant his election to treat the tenancy as continuing, or does any act which recognises the existence of the tenancy or is inconsistent with its determination, he is deemed to have waived the forfeiture. It is for the lessee to establish the facts which in law constitute the waiver." (*David Blackstone Ltd v Burnetts (West End) Ltd* [1973] 3 All E.R. 782, per Swanwick J at 790f.)

There is no waiver if at the time of the landlord's act he has no actual or implied knowledge of the breach (see *Official Custodian for Charities v Parway Estates Development Ltd* [1984] 3 All E.R. 679). The landlord must have knowledge of the breach before he can be said to have waived his right to forfeit. The knowledge required to put the landlord to his election is the knowledge of *the basic facts*, which in law constitute the breach of covenant entitling him to forfeit the lease. Once he or his agent, such as an employee working at the premises, knows the facts, any appropriate act by the landlord or his agent will in law effect a waiver or a forfeiture (*David Blackstone Ltd v Burnetts (West End) Ltd* [1973] 3 All E.R. 782; *Metropolitan Properties Co Ltd v Cordery* [1979] 2 E.G.L.R. 78).

"It is also clear ... that a principal is affected by the knowledge of his agent and that he cannot escape the consequences of an act done by one agent by saying that it was not that agent but another that had the actual knowledge.

... the knowledge required to put a landlord to his election is knowledge of the basic facts that in law constitute a breach of covenant entitling him to forfeit the lease. Once he or his agent knows these facts, an appropriate act by himself or any agent will in law effect a waiver or a forfeiture. His knowledge or ignorance of the law is ... irrelevant." (*David Blackstone Ltd v Burnetts (West End) Ltd* [1973] 3 All E.R. 782, per Swanick J at p.789h.)

The landlord does not need to know all the facts. It is sufficient if he knows that there has been a breach, or if he is aware of facts that pointed to a breach of covenant or which should put him on inquiry as to the nature of the breach (*Metropolitan Properties Ltd v Cordery; Cornillie v Saha* (1996) 72 P.&C.R. 147). Where the tenant has sublet the landlord need know only that there has been a subletting or parting with possession. He does not need to know the name of the sub-tenant or the length of the term, nor the rent payable (*Cornillie v Saha*).

However, simply allowing the tenant to commit the breach without doing anything to prevent it is not sufficient to amount to a waiver (*Perry v Davis* (1858) C.B. NS 769).
To constitute a waiver the election must be communicated to the tenant.

> "The landlord has an election whether to waive or to forfeit, and it seems to me as at present advised, that a statement or act by the landlord which is neither communicated to the tenant nor can have any impact on the tenant should not be taken to be an election to waive the forfeiture" (*London & County (A&D) Ltd v Wilfred Sportsman Ltd* [1971] 1 Ch. 764, per Russell LJ at 782A; see also Swanick J at 793c in *David Blackstone Ltd v Burnetts (West End) Ltd* [1973] 3 All E.R. 782.)

"Continuing" and "once and for all" breaches

7–15   In considering whether or not a breach has been waived it is necessary to distinguish between "continuing" and "once and for all breaches". If the breach is a "once and for all breach" the right to forfeit is lost once the landlord does an act recognising the continuation of the tenancy. Where the breach is a continuing one (e.g. where the tenant is failing to keep the premises in good repair), the landlord will not be able to forfeit in respect of the earlier stage of the breach that he has waived but he may forfeit for any continuation of the breach that has occurred since the waiver. Thus, if the tenant continues to fail to repair the premises after the waiver, the landlord may forfeit. If a notice under s.146 of the Law of Property Act 1925 has previously been served in respect of the breach, there is no need to serve a further notice if there has been no change in the condition of the premises (*Greenwich LBC v Discreet Selling Estates Ltd* [1990] 2 E.G.L.R. 65).

In most cases there is no difficulty in distinguishing between continuing and once and for all breaches. For example, failure to pay rent is a "once and for all" breach that can be waived by subsequent action (*Church Commissioners for England v Nodjoumi* (1985) 51 P.&C.R. 155). Breach of the covenant to repair is a continuing breach (*Penton v Barnett* [1898] 1 Q.B. 276; *Greenwich LBC v Discreet Selling Estates Ltd* [1990] 2 E.G.L.R. 65); as is breach of the covenant to use the premises as a private residence (*Segal Securities v Thoseby* [1963] 1 Q.B. 887) or only for business use (*Cooper v Henderson* (1982) 263 E.G. 592 at 594). If a covenant is one to do something by a particular date, including a covenant to repair by such a date, that is a covenant which can be broken only once. The same applies to a covenant to do something within a reasonable time (*Farimani v Gates* [1984] 2 E.G.L.R. 66 applied). *Channel Hotels and Properties (UK) Ltd v Tamimi* [2004] EWCA Civ 1072 was concerned with the development of the roof space above a block of flats. A breach of a covenant to carry out the development as expeditiously as possible was a once and for all breach as it was possible to point to a time by which the works, if carried out and completed as expeditiously as possible, should have been completed.

The landlord may of course forfeit in respect of any breach that has occurred since the waiver whether the new breach is continuing or is a once and for all breach. Waiver of the breach does not waive the existence of the covenant see below, para.7–27.

Waiver by acceptance etc of rent

Acceptance of rent

Acceptance of rent payable in arrears, as a matter of law, **7–16** waives the right to forfeit. The landlord may not protect his position by accepting the rent "without prejudice" to that right. He must make an election: forfeiture or acceptance of the rent. He cannot have both (*Segal Securities v Thoseby* [1963] 1 Q.B. 887 at 898).

Acceptance of future rent payable in advance waives a once and for all breach which has occurred in the past as well as (apparently) a breach that occurs in the period covered by the rent (*Segal Securities* at 901). So far as continuing breaches are concerned, the acceptance of rent in advance can waive only those breaches that are at the time of the demand known to be continuing and will waive them only for such periods as it is definitely known they will continue (*Segal Securities* at 901).

> " . . . I now turn to the important and decisive question as to the circumstances in which a demand for or acceptance of rent payable in advance constitutes a waiver of breaches during the period covered by the rent demanded. Clearly it cannot be a waiver of future breaches of which the landlord has no advance knowledge . . . Equally clearly, an acceptance of rent in advance does waive a once and for all—that is to say, a non-continuing—breach in the past: such a waiver applies both to the past and to the period covered by the rent.

> As regards continuing breaches, it seems to me that, in the absence of express agreement, the acceptance of rent in advance can at highest only waive those breaches that are at the time of demand known to be continuing, and to waive them for such period as it is definitely known they will continue." (*Segal Securities Ltd v Thoseby* [1963] 1 Q.B. 887, per Sachs J at 901.)

Where rent is due in respect of two or more periods, a demand for rent in respect of the later period waives the breach in respect of the earlier period. For example, if the tenant fails to pay rent on the September quarter day and on the December quarter day a demand for both lots of rent will waive the right to forfeit in respect of the failure to pay the September quarter. However, the demand for the December quarter will not waive the right to forfeit in respect of the failure to pay that sum. The landlord may demand and bring proceedings in respect of the rent for that quarter and obtain judgment for it; and if the tenant fails to pay still forfeit in respect of it (*In Re Debtors Nos 13AI0 and 14AI0 of 1995* [1996] 1 All E.R. 691 Ch D).

> "In my judgment, in the context of a lease containing a right of re-entry in the common form, as that in the present case, once an instalment of rent has not been paid in the period allowed by the lease for payment, there is nothing inconsistent between the landlords re-entering and their claiming or receiving the rent concerned. Their right of re-entry arises once the rent is unpaid within the specified period and by virtue of that non-payment. It is unaffected

by demand for or acceptance of that instalment of rent outside the period permitted for payment" (per Rattee J at 697b).

(See further para.8-04: "Appropriation of payment to specific debt".)

It is important to note that acceptance *after* the event giving the landlord the right to forfeit for rent that *accrued prior* to that date does not waive the right to forfeit in respect of that breach, i.e. you can accept the old rent but not the new (*Stephens v Junior Army and Navy Stores Ltd* [1914] 2 Ch. 516 at 523).

Acceptance of a cheque tendered by the tenant in part to secure the dismissal of bankruptcy proceedings, did not amount to an act of waiver of the right to forfeit (*Osibanjo v Seahive Investments Ltd* [2008] EWCA Civ 1282).

Where, in order to avoid waiver of the breach, the landlord refuses to accept rent he will subsequently be able to claim mesne profits (damages for use and occupation) in proceedings for possession (para.7-54) and, may in those proceedings, seek an order for an interim payment (CPR 25.7(1)(d); PD 25B).

Demand for rent

An unambiguous demand for rent that has accrued since the right to forfeit has arisen is no different from acceptance of rent. It amounts in law to an election to treat the tenancy as continuing and waives the right to forfeit if at the time it is made the landlord has sufficient knowledge (see above) of the facts to put him to his election. It does not matter that the demand was sent by mistake by a person employed by the landlord or his agent who has no personal knowledge of the breach. Likewise, the mere fact that the landlord did not intend to waive the breach is irrelevant (*David Blackstone Ltd v Burnetts (West End) Ltd* [1973] 3 All E.R. 782; *Central Estates (Belgravia) Ltd v Woolgar (No.2)* [1972] 3 All E.R. 610).

7-17

Distraint for rent

The general rule is that a distraint for rent does waive a prior breach (*Doe d. David v Williams* (1835) 7 C.&P. 322). However,

7-18

where the lease provides that a landlord may not forfeit for non-payment of rent until he has attempted to distrain for the rent, any such act of distraint does not operate as a waiver (*Shepherd v Berger* [1891] 1 Q.B. 597). In that case part of the arrears were recovered by the distraint but that did not prevent the landlord from being able to forfeit in respect of the balance. (See also s.139(1) of the County Courts Act 1984 (para.12-03) and s.210 of the Common Law Procedure Act 1852 (para.12-15).)

Proceedings for rent

7-19 To bring a straightforward claim for rent is clearly no different from a demand for rent and thus waives the right to forfeit (*Dendy v Nicholl* (1856) 4 C.B. NS 376).

However, it often occurs that the tenant is in breach of covenant. The landlord serves a notice under s.146 of the Law of Property Act 1925 but before he commences proceedings a further instalment of rent falls due. If the rent is tendered and accepted, the landlord waives the right to forfeit. If no rent is tendered, may the landlord seek to forfeit in respect of both the earlier breach and the non-payment of rent and may he claim the arrears in the proceedings? The arguments each way are as follows:

(1) That the service of proceedings for possession is an unequivocal election to forfeit and that anything else done or claimed in the proceedings cannot amount to a waiver (see para.7-12).

(2) On the other hand, a claim based upon non-payment of rent implies that the landlord considers the lease to be in existence on the date upon which the rent falls due. Such a claim is therefore inconsistent with an election to treat the lease as forfeited.

The decision in *Dendy v Nicholl* is sometimes cited as authority for the proposition that one may not make a claim for possession based upon forfeiture and claim arrears of rent. However, in *Penton v Barnett* [1898] 1 Q.B. 276 it was stated that *Dendy v Nicholl* is simply authority for the proposition that an action for rent is as good as a waiver of forfeiture as an action for possession is a forfeiture of the tenancy. In *Penton v Barnett* the lease contained a covenant to repair and the landlord served a s.146 notice requiring the tenant to repair within three months. Three days after the expiration of the notice a quarter's rent became due. No repairs having been carried out, the landlord brought an action for possession based on the breach of covenant and non-payment of rent and in the proceedings claimed the quarter's rent. (The defendant paid the rent into court.) The Court of Appeal held that, as the breach of covenant was a continuing one, the claim for rent did not affect the right to possession in respect of non-repair after the date when the rent fell due. The implication is that the claim for rent in the proceedings did waive the failure to repair up to the date upon which the rent fell due and that, if the breach had been a once and for all breach, the claim for rent would have waived the breach.

> "The position on January 14, 1897 would be that as nothing had been done since the notice as to repairs, the plaintiff had the right to determine the tenancy by the issue of the writ, and to sue in respect of such rights as had accrued to him during the tenancy. . . . Then he brought his action for possession, and in it he claimed for a quarter's rent due on the previous December 25. In my opinion, this claim does not constitute a waiver of the forfeiture. All that was laid down in *Dendy v Nicholl* was that an action for rent was as good as a waiver of forfeiture as an action of ejectment was as a determination of the tenancy. *If there had not been a recurring breach, but something which had happened once for all, the state of things might have been different,* but in this case, in my opinion, there is nothing in the statement of claim inconsistent with an election to determine the lease from December 25." (*Penton v Barnett* [1898] 1 Q.B. 276, per Rigby LJ at 280–1.)

In conclusion therefore it would seem that a claim for arrears of rent that is included in proceedings for possession based upon forfeiture for breach of covenant will waive the breach if it is a once and for all breach but not if it is a continuing breach. (See also the discussion of *Penton v Barnett* in *Greenwich LBC v Discreet Selling Estates Ltd* [1990] 2 E.G.L.R. 65.)

After re-entry has occurred the landlord is entitled to bring a claim for the rent that accrued prior to the re-entry (*Hartshorne v Watson* (1838) 4 Bing. N.C. 178). Perhaps, therefore, the solution is to commence proceedings for possession based upon forfeiture for the breach of covenant with an alternative claim based upon forfeiture for non-payment of rent but not to include a claim for those arrears. Once those proceedings have been served (i.e. once the re-entry is deemed to have taken place), a claim for rent up to the date of service of the proceedings (i.e. the date of re-entry) and for mesne profits thereafter can be issued and served. The two actions can then be consolidated. In some cases an application for an interim payment may provide a suitable remedy (see para.7–16).

Waiver by other means

7-20   Where no demand for rent is involved, different considerations apply. The general principle was set out in *Expert Clothing Service and Sales Ltd v Hillgate House Ltd* [1985] 2 All E.R. 998.

> "In cases where no demand for rent is involved the court is free to look at all the circumstances of the case to consider whether the landlord's act was so unequivocal that, when considered objectively, it could only be regarded as having been done consistently with the continued existence of the tenancy." (*Expert Clothing Service and Sales Ltd v Hillgate House Ltd* [1985] 2 All E.R. 998, per Slade LJ at 1012c.)

This general principle should always be borne in mind but there are also authorities dealing with particular circumstances.

Service of a notice to quit

7-21   Service of a *valid* notice to quit recognises the continuing existence of the lease and thus waives the right to forfeit (*Marche v Christodoulakis* (1948) 64 T.L.R. 466).

Service of a s.146 notice

7-22   As the purpose and effect of a s.146 notice is to operate as a preliminary to actual forfeiture (see para.9–02), service of such a notice cannot be an unequivocal affirmation of the existence of the lease and therefore does not operate to waive a right to forfeit (*Church Commissioners for England v Nodjoumi* (1985) 51 P. & C.R. 155); but a notice served under s.146 should not contain a demand for arrears of rent accruing since the breach complained of in the notice because (it is submitted) the demand will waive that breach, it not being necessary to serve a s.146 notice in respect of arrears of rent.

Negotiations that recognise the continued existence of the tenancy

In *Expert Clothing*, the sending of a letter enclosing a proposed **7–23** deed of variation was not, on the facts, regarded as a waiver but it was recognised that in certain circumstances the proffering of a mere negotiating document might amount to an unequivocal recognition of the existence of a presently subsisting tenancy (at p.1012). But it seems that it will be necessary to know the terms of the negotiations before it will be held that the right to forfeit has been waived. The mere fact that negotiations have taken place will be insufficient and the court will not have regard to the contents of "without prejudice" negotiations (*National Jazz Centre Ltd, Re* [1988] 2 E.G.L.R. 57).

> " . . . The test that was adopted by Slade L.J. in *Expert Clothing* . . . was whether the sending of a letter in the course of negotiations could be reasonably understood as unequivocally indicating the landlord's intention to treat the lease as subsisting on the date of the letter.
>
> The facts of that case were much stronger than the present case in favour of the tenant's submission of the existence of the lease, in that a draft had been proferred which referred to the continuation of a lease. Nevertheless, the Court of Appeal held that there had been no such waiver. That case in itself demonstrates that the mere existence of negotiations is not sufficient to show that the landlord participating in the negotiations is accepting that the tenancy does not exist and that there has been no forfeiture. It is true that if rent is proferred and accepted without prejudice, the court will look at the fact of acceptance of the rent and will hold that is sufficient to constitute an admission of the existence of the lease and a waiver of any forfeiture said to have occurred prior to that date. But I cannot see that there is any similarity between the acceptance of a rent without prejudice and the mere entering into of negotiations. It is impossible, in my judgment, to reach a conclusion that there has been an unequivocal acceptance of the existence of a lease by the entering into of negotiations,

> without looking at what occurred in the [*without prejudice*] negotiations themselves, and that, it is quite clear ... is something which the court cannot do." (*National Jazz Centre Ltd, Re* [1988] 2 E.G.L.R. 57, per Gibson J at 58H.)

For the most recent House of Lords authority on "without prejudice" negotiations see (*Ofulue v Bossert* [2009] UKHL 16).

Agreement to voluntary arrangement

7-24   The landlord does not waive his right to forfeit if he agrees to a voluntary arrangement pursuant to s.258 of the Insolvency Act (*Naeem (A Bankrupt), Re* [1990] 1 W.L.R. 48); although relief from forfeiture will probably be granted on terms that the tenant pay the amount agreed under the arrangement (see para.7-50).

Grant of a reversionary lease

7-25   The grant of a reversionary lease "subject to and with the benefit" of the tenant's lease does not waive the right to forfeit. It is not an unequivocal act of recognition of the pre-existing lease and as a statement or act which is neither communicated to nor could have any impact on the tenant is not an election to waive a right to forfeit (*London & County (A&D) Ltd v Wilfred Sportsman Ltd* [1971] 1 Ch. 764).

Court proceedings; injunction claim

7-26   A claim in forfeiture proceedings for possession *and* an injunction restraining the tenant from continuing with the breaches will waive the right to forfeit. However, the landlord may seek an injunction in the alternative without waiving the right to forfeit (*Calabar Properties Ltd v Seagull Autos Ltd* [1969] 1 Ch. 451). For examples of cases where the landlord waived his right to forfeit by seeking an injunction see *Iperion Investments Corp v Broadwalk House Residents Ltd* [1992] 2 E.G.L.R. 235) and *Comillie v Saha* (1996) 72 P. & C.R. 147.

Waiver of breach does not waive the covenant

7-27   It is sometimes thought that a waiver of the breach amounts to a waiver of the covenant. For example, that a waiver by the landlord of a particular subletting in breach of covenant prevents the landlord from complaining about sublettings that may occur in the future. This view is incorrect. Section 148 of the Law of Property Act 1925 expressly provides that this is not so, "unless a contrary intention appears".

Law of Property Act 1925, s.148(1)

148.–(1) Where any actual waiver by a lessor or the persons deriving title **7–28**
under him of the benefit of any covenant or condition in any lease is
proved to have taken place in any particular instance, such waiver shall
not be deemed to extend to any instance, or to any breach of covenant
or condition save that to which such waiver specially relates, nor operate
as a general waiver of the benefit of any such covenant or condition.
(2) This section applies unless a contrary intention appears . . .

However, circumstances may arise where the landlord is estopped from relying on a term of the lease (*Central London Property Trust Ltd v High Trees House Ltd* [1947] K.B. 130; *Brikom Investments Ltd v Carr* [1979] 2 All E.R. 753).

Clauses that attempt to avoid waiver

Some leases contain a proviso to the effect that the right to **7–29**
forfeit will continue notwithstanding the acceptance of or demand for rent by the landlord with knowledge of the breach. However, the consequences of an act, relied on by a tenant as a waiver, are a matter of law and not of intention (*David Blackstone v Burnetts (West End) Ltd* [1973] 3 All E.R. 782 at 789h). It is therefore submitted that any clause in a lease that seeks to permit the landlord to forfeit, notwithstanding an act waiving the breach is of no effect.

After service of proceedings

Once the landlord has unequivocally elected to re-enter, **7–30**
whether by service of a claim for possession or otherwise, no subsequent act will be treated as waiving the right to forfeit (*Civil Service Co-operative Society v McGrigor's Trustee* [1923] 2 Ch. 347 at 358). Further receipt of "rent" may however give rise to an inference that a new tenancy has been created (*Evans v Wyatt* (1880) 43 L.T. 176).

The landlord should not therefore accept any monies until after he has served his claim form and if he does so he is best advised to accept expressly on the basis that the payments are being accepted as mesne profits (damages for occupation) and that there is no intention to create a new tenancy. (For a specimen letter see Form 2, para.7–31.) Receipt of monies in such circumstances does not create a new tenancy because there is no intention to create legal relations (see discussion of *Street v Mountford*, para.6–02). See also the ability to apply for interim payments in respect of mesne profits para.7–16.

Form 2: Letter accepting mesne profits

7–31

> Dear
>
> RE ....
> Please find enclosed a claim form claiming possession of the property which you occupy at ....
>
> All further payments in respect of your occupation of the property should be sent to .... at .... These payments will be accepted by your landlord as damages for your use and occupation of the property whilst the proceedings continue. The acceptance by the landlord of such sums will not give rise to the creation of a new tenancy.
>
> Yours etc.

Forfeiture proceedings

7–32 Chapter 23 deals with proceedings for possession generally. This section deals with specific requirements where the claim is based upon forfeiture of the lease.

The claim form/particulars of claim

7–33 The particulars of claim must be endorsed with the name and address of any person entitled to claim relief against forfeiture as undertenant including a mortgagee; and where such particulars are stated an extra copy of the particulars of claim should be filed with the court for service on that person (PD 55.4, para.2.4; para.23–93).

Where the person concerned is a sub-tenant in occupation, the landlord may well wish to join him as a party to the proceedings in any event (see further para.23–13).

The claim form should not include a claim for an injunction *in addition* to the claim for possession as this may be construed as a waiver of the right to forfeit, although a claim in the alternative may be added (see above, para.7–26). Where possession is claimed in respect of non-payment of rent and the property includes a dwelling, (see paras 23–29 and 23–30).

Registration of the action

Where the land is registered, the action may be protected by entry of a notice (Land Registration Act 2002 s.34 and s.87(1)(a)). Where it is unregistered, a claim for the forfeiture of a lease is a "pending land action" within the meaning of s.17(1) of the Land Charges Act 1972 and is therefore registerable as a "pending action" under s.5(2) of the 1972 Act (*Selim Ltd v Bickenhall Engineering Ltd* [1981] 3 All E.R. 210). **7–34**

Consequences of service of the proceedings

Where the landlord elects to determine the lease by proceedings it is the *service* of the claim form (not its issue) that operates as the decisive election to forfeit and that is equivalent to re-entry (see para.7–12). The following consequences result from the rule that it is the service of the proceedings that brings the lease to an end: **7–35**

(1) Rent is payable by the tenant up until the date of service of the proceedings. From that date the landlord is entitled to recover payments for the occupation of the land from the ex-tenant as trespasser, as mesne profits (damages for use and occupation): *Canas Property Co Ltd v K L Television Services Ltd* [1970] 2 All E.R. 795 CA. See further para.7–54.

(2) From the date of service of the writ, the tenant is no longer bound by any of the other covenants in the lease such as the covenant to repair. If after that date the ex-tenant damages the property the landlord's remedy will be in tort (*Associated Deliveries Ltd v Harrison* (1984) 50 P. & C.R. 91 CA).

" . . . in appropriate proceedings it seems to me that the landlord could well have a very adequate remedy in a claim for damages for wrongful occupation of the land . . . the authorities seem to indicate that in appropriately constituted proceedings the damages recoverable could extend beyond mere payment for the use and occupation of land, to include any loss within the ordinary rules of remoteness of damage which the plaintiff has suffered from being denied possession of the property and so unable to secure and occupy the property for his own purposes." (*Associated Deliveries Ltd v Harrison* (1984) P. & C.R. 91, per Dillon J at p.103.)

(3) The fact that the tenancy has been determined also means that the landlord will be unable to invoke the provisions of a rent review clause. However, if the tenant subsequently applies for relief from forfeiture, the court should give consideration to the inclusion of a condition to the grant of relief, which will preserve the right of the landlord to bring the rent review provision into operation (*Soteri v Psylides* [1991] 1 E.G.L.R. 138).

Between service of the proceedings and the final conclusion of the action there is a "twilight period" during which it is not clear whether the forfeiture is going to be effective. It may be that the landlord will not establish his allegations or that the tenant will succeed in an application for relief from forfeiture. As will be seen in Ch.12, if relief from forfeiture is granted the tenant is restored to his original position as if the lease had never been forfeited. In *Meadows v Clerical, Medical and General Life Assurance Society* [1980] 1 All E.R. 454 it was held that, during the period while an application for relief against forfeiture is pending (i.e. during the "twilight period"), the tenant has sufficient standing to apply under Pt II of the Landlord and Tenant Act 1954 for the grant of a new tenancy. The tenant (who has not elected to determine the tenancy) can also enforce the landlord's covenants during this period if he is claiming relief (*Peninsular Maritime Ltd v Padseal Ltd* (1981) 259 E.G. 860).

The landlord is not precluded by service of forfeiture proceedings from serving a notice to terminate the tenancy under s.25 of the Landlord and Tenant 1954 Act (see Ch.14). If as a result of that notice the lease comes to an end before the forfeiture proceedings have been completed, the landlord can seek possession on the basis of that notice (*Baglarbasi v Deed Method Ltd* [1991] 29 E.G. 137).

Summary judgment

A very important case of which representatives of tenants should be aware is *Liverpool Properties Ltd v Oldbridge Investments Ltd* [1985] 2 E.G.L.R. 111 where it was held that a claim for relief is inextricably linked to the landlord's claim for possession and that if genuine and arguable it amounts to a defence precluding the making of an order for possession on an application for summary judgment. No doubt the same principles apply under Pt 24 in which the court will consider whether there is a real prospect of success (CPR Pt 24.2).

7–36

> "Although the right to claim relief against forfeiture is now statutory, it is in origin an equitable defence. It was a means by which equity stepped in to prevent the enforcement of a legal right. It is inextricably mixed with the claim for forfeiture, and it is, in my judgment, a true equitable defence to the legal claim for forfeiture. In those circumstances, it is something which should be viewed quite without regard to the words of Order 14, rule 3 upon which the judge relied. It is a counterclaim which ought to result in unconditional leave to defend being given . . .
>
> I would for my part, if I had not come to the conclusion that the order was justified because it was an equitable counterclaim inextricably involved in the claim, also have come to the conclusion, as did the learned judge, that there ought to be unconditional leave to defend under Order 14, rule 3. I cannot see that it would serve the ends of justice if claims of this sort were to result in orders for possession. It would put tenants in a position which would be wholly untenable.
>
> It was submitted on behalf of the plaintiffs that, if this were so, no landlord would ever be able to get an order for possession, for all that would be needed would be that the tenant should counterclaim for relief. That may be so, but if the counterclaim for relief is a genuine claim which might succeed, I see no reason why the landlord should have a claim to possession immediately. If the tenant has got an arguable claim for relief which he desires to pursue, and which, if successful, will result in the lease never being truly determined, then I see no reason why a landlord

> should have judgment under Order 14." (*Liverpool Properties Ltd v Oldbridge Investments Ltd* [1985] 2 E.G.L.R. 111, per Parker LJ)

There will be few cases where the court comes to the conclusion that the tenant's application for relief is bound to fail (*Sambrin Investments Ltd v Taborn* [1990] 1 E.G.L.R. 61).

> "She (*counsel for the landlord*) boldly submitted that on the facts of the present case there was no prospect of relief being granted. She pointed to the long history of failures by the defendants to honour their contractual obligations to repair the premises and, in particular, to the fact that a schedule of dilapidation had been served as long ago as 1986, and she submitted that even now [1990], there is no evidence that all the repairs have been completed.
>
> I must, in considering this point, bear in mind the width of the discretion conferred by section 146(2) of the Law of Property Act 1925 on the court when it considers whether or not relief from forfeiture should be granted. . . .
>
> So wide is the discretion that, in my judgment it will be a fairly rare case where the court will be able to say that a genuine claim for relief from forfeiture is bound to fail." (*Sambrin Investments Ltd v Taborn* [1990] 1 E.G.L.R. 61, per Gibson J at 62H.)

Unfortunately for many tenants these cases do not appear to be widely known. It is common for the court to give judgment for possession and to adjourn the application for relief. It will usually grant a stay of execution pending that application. If a practitioner is presented with a case (perhaps initially dealt with by the client in person) where judgment has been given for possession and the claim for relief adjourned, the first step to take is to see whether a stay of execution has been granted. If not it should be applied for immediately, if necessary in the first instance without notice. If no application for relief has been issued, such an application should be issued immediately. If the basis upon which the forfeiture claim was made was for breach of a covenant other than for non-payment of rent and the landlord has already re-entered pursuant to the order, the tenant will have lost his right to apply for relief (para.12-18).

Form 3 at para.7–38 is a suitable form of witness statement for use in an application for a stay.

See further para.22–46 in relation to summary judgment in possession claims.

Company in liquidation: the "Blue Jeans" order

Where a company is in liquidation under a winding up order and **7–37** has no defence to a claim for possession based upon forfeiture, the landlord may, instead of issuing a claim (which would require leave from the companies court) and making an application for summary judgment, seek an order for possession in the winding up (*Blue Jeans Sales Ltd, Re* [1979] 1 All E.R. 641—possession was sought on the ground that the lease was forfeit by reason of non-payment of rent. It was not disputed that there were substantial arrears).

In *Blue Jeans Sales Ltd, Re* the company had sublet and there were sub-tenants in occupation. The question arose as to their protection as they were obviously not party to the proceedings. The court held that the parties in actual occupation were protected by RSC Ord 45, r.3 (which is now CPR 83.13, see para.23–69), which precludes the Companies Registrar from giving leave to issue a claim of possession until notice to the occupiers has been given enabling them to apply for relief from forfeiture.

Landlord seeking to withdraw the claim

Where a landlord serves a claim unequivocally electing to forfeit **7–38** a lease and the landlord's claim is admitted by the tenant the landlord cannot subsequently withdraw the claim and argue that the lease remains in existence (*GS Fashions Ltd v B & Q plc* [1995] 4 All E.R. 899 Ch D; see also *Kingston upon Thames Royal London Borough Council v Marlow* [1996] 17 E.G. 187 QBD where the tenant vacated and handed the keys to the landlord). In an appropriate case the landlord will be able to avoid the problem by claiming an injunction as an alternative to forfeiture because proceedings making such a claim do not constitute an unequivocal election to determine the lease (para.7–26).

"In this case the landlord by its writ, after pleading a breach of the covenant against parting with possession, made the immediate election to forfeit. In law this was equivalent of the landlord peaceably re-entering and taking possession. Thereupon the tenant by its defence admitted and agreed the commission of the breach and the forfeiture, and the landlord's right to possession, and made no claim to relief. It seems to me that at this stage on the pleadings alone there is agreement resolving or obviating any dispute as to the landlord's entitlement to forfeit, and the forfeiture effected by service of the writ no longer remained open to challenge or question by the landlord. The lease is to be treated as determined by forfeiture as the parties intended." (*GS Fashions Ltd v B & Q plc*, per Lightman J at 904.)

The limitations of the decision in *GS Fashions Ltd* were set out by Lightman J at p.906d:

"I should emphasise certain limitations on the proposition of law on which I have founded this judgment. (1) I am concerned only with the rights inter se as between lessor and lessee. I am not here concerned only with the situation where there is a sub-tenant or mortgagee of the lease. Confirmation or validation of a forfeiture by the lessee alone may not prejudice the entitlement of a sublessee or mortgagee to challenge the validity of the forfeiture and accordingly to maintain the continued subsistence of their interests. (2) I do not have to consider the position where after service of the writ the lessee in its defence denies the entitlement to forfeit and how far it is open to the parties and in particular the lessor to challenge his pleadings and position thereafter. But as it seems to me, by parity of reasoning, if the lessee alleges that the forfeiture was invalid, the lessor should be able to concede and agree the lessee's contention and on that basis withdraw his claim to forfeiture. (3) The lessor can avoid the situation arising in this case by claiming in the alternative in his writ forfeiture and relief (e.g. an injunction restraining or remedying breaches of covenant) which presupposes the continued existence of the lease, leaving his election between remedies (unless previously exercised) to the trial."

Form 3: Witness statement seeking stay of execution

IN THE HIGH COURT
OF JUSTICE

Queen's Bench/
Chancery Division

[Name and number
of statement.
dated ....

Filed on behalf of the Claimant

7–38

[*The Landlord*]

Claimant

-and-

[*The Tenant*]

Defendant

I, [*name of solicitor*], Solicitor, of [*address*] hereby state as follows:

1. I am a partner in the firm of ...., solicitors for the Defendant, and have the conduct of this matter on behalf of the Defendant. This statement is made in support of the Defendant's application to stay execution of an order for possession made in favour of the Claimant on .... I make this statement with the authority of the Defendant and from information supplied to me by the Defendant, which I believe to be true, and from the documents exhibited to this statement. A bundle containing relevant documentation is now produced and shown to be marked " . . . 1".

2. The Claimant's claim for possession was based upon forfeiture of a lease of commercial premises held by the Defendant at [*address of property*]. The Claimant sought to forfeit the lease and to obtain an order for possession for breach of [*set out brief details of breach*]. The Claimant applied for summary judgment and on .... Master ..... made an order for possession (p.1 of "..1"). At that stage the Defendant was acting in person but the next day he instructed me to act on his behalf.

3. Yesterday my firm took out an application seeking relief from forfeiture (p.2 of "..1"). The application was served by hand yesterday afternoon on the Claimant's solicitors and is due to be heard on .... I have not yet had time to prepare a full statement in support of the Defendant's application for relief but the basic grounds for the claim for relief are that [*briefly set out the basis of the claim for relief, e.g.* that the breach has been substantially remedied etc.].

4. In my letter to the Claimant's solicitors enclosing the application for relief I asked for an undertaking to be given by noon today that the Claimant would not seek to enforce the order for possession pending the hearing of the Defendant's application for relief. I do not know whether or not they have yet applied for leave, which of course may be sought without notice.

5. The Claimant's solicitors have failed to give the undertaking requested and I therefore request that the court stay execution of the order for possession until after the hearing of the Defendant's application for relief. The Defendant has an appointment to see me at 10 a.m. tomorrow morning to give me full instructions so that I can prepare a full statement in support of the application for relief.

Statement of Truth

Dismissal of a forfeiture claim

7-40   The dismissal of a forfeiture claim, whether by compromise or otherwise, has the consequence that the forfeiture has not been established and the lease whatever its status might have been during the action is fully restored (*Hynes v Twinsectra Ltd* [1995] 2 E.G.L.R. 69 CA):

> "The order made was that that action should be dismissed, and it seems to me impossible to contend, once that has happened, that any conclusion follows other than that the forfeiture has not been established. The lease, whatever may have been its status pending that action, must, in my judgment, be taken to have been fully restored when the action was dismissed ... In my view, once the forfeiture proceedings were dismissed, the contention that the lease did not exist cannot be accepted. There was no need for a grant of relief to restore the lease from the shadowy state it had enjoyed to a full existence; the dismissal of the claim that had driven it into the shadows had that effect" (per Hutchison LJ at p.73D).

> " ... the authorities establish that service of proceedings for possession is an election by the lessor to treat the lease as forfeited. Further, it is to be taken as notional re-entry and thus forfeiture; but the act of forfeiture is subject to determination by the court of the validity of the claim. The lease is potentially good and the process of forfeiture is not complete until the proceedings are determined, which may include determination of an application for relief from forfeiture, but it will be a nullity if the proceedings do not succeed, or there is relief from forfeiture" (per Aldous LJ at 73K).

See also the more recent case of *Mount Cook Ltd v The Media Business Centre Ltd* [2004] EWHC 346 Ch where the court applied the principle to a case where the landlord unilaterally discontinued the claim before it had been dealt with.

Insolvency of the tenant

7-41   This section considers the affect of the insolvency of the tenant on the ability of the landlord to forfeit the lease. It also deals with insolvency as a reason for forfeiture.

Companies

Administration

The primary objective of administration is to rescue the company as a going concern. If that is not possible the objective is to get a better result from the creditors than is likely to result from liquidation; or, if that is not possible, to realise the property of the company to distribute to secured creditors: see para.3 of Sch.B1 of the Insolvency Act 1986 (as amended by the Insolvency Act 2000 and the Enterprise Act 2002). The 1986 Act imposes restrictions on forfeiture, whether by peaceable re-entry or by proceedings, against companies that are in administration. Where the tenant is a company in administration, or in respect of which an application for administration is made, the restrictions are to be found in paras 43 and 44 of Sch.B to the 1986 Act:

7–42

Insolvency Act 1986 Sch.B1 paras 43 and 44

43.–(1) This paragraph applies to a company in administration.
(2) No step may be taken to enforce security over the company's property except—

7–43

> (a)   with the consent of the administrator, or
> (b)   with the permission of the court.

(3)
(4) A landlord may not exercise a right of forfeiture by peaceable re-entry in relation to premises let to the company except—

> (a)   with the consent of the administrator, or
> (b)   with the permission of the court.

(5)
(6) No legal process (including legal proceedings, execution, distress and diligence) may be instituted or continued against the company or property of the company except—

> (a)   with the consent of the administrator, or
> (b)   with the permission of the court.

[(6A) . . .
(7) Where the court gives permission for a transaction under this paragraph it may impose a condition on or a requirement in connection with the transaction.
(8) In this paragraph "landlord" includes a person to whom rent is payable.

44.–(1) This paragraph applies where an administration application in respect of a company has been made and—

> (a)   the application has not yet been granted or dismissed, or

    (b)   the application has been granted but the administration order has not yet taken effect.

(2) This paragraph also applies from the time when a copy of notice of intention to appoint an administrator under paragraph 14 is filed with the court until—

    (a)   the appointment of the administrator takes effect, or
    (b)   the period of five business days beginning with the date of filing expires without an administrator having been appointed.

(3) Sub-paragraph (2) has effect in relation to a notice of intention to appoint only if it is in the prescribed form.

(4) This paragraph also applies from the time when a copy of notice of intention to appoint an administrator is filed with the court under paragraph 27(1) until—

    (a)   the appointment of the administrator takes effect, or
    (b)   the period specified in paragraph 28(2) expires without an administrator having been appointed.

(5) The provisions of paragraphs 42 and 43 shall apply (ignoring any reference to the consent of the administrator).

(6) If there is an administrative receiver of the company when the administration application is made, the provisions of paragraphs 42 and 43 shall not begin to apply by virtue of this paragraph until the person by or on behalf of whom the receiver was appointed consents to the making of the administration order.

(7) . . .

It will be seen from these provisions that the consent of the administrator or permission of the court is required before various steps can be taken. For the general principles that the court will take into account when deciding whether or not to grant permission see the judgment of Nicolls LJ (at p.542) in *In re Atlantic Computer Systems plc* [1992] Ch. 505; the key points of which can be summarised as follows:

(1)   The burden of proof is on the landlord to persuade the court to grant permission.

(2)   If granting permission to the landlord to exercise his proprietary rights and repossess his land is unlikely to impede the achievement of that purpose, permission should normally be given.

(3)   In other cases when a landlord seeks possession the court has to carry out a balancing exercise, balancing the legitimate interests of the landlord and the legitimate interests of the other creditors of the company.

(4)   In carrying out the balancing exercise great importance is normally to be given to the proprietary interests of the landlord.

(5) Thus it will normally be a sufficient ground for the grant of permission if significant loss would be caused to the landlord by a refusal. For this purpose loss comprises any kind of financial loss, direct or indirect, including loss by reason of delay, and may extend to loss which is not financial. But if substantially greater loss would be caused to others by the grant of permission, or loss which is out of all proportion to the benefit which permission would confer on the landlord, that may outweigh the loss to the landlord caused by a refusal. In considering these matters it will often be necessary to assess how probable the suggested consequences are.

(6) There are many factors that may be relevant. For example, the conduct of the parties might be a relevant factor.

Permission to bring proceedings

These principles were applied in *Innovate Logistics Ltd (in administration) v Sunberry Properties Ltd* [2008] EWCA Civ 1321 where it was held that in considering whether or not to give permission to a landlord to commence proceedings against a company in administration the court must balance the need of the administrator to conduct the administration in the interests of all the creditors against the interests of individual creditors. It is for the applicant seeking permission to show that it is equitable for permission to be given. Stanley Burnton LJ at para.66:

7–44

> "As to the exercise by the Court of its discretion under paragraph 43 of Schedule B1 to the Insolvency Act 1986, it is inherent in the provisions of subparagraphs (4) and (6) that administration may preclude a landlord from enforcing the terms of his lease. He can enforce them only with the consent of the administrator or the permission of the court. When considering whether to grant or to refuse leave, the court has regard to the consequences of the administration and of the order sought for the persons affected by them: in other words, it follows the guidance given in *Atlantic Computers*."

The landlord in *Innovate* wanted permission to require the administrator of the tenant to terminate a licence, that had been granted in breach of covenant, to a purchaser of the tenant's business. The administrator had agreed to sell the business as a going concern so that outstanding contracts could be fulfilled and substantial debts recovered. The lease was excluded from the sale, but the administrators granted the purchaser an occupational licence of the demised premises for a short period for these purposes. The licence fees were to be passed onto the landlord. The judge at first instance granted the landlord permission to bring proceedings to require the tenant/administrator to bring the licence to an end. However, the decision was overturned on appeal. Although permission to bring proceedings would normally be given to a landlord to exercise its proprietary rights if this was unlikely to impede the statutory purpose of the administration, the court nevertheless had to balance the legitimate interests of the landlord against those of tenant's other creditors. It was in their interests to allow collection by the purchase of the book debts (which ran into millions of pounds) to continue. In order to achieve that it was essential for the purchaser to occupy the property and perform the existing contracts. On the other hand the order sought by the landlord to terminate licence and end the occupation of the property of the purchaser would prevent the debt collection and thus prejudice the interests of unsecured creditors. The landlord would not be prejudiced. In fact it would benefit financially from a continuation of the purchaser's occupation of the premises since the tenant was unable to pay the rent.

In *Lazari GP Ltd v Jervis* [2012] EWHC 1466 the court gave permission because it took the view that the forfeiture would not interfere with the administration of the company. Shortly after the company went into administration the administrator agreed to sell the business, with the buyers going into occupation under a licence and taking the risk of the consequences if the landlord forfeited. Briggs J:

> "It matters not for the beneficial realisation of [T's] property in the administration whether the landlord is or is not able to exercise its proprietary rights by seeking recovery of possession of the property, because, the buyer having taken the full risk of the exercise of those rights, there will be no adverse consequences for the administration."

Rent as an expense in the administration

Where a tenant enters into administration or winding-up, the **7-45**
administrator or liquidator will be liable to pay rent for the
period during which the premises are used for the purposes of
the administration or winding-up. It does not matter whether
the rent was payable in advance or in arrears under the terms
of the lease, the rent is treated as accruing from day to day. The
duration of the period is a question of fact. (*Re Games Station
Ltd; Jervis v Pillar Denton Ltd* [2014] EWCA Civ 180).

Company voluntary arrangements

A company voluntary arrangement ("CVA") is an arrangement **7-46**
entered into between a company and some or all of its
creditors, for the payment of the company's debts, following
meetings between the company and the creditors. Although
initiated by the company, the CVA is supervised by an
insolvency practitioner. The purpose of the CVA is to allow the
company to make a binding agreement with its creditors, which
will then allow the company to deal with its financial problems
and survive into the future. Once the CVA is entered into the
landlord is bound by its terms whether or not the landlord
attended the creditors' meeting and voted and whether or not
the landlord was notified of the meeting (1986 Act ss.4A and
5).

A landlord is a creditor who should receive notice of the
creditors' meeting at which the proposed voluntary
arrangement is to be discussed. If notice is not received the
landlord has 28 days from becoming aware of the notice to
challenge the CVA.

The challenge may be successful where the landlord is unfairly
prejudiced or there is a material irregularity (1986 Act, s.6;
Prudential Assurance Co Ltd v PRG Powerhouse Ltd [2007]
EWHC 1002 Ch—CVA successfully challenged by landlord on
the grounds of unfair prejudice where the effect of the CVA was
to deprive the landlord of its guarantees in circumstances
where all the other creditors were to be paid in full.

A CVA can have an important affect on a landlord's rights. In
Thomas v Ken Thomas Ltd [2006] EWCA Civ 1504 Neuberger LJ

stated (obiter but after reviewing the earlier authorities) that he considered that where there is a CVA the landlord is not only prevented from claiming *past* rent (which is included in the CVA) but also from forfeiting in respect of that rent. Neuberger LJ at paras 47 to 49:

> "[The landlord] is not being deprived of his right to forfeit: he is merely unable to forfeit for rent which he can no longer claim for, because it has been replaced by debt under, and pursuant to the terms of, the CVA. In any event, the landlord is not deprived of his right to forfeit the lease if, as in this case, as under any well-drafted lease, he has the right to forfeit in the event of insolvency including the proposing of the CVA, or any other act of insolvency, and he does not waive it. Furthermore, although the landlord, like any other creditor, might feel prejudiced by CVA, particularly, as in this case, if it is one which he has opposed, that is a problem faced by any creditor on the company of the CVA and it is part of the price of the rescue culture."

However, he considered that a CVA would not prevent the landlord from forfeiting in respect of rent that accrues after the date of the CVA. Neuberger LJ at para.34:

> "As at present advised, it appears to me that the rent falling due after the CVA should by no means necessarily be expected to be caught by the terms of the CVA, even if it is capable of being so caught (as was held first instance in *Cancol Ltd, Re* (1996) 1 All E.R. 37). It strikes me that, at least normally, it would seem wrong in principle that a tenant should be able to trade under a CVA for the benefit of its past creditors, at the present and future expense of its landlord. If the tenant is to continue occupying the landlord's property for the purposes of trading under the CVA (and hopefully trading out of the CVA) he should normally, as it currently appears to me, expect to pay the full rent to which the landlord is contractually entitled . . . . Therefore as at present advised, I consider that a CVA should so provide, or if it does not provide, in the absence of special circumstances the landlord may well be entitled to object to the proposals as unreasonable."

Moratorium for small companies

In the case of a "small company" (as defined in Sch.A1 of the 1986 Act) where there is a moratorium in force the landlord cannot forfeit, whether by peaceable re-entry or proceedings, without permission of the court (Sch.A1 para.12). This is similar to the position in relation to interim orders for individuals seeking enter into a voluntary arrangement (see below).

7-47

Insolvency Act 1986 Sch.A1 para.12

12.–(1) During the period for which a moratorium is in force for a company—

7-48

- (f) no landlord or other person to whom rent is payable may exercise any right of forfeiture by peaceable re-entry in relation to premises let to the company in respect of a failure by the company to comply with any term or condition of its tenancy of such premises, except with the leave of the court and subject to such terms as the court may impose,
- (g) no other steps may be taken to enforce any security over the company's property, or to repossess goods in the company's possession under any hire-purchase agreement, except with the leave of the court and subject to such terms as the court may impose, and
- (h) no other proceedings and no execution or other legal process may be commenced or continued, and no distress may be levied, against the company or its property except with the leave of the court and subject to such terms as the court may impose.

Forfeiting after liquidation

See para.23-15 for the position after a winding up petition has been presented and after a winding up order has been made or a provisional liquidator has been appointed (ss.126 and 130 of the Insolvency Act 1986). See also para.7-37 in relation to *Blue Jeans* orders, that is an order for possession in the winding up proceedings.

7-49

The fact that a company is being wound up is not a reason for refusing relief (*Brompton Securities Ltd (No.2), Re* [1988] 3 All E.R. 677—non-payment of rent case; see para.12-11). The application for relief may be made in the winding up proceedings (*Brompton, Re*).

Individuals

Individual voluntary arrangements; interim orders

7-50 Under s.253 of the Insolvency Act 1986 an application for:

> "an interim order may be made where the debtor intends to make a proposal to his creditors for a composition in satisfaction of his debts or a scheme of arrangement of his affairs".

Sections 252 and 254 set out restrictions that apply where an application for an interim order is pending or where such an order is made.

Insolvency Act 1986 ss.252, 254(1)

7-51 **252.**–(1) In the circumstances specified below, the court may in the case of a debtor (being an individual) make an interim order under this section.

(2) An interim order has the effect that, during the period for which it is in force–

(a)   no bankruptcy petition relating to the debtor may be presented or proceeded with,

[(aa) no landlord or other person to whom rent is payable may exercise any right of forfeiture by peaceable re-entry in relation to premises let to the debtor in respect of a failure by the debtor to comply with any term or condition of his tenancy of such premises, except with the leave of the court] and

(b)   no other proceedings, and no execution or other legal process, may be commenced or continued [and no distress may be levied] against the debtor or his property except with the leave of the court.

254.–(1) At any time when an application under section 253 for an interim order is pending,

[(a)   no landlord or other person to whom rent is payable may exercise any right of forfeiture by peaceable re-entry in relation to premises let to the debtor in respect of a failure by the debtor to comply with any term or condition of his tenancy of such premises, except with the leave of the court, and

(b)]   the court may [forbid the levying of any distress on the debtor's property or its subsequent sale, or both, and] stay any action, execution or other legal process against the property or person of the debtor.

The fact that an individual voluntary arrangement has been agreed upon and the landlord has been a party to it under s.258 of the 1986 Act does not prevent him from forfeiting the lease, although in a rent case the tenant is likely to be granted relief from forfeiture upon terms that he pays the amount required by the arrangement (*Naeem (A Bankrupt), In re* [1990] 1 W.L.R.; see further para.7–24).

Forfeiting after bankruptcy

At any time when proceedings on a bankruptcy petition are pending or an individual has been adjudged bankrupt, the court may stay any action, execution or other legal process against "the property or person of the debtor or, as the case may be of, the bankrupt" (s.285 of the Insolvency Act 1986). Section 285(3) of the 1986 Act also provides that after the making of a bankruptcy order no person who is a creditor of the bankrupt in respect of a debt provable in the bankruptcy shall have any remedy against "the property or person of the bankrupt" in respect of the debt except with the leave of the court (para.23–19).

7–52

However, it has been held that a claim for possession based on forfeiture is not a remedy against the person or property of the bankrupt in respect of the debt. Thus, it was not necessary to obtain the court's leave under the predecessor of s.285(3) where a bankruptcy order had been made (*Ezekiel v Orakpo* [1976] 3 All E.R. 659).

> "In our view, an action for possession following the forfeiture of a lease is not within the terms of the section, and this is so whatever the ground of forfeiture to which the lessor has recourse under the covenants in the lease. The nature of the action is the same in every case, namely that the right and interest of the lessee to possession has been terminated before its natural expiry in pursuance of a contractual provision in his lease so that he becomes a trespasser if he continues in occupation of the premises. The obverse of this situation is that the lessor becomes entitled to possession on forfeiture of the lessee's interest. The action for re-entry is in the nature of an action in trespass. It is not a remedy against the property of the debtor in respect of a debt, notwithstanding that the occasion of the forfeiture is default in payment of the rent reserved by the lease. The consequence of forfeiture,

subject to the power of the court to grant relief, is to determine the lessee's interest. It is not a remedy enforcing payment of the rent due ... " (per Shaw LJ at 663e–g).

The same applies in respect of debt relief orders (see *Sharples v Places for People Homes Ltd* [2011] EWCA Civ 813).

Forfeiting because of bankruptcy or winding up

Law of Property Act 1925 s.146(9) and (10)

7-53   **146.**–(9) This section does not apply to a condition for forfeiture on the bankruptcy of the lessee or on taking in execution of the lessee's interest if contained in a lease of–

  (a)   Agricultural or pastoral land;
  (b)   Mines or minerals;
  (c)   A house used or intended to be used as a public-house or beership;
  (d)   A house let as a dwelling-house, with the use of any furniture, works of art, or other chattels not being in the nature of fixtures;
  (e)   Any property with respect to which the personal qualifications of the tenant are of importance for the preservation of the value or character of the property, or on the ground of neighbourhood to the lessor, or to any person holding under him.

   (10) Where a condition of forfeiture on the bankruptcy of the lessee or on taking in execution of the lessee's interest is contained in any lease, other than a lease of any of the classes mentioned in the last subsection then–

  (a)   if the lessee's interest is sold within one year from the bankruptcy or taking in execution, this section applies to the forfeiture condition as aforesaid;
  (b)   if the lessee's interest is sold before the expiration of that year, this section only applies to the forfeiture condition aforesaid during the first year from the date of the bankruptcy or taking in execution.

Most leases contain a provision entitling the landlord to forfeit in the event of the bankruptcy or winding up of the tenant (see the example at para.7–03). Where he wishes to do so, s.146(9) and (10) are relevant. Where the tenant is a corporation, the term "bankruptcy" in the subsections means the winding up of the company (s.205(1) of the Law of Property Act 1925). The effect of those subsections is that, save in the limited circumstances set out in subs.(9), s.146 applies:

(a)   forever, if the lease is sold within one year from the bankruptcy or winding up;

(b)   for a period of one year only, if the lease is not sold within that year.

Nothing in subs.(9) or (10) affects the right of sub-tenants to apply for an order under s.146(4) (s.1 Law of Property (Amendment) Act 1929, as to which see para.12–36).

An example of a s.146 notice that may be used on the winding up of a company is shown below (see Form 4; para.7–51).

For an example of a case where the court considered whether or not the personal qualifications of the tenant were important for the purposes of s.146(9)(e), see *Hockley Engineering Co Ltd v V & P Midlands Ltd* [1993] 1 E.G.L.R. 76 Ch D.

A landlord claiming to forfeit the lease on the bankruptcy of a surety is first required to serve a s.146 notice on the tenant specifying the bankruptcy of the surety as the breach of condition complained of (*Halliard Property Co Ltd v Jack Segal Ltd* [1978] 1 All E.R. 1219).

Mesne profits

7–54

Where a party has remained in occupation of property without any right to do so, the landlord has a choice in seeking pecuniary compensation between a restitutionary remedy and a claim for damages. Once the landlord has elected which remedy to pursue, that should dictate the method of assessment (*Shi v Jiangsu Native Produce Import & Export Corp* [2010] EWCA Civ 1582; in which the first instance judge had wrongly approached the matter on a restitutionary basis when the landlord had pleaded a claim for damages).

In order to claim mesne profits by way of damages (damages for use and occupation) it is not necessary to show that the property would have been let to another person had the defendant vacated and the amount awarded is usually the same as the amount of rent (*Swordheath Properties Ltd v Tabet* [1979] 1 All E.R. 240).

> " . . . the plaintiff, when he has established that the
> defendant has remained on as a trespasser in residential
> property, is entitled, without bringing evidence that he
> could or would have let the property to someone else in
> the absence of the trespassing defendant, to have as
> damages for the trespass the value of the property as it
> would fairly be calculated; and, in the absence of
> anything special in the particular case it would be the
> ordinary letting value of the property that would
> determine the amount of damages." (*Swordheath
> Properties Ltd v Tabet* [1979] 1 W.L.R. 285 at 288E;
> [1979] 1 All E.R. 240.)

However, the landlord is entitled to the true value of the
property. He may therefore claim such sum as he is able to
prove is equivalent to a market rent for the property even if this
is higher than the rent originally payable (*Clifton Securities v
Huntley* [1948] 2 All E.R. 283). If the tenant wishes to argue
that the market value was less than the rent he previously paid,
the burden will be upon him to prove it (*Ministry of Defence v
Ashman* [1993] 2 E.G.L.R. 102 CA).

A restitutionary remedy is one where the sum awarded is
equivalent to the amount of the benefit to the *defendant*, which
may not necessarily be the same as the rent he was paying,
particularly where that rent was a concessionary one. (See
Ministry of Defence v Ashman and *Ministry of Defence v
Thompson* [1993] 2 E.G.L.R. 107—servicemen paying
concessionary rent required to pay greater sums in respect of
mesne profits):

> "The principles in *Ashman* may, in my judgment, be
> summarised as follows: first, an owner of land which is
> occupied without his consent may elect whether to claim
> damages for the loss which he has been caused or
> restitution of the value of the benefit which he has
> received.

> Second, the fact that the owner, if he had obtained
> possession, would have let the premises at a
> concessionary rent, or even would not have let them at all,
> is irrelevant to the calculation of the benefit for the
> purposes *of a restitutionary claim*. What matters is the
> benefit which the defendant has received.

Third, a benefit may be worth less to an involuntary recipient than to one who has a free choice as to whether to remain in occupation or move elsewhere.

Fourth, the value of the right of occupation to a former licensee who has occupied at a concessionary rent and who has remained in possession only because she could not be rehoused by the local authority until a possession order has been made would ordinarily be whichever is the higher of the former concessionary rent and what she would have paid for local authority housing for her needs, if she had been rehoused at the time when the notice expired." (per Hoffman LJ in *Ministry of Defence v Thompson* at 149; but compare the approach adopted by Kennedy LJ and Lloyd LJ in *Ashman*.)

In *Viscount Chelsea v Hutchinson* [1994] 43 E.G. 153 CA (a case concerning residential premises) the landlord was held to be entitled to mesne profits from the tenant assessed by reference to the letting value of the property even though the flats were sublet to a long leaseholder. The tenant had argued that they were not therefore available for letting. However, technically the subleases came to an end on the forfeiture and could not be restored until a vesting order had been made and even then only from the date of the order.

And in *Inverugie Investments Ltd v Hackett* [1995] 3 All E.R. 841 PC it was held that the plaintiff was still entitled to recover a reasonable rent for the wrongful use of his property by the defendants even though the claimant might not have suffered any actual loss by being wrongly deprived of his property and the defendants might not have derived any actual benefit from the use of the property (*Swordheath v Tabet* and *Stoke on Trent City Council v W&J Wass Ltd* [1988] 3 All E.R. 394 applied).

Form 4: Section 146 notice on liquidation

7-51

**NOTICE FROM LANDLORD TO TENANT OF BREACH OF COVENANT
SERVED PURSUANT TO SECTION 146 OF THE LAW OF
PROPERTY ACT 1925**

PROPERTY   [*Address of property*]

LEASE   Dated .... for a term of .... years
commencing on .... and terminating on ....

LANDLORD   [*Name and address of landlord*]

TENANT   [*Name and address of tenant*]

TO: The above named Tenant.

We, [*name of landlord's solicitors*], Solicitors, of [*address*] acting for and on behalf of and with the authority of the above named Landlord, hereby give you notice as follows:

1. The Lease contains a proviso for re-entry by the Landlord in the event of the Tenant entering into voluntary or compulsory liquidation (Clause....................).

2. The Tenant has entered into voluntary liquidation and the first meeting of creditors is due to take place on ....

3. Upon the expiration of 14 days from the date of this notice the Landlord intends to re-enter the Property pursuant to Clause.................... and will thereby forfeit the Lease.

DATED ......20--.

[*Signed*]

....

Chapter 8

NON-PAYMENT OF RENT

. . . .

This chapter deals with various matters that arise where the landlord seeks to forfeit the lease for non-payment of rent.   **8–01**

The effect of assignment of the landlord's interest on the rent claim is dealt with in Ch.5. Mesne profits are dealt with in Ch.7 (see para.7–54). Relief from forfeiture is dealt with in Ch.12. Rights against third parties are dealt with in Ch.13.

Rent payable in advance/arrears

Rent is payable in arrears unless there is an express agreement that it should be paid in advance.   **8–02**

Where the rent is payable in *arrears* the landlord is entitled to rent only up until the date the tenancy is determined. The date of termination is the date upon which the landlord re-enters the premises. If he re-enters by service of proceedings (see para.7–35), rent is calculated up to the date of service. If the tenancy is determined in the middle of a rent period, it is necessary to calculate, on a daily basis, the proportion of rent that is due from the last rent day until the date of service (Apportionment Act 1870 s.2). The landlord is entitled to mesne profits thereafter (*Canas Property Co Ltd v K L Television Services Ltd* [1970] 2 All E.R. 795 CA).

Where the rent is payable in *advance*, the landlord is entitled to the whole of the rent that was due on the last rent day before termination even though the tenancy has come to an end in the middle of the rent period (*Ellis v Rowbotham* [1900] 1 Q.B. 740). Mesne profits should be claimed from what would have been the next rent day had the tenancy not been forfeited (*Canas Property Co Ltd*; see further para.7–54).

It is important therefore to ascertain the rent days and to see whether the re-entry occurred before or after that date. If the rent was payable quarterly, the quarters are calculated from the date of the agreement unless the lease states that the rent is paid on the usual quarter days, which are:

- Lady day—March 25
- Midsummer—June 24
- Michaelmas—September 29
- Christmas Day—December 25.

If the rent is payable in advance the tenant is not liable for the rent unless the tenancy has continued up until the end of the rent day (*Aspinall, Re* [1961] Ch. 526).

Deemed rent payments: service charges, insurance etc

8–03   Many leases contain covenants requiring the tenant to contribute to the cost of insuring the building of which the demised premises forms part, to pay service charges etc. and these payments are deemed by the lease to be payable as rent. They are normally called "insurance rent", "additional rent" etc. Each covenant of this type and its relationship to the forfeiture clause must be construed according to the terms of the lease (*Escalus Properties Ltd v Robinson* [1995] 4 All E.R. 852 at 857 CA), but the effect is often that the landlord will not have to serve a notice under s.146 of the Law of Property Act 1925 in respect of the failure to pay these sums and that the relief provisions relating to non-payment of rent will apply, rather than s.146(2) of the 1925 Act, which deals with relief in other cases (see Ch.9). A s.146 notice, where these sums are not payable as rent, is to be found at para.9–06 (Form 5).

A standard form service charge clause entitling the landlord to recover the costs of management and administration, including the costs of collecting rents, does not entitle the landlord to recover from the tenant legal costs in suing other tenants. Clear words are required in the lease to entitle him to do so (*Sella House Ltd v Mears* [1989] 1 E.G.L.R. 65).

The provisions of the Landlord and Tenant Act 1985 ss.18–30 (as amended), which provide protection to tenants of "dwellings" in relation to service charges, do not apply to business premises.

Appropriation of payment to specific debt

The basic principle in respect of appropriation of payments is as follows:

8–04

> "Where several separate debts are due from the debtor to the creditor, the *debtor* may, when making a payment, appropriate the money paid to a particular debt or debts, and if the creditor accepts the payment so appropriated, he must apply it in the manner directed by the debtor".
> (*Chitty on Contracts*)

If the debtor does not make an appropriation at the time when he makes the payment the right of appropriation devolves on the creditor. The principle, as it applies to the relationship between a landlord and tenant, was expressed in the following way by Neuberger LJ in *Thomas v Ken Thomas Ltd* [2006] EWCA Civ 1504 at para.28:

> " . . . (4) That law, properly applied, shows that, if he exercises the right, it is the tenant debtor who can appropriate, and that it is only if he does not do so that the creditor landlord is entitled to appropriate. (5) If the creditor landlord is unhappy with the appropriation to the extent of not being prepared to accept the money on the basis that it is offered, he can refuse it or if, as in this case, it is paid by CHAPS or a similar system, he can return it within a reasonable time. (6) Once the money is accepted or retained on the basis selected by the tenant, then, subject to any question of contrary agreement, estoppel or the like, the recipient of the money, the landlord, is as a matter of law fixed with the appropriation . . . and with its consequences in terms of waiver of forfeiture, which do not depend on what he intended."

The facts of *Thomas v Ken Thomas Ltd* [2006] EWCA Civ 1504 provide an illustration of what can go wrong for a landlord:

- The rent was payable monthly.
- The rent, which fell due on *November 1*, 2004, was not paid.
- On December 3, 2004 a letter was written on behalf of the tenant to the landlord stating that the tenant proposed making two payments on December 7 and 14, in respect of the rent due on *December* 2004. The letter stated that the

rent due for November (and some outstanding VAT on earlier rent payments) would go into a company voluntary arrangement as an unsecured amount.

- In a telephone conversation the landlord made it clear that he would not accept the appropriation made on behalf of the tenant but would only accept the money on the basis that the payment was made in respect of the rent due on November 1, 2004. The sums were paid by CHAPS directly into the landlord's bank account. They were not returned.
- By a letter dated December 31, 2004 the tenant stated that the January rent would be paid weekly, rather than monthly.
- On January 1, 2005 the landlord sent a rent demand for the rent due on January 1, 2005. Weekly payments were then made as stated in the letter of the previous day and were accepted.
- On February 1, 2005 the landlord commenced forfeiture proceedings in respect of one month's rent.

The tenant argued that the landlord had waived the breach. As a consequence of the tenant's appropriation the rent outstanding was that due for November 1, 2004. By accepting the rent for December 2004 and January 2005 the landlord had waived the right to forfeit in respect of the failure to pay the rent for November 2004. The landlord argued that it had made clear that it had not accepted the appropriation that the tenant purported to make so that the rent outstanding when the proceedings were issued was the rent for January 2005—which had not therefore been paid.

The problem with the landlord's argument was that a creditor cannot unilaterally reject an appropriation made by a debtor. If he does not accept the appropriation he must return the money. In the case of a CHAPS payment this means that he must repay it as quickly as the circumstances permit. The landlord had failed to do so. The right to forfeit was therefore lost.

Payment by a surety

8–05   Payment by a surety of the tenant's rent discharges the tenant from liability to pay the rent (*Milverton Group Ltd v Warner World Ltd* [1995] 32 E.G. 70 CA).

Assignment by the tenant

A landlord has no right to sue the assignee for arrears incurred **8-06**
by an assignor (*Parry v Robinson-Wyllie Ltd* [1987] 2 E.G.L.R.
133; s.23(1) of the Landlord and Tenant Covenants Act 1995 in
relation to "new" tenancies—see para.13-02)). Nor may he
distrain against the goods of the assignee in respect of those
arrears (*Wharfland Ltd v South London Co-operative Building
Co Ltd* [1995] 2 E.G.L.R. 21 QBD). However, the landlord will be
entitled to forfeit in respect of any breaches that have not been
remedied or waived and the new tenant will have to apply for
relief from forfeiture (*Parry v Robinson-Wyllie Ltd*).

Effect of paying rent in advance

A payment of rent before it is due is not a fulfilment of an **8-07**
obligation to make that payment (*Altonwood Ltd v Crystal
Palace FC (2000) Ltd* [2005] EWHC 292 Ch). If by mistake a
payment is made in advance of the due date it will not count
towards payment of the rent unless there is agreement to that
effect, express or inferred. In most cases of standard payment
of rent the principle is not likely to have any practical effect.
However, in *Altonwood* it was important on the context of a
turnover rent which was a separate payment from the basic
rent. Lightman at para.34:

> "The third question raised is whether CPFC is likewise
> entitled to credit for and to deduct any overpayment of
> Turnover Rent in respect of its liability to make any
> subsequent payment of Basic Rent. The principle is long
> established that a payment of rent before it is due is not
> a fulfilment of an obligation to make that payment. There
> may however be an agreement (and the payment in
> appropriate circumstances may evidence an agreement)
> between the landlord and tenant that on the day that the
> rent becomes due the payment shall be treated as a
> fulfilment of the obligation to pay the rent, and in such a
> case on the day that the rent becomes due the landlord is
> bound to treat payment in this way: see, e.g. *De Nicholls
> v Saunders* (1870) 5 L.R.C.P. 589 and *Lord Ashburton v
> Nocton* [1915] 1 Ch. 274 at 290 per Swinfen Eady LJ There
> is no such agreement in this case, and none is alleged.
> Accordingly the erroneous payment in respect of Turnover

Rent cannot be treated as a prepayment of or discharge of the future obligation to pay Rent and in particular the Basic Rent. For all purposes of the Lease the full amount of the monthly instalments of Basic Rent continue to be payable and the sanctions for non-payment become enforceable as and when the monthly payments accrue due and are undischarged. CPFC's rights are confined to claiming credit in respect of future liabilities for Turnover Rent and to making a claim in restitution for repayment. This result, as it seems to me, is fully in accord with the evident intention of the parties who have excluded all rights of deduction and set-off and limited the right to credit for overpayments to credit in subsequent payments of Turnover Rent."

A more likely circumstance where the tenant might end up paying rent twice is if he pays rent in advance and before the rent day the landlord assigns the reversion. Although under s.151 of the Law of Property Act, the tenant can carry on paying rent to the old landlord until he receives notice of the assignment (para.5–05), if the notice is given to him prior to the rent day he will (it is suggested) be liable to pay the rent to the new landlord once it falls due.

Rent review clauses

8–08   A full discussion of rent review clauses is beyond the scope of this book. However, it may be necessary to consider such a clause in a claim for possession based upon foreefiture for non-payment of rent. This is because such claims sometimes come about where there is a dispute between the parties as to whether or not the landlord has successfully invoked such a clause. When the tenant refuses to pay the increased rent, which the landlord claims is now due the landlord commences proceedings for possession.

This situation often arises where the lease provides for service by the landlord of a "rent review notice", which notice is to specify the amount the landlord believes to be the current market rent. This type of clause often requires the tenant to serve a counter-notice within a certain period if he objects to an increase to the amount specified as being the current market rent. If the tenant serves a counter-notice, the dispute is referred (under the terms of the lease) to arbitration or to an expert for determination. If the tenant fails to serve a counter-notice the sum specified in the landlord's notice becomes the rent payable. The following issues often arise in these cases.

"Subject to contract" and "without prejudice" notice

Some landlords head their rent review notice with the phrases **8–09** "subject to contract" and/or "without prejudice". However, these phrases are inappropriate to a rent review notice. The phrase "subject to contract" is inappropriate because the parties are not negotiating a contract. They are invoking a procedure previously set out under the terms of a lease. So far as the phrase "without prejudice" is concerned, there is no previous dispute between the parties to which the words "without prejudice" can be relevant. These phrases are therefore meaningless in this context. The courts have held that this ambiguity affects the whole notice and deprives it of sufficient certainty to trigger the rent review provision. The tenant is not liable to pay the increased rent specified in the notice (see *Shirlcar Properties Ltd v Heinitz* (1983) 268 E.G. 362 where the phrase "subject to contract" was used; and *Norwich Union Life Insurance Society v Tony Waller Ltd* (1984) 128 S.J. 300 where the phrase "without prejudice" was used).

Late service of the trigger notice

Sometimes the landlord can be late in serving a trigger notice. **8–10** However, unless time is of the essence service of the notice will still be regarded as valid. In *Lancecrest Ltd v Asiwaju* [2005] EWCA Civ 117, a trigger notice served by a landlord to implement a rent review was held to be valid, notwithstanding the fact that it was served 54 weeks later than the cut-off date envisaged by the rent review clause. It was valid because time was not of the essence:

> "Apart from the fact that there is nothing in that sub clause expressly stating or even implying that time is to be of the essence, there is the fairly telling point that, by contrast, there is the express provision that time is to be of the essence in respect of the counter-notice prescribed by the following provision . . . " (Neuberger LJ).

There was really no prejudice to the tenant because:

> "the day after the review date, the tenant can make time of the essence for the service of a trigger notice. Accordingly, while it might seem a commercially unrealistic solution to many people, and not what the parties to the lease envisaged, the tenant's right to make time of the essence for the service of a trigger notice means that he need suffer very little delay beyond the time limit contemplated by clause 5.1(b)."

Is tenant's letter sufficiently clear to be a counter-notice?

8-11   The tenant's "counter-notice should be in terms which are sufficiently clear to bring home to the ordinary landlord that the tenant is purporting to exercise his right" under the clause to challenge the landlord's proposed rent (Neuberger LJ in *Lancecrest Ltd v Asiwaju* [2005] EWCA Civ 117 citing the test laid down by Sir Nicolas Browne-Wilkinson, V.-C. in *Nunes v Davies Laing & Dick Ltd* (1985) 51 P. & C.R. 310 at 314). In *Lancrest* the tenant's letter said: "Your notice or demand is invalid . . . Until you serve me with a valid one-year notice about future rent review . . . I will not enter into any arbitration." The Court of Appeal held (2–1) that the letter was sufficient to operate as a counter-notice within the rent review clause.

Late service of counter-notice

8-12   A second common event is that the tenant serves his counter-notice out of time but argues that time is not of the essence of the contract. Is he entitled to do so? If not, the landlord is entitled to the increased rent specified in the notice even if it in fact bears no relation to the true market rent. The leading case is *United Scientific Holdings Ltd v Burnley BC* [1978] A.C. 904 HL in which Lord Diplock stated:

> " . . . in the absence of any contra-indications in the express words of the lease or in the inter-relation of the rent review clause itself and other clauses in the surrounding circumstances the presumption is that the timetable specified in a rent review clause for completion of the various steps for determining the rent payable in respect of the period following the review date is not of the essence of the contract".

However, this presumption can be displaced if there is a clear contra-indication in the working of the rent review clause. A deeming provision, which expresses a clear intention as to the consequences of a party's failure to comply with a prescribed timetable, will make time of the essence (*Starmark Enterprises Ltd v CPL Distribution Ltd* [2001] EWCA Civ 1252—the lease stated that if the tenants failed to serve a counter-notice within one month "they shall be deemed to have agreed to pay the increased rent specified in the rent notice"; the presumption had been displaced).

For the possibility of applying to the court for an extension of time for the matter to be referred to arbitration pursuant to s.12 of the Arbitration Act 1996, where the lease provides for arbitration in default of agreement see *Pittalis v Sherefettin* [1986] 2 All E.R. 227 CA.

Formal demands for rent

The common law requires a formal demand to be made for the rent before the landlord can forfeit in respect of non-payment unless the lease dispenses with this requirement. The modern forfeiture clause in dealing with non-payment of rent does dispense with the requirement for a formal demand. It provides for re-entry if the rent is more than, say, 14 days in arrears whether or not the landlord has made a formal demand for overdue rent (see the example on para.7–03).

8–13

If the forfeiture clause does not dispense with the requirement for a formal demand, such a demand must be made at the place specified in the lease or, if none is specified, at the demised premises. It must be made before sunset on the last day for payment and should relate only to the sum due in respect of the last rental period. The strict common law position is ameliorated by statute where there is *one half year's rent in arrears* and an attempt to distrain is made but *insufficient distress* is found on the premises. In the County Court service of the claim form will stand in lieu of the demand and re-entry so long as the rent was six months in arrears when the action was commenced (County Courts Act 1984 s.139(1); see para.12–03). Where proceedings for possession are commenced in the High Court, service of the claim form will stand in lieu of a formal demand and re-entry where the half year's rent was due before the claim form was served (s.210 of the Common Law Procedure Act (see para.12–15)).

Waiver

8–14 The question of waiver does not usually arise in rent cases. However, failure to pay rent is a once and for all breach that can be waived by subsequent action (*Church Commissioners for England v Nodjoumi* (1985) 51 P. & C.R. 155). For a full discussion of waiver of the right to re-enter and forfeit the lease see Ch.7 para.7–14.

Limitation period

8–15 The landlord may not recover rent that is more than six years in arrears (Limitation Act 1980 s.22).

Landlord under no duty to mitigate

8–16 A landlord's claim for rent is a debt claim and not a claim for damages; and there is no duty on the landlord to mitigate by seeking to find a new tenant if the tenant has left during the period of the tenancy with accruing rent arrears (*Reichman v Beveridge* [2006] EWCA Civ 1659). It is only where it would be "wholly unreasonable" to allow an innocent party to enforce its full contractual rights that the court might interfere and it "would have to be a most extraordinary case for a tenant to show that the landlord's conduct could properly be characterised in this way" (Lloyd LJ at para.40). Further, in order to establish such a claim against the landlord the tenant would also have to show that damages would be an adequate alternative remedy. This would not be the case in a rent arrears matter as should the landlord take back the premises and then be unable to re-let at the full rental level under the old lease, he would not be able to recover damages to compensate for the difference between the two rental levels.

The particulars of claim

8–17 See para.23–27 and 23–29.

Proving the arrears: evidence

Rent arrears are often proved by the production of business records. These documents are admissible in evidence by virtue of s.9 of the Civil Evidence Act 1995. The claimant should prove that the document is part of the business records by producing a certificate to that effect in accordance with s.9(2).

8–18

Civil Evidence Act 1995 s.9

9.–(1) A document which is shown to form part of the records of a business or public authority may be received in evidence in civil proceedings without further proof.

8–19

(2) A document shall be taken to form part of the records of a business or public authority if there is produced to the court a certificate to that effect signed by an officer of the business or authority to which the records belong.

For this purpose—

  (a) a document purporting to be a certificate signed by an officer of a business or public authority shall be deemed to have been duly given by such an officer and signed by him; and

  (b) a certificate shall be treated as signed by a person if it purports to bear a facsimile of his signature.

(3) The absence of any entry in the records of a business or public authority may be proved in civil proceedings by affidavit of an officer of the business or authority to which the records belong.

(4) In this section—

"records" means records in whatever form;

"business" includes any activity regularly carried on over a period of time, whether for profit or not, by any body (whether corporate or not) or by an individual;

"officer" includes any person occupying a responsible position in relation to the relevant activities of the business or public authority or in relation to its records; and

"public authority" includes any public or statutory undertaking, any government department and any person holding office under Her Majesty.

(5) The court may, having regard to the circumstances of the case, direct that all or any of the provisions of this section do not apply in relation to a particular document or record, or description of documents or records.

Interest

Interest prior to judgment

By virtue of s.69 of the County Courts Act 1984 the landlord is entitled to claim interest on the rent and (it is submitted) mesne

8–20

profits outstanding. He may also have a right to claim such interest by reason of the tenancy agreement. However, any claim for interest, whether under the Act or the agreement, must be pleaded in the detail required by CPR 16.4(2).

The particulars of claim should show the amount of interest claimed at the rate at which it is claimed.

If pleaded, interest will usually be awarded. The burden is upon the tenant to show why interest should not be awarded (*Allied London Investments Ltd v Hambro Life Assurance Ltd* (1985) 50 P. & C.R. 207 CA). It is submitted that the absence of a clause in a written tenancy agreement entitling the landlord to interest is not a good reason for depriving him of interest under s.69.

County Courts Act 1984 s.69

8–21

69.–(1) Subject to county court rules, in proceedings (whenever instituted) before a county court for the recovery of a debt or damages there may be included in any sum for which judgment is given simple interest, at such rate as the court thinks fit or as may be prescribed, on all or any part of the debt or damages in respect of which judgment is given, or payment is made before judgment for all or any part of the period between the date when the cause of action arose and—

    (a)   in the case of any sum paid before judgment, the date of the payment; and

    (b)   in the case of the sum for which the judgment is given, the date of the judgment.

(2) . . .

(3) Subject to county court rules, where—

    (a)   there are proceedings (whenever instituted) before a county court for the recovery of a debt; and

    (b)   the defendant pays the whole debt to the plaintiff (otherwise than in pursuance of a judgment in the proceedings).

the defendant shall be liable to pay the plaintiff simple interest, at such rate as the court thinks fit or as may be prescribed, on all or any part of the debt for all or any part of the period between the date when the cause of action arose and the date of the payment.

(4) Interest in respect of a debt shall not be awarded under this section for a period during which, for whatever reason, interest on the debt already runs.

(5) Interest under this section may be calculated at different rates in respect of different periods.

(6) In this section "plaintiff" means the person seeking the debt or damages and "defendant" means the person from whom the plaintiff seeks the debt or damages . . .

(8) In determining whether the amount of any debt or damages exceeds that prescribed by or under any enactment, no account shall be taken of

any interest payable by virtue of this section except where express provision to the contrary is made by or under this or any other enactment.

Interest on judgment debts

In the High Court interest on a judgment debt is recoverable   **8–22** pursuant to s.17(1) of the Judgments Act 1838. The rate is prescribed from time to time and may not be varied by the court. See further the notes in the *White Book* to CPR 40.8.

Although as a general rule a claimant in the County Court may recover interest on a judgment debt for a sum of not less than £5,000, such interest is not payable where the relevant judgment grants the landlord of a dwelling house a suspended order for possession (s.74 of the County Courts Act 1984 and The County Courts (Interest on Judgment Debts) Order 1991 (SI 1991/1184).

Tenant's counter-claim and set-off

Where the landlord is in breach of covenant the tenant may   **8–23** have a counter-claim that he can set-off against the amount of rent due, particularly where the landlord is in breach of the covenant to repair (*Lee-Parker v Izzet* [1971] 3 All E.R. 1099; *British Anzani v International Marine* [1979] 2 All E.R. 1063). If the set-off is equal to or greater than the amount of rent claimed, the landlord will have lost the ground upon which he claims possession (for an example see *Televantos v McCulloch* [1991] 1 E.G.L.R. 123 CA—a tenant successfully resisted a claim for possession based upon non-payment of rent by setting off a counterclaim for damages for failure to repair).

Anti-set-off clauses—"without any deduction"

Many leases seek to prevent the tenant from deducting sums   **8–24** from the rent by stating that it must be paid "without deductions". However, these words will not normally be sufficient to exclude the equitable right of set-off. Clear words are required (*Connaught Restaurants Ltd v Indoor Leisure Ltd* [1994] 1 W.L.R. 501). The decision in *Connaught Restaurants* was confirmed by the Court of Appeal in *Edlington Properties Ltd v JH Fenner & Co Ltd* [2006] EWCA Civ 403. Neuberger LJ at para.75:

> "The point is a difficult one and I am not sure that I would have decided it the same way as the judge in the absence of the decision in *Connaught*. However I consider it would be wrong for this court to depart from the strict approach it adopted in that case, that approach being to hold that the right of set-off against rent in a lease is not to be excluded except by words which cannot sensibly be interpreted as not extending to set-off. In my judgment the effect of the decision of the court in *Connaught* was almost this: that at least in the absence of any clear indication to the contrary in the lease, a covenant or other provision relating to the payment of rent will not exclude the tenant's normal right to claim equitable set-off, save where the word 'set-off' is specifically used."

On the other hand a provision requiring payment "without any deduction or set off whatsoever" (and thus using the word set-off) has been held sufficient to exclude any right of deduction or set-off (*Star Rider Ltd v Inntrepreneur Pub Co* [1998] 1 E.G.L.R. 53); and in *Altonwood Ltd v Crystal Palace FC (2000) Ltd* [2005] EWHC 292 Ch, the court held that the words "without any deduction or set-off", omitting the word "whatsoever", were "likewise clear and sufficient (if less emphatic) to exclude any right of deduction or set-off."

If the words are sufficiently clear the Unfair Contract Terms Act 1977 does not apply (*Electricity Supply Nominees v IAF Group* [1993] 3 All E.R. 372 QBD.

Claim by new landlord—tenant seeking to set-off claim against old landlord

8–25 Where the tenancy is a new lease (i.e. generally one granted on or after January 1, 1996—see further para.13–02) the tenant is not entitled to set-off a damages claim he has against the previous landlord against the rent being claimed by the new landlord (*Edlington Properties Ltd v JH Fenner & Co Ltd* [2006] EWCA Civ 403). Neuberger LJ at para.64:

> "Where the reversion to a lease is transferred, a tenant cannot set off, against rent falling due after the transfer, a claim for damages he has arising out of a breach by his original landlord of the lease, let alone of the agreement

pursuant to which the lease was granted, unless of course the lease specifically provides that he should have that right.".

(Note that where the tenancy is a new tenancy—see para.13-02—it not possible for the new landlord to sue for rent that fell due prior to assignment of the reversion to him; para.5-06)

CHAPTER 9

FORFEITURE: OTHER COVENANTS (GENERAL)

· ·

Law of Property Act 1925 s.146

9–01   **146.**–(1) A right of re-entry or forfeiture under any proviso or stipulation in a lease for a breach of any covenant or condition in the lease shall not be enforceable by action or otherwise, unless and until the lessor serves on the lessee a notice—

(a)   specifying the particular breach complained of; and

(b)   if the breach is capable of remedy, requiring the lessee to remedy the breach; and

(c)   in any case requiring the lessee to make compensation in money for the breach;

and the lessee fails, within a reasonable time thereafter, to remedy the breach, if it is capable of remedy, and to make reasonable compensation in money, to the satisfaction of the lessor, for the breach.

. . .

(5) For the purposes of this section—

(a)   "Lease" includes an original or derivative under-lease; also an agreement for a lease where the lessee has become entitled to have his lease granted; also a grant at a fee farm rent, or securing a rent by condition;

(b)   "Lessee" includes an original or derivative under-lessee, and the persons deriving title under a lessee; also a guarantee under any such grant as aforesaid and the persons deriving title under him;

(c)   "Lessor" includes an original or derivative under-lessor, and the persons deriving title under a lessor; also a person making such grant as aforesaid and the persons deriving title under him;

(d)   "Under-lease" includes an agreement for an under-lease where the under-lessee has become entitled to have his under-lease granted;

(e)   "Under-lessee" includes any person deriving title under an under-lessee.

. . .

(7) For the purposes of this section a lease limited to continue as long only as the lessee abstains from committing a breach of covenant shall be and take effect as a lease to continue for any longer term for which it

could subsist, but determinable by a proviso for re-entry on such a breach.

...

(11) This section does not, save as otherwise mentioned, affect the law relating to re-entry or forfeiture or relief in case of non-payment of rent.

(12) This section has effect notwithstanding any stipulation to the contrary.

Section 146 notices: introduction

If a tenant is in breach of covenant (other than a covenant to pay rent: s.146(11) of the Law of Property Act 1925), the landlord cannot (subject to certain limited exceptions set out in s.146(9) of the 1925 Act; para.7–53) exercise any right of re-entry in the lease in respect of that breach unless he has first served a notice under s.146(1) of the 1925 Act. The notice must be in writing (s.196(1) of the 1925 Act para.9–12).

9–02

Any stipulation purporting to exclude the requirement of a s.146 notice is of no effect (s.146(12)). A forfeiture clause dressed up as a surrender or a termination by notice remains a forfeiture clause subject to the provisions of the Act (*Plymouth Corp v Harvey* [1971] 1 W.L.R. 549; *Richard Clarke & Co Ltd v Widnall* [1976] 1 W.L.R. 845).

As the purpose and effect of a s.146 notice is to operate as a preliminary to actual forfeiture, service of such a notice cannot be an unequivocal affirmation of the existence of the lease and therefore does not operate to waive a right to forfeit (*Church Commissioners for England v Nodjoumi* (1985) 51 P. & C.R. 155; see para.7–22); but a notice served under s.146 should not contain a demand for arrears of rent accruing since the breach complained of in the notice. This is because the demand may possibly waive that breach, it not being necessary to serve a s.146 notice in respect of arrears of rent.

Where the breach of covenant is a continuing one (see para.7–15), e.g. where the tenant is failing to keep the premises in good repair and the landlord has waived the right to forfeit in respect of the earlier stages of the breach but is seeking to forfeit in respect of the stages that have occurred since the waiver, he does not need to serve a fresh s.146 notice if such a notice was served prior to the waiver if there has been no change in the condition of the premises (*Greenwich LBC v Discreet Selling Estates Ltd* [1990] 2 E.G.L.R. 65).

"It seems to me that a notice under section 146 asserts not only that the tenant is presently in breach but also that he will continue to be in breach unless and until he carried out the repairs required. It must necessarily assert that, if the landlord is to be able to rely at the trial on further delay which will have occurred up to the commencement of proceedings. In those circumstances I see no practical need for any fresh notice if a landlord wishes to rely on the continuing breach as a ground for forfeiture in the future and no legal reason why a fresh notice should be required in respect of the same defects." (*Greenwich LBC v Discreet Selling Estates Ltd* [1990] 2 E.G.L.R. 65, per Staughton LJ at 68C.)

A particular type of s.146 notice is required in a repairing case (see para.11–04).

Contents of the notice

9–03   Section 146(1) of the Law of Property Act 1925 requires that the notice should:

(a)   specify the breach complained of; and
(b)   if the breach is capable of remedy, require the tenant to remedy it; and
(c)   in any case, require the tenant to make compensation in money for the breach.

The notice does not need to refer to the statute (*Van Haarlam v Kasner* [1992] 2 E.G.L.R. 59 Ch D).

A s.146 notice must be served even if the breach is not capable of remedy. The notice has a two-fold purpose:

(1)   to give the tenant the opportunity to remedy the breach, if it is capable of remedy, before the landlord forfeits; and
(2)   to give the tenant the opportunity to apply to the court for relief (*Expert Clothing and Sales Ltd v Hillgate House Ltd* [1985] 2 All E.R. 998).

"In a case where the breach is 'capable of remedy' . . . the principal object of the notice procedure . . . is to afford the lessee two opportunities before the lessor actually proceeds to enforce his right of re-entry, namely (1) the opportunity to remedy the breach within a reasonable time after service of the notice and (2) the opportunity to apply to the court for relief from forfeiture. In a case where the breach is not 'capable of remedy', there is clearly no point in affording the first of these two opportunities; the object of the notice procedure is thus simply to give the lessee the opportunity to apply for relief." (*Expert Clothing Service and Sales Ltd v Hillgate House Ltd* [1985] 2 All E.R. 998, per Slade LJ at 1005c.)

Each of the three requirements will be looked at in turn. An example of a s.146 notice is to be found at para.9–06, Form 5. In cases of disrepair in some circumstances the notice must also comply with the Leasehold Property (Repairs) Act 1938 (see para 11–05).

Specify the breach

The breach complained of should clearly be set out in the **9–04** notice. The usual practice is to set out the terms of the lease that have allegedly been breached and then to give details of the breach by reference to those terms. The notice will be invalid if it refers to the wrong covenant (*Jacobs v Down* [1900] 2 Ch. 156).

The importance of accurately specifying the breach is starkly demonstrated by *Akici v LR Butlin Ltd* [2005] EWCA Civ 1296 where the judge found that the tenant had shared possession with a company, and that represented a breach of the covenant. However, the s.146 notice that was served by the landlord did not allege that the tenant was *sharing possession.* It only alleged that the tenant had *parted with possession* to the company. It was therefore an ineffective notice and the landlord's re-entry was unlawful. Neuberger LJ:

> "54. I accept the submission that the approach of the majority of the House of Lords in *Mannai* to contractual notices would apply to section 146 notices . . . However, I have nonetheless come to the conclusion that Mr Lloyd's defence of the notice cannot stand. Even applying *Mannai*, the notice has to comply with the requirements of section 146(1) of the 1925 Act, and if, as appears pretty plainly to be the case, it does not specify the right breach, then nothing in *Mannai* can save it.

55. Quite apart from this, if, on its true construction, the section 146 notice did not specify sharing possession as a breach complained of, it can be said with considerable force that it neither informed the recipient of the breach complained of, nor indicated to him whether, and if so how, he must remedy any breach. On the basis that there was a sharing of possession, a reasonable recipient of the section 146 notice would have been entitled to take the view that he need do nothing, because the lessors were only complaining about the presence of the company if there was a parting with of possession (or assigning or underletting) by Mr Akici to it.

56. Accordingly, a reasonable recipient in this case (and it is the understanding of such a hypothetical person by reference to which the validity of the notice is to be assessed according to *Mannai*) could, to put it at its lowest, reasonably have taken the view that the lessors were not objecting to any sharing of possession, and consequently that no steps need to be taken, either with a view to remedying the breach or with a view to improving the prospects of obtaining relief from forfeiture . . . "

Remedy the breach; time given

9-05   If a breach can be remedied, remedial action must be required of the tenant in the notice but, notwithstanding the wording of s.146, it is not necessary to require the tenant to remedy the breach if it is not capable of remedy within a reasonable time after service of the notice (*Expert Clothing* at 1009f).

Whether a breach of covenant is "capable of remedy" for the purposes of s.146(1)(b) depends on whether the harm suffered by the landlord by the relevant breach is capable of being remedied in practical terms. The breach of a positive covenant, whether continuous or once and for all, is ordinarily remediable provided the remedy is carried out within a reasonable time. The amount of time that is to be regarded as reasonable will depend on the particular circumstances of the case (*Expert Clothing* at 1008c).

The position so far as negative covenants are concerned is not quite so clear. Although there may be negative covenants that are capable of being remedied (*Scala House and District Property Co Ltd v Forbes* [1974] Q.B. 575 at 585) they are less likely to be remediable than positive ones (cf. *Bass Holdings Ltd v Morton Music Ltd* [1987] 3 W.L.R. 543). Fortunately, there are authorities in respect of some negative covenants. For example, if the tenant assigns, sublets or parts with possession in breach of covenant he commits an act which is incapable of remedy (*Scala House v Forbes*). Breach of a covenant not to use the premises for illegal or immoral purposes is a breach that is incapable of remedy if a stigma is thereby attached to the premises (*Rugby School (Governors) v Tannahill* [1935] 1 K.B. 87; *British Petroleum Pension Trust Ltd v Behrendt* (1985) 276 E.G. 199); but for the position where the sub-tenant has used the premises in an immoral or illegal way without the knowledge of the tenant see *Glass v Kencakes Ltd* [1966] 1 Q.B. 611; and more recently *CB Patel & Patel v K&J Restaurants Ltd* [2010] EWCA Civ 1211. If the mischief caused by the breach can be removed the breach is capable of remedy for the purposes of the section. Thus, a covenant not to display trade or business signs can be remedied by taking down the sign (*Savva v Housein*) [1996] 2 E.G.L.R. 65 CA).

In the absence of special circumstances, a breach of covenant against parting with possession or sharing possession, falling short of creating or transferring a legal interest, are breaches of covenant which are capable of remedy (*Akici v LR Butlin Ltd* [2005] EWCA Civ 1296—lessee who had permitted a company, in which he had an interest, to occupy the demised premises for the purpose of its business was sharing possession—the breach was remedied by the lessee acquiring all the shares in, and becoming the sole director of, the company.)

If the landlord is not sure whether the breach is one that is capable of remedy, he should require the tenant to remedy it "if it is capable of remedy" (*Glass v Kencakes Ltd* and see Form 5 below).

Although not required by s.146(1), it is common practice to state the time in which the breach is to be remedied, which must be a reasonable one. Three months will be sufficient in most cases (see *Gulliver Investments v Abbott* [1966] E.G.D. 299—a repairs case; see further Ch.11) but obviously every case will depend upon its own facts and in many cases a much shorter period will be all that is required. Where the breach is incapable of remedy and the only purpose of the notice is to give the tenant the opportunity to apply for relief an extended period will not be necessary.

Form 5: Section 146 notice

9-06

NOTICE FROM LANDLORD TO TENANT OF BREACH OF COVENANT SERVED PURSUANT TO SECTION 146 OF THE LAW OF PROPERTY ACT 1925

PROPERTY   *[Address of property]*

LEASE   Dated .... for a term of .... years commencing on .... and terminating on ....

LANDLORD   *[Name and address of landlord]*

TENANT   *[Name and address of tenant]*

TO: The above named Tenant.

I, the above named Landlord, hereby give you, the Tenant under the above mentioned Lease, notice as follows:

1.   The Lease under which you hold the Property contains the following COVENANTS:

(1) (*Set out the clauses that have been breached*)

(2) To pay the Landlord all costs charges and expenses (including legal costs and surveyors fees) incurred by the Landlord in or in contemplation of any proceedings under sections 146 and 147 of the Law of Property Act 1925 or any statutory re-enactment thereof notwithstanding that forfeiture shall be avoided otherwise than by relief granted by the court (Clause .....).

2.   By Clause .... of the Lease it is provided that if the Tenant fails to observe or perform any of the Tenant's covenants it is lawful for the Landlord at any time thereafter to re-enter the Property or any part thereof in the name of the whole and that thereupon the demise granted by the Lease will absolutely determine.

3.   IN BREACH of the said covenants you have

(1) [*When setting out the breaches make it clear in relation to each breach the covenant which it is alleged has been broken*]

4.   I hereby require you to REMEDY the said breaches within [*specify a reasonable period*] of the date of this notice [if the same are capable of remedy].

5.   I further require you to pay me reasonable COMPENSATION for your breaches in the sum of £..... being ....

6.   I further require you to pay me the sum of £..... pursuant to clause ..... of the Lease being the COSTS of my surveyor and solicitors incurred in contemplation of and incidental to the preparation and service of this notice.

7.   I require you to pay the above sums to my solicitors .... of .... within the said period of ....

IF YOU FAIL TO COMPLY WITH THE REQUIREMENTS OF THIS NOTICE YOUR LEASE WILL BE FORFEIT AND I SHALL EXERCISE MY RIGHT TO RE-ENTER THE PROPERTY [BY TAKING PROCEEDNGS FOR POSSESSION] AND SHALL ALSO CLAIM DAMAGES

DATED .... 20...... SIGNED ....

Compensation

Notwithstanding the terms of s.146(1)(c), the landlord need not include a provision in the notice requiring compensation if he does not in fact desire to be compensated (*Rugby School (Governors) v Tannahill*) but, if he does not ask for it in the notice, he will not be entitled to recover compensation in the proceedings (*Lock v Pearce* [1893] 2 Ch. 271).

9–07

Surveyors' and solicitors' costs

Many leases contain specific provision for payment of professional fees incurred in preparation and service of a s.146 notice even if the forfeiture of a lease is avoided without a court order. Each case will turn upon the wording of the lease and will usually be successful. However, in *Agricullo Ltd v Yorkshire Housing Ltd* [2010] EWCA Civ 229 the landlord's claim failed on this point because on a proper construction of the lease the court held the provision did not entitle the landlord to recover the costs of service of the s.146 notice where the dispute had been resolved by negotiation (see paras 20 and 21 of the judgment). If there is no clause that will assist, the landlord might still be able to rely upon s.146(3), which provides for recovery of costs where there is waiver or relief.

9–08

Law of Property Act 1925 s.146(3)

146.–(3) A lessor shall be entitled to recover as a debt due to him from a lessee, and in addition to damages (if any), all reasonable costs and expenses properly incurred by the lessor in the employment of a solicitor and surveyor or valuer, or otherwise, in reference to any breach giving rise to a right of re-entry or forfeiture which, at the request of the lessee, is waived by the lessor, or from which the lessee is relieved, under the provisions of this Act.

For disrepair cases in which the Leasehold Property (Repairs) Act 1938 is engaged this section may be dis-applied (see further para.11–09).

9–09

Service of the notice: upon whom

The notice should be served upon the tenant. If there is more than one tenant all the tenants must be served (*Blewett v Blewett* [1936] 2 All E.R. 188). Where the lease has been assigned, the notice should be served on the assignee and not

9–10

the assignor, even if the assignment is unlawful. This is so because the assignment, although unlawful, is effective to transfer the tenancy to the assignee. He is now the tenant and the person who is interested in avoiding the forfeiture (*Old Grovebury Manor Farm Ltd v W Seymour Plant Sales and Hire Ltd (No.2)* [1979] 1 W.L.R. 1397). However, where the lease is required to be registered (generally where it is for a term of seven years or more from grant), the assignee will not take legal title until they are registered as proprietor (see ss.27 (1) and (2) Land Registration Act 2002). If the assignee does not have legal title, then the notice should be served on the assignor.

It is not necessary to serve the notice on sub-tenants or mortgagees (*Egerton v Jones* [1939] 2 K.B. 702; *Church Commissioners for England v Ve-Ri-Best Manufacturing Co Ltd* [1957] 1 Q.B. 238); even in the case of a mortgagee in possession (*Smith v Spaul* [2002] EWCA Civ 1830). See further Ch.10 para.10-03.

Mode of service

9-11   Having said that the landlord must serve the notice on the tenant, it is not in fact necessary actually to search out the tenant and place the notice in his hand. The provisions of s.196 of the Law of Property Act 1925 (see para.9-12), as extended by s.1 of the Recorded Delivery Service Act 1962, apply. The effect of these sections is as follows:

(1) A s.146 notice is sufficiently served if it is sent by recorded delivery addressed to the tenant by name at the tenant's last known place of abode or business in the United Kingdom. If the letter is not returned through the post office undelivered, service is deemed to be made at the time at which the letter would in the ordinary course of post be delivered (s.196(4); *WX Investments v Begg* [2002] EWHC 925 Ch). To prove service the landlord need only show that the letter was prepaid, properly addressed and actually posted.

(2) The landlord may also serve the s.146 notice by leaving it at the tenant's last known place of abode or business in the United Kingdom or affixing it or leaving it for him on the land or on any house or building comprised in the

lease (s.196(3)). If this method is used it is sufficient if it is addressed to "the lessee" (s.196(2)).

In either of the above two cases the landlord will not need to show that the tenant actually received the s.146 notice (*88 Berkeley Road, London NW9, Re* [1971] Ch. 648). In *Van Haarlam v Kasner* [1992] 2 E.G.L.R. 59 a notice, which was served at the property pursuant to s.196(3), was held to be good service even though at the date of service the landlord knew that the tenant was in prison and unlikely to receive it. See also *Blunden v Frogmore Investments Ltd* [2002] EWCA Civ 573—where the building was destroyed by a bomb and the notices sent to various addresses by recorded delivery were returned. Nevertheless service was good.

The methods of service set out in s.196 are permissive. They do not have to be used. If the notice is in fact served by some other method and it can be proved, that will be sufficient.

The notice may also be left at the tenant's property with some person provided that it is reasonable to suppose that it will be passed on to the tenant (*Cannon Brewery Co Ltd v Signal Press Ltd* (1928) 139 L.T. 384).

The landlord should plead service of the notice as a matter of good pleading but he will not be prejudiced if he fails to do so (*Gates v WA and RJ Jacobs Ltd* [1920] 1 Ch. 567).

Law of Property Act 1925 s.196

196.—(1) Any notice required or authorised to be served or given by this Act shall be in writing.

(2) Any notice required or authorised by this Act to be served on a lessee or mortgagor shall be sufficient, although only addressed to the lessee or mortgagor by the designation, without his name, or generally to the persons interested, without any name, and notwithstanding that any person to be affected by the notice is absent, under disability, unborn, or unascertained.

(3) Any notice required or authorised by this Act to be served shall be sufficiently served, if it is left at the last-known place of abode or business in the United Kingdom of the lessee, lessor, mortgagee, mortgagor, or other person to be served, or, in the case of a notice required or authorised to be served on a lessee or mortgagor, is affixed or left for him on the land or any house or building comprised in the lease or mortgage,

9–12

or, in case of a mining lease, is left for the lessee at the office or counting-house of the mine.

(4) Any notice required or authorised by this Act to be served shall also be sufficiently served, if it is sent by post in a registered letter addressed to the lessee, lessor, mortgagee, mortgagor, or other person to be served, by name, at the aforesaid place of abode or business, office, or counting-house, and if that letter is not returned through the post-office undelivered; and that service shall be deemed to be made at the time at which the registered letter would in the ordinary course of post be delivered.

(5) The provisions of this section shall extend to notices required to be served by an instrument affecting property executed or coming into operation after commencement of this Act unless a contrary intention appears.

(6) This section does not apply to notice served in proceedings in the court.

Tenant's action on receipt of notice

9-13 A tenant in receipt of a s.146 notice (who wishes to retain his lease) has three choices:

(1) He may remedy the breach complained of within the time stated, if the breach is capable of remedy.
(2) He may apply to the court for an injunction to prevent the landlord from re-entering the property. He may wish to do so where he denies that he is in breach of covenant at all or where the landlord specifies a time in which to remedy the breach which the tenant considers to be unreasonably short.
(3) He may apply for relief from forfeiture. He is entitled to make the application immediately on receipt of the notice and does not need to wait for the landlord to commence proceedings for possession (see para.12-18).

Depending upon the circumstances, the tenant may wish to combine two or more of these three courses. Where it is clear that the landlord will forfeit only by taking proceedings it will not be necessary to seek an injunction or to apply for relief prior to service of those proceedings. However, one can never be sure that the landlord will not seek to forfeit by actually re-entering. If the landlord does forfeit by actual re-entry, the tenant will not lose his right to apply (para.12-18) but the inconvenience and cost caused by the disturbance is likely to be substantial. A letter to the landlord seeking clarification of his intentions should therefore be written.

Where the tenant accepts that he is in breach and accepts the validity of the s.146 notice the letter should offer to remedy the breach and to pay the landlord's reasonable costs incurred to date. The tenant should immediately commence any action required to remedy the breach. The letter should seek an undertaking not to forfeit otherwise than by proceedings and should invite the landlord to withdraw the notice on completion of the remedial action. Such a letter and any response will help the tenant to decide whether or not to take any further steps immediately and will also assist on any question of costs should an application for relief or an injunction have to be made. (See further para.12–31 in relation to costs on an application for relief.) An example of a letter that might be used is set out at para.9–15.

Tenant's failure to comply with notice

If the tenant fails, within a reasonable time of service of the **9–14** notice, to remedy the breach (if it is capable of remedy) and to make reasonable compensation in money to the landlord's satisfaction (if the landlord has required compensation), the landlord may re-enter the property and thereby forfeit the lease. He may do so by peaceable re-entry, the issue *and* service of proceedings, or (in certain circumstances) by re-letting the property to the tenant's sub-tenant or other existing occupier (see para.7–09 for a full discussion of re-entry). The landlord must not re-enter by any method until a reasonable time has elapsed. This is the position even where the breach is incapable of remedy for even in these circumstances the tenant needs time to consider his position and to decide whether to apply for, and to take such action as will assist his claim for, relief (*Scala House*—14 days held sufficient in the circumstances of the case; and see *Expert Clothing* above).

If the tenant has obtained an injunction preventing re-entry without the service of proceedings, he will have to decide whether or not to apply to set aside the injunction (if it was obtained without notice) and/or will have to seek to re-enter by service of proceedings.

Form 6: Letter to landlord before application for relief

9-15

Dear Sirs

Re: _____

We act for ...., the lessee of the above premises.

We are in receipt of your s.146 notice dated .... 20 . .
Our client acknowledges that he has breached the covenants in the lease in the manner set out in your s.146 notice.

He apologises for the breaches and is prepared to remedy them by taking the following steps: [*List the steps*] He has begun doing so by ....

He is also prepared to pay the reasonable costs of preparing and serving the s.146 notice.

In the circumstances we do not consider that you are entitled to forfeit the lease. Alternatively, we consider that our client will obtain relief from forfeiture.

We therefore invite you to withdraw your s.146 notice upon being satisfied that the breach has been remedied. In the meantime please give us your undertaking that you will not in any circumstances seek to forfeit by peaceably re-entering and that if you decide to seek to forfeit the lease that you will only do so by taking proceedings for possession. In the absence of such an undertaking we will have to consider seeking an injunction.

If you decide to issue proceedings or we are forced to seek an injunction we shall bring this letter to the attention of the court on the question of costs.

Yours faithfully

CHAPTER 10

ASSIGNMENT, SUBLETTING AND PARTING WITH POSSESSION

. . . .

This chapter deals with various matters that may arise in connection with a decision by a landlord to forfeit for breach of the covenant against assigning, subletting or parting with possession. It is not confined to matters directly relating to forfeiture but includes other matters that might arise, for example the landlord's duty to deal with applications or assignments, subletting etc promptly.

10–01

Introduction: types of covenant

There are two types of covenant against assigning, underletting, charging or parting with possession:

10–02

(1) Absolute covenants: i.e. covenants that prevent the tenant from assigning, subletting, charging or parting with possession of the property in any circumstances. A typical covenant would simply say "The tenant covenants and agrees not to assign, underlet, charge or part with possession of the demised premises or any part thereof".

(2) Qualified covenants: i.e. covenants that prevent the tenant from assigning, underletting, charging or parting with possession without the consent of the landlord. There are often other conditions that the tenant is required to comply with before a consent will be given, e.g. to include in a sub-lease a covenant against assigning, underletting, charging or parting with possession without the consent of the headlandlord.

In many cases the covenant will be "fully qualified", i.e. there will be an express term that the landlord's consent will not be unreasonably withheld. However, even if there is no express term to that effect s.19(1) of the Landlord and Tenant Act 1927 implies such a term (para.10-09). Further, by virtue of the Landlord and Tenant Act 1988 the landlord is under a duty to come to a decision about whether or not to consent and, if he does consent, whether or not to impose conditions on that consent "within a reasonable time".

Where the landlord refuses his consent or simply fails to deal with the tenant's application for consent the tenant has three choices:

(1) The tenant may apply to the court for a declaration that consent is being unreasonably withheld. The application may be made in the County Court whatever the rateable value of the property (Landlord and Tenant Act 1954 s.53 (as amended); *Mills v Cannon Brewery Co* [1920] 2 Ch. 38). Such an application can obviously take time and in most cases the parties to the proposed assignment etc. are not likely to have the patience to wait for the outcome of such an application.

(2) The tenant may sue the landlord for damages pursuant to the Landlord and Tenant Act 1988. (See para.10-14.)

(3) The tenant can assign, underlet, charge or part with possession of the property without the landlord's consent on the basis that the landlord's withholding of consent is unreasonable. The legal interest in the lease will pass as intended (*Old Grovebury Manor Farm Ltd* v *Seymour Plant Sales & Hire Ltd (No.2)* [1979] 1 W.L.R. 1397). However, this is obviously a high risk strategy and may lead to forfeiture. A tenant contemplating this step will need to anticipate a physical re-entry and should consider requesting the landlord to confirm that it will not do so and/or applying for an injunction to prevent physical re-entry until the question of whether the assignment is in breach of covenant has been determined by the court. The other risk is that the landlord may be able to obtain an order requiring the assignee or sub-tenant to give the property back (see para.10-06). However, if the landlord has acted unreasonably, the tenant will have a defence to the landlord's action (*Treloar v Bigge* (1874) L.R. 9 Ex. 151). The tenant must remember to ask for consent before he assigns, sublets, or parts with possession. If he fails to do

so he will be in breach of covenant whether or not the landlord's refusal, if he had given it, would have been unreasonable.

Proceedings by the landlord

Forfeiture: s.146 notices

If the tenant does decide to assign, underlet charge or part with **10–03** possession of the property without the landlord's consent and without applying to the court for a declaration that the landlord is acting unreasonably and the landlord wishes to forfeit, the landlord must first serve a s.146 notice (see para.9–02). In an assignment case the notice should be served on the assignee and not the assignor. This is because the assignment, although unlawful, is effective to transfer the tenancy to the assignee. He is now the tenant and the person who is interested in avoiding the forfeiture (para.9–10). It is not necessary to serve the notice on sub-tenants or mortgagees (see para.9–10).

There will be many cases where the landlord does not know whether or not there has been an effective assignment. However, the clause being relied upon by the landlord will usually be one against assigning or parting with possession. The problem will therefore be solved by relying upon a s.146 notice that relies upon assignment and parting with possession in the alternative and which is served on the tenant and on the person who is believed to be the assignee. It is also possible to serve a s.146 notice addressed to "the lessee" (s.196(2) of the Law of Property Act 1925; see para.9–12) by leaving it at or affixing it to the property (s.196(3)). See also para.9–04.

Form 7: Particulars of claim—unlawful subletting

10-04

IN THE   COUNTY COURT   Case No.

Between:

[The Landlord]

Claimant

-and-

(1) *[The Tenant]*
(2) *[The Tenant's unlawful sub-tenant]*

Defendants

PARTICULARS OF CLAIM

1. The Claimant is the freehold/leasehold *[state which]* owner and is entitled to possession of the building known as *[address of the building of which the demised premises forms part]*. The building is an office block.

2. By a Lease dated .... 20 .... made between the Claimant and the Defendant, the Claimant leased to the First Defendant the office premises at the building known as Suite .... for a term of ...... years from .... 20 ..... at a rent of £...... per annum payable in advance by equal quarterly instalments on the usual quarter days.

3. By Clause ...... of the Lease the First Defendant covenanted:
   (1) Not to underlet or part with possession or occupation of Suite .... as a whole or any part thereof, and not to share possession or occupation of Suite .... with any other person (Clause ......).
   (2) To pay all proper and reasonable expenses incidental to the preparation and service of a notice under s.146 of the Law of Property Act 1925 notwithstanding that forfeiture is avoided otherwise than by relief granted by the court and to pay Value Added Tax thereupon (Clause ......).

4. The Lease contains a proviso for re-entry entitling the Claimant to forfeit the term and re-enter the Suite if the First Defendant should at any time fail or neglect to perform or observe any of the covenants conditions or agreements contained in the Lease (Clause ....).

5. In breach of the Lease the First Defendant has sublet part of the Suite, namely rooms .... to the Second Defendant, or, in the alternative, has permitted the Second Defendant to share possession or occupation of the Suite with the First Defendant.
6. On .... 20 ..... the Claimant, by its solicitors, served on the First Defendant a notice in writing under s.146 of the Law of Property Act 1925 specifying the breach referred to in para.5 and calling upon the First Defendant to remedy the said breach within 14 days if the same was capable of remedy.

cont

cont

By the said notice, the Claimant also required the First Defendant to pay the sum of £690 (inclusive of Value Added Tax) to the Claimant in respect of the costs incurred in preparing and serving the said notice.

7. The said breach is incapable of remedy. Further or in the alternative, the First Defendant has failed within the said period of 14 days to remedy the said breach and has failed to pay the said sum of £690.

8. By reason of the matters aforesaid the Lease has become liable to be forfeited to the Claimant and is by service of these proceedings forfeited so that the Claimant is entitled to possession of the Suite.

9. The Suite was let to the First Defendant so that he could carry on a business there and is occupied by the First Defendant for the purposes of a business. In the premises the provisions of the Rent Act 1977 [*or the Housing Act 1988, if the lease was granted on or after January 15, 1989*] do not apply.

10. The Claimant does not know the name of any person who may claim relief from forfeiture as under-tenant or mortgagee other than the Second Defendant [see para.7-32].

AND the Claimant claims:
   (1) Possession of the Suite;
   (2) Mesne profits at the rate of £...... from .... 20..... until possession be delivered up.

Statement of truth

Forfeiture: proceedings and relief

Upon receipt of the notice the tenant (i.e. the assignee in an assignment case; see above) should consider immediately applying to the court seeking relief from forfeiture and if he thinks there is any danger of the landlord peaceably re-entering the property he should apply for an injunction to prevent him from forfeiting otherwise than by court proceedings. See further para.9-13 for the actions that a tenant should take on receipt of a s.146 notice.   **10-05**

An example of a Particulars of Claim to be used where the landlord wishes to forfeit by reason of the tenant's subletting in breach of covenant is to be found at para.10-04.

Unlawful assignees and sub-tenants may apply for relief from forfeiture (*Southern Depot Co Ltd v British Railways Board* [1990] 2 E.G.L.R. 39 at 42M-43A). As to applications for relief from forfeiture generally see para.12-16 and para.12-32.

Injunction and damages

10-06   If the landlord does not wish to forfeit the lease, he may seek an injunction either in anticipation of an intended breach or in some cases afterwards. In *Hemingway Securities v Dunraven Ltd* [1995] 1 E.G.L.R. 61 an injunction was granted against a tenant and subtenant for breach of the covenant against subletting. The sub-tenant was ordered to surrender the tenancy. See also *Crestfort Ltd v Tesco Stores Ltd* [2005] EWHC 805 Ch where it was held that it was possible to grant a mandatory injunction against the sub-tenant requiring it to give up the sub-lease because by agreeing to take the sublease it had committed the tort of wrongful interference with a contract. It was right to grant the injunction because the interference had been done knowingly and intentionally in the financial interests of the tenant and the subtenant. The judge also awarded damages against both the tenant and the subtenant, to be assessed by reference to the sum the landlord might reasonably have demanded at the date of the breach of covenant, or commission of the tort, for relaxing the alienation covenant so as to permit the underletting. He said this at para.75:

> "Tesco then took the point that the experts in their joint report contemplate the award of damages in lieu of and not in addition to an injunction. This is correct, but the failure to contemplate the eventuality of an award of damages in addition should not preclude such an award unless to make such an award would occasion injustice to the Defendants. It has not been suggested that the award would occasion any injustice. No injustice can be occasioned so long as the Defendants are afforded the protection which they are afforded by this judgment."

Landlord's duty not unreasonably to withhold consent

10-07   Most *qualified* covenants against assigning etc. provide that the landlord's consent is not to be unreasonably withheld. A typical covenant would be in the following terms.

Qualified covenant against assignment etc

10-08   The Tenant covenants not to assign, underlet, charge or part with possession of the demised premises without the consent in writing of the Landlord, *such consent not to be unreasonably withheld.*

However, even if there is no such express provision in the lease the requirement not unreasonably to withhold consent is implied by statute (Landlord and Tenant Act 1927 s.19).

Landlord and Tenant Act 1927 s. 19

19.–(1) In all leases whether made before or after the commencement of this Act containing a covenant condition or agreement against *assigning, underletting, charging or parting with the possession* of demised premises *or any part thereof without licence or consent*, such covenant condition or agreement shall, notwithstanding any express provision to the contrary, be deemed to be subject—

10–09

    (a)   to a proviso to the effect that such licence or consent is *not to be unreasonably withheld,* but this proviso does not preclude the right of the landlord to require payment of a reasonable sum in respect of any legal or other expenses incurred in connection with such licence or consent; and

    (b)   (if the lease is for more than forty years, and is made in consideration wholly or partially of the erection, or the substantial improvement, addition or alteration of buildings, and the lessor is not a Government department or local or public authority, or a statutory or public utility company) to a proviso to the effect that in the case of any assignment, underletting, charging or parting with the possession (whether by the holders of the lease or any undertenant whether immediate or not) effected more than seven years before the end of the term no consent or licence shall be required, if notice in writing of the transaction is given to the lessor within six months after the transaction is effected. (*Emphasis added.*)

Whether or not the landlord's refusal to give consent is unreasonable or not is often a difficult question, which is why most tenants will be well advised not simply to assign etc. without either first obtaining that consent or applying to the court for a declaration that the landlord's refusal is unreasonable. There are many cases dealing with the issue but in *International Drilling Fluids Ltd v Louisville Investments (Uxbridge) Ltd* [1986] 1 All E.R. 321 CA the court reviewed the authorities and in relation to a covenant against assignment set out guidance for determining the issue:

"(1) The purpose of a covenant against assignment without the consent of the landlord, such consent not to be unreasonably withheld, is to protect the lessor from having his premises used or occupied in an undesirable way or by an undesirable tenant or assignee.

(2) As a corollary . . . , a landlord is not entitled to refuse his consent to an assignment on grounds which have nothing to do with the relationship of landlord and tenant in regard to the subject matter of the lease.

(3) The onus of proving that consent has been unreasonably withheld is on the tenant. [But see note (1) below.]

(4) It is not necessary for the landlord to prove that the conclusions which led him to refuse consent were justified, if they were conclusions which might be reached by a reasonable man in the circumstances.

(5) It may be reasonable for the landlord to refuse his consent for an assignment on the ground of the purpose for which the proposed assignee intends to use the premises, even though that purpose is not forbidden by the lease.

(6) There is a divergence of authority on the question, in considering whether the landlord's refusal of consent is reasonable, whether it is permissible to have regard to the consequences to the tenant if consent to the proposed assignment is withheld. . . . A proper reconciliation of the . . . [authorities] can be achieved by saying that while a landlord need usually only consider his own relevant interests, there may be cases where there is such a disproportion between the benefit to the landlord and the detriment to the tenant if the landlord withholds his consent to an assignment, that it is unreasonable for the landlord to refuse consent.

(7) Subject to the propositions set out above, it is, in each case a question of fact, depending on all the circumstances, whether consent is being unreasonably withheld." (*International Drilling Fluids Ltd v Louisville Investments (Uxbridge) Ltd* [1986] 1 All E.R. 321 CA, per Balcombe J at 325.)

Notes:
(1) The effect of the 1988 Act is to reverse the burden of **10–10** proof. It is now for the landlord to show that his refusal was reasonable (see s.1(6)(*c*); *Midland Bank plc v Chart Enterprises Inc* [1990] 2 E.G.L.R. 59; *Air India v Balabel* [1993] 2 E.G.L.R. 66 CA at 69, *Kened Ltd v Connie Investments Ltd* [1997] 04 E.G. 141 at 142).

(2) When a court is determining whether or not a landlord's consent was reasonable, the landlord cannot rely upon matters that did not influence him at the time he refused his consent. The time at which the landlord's refusal must be judged is the time at which he refuses consent (*CIN Properties v Gill* [1993] 2 E.G.L.R. 97 *Go West Ltd v Spigarolo* [2003] EWCA Civ 17). However, he may elaborate a reason already given (*Ashworth Frazer v Gloucester City Council (No.2)* [2001] UKHL 59; *The Royal Bank of Scotland v Victoria Street (No.3) Ltd* [2008] EWHC 3052 Ch). Morgan J at para.37:

"That brings me to the letter of refusal, which I have read. The letter is brief, but as explained by Lord Rodger in the *Ashworth Frazer* case . . . a landlord is entitled to *elaborate a reason which is stated* concisely in a letter of refusal, without going outside what is permitted by s.1 of the Landlord and Tenant Act 1988. In my judgment, the essential distinction in this area is between something which is an elaboration of the reasons stated in the letter, which is permitted, and *something which is a different reason* to that stated in the letter, which is not permitted." (*Emphasis added*).

(3) The rule that a landlord who refuses consent has to establish only that his grounds for so doing are reasonable and not that they are true (*International Drilling Fluids Ltd v Louisville Investments (Uxbridge) Ltd* [1986] 2 W.L.R. 581) is not affected by the Landlord and Tenant Act 1988 (*Air India v Balabel* at 69F).

(4) The landlord does not have to have the full terms of the underlease before deciding whether or not to consent. However, it may be reasonable to impose conditions as to the terms of the underletting (*Dong Bang Minerva (UK) Ltd v Davina Ltd* [1995] 1 E.G.L.R. 41 Ch D).

(5) Contrary to popular belief, there is no absolute rule that a landlord is entitled to refuse consent while the tenant is in arrears or otherwise in breach of covenant. Each case

will depend on its own facts. It is submitted that the refusal is likely to be reasonable only where the breach is serious and is likely to be continued after the assignment. For an example see *F W Woolworth plc v Charlwood Alliance Properties Ltd* [1987] 1 E.G.L.R. 53 Ch D—breach of user covenant continuing after assignment.

(6) It is not reasonable to demand an undertaking as to costs before consenting (*Dong Bang Minerva (UK) Ltd v Davina Ltd*). Rather the landlord should make it a condition of the consent that his reasonable costs will be paid and/or should subsequently seek to recover costs pursuant to any relevant express term in the lease dealing with them.

(7) A refusal to give consent to an assignment on the ground that the intended use by the assignee would be a breach of covenant is not automatically unreasonable. It is necessary to consider what the reasonable landlord would do in the particular circumstances of the case (*Ashworth Frazer Ltd v Gloucester City Council (No.2)* [2001] U.K.H.L. 59).

(8) The fact that the original tenant is still liable under the lease does not prevent a landlord from objecting to the covenant strength of the assignee where the landlord is concerned in a practical way about the payment of rent and the performance and observance of the covenants (*The Royal Bank of Scotland v Victoria Street (No. 3) Ltd* [2008] EWHC 3052 Ch).

(9) A landlord imposing a condition can only rely upon written reasons given within a reasonable time of receiving the tenant's application and within a reasonable time of imposing the condition. The question of reasonableness is determined by the information available to the landlord at the time he imposed the condition. (*London & Argyll Developments Ltd v Mount Cook Land Ltd* [2002] 50 EG 111 Ch D).

Effect of Landlord and Tenant (Covenants) Act 1995

10–11 The position was altered by the Landlord and Tenant (Covenants) Act 1995. In respect of all "new tenancies" (generally those granted on or after January 1, 1996; see para.13–02), the landlord and tenant may enter into a lease specifying the circumstances in which the landlord may withhold his consent to an assignment specifying conditions subject to which any such consent may be granted. Unless the circumstances are met or the conditions are fulfilled, the landlord will be able to withhold his consent (s.19(1A)–(1E) of the Landlord and Tenant Act 1927, as introduced by s.22 of the 1995 Act).

Note that these provisions only apply to assignments and parting with possession (s.19(1E)(b))–not to sublettings.

Where these provisions do apply whether the landlord is entitled to withhold consent will depend upon a construction of the "circumstances" specified in the lease. However, it is to be noted that the provisions are strict. They relate to "any circumstances" specified in the lease. There is no "reasonableness requirement". Thus, where the circumstances relate to performance by the tenant of the covenants in the lease even small technical breaches of the terms of a lease will permit the landlord to refuse consent unless e.g. the lease specified that consent may only be refused in the case of substantial or material breaches. (But see s.19(1C) where any circumstances or conditions specified in the lease are framed by reference to any matter falling to be determined by the landlord or some other person in which case that person's power must be exercised reasonably or the matter must be determined by an independent person.)

Landlord and Tenant Act 1927 s.19(1A)–(1E)

19.–(1A) Where the landlord and the tenant under a qualifying lease have entered into an agreement specifying for the purpose of this subsection– **10-12**

    (a)   any circumstances in which the landlord may withhold his licence or consent to an assignment of the demised premises or any part of them, or

    (b)   any conditions subject to which any such licence or consent may be granted, then the landlord–

        (i) shall not be regarded as unreasonably withholding his licence or consent to any such assignment if he withholds it on the ground (and it is the case) that any such circumstances exist, and

       (ii) if he gives any such licence or consent subject to any such conditions, shall not be regarded as giving it subject to unreasonable conditions;

and section 1 of the Landlord and Tenant Act 1988 (qualified duty to consent to assignment etc. shall have effect subject to the provisions of this subsection.

(1B) Subsection (1A) of this section applies to such an agreement as is mentioned in that subsection—

(a)   whether it is contained in the lease or not, and

(b)   whether it is made at the time when the lease is granted or at any other time falling before the application for the landlord's licence or consent is made.

(1C) Subsection (1A) shall not, however, apply to any such agreement to the extent that any circumstances or conditions specified in it are framed by reference to any matter falling to be determined by the landlord or by any other person for the purposes of the agreement, unless under the terms of the agreement—

(a)   that person's power to determine that matter is required to be exercised reasonably, or

(b)   the tenant is given an unrestricted right to have any such determination reviewed by a person independent of both landlord and tenant whose identity is ascertainable by reference to the agreement,

and in the latter case the agreement provides for the determination made by any such independent person on the review to be conclusive as to the matter in question.

(1D) In its application to a qualifying lease, subsection (1)(b) of this section shall not have effect in relation to any assignment of the lease.

(1E) In subsections (1A) and (1D) of this section—

(a)   "qualifying lease" means any lease which is a new tenancy for the purposes of section 1 of the Landlord and Tenant (Covenants) Act 1995 other than a residential lease, namely a lease by which a building or part of a building is let wholly or mainly as a single private residence; and

(b)   references to assignment include parting with possession on assignment.

Impact of absolute provisos

10–13   The 1995 Act only applies to new leases. However, it can often be the case that an alienation covenant (whether in a new or old lease), which on the face of it seems qualified, has a proviso that amounts to a condition precedent that must be satisfied before the landlord is even required to consider the application for consent. Any such proviso is valid (*Bocard SA v S&M Hotels Ltd* [1980] 1 W.L.R. 17—proviso requiring the tenant to offer to surrender the lease to the landlord first; *Allied Dunbar Assurance PLC v Homebase Ltd* [2002] L.&T.R. 27, at para.16 and 17—proviso that rent in sublease be reviewed to full market rent not met by fixed rent agreed between tenant and proposed subtenant; *Crestfort Ltd v Tesco Stores Ltd* [2005] EWHC 805 Ch proviso that any underlease be "subject to like covenants" to that in the headlease). In *Crestfort* the position was explained thus:

> "Accordingly by reason of the absence of a like repairing covenant in the Underlease the condition precedent to the existence of any obligation on the part of the Landlords *to consider the application* for consent to the grant of the Underlease to Magspeed was never satisfied. Tesco at all times therefore remained subject to an absolute obligation not to underlet and the Landlords at no time were under any obligation to consider Tesco's application for consent to underlet, section 1 of the Landlord and Tenant Act 1988 had no application and the grant of the Underlease to Magspeed constituted a breach of covenant by Tesco". (*Emphasis added*).

By way of further example, a requirement for a prospective assignee to offer a guarantor is often included in a lease as an absolute requirement in what is otherwise a fully qualified alienation covenant. There is no need for the landlord to be reasonable in that regard. The most that can be said is that there is an implied term that any request for a guarantor must be genuinely for the purpose of improving the landlord's financial security (*Mount Eden v Towerstone* [2002] 31 E.G. 97; [2003] L.&T.R. 4).

Compare *Mount Eden Land Ltd v Folia Ltd* [2003] EWHC 1815 Ch for a case in which the judge considered on a construction of the particular lease that there was no condition precedent that precluded him from considering the reasonableness of the landlord's refusal to grant consent.

Duty to deal in writing with application expeditiously: damages for breach

As stated above the Landlord and Tenant Act 1988 imposes obligations on a landlord to deal expeditiously with a tenant's applications for consent. If he fails to do so he will be liable to the tenant for damages under the Act. The text of the Act is to be found below (see para.10–15). The following points in particular should be noted:

10–14

(1) The core of the Act is contained in s.1(3), which imposes the duty, within a reasonable time—
   (a) to give consent in writing; or
   (b) to state in writing that consent is being given with conditions and to state those conditions; or
   (c) if no consent is given to state in writing the reasons for the refusal.

(2) Usually one is concerned with the landlord, but the Act applies to any person who under the tenant's covenant is to be asked for his consent, e.g. a superior landlord (s.1(2)(b)). A duty is also imposed upon a person, such as an immediate landlord, receiving an application to pass it on to any other person, such as a superior landlord, who is or may be the person whose consent to the transaction is required (s.2). (See also s.3 where a tenant has covenanted with his landlord not to permit his sub-tenant to assign, underlet, charge or part with possession without the consent of his landlord, which said consent is not to be unreasonably withheld. The qualification must be expressed. Section 19(1) of the Landlord and Tenant Act 1927 does not apply.)

(3) The burden of proof on any particular issue is on the landlord or such other person who has been asked for consent pursuant to the tenant's covenant (s.1(6)).

(4) In *NCR Ltd v Riverland Portfolio No.1 Ltd (No.2)* [2005] EWCA Civ 312 the judge considered that a period of two weeks was sufficient time for a decision once all the relevant information was available. This was criticised by Carnwarth LJ in the Court of Appeal, at para.21:

> "In my view, whatever earlier discussions there had been, Riverland was entitled to adequate time following receipt of the completed application to consider the serious financial and legal implications of a refusal with its advisers, and if necessary to report to the relevant Board. In the absence of special exceptional circumstances, a period of less than three weeks (particularly in the holiday period) cannot in my view be categorised as inherently unreasonable for that process."

And in *E.ON UK plc v Gilesports Ltd* [2012] EWHC 2172 it was held that eleven working days was not a reasonable time. It was a short period, it crossed a half-term break, the transaction had not been stated to be urgent and, although it was not complicated, it did require the landlord to consider a guarantee and an application for a change of use (see para.[59]).

(5) Section 5(2) specifies that an application or notice is "treated as served for the purposes of this Act" if served in any manner specified in the tenancy (which may well have incorporated the provisions of s.196 of the Law of Property Act 1925—see para.9–12) or if the tenancy makes no provision if served in any manner provided by s.23 of the Landlord and Tenant Act 1927 (see para.14–23). Although service outside those provisions is always possible (e.g. on an agent for the landlord who has authority to accept service) there are dangers in not using one of the methods referred to in s.5(2) (e.g. see *Norwich Union Linked Life Assurance Ltd v Mercantile Credit Co Ltd* [2003] EWHC 3064 Ch—service on landlord's solicitor who may not have had authority to accept service of the application). See also *E.ON UK plc v Gilesports Ltd* [2012] EWHC 2172 where the sub-lease incorporated s196. An application by email was ineffective.

(6) Once the landlord has given written notice with reasons refusing consent the period of reasonable time for giving consent has passed. The landlord cannot subsequently change his mind and say that the change has occurred within a reasonable time of the request. The fact that there were subsequent attempts to negotiate permission to assign did not deprive the tenant on the facts to its rights under the 1988 Act (*Go West Ltd v Spigarolo* [2003] EWCA Civ 17). Pill LJ at para.80:

"The expression 'within a reasonable time' may have entitled the landlords to a longer period in which to serve the notice than in fact they chose to take. Having chosen to serve a notice, however, they cannot subsequently be allowed to say, because they could have taken more time, that their refusal was ineffective as a refusal under the section. The purpose of written statutory notices such as those required by section 1(3) is to ensure that each party knows where the other stands and the refusal must be treated as such."

(7) If there is a breach of duty the tenant is entitled to damages under s.4 which can include exemplary damages (*Design Progression Ltd v Thurloe Properties Ltd* [2004] EWHC 324 where the damages awarded

included £25,000 exemplary damages, £75,000 for loss of a premium and a sum for loss of goodwill and turnover).

Landlord and Tenant Act 1988 ss.1-6

10-15   **1. Qualified duty to consent to assigning, underletting, charging or parting with possession of premises**—(1) This section applies in any case where—

- (a) a tenancy includes a covenant on the part of the tenant not to enter into one or more of the following transactions, that is—
  - (i) assigning,
  - (ii) underletting,
  - (iii) charging, or
  - (iv) parting with possession of

  the premises comprised in the tenancy or any part of the premises without the consent of the landlord or some other person, *but*
- (b) the covenant is subject to the qualification that the consent is not to be unreasonably withheld (whether or not it is also subject to any other qualification).

(2) In this section and section 2 of this Act—

- (a) references to a proposed transaction are to any assigning, underletting, charging or parting with possession to which the covenant relates, and
- (b) references to the person who may consent to such a transaction are to the person who under the covenant may consent to the tenant entering into the proposed transaction.

(3) Where there is served on the person who may consent to a proposed transaction a written application by the tenant for consent to the transaction, he *owes a duty to the tenant within a reasonable time*—

- (a) to give consent, except in a case where it is reasonable not to give consent,
- (b) to serve on the tenant *written notice* of his decision whether or not to give consent specifying in addition—
  - (i) if the consent is given *subject to conditions*, the conditions,
  - (ii) if the consent is withheld, the *reasons for withholding* it.

(4) Giving consent subject to any condition that is not a reasonable condition does not satisfy the duty under subsection (3)(*a*) above.

(5) For the purposes of this Act it is reasonable for a person not to give consent to a proposed transaction only in a case where, if he withheld consent and the tenant completed the transaction, the tenant would be in breach of a covenant.

(6) It is for the person who owed any duty under subsection (3) above—

- (a) if he gave consent and the question arises whether he gave it within a reasonable time, to show that he did,

(b) if he gave consent subject to any condition and the question arises whether the condition was a reasonable condition, to show that it was,

(c) if he did not give consent and the question arises whether it was reasonable for him not to do so, to show that it was reasonable,

and if the question arises whether he served notice under that subsection within a reasonable time, to show that he did.

2. Duty to pass on applications—(1) If, in a case where section 1 of this Act applies, any person receives a written application by the tenant for consent to a proposed transaction and that person—

(a) is a person who may consent to the transaction or (though not such a person) is the landlord, and

(b) believes that another person, other than a person who he believes has received the application or a copy of it, is a person who may consent to the transaction,

he owes a duty to the tenant (whether or not he owes him any duty under section 1 of this Act) to take such steps as are reasonable to secure receipt within a reasonable time by the other person of a copy of the application.

(2) The reference in section 1(3) of this Act to the service of an application on a person who may consent to a proposed transaction includes a reference to the receipt by him of an application or a copy of an application (whether it is for his consent or that of another).

3. Qualified duty to approve consent by another—(1) This section applies in a case where—

(a) a tenancy includes a covenant on the part of the tenant not without the approval of the landlord to consent to the sub-tenant—

  (i) assigning,

  (ii) underletting,

  (iii) charging, or

  (iv) parting with possession of,

the premises comprised in the sub-tenancy or any part of the premises, but

(b) the covenant is subject to the qualification that the approval is not to be unreasonably withheld (whether or not it is also subject to any other qualification).

(2) Where there is served on the landlord a written application by the tenant for approval or a copy of a written application to the tenant by the sub-tenant for consent to a transaction to which the covenant relates the landlord owes a duty to the tenant within a reasonable time—

(a) *to give approval, except* in a case where it is reasonable not to give approval,

(b) to serve on the tenant and the sub-tenant written notice of his decision whether or not to give approval specifying in addition—

  (i) if approval is given *subject to conditions*, the conditions;

  (ii) if approval is withheld, the reasons *for withholding it*.

(3) Giving approval subject to any condition that is not a reasonable condition does not satisfy the duty under subsection (2)(*a*) above.

(4) For the purposes of this section it is reasonable for the landlord not to give approval only in a case where, if he withheld approval and the tenant gave his consent, the tenant would be in breach of a covenant.

(5) It is for the landlord who owed any duty under subsection (2) above—

(a) if he gave approval and the question arises whether he gave it within a reasonable time, to show that he did;

(b) if he gave approval subject to any condition and the question arises whether the condition was a reasonable condition, to show that it was;

(c) if he did not give approval and the question arises whether it was reasonable for him not to do so, to show that it was reasonable;

and if the question arises whether he served notice under that subsection within a reasonable time, to show that he did.

10–16   **4. Breach of duty**—A claim that a person has broken any duty under this Act may be made the subject of civil proceedings in like manner as any other claim in tort for breach of statutory duty.

5. Interpretation—(1) In this Act—

"covenant" includes condition and agreement,
"consent" includes licence,
"landlord" includes any superior landlord from whom the tenant's immediate landlord directly or indirectly holds,
"tenancy" subject to subsection (3) below, means any lease or other tenancy (whether made before or after the coming into force of this Act) and includes—

(a) a subtenancy, and

(b) an agreement for a tenancy

and references in this Act to the landlord and to the tenant are to be interpreted accordingly, and "tenant", where the tenancy is affected by a mortgage (within the meaning of the Law of Property Act 1925) and the mortgagee proposes to exercise his statutory or express power of sale includes the mortgagee.

(2) An application or notice is to be treated as served for the purposes of this Act if—

(a) served in any manner provided in the tenancy, and

(b) in respect of any matter for which the tenancy makes no provision served in any manner provided by section 23 of the Landlord and Tenant Act 1927.

(3) This Act does not apply to a secure tenancy (defined in section 79 of the Housing Act 1985).

(4) This Act applies only to applications for consent or approval served after its coming into force (the Act came into force on 29 September 1988).

6. Application to Crown—This Act binds the Crown; but as regards the Crown's liability in tort shall not bind the Crown further than the Crown is made liable in tort by the Crown Proceedings Act 1947.

Consent granted by mistake!

It might seem odd but a landlord can inadvertently consent to   **10-17**
an assignment or subletting. If he has done so he will not subsequently be able to complain that the disposition has taken place without his consent and thus in breach of covenant. This can occur where the landlord writes a letter headed "subject to licence". If the body of the letter constitutes the granting of consent the words "subject to licence" will have no meaning (*Prudential Assurance Co v Mount Eden Land* [1997] 1 E.G.L.R. 37 CA, and *Aubergine Enterprises Ltd v Lakewood International Ltd* [2002] EWCA Civ 177). Auld LJ in the *Aubergine* case at para.43 citing the *Prudential* case:

> "The landlord's solicitors' heading of a number of their letters 'subject to licence', coupled with a statement of conditions, did not qualify the plain indication of consent in the body of the letters so as to make it equivocal or uncertain. This follows from the reasoning in [*Mount Eden v Prudential*] . . . In that case . . . Morritt L.J. . . . said . . .
>
> > 'I do not accept that it is legitimate to extend the principle . . . from the field of bilateral negotiations to that of a unilateral act . . . In cases requiring a unilateral act the only question is whether the act occurred. In truth the heading 'subject to licence' added little to the condition expressed in the body of the letter and could not qualify the unambiguous expression of consent it contained."

Even more dramatically in *Alchemy Estates Ltd v Astor* [2008] EWHC 2675 Ch the judge held that an email that said that the landlord's consented to the assignment "in principle" subject to certain conditions had in fact constituted consent, even though the e-mail specifically went on to state:

> "Please note that this correspondence does not constitute the provision of consent by our client. Such consent will only be provided on the completion and delivery of a formal Licence executed as a Deed. Please also note that

our client reserves the right to change the form of the draft Licence submitted herewith and to impose new conditions to the grant of their licence in light of any further information received".

Has there been an assignment?

10-18 To be effective to pass the legal estate an assignment must be made by deed (s.52(1) of the Law of Property Act 1925) even where the tenancy is a yearly or other periodic tenancy (*Crago v Julian* [1992] 1 All E.R. 744).

An assignment of a registered leasehold interest is not effective to pass the legal estate until it is registered (ss.6, 27 of the Land Registration Act 2002); and if the registration is not effected within two months the transfer is void (s.7). Thus, in *E.ON UK plc v Gilesports Ltd* [2012] EWHC 2172 the original sub-tenant remained liable for the performance of the sub-tenant covenants in circumstances where the assignment of the sub-lease had not been registered. (See also para.5–18).

It has also been held that a person who has entered into an agreement to take an existing lease from a tenant, but who has not yet obtained the legal estate, is entitled to apply for relief from forfeiture (see para.12–19).

CHAPTER 11

FORFEITURE: REPAIRS

. . . .

Leasehold Property (Repairs) Act 1938 s.1–3, 7

1.—(1) Where a lessor serves on a lessee under subsection (1) of section 146 of the Law of Property Act 1925, a notice that relates to a breach of covenant or agreement to keep or put in repair during the currency of the lease all or any of the property comprised in the lease and at the date of the service of the notice *three years or more* of the term of the lease remain unexpired, the lessee may within *28 days* from the date serve on the lessor a *counter-notice* to the effect that he claims the benefit of this Act.

(2) A right to *damages* for a breach of such a covenant as aforesaid shall not be enforceable by action commenced at any time at which three years or more of the term of the lease remain unexpired unless the lessor has served such a notice as is specified in subsection (1) of section 146 of the Law of Property Act 1925 and where a notice is served under this subsection, the lessee may, within 28 days from the date of the service thereof, serve on the lessor a counter-notice to the effect that he claims the benefit of this Act.

(3) Where a *counter-notice is served* by a lessee under this section, then, notwithstanding anything in any enactment or rule of law, *no proceedings by action or otherwise* shall be taken by the lessor for the enforcement of any right of re-entry or forfeiture under any proviso or stipulation in the lease for breach of the covenant or agreement in question, or for damages for breach thereof, otherwise than with the leave of the court.

(4) A notice served under subsection (1) of s.146 of the Law of Property Act 1925 in the circumstances specified in subsection (1) of this section, and a notice served under subsection (2) of this section shall not be valid unless it contains a statement, *in characters not less conspicuous* than those used in any other part of the notice, to the effect that the *lessee is entitled* under this Act *to serve on the lessor a counter-notice* claiming the benefit of this Act, and a statement in the like characters specifying the time within which, and the manner in which, under this Act a counter-notice may be served specifying the name and address for service of the lessor.

(5) *Leave* for the purposes of this section shall not be given unless the lessor proves—

    (a)   that the immediate remedying of the breach in question is requisite or preventing *substantial diminution* in the value of his reversion, or that the value thereof has been substantially diminished by the breach;

(b)   that the immediate remedying of the breach is required for giving effect in relation to the premises to the purposes of any *enactment*, or any byelaw or other provision having effect under any enactment or for giving effect to any *order of a court* or requirement of any authority under any enactment or any such byelaw or other provision as aforesaid;

(c)   in a case in which the *lessee is not in occupation of the whole* of the premises as respects which the covenant or agreement is proposed to be enforced, that the immediate remedying of the breach is required in the interests of the occupier of those premises or of part thereof;

(d)   that the breach can be immediately remedied at an *expense that is relatively small in comparison* with the much greater expense that would probably be occasioned by postponement of the necessary work; or

(e)   *special circumstances* which in the opinion of the court, render it just and equitable that leave should be given.

(6) The court may in granting or in refusing leave for the purposes of this section, impose such terms and conditions on the lessor or on the lessee as it may think fit.

2. A lessor on whom a counter-notice is served under the preceding section shall not be entitled to the benefit of subsection (3) of section 146 of the Law of Property Act 1925 (which relates to costs and expenses incurred by a lessor in reference to breaches of covenant) so far as regards any costs or expenses incurred in reference to breaches in question, unless he makes an application for leave for the purposes of the preceding section, and on such an application the court shall have power to direct whether and to what extent the lessor is to be entitled to the benefit thereof.

3. This Act shall not apply to a breach of a covenant or agreement in so far as it imposes on the lessee an obligation to put premises in repair that is to be performed upon the lessee taking possession of the premises or within a reasonable time thereafter.

. . .

7.–(1) In this Act the expressions "lessor", "lessee" and "lease" have the same meanings assigned to them respectively by sections 146 and 154 of the Law of Property Act 1925 [see para.9–01], except that they do not include any reference to such a grant as is mentioned in the said section 146, or to the person making, or to the grantee under such a grant, or to persons deriving title under such a person; and "lease" means a lease for a *term of seven years or more*, not being a lease of an agricultural holding within the meaning of the Agricultural Holdings Act 1986.

(2) The provisions of section 196 of the said Act [i.e. Law of Property Act 1925] (which relate to the service of notices) shall extend to notices and counter-notices required or authorised by this Act.

Landlord and Tenant Act 1954 s.51

11-02   . . .

(3) The said Act of 1938 shall apply where there is an interest belonging

to Her Majesty in right of the Crown or to a Government department, or held on behalf of Her Majesty for the purposes of a Government department, in like manner as if that interest were in interest not so belonging or held.

Introduction

Particular rules apply where the landlord is seeking to forfeit for breach of the covenant to repair: **11–03**

(1) There are rules about the content of the notice.
(2) In all cases special rules apply in relation to *service* of s.146 notices.
(3) Where the tenancy was *granted for a term of seven years or more* and in respect of which *three years or more remain unexpired* at the date of service of the s.146 notice the landlord's right to recover possession (or claim damages) is limited by the provisions of the Leasehold Property (Repairs) Act 1938.

Section 146 notices in repair cases

All repairing cases

All s.146 notices in repair cases must, in accordance with the usual requirement to specify the breach complained of, give details of the repairs that have not been carried out. The usual and most sensible practice is to attach a schedule of dilapidations prepared by a surveyor to the notice. However, it is not necessary to specify in the minutest detail the items that need to be repaired so long as the tenant clearly knows what he has to do to avoid forfeiture. The schedule of dilapidations will normally set out the work that is required to put the property into good repair but it is not in fact necessary to specify the acts required to remedy the breach (*Fox v Jolly* [1916] 1 A.C. 1). The notice is not invalid if it alleges some breaches that were not in fact committed (*Blewett v Blewett* [1936] 2 All E.R. 188). **11–04**

Cases where the Leasehold Property (Repairs) Act 1938 applies

Where the 1938 Act applies (see above and s.1(1) of the Act), the landlord must serve the s.146 notice at least one month **11–05** before he intends to re-enter. In many cases it should be served further in advance than that. Section 146 notices in repairs cases often specify three months. However, each case will very much depend on its own facts. The landlord must always leave sufficient time: see para.9–05 and must inform the tenant in the notice of his right to serve a counter-notice. If the tenant does serve a counter-notice, the landlord may not forfeit without the leave of the court (s.1 of the 1938 Act). As to the application for leave see para.11–08.

It is possible to waive a defect in a s.146 notice. However, it would seem that this is possible only where the tenant makes some promise or representation that he will not take any point on the invalidity of the notice and the landlord acts upon it (*BL Holdings Ltd v Marcoult Investments Ltd* [1979] 1 E.G.L.R. 97 CA—mere service of a counter-notice by the tenant (see para.11–07) did not amount to such a representation).

Service of the notice

Landlord and Tenant Act 1927 s.18

11–06   18. . . .
     (2) A right of re-entry or forfeiture for a breach of any such covenant or agreement as aforesaid [i.e. *any covenant or agreement to keep or put premises in repair during the currency of a lease, or to leave or put premises in repair at the termination of a lease: see s.18(1) below*] shall not be enforceable, by action or otherwise, unless the lessor proves that the fact that such a notice as is required by section 146 of the Law of Property Act 1925, has been served on the lessee was known either—

    (a)   to the lessee; or
    (b)   to an underlessee holding under an underlease which reserved a nominal reversion only to the lessee; or
    (c)   to the person who last paid the rent due under the lease either on his own behalf or as agent for the lessee or underlessee,

and that a time reasonably sufficient to enable the repairs to be executed had elapsed since the time when the fact of the service of the notice came to the knowledge of any such person.
     Where a notice has been sent by registered post addressed to a person at his last known place of abode in the United Kingdom then, for the purposes of this subsection, that person shall be deemed, unless the contrary is proved, to have knowledge of the fact that the notice had been served as from the time at which the letter would have been delivered in the ordinary course of post.

This subsection shall be construed as one with s.146 of the Law of Property Act 1925.

Service of s.146 notices was dealt with in general terms at para.9–11. However, where one is concerned with breach of a repairing covenant, there are further requirements imposed on the landlord in relation to service of the notice (s.18 of the Landlord and Tenant Act 1927). He may not exercise his right to re-enter unless he proves that service of the notice was known either:

(a) to his tenant;
(b) to a sub-tenant holding under a sub-lease which reserved only a nominal reversion to the tenant; or
(c) to the person who last paid the rent;

and that a reasonable time has elapsed since the time when the fact of service was known to such a person.

However, the landlord's position is ameliorated by the fact that where the notice is sent by recorded delivery to a person at his last known place of abode in the United Kingdom, proof of posting means that the notice is deemed to have come to his knowledge in the ordinary course of post unless the contrary is proved (s.18(2) of the 1927 Act; s.1(1) of the Recorded Delivery Service Act 1962).

Tenant's action on receipt of the notice: counter-notice

The tenant has 28 days in which to serve a counter-notice. If he **11–07** serves the counter-notice within this period the landlord will have to apply to the court for leave to enter the property, which the court will grant only in limited circumstances (see below). If the tenant fails to serve a counter-notice within this period he will lose his rights under the Act. The counter-notice should inform the landlord that he claims the benefit of the 1938 Act. There is no prescribed form and a simple letter will suffice.

Section 23(2) of the Landlord and Tenant Act 1927, which authorises a tenant to serve documents on the person to whom he has been paying rent, applies in relation to service of the counter-notice (s.5(4) of the Landlord and Tenant Act 1954).

As to the actions of a tenant generally on receipt of a s.146 notice see para.9–13.

A mortgatgee, even in possession, has no right to serve a counter-notice (*Smith v Spaul* [2002] EWCA Civ 1830).

Landlord's application for leave to enforce right of re-entry

11–08   As stated above, if the tenant serves a counter-notice the landlord must apply for leave to forfeit the lease (s.1(3) of the 1938 Act). The landlord will be granted leave to re-enter the property (whether by proceedings or otherwise: s.1(3)) only if the landlord proves one of the five grounds set out in s.1(5) of the 1938 Act. The full subsection is at para.11–01. The grounds may be summarised as follows:

(1) Immediate remedying of the breach is required to prevent substantial diminution of value of reversion, or substantial diminution has occurred.
(2) Immediate remedying of the breach is required to comply with statute, bye-law, court order etc.
(3) Immediate remedying of the breach is required in interests of occupiers other than the tenant.
(4) Immediate remedying of the breach is cheap compared to result of delay.
(5) Special circumstances.

The application is made generally in the County Court under CPR Pt 8. See Form 8 for the main body of the Part 8 claim form, at para.11–11 (PD 56 para.1); 56.2, PD 56 para.2.2).

The witness statement in support is usually made by the landlord's surveyor who will exhibit his original schedule of dilapidations that was served with the s.146 notice. The statement should state the grounds in s.1(5) of the 1938 Act relied upon and the facts and matters relied upon to establish those grounds. See Form 9 for a precedent at para.11–12.

It is not good enough for the landlord to show that he has an arguable or prima facie case. He must prove on a balance of probabilities that one or more of the grounds set out in s.1(5) of the 1938 Act applies (*Associated British Ports v CH Bailey plc*

[1990] 1 All E.R. 929 HL). Thus, if a dispute arises as to whether or not any of the grounds apply, it will be necessary to have a full trial of the issue with oral evidence given. The date for determining whether or not the ground is made out is the date of the hearing (*Landmaster Properties Ltd v Thackeray Property Services* [2003] EWHC 959).

The court may, in granting or in refusing leave, impose on the landlord or the tenant such terms and conditions as it thinks fit (s.1(6)).

An application under the 1938 Act for leave to commence proceedings for forfeiture of a lease is a "pending land action" within the meaning of s.17(1) of the Land Charges Act 1972 and is therefore registrable as a "pending action" under s.5(2) of the 1972 Act (*Selim Ltd v Bickenhall Engineering Ltd* [1981] 3 All E.R. 210). Where the land is registered the action is protected by entry of a notice (Land Registration Act 2002, s.34 and s.87(1)(a)).

Recovery of landlord's costs

Section 146(3) of the Law of Property Act 1925 gives the landlord the right to recover as a debt due to him all reasonable costs and expenses properly incurred in the employment of a solicitor and surveyor or valuer in reference to any breach giving rise to a right of re-entry that, at the request of the tenant, is waived by the landlord or from which the tenant is relieved under the provisions of s.146(4) of the 1925 Act (see para.9–08). However, a landlord on whom a counter-notice has been served under s.1 of the 1938 Act may not rely on s.146(3) unless he makes an application for leave under that section (s.2 of the 1938 Act; para.11–01).   **11–09**

Leases often contain express terms as to recovery of costs giving the landlord the right to forfeit where the tenant fails to pay. These clauses are not ousted by s.146(3) and are not affected by the provisions of the 1938 Act (*Bader Properties Ltd v Linley Property Investments Ltd* (1968) 19 P. & C.R. 620; *Middlegate Properties Ltd v Gidlow-Jackson* (1977) 34 P. & C.R. 4).   **11–10**

11-11   **Form 8: Part 8 claim form for leave under 1938 Act**

IN THE HIGH COURT OF JUSTICE   20.........

[Chancery/Queen's] Bench Division
BETWEEN:

[*Name of the Landlord*]

Claimant

-and-

[*Name of the Tenant*]

Defendant

The claim is for:

(1) Leave under s.1 of the Leasehold Property (Repairs) Act 1938 to take proceedings for the enforcement of its right of re-entry by reason of breaches of the repairing covenants contained in a Lease now held by the Defendant and made on .... between the claimant's predecessor in title [*name of predecessor*] and the Defendant's predecessor in title [*name of predecessor*] whereby the Property known as [*address of demised premises*] was demised to the Defendant's predecessor in title for a term of .... years from ....;

(2) Leave under s.1 of the 1938 Act to take proceedings for damages for breaches of the said repairing covenants;

(3) A direction under s.2 of the 1938 Act that the Claimant do have the benefit of s.146(3) of the Law of Property Act 1925 in relation to the costs and expenses incurred in reference to the said breaches; and

(4) An order that the Defendant do pay the costs of this application.

11-12   **Form 9: Witness statement in support of application for leave—1938 Act**

[*Name*] (1)
Dated ....
Filed on behalf of the Claimant

IN THE HIGH COURT OF JUSTICE   20....

[Chancery/Queen's] Bench Division

BETWEEN:

[*Name of the Landlord*]

Claimant

-and-

[*Name of the Tenant*]

Defendant

cont

cont

I, [*name of the landlord's surveyor*] F.R.I.C.S., Chartered Surveyor, of [*address*] hereby say as follows:

1.   I make this affidavit with the authority of the Claimant and in support of its application for permission to take the proceedings referred to in the claim form dated .... and for the other orders sought in that claim form. I have been a qualified surveyor for ..... years and am a partner in the firm of ...., Chartered Surveyors, of .... Save where otherwise appears the facts stated herein are within my own knowledge and belief.

2.   The counter-part of the Lease dated .... between .... and .... referred to in the Claim form is attached and marked ".... 1". Under the terms of the Lease the landlord granted the tenant a tenancy of the Property known as .... for a term of .... years from .... I am informed by Mr ...., the Claimant's managing director, and believe that the Claimant is the successor in title to the landlord's interest.

3.   By Clause .... of the Lease, the tenant covenanted with the landlord to keep the Property in good and proper repair. By Clause .... of the Lease the tenant covenanted to pay to the landlord the legal costs and surveyor's fees incurred by the landlord in preparing a notice under s.146 of the Law of Property Act 1925.

4.   On .... I visited the Property and subsequently prepared a Schedule of Dilapidation. I confirm that it is necessary to carry out the remedial works listed in the Schedule. I am informed by the Claimant's solicitors and believe that they served a copy of my Schedule together with a notice under s.146 of the Law of Property Act 1925 and s.1 of the Leasehold Property (Repairs) Act 1938 upon the Defendant by recorded delivery on .... A copy of the notice and attached Schedule are attached and marked ".... 2". A counter notice was served by the Defendant on .... A copy of that notice is attached and marked ".... 3".

5.   There are a large number of items in the Schedule. The items upon which the Claimant relies for the purpose of this application are marked with an asterisk on the copy exhibited to this affidavit. *All the items so marked relate to dampness. The Property is being severely damaged by the ingress of water through the roof, and by rising damp around the foundations. If the remedial works are not carried out immediately there is a grave risk that the structural timbers could be affected by the damp penetration. It is therefore most urgent that steps are taken to eliminate damp penetration. The cost of the works listed in the Schedule connected with remedying the problem of damp is approximately £..... If the works are left for any period and the structural timbers are affected the cost of remedying the defects will be greatly increased.*

6.   Having regard to the above, I consider that subsections (a) and (d) of s.1(5) of the Leasehold Property (Repairs) Act 1938 apply, namely:

(a) That the breaches must be remedied immediately in order to prevent substantial diminution in the value of the Claimant's reversion; and

(b) That the breach can be immediately remedied at an expense that is relatively small in comparison with a much greater expense that would probably be

---

cont

occasioned by postponement of the necessary work.

7. On .... I returned to the Property. Notwithstanding service of the notice, the necessary repairs have not been carried out.

Statement of truth

Damages for failure to repair

11-13 Where the landlord forfeits for breach of the repairing covenant, it is also likely that he will wish to recover damages for breach of that covenant. A full discussion of the subject is beyond the scope of this book but the following points are particularly worth noting.

Heads of damage

11-14 There are two stages when assessing damages in any dilapidations claims. First, one must calculate the amount that the landlord would be entitled to recover at common law. Secondly, one must look to see whether or not those damages are to be capped by virtue of s.18 of the Landlord and Tenant Act 1927 (below). The main headings under which damages may be claimed at common law are:

- Cost of repairs.
- Professional fees in connection with the work.
- Loss of rent during repairs work

Cost of repairs

11-15 The basic statement of principle is contained in the judgment of Lord Esher in *Joyner v Weeks* [1891] 2 Q.B. 31. Lord Esher:

> "The rule is that, when there is a lease with a covenant to leave the premises in repair at the end of the term, and such covenant is broken, the lessee must pay what the lessor proves to be *a reasonable and proper amount* for putting the premises into the state of repair in which they ought to have been left". (Emphasis added).

The following particular points are worth noting:

- Betterment: There is no discount for betterment where it is necessary to do the works to put the claimant back into the position he should be in (*Harbutt's Plasticene Ltd v Wayne Tank & Pump Ltd* [1970] 1 Q.B. 447—in the first instance decision; *McGreal v Wake* (1984) 13 H.L.R. 197). The following example is given in *Dilapidations by Dowding and Reynolds* (Sweet & Maxwell):

  "For example, it will not generally be possible to repair a rotten window frame without cutting out the rot and joining in new wood, or, where the rot is serious, replacing the entire frame. In such cases the damages should not be reduced because the landlord is getting back a new frame in place of the old".

- However, where the work can be done in different ways some of which don't involve betterment then the cheaper method will be used to assess damages (e.g. see *Riverside Property Investments v Blackhawk* [2005] 1 E.G.L.R. 114—patching of roof ok where it would give 10 years of life to the roof and three years left on lease when work done—T not required to pay L cost of replacing the roof at expiry of term).

Professional fees

Professional fees reasonably incurred and reasonable in amount in connection with the work are recoverable, e.g. the specification of works, drawings, supervision. But note that the cost of the schedule of dilapidations is not recoverable as damages (*Lloyds Bank Ltd v Lake* [1961] 1 W.L.R. 884). This is why most leases make such sums expressly recoverable under the terms of the lease.

11–16

Rent

In order to recover loss of rent as part of his damages the landlord must show that he was unable to relet the premises because of the works. If the landlord would not have been able to relet even if they had been handed back in good repair he will not be able to claim loss of rent. It is:

11–17

"an essential prerequisite that it should be demonstrated on the balance of probabilities that the carrying out of those repairs after the end of the term has prevented or

will prevent the letting of the premises for that period"
(*Scottish Amicable Life Assurance Society v British
Telecommunications plc* (Deputy OR, unreported, March
18, 1994—cited in *Dilapidations by Dowding &
Reynolds*).

Limitation on amount of damages

11–18 The sum that the landlord may recover for damages for breach
of covenant to repair is limited by s.18(1) of the Landlord and
Tenant Act 1927—often referred to as the "s.18 cap". There are
two limbs to this subsection. Under the first limb the damages
are limited to the amount by which the value of the landlord's
interest in the property is damaged by the breach. The second
limb precludes the landlord from recovering damages if the
landlord intended to pull down the premises or make structural
alterations which would render the repairs valueless.

Landlord and Tenant Act 1927 s.18

11–19 **18.**—(1) Damages for breach of a covenant or agreement to keep or put
premises in repair during the currency of a lease, or to leave or put
premises in repair at the termination of a lease, whether such covenant
or agreement is expressed or implied, and whether general or specific,
shall in no case exceed the amount (if any) by which the *value of the
reversion* (whether immediate or not) in the premises is diminished owing
to the breach of such covenant or agreement as aforesaid; and in
particular no damage shall be recovered for a breach of any such
covenant or agreement to leave or put premises in repair at termination
of a lease, if it is shown that the premises, in whatever state of repair they
might be, would at or shortly after the termination of the tenancy have
been pulled down, or such structural alterations made therein as would
render valueless the repairs covered by the covenant or agreement.
(*Emphasis added.*)

A covenant to decorate is a covenant to repair and so is subject
to the s.18 cap (*Latimer v Carney* [2006] EWCA Civ 1417).

Limb 1: Diminution in value

11–20 If appropriate, the cost of repairs may be used as a guide to the
amount of the diminution in value of the property (*Jones v
Herxheimer* [1950] 2 K.B. 106) but, if the repairs are not
actually going to be carried out, the cost of them is unlikely to
be a good guide (*Smiley v Townshend* [1950] 2 K.B. 311).
However, it does not necessarily follow that where repairs are
not going to be done that the damages will be nominal

(*Culworth Estates Ltd v Society of Licensed Victuallers* [1991] 2 E.G.L.R. 54). (see also *Craven/Builders) Ltd v Secretary of State for Health* [2000] 1 E.G.L.R. 128 and *Ultraworth Ltd v General Accident Fire and Life* [2000] E.G.L.R. 115).

In *Latimer v Carney* [2006] EWCA Civ 1417 the Court of Appeal held that an *estimated* cost of repairs in a schedule of dilapidations could be used to establish diminution in value. The landlord had obtained a schedule of dilapidations from a surveyor, which set out an estimate of what it would cost to put the premises in repair by reason of the defects. However, the landlord did not actually carry out the works specified in the report. Rather, the landlord refurbished the property to meet the needs of an incoming tenant. Even though there was no expert evidence, the judge could have drawn the inference that the cap was not exceeded from the fact that the landlords had to do some repairs to the roof of the premises before they could be relet, and had to execute the other repairs before the new tenant would take his lease. Arden LJ:

> "46. It is clear from the *Jones* case that expert evidence is not required and that in an appropriate case the court can infer that there has been a diminution in the value of the reversion, and the amount of such diminution, from the fact that the landlords have had to carry out certain repairs. But this is not the only circumstance in which diminution will be found. It may be found where for instance the landlord has not carried out the repairs through lack of funds. In my judgment the judge was in error in thinking that if the repairs had actually been carried out he could not infer that damage to the reversion had occurred from the fact of those repairs unless he had the actual cost of those repairs. In my judgment he could make that inference from an estimate of those costs if he was satisfied the estimated costs were reasonable. In an ideal world every landlord will come to court with the appropriate valuations but where this does not happen the landlord should not fail to make any recovery if it is clear that breaches occurred, that the repair work had to be done and that damage to the reversion as a result of the breaches is proved in other ways . . . "

However, it is to be noted that the estimated costs of remedying the other breaches was made subject to a discount of 60 per cent to take account of the uncertainty as to the extent that the disrepair affected the value of the reversion. Arden LJ:

> "51. The position therefore, is this. The landlords were obliged to do the repairs. But they went further than simply doing the repairs. They carried out improvements at the same time. In fairness to the outgoing tenants, there is the possibility that the landlords' work rendered some of the work required to remedy the breaches of covenant by the outgoing tenants futile and that some of the improvements rendered some of the work of repair unnecessary . . . .
>
> 52. In all the circumstances, the right course in my judgment was for the judge to have inferred diminution in value to the reversion from the estimated costs of any repairs required to be done by the outgoing tenant which the landlord could actually show they had done. This would include damage to the roof. In the case of other repairs, the judge should have applied a discount to take account of the possibilities referred to above. . . . In my judgment, the discount should be 60%."

A 60 per cent discount is a very large one. The lessons seem to be this:

* The tenant should not assume that a landlord will be awarded nothing just because there is no expert evidence.
* There should always be expert evidence dealing with diminution in value of the reversion—especially where the landlord does not carry out the works listed in his costed schedule of dilapidations. The landlord may get something but his damages may also suffer an unwarranted discount that the judge plucks out of the air "doing the best he can" on the facts of the case.

There is nothing in principle against there being a negative value of the reversion (*Shortlands Investments Ltd v Cargill Plc* [1995] 1 E.G.L.R. 51). Judge Bowsher QC:

> "At the heart of this case, as it seems to me, there is a point of principle which arises out of the implicit assumption of Mr Lyall and the defendants that it is impossible to accept that one negative value can be worse or better than another negative value. The point never came out into the open in express terms, but it seems to

have been assumed by Mr Lyall that once the value of a property gets down to £nil there cannot be any diminution in value. That may be true in many or perhaps most cases of chattels. It is quite a different situation where an owner of a leasehold property has an onerous interest which he wishes to transfer. Such an interest is transferable on the market if not 'saleable'. If one assumes a willing transferor and a willing transferee, there will be a point in negotiations for a payment from the transferor where the parties are willing to do a deal."

Limb 2: No damages

Under the second limb: **11–21**

"no damage shall be recovered . . . if it is shown that the premises, in whatever state of repair they might be, would at or shortly after the termination of the tenancy have been pulled down or such structural alterations made therein as would render valueless the repairs . . . ".

This second limb is awkward in its wording and will often be difficult to establish even where it seems clear that the property was ripe for development at the end of the lease. It depends upon the intention of the landlord at the date of termination (sometimes the intention of a third party) and it can often be difficult to show an intention to pull down/carry out structural alterations "at or shortly after the termination".

Property ripe for development

Although it may be difficult for the tenant to establish that the   **11–22**
second limb applies he may still be able to rely upon the first limb if the evidence establishes that the property was ripe for development at the termination of the lease (*Ravengate Estates Ltd v Horizon Housing Group Ltd* [2007] EWCA Civ 1368).

In *Ravengate* the judge found that:

(i) the premises were ripe for development,
(ii) any potential purchaser would give effect to development and

(iii) that development would render otiose the carrying out of most of the repairs claimed by the landlord.

The Court of Appeal considered that "the judge was right to find that any purchaser of these premises would purchase with an eye to redevelopment. That means that any purchaser would not need, require or expect a reduction in respect of a large part of the repairs". The consequence of this was that:

" . . . the judge was right to find that the amount of the diminution in the value of the reversion brought about by the want of repair was less than the cost of repairs, and therefore to apply that as the relevant measure of damage. He was also right to assess that value by reference to the amount which a developer purchaser (in effect the only likely purchaser) would require to be deducted from the purchase price, which in turn is to be assessed by reference to items of repair which the developer would have to carry out himself."

The landlord was therefore only entitled to the small sum representing the few repairs that the developer would require to the common parts.

A good tactic for the tenant to use sometimes (where he is not contracted out of the security provisions of the Act; see Ch.3) and where he thinks that the landlord may be intending to redevelop (or sell onto someone else who will wish to redevelop) is to serve a request for a new tenancy under s.26, even if he does not actually wish to have a new tenancy. The notice will be valid (*Sun Life Assurance plc v Thales Tracs Ltd;* see para.15–05) and will preserve the tenant's right to compensation under Pt II of the 1954 Act if the landlord does wish to redevelop (Ch.27, para.27–10 onwards). More importantly for present purposes, it will put the landlord on the spot. If he wishes to preserve his position the landlord will need to serve a counter-notice specifying the redevelopment ground (s.30(1)(f); para.17–10) within two months (s.26(6); para.15–13). Service of a counter-notice will not be conclusive evidence that the landlord intends to redevelop. He may just be preserving his position. However, it is clearly a bit of good evidence that that is indeed what he intends to do and will usually put the tenant into a very good bargaining position. See also para.11–24.

Date at which damages are assessed

Where the landlord has forfeited the lease by proceedings and   **11–23**
is claiming damages for failure to deliver up the property in
good repair, the date at which damages are assessed is the
date upon which the claim in the forfeiture action was served.
This is because the lease (and the covenants contained therein)
came to an end on that date and thereafter the ex-tenant
remained in occupation as a trespasser. If the ex-tenant has
caused further damage after service of the claim, the landlord
should seek to recover his loss by claiming damages in tort.
(*Associated Deliveries Ltd v Harrison* (1984) 50 P. & C.R. 91 CA;
see also para.7–35 above.)

Damages where the landlord has previously indicated by service of a s.25 notice of an intention to demolish

It sometimes occurs that the landlord will serve a notice under   **11–24**
s.25 of the Landlord and Tenant Act 1954 terminating the
tenancy and stating that he intends to rely upon s.30(1)(f) in
opposition to any application that the tenant may make in
respect of a new tenancy, i.e. that he intends to demolish or
reconstruct (see Ch.17, para.17–10). Subsequently, he changes
his mind and expresses his willingness to grant a lease.
However, the tenant has found alternative accommodation and
gives up occupation. The landlord then serves a Schedule of
Dilapidations on the tenant who objects and relies upon the
second limb of s.18(1). Is he permitted to do so?

The time for determining whether or not the landlord intended
to pull down the property or make structural alterations is the
date upon which the tenancy came to an end (*Salisbury v
Gilmore* [1942] 2 K.B. 38; *Mather v Barclays Bank* [1987] 2
E.G.L.R. 254). The landlord will not therefore be precluded from
recovering damages by the second limb in s.18(1) if at that date
(see para.27–02) he no longer intends to demolish or
reconstruct. See also para.11–22.

Sub-tenants in occupation at end of lease

Where the property is sublet the property must be valued   **11–25**
subject to those sub-tenancies if they are to become binding on
the landlord, e.g. sub-tenants with 1954 Act rights (*Family*

Management Ltd v Gray (1979) 253 E.G. 369). In that case, the repairing covenants in the head lease and the sub-tenancies were similar and the whole of the property was sublet. It was therefore held that there was no diminution in the value of the reversion because one had to proceed on the basis that the sub-tenants would comply with the repairing obligations. However, it is necessary to be careful. The case is not authority for the proposition that wherever there are sub-tenants there will never be a diminution in the value of the reversion. For example, if the repairing covenants were different or the sub-tenant was of less financial strength than the outgoing tenant the position might be different. Each case will depend on the facts and the valuation evidence. (For a recent example see *Lyndendown Ltd v Vitamol Ltd* [2007] EWCA Civ 826).

Other covenants

11–26   Other covenants, such as the covenant to re-instate or the covenant to comply with statutory obligations, are not covenants to repair and so are not subject to the s.18 cap. However, it is quite likely that even at common law the courts might now adopt similar principles to those in s.18 where they are considering these other covenants. See *Ruxley v Forsyth* [1996] A.C. 344—the swimming pool case where the House of Lords held that where the expenditure required to be done to an asset to remedy a breach of contract is out of all proportion to the benefit to be obtained, the appropriate measure of damages will be the diminution in value of the asset rather than the expenditure. See also the comments of Arden LJ in *Latimer v Carney* [2006] EWCA Civ 1417 at paras 24 and 60 which suggest that these principles would apply to non-repairing covenants in leases:

> "The basic measure of damages for breach of the covenant to repair is the reasonable costs of executing the repairs required to fulfil the covenant (see *Hanson v Newman* [1934] Ch. 298). This general rule is subject to the statutory cap in section 18(1) of the 1927 Act, set out above. It is also subject to general principles of law, including the principle established in *Ruxley v Forsyth* [1996] A.C. 344. In that case the House of Lords held that, where the expenditure required to be done to an asset to remedy a breach of contract is out of all proportion to the benefit to be obtained, the appropriate measure of damages will be the diminution in value of the asset rather

than the expenditure. In *Ruxley,* the owner of the asset had no intention of expending the money required to remedy the defect and this point raises the question of the extent to which the subjective intention of the claimant is relevant. However, it is unnecessary to deal with that point in this case as the landlords have executed the repairs, that is, they have done works which are or supersede the repairs the respondents were bound to effect. Although courts are not normally concerned with what a claimant does with his damages, a landlord's conduct in taking steps or not taking steps to remedy a breach of the covenant to repair may throw light on the question whether the repairs are reasonably necessary, and thus on the question whether there was any diminution in value of the reversion as a result of the disrepair.

... Parliament enacted the cap in section 18(1) to meet the rigour of the measure of damages for breach of the repair covenant at common law. It may be that the courts would not apply the common law measure of damages in all cases today: I would accept the argument of counsel for the second respondent (Mr Matthew Hall) that, if the common law measure alone were relevant to a landlord's claim, the courts today might in an appropriate case adopt the measure of damages in section 18(1) in preference to that which has previously been held to be the measure at common law (see generally *Ruxley v Forsyth*)."

And see also *Sunlife Europe Properties v Tiger Aspect Holdings* [2013] EWHC 463 (TCC)–para.[24] where at first instance judge said that *Ruxley v Forsyth* [1996] 1 AC 344 "shows that the general rule that the cost of re-instatement is the appropriate measure of damages does not apply if the expenditure would be out of all proportion to the benefit obtained". It does therefore seem reasonably certain that the *Ruxley* principles have become established in relation to re-instatement claims. (The case went to appeal on other points).

Costs of proceedings

Where a landlord exaggerates his claim for damages for disrepair he may end up paying the tenant damages on an indemnity basis even if he does recover a sum greater than that

11–27

offered by the tenant (*Business Environment Bow Lane Ltd v Deanwater Estates Ltd* [2008] EHCC 2003 TCC). In that case the landlord originally claimed £557,483.97. That sum was whittled down at various stages of the proceedings until the landlord eventually made a Pt 36 offer stating that it would accept £1,073.50. Even though a consent order was made for that sum and tenant had not previously offered that or more the landlord was ordered to pay the tenant's costs on an indemnity basis (see in particular paras 104, 105 and 109 of the judgment).

Entry by landlord to repair: an alternative remedy

11–28   Many leases contain a clause entitling the landlord to enter the property to view its state of repair and to serve a notice of defects. The tenant is then obliged to carry out the repairs within a specified period. If he fails to do so, the landlord may enter the property himself, carry out the repairs and demand repayment of the cost from the tenant. If the tenant fails to pay and the landlord decides to sue for the sum expended or to forfeit for breach of the tenant's obligation to pay that sum, the provisions of the 1938 Act do not apply. Thus, no special s.146 notice is required and the leave of the court to commence proceedings is not required. The tenant's liability to reimburse the landlord for his expenditure on repairs is not a liability in damages but is for a debt (*Jervis v Harris* [1996] 1 All E.R. 303).

> " . . . the question is: does the section [i.e. *s.1 of the 1938 Act*] require him to obtain the leave of the court after having carried out the repairs and before demanding reimbursement? But this claim cannot sensibly be described as a claim to damages for breach of the tenant's repairing covenant. That breach has been remedied. The landlord sues in respect of an altogether different breach which occurs when the tenant fails to repay to the landlord on demand the amount which he promised to pay.
>
> The landlord's claim is not triggered by the tenant's breach of covenant but by his own expenditure on carrying out repairs" (per Millett LJ at 308j to 309a).

Use of a *Jervis v Harris* clause (as they have become known) therefore has obvious attractions. However, there are real dangers in their use:

- The landlord actually has to pay out the sums required to do the works before he recovers from the tenant.
- There may be disputes with the tenant as to what works are actually required. If the tenant turns out to be correct the landlord may not recover all its costs.
- *Jervis v Harris* clauses contain specific procedures to be followed by the landlord relating to notice etc. before entry can be made. If the landlord gets the procedure wrong any entry by him will be a trespass, which might lead to a claim for damages. If the works interfere with the tenant's business these could be high.
- There may be disputes as to whether or not the works have been carried out in a reasonable manner, which once again could lead to the tenant bringing a damages claim.
- The tenant's co-operation in terms of access, use of facilities, electricity and other services will be required.

Improvements

Where a landlord is seeking to forfeit for breach of covenant **11–29** against making improvements without licence or consent, it should be remembered that such covenants are subject to a statutory proviso that such licence or consent will not be unreasonably withheld (s.19(2) of the Landlord and Tenant Act 1927).

Landlord and Tenant Act 1927 s.19

19.– . . .   **11–30**
    (2) In all leases whether made before or after the commencement of this Act containing a covenant or agreement against the making of improvements without licence or consent, such covenant condition or agreement shall be deemed, notwithstanding any express provision to the contrary, to be subject to a proviso that such licence or consent is not to be unreasonably withheld; but this proviso does not preclude the right to require as a condition of such licence or consent the payment of a reasonable sum in respect of any damage to or diminution in the value of the premises or any neighbouring premise belonging to the landlord, and of any legal or other expenses properly incurred in connection with such licence or consent nor, in the case of an improvement which does not add to the letting value of the holding, does it preclude the right to require as a condition of such licence or consent, where such a requirement would

be reasonable, an undertaking on the part of the tenant to reinstate the premises in the condition in which they were before the improvement was executed.

. . .

(4) This section shall not apply to leases of agricultural holdings within the meaning of the Agricultural Holdings Act 1986 and paragraph (b) of subsection (1), subsection (2) and subsection (3) of this section shall not apply to mining leases.

See also *Iqbal v Thakrar* [2004] EWCA Civ 592 and *Sargeant v Macepark (Whittlebury) Ltd* [2004] EWHC 1333 Ch where it was held that the principles in *International Drilling* (para.10-09) suitably adapted to the situation apply where it is suggested that the landlord has unreasonably refused to consent to alterations.

CHAPTER 12

RELIEF FROM FORFEITURE

. . . .

Rent cases: County Court

Sections 138 to 140 of the County Courts Act 1984 (as amended) contain the rules relating to relief from forfeiture where proceedings are brought in the County Court. Section 138 applies where the landlord has commenced proceedings for possession. Section 139(2) applies where the landlord has re-entered the property without taking proceedings.

12–01

County Courts Act 1984 ss.138–40

138.–(1) This section has effect where a lessor is proceeding by action in a county court (being an action in which the county court has jurisdiction) to enforce against a lessee a right of re-entry or forfeiture in respect of any land for non-payment of rent.

12–02

(2) If the lessee pays into court not less than 5 clear days before the return day all the rent in arrear and the costs of the action, the action shall cease, and the lessee shall hold the land according to the lease without any new lease.

(3) If—

   (a)   the action does not cease under subsection (2); and
   (b)   the court at the trial is satisfied that the lessor is entitled to enforce the right of re-entry or forfeiture, the court shall order possession of the land to be given to the lessor at the expiration of such period, not being less than 4 weeks from the date of the order, as the court thinks fit, unless within that period the lessee pays into court all the rent in arrear and the costs of the action.

(4) The court may extend the period specified under subsection (3) at any time before possession of the land is recovered in pursuance of the order under that subsection.

(5) If—

   (a)   within the period specified in the order; or
   (b)   within that period as extended under subsection (4), the lessee pays into court—

      (i)   all the rent in arrear; and
      (ii)   the costs of the action,

he shall hold the land according to the lease without any new lease.

(6) Subsection (2) shall not apply where the lessor is proceeding in the same action to enforce a right of re-entry or forfeiture on any other ground as well as for non-payment of rent, or to enforce any other claim as well as the right of re-entry or forfeiture and the claim for arrears of rent.

(7) If the lessee does not—

(a)   within the period specified in the order; or
(b)   within that period as extended under subsection (4), pay into court—
  (i) all the rent in arrear; and
  (ii) the costs of the action,

the order shall be enforceable in the prescribed manner and so long as the order remains unreversed the lessee shall, subject to subsections (8) and (9A), be barred from all relief.

(8) The extension under subsection (4) of a period fixed by a court shall not be treated as relief from which the lessee is barred by subsection (7) if he fails to pay into court all the rent in arrear and the costs of the action within that period.

(9) Where the court extends a period under subsection (4) at a time when—

(a)   that period has expired; and
(b)   a warrant has been issued for the possession of the land,

the court shall suspend the warrant for the extended period; and, if, before the expiration of the extended period, the lessee pays into court all the rent in arrear and all the costs of the action, the court shall cancel the warrant.

(9A) Where the lessor recovers possession of the land at any time after the making of the order under subsection (3) (whether as a result of the enforcement of the order or otherwise) the lessee may, at any time within 6 months from the date on which the lessor recovers possession, apply to the court for relief; and on any such application the court may, if it thinks fit, grant to the lessee such relief, subject to such terms and conditions, as it thinks fit.

(9B) Where the lessee is granted relief on application under subsection (9A) he shall hold the land according to the lease without any new lease.

(9C) An application under subsection (9A) may be made by a person with an interest under a lease of the land derived (whether immediately or otherwise) from the lessee's interest therein in like manner as if he were the lessee; and on any such application the court may make an order which (subject to such terms and conditions as the court thinks fit) vest the land in such a person, as lessee of the lessor, for the remainder of the term of the lease under which he has any such interest as aforesaid, or for any lesser term.

In this subsection any reference to the land includes a reference to part of the land.

(10) Nothing in this section or section 139 shall be taken to affect—

(a)   the power of the court to make any order which it would otherwise have power to make as respects a right of re-entry or forfeiture on any ground other than non-payment of rent; or

(b) section 146(4) of the Law of Property Act 1925 (relief against forfeiture).

139.–(1) In a case where section 138 has effect, if–

(a) one-half year's rent is in arrear at the time of the commencement of the action; and

(b) the lessor has a right to re-enter for non-payment of that rent; and

(c) no sufficient distress is to be found on the premises countervailing the arrears then due,

the service of the summons in the action in the prescribed manner shall stand in lieu of a demand and re-entry.

(2) Where a lessor has enforced against a lessee, by re-entry without action, a right of re-entry or forfeiture as respects any land for non-payment of rent, the lessee may, at any time within six months from the date on which the lessor re-entered apply to the county court for relief, and on any such application the court may, if it thinks fit, grant to the lessee such relief as the High Court could have granted.

(3) Subsections (9B) and (9C) of section 138 shall have effect in relation to an application under subsection (2) of this section as they have effect in relation to an application under subsection (9A) of that section.

140. For the purposes of sections 138 and 139–
"lease" includes–

(a) an original or derivative underlease;

(b) an agreement for a lease where the lessee has become entitled to have his lease granted; and

(c) a grant at a fee farm rent, or under a grant securing a rent by condition;

"lessee" includes–

(a) an original or derivative under lessee;

(b) the persons deriving title under a lessee;

(c) a grantee under a grant at a fee farm rent, or under a grant securing a rent by condition; and

(d) the persons deriving title under such a grantee;

"lessor" includes–

(a) an original or derivative under lessor;

(b) the persons deriving title under a lessor;

(c) a person making a grant at a fee farm rent, or a grant securing a rent by condition; and

(d) the persons deriving title under such a grantor;

"under-lease" includes an agreement for an under lease where the under-lessee has become entitled to have his under-lease granted; and

"under-lessee" includes any person deriving title under an under lessee.

12-05 Particular points to note are as follows:

(1) Relief granted by virtue of s.138 is restricted to cases of forfeiture for non-payment of rent. It has no application where there are arrears of service charge which are *not* deemed by the lease to be payable as additional rent (*Escalus Properties Ltd v Robinson* [1995] 4 All E.R. 852 CA).

(2) There is an automatic grant of relief if all the arrears and costs are paid into court not less than five clear days before the return date (s.138(2)). The words "all rent in arrears" includes the rent that has accrued since the proceedings began (see *Maryland Estates Ltd v Joseph* [1999] 1 W.L.R. 83 CA—a case on sub-section (3) but which surely applies to this subsection). Relief is retrospective and the tenant is not obliged to pay anything further, such as mesne profits (*United Dominions Trust Ltd v Shellpoint Trustees* [1993] 4 All E.R. 310 CA; *Escalus Properties Ltd v Robinson* [1995] 4 All E.R. 852 CA).

(3) The "return day" referred to in s.138(2) is the date stated on the claim form for the hearing of the claim for possession. Thus, if the hearing does not go ahead on that date, the tenant may not take advantage of this provision by paying the arrears and fixed court fee and fixed solicitor's costs not less than five clear days prior to the actual hearing (*Swordheath Properties Ltd v Bolt* [1992] 2 E.G.L.R. 68 CA). He will have to rely upon the other relief provisions in the section and pay any further costs that have been incurred in the meantime and that he may be ordered to pay.

(4) Where the money is not paid into court more than five clear days prior to the return day so that the case proceeds, the court must make an order giving the tenant at least four weeks to pay the arrears and costs (s.138(3)). The phrase "all rent in arrear" in s.138(3) includes an amount for the period between service of the claim and the date of the order for relief (*Maryland Estates Ltd v Joseph*).

(5) An application for an extension under s.138(4) should be made on notice (CPR Pt 23).

(6) The words "the lessee shall be barred from all relief" in s.138(7) mean barred from relief in all courts. The tenant may not therefore attempt to obtain relief in the High

216

Court relying upon that court's inherent jurisdiction (*Di Palma v Victoria Square Property Co Ltd* [1985] 2 All E.R. 676); but by virtue of s.138(9A) the tenant may apply for relief in the county court at any time within six months from the date on which the landlord recovers possession.

(7) For the exercise of the discretion in cases where an application is made under s.138(9A) or s.139(2), see the cases mentioned below in relation to High Court applications for relief (para.12-11).

(8) Where relief is granted pursuant to s.138(9A) and (9B), the order is retrospective. The effect is that the tenant is obliged to pay only the arrears of rent and costs. The court will not order the tenant to pay mesne profits from the date the proceedings were served (*United Dominions Trust Ltd v Shellpoint Ltd* [1993] 4 All E.R. 310 CA; *Escalus Properties Ltd v Robinson* [1995] 4 All E.R. 852 CA).

(9) Subtenants and mortgagees may apply for relief under s.138(9C)—see further para.12-32.

(10) Where the tenancy is in joint names, it is probably necessary for any application under s.138(9C) or by a tenant pursuant to s.139(2) to be made by all the joint tenants (see *T M Fairclough & Sons Ltd v Berliner* [1931] 1 Ch. 60; *Jacobs v Chaudhuri* [1968] 2 Q.B. 470).

(11) If a party cannot claim relief pursuant to s.138 or s.146 of the Law of Property Act 1925 proceedings can be transferred to the High Court, where the court can exercise its inherent jurisdiction to grant relief (s.42 of the County Courts Act 1984 and *Bland v Ingrams Estates Ltd* [2001] 2 W.L.R. 1638 CA—a charging order case).

(12) Where the landlord has peaceably re-entered and the tenant wishes to make a claim for relief from forfeiture, CPR Pt 55 applies and he must use claim form N5A. Note in particular r.55.3(1) and PD 55 para.1 which require the claim to be made in the county court in nearly all cases.

Rent cases: High Court

Introduction

There are two statutory provisions concerned with relief against forfeiture for non-payment of rent where the proceedings are in

12-06

the High Court. The oldest is the Common Law Procedure Act 1852, the relevant provisions of which are set out at para.12–15. The most recent statutory provision is s.38 of the Senior Court Act 1981.

Senior Court Act 1981 s.38

12–07   **38.**–(1) In any action in the High Court for the forfeiture of a lease for non-payment of rent, the court shall have power to grant relief against forfeiture *in a summary manner*, and may do so subject to the same terms and conditions as to the payment of rent, costs or otherwise as could have been imposed by it in such an action immediately before the commencement of this Act.

(2) Where the lessee or a person deriving title under him is granted relief under this section, he shall hold the demised premises in accordance with the terms of the lease without the necessity for a new lease.

Time limits for applications

12–08   Where there is at least six months rent in arrears, if at any time before the trial of the landlord's claim for possession the tenant pays or tenders to the landlord or pays into court all the rent and arrears due together with the costs, the proceedings are automatically discontinued; and the tenant holds the property without any need for a new lease (Common Law Procedure Act 1852 s.212; *Standard Pattern Co Ltd v Ivey* [1962] Ch. 432).

If the tenant fails to pay this sum before trial, he may apply for relief thereafter (Senior Court Act 1981 s.38). The application must however be made within six months of the order for possession being executed. After six months have elapsed, he is barred from applying for relief (Common Law Procedure Act 1852 s.210: set out at para 12–15 below).

Where the tenant owes less than six months rent or the landlord has re-entered without the benefit of a court order, the tenant may apply for relief at any time after the order has been made. There is no six-month time limit but the court will take into account any delay when deciding whether or not relief should be granted (*Thatcher v Pearce & Sons* [1968] 1 W.L.R. 748).

Method of application

12–09   Where the landlord has brought proceedings for possession the application for relief may be made by way of counter-claim or application in the landlord's proceedings or informally during the course of the hearing of the landlord's claim (*Lam Kee Ying Sdn Bhd v Lam Shes Tong* [1974] 3 All E.R. 137). Alternatively, the tenant may commence his own proceedings using Pt 55. This is also the procedure to adopt if the landlord re-enters otherwise than by court proceedings. See para.12–05, note (12) and para.12–20.

Where the tenancy is in joint names, it is probably necessary for all the joint tenants to join in the application for relief together (see *T M Fairclough & Sons Ltd v Berliner* [1931] 1 Ch. 60; *Jacobs v Chaudhuri* [1968] 2 Q.B. 470).

Summary judgment for possession

Most claims for possession in the High Court based upon forfeiture for non-payment of rent proceed by way of summary judgment. Unless the tenant raises an arguable defence to the claim the landlord will be entitled to judgment. However, a genuine claim for relief amounts to an arguable defence to the claim for possession (*Liverpool v Oldridge*, see para.7–36). Thus, if the landlord has not yet obtained an order for possession, a genuine claim for relief will prevent summary judgment being given. Where summary judgment for possession has been given the tenant should apply for relief. **12–10**

Exercise of discretion to grant relief

The court may grant relief on such terms and conditions as to the payment of rent, costs or otherwise as the court thinks fit (Senior Court Act 1981 s.38). It is settled law that the purpose of including in a lease a right of re-entry for non-payment of rent is to secure payment of rent and that: **12–11**

> " . . . save in exceptional circumstances, the function of the court in exercising this equitable jurisdiction is to grant relief when all that is due for rent and costs has been paid up, and (in general) to disregard any other causes of complaint that the landlord may have against the tenant" (*Gill v Lewis* [1956] 2 Q.B. 1 at p.13).

The fact that the tenant has been a bad payer in the past is not even a good reason for refusing relief; nor is the fact that the tenant is insolvent (*Brompton Securities Ltd (No.2), Re* [1988] 3 All E.R. 677 Ch D).

"The case for Langham House [*the landlord*], in substance, is that it is unfair and unjust that Langham House should have to continue to look for payment of rent and performance of the other covenants in the lease to a company which is admittedly insolvent and which is, in effect, a trustee of the benefit of the lease for another. I do not think that that is a ground for refusing relief. Once arrears are brought up to date Langham House will be in no different position from any other lessor with an impecunious tenant. It would be an entirely new departure for the court to decline to grant relief on the ground that a tenant has been a bad payer in the past and is likely to continue to be a bad payer in the future" (per Vinelott J. at 680j). (*Emphasis added.*)

However, where the parties have altered their position prior to the application for relief the court may well refuse relief particularly where third parties have acquired rights and the effect of the order would be to defeat those rights or would be unfairly prejudicial to the landlord (*Gill v Lewis* [1956] 2 Q.B. 1; *Silverman v Afco (UK) Ltd* [1988] 1 E.G.L.R. 51 CA).

" ... where parties have altered their position in the meantime, and in particular where the rights of third parties have intervened, relief ought not to be granted where the effect of it would be to defeat the new rights of third parties or be unfair to the landlord having regard to the way in which he has altered his position." (*Gill v Lewis*, per Jenkins LJ at p.10.)

Where the court considers it appropriate to grant relief notwithstanding a grant of a new tenancy by the landlord to a third party, the tenant (who has applied for relief) will be put into the position of immediate reversioner on the new tenant's lease and entitled to payment of rent from the new tenant (*Fuller v Judy Properties Ltd* [1992] 1 E.G.L.R. 75 CA). Compare *Bank of Ireland Home Mortgages v South Lodge Developments* [1996] 14 E.G. 92 where Lightman J. took the view that *Fuller v Judy Properties* was authority for the proposition that relief may be granted "either in reversion upon the new lease or with priority to and unencumbered by the new lease". In deciding what is appropriate the court in each case has regard to whether or not the new tenant had or should have had notice of the application for relief. In *Khar v Delbounty Ltd* [1996] E.G.C.S. 183 CA, the court ordered the original tenant's lease to be sold with the landlord taking the amount due to him out of the proceeds of sale and paying the balance to the tenant. The sale was postponed while the new tenant, who had an assured shorthold tenancy, remained in occupation.

See also *Bland v Ingram Estates (No.2)* [2001] EWCA Civ 1088 CA where it was held that the consequence of the grant of relief was that the new lease took effect as a lease of the reversion and the new tenants were interposed as the intermediate landlord between the landlord and the original tenant. It was therefore the new tenants who were entitled to receive the rent arrears which had accrued since the new lease was granted. In deciding how much to pay to the new tenants, credit was given for the fact that they had enjoyed occupation of the premises from the date of the new lease until the date of the grant of relief. The amount of credit they had to give was a full occupation rent and this cancelled out the rent due from the date of the new lease.

Effect of relief: mesne profits

Where relief is granted the order is retrospective. The tenant holds the demised premises in accordance with the terms of the lease and without the necessity for a new lease (Common Law Procedure Act 1852 s.212; Senior Court Act 1981 s.38). The effect is that the tenant is only obliged to pay the arrears of rent and costs. He will not be ordered to pay mesne profits (*United Dominions Trust Ltd v Shellpoint Ltd* [1993] 4 All E.R. 310 CA; *Escalus Properties Ltd v Robinson* [1995] 4 All E.R. 852 CA). **12–12**

Compensation to tenant who obtains relief

If the landlord obtains judgment for possession and re-enters the property and the tenant thereafter obtains relief the landlord must give credit for any sums made on the premises whilst in possession; but in the absence of fraud, deceit or wilful neglect his liability is limited to the sums so made (Common Law Procedure Act 1852 s.211; para.12–15). **12–13**

12–14   ## Form 10: Order granting relief from forfeiture

IN THE HIGH COURT OF JUSTICE

[QUEEN'S BENCH/CHANCERY] DIVISION

Between:

[Name of the Landlord]

Claimant

-and-

[Name of the Tenant]

Defendant

Upon the application of the Defendant[1] for relief from forfeiture dated ....

And upon hearing Counsel for the Claimant and for the Defendant

It is ordered that:

1. Upon payment by the Defendant to the Claimant of the sums referred to below on or before .... 20.... the Defendant be granted relief from forfeiture of the lease dated .... 20.... of the premises known as .... and that the Defendant do thereafter hold the premises according to the lease without the grant of a new lease. The sums referred to are as follows:

1.1. £...... in respect of arrears of rent that accrued up to ...... and including ......; and

1.2. £.......... on account[2] of the Claimant's costs of the claim including the costs occasioned by the Defendant's application for relief from forfeiture.

2. The Defendant do pay the Claimant's costs of the application for relief to be summarily assessed if not agreed.[3]

3. If the Defendant fails to pay the sums referred to in paragraph 1 to the Claimant by the said date (or within such further period or periods as the parties may agree or the Court may allow) the Defendant's application for relief from forfeiture shall stand dismissed and the defendant shall pay the Claimant's costs of and occasioned by the said application to be summarily assessed if not agreed.

DATED

---

1   This form assumes that the landlord has obtained an order for possession and that the application is being made in those proceedings. If made before that time or in separate proceedings the form will need to be adapted accordingly.
2   This provision allows for relief to take effect without waiting for an assessment of the landlord's costs.
3   As the landlord will have obtained an order for costs in the possession claim it is not necessary to make an order for such costs here.

Common Law Procedure Act 1852 ss.210–222

210. Proceedings in ejectment by landlord for non-payment of **12–15**
rent—In all cases between landlord and tenant, as often as it shall happen
that *one half year's rent* shall be in arrear and the landlord or lessor, to
whom the same is due, hath right by law to re-enter for the non-payment
thereof, such landlord or lessor shall and may, *without any formal demand*
or re-entry, serve a writ in ejectment for the recovery of the demised
premises, ... which service ... shall stand in the place and instead of a
demand and re-entry;

and in case of judgment against the defendant for nonappearance, if it
shall be made to appear to the court where the said action is depending,
by affidavit, or be proved upon the trial in case the defendant appears,
that *half a year's rent* was due before the *said writ was served*, and that
no sufficient distress was to be found on the demised premises,
countervailing the arrears then due, and that the lessor had power to
re-enter, then and in every such case the lessor shall recover judgment
and execution, in the same manner as if the rent in arrear had been legally
demanded, and a re-entry made;

[*Lessee barred from relief unless he seeks relief within six months of
execution*] and in case the lessee or his assignee, or other person
claiming or deriving under the said lease, shall permit and suffer judgment
to be had and recovered on such trial in ejectment, and execution to be
executed thereon, without paying the rent and arrears, together with full
costs, *and without proceeding for relief in equity within six months after
such execution* executed, then and in such case the said lessee, his
assignee, and all other persons claiming and deriving under the said lease,
shall be barred and foreclosed from all relief or remedy in law or equity
other than by bringing error for reversal of such judgment, in case the
same shall be erroneous, and the said landlord or lessor shall from
thenceforth hold the said demised premises discharged from such
lease; ...

provided that nothing herein contained shall extend to bar the right of
any *mortgagee* of such lease, or any part thereof, who shall not be in
possession, so as much mortgagee shall and do, within six months after
such judgment obtained and execution executed pay all rent in arrear, and
all costs and damages sustained by such lessor or person entitled to the
remainder or reversion as aforesaid, and perform all the covenants and
agreements which, on the part and behalf of the first lessee, are and
ought to be performed.

**211. Lessee proceeding in equity not to have injunction or relief
without payment of rent and costs**—In case the said lessee, his
assignee, or other person claiming any right, title, or interest, in law or
equity, of, in, or to the said lease, shall, *within the time aforesaid*, proceed
for relief in any court of equity, such person shall not have or continue any
injunction against the proceedings at law on such ejectment, unless he
does or shall, *within forty days next after a full and perfect answer shall
be made by the claimant* in such ejectment, *bring into court*, and lodge
with the proper officer *such sum and sums of money as the lessor or
landlord shall in his answer swear to be due and in* arrear over and above
all just allowances, *and also the costs taxed* in the said suit, there to

remain till the hearing of the cause, or to be paid out to the lessor or landlord on good security, subject to the decree of the court;

[*If lessor re-enters, he is only liable for what he made from the demised premises; if that is less than the rent lessee obliged to pay the balance*]

and in case such proceedings for relief in equity shall be taken within the time aforesaid, and after execution is executed, the lessor or *landlord shall be accountable only for so much and no more as he shall really and bona fide, without fraud, deceit, or wilful neglect, make of the demised premises from the time of his entering into the actual possession* thereof; and if what shall be so made by the lessor or landlord happen to be less than the rent reserved on the said lease, then the said lessee or his assignee, before he shall be restored to his possession, shall pay such lessor or landlord what the money so by him made *fell short* of the reserved rent for the time such lessor landlord held the said lands.

212. Tenant paying all rent, with costs, proceedings to cease—If the tenant or his assignee do or shall, *at any time before the trial* in such ejectment, *pay* or tender to the lessor landlord, his executors or administrators, or his or their attorney in that cause, or *pay into the court* where the same cause is depending, all the *rent and arrears, together with the costs,* then and in such case all further proceedings on the said ejectment shall cease and be discontinued; and if such lessee, his executors, administrators, or assigns, shall, upon such proceedings as aforesaid, be relieved in equity, he and they shall have, hold, and enjoy the demised lands, according to the lease thereof made, without any new lease. (*Emphasis added.*)

Other breaches

12–16   Where the landlord brings proceedings, whether in the County Court or the High Court, for forfeiture of a lease or forfeits by actual re-entry in respect of a breach of covenant other than by non-payment of rent, the tenant may apply for relief pursuant to s.146(2) of the Law of Property Act 1925. Where relief is granted to the tenant the relief reinstates the lease as if there had never been a forfeiture (*Official Custodian for Charities v Mackey* [1984] 3 All E.R. 689 at 694f).

Law of Property Act 1925 s.146(2), (13)

12–17   146.– . . .

(2) Where a lessor *is proceeding,* by action *or otherwise,* to enforce such a right of re-entry or forfeiture, the lessee may, in the lessor's action, if any, or in any action brought by himself, apply to the court for relief; and the court may grant or refuse relief, as the court, having regard to the proceedings and conduct of the parties under the foregoing provisions of this section, and to all the other circumstances, thinks fit; and in case of relief may grant it on such *terms,* if any, as to costs, expenses, damages, compensation, penalty, or otherwise, including the granting of any

injunction to restrain any like breach in the future, as the court, in the circumstances of each case, thinks fit.

. . .

(13) The county court has jurisdiction under this section.

Time for applying

The wording of s.146(2) states that the tenant may apply for relief where the landlord "is proceeding by action or otherwise to enforce" his right of re-entry. The landlord is proceeding the moment he serves his s.146 notice (*Pakwood Transport Ltd v 15 Beauchamp Place Ltd* (1977) 245 E.G. 309 CA). The tenant may therefore apply for relief upon receipt of the notice.

12-18

In *Rogers v Rice* [1892] 2 Ch. 170 the landlord had forfeited by bringing proceedings. It was held that the words "is proceeding" mean that the tenant may apply for relief at any time up until the time the landlord has actually re-entered pursuant to the order for possession. After that date it is no longer possible to make an application under s.146(2). It is therefore very important that an application is made before that time. If the landlord has obtained a judgment for possession but has not actually re-entered, the landlord is still "proceeding" and the tenant may still apply for relief (*Egerton v Jones* [1939] 2 K.B. 702).

The decision in *Rogers v Rice* does not apply where the landlord has forfeited by peaceable re-entry, in which case the tenant may apply for relief after actual re-entry (*Billson v Residential Apartments Ltd* [1992] 1 All E.R. 141 HL).

A tenant who has received a s.146 notice is always well advised to act promptly in making his application for relief (see para.9-13: "Tenant's action on receipt of notice"). It is very important that he should never assume that the landlord will forfeit by taking proceedings. The landlord may simply re-enter. The tenant retains his right to claim relief but his business will suffer substantial loss and inconvenience.

Joint tenants and equitable assignees

Where the lease is in joint names all the tenants must join in the application for relief (*TM Fairclough & Sons Ltd v Berliner* [1931] 1 Ch. 60).

12-19

An equitable assignee (i.e. a person who has agreed to take the lease from an existing tenant) as well as the assignor is entitled to apply for relief (*High Street Investments Ltd v Bellshore Property Investments Ltd* [1996] 2 E.G.L.R. 40.

Method of application

12-20   The tenant may apply for relief by the following methods:

(1) By claim from N5A under Pt 55.2(1)(c)—usually in the County Court (Pt 55.3(1) and PD 55 para.1).
(2) By application in the landlord's proceedings (CPR Pt 23).
(3) By Pt 20 claim in the landlord's claim for possession.
(4) By application at the hearing of the landlord's claim for possession (*Lam Kee Ying Sdn Bhd v Lam Shes Tong* [1974] 3 All E.R. 137).
(5) If the landlord is proceeding by way of summary judgment, the tenant may apply for relief on the landlord's application. If the tenant can show that he has relief he has a defence to the landlord's claim for possession and he should be given a real prospect of obtaining leave to defend (see further para.7-36).

Exercise of discretion to grant relief to the tenant

12-21   The first point to have in mind when considering whether or not a tenant is likely to be granted relief is the width of the discretion granted to the court by s.146(2). The position was clearly stated by the Lord Chancellor, Lord Loreborn, in the leading case of *Hyman v Rose* [1912] A.C. 623 (in relation to the statutory predecessor to s.146):

> " . . . the discretion given by the section is very wide. The court is to consider all the circumstances and the conduct of the parties. Now it seems to me that when the Act is so express to provide a wide discretion, meaning, no doubt, to prevent one man from forfeiting what in fair dealing belongs to someone else, by taking advantage of a breach from which he is not commensurately and irreparably damaged, it is not advisable to lay down any rigid rules for guiding that discretion . . . It is not safe I think to say that the court must and always will insist upon certain things when the Act does not require them, and the facts of some

unforeseen case may make the court wish it had kept a free hand." (*Hyman v Rose* [1912] A.C. 623, per Lord Loreborn at p.631.)

Some of the reported cases (including some referred to below) come close to losing sight of this general principle and this needs to be borne in mind when looking at the authorities. For a more recent case in which the above statement of Lord Loreborn was considered and applied see *Southern Depot Co Ltd v British Railways Board* [1990] 2 E.G.L.R. 39—referred to below, para.12-23.

Remedying the breach as a condition of relief

"In the ordinary way relief is almost always granted to a person who makes good the breach of covenant and is able and willing to fulfil his obligations in the future" (*Bathurst (Earl) v Fine* [1974] 2 All E.R. 1162, per Lord Denning at 1162h).

12-22

In accordance with the principle that the court's discretion under s.146(2) is unfettered, there is no rule of law that the breach must be remedied prior to the hearing of the application for relief. However, unless there is some good reason why the breach has not been remedied by that date or, at least, that all reasonable steps have been taken to remedy the breach, the court will usually take a dim view of the tenant's case and may exercise its discretion in refusing to grant relief. It will almost invariably require the breach to be remedied as a condition precedent to relief. See *Cremin v Barjack Properties Ltd* [1985] 1 E.G.L.R. 30 CA where the following passage in *Woodfall: Landlord and Tenant,*, was cited with approval by Slade LJ:

"As a general principle the remedying of the breach is undoubtedly required as a condition precedent to relief. In the ordinary way relief is almost always granted to a person who makes good the breach of covenant and is able and willing to fulfil his obligations in future."

St Marylebone Property Co v Tesco Stores [1988] 2 E.G.L.R. 40 is an example of a case where the court refused to grant relief because the tenant was unable to remedy the breach. Tesco (the tenant) was granted a licence to assign to sublet shop premises. The licence required that the sub-lease be made subject to the covenants and conditions in the lease, one of which was that the property should not be used for any business other than that of "grocers provisions wine spirit and beer merchants" without consent. Tesco subsequently sublet the property "with (apparent) total disregard of all the covenants which they had given in the licence". The sub-lease was later assigned, without consent of the landlord, and as time went on an increasing number of items were sold that were not permitted by the headlease. The assignee refused to stop selling the offending lines after being asked to do so. The landlord forfeited. Tesco and the assignee of the sub-lease applied for relief. Both applications were refused. The following passage appears in the judgment of Hoffman J. at p.42k:

> "It is clear that relief cannot be granted except upon terms that the tenant will, so far as possible, remedy the breach and not commit any further breaches thereafter. Tesco, however, by granting the underlease in the terms in which they did in 1981, have put it altogether out of their power to ensure that their undertaking does comply with the lease in the future. On that ground alone it would seem to me that they do not qualify for relief."

"Wilful" breaches

12-23 It is sometimes argued that the court will not grant relief against forfeiture to a tenant who is in "wilful breach" except in exceptional circumstances (e.g. see *Ropemaker Properties Ltd v Noonhaven Ltd* [1989] 2 E.G.L.R. 50). The following passage of Lord Wilberforce in *Shiloh Spinners v Harding* [1973] A.C. 691 at 723 is relied upon.

> "Established and, in my opinion, sound principle requires that wilful breaches should not, or at least should only in exceptional cases, be relieved against, if only for the reason that the assignor should not be compelled to remain in a relation of neighbourhood with a person in deliberate breach of his obligations."

However, *Shiloh Spinners v Harding* was not a case concerned with relief from forfeiture of a lease and in *Southern Depot Co Ltd v British Railways Board* [1990] 2 E.G.L.R. 39 Morritt J. refused to hold that relief was confined to exceptional cases where the tenant had been in wilful breach. The court granted relief on stringent terms which included payment of the landlord's costs of the action on an indemnity basis.

"There can be no doubt that the wilfulness of the breach is a relevant consideration and that the court should not in exercising its discretion encourage a belief that parties to a lease can ignore their obligations and buy their way out of any consequential forfeiture. But to impose a requirement that relief under section 146(2) should be granted only in an exceptional case seems to me to be seeking to lay down a rule for the exercise of the court's discretion which the decision of the House of Lords in *Hyman v Rose* [1912] A.C. 623 said should not be done. Certainly Lord Wilberforce in *Shiloh Spinners v Harding* did not purport to do so in cases under the statute.

Accordingly, in my judgment, although I should give considerable weight to the fact that two out of the three breaches were wilful, I am not required to find an exceptional case before granting relief from forfeiture." (*Southern Depot Co Ltd v British Railways Board* [1990] 2 E.G.L.R. 39, per Morritt J. at 43M to 44A.)

For a case where *Southern Depot* was applied see *Mount Cook Land Ltd v Hartley* [2000] E.G.C.S. 26 where it was held that consideration should be given to the proportionality between the extent of the breach and the potential windfall for the landlord.

Serious breaches

12–24 Relief may be granted where a serious breach is involved such as using the premises as a brothel in breach of a covenant against immoral user (*Central Estates (Belgravia) Ltd v Woolgar (No.2)* [1972] 1 W.L.R. 1048). It has been stated that it is the established practice of the court not to grant relief in cases where the breach involves immoral user "save in very exceptional circumstances" (*GMS Syndicate Ltd v Gary Elliott Ltd* [1982] Ch. 1); although to be quite so definite may be to lay down a "rigid rule" that fetters the court's discretion (see *dicta* of Lord Loreborn in *Hyman v Rose* at para.12–21 above).

And in the recent case of *CB Patel & PC Patel v K & J Restaurants Ltd* [2010] EWCA Civ 1211 relief was granted where the premises had been used as a brothel by a sub-tenant.

Personal qualifications of the tenant

12-25   Where the personal qualifications of the tenant are of importance for the preservation of the value or character of the property, those qualifications may be taken into account by the court in determining whether to exercise its discretion to grant relief against forfeiture (*Earl Bathurst v Fine* [1974] 2 All E.R. 1160).

Relief in respect of part of the premises

12-26   The court has power to grant relief in respect of part only of the premises (*GMS Syndicate Ltd*, the tenant was not granted relief in respect of the other part used by sub-tenants for immoral purposes).

Tenant altering position and third parties affected

12-27   Where the landlord has altered his position before the application for relief or where a third party has acquired an interest in the property prior to that date, relief will invariably not be granted if the landlord or the third party would be unfairly prejudiced by the order (*Gill v Lewis* [1956] 2 Q.B. 1—a rent case; see further at para. 12-11 above, where this point is more fully discussed).

Where a landlord has recovered possession pursuant to a court order and the tenant subsequently has the order set aside or successfully appeals and makes an application for relief in the continuing proceedings the court, in deciding whether or not to grant relief, will take into account any consequences of the original order and repossession and any delay on the part of the tenant (*Billson v Residential Apartments Ltd* [1992] 1 All E.R. 141 HL).

Terms and conditions of relief

12-28   The court may (and usually does) grant relief on such terms as to costs, expenses, damages, compensation, penalty or otherwise, including the grant of an injunction to restrain any like breach in the future, as the court thinks fit (s. 146(2) of the Law of Property Act 1925). See Form 11 below for a specimen order. Different parties may be granted relief on different terms (*Duke of Westminster v Swinton* [1948] 1 K.B. 524).

Where relief is granted under s.146(2) of the 1925 Act, the order is retrospective and is by reinstatement of the lease. The effect is that the tenant is obliged to pay only the arrears of rent and costs. He will not be required to pay mesne profits (which could be higher than the rent) as a condition of relief (*Escalus Properties Ltd v Robinson* [1995] 4 All E.R. 852 CA).

Where relief is granted subject to a condition as to the doing of something within a certain time, the court may extend the time for compliance (*Starside Properties Ltd v Mustapha* [1974] 1 W.L.R. 816). Where the parties have entered into a consent order specifying terms and conditions for relief, the court has jurisdiction to vary the terms but will do so only in exceptional circumstances (*Fivecourts Ltd v JR Leisure Development Co Ltd* [2001] L.&T.R. 47 HC; *Ropac v Inntrepreneur* [2001] L.&T.R. 93 HC). Where the landlord alleges that the tenant has failed to comply with the condition, he may not apply for leave to enforce the order for possession without notifying the tenant of the application (see para.23–69).

Form 11: Order granting tenant relief—other breaches   12–29

IN THE HIGH COURT OF JUSTICE   20....

[QUEEN'S BENCH/CHANCERY] DIVISION

Between:

[Name of the Landlord]

-and-   Claimant

[Name of Tenant]

Defendant

Upon the application of the Defendant[1] for relief from forfeiture dated ....

And upon hearing Counsel for the Claimant and for the Defendant

It is ordered that:

1. If the Defendant do comply with the following conditions on or before .... 20.... he do be granted relief from forfeiture of the lease dated .... 20 .... of the premises known as .... and that he do thereafter hold the premises according to the lease without the grant of a new lease. The conditions are that the defendant do:

cont

---

cont

1.1. [*Remedy the matter complained of, presuming that he has not already done so*]; and

1.2. Pay the Claimant's solicitors and surveyors costs referred to in paragraph .... of the Statement of Claim [incurred in preparation and service of the s.146 notice]; and

1.3. Pay the Claimant £.......... on account[2] of the Claimant's costs of the action including the costs occasioned by the defendant's application for relief from forfeiture;

2. The defendant do pay the Claimant's costs of the action including the Defendant's application for relief to be taxed if not agreed.

3. If the Defendant fails to comply with the conditions referred to in paragraph 1 or to any of them by the said date (or within such further period or periods as the parties may agree or the Court may allow) the Defendant's application for relief from forfeiture shall stand dismissed and the Defendant shall pay the Claimant's costs of and occasioned by the said application to be summarily assessed if not agreed.

DATED

---

1 This form assumes that the application is being made in the landlord's proceedings for possession. If made before that time or in separate proceedings it will need to be adapted accordingly.
2 This provision allows for relief to take effect without waiting for an assessment of the landlord's costs.

Exercise of discretion on an appeal

12–30 On an appeal from a Master to a judge against an order refusing or granting an application for relief the court must consider the case on the facts as they appear at the date of the appeal (*Cremin v Barjack Properties Ltd* (1985) 273 E.G. 299). But on an appeal to the Court of Appeal the court will exercise the discretion only if there has been a change in circumstances (*Darlington BC v Denmark Chemists Ltd* [1993] 1 E.G.L.R. 62 CA).

Costs

12–31 Where relief from forfeiture is granted, the tenant should normally be required to pay the landlord's costs on an indemnity basis as a condition for relief (*CB Patel & PC Patel v K&J Restaurants Ltd* [2010] EWCA Civ 1211 at paras 98 and 104). However, if the landlord unsuccessfully resists the tenant's application for relief, he will usually be obliged to pay the extra costs incurred in so doing. The tenant can improve his position on costs by making an offer, either on an open basis or on a "Calderbank" basis, preferably no later than the date upon which he serves his application, setting out his proposed terms which should include an offer to pay the costs to date. (See further para.9–13).

Sub-tenants and mortgagees: rent and other covenants

Introduction

Forfeiture of a lease brings any sub-lease or other derivative interest to an end. Where an order is made granting the tenant relief from forfeiture, all derivative interests are automatically reinstated (*Dendy v Evans* [1910] 1 K.B. 263). Where, however, the tenant has not been granted or has not applied for relief, the sub-tenant may wish to make his own application. If the lease was subject to a mortgage, the mortgagee will also wish to make an application for relief.

12–32

Depending on the circumstances, relief may be obtained under s.138 of the County Courts Act 1984 (rent cases only), s.38 of the Senior Court Act 1981 (rent cases only, High Court) or s.146 of the Law of Property Act 1925 (rent and other covenants, either court).

County Court: rent cases

Where proceedings have been commenced in the County Court based upon non-payment of rent a sub-tenant may obtain automatic relief by the payment of arrears of rent and costs pursuant to s.138(2) or (5) (see para.12–02) even though the landlord has brought the action against the tenant and the sub-tenant is not itself a party to the proceedings (*United Dominions Trust Ltd v Shellpoint Trustees Ltd* [1993] 4 All E.R. 310 CA, because the term "lessee" in s.138(2), (5), by virtue of s.140, includes an underlessee). If automatic relief is granted

12–33

by reason of payment by the sub-tenant of the rent and costs, *all* the leasehold interests in the property, including the tenant's, are restored unconditionally. The sub-tenant is not required to pay mesne profits to the landlord for the period between service of the proceedings and the date of the order. This is a consequence of the lease being restored (*United Dominions Trust Ltd* at pp.316f and 318j; *Escalus Properties Ltd v Robinson* [1995] 4 All E.R. 853 at 858d).

If automatic relief has not been obtained by the tenant or a sub-tenant pursuant to s.138(2) or (5) and the landlord obtains possession, an application for a *vesting order* may be made pursuant to s.138(9C) at any time within six months from the date on which the landlord recovers possession (see para.12–02). The court's power to make an order under this section is discretionary. If made, a vesting order does *not* reinstate the interests derived from the original underlease or mortgage but gives rise to a new interest (see further below in relation to vesting orders made under s.146(4)). If the sub-tenant fails to make an application within the six months time limit he will thereafter be barred from all relief in both the County Court and High Court (s.138(7); *United Dominions Trust Ltd v Shellpoint Trustees Ltd*).

High Court: rent cases

12–34   Relief may be sought in the High Court, in a rent case, pursuant to s.38 of the Senior Court Act 1981, (para.12–07). The application may be made after the landlord has enforced the order but if the rent is six months or more in arrears s.210 of the Common Law Procedure Act 1852 applies so that the application must be made within six months of the date of execution.

If relief is granted by reason of payment the rent and costs, and *all* the leasehold interests in the property, including the tenant's, are restored unconditionally. The sub-tenant cannot be required to pay mesne profits to the landlord for the period between the service of the writ and the date of the order as a condition of relief (*Escalus Properties Ltd v Robinson* [1995] 4 All E.R. 853 at 859).

County Court or High Court: rent or other covenants

Application under s.146(4)

A vesting order may also be sought pursuant to s.146(4) of the Law of Property Act 1925 both in the County Court and in the High Court. This subsection applies to rent cases as well as to breaches of other covenants.

12–35

Law of Property Act 1925 s.146(4)

146.–(4) Where a lessor *is proceeding* by action *or otherwise* to enforce a right of re-entry or forfeiture under any covenant, proviso, or stipulation in a lease, or *for non-payment of rent*, the court may on application by any person claiming as under-lessee any estate or interest in the property comprised in the lease or any part thereof, either in the lessor's action (if any) or in any action brought by such person for that purpose, make an order *vesting*, for the whole term of the lease or any less term, the property comprised in the lease or any part thereof in any person entitled as under-lessee to any estate or interest in such property upon such conditions as to execution of any deed or other document, payment of rent, costs, expenses, damages, compensation, giving security, or otherwise, as the court in the circumstances of each case may think fit, but in no case shall any such under-lessee be entitled to require a lease to be granted to him for any longer term than he had under his original sub-lease.

12–36

An order made pursuant to s.146(4) does not restore the original underlease. A new lease is created and vested in the sub-tenant (see *Cadogan v Dimovic* [1984] 2 All E.R. 168 to 172). The position is the same where a mortgagee is granted a new lease under s.146(4) save that the new lease is held subject to the equity of redemption in the mortgagor (*Chelsea Estates Investment Trust Co Ltd v Marche* [1955] 1 All E.R. 195).

Alternative application under s.146(2)

A sub-tenant may also apply for relief pursuant to s.146(2) of the 1925 Act (see para.12–17). The subsection although usually used by tenants also applies to sub-tenants. If relief is granted pursuant to this subsection the order is retrospective and operates by reinstatement of the lease. There is therefore no requirement made to pay mesne profits as a condition of relief (*Escalus Properties Ltd v Sinclair* [1995] 4 All E.R. 853 CA). If the application is made under s.146(4) the court is likely to make an order that it be a condition of the grant of a vesting

12–37

order that mesne profits be paid in respect of the period between service of the proceedings and the date of order. If the amount of the market rent is greater than the current rent the tenant may therefore wish to make the application under s.146(2) with an alternative application for a vesting order under s.146(4). The effect of an order under s.146(2) is that the lease is restored to the lessee (even though he has made no application) and the underlease is restored to the sub-tenant (*United Dominion Trust* pp.316f and 318j; *Escalus*, see 864c). In this situation the sub-tenant is reliant on the tenant continuing to comply with the obligations under the lease or must fulfil those obligations himself. The advantage of having a vesting order is that on the grant of the new lease to the sub-tenant he has a clear interest and the tenant goes out of the picture.

If the sub-tenant does make an alternative application under s.146(2) the court has a discretion to choose between ordering relief under that subsection or making a vesting order under s.146(4); and where a vesting order together with an order for mesne profits would give the landlord a windfall the court is likely to make an order for relief under s.146(2) (*Escalus Properties Ltd v Sinclair*).

Time for the application

12–38 The decision of the House of Lords in *Billson v Residential Apartments Ltd* [1992] 1 All E.R. 141 (see para.12–18), that a tenant may apply for relief after peaceable re-entry but not after a landlord has recovered possession pursuant to a court order (unless that order is set aside), applies to applications made pursuant to s.146 by "any person claiming as under-lessee" (*Rexhaven Ltd v Nurse* [1995] E.G.C.S. 125, Judge Colyer Q.C. sitting as a judge of the Chancery Division). Thus, if a sub-tenant or mortgagee is served with proceedings (see para.7–33) or otherwise discovers that the landlord has served a s.146 notice on the tenant he will usually be best advised to make an application under s.146(4) immediately—see further under para.12–43.

If an order for possession is obtained and executed without the sub-tenant or mortgagee knowing about it an application to be joined in the proceedings (para.23–65) and for the order for possession and execution thereon to be set aside, will need to be applied for. However, in *Rexhaven v Nurse* (above) it was held that it will be a rare case in which it will be appropriate to exercise the court's discretion to set aside a regular judgment and special circumstances need to be shown. This would appear to be a particularly harsh judgment and it should be noted that the mortgagee in that case had been sent a copy of the writ seeking possession but had mistakenly filed it away. The court would presumably be more sympathetic in a case where the sub-tenant or mortgagee had never been served with the proceedings.

Exercise of court's discretion under s.146(4)

The court's power under s.146(4) is discretionary. When making an order under s.146(4), the court's discretion is very wide and the new lease may be different from that which he originally held. The position is explained by Warner J. in *Hammersmith and Fulham LBC v Top Shop Centres Ltd* [1989] 2 All E.R. 655, at 664–665:

12–39

> "The court may not under that subsection vest in the applicant a new lease beginning before the date of its order or ending later than the original underlease would have done; but the discretion is otherwise unfettered. The term may within those parameters, be of any length and the rent and other terms may not necessarily be the same. . . . Thus the court may, under s.146(4), order that the new lease should be at a rent different from that reserved by the original underlease. . . . It may order that the new lease should be for a term ending sooner than the term granted by the original underlease. It may order that the new lease should contain different covenants and it may, on my reading of the subsection order that the new lease should comprise a lesser part of the property demised by the forfeited lease than was comprised in the original underlease."

However, the court is unlikely to grant a lease containing terms less stringent than those in the head-lease (*Hill v Griffin* [1987] 1 E.G.L.R. 81—vesting order refused because the sub-tenant was not prepared to accept a lease containing a repairing covenant which was as onerous as in the headlease). There is sometimes a reluctance to grant relief to a sub-tenant "because it thrusts upon the landlord a person whom he has never accepted as tenant and creates . . . a contract between them" (*Fivecourts Ltd v JR Leisure Development Co Ltd* [2001] L.&T.R.

47) although such an argument will have less weight where the landlord granted consent to the sub-tenancy.

For a case in which the court refused to make an order under s.146(4) see *St Marylebone v Tesco Stores* [1988] 2 E.G.L.R. 40. The court (having refused to grant relief to the tenant; see para.12–22) refused to grant relief to an assignee of a sub-tenant who was in occupation of shop premises without the landlord's consent and who had been trading in breach of terms in the headlease. The particular factors that the court took into account were that:

- The assignee had been guilty of continuing to trade in breach of restrictions after promising not to do so.
- He was likely to be in financial difficulty if he operated in accordance with the restrictions.
- It was unfair on the landlord to require them to accept the assignee as a tenant by way of relief when the had never accepted him as a tenant in the first place.
- It is an invariable condition that the sub-tenant pay the landlord's costs of the proceedings, on a standard basis (para.12–31); although this might not be the case if an appropriate Pt 36 offer is made at an early stage (para.12–31).

Persons who may apply: sub-tenants, mortgagees and sub-undertenants

Sub-tenants

12–40 Sub-tenants may clearly apply for relief under the various provisions; including unlawful sub-tenants (*Southern Depot Co Ltd v British Railways Board* [1990] 2 E.G.L.R. 39 at 42M–43A).

An equitable assignee of an underlease (i.e. a person who has agreed to take the underlease from the existing sub-tenant) as well as the assignor is entitled to apply for relief (*High Street Investments Ltd v Bellshore Property Investments Ltd* [1996] 2 E.G.L.R. 40 CA.

Mortgagees

12–41 Mortgagees, whether legal or equitable, of the tenant's interest are persons who derive title under a tenant and so may apply for relief (s.140 of the 1984 Act; s.38 of the 1981 Act; s.146(4) of the 1925 Act; see *Belgravia Insurance Co Ltd v Meah* [1963] 3 All E.R. 828—general principles and legal mortgages; *Good v Wood* [1954] 1 All E.R. 275—equitable mortgages). Mere equitable chargees, such as a person who has obtained a charging order against the tenant's interest under the Charging Orders Act 1979 may apply (*Croydon (Unique) Ltd v Wright* [2001] Ch. 318 and *Bland v Ingram's Estates Ltd* [2001] 24 E.G. 163—see further para.22-32). See Forms 12 and 13 (paras 12-45 and 12-46) for an application for relief and witness statement in support to be used by a mortgagee. (See Form 14 for an order, para.12-47.)

Where the landlord has forfeited for non-payment of rent and the sub-tenant or mortgagee applies for relief under the Senior Court Act 1981 he should join the original tenant in the proceedings (or, if the lease was assigned, the assignee) or if it is not possible to do so the absence of that party should be explained (*Hare v Elms* [1893] 1 Q.B. 604; *Humphrey v Morten* [1905] Ch. 739; and see *Escalus Properties Ltd v Robinson* [1995] 4 All E.R. 852, per Nourse LJ at 859f). Lord Denning has stated, obiter, that it is not necessary to join the tenant (or his assignee) where the sub-tenant claims relief under s.146(4) of the Law of Property Act 1925 (*Belgravia Insurance Co Ltd* at 832H) but it is advisable to do so (or at least to notify him of the application) unless it is not possible in which case his absence should be explained.

Sub-undertenants

As the vesting of a new lease in an undertenant or mortgagee, **12-42** pursuant to s.146(4) of the 1925 Act or s.138(9C) of the 1984 Act, does *not* reinstate the interests derived from the underlease or mortgage any sub-undertenant must make his own application for a vesting order even if the sub-tenant has made an application (*Hammersmith and Fulham LBC v Top Shop Centres Ltd* [1989] 2 All E.R. 655).

Court procedure

A sub-tenant or mortgagee who has been joined by the landlord **12-43** as a party to the claim for possession may make an application for relief by way of Pt 20 or by application in the landlord's claim (see Form 12 para.12-45). If he is not an original defendant he may apply to be joined as a party and then apply by counter-claim or application. Alternatively, he may issue his own Pt 8 claim. This is the way to proceed if the sub-tenant or mortgagee discovers that the landlord has served a s.146 notice on the tenant but proceedings have not yet been commenced.

The applicant should support his application by a witness statement setting out his case which should be served with the claim. See Form 13 para.12-46

As stated above (para.12-38), if the landlord re-enters the property pursuant to an order for possession made after service of a s.146 notice (i.e. for breach of covenant other than payment of rent) any such sub-tenant or mortgagee has no right to apply for relief until he has had that order set aside (*Billson v Residential Apartments Ltd*). Nor may he apply under s.138(9C) in a rent case outside the six-month time limit (para.12-02). If the landlord does manage to obtain and enforce an order for possession in the County Court without the knowledge of the sub-tenant or a mortgagee any such person should apply to have the order for possession and the execution set aside (see para.23-65), to be joined in the action and for an order pursuant to s.146(4) in the continuing proceedings.

High Court

12-44 Where the landlord has proceeded in the High Court and has obtained an order for possession, he may not enforce the order without leave and leave will not be given unless it is shown that every person in actual possession has sufficient notice of the proceedings to enable him to apply for relief (CPR 83.13 (8); see further para.23-69). The sub-tenant will therefore have an opportunity to make an application for relief. (There is no equivalent provision in the County Court.) As stated above, if the landlord re-enters the property pursuant to an order for possession made after service of a s.146 notice (i.e. for breach of covenant other than payment of rent), any such sub-tenant or mortgagee has no right to apply for relief unless the order is set aside, which may not be easy (see para.12-38). Thus, if the sub-tenant or mortgagee is notified of the order pursuant to CPR 83.13 (8), he should immediately make an application for relief.

Form 12: Application for vesting order—mortgagee 12–45

IN THE COUNTY COURT

BETWEEN:

[Name of the Landlord]

-and- *Claimant*

[Name of the Tenant]

Defendant

FOOLISH LENDING BANK PLC ("the Bank") wishes to apply for:

(1) An order that it be joined in these proceedings; and
(2) An order that [*the property referred to in the Particulars of Claim*] be vested in the Bank pursuant to s.146(4) of the Law of Property Act 1925.

The grounds upon which the Bank makes the application are that it is a mortgagee of the said property under a first charged dated ...., that it is entitled to make this application under the said statutory provisions and that it is willing to comply with such conditions as the court may think fit.

Form 13: Witness statement by mortgagee seeking 12–46
vesting order

Witness statement of .... (1)
Filed on behalf of Foolish Lending Bank plc
dated .... 20 ....

IN THE COUNTY COURT

BETWEEN:

[Name of the Landlord]

-and- *Claimant*

[Name of Tenant]

Defendant

WITNESS STATEMENT

I, [*name*], Solicitor, of [*address*] hereby MAKE OATH and say as follows:

cont

---

cont

1. I am the solicitor acting on behalf of the Foolish Lending Bank plc ("the Bank"). I make this statement, with due authority from my client, in support of the Bank's application to be joined in these proceedings and for a vesting order pursuant to section 146(4) of the Law of Property Act 1925. Save where otherwise appears the facts stated herein are within my own knowledge and belief.

2. The claim is for possession of the premises known as [*address*]. The property is held by the Defendant under a lease for a term of 25 years granted to him by the Claimant on .... A copy of the lease is attached and marked "1". This lease is subject to an all monies charged in favour of the Bank. A copy of the Charge Certificate is attached and marked "2".

3. I am informed by .... and believe that the Defendant is indebted to the Bank in the sum of £.... and that the Bank took possession on .... 20.... pursuant to an order for possession in this court dated .... 20..... The Bank is in the process of selling the lease although a buyer has not yet been found.

4. The Bank has been served with these proceedings pursuant to PD 55.4 para.2–4. It is in these circumstances that the Bank applies to be joined in the proceedings and seeks a vesting order pursuant to the statutory provisions referred to in the application. The Bank is ready, able and willing to comply with such conditions as the court may consider it proper to impose.

STATEMENT OF TRUTH

12–47   **Form 14: Order granting mortgagee vesting order**

IN THE COUNTY COURT

BETWEEN:

[*Name of Landlord*]

-and-   *Claimant*

(1) [*Name of Tenant*]

(2) [FOOLISH LENDING BANK PLC]

Defendants

ORDER

UPON the application of the Foolish Lending Bank plc

cont

cont

AND UPON HEARING solicitors for the Claimant and for the Foolish Lending Bank plc

IT IS ORDERED THAT:

1. The Foolish Lending Bank plc be joined as a second Defendant to these proceedings.

2. The property known as [*address*] be vested in the Second Defendant pursuant to s.146(4) of the Law of Property Act 1925 upon the terms of the draft lease attached to this Order provided that the Second Defendant do within 28 days hereof:

   (1) Pay to the Claimant the sum of £........... in respect of rent and service charges outstanding at .... 20....

   (2) Pay the Claimant £........... in respect of the costs of its claim against the First Defendant and the costs of and occasioned by the Second Defendant's application dated ....

   (3) Pay mesne profits of £........... in respect of the period from .... to the date of this order. [*See comment on para. 12–37*]

   (4) Execute a Lease in the terms of the draft annexed hereto.

3. If the Second defendant fails to comply with any of the said conditions within the said period of 28 days or within such further period or periods as the parties may agree or the Court may allow IT IS ORDERED THAT the Second Defendant's application for a vesting order shall stand dismissed and the second Defendant shall pay the Claimant's costs of and occasioned by the Second Defendant's application to be summarily assessed if not agreed.

4. Liberty to apply.

DATED

CHAPTER 13

CLAIMS AGAINST THIRD PARTIES

. . . .

13–01 Forfeiture of the lease may not solve the landlord's problems. He may still be owed a large sum in arrears of rent or the property may still require expenditure to put it into repair. If the tenant is unable to meet the liability the landlord will want to look elsewhere for recovery. In deciding whether or not to terminate the tenancy the landlord should have regard to the potential liabilities of the original tenant, any intermediate assignees and any sureties. He should also consider the possibility of recovering any arrears of rent from sub-tenants.

This chapter considers the rights of the landlord against these persons and the rights they may have if the landlord makes a claim against them. For example, the landlord may sue the surety if the tenant has failed to pay the rent. The surety will then wish to know what rights he has against the tenant. Alternatively, the landlord may sue the original tenant who in turn will wish to know whether he has any rights against subsequent assignees or their sureties.

The 1995 Act: "new tenancies"

13–02 As will be seen much of the law covered by this chapter has been affected by the Landlord and Tenant (Covenants) Act 1995 ("the 1995 Act"), which came into force on January 1, 1996. Some of its provisions apply only to "new tenancies", others apply to all tenancies (s.1 of the 1995 Act).

Generally speaking, a tenancy is a "new tenancy" if it was granted on or after January 1, 1996, the day upon which the Act came into force (s.1(3)).

However, the tenancy will not be a new tenancy if it was granted on or after that date in pursuance of:

(a) an agreement entered into before that date;

(b) an order of a court made before that date (for example an order for a new lease under Pt II of the Landlord and Tenant Act 1954); or

(c) in pursuance of an option or right of first refusal granted before that date (s.1(3), (6), (7)).

The lease will not necessarily state that the tenancy was granted pursuant to one of these events and so it may well be necessary to make suitable enquiries in order to ascertain whether or not the tenancy is a "new tenancy", particularly in the case of leases granted in the early part of 1996.

The same rules apply where there has been a surrender and regrant of a tenancy by virtue of a variation in the tenancy (s.1(5)). Thus, if the variation giving rise to the surrender and regrant took place on or after January 1, 1996 the tenancy will be a new tenancy unless the variation took place pursuant to an agreement entered into before that date. (It should be noted that there are not many circumstances where a variation will give rise to a surrender and regrant (see para.19–07).)

As will be seen below, the 1995 Act introduced a new right for a former tenant who has had to pay rent, or other arrears that have accrued during an assignee's occupancy to acquire an overriding lease of the property (see para.13–54). Where the lease is an overriding lease, it will be a "new tenancy" only if the tenancy in respect of which the tenant of the overriding lease was required to pay the arrears was itself a new tenancy (ss.1(4) and 20(1)).

Although not a statutory term, in this chapter tenancies that are not new tenancies are referred to for convenience as "old tenancies".

Landlord and Tenant (Covenants) Act 1995 ss.1 and 20(1)

1.–(1) Sections 3 to 16 and 21 apply only to new tenancies.　　　　**13–03**
　　(2) Sections 17 to 20 apply to both new and other tenancies.
　　(3) For the purposes of this section a tenancy is a new tenancy if it is granted on or after the date on which this Act comes into force otherwise than in pursuance of—

　　　　(a)　an agreement entered into before that date, or
　　　　(b)　an order of a court made before that date.

　　(4) Subsection (3) has effect subject to section 20(1) in the case of overriding leases granted under section 19.

(5) Without prejudice to the generality of subsection (3), that subsection applies to the grant of a tenancy where by virtue of any variation there is a deemed surrender and regrant as it applies to any other grant of a tenancy.

(6) Where a tenancy granted on or after the date on which this Act comes into force is so granted in pursuance of an option granted before that date, the tenancy shall be regarded for the purposes of subsection (3) as granted in pursuance of an agreement entered into before that date (and accordingly is not a new tenancy), whether or not the operation was exercised before that date.

(7) In subsection (6) "option" includes the right of first refusal.
. . .

20.–(1) For the purpose of section 1 an overriding lease shall be a new tenancy only if the relevant tenancy (see para.13–56) is a new tenancy.

General principles

13-04 In order to understand the rules in this chapter, it is necessary to understand the following principles and how they have been affected by the 1995 Act.

Privity of contract

13-05 As between the original landlord and the original tenant there is a direct contractual relationship. Other persons who may be liable in contract are parties to a licence to assign or to a deed of assignment such as assignees and sureties.

As will be seen below, the original parties to a lease created before the 1995 Act came into force (January 1, 1996) continue to be liable in contract notwithstanding one or more assignments of the lease or the reversion. However, where the tenancy has been created on or after that date the position is substantially different. On assignment of the tenancy, the tenant will (generally) cease to be liable to the landlord; and on an assignment of the landlord's interest the landlord can apply to have his liability extinguished (see para.5–15). It is not possible to contract out of the provisions of the Act (s.25; see para.13–09).

Privity of estate

13-06 Once a lease has been assigned there is no longer any direct contractual relationship between the person who holds the lease and the landlord. The principle upon which the landlord and the current tenant are liable to each other is known as "privity of estate". Prior to the 1995 Act, they were liable to each other under this principle only in respect of covenants in the lease that were said to "touch and concern" the land (see *P & A Swift Investments v Combined English Stores Group plc* [1988] 2 All E.R. 885 HL per Lord Oliver at 890j for a recent exposition of the test for determining whether covenants touch and concern the land). Applying the test, the usual covenants as to payment of rent, repair, insurance and user "touch and concern" the land.

In relation to new tenancies, the benefit and burden of all landlord and tenant covenants generally bind successors in title "whether or not the covenant has reference to the subject matter of the tenancy" (ss.2 and 3 of the 1995 Act). A covenant that is expressed to be personal to any person will not be enforceable by or against any other person. The provisions relevant to the situation where the landlord assigns the reversion are to be found in Ch.5. The provisions that apply where a tenant assigns are set out below.

Landlord and Tenant (Covenants) Act 1995 ss.2, 3 and 23

2.–(1) This Act applies to a landlord and tenant covenant of a tenancy–   **13–07**

- (a) whether or not the covenant has reference to the subject matter of the tenancy, and
- (b) whether the covenant is express, implied or imposed by law, but does not apply to a covenant falling within subsection (2).

(2) [*Not relevant to commercial premises.*]

3.–(1) The benefit and burden of all landlord and tenant covenants of a tenancy–

- (a) shall be annexed and incident to the whole, and to each and every part, of the premises demised by the tenancy and of the reversion in them, and
- (b) shall in accordance with this section pass on an assignment of the whole or any part of those premises or of the reversion in them.

(2) Where the assignment is by the tenant under the tenancy, then as from the assignment the assignee–

- (a) becomes bound by the tenant covenants of the tenancy except to the extent that–
  - (i) immediately before the assignment they did not bind the assignor, or

  (ii) they fall to be complied with in relation to any demised premises not comprised in the assignment; and

 (b) becomes entitled to the benefit of the landlord covenants of the tenancy except to the extent that they fall to be complied with in relation to any such premises.

(3) . . .

(4) In determining for the purposes of subsection (2) or (3) whether any covenant bound the assignor which (in whatever) terms is expressed to be personal to the assignor shall be disregarded.

(5) Any landlord or tenant covenant which is restrictive of the user of land shall, as well as being capable of enforcement against an assignee, be capable of being enforced against any other person who is the owner or occupier of any demised premises to which the covenant relates, even though there is no express provision in the tenancy to that effect.

(6) Nothing in this section shall operate—

 (a) in the case of a covenant which (in whatever terms) is expressed to be personal to any person, to make the covenant enforceable by or (as the case may be) against any other person; or

 (b) to make a covenant enforceable against any person if, apart from this section, it would not be enforceable against him by reason of its not having been registered under the Land Registration Act 1925 or the Land Charges Act 1972.

(7) . . .

23.—(1) Where as a result of an assignment a person becomes, by virtue of this Act, bound by or entitled to the benefit of any covenant, he shall not by virtue of this Act have any liability or rights under the covenant in relation to any time falling before the assignment.

(2) Subsection (1) does not preclude any such rights being expressly assigned to the person in question.

30.—(4) In consequence of this Act nothing in the following provisions, namely—

 (a) sections 78 and 79 of the Law of Property Act 1925 (benefit and burden of covenants relating to land), and

 (b) sections 141 and 142 of that Act (running of benefit and burden of covenants with reversion).

shall apply in relation to new tenancies.

Equitable indemnity and subrogation

13–08 These principles apply where there are two persons liable for a debt but one is considered to have a greater liability than the other. For example, as will be seen below, both the original tenant and the present tenant are liable to the landlord under the terms of the lease. The present tenant is considered to have the primary, or ultimate, liability and is under a duty to indemnify the original tenant if the latter is required to make payment to the landlord. The person who is required to pay the debt is also entitled to be subrogated to the rights and securities of the person to whom he pays the debt. Thus, the original tenant is entitled to exercise the rights of the landlord against the present tenant. This principle is well established and was expressed by Sir John Pennycuick V.C. in *Downer Enterprises Ltd, Re* [1974] 2 All E.R. 1074.

> "The general principle here, I think, is not in doubt, that if A and B are liable to a creditor for the same debt in such circumstances that the ultimate liability falls on A, and if in fact B pays the debt to the creditor, then B is entitled to be reimbursed by A, and likewise is entitled to take over by subrogation any securities or rights which the creditor may have against A, and I can see no reason why such rights should not include the right to be paid rent in full in circumstances such as the present . . . " (1082b). (*Downer Enterprises Ltd, Re* [1974] 2 All E.R. 1074, per Sir John Pennycuick V.C.)

For the principle of equitable indemnity to apply the person who pays the debt must be under a liability to do so. If one person makes a voluntary payment on behalf of another he is not entitled to an indemnity from the principal debtor unless the principal debtor has authorised or (perhaps) subsequently ratified the payment (*Electricity Supply Nominees Ltd v Thorn EMI Retail Ltd* (1991) 35 E.G. 114).

Agreements attempting to frustrate the 1995 Act

It is not possible to contract out of the provisions of the 1995 Act. Any agreement that seeks to have that effect is void (s.25). (But note the *Avonridge* case referred to at para.5–17.) **13–09**

Landlord and Tenant (Covenants) Act 1995 s.25

25.—(1) Any agreement relating to a tenancy is void to the extent that— **13–10**

    (a)   it would apart from this section have effect to exclude, modify or otherwise frustrate the operation of any provision of this Act, or

    (b)   it provides for—

        (i) the termination or surrender of the tenancy, or

        (ii) the imposition on the tenant of any penalty, disability, or liability, in the event of the operation of any provision of this Act, or

(c) it provides for any of the matters referred to in paragraph (b)(i) or (ii) and does so (whether expressly or otherwise) in connection with, or in consequence of, the operation of any provisions of this Act.

(2) To the extent that an agreement relating to a tenancy constitutes a covenant (whether absolute or qualified) against the assignment, or parting with the possession of the premises demised by the tenancy or any part of them—

(a) the agreement is not void by virtue of subsection (1) by reason only of the fact that as such the covenant prohibits or restricts any such assignment or parting with possession; but

(b) paragraph (a) above does not otherwise affect the operation of that subsection in relation to the agreement (and in particular does not preclude its application to the agreement to the extent that it purports to regulate the giving of, or the making of any application for, consent to any such assignment or parting with possession).

(3) In accordance with section 16(1) nothing in this section applies to any agreement to the extent that it is an authorised guarantee agreement; but (without prejudice to the generality of subsection (1) above) an agreement is void to the extent that it is one falling within section 165(4)(a) or (b).

(4) This section applies to an agreement relating to a tenancy whether or not the agreement is—

(a) contained in the instrument creating the tenancy; or
(b) made before the creation of the tenancy.

Original tenant: old tenancies

The rule

13-11 The original tenant under an old tenancy (i.e. generally one granted before January 1, 1996 when the 1995 Act came into force; see para.13-02) remains liable to the landlord throughout the term. The basis of the liability is the original contract entered into between the landlord and the tenant by the grant and taking of the lease:

"Generally speaking, an original lessee *prima facie* remains liable to the reversioner for payment of the rent throughout the term, ever after it has been assigned. This is a direct and primary liability, though after an assignment it is normally accompanied by rights of indemnity against the first assignee, and also, where there have been further assignments, against the assignee in whom the lease is for the time being vested." (*Wamford Investments Ltd v*

Duckworth [1978] 2 All E.R. 517, per Megarry V.C. at p.525e.)

The landlord's claim for arrears of rent is a claim for a debt and not damages. He is therefore under no duty to mitigate his loss. Nor is he under any duty to the original tenant to ensure that future assignees are of worth or to pursue a remedy against the current tenant or any other person before suing the original tenant (*Norwich Union Life Insurance Society v Low Profile Fashions Ltd* [1992] 1 E.G.L.R. 86 CA):

> "[T]he remedies available to the landlord are against different persons and are cumulative and not alternative. I can see no equity in requiring the landlord to pursue one rather than another means of seeking to recover his loss or requiring him to run the risk that by pursuing one party he may jeopardise his chances of recovering against another. It has long been the law that the landlord may sue either the original lessee or the assignee, or both at the same time." (*Norwich Union*, per Beldam LJ at 88H.)

Where the lease requires the tenant to pay service charges as rent, the original tenant retains the obligation to pay those service charges after an assignment in the same way that he continues to be liable to pay the rent (*Royton Industries v Lawrence* [1994] E.G. 151.)

Where the reversion has been assigned, the original tenant is liable to the assignee of the reversion (see para.5-04).

Notice of intention to recover the arrears

By virtue of s.17 of the 1995 Act (which applies to all tenancies, whether new or old; s.1(1), para.13-02), the landlord must give notice to the original tenant of his intention to recover arrears of rent and other "fixed charges". If he fails to do so within six months, they will be irrecoverable (see further para.13-41). **13-12**

Variation of the lease

The original tenant's liability may be limited if the landlord and an assignee agree a variation in the terms of the lease (s.18 of the 1995 Act that applies to all tenancies whenever granted; see para.13-39). **13-13**

Extension of the lease

13-14 An original tenant who has contracted to pay the rent throughout "the term" and who has subsequently assigned is not liable during any statutory continuation of the tenancy under s.24 of the 1954 Act (*London City Corp v Fell* [1993] 4 All E.R. 968 HL—as to s.24 see para.1-02). It follows that the original tenant will not be liable under a new lease granted pursuant to Pt II of the 1954 Act. (See also *Herbert Duncan Ltd v Cluttons* [1993] 2 All E.R. 449 CA.)

At common law the original tenant remained liable under the lease if it was extended by an assignee (*Baker v Merckel* [1961] 1 All E.R. 668). However, this rule has probably been revoked by s.18(2) of the 1995 Act (see para.13-40) that applies to all tenancies whenever granted (s.1(2), para.13-03)).

Disclaimer

13-15 Where the present assignee of the lease goes bankrupt (or, if it is a company, goes into liquidation) and the trustee in bankruptcy (liquidator) disclaims the lease the original tenant remains liable for the rent accruing after the disclaimer. For a full discussion of the effects of disclaimer see Ch.20.

Compromise and voluntary arrangements

13-16 Where the landlord and the ultimate assignee enter into a compromise whereby the debt is released the original tenant is released from liability (*Deanplan v Mahmoud* [1992] 3 All E.R. 945):

> "From this long review of the cases, I draw the following conclusions. First, a release of one joint contractor releases the others. There is only one obligation . . . It is a question of construction of the contract between the creditor and joint debtor in the light of the surrounding circumstances whether the contract amounts to a release or merely to a contract not to sue. Secondly, the same principles apply to a contract between the creditor and of joint and several debtors. If one joint and several covenantor is released by accord and satisfaction, all are released." (Judge Paul Baker at 959-960).

The judge speculated on the reasons for the rule and specified two in particular:

"First, that where the obligations are non-cumulative, *i.e.* the obligation of each is to perform in so far as it had not been performed by any other party, the acceptance of some other performance in lieu of the promised performance relieves the others. The covenantee cannot have both the premised performance and some other performance which he agrees to accept. Second, unless the covenantors were released following an accord and satisfaction, they could claim contribution or indemnity from the one released. Thus, by suing the co-contractor the creditor commits a breach of the contract with the released covenantor, for such an action would inevitably lead to the very claim from which the release has been purchased by accord and satisfaction."

In *Friends' Provident Life Office v British Railways Board* [1996] 1 All E.R. 336 it was held that a deed of variation, which substituted a different rental obligation, could not be construed as granting an assignee, and therefore a tenant, a release from the obligation to pay rent. (See also para.19–07).

The principle does not automatically apply to insolvency arrangements made under the Insolvency Act 1986 in which agreement is reached as to the payment of creditors. The original tenant may not therefore take advantage of a voluntary arrangement (an "IVA") entered into by an assignee which is binding on the landlord by virtue of s.5(2) of the Insolvency Act 1986 (*RA Securities Ltd v Mercantile Credit Co Ltd* [1995] 3 All E.R. 581 Ch D; *Burford Midland Properties Ltd v Marley Extrusions Ltd* [1995] 2 E.G.L.R. 15 Ch D; *Mytre Investments Ltd v Reynolds* [1995] 3 All E.R. 588 Ch D).

For example, if an assignee who is liable to the landlord for £100,000 arrears of rent enters into a voluntary arrangement with his creditors containing a clause whereby he is required to pay his landlord only £50,000, the landlord may recover the balance from the original tenant:

" . . . the entry into an IVA which makes no provision for the forfeiture or the disclaimer or the variation of the lease and which on its face makes no express provision in relation to the original lessees, does indeed leave open the right to the landlord to recover against the original lessees, that it is only the claim against the existing lessee that is affected by the IVA" (*Mytre Investments Ltd v Reynolds*, per Michael Burton, sitting as deputy High Court Judge in the QBD).

If an original tenant is held to be liable, he can recover from the assignee notwithstanding the IVA unless he was a party to the IVA (i.e. given notice of the creditors meeting). It has therefore been suggested that original tenants should be given notice of creditors' meetings so that their right to an indemnity from the debtor can be taken into account when the voluntary arrangement is drawn up and approved (*Mytre Investments Ltd* at p.596h).

Release of and payment by surety

13-17 The original tenant is not released from his liability by the landlord releasing the current tenant's surety (*Allied London Investments Ltd v Hambro Life Assurance Ltd* (1985) 50 P. & C.R. 207).

Where a surety pays a particular instalment of rent that same instalment cannot be claimed from the original tenant. However, the landlord may accept payment from the surety of a lump sum in lieu of all future liability without affecting his right to recover rent from the original tenant so long as no part of the payment is appropriated to the debt being claimed against the original tenant (*Milverton Group Ltd v Warner World Ltd* [1995] 32 E.G. 70; see para.8-04 in relation to appropriation of rent payments).

Effect of forfeiture or surrender

13-18 The original tenant ceases to be liable if the landlord forfeits or takes a surrender of the lease but merely locking the premises for security purposes after the tenant has abandoned them is not sufficient to constitute a forfeiture or surrender (*Relvock Properties Ltd v Dixon* (1973) 25 P. & C.R. 1—a surrender case; para.18-08 and see para.7-11 on forfeiture). Once a landlord has taken sufficient steps to constitute a forfeiture, he cannot change his mind and argue that the forfeiture has not taken place (see paras 7-11 and 7-38).

Original tenant: new tenancies

The new rule

t1 Where a tenant assigns a new tenancy (generally one granted on or after January 1, 1996; see para.13-01) he is "released from the tenant covenants of the tenancy" (and ceases to be entitled to the benefit of the landlord covenants) as from the assignment (s.5 of the 1995 Act).   **13-19**

Certain assignments ("excluded assignments") are excluded from this rule, namely assignments in breach of covenant or assignments by operation of law (eg where a lease vests in the Crown following a disclaimer: *RVB Investments Ltd v Bibby* [2013] EWHC 65 (Ch)). In the case of an excluded assignment s.5 has effect from the next assignment (if any) of the premises assigned by him which is not an excluded assignment (s.11(1), (2)).

The release of the original tenant from his obligations under the tenancy that takes place when he assigns, does not affect any liability of his arising from a breach of the covenant occurring before the release (s.24).

Where the tenant assigns only part of the property, see s.9 of the 1995 Act and Form 7 of the Landlord and Tenant (Covenants) Act 1995 (Notices) Regulations 1995 (SI 1995/2964) (not set out in this book).

Landlord and Tenant (Covenants) Act 1995 ss.5, 24

5.—(1) This section applies where a tenant assigns premises demised to   **13-20**
him under a tenancy.
    (2) If the tenant assigns the whole of the premises demised to him, he—

    (a)   is released from the tenant covenants of the tenancy, and
    (b)   ceases to be entitled to the benefit of the landlord covenants of the tenancy,

as from the assignment.
    (3) If the tenant assigns part only of the premises demised to him, then as from the assignment he—

    (a)   is released from the tenant covenants of the tenancy, and
    (b)   ceases to be entitled to the benefit of the landlord covenants of the tenancy,

only to the extent that those covenants fall to be complied with in relation to that part of the demised premises.

(4) This section applies as mentioned in subsection (1) whether or not the tenant is tenant of the whole of the premises comprised in the tenancy.

. . .

24.–(1) Any release of a person from a covenant by virtue of this Act does not affect any liability of his arising from a breach of the covenant occurring before the release.

. . .

Authorised guarantee agreements

13-21 Although s.5 releases the tenant from his covenants on an assignment there is nothing in the Act to preclude him from entering into an agreement ("an authorised guarantee agreement") guaranteeing the performance of the relevant covenant by the assignee provided that the provisions of s.16 of the Act are complied with. Thus, if there is an absolute or qualified covenant against assignment the landlord can require the tenant to enter into an authorised guarantee agreement before giving his consent to the assignment (in the latter case if the requirement is reasonable or if there is a contractual right entitling him to do so (s.16(3)(b)) *Wallis Fashion Group Ltd v Life Assurance Ltd* [2000] 2 E.G.L.R. 49; see further Ch.10).

If the tenant has assigned only part of the property, see s.28(2), (3) of the 1995 Act.

Landlord and Tenant (Covenants) Act 1995 s.16

13-22 **16.**–(1) Where on an assignment a tenant is to any extent released from a tenant covenant of a tenancy by virtue of this Act ("the relevant covenant"), nothing in this Act (and in particular section 25) shall preclude him from entering into an authorised guarantee agreement with respect to the performance of that covenant by the assignee.

(2) For the purposes of this section an agreement is an authorised guarantee agreement if—

(a)   under it the tenant guarantees the performance of the relevant covenant to any extent by the assignee; and

(b)   it is entered into in the circumstances set out in subsection (3); and

(c)   its provision conform with subsections (4) and (5).

(3) Those circumstances are as follows—

(a)   by virtue of a covenant against assignment (whether absolute or qualified) the assignment cannot be effected without the consent of the landlord under the tenancy or some other person;

(b)   any such consent is given subject to a condition (lawfully imposed) that the tenant is to enter into an agreement guaranteeing the performance of the covenant by the assignee; and

(c)   the agreement is entered into by the tenant in pursuance of that condition.

(4) An agreement is not an authorised guarantee agreement to the extent that it purports—

(a)   to impose on the tenant any requirement to guarantee in any way the performance of the relevant covenant by any person other than the assignee; or

(b)   to impose on the tenant any liability, restriction or other requirement (of whatever nature) in relation to any time after the assignee is released from that covenant by virtue of this Act.

(5) Subject to subsection (4), an authorised guarantee agreement may—

(a)   impose on the tenant any liability as sole or principal debtor in respect of any obligation owed by the assignee under the relevant covenant;

(b)   impose on the tenant liabilities as guarantor in respect of the assignee's performance of that covenant which are no more onerous than those to which he would be subject in the event of his being liable as sole or principal debtor in respect of any obligation owed by the assignee under that covenant;

(c)   require the tenant, in the event of the tenancy assigned by him being disclaimed, to enter into a new tenancy of the premises comprised in the assignment—

    (i) whose term expires not later than the tenant of the tenancy assigned by the tenant, and

    (ii) whose tenant covenants are no more onerous than those of that tenancy;

(d)   make provision incidental or supplementary to any provision made by virtue of any of paragraphs (a) to (c).

. . .

(8) It is hereby declared that the rules of law relating to guarantees (and in particular those relating to release of Sureties) are, subject to its terms, applicable in relation to any authorised guarantee agreement as in relation to any other guarantee agreement.

Intermediate assignee

Old tenancies

As a matter of general principle, an assignee of a lease is liable only on the leasehold covenants, pursuant to the principle of privity of estate (see para.13-06), while he holds the lease. However, where on each successive assignment the assignee   **13-23** has covenanted (usually in a licence to assign) that he will, during the residue of the term, pay the rent and observe the covenants and conditions on the part of the tenant contained in the lease, each successive assignee remains liable under the covenant until the end of the term (*J Lyons & Co v Knowles* [1943] 1 K.B. 366; and see *Estates Gazette Ltd v Benjamin Restaurants Ltd* [1995] 1 All E.R. 129 CA—covenant "to pay the rents reserved by the lease at the time and in the manner therein provided for and to observe and perform all the covenants on the lessee's part therein contained").

For the effect of disclaimer, by the liquidator or trustee of the final assignee, on an intermediate assignee who has entered into a direct contractual relationship with the landlord pursuant to a licence to assign see Chapter 20, para.20–22.

New tenancies

13–24   Section 28(1) of the 1995 Act provides that "tenant" in relation to a tenancy means the person for the time being entitled to the term of the tenancy. Thus, s.5 (release of tenants from liability on assignment; see para.13–19) applies to all former tenants including assignees.

Notice of intention to recover arrears

13–25   The rule which provides for the provision of service of notices in respect of arrears of rent and other "fixed charges" applies to all former tenants. Thus an assignee who has assigned the lease will not be liable for the arrears unless a notice in the prescribed form has been served on him within the statutory period (see further para.13–41).

Sureties

Introduction

13–26   Most leases of business premises contain a surety provision, that is a clause whereby a third person covenants that the tenant will pay the rent and perform the other covenants in the lease and that, if the tenant defaults in any respect, the surety will indemnify the landlord in respect of any losses thereby incurred. This is particularly true where the tenant is a limited liability company. An example of a surety covenant is to be found in the Law Society's business lease, below.

The Law Society Business Lease

"Guarantee Box"

The terms in this box only take effect if a guarantor is named and then only until the Tenant transfers this lease with Landlord's written consent. The guarantor must sign this lease.

13–27

> 'Guarantor"...........................: of .... agrees to compensate the Landlord for any loss incurred as a result of the Tenant failing to comply with an obligation in this lease during the lease period or any statutory extension of it. If the Tenant is insolvent and this lease ends because it is disclaimed, the Guarantor agrees to accept a new lease, if the Landlord so requires, in the same form but at the rent then payable. Even if the Landlord gives the tenant extra time to comply with an obligation, or does not insist on strict compliance with the terms of this lease, the Guarantor's obligation remains fully effective.

If the lease is assigned the landlord will also usually ask a surety to guarantee that the assignee will comply with the terms of the lease. The landlord's agreement to the assignment is usually contained in a licence to assign, to which the surety will be a party. The landlord is under no obligation to require payment from the tenant before pursuing the surety (*Wright v Simpson* (1802) 31 E.R. 1272 at 1282).

Notice of intention to recover arrears

The rule that provides for the provision of service of notices in respect of arrears of rent and other "fixed charges" applies to sureties (s.17(3); see para.13–42). Thus a surety will not be liable for the arrears unless a notice in the prescribed form has been served on him within the statutory period. (see further para.13–41).

13–28

Limit of surety's liability

The extent to which the surety's liability continues varies depending upon the different circumstances of the case.

13–29

Introduction

13-30 By virtue of s.24 of the 1995 Act, a surety is released from his covenant in any circumstances in which the tenant is *by reason of the Act* released from his liability.

Landlord and Tenant (Covenants) Act 1995 s.24

13-31 **24.**–(2) Where–

    (a) by virtue of this Act a tenant is released from a tenant covenant of a tenancy, and

    (b) immediately before the release another person is bound by a covenant of the tenancy imposing any liability or penalty in the event of a failure to comply with that tenant covenant, then, as from the release of the tenant, that other person is released from the covenant mentioned in paragraph (b) to the same extent as the tenant is released from that covenant.

Position of surety of original tenant after assignment

13-32 The original tenant under an old tenancy (generally one entered into before January 1, 1996; see para.13–02) remains liable on the covenants throughout the term (para.13–11). A consequence of that fact is that the surety's obligation also continues after an assignment of the lease by the original tenant, unless he has agreed to be bound only during the period in which the tenancy is vested in the original tenant (see Law Society's Business Lease, Guarantee Box; para.13–27).

However, where the tenancy is a new tenancy (i.e. generally one granted on or after January 1, 1996; see para.13–02), the original tenant will cease to be liable after the lease has been assigned (para.13–19); and the surety's liability will likewise come to an end (s.24(2)(b)). Under s16 of the 1995 Act the landlord is entitled to require the outgoing tenant to enter into an authorised guarantee agreement guaranteeing the performance of the tenant covenants by the assignee until the next lawful assignment (para.13–21). However, there is no similar provision for guarantors. Any guarantee given by the guarantor of an assignor to guarantee the assignee's obligations under a lease is void under the provisions of s.25 of the 1995 Act; para.13–10 (*K/S Victoria Street v House of Fraser (Stores Management) Ltd* [2011] EWCA Civ 904).

Liability of surety of intermediate assignee

Where the tenancy is an old tenancy, the surety of an assignee **13-33** ceases to be liable to the landlord unless (as is usual) he has covenanted to ensure that the rent is paid and the covenants are performed throughout the term.

As above, here the tenancy is a new tenancy, the surety will cease to be liable after the assignee has himself assigned (s.24(2)(b)).

Liability of surety if tenant dies

On the death of an individual tenant, the estate vests in his **13-34** personal representatives who will be under a continuing obligation to pay the rent (*Youngmin v Heath* [1974] 1 W.L.R. 135). The surety's obligations will therefore also continue.

Liability of surety on disclaimer

See Ch.20, para.20-22. **13-35**

Liability of surety on forfeiture of the lease

If the landlord forfeits the lease, the term comes to an end. **13-36** Thus, no new rent accrues and the surety's obligation to pay continuing rent comes to an end. He will of course remain liable to indemnify the landlord in respect of any rent that accrued prior to the re-entry and for any breaches that occurred prior to that date. The surety will also remain liable for mesne profits if the tenant fails to give up possession because failure to do so is a breach of the covenant to yield up at the end of the term (*Associated Dairies v Pierce* (1983) 265 E.G. 127).

Variation of the lease

Prior to the 1995 Act it had been held that a variation in the **13-37** lease would absolve the surety of liability unless the variation was clearly insubstantial or could not prejudice him (*Howard De Walden Estates Ltd v Pasta Place Ltd* [1995] 1 E.G.L.R. 79; *Metropolitan Properties Co (Regis) Ltd v Bartholomew* [1995] 1 E.G.L.R. 65 CA).

Section 18(3) of the Act also now provides that the surety of a former tenant will cease to be liable where a variation to which the section applies has taken place (see para.13-40).

Other defences of surety

13-38 There are a number of other general defences that a surety may be able to rely on in defence to an action brought by a landlord in addition to those referred to above. They include the giving of time, or surrendering the lease (*Holme v Brunskill* (1877) 3 Q.B.D. 495 and *Topland Portfolio v Smiths News Trading Ltd* [2014] EWCA Civ 18). See generally *Atkin's Court Forms* (Butterworths) Vol.21, [6] (132). But note that a surety may agree to remain liable notwithstanding the giving of time etc. (*Perry v National Provincial Bank of England* [1910] 1 Ch. 464 at 473).

A claim by a landlord against a surety is governed by s.19 of the Limitation Act 1980 (rather than s.8) so that any such claim is statute barred after six years after the rent has accrued, not 12 (*Romain v Scuba TV Ltd* [1996] 2 All E.R. 377 CA).

Variation of lease: effect on liability

13-39 A former tenant (i.e. the original tenant or an earlier assignee) is not liable for any amount "to the extent that the amount is referable to any relevant variation of the tenant covenants of the tenancy" (s.18 of the 1995 Act). A variation is a "relevant variation" if the landlord, at the time of the variation, has an absolute right to refuse to allow it (s.18(4)(a); see further s.18(4)(b)). A "variation" means a variation whether effected by deed or otherwise.

This rule applies to both new and old tenancies (s.1(2); para.13-03). Thus, a new rent determined in accordance with a rent review clause will be binding on the former tenant because the landlord does not have the absolute right to refuse to allow the variation. However, a variation outside the terms of the rent review clause would not bind a former tenant.

Although s.18 applies to new and old tenancies, nothing in the section applies to any variation of the tenant covenants effected before the date on which the Act came into force (s.18(6)). However, the decision in *Friends' Provident Life Office v British Railways Board* [1996] 1 All E.R. 336 CA should be noted. In that case it was held (prior to the 1995 Act) that the obligations accepted by a former tenant cannot be varied or increased by a subsequent agreement made between the landlord and the current tenant. A deed of variation had been entered into that substantially increased the rent and made it payable in advance rather than in arrears and altered the covenants as to user and alienation. That variation was not binding on the former tenant. See also para.19–07.

Landlord and Tenant (Covenants) Act 1995 s.18

18.–(1) This section applies where a person ("the former tenant") is as a result of an assignment no longer a tenant under a tenancy but— **13–40**

- (a)   (in the case of a new tenancy) he has under an authorised guarantee agreement guaranteed the performance by his assignee of any tenant covenant of the tenancy; or
- (b)   (in the case of any tenancy) he remains bound by such a covenant.

(2) The former tenant shall not be liable under the agreement or (as the case may be) the covenant to pay any amount in respect of the covenant to the extent that the amount is referable to any relevant variation of the tenant covenants of the tenancy effected after the assignment.

(3) Where a person ("the guarantor") has agreed to guarantee the performance by the former tenant of a tenant covenant of the tenancy, the guarantor (where liability to do so is not wholly discharged by any such variation of the tenant covenants of the tenancy) shall not be liable under that agreement to pay any amount in respect of the covenant to the extent that the amount is referable to any such variation.

(4) For the purposes of this section a variation of the tenant covenants of a tenancy is a "relevant variation" if either—

- (a)   the landlord has, at the time of the variation, an absolute right to refuse to allow it; or
- (b)   the landlord would have had such a right if the variation had been sought by the former tenant immediately before the assignment by him but, between the time of that assignment and the time of the variation, the tenant covenants of the tenancy have been so varied as to deprive the landlord of such a right.

(5) In determining whether the landlord has or would have had such a right at any particular time regard shall be had to all the circumstances (including the effect of any provision made by or under any enactment).

(6) Nothing in this section applies to any variation of the tenant covenants of a tenancy effected before the date on which this Act comes into force.

(7) In this section "variation" means a variation whether effected by deed or otherwise.

Notice of intention to recover arrears: the six-month rule

13-41 Prior to the 1995 Act, one of the most difficult things for former tenants and their sureties to understand was how landlords could be permitted to allow large arrears to accrue over a long period of time without telling them and then be able to demand that they pay up. That situation was remedied by s.17 of the 1995 Act, which requires the landlord to serve notice of his intention to recover the arrears upon the former tenant or his surety. He must serve the notice within six months beginning with the date when the amount payable became due. If the landlord fails to do so, the amount sought will not be recoverable.

Landlord and Tenant Act 1995 s.17

13-42   **17.**–(1) This section applies where a person ("the former tenant") is as a result of an assignment no longer a tenant under a tenancy but—

(a)   (in the case of a tenancy which is a new tenancy he has under an authorised guarantee agreement guaranteed the performance by his assignee of a tenant covenant of the tenancy under which any fixed charge is payable [*see para.13-21*]; or

(b)   in the case of any tenancy) he remains bound by such a covenant.

(2) The former tenant shall not be liable under that agreement or (as the case may be) the covenant to pay any amount in respect of any fixed charge payable under the covenant unless, within the period of six months beginning with the date when the charge becomes due, the landlord serves on the former tenant a notice informing him—

(a)   that the charge is now due; and

(b)   that in respect of the charge the landlord intends to recover from the former tenant such amount as is specified in the notice and (where payable) interest calculated on such basis as is so specified.

(3) Where a person ("the guarantor") has agreed to guarantee the performance by the former tenant of such a covenant as is mentioned in subsection (1), the guarantor shall not be liable under the agreement to pay any amount in respect of any fixed charge payable under the covenant unless, within the period of six months beginning with the date when the charge becomes due, the landlord serves on the guarantor a notice informing him—

(a)   that the charge is now due; and

(b)   that in respect of the charge the landlord intends to recover from the guarantor such amount as is specified in the notice and (where payable) interest calculated on such basis as is so specified.

(4) Where the landlord has duly served a notice under subsection (2) or (3), the amount (exclusive of interest) which the former tenant or (as the case may be) the guarantor is liable to pay in respect of the fixed charge in question shall not exceed the amount specified in the notice unless—

    (a)   his liability in respect of the charge is subsequently determined to be for a greater amount,

    (b)   the notice informed him of the possibility that liability would be so determined, and

    (c)   within the period of three months beginning with the date of determination, the landlord serves on him a further notice informing him that the landlord intends to recover that greater amount from him (plus interest, where payable).

(5) For the purposes of subsection (2) or (3) any fixed charge which has become due before the date on which this Act comes into force shall be treated as becoming due on that date; but neither of those subsections applies to any such charge if before that date proceedings have been instituted by the landlord for the recovery from the former tenant of any amount in respect of it.

(6) In this section—

"fixed charge", in relation to a tenancy, means—

    (a)   rent

    (b)   any service charge as defined by section 18 of the Landlord and Tenant Act 1985 (the words "of a dwelling" being disregarded for this purpose), and

    (c)   any amount payable under a tenant covenant of the tenancy providing for the payment of a liquidated sum in the event of a failure to comply with any such covenant;

"landlord", in relation to a fixed charge, includes any person who has a right to enforce a payment of the charge.

Notes:

(1)   The rule applies to rent, service charges and interest and to any other liquidated sum which is payable as a result of a breach of covenant (s.17(6)—for example, the cost of repairs carried out by a landlord pursuant to a right to enter and repair; see para.11-28). The amount due is known as a "fixed charge".   **13-43**

(2)   It is not possible to sue for the arrears within the six months without serving a notice. A s.17 notice must be served in all cases otherwise the arrears will not be recoverable (s.17(2)).

(3)   The notice must be in prescribed form (s.27(1); Form 1 of The Landlord and Tenant (Covenants) Act 1995 (Notices) Regulations, 1995/2964): see Form 15, para.13-44.

(4)   The notice should not be served before the date upon which the sum becomes due (s.17(2)(a)). It should also not necessarily be served too soon in the six-month

period where the former tenant is not necessarily a person who the landlord would want to be his tenant under an overriding lease (see further note (9)).

(5) The rule applies to all former tenants (s.17(1)) and their guarantors (s.17(3)). It does not apply to the guarantor of the present tenant.

(6) The notice may specify the possibility that the liability may be subsequently determined to be for a greater amount than the amount specified in the notice as being due. If so, the landlord may recover the greater amount so long as he serves a further notice stating that he intends to recover the greater amount (see s.17(4)). For example, the amount of service charge due may not be certain or there may be an outstanding rent review. See Form 16, para.13-45. Where there are arrears that have accrued following a rent review the landlord does not have to serve a Form 1 notice (Form 15, para.13-44) at each of the normal rent payment dates between the review date and the actual review; and then serve a Form 2 notice (Form 16) after the rent review has been completed (as envisaged by para.4 of the Form 1 notice and the note to that paragraph on the form—Form 15, para.13-44). It is sufficient for the landlord to wait until the rent is determined after the rent review and then only serve a Form 1 notice. The date that the additional rent under a rent review clause "becomes due" is the date when the increase has been agreed or determined. (*Scottish & Newcastle v Raguz* [2008] UKHL 65—the House considered that it was hard to attribute to Parliament the intention that landlords had to serve a s.17 notice within six months after every rent payment date specifying the amount due as "nil" if they wanted to preserve their rights against former tenants pending a rent review; see in particular Lord Hoffmann at para.13).

(7) The six-month rule applies to arrears that accrued prior to the coming into force of the 1995 Act unless proceedings had already been instituted in respect of them. However, the period of six months is calculated from January 1, 1996 (s.17(5)).

(8) Section 23 of the Landlord and Tenant Act 1927 applies in relation to the service of notices (s.27(5) of the 1995 Act; para.14-23).

(9) As will be seen below, a person who pays the arrears pursuant to a s.17 notice may acquire an overriding lease

of the property (para.13–54). Where more than one person has been served with a s.17 notice (for example an original tenant and an intermediate assignee), the person who makes the first request is entitled to the overriding lease (s.19(7)(b)). A landlord may therefore consider it advantageous to serve his first s.17 notice on the person who he considers will be the most secure tenant (or in the language of the business "the best covenant"). For example, if the original tenant was a substantial company and the first assignee is a much smaller company, the landlord should perhaps serve a s.17 notice on the larger company stating that they are the first to be served and giving them a short period to make a request for an overriding lease before any other former tenant is to be served with a s.17 notice. Whatever the landlord does however he should make sure that he serves any s.17 notice within the six-month time period.

(10) Section 17(3) does not require a notice to be served before a landlord can seek to enforce a covenant requiring a surety to accept a new lease for the residue of the term following disclaimer or foreiture. Nor would it prevent a claim for damages for breach of, or in lieu of an order for specific performance of such a covenant (*RVB Investments Ltd v Bibby* [2013] EWHC 65 (Ch).

13–44   **Form 15: Notice to former tenant or guarantor of intention to recover fixed charge (Landlord and Tenant (Covenants) Act 1995 s.17)**

To [name and address]: ....

....

> IMPORTANT—THE PERSON GIVING THIS NOTICE IS PROTECTING THE RIGHT TO RECOVER THE AMOUNT(S) SPECIFIED FROM YOU NOW OR AT SOME TIME IN THE FUTURE. THERE MAY BE ACTION WHICH YOU CAN TAKE TO PROTECT YOUR POSITION. READ THE NOTICE AND ALL THE NOTES OVERLEAF CAREFULLY. IF YOU ARE IN ANY DOUBT ABOUT THE ACTION YOU SHOULD TAKE, SEEK ADVICE IMMEDIATELY, FOR INSTANCE FROM A SOLICITOR OR CITIZENS ADVICE BUREAU.

1. This notice is given under s.17 of the Landlord and Tenant (Covenants) Act 1995. [*see Note 1*]

2. It relates to (address and description of property) ....

....

let under a lease date .... and made between ....

....

[of which you were formerly tenant] [in relation to which you are liable as guarantor of a person who was formerly tenant].[2]

3. I/we as landlord[3] hereby give you notice that the fixed charge(s) of which details are set out in the attached Schedule[4] is/are now due and unpaid, and that I/we intend to recover from you the amount(s) specified in the Schedule [and interest from the date and calculated on the basis specified in the Schedule][5]. [*see Notes 2 and 3*]

4.[6] There is a possibility that your liability in respect of the fixed charge(s) detailed in the Schedule will subsequently be deterimined to be for a greater amount. [*see Note 4 below*]

5. All correspondence about this notice should be sent to the landlord/landlord's agent at the address given below.

   Date .... Signature of landlord/landlord's agent ....

   Name and address of landlord ....

                                                                                        cont

268

---

cont

....

[Name and address of agent ....

....

....]

NOTES

1. The person giving you this notice alleges that you are still liable for the performance of the tenant's obligations under the tenancy to which this notice relates, either as a previous tenant bound by privity of contract or an authorised guarantee agreement, or because you are the guarantor of a previous tenant. By giving you this notice, the landlord (or other person entitled to enforce payment, such as a management company) is protecting his right to require you to pay the amount specified in the notice. There may be other sums not covered by the notice which the landlord can also recover because they are not fixed charges (for example in respect of repairs or costs if legal proceedings have to be brought). If you pay the amount specified in this notice in full, you will have the right to call on the landlord to grant you an "overriding lease", which puts you in the position of landlord to the present tenant. There are both advantages and drawbacks to doing this, and you should take advice before coming to a decision.

Validity of notice
2. The landlord is required to give this notice within six months of the date on which the charge or charges in question became due (or, if it became due before 1 January 1996, within six months of that date). If the notice has been given late, it is not valid and the amount in the notice cannot be recovered from you. The date of the giving of the notice may not be the date written on the notice or the date on which you actually saw it. It may, for instance, be the date on which the notice was delivered through the post to your last address known to the landlord. If you are in any doubt, you should seek advice immediately.

Interest
3. If the interest is payable on the amount due, the landlord does not have to state the precise amount of interest, but he must state the basis on which the interest is calculated to enable you to work out the likely amount, or he will not be able to claim interest at all. This does not include interest which may be payable under rules of court if legal proceedings are brought.

Change in amount due
4. Apart from interest, the landlord is not entitled to recover an amount which

cont

---

cont

is more than he has specified in the notice, with one exception. This is where the amount cannot be finally determined within six months after it is due (for example, if there is dispute concerning an outstanding rent review or if the charge is a service charge collected on account and adjusted following final determination). In such a case, if the amount due is eventually determined to be more than originally notified, the landlord may claim the larger amount *if and only if* he completes the paragraph giving notice of the possibility that the amount may change, and gives a further notice specifying the larger amount within three months of the final determination.

The Act defines a fixed charge as (a) rent, (b) any service charge (as defined by s.18 of the Landlord and Tenant Act 1985, disregarding the words "of a dwelling") and (c) any amount payable under a tenant covenant of the tenancy providing for payment of a liquidated sum in the event of failure to comply with the covenant.

2   Delete alternative as appropriate.
3   "Landlord" for these purposes includes any person who has the right to enforce the charge.
4   The Schedule must be in writing, and must indicate in relation to each item the date on which it became payable, the amount payable and whether it is rent, service charge or a fixed charge of some other kind (in which case particulars of the nature of the charge should be given). Charges due before 1 January 1996 are deemed to have become due on that date, but the actual date on which they became due should also be stated.
5   Delete words in brackets if not applicable. If applicable, the Schedule must state the basis on which interest is calculated (for example, rate of interest, date from which it is payable and provision of Lease or other document under which it is payable).
6   Delete this paragraph if not applicable. If applicable (for example, where there is an outstanding rent review or service charge collected on account) a further notice must be served on the former tenant or guarantor within three (3) months beginning with the date on which the greater amount is determined. If only applicable to one or more charge of several, the Schedule should specify which.

Form 16: Further notice to former tenant or guarantor of revised amount due in respect of a fixed charge (Landlord and Tenant (Covenants) Act 1995 s.17)

13–45

To [name and address]: ....

....

> IMPORTANT—THE PERSON GIVING THIS NOTICE IS PROTECTING THE RIGHT TO RECOVER THE AMOUNT(S) SPECIFIED FROM YOU NOW OR AT SOME TIME IN THE FUTURE. THERE MAY BE ACTION WHICH YOU CAN TAKE TO PROTECT YOUR POSITION. READ THE NOTICE AND ALL THE NOTES OVERLEAF CAREFULLY. IF YOU ARE IN ANY DOUBT ABOUT THE ACTION YOU SHOULD TAKE, SEEK ADVICE IMMEDIATELY, FOR INSTANCE FROM A SOLICITOR OR CITIZENS ADVICE BUREAU.

1. This notice is given under section 17 of the Landlord and Tenant (Covenants) Act 1995. [*see Note 1*]

2. It relates to (address and description of property) ....

   ....

   let under a lease date .... and made between ....

   ....

   [of which you were formerly tenant] [in relation to which you are liable as guarantor of a person who was formerly tenant].[2]

   You were informed on .... (date of original notice) of the amount due in respect of a fixed charge or charges, and of the possibility that your liability in respect of the charge(s) might subsequently be determined to be for a greater amount.

4. I/we as landlord[3] hereby give you notice that the fixed charge(s) of which details are set out in the attached Schedule[4] has/have now been determined to be for a greater amount than specified in the original notice, and that I/we intend to recover from you the amount(s) specified in the Schedule [and interest from the date and calculated on the basis specified in the Schedule][5]. [*see Notes 2 and 3*]

5. All correspondence about this notice should be sent to the landlord/landlord's agent at the address given below.

   Date .... Signature of landlord/landlord's agent ....

   Name and address of landlord ....

   cont

---

cont

....

....

[Name and address of agent ....

....

....]

NOTES

1. The person giving you this notice alleges that you are still liable for the performance of the tenant's obligations under the tenancy to which this notice relates, either as a previous tenant bound by privity of contract or an authorised guarantee agreement, or because you are the guarantor of a previous tenant. You should already have been given a notice by which the landlord (or other person entitled to enforce payment, such as a management company) protected his right to require you to pay the amount specified in that notice. The purpose of this notice is to protect the landlord's right to require you to pay a larger amount, because the amount specified in the original notice could not be finally determined at the time of the original notice (for example, because there was a dispute concerning an outstanding rent review or if the charge was a service charge collected on account and adjusted following final determination).

Validity of notice
2. The notice is not valid unless original notice contained a warning that the amount in question might subsequently be determined to be greater. In addition, the landlord is required to give this notice within three months of the date on which the amount was finally determined. If the original notice did not include that warning, or if this notice has been given late, then this notice is not valid and the landlord cannot recover the greater amount, but only the smaller amount specified in the original notice. The date of the giving of this notice may not be the date written on the notice or the date on which you actually saw it. It may, for instance, be the date on which the notice was delivered through the post to your last address known to the person giving notice. If you are in any doubt, you should seek advice immediately.

Interest
3. If interest is chargeable on the amount due, the landlord does not have to state the precise amount of interest, but he must have stated the basis on which the interest is calculated, or he will not be able to claim interest at all.

> *cont*
> ———————
> 1 The Act defines a fixed charge as (a) rent, (b) any service charge (as defined by section 18 of the Landlord and Tenant Act 1985, disregarding the words "of a dwelling") and (c) any amount payable under a tenant covenant of the tenancy providing for payment of a liquidated sum in the event of failure to comply with the covenant.
> 2 Delete alternative as appropriate.
> 3 "Landlord" for these purposes includes any person who has the right to enforce the charge.
> 4 The Schedule can be in any form, but must indicate in relation to each item the date on which it was revised, the revised amount payable and whether it is rent, service charge or a fixed charge of some other kind (in which case particulars of the nature of the charge should be given).
> 5 Delete words in brackets if not applicable. If applicable, the Schedule must state the basis on which interest is calculated (for example, rate of interest, date from which it is payable and provision of Lease or other document under which it is payable).

Remedies of persons with secondary liability

A person with a secondary liability who is required to pay the landlord will wish to recover the sums paid from the person with the ultimate liability. If the person with the secondary liability is sued by the landlord he should consider joining the person with ultimate liability as a third party to the action with a view to seeking an indemnity from him.   **13–46**

The original tenant

Where the tenancy is a *new tenancy* (see para.13–02), the original tenant ceases to be liable to the landlord under the tenancy (s.5 of the 1995 Act; see para.13–20) and so he has no need of an indemnity from subsequent assignees. (The provisions of the 1925 legislation referred to below do not apply to new tenancies: s.30 of the 1995 Act.) The original tenant will be under a continuing liability only if he has entered into an authorised guarantee agreement guaranteeing performance of the covenants by the assignee (para.13–21), in which case he will have the same right of indemnity against the assignee as any other surety would have against a principal debtor (s.16(8); and see para.13–22).   **13–47**

Where, however, the original tenant is a tenant under an *old tenancy* (para.13–02) there are three bases upon which he may seek an indemnity from persons who have the ultimate liability to pay the rent:

(1) *Direct covenant:* so far as the first assignee is concerned (i.e. the assignee to whom the original tenant sold his lease) there is probably an express covenant in the Deed of Assignment whereby the assignee covenanted to indemnify the tenant.

(2) *Implied covenant:* if there is no express covenant in the Deed of Assignment, s.77(1)(c) of the Law of Property Act 1925 will usually apply. This section imposes an implied obligation on the assignee to indemnify the original tenant in certain circumstances. Note in particular that there must be a conveyance for valuable consideration. Note also that the assignees are liable for breaches by "persons deriving title under them". A similar covenant would have been implied where the leasehold interest transferred is registered (Land Registration Act 1925, s.24(1)(b)).

Law of Property Act 1925 s.77(1) and Sch.2

13-48

77.–(1) In addition to the covenants implied under the last preceding section, there shall in the several cases in this section mentioned, be deemed to be included and implied, a covenant to the effect in this section stated, by and with such persons as are hereinafter mentioned, that is to say—

. . .

(C) In a conveyance for valuable consideration, other than a mortgage, of the entirety of the land comprised in a lease, for the residue of the term or interest created by the lease, a covenant by the assignee or joint and several covenants by the assignees (if more than one) with the conveying parties and with each of them (if more than one) in the terms set out in Part IX of the Second Schedule to this Act. Where a rent has been apportioned in respect of any land, with the consent of the lessor, the covenants in this paragraph shall be implied in the conveyance of that land in like manner as if the apportioned rent were the original rent reserved, and the lease related solely to that land.

SCHEDULE 2

PART IX: COVENANT IN A CONVEYANCE FOR VALUABLE CONSIDERATION, OTHER THAN A MORTGAGE, OR THE ENTIRETY OF THE LAND COMPRISED IN A LEASE FOR THE RESIDUE OF THE TERM OR INTEREST CREATED BY THE LEASE.

That the assignees, or the persons deriving title under them, will at all times, from the date of the conveyance or other date therein stated, duly pay all rent becoming due under the lease creating the term or interest for which the land is conveyed, and observed and perform all the covenants, agreements and conditions therein contained and thenceforth on the part of the lessees to be observed and performed.

And also will at all times, from the date aforesaid, save harmless and keep indemnified the conveying parties and their estates and effects, from and against all proceedings, costs, claims and expenses on account of any omission to pay the said rent or any breach of any of the said covenants, agreements and conditions.

Land Registration Act 1925 s.24(1)(b)

24.–(1) On the transfer, otherwise than by way of underlease, of any leasehold interest in land under this Act, unless there be an entry on the register negativing such implication, there shall be implied— **13–49**

. . .

(b)   on the part of the transferee, a covenant with the transferor, that during the residue of the term the transferee and the persons deriving title under him will pay, perform, and observe the rent, covenants, and conditions by and in the registered lease reserved and contained, and on the part of the lessee to be paid, performed, and observed, and will keep the transferor and the person deriving title under him indemnified against all actions, expenses, and claims on account of the non-payment of the said rent or any part thereof, or the reach of the said covenants or conditions or any of them.

(3) *Equitable indemnity:* In addition to any express or statutorily **13–50** implied covenant the original tenant may wish to rely upon the implied indemnity on the part of each successive assignee to indemnify the original tenant. This is based upon the equitable principle explained in *Downer Enterprises Ltd, Re* (para.13–08). The final assignee has the ultimate liability as against the original tenant (*Moule v Garrett* (1872) L.R. Exch. 101; *Beckton Dickinson UK Ltd v Zwebner* [1989] 1 E.G.L.R. 72; [1989] Q.B. 208). Where the original tenant and the assignee agreed to exclude the covenant implied by s.77 of the 1925 Act (see above) the tenant can nevertheless rely upon the equitable indemnity (*Healing Research Trustee Co Ltd, Re* [1992] 2 All E.R. 481 Ch D).

Whether the intermediate assignees remain liable under this principle to the original tenant for breaches that occur after they have divested themselves of the tenancy is not clear (*Selous Street Properties Ltd v Oronel Fabrics Ltd* (1984) 270 E.G. 643 at p.748); although the immediate assignee would be liable under the covenant implied by s.77 of the 1925 Act (see above). If the assignee had entered into a covenant with the landlord in a licence to assign or other document, the original tenant would be entitled to be subrogated to the rights of the landlord (para.13–08).

As between the original tenant and the present assignee's surety, the ultimate liability rests upon the latter. The original tenant is entitled to be subrogated to the rights of the landlord against the surety (*Kumar v Dunning* [1987] 2 All E.R. 801; *Beckton Dickinson v Zwebner*). Some doubt has been thrown on the propositions set out in *Selous* and *Beckton*—see Subrogation and non-payment of rent, Pawlowski [2007] L&TR 181.

Assignees

13-51 Where the tenancy is a new tenancy (see para.13-02), the position of an assignee who has himself assigned is the same as that of an original tenant. He ceases to be liable to the landlord under the tenancy (s.5 of the 1995 Act; see para.13-20) and so has no need of an indemnity from subsequent assignees. The assignee will be under a continuing liability only if he has entered into an authorised guarantee agreement guaranteeing performance of the covenants by the assignee, in which case he will have the same right of indemnity against the assignee as any other surety would have against a principal debtor (s.16(8)).

Where the assignee was a tenant under an old tenancy he may seek an indemnity from subsequent assignees upon the same three bases upon which an original tenant may seek an indemnity:

(1) Any direct covenant that was entered into by the assignee who took the lease from him when he assigned.
(2) The covenant implied by s.77 of the Law of Property Act 1925 or s.24(1) of the Land Registration Act 1925. This will be available only against the next assignee.
(3) The equitable indemnity explained in *Downer Enterprises Ltd, Re* (para.13-08). Presumably, as between an intermediate assignee and the final assignee, ultimate liability rests on the latter. Query the position between two intermediate assignees who had no direct relationship; is the ultimate liability on the latter?

Original tenant's surety

13-52 The original tenant's surety is no worse position than the original tenant and, in so far as he is obliged to pay the landlord, he is entitled to be subrogated to the landlord's rights and is entitled to an indemnity from the person with ultimate liability (*Selous Street Properties Ltd v Oronel Fabrics Ltd* (1984) 270 E.G. 643 at 748; see the position of Mr Morgan who was the original tenant's surety in that case). For what it is worth, he also has a right of indemnity as against the original tenant pursuant to the normal rule that the principal debtor is liable to indemnify the surety.

Contribution between sureties

If one surety pays out to the landlord, he is entitled to a contribution from his co-sureties.

13–53

Right to an overriding lease: s.19 of the 1995 Act

Section 19 of the 1995 Act deals with one of the most unsatisfactory effects of the privity of contract rule in relation to leases, i.e. the liability of the former tenant or his surety for the arrears but his inability to have possession of the property. The position now is that any person who makes full payment of an amount demanded in accordance with s.17 together with any interest payable (para.13–41) is entitled to have an overriding lease of the premises granted to him. This will allow him to obtain the property and market it. A claim to exercise the right to an overriding lease is made by a request to the landlord in writing specifying the payment by virtue of which the claimant claims to be entitled to the lease (s.19(5)). The request must be made within 12 months of the payment (s.19(5)).

13–54

Landlord and Tenant (Covenants) Act 1995 ss.19 and 20

19.–(1) Where in respect of any tenancy ("the relevant tenancy") any person ("the claimant") makes full payment of an amount which he has been duly required to pay in accordance with section 17, together with any interest payable, he shall be entitled (subject to and in accordance with this section) to have the landlord under that tenancy grant him an overriding lease of the premises demised by the tenancy.

13–55

(2) For the purposes of this section "overriding lease" means a tenancy of the reversion expectant on the relevant tenancy which—

    (a)   is granted for a term equal to the remainder of the term of the relevant tenancy plus three days or the longest period (less than three days) that will not wholly displace the landlord's reversionary interest expectant on the relevant tenancy, as the case may require; and

(b)   (subject to subsections (3) and (4) and to any modifications agreed to by the claimant and the landlord) otherwise contains the same covenants as the relevant tenancy, as they have effect immediately before the grant of the lease.

(3) An overriding lease shall not be required to reproduce any covenant of the relevant tenancy to the extent that the covenant is (in whatever terms) expressed to be a personal covenant between the landlord and the tenant under that tenancy.

(4) If any right, liability or other matter arising under a covenant of the relevant tenancy falls to be determined or otherwise operates (whether expressly or otherwise) by reference to the commencement of that tenancy—

(a)   the corresponding covenant of the overriding lease shall be so framed that that right, liability or matter falls to be determined or otherwise operates by reference to the commencement of that tenancy; but

(b)   the overriding lease shall not be required to reproduce any covenant of that tenancy to the extent that it has become spent by the time that that lease is granted.

(5) A claim to exercise the right to an overriding lease under this section is made by the claimant making a request for such a lease to the landlord; and any such request—

(a)   must be made to the landlord in writing and specify the payment by virtue of which the claimant claims to be entitled to the lease ("the qualifying payment"); and

(b)   must be so made at the time of making the qualifying payment or within the period of 12 months beginning with the date of that payment.

(6) Where the claimant duly makes such a request—

(a)   the landlord shall (subject to subsection (7)) grant and deliver to the claimant an overriding lease of the demised premises within a reasonable time of the request being received by the landlord; and

(b)   the claimant—

    (i)   shall thereupon deliver to the landlord a counterpart of the lease duly executed by the claimant, and

    (ii) shall be liable for the landlord's reasonable costs of and incidental to the grant of the lease.

(7) The landlord shall not be under any obligation to grant an overriding lease of the demised premises under this section at a time when the relevant tenancy has been determined; and a claimant shall not be entitled to the grant of such a lease if at the time when he makes his request—

(a)   the landlord has already granted such a lease and that lease remains in force; or

    (b)   another person has already duly made a request for such a lease to the landlord and that request has been neither withdrawn nor abandoned by that person.

(8) Where two or more requests are duly made on the same day, then for the purposes of subsection (7)—

    (a)   a request made by a person who was liable for the qualifying payment as a former tenant shall be treated as made before a request made by a person who was so liable as a guarantor; and

    (b)   a request made by a person whose liability in respect of the covenant in question commenced earlier than any such liability of another person shall be treated as made before a request made by that other person.

(9) Where a claimant who has duly made a request for an overriding lease under this section subsequently withdraws or abandons the request before he is granted such a lease by the landlord, the claimant shall be liable for the landlord's reasonable costs incurred in pursuance of the request down to the time of its withdrawal or abandonment; and for the purposes of this section—

    (a)   a claimant's request is withdrawn by the claimant notifying the landlord in writing that he is withdrawing his request; and

    (b)   a claimant is to be regarded as having abandoned his request if—

        (i)   the landlord has requested the claimant in writing to take, within such reasonable period as is specified in the landlord's request, all or any of the remaining steps required to be taken by the claimant before the lease can be granted, and

       (ii)   the claimant fails to comply with the landlord's request,

and is accordingly to be regarded as having abandoned it at the time when that period expires.

(10) Any request or notification under this section may be sent by post.

(11) The preceding provisions of this section shall apply where the landlord is the tenant under an overriding lease granted under this section as they apply where no such lease has been granted; and accordingly there may be two or more such leases interposed between the first such lease and the relevant tenancy.

20.—(1) For the purposes of section 1 an overriding lease shall be a new tenancy only if the relevant tenancy is a new tenancy. **13–56**

(2) Every overriding lease shall state—

    (a)   that it is a lease granted under section 19, and

    (b)   whether it is or is not a new tenancy for the purposes of section 1;

and any such statement shall comply with such requirements as may be prescribed by land registration rules under the Land Registration Act 2002.

(3) A claim that the landlord has failed to comply with subsection (6)(a) of section 19 may be made the subject of civil proceedings in like manner

as any other claim in tort for breach of statutory duty; and if the claimant under that section fails to comply with subsection (6)(b)(i) of that section he shall not be entitled to exercise any of the rights otherwise exercisable by him under the overriding lease.

(4) An overriding lease—

(a)   shall be deemed to be authorised as against the persons interested in any mortgage of the landlord's interest (however created or arising); and

(b)   shall be binding on any such persons;

and if any such person is by virtue of such a mortgage entitled to possession of the documents of title relating to the landlord's interest—

(i)   the landlord shall within one month of the execution of the lease deliver to that person the counterpart executed in pursuance of section 19(b)(i); and

(ii)   if he fails to do so, the instrument creating or evidencing the mortgage shall apply as if the obligation to deliver a counterpart were included in the terms of the mortgage as set out in that instrument.

(5) It is hereby declared—

(a)   that the fact that an overriding lease takes effect subject to the relevant tenancy shall not constitute a breach of any covenant of the lease against subletting or parting with possession of the premises demised by the lease or any part of them; and

(b)   that each of sections 16, 17 and 18 applies where the tenancy referred to in subsection (1) of that section is an overriding lease as it applies in other cases falling within that subsection.

(6) No tenancy shall be registrable under the Land Charges Act 1972 or be taken to be an estate contract within the meaning of that Act by reason of any right or obligation that may arise under section 19, and any right arising from a request made under that section shall not be capable of falling within paragraph 2 of Schedule 1 or 3 of the Land Registration Act 2002; but any such request shall be registrable under the Land Charges Act 1972, or may be the subject of a notice or caution under the Land Registration Act 2002, as if it were an estate contract.

(7) In this section—

(a)   "mortgage" includes "charge"; and

(b)   any expression which is also used in section 19 has the same meaning as in that section.

Sub-tenants: s.6 of the Law of Distress Amendment Act 1908

13-57   If the landlord does not wish to forfeit the lease, another person from whom he may obtain funds in discharge of arrears of rent is the sub-tenant. Section 6 of the Law of Distress Amendment Act 1908 entitles the landlord to serve a notice on the sub-tenant requiring that person to pay his rent to the landlord until the arrears have been paid.

Law of Distress Amendment Act 1908 s.6

In cases where the rent of the immediate tenant of the superior landlord is in arrear it shall be lawful for such superior landlord to serve upon any under tenant or lodger a notice (by registered post addressed to such under tenant or lodger upon the premises) stating the amount of such arrears of rent, and requiring all future payments of rent, whether the same has already accrued due or not, by such under tenant or lodger to be made direct to the superior landlord giving such notice until such arrears shall have been duly paid, and such notice shall operate to transfer to the superior landlord the right to recover, receive, and give a discharge for such rent.

Part 3

Termination by Notice

CHAPTER 14

LANDLORD'S NOTICES TO TERMINATE

. . . .

Where Pt II of the 1954 Act applies to the tenancy, the method **14–01** by which it is brought to an end is service of a notice under s.25. As will be seen, the notice is served by "the competent landlord", who is not necessarily the tenant's immediate landlord. Where a tenancy has continued under s.24 of the Act but has ceased to be a tenancy to which the Act applies (perhaps because the tenant has sublet the whole; see para.2-06), the tenancy is determined in accordance with s.24(3)(a) (see para.14-27 below).

Where the Landlord does serve a s25 notice it will be necessary to state whether they are seeking to oppose the grant of a new tenancy and if so, which of the statutory grounds they rely upon (the grounds are dealt with in Chapter 17).

Where the 1954 Act has never applied and the tenancy is a periodic tenancy, the common law rules relating to notices to quit apply (para.14-28 below). Break clauses are dealt with at para.14-43.

Section 25 notices

A lease of business premises to which Pt II of the Landlord and **14–02** Tenant Act 1954 applies may be brought to an end by the landlord by a termination notice served pursuant to s.25 of the 1954 Act. The s.25 notice does not of itself bring the tenancy to an end. The tenancy is continued by virtue of s.24 (para.1-02) until the tenancy is brought to an end by order of the court. However, once a landlord has served a s.25 notice, he may apply to the court for the continuation tenancy to be terminated (see Ch.22) if he has a ground for termination under s.30 (Ch.17). Alternatively, if he wants to keep the tenant but on new terms, the landlord can apply to the court for a new tenancy to be ordered (Ch.24).

Where a s.25 notice is served, the tenant may apply to the court for a new tenancy but must do so by the date specified as the termination date in the s.25 notice or by any agreed extension of that date. If the tenant fails to make an application in time, the tenancy will come to an end on the date specified as the termination date in the notice (or agreed extension date) and the landlord will be entitled to possession. (See further para.24–08.)

If the tenant makes an application to the court within the times specified, the tenancy will continue pursuant to s.24 of the 1954 Act, as a continuation tenancy, until three months after the claim for a new lease has finally been disposed of (ss.25(1) and 64; as to the continuation tenancy see para.1–01).

The landlord may not serve a s.25 notice if the tenant has made a request for a new tenancy by service of a notice pursuant to s.26 of the 1954 Act (s.26(4)).

The landlord is not prevented from serving a s.25 notice by prior service of forfeiture proceedings. If as a result of the notice the lease comes to an end before the forfeiture proceedings have been completed, the landlord can seek possession on the basis of that notice (*Baglarbasi v Deed Method Ltd* [1991] 2 E.G.L.R. 71).

Landlord and Tenant Act 1954 s.25

14–03   **25.**–(1) The landlord may terminate a tenancy to which this Part of this Act applies by a notice given to the tenant in the prescribed form specifying the date at which the tenancy is to come to an end (hereinafter referred to as "the date of termination"):

    Provided that this subsection has effect subject to the provisions of section 29B(4) of this Act and Part IV of this Act as to the interim continuation of tenancies pending the disposal of applications to the court.

    (2) Subject to the provisions of the next following subsection, a notice under this section shall not have effect unless it is given not more than twelve nor less than six months before the date of termination specified therein.

(3) In the case of a tenancy which apart from this Act could have been brought to an end by notice to quit given by the landlord—

(a) the date of termination specified in a notice under this section shall not be earlier than the earliest date on which apart from this Part of this Act the tenancy could have been brought to an end by notice to quit given by the landlord on the date of the giving of the notice under this section; and

(b) where apart from this Part of this Act more than six months' notice to quit would have been required to bring the tenancy to an end, the last foregoing subsection shall have effect with the substitution for twelve months of a period six months longer than the length of notice to quit which would have been required as aforesaid.

(4) In the case of any other tenancy, a notice under this section shall not specify a date of termination earlier than the date on which apart from this Part of this Act the tenancy would have come to an end by effluxion of time.

Prescribed forms

There are a number of new prescribed forms (made under s.66 **14–04** of the 1954 Act) dealing with various different situations (The Landlord and Tenant Act 1954 Pt 2 (Notices) (England and Wales) Regulations 2004). A full list is set out in Sch.1 to these regulations (see Appendix 2); and the forms themselves are in Sch.2. To obtain a copy of any of these forms using the internet simply type in the name of the regulations into a search engine. The two main forms that will be used in most cases are:

- Form 1—To be used where the landlord is *not* opposed to the grant of a new tenancy (para.14–05; Form 17 of this book).
- Form 2—To be used where the landlord *is opposed* to the grant of a new tenancy (para.14–06, Form 18 of this book).

The landlord must use the appropriate form listed in the Schedule or "a form substantially to the same effect" (reg.2(2)). The notes on the back of each form are part of the prescribed form and must be used. If they are omitted they will not be regarded as being in "a form substantially to same effect". These are important parts of the form and must be included. The fact that the tenant is not misled by their omission is irrelevant (*Sabella Ltd v Montgomery* [1998] 1 E.G.L.R. 65 CA).

14–05

Form 17

Form 1

LANDLORD'S NOTICE ENDING A BUSINESS TENANCY WITH PROPOSALS FOR A NEW ONE

Section 25 of the Landlord and Tenant Act 1954

IMPORTANT NOTE FOR THE LANDLORD: If you are willing to grant a new tenancy, complete this form and send it to the tenant. If you wish to oppose the grant of a new tenancy, use form 2 in Schedule 2 to the Landlord and Tenant Act 1954, Part 2 (Notices) Regulations 2004 or, where the tenant may be entitled to acquire the freehold or an extended lease, form 7 in that Schedule, instead of this form.

To:

....

....

....

(*insert name and address of tenant*)

From:

....

....

....

(*insert name and address of landlord*)

1. This notice applies to the following property: (*insert address or description of property*)

....

2. I am giving you notice under section 25 of the Landlord and Tenant Act 1954 to end your tenancy on (*insert date*).

....

3. I am not opposed to granting you a new tenancy. You will find my proposals for the new tenancy, which we can discuss, in the Schedule to this notice.

cont

---

cont

4. If we cannot agree on all the terms of a new tenancy, either you or I may ask the court to order the grant of a new tenancy and settle the terms on which we cannot agree.

5. If you wish to ask the court for a new tenancy you must do so by the date in paragraph 2, unless we agree in writing to a later date and do so before the date in paragraph 2.

6. Please send all correspondence about this notice to:

Name:

....

Address:

....

....

Signed: ....   Date: ....

*[Landlord] *[On behalf of the landlord]

*[Mortgagee] *[On behalf of the mortgagee]

(delete if inapplicable)

SCHEDULE

LANDLORD'S PROPOSALS FOR A NEW TENANCY

(*attach or insert proposed terms of the new tenancy*)

IMPORTANT NOTE FOR THE TENANT

This Notice is intended to bring your tenancy to an end. If you want to continue to occupy your property after the date specified in paragraph 2 you must act quickly. If you are in any doubt about the action that you should take, get advice immediately from a solicitor or a surveyor.

cont

cont

The landlord is prepared to offer you a new tenancy and has set out proposed terms in the Schedule to this notice. You are not bound to accept these terms. They are merely suggestions as a basis for negotiation. In the event of disagreement, ultimately the court would settle the terms of the new tenancy.

It would be wise to seek professional advice before agreeing to accept the landlord's terms or putting forward your own proposals.

NOTES

The sections mentioned below are sections of the Landlord and Tenant Act 1954, as amended, (most recently by the Regulatory Reform (Business Tenancies) (England and Wales) Order 2003).

Ending of tenancy and grant of new tenancy

This notice is intended to bring your tenancy to an end on the date given in paragraph 2. Section 25 contains rules about the date that the landlord can put in that paragraph.

However, your landlord is prepared to offer you a new tenancy and has set out proposals for it in the Schedule to this notice (section 25(8)). You are not obliged to accept these proposals and may put forward your own.

If you and your landlord are unable to agree terms either one of you may apply to the court. You may not apply to the court if your landlord has already done so (section 24(2A)). If you wish to apply to the court you must do so by the date given in paragraph 2 of this notice, unless you and your landlord have agreed in writing to extend the deadline (sections 29A and 29B).

The court will settle the rent and other terms of the new tenancy or those on which you and your landlord cannot agree (sections 34 and 35). If you apply to the court your tenancy will continue after the date shown in paragraph 2 of this notice while your application is being considered (section 24).

If you are in any doubt about what action you should take, get advice immediately from a solicitor or a surveyor.

Negotiating a new tenancy

Most tenancies are renewed by negotiation. You and your landlord may agree in writing to extend the deadline for making an application to the court while negotiations continue. Either you or your landlord can ask the court to fix the rent that you will have to pay while the tenancy continues (sections 24A to 24D).

You may only stay in the property after the date in paragraph 2 (or if we have agreed in writing to a later date, that date), if by then you or the landlord has asked the court to order the grant of a new tenancy.

If you do try to agree a new tenancy with your landlord remember:

cont

cont

- that your present tenancy will not continue after the date in paragraph 2 of this notice without the agreement in writing mentioned above, unless you have applied to the court or your landlord has done so, and

- that you will lose your right to apply to the court once the deadline in paragraph 2 of this notice has passed, unless there is a written agreement extending the deadline.

Validity of this notice

The landlord who has given you this notice may not be the landlord to whom you pay your rent (sections 44 and 67). This does not necessarily mean that the notice is invalid.

If you have any doubts about whether this notice is valid, get advice immediately from a solicitor or a surveyor.

Further information

An explanation of the main points to consider when renewing or ending a business tenancy, "Renewing and Ending Business Leases: a Guide for Tenants and Landlords", can be found at http://www.odpm.gov.uk/ Printed copies of the explanation, but not of this form, are available from 1st June 2004 from Free Literature, PO Box 236, Wetherby, West Yorkshire, LS23 7NB (0870 1226 236).

Form 18   14–06

Form 2

LANDLORD'S NOTICE ENDING A BUSINESS TENANCY AND REASONS FOR REFUSING A NEW ONE

Section 25 of the Landlord and Tenant Act 1954

IMPORTANT NOTE FOR THE LANDLORD: If you are willing to grant a new tenancy, complete this form and send it to the tenant. If you wish to oppose the grant of a new tenancy, use form 2 in Schedule 2 to the Landlord and Tenant Act 1954, Part 2 (Notices) Regulations 2004 or, where the tenant may be entitled to acquire the freehold or an extended lease, form 7 in that Schedule, instead of this form.

To:

....

....

cont

cont

....

(*insert name and address of tenant*)

From:

....

....

....

(*insert name and address of landlord*)

1. This notice applies to the following property: (*insert address or description of property*)

....

2. I am giving you notice under section 25 of the Landlord and Tenant Act 1954 to end your tenancy on (*insert date*).

....

3. I am opposed to the grant of a new tenancy.

4. You may ask the court to order the grant of a new tenancy. If you do, I will oppose your application on the ground(s) mentioned in paragraph(s)* of section 30(1) of that Act. I draw your attention to the Table in the Notes below, which sets out all the grounds of opposition.

*(*insert letter(s) of the paragraph(s) relied on*)

....

5. If you wish to ask the court for a new tenancy you must do so before the date in paragraph 2 unless, before that date, we agree in writing to a later date.

6. I can ask the court to order the ending of your tenancy without granting you a new tenancy. I may have to pay you compensation if I have relied only on one or more of the grounds mentioned in paragraphs (e), (f) and (g) of section 30(1). If I ask the court to end your tenancy, you can challenge my application.

7. Please send all correspondence about this notice to:

Name:

....

cont

cont

Address:

....

....

Signed: .... Date: ....

*[Landlord] *[On behalf of the landlord]

*[Mortgagee] *[On behalf of the mortgagee]

(delete if inapplicable)

IMPORTANT NOTE FOR THE TENANT

This notice is intended to bring your tenancy to an end on the date specified in paragraph 2.

Your landlord is not prepared to offer you a new tenancy. You will not get a new tenancy unless you successfully challenge in court the grounds on which your landlord opposes the grant of a new tenancy.

If you want to continue to occupy your property you must act quickly. The notes below should help you to decide what action you now need to take. If you want to challenge your landlord's refusal to renew your tenancy, get advice immediately from a solicitor or a surveyor.

NOTES

The sections mentioned below are sections of the Landlord and Tenant Act 1954, as amended, (most recently by the Regulatory Reform (Business Tenancies) (England and Wales) Order 2003).

Ending of your tenancy

This notice is intended to bring your tenancy to an end on the date given in paragraph 2. Section 25 contains rules about the date that the landlord can put in that paragraph.

Your landlord is not prepared to offer you a new tenancy. If you want a new tenancy you will need to apply to the court for a new tenancy and successfully challenge the landlord's grounds for opposition (see the section below headed "*Landlord's opposition to new tenancy*"). If you wish to apply to the court you must do so before the date given in paragraph 2 of this notice, unless you and your landlord have agreed in writing, before that date, to extend the deadline (sections 29A and 29B).

cont

If you apply to the court your tenancy will continue after the date given in paragraph 2 of this notice while your application is being considered (section 24). You may not apply to the court if your landlord has already done so (section 24(2A) and (2B)).

You may only stay in the property after the date given in paragraph 2 (or such later date as you and the landlord may have agreed in writing) if before that date you have asked the court to order the grant of a new tenancy or the landlord has asked the court to order the ending of your tenancy without granting you a new one.

If you are in any doubt about what action you should take, get advice immediately from a solicitor or a surveyor.

Landlord's opposition to new tenancy

If you apply to the court for a new tenancy, the landlord can only oppose your application on one or more of the grounds set out in section 30(1). If you match the letter(s) specified in paragraph 4 of this notice with those in the first column in the Table below, you can see from the second column the ground(s) on which the landlord relies.

Paragraph of section 30(1)	Grounds
(a)	Where under the current tenancy the tenant has any obligations as respects the repair and maintenance of the holding, that the tenant ought not to be granted a new tenancy in view of the state of repair of the holding, being a state resulting from the tenant's failure to comply with the said obligations.
(b)	That the tenant ought not to be granted a new tenancy in view of his persistent delay in paying rent which has become due.
(c)	That the tenant ought not to be granted a new tenancy in view of other substantial breaches by him of his obligations under the current tenancy, or for any other reason connected with the tenant's use or management of the holding.
(d)	That the landlord has offered and is willing to provide or secure the provision of alternative accommodation for the tenant, that the terms on which the alternative accommodation is available are reasonable having regard to the terms of the current tenancy and to all other relevant circumstances, and that the accommodation and the time at which it will be available are suitable for the tenant's requirements (including the requirement to preserve *cont*

cont

goodwill) having regard to the nature and class of his business and to the situation and extent of, and facilities afforded by, the holding.

(e) Where the current tenancy was created by the sub-letting of part only of the property comprised in a superior tenancy and the landlord is the owner of an interest in reversion expectant on the termination of that superior tenancy, that the aggregate of the rents reasonably obtainable on separate lettings of the holding and the remainder of that property would be substantially less than the rent reasonably obtainable on a letting of that property as a whole, that on the termination of the current tenancy the landlord requires possession of the holding for the purposes of letting or otherwise disposing of the said property as a whole, and that in view thereof the tenant ought not to be granted a new tenancy.

(f) That on the termination of the current tenancy the landlord intends to demolish or reconstruct the premises comprised in the holding or a substantial part of those premises or to carry out substantial work of construction on the holding or part thereof and that he could not reasonably do so without obtaining possession of the holding.

(g) On the termination of the current tenancy the landlord intends to occupy the holding for the purposes, or partly for the purposes, of a business to be carried on by him therein, or as his residence.

In this Table "the holding" means the property that is the subject of the tenancy.

In ground (e), "the landlord is the owner of an interest in reversion expectant on the termination of that superior tenancy" means that the landlord has an interest in the property that will entitle him or her, when your immediate landlord's tenancy comes to an end, to exercise certain rights and obligations in relation to the property that are currently exercisable by your immediate landlord.

If the landlord relies on ground (f), the court can sometimes still grant a new tenancy if certain conditions set out in section 31A are met.

If the landlord relies on ground (g), please note that "the landlord" may have an extended meaning. Where a landlord has a controlling interest in a company then either the landlord or the company can rely on ground (g). Where the landlord is a company and a person has a controlling interest in that company then either of them can rely on ground (g) (section 30(1A) and (1B)). A person has a "controlling interest" in a company if, had he been a company, the other company would have been its subsidiary (section 46(2)).

cont

---

cont

The landlord must normally have been the landlord for at least five years before he or she can rely on ground (g).

Compensation

If you cannot get a new tenancy solely because one or more of grounds (e), (f) and (g) applies, you may be entitled to compensation under section 37. If your landlord has opposed your application on any of the other grounds as well as (e), (f) or (g) you can only get compensation if the court's refusal to grant a new tenancy is based solely on one or more of grounds (e), (f) and (g). In other words, you cannot get compensation under section 37 if the court has refused your tenancy on *other* grounds, even if one or more of grounds (e), (f) and (g) also applies.

If your landlord is an authority possessing compulsory purchase powers (such as a local authority) you may be entitled to a disturbance payment under Part 3 of the Land Compensation Act 1973.

Validity of this notice

The landlord who has given you this notice may not be the landlord to whom you pay your rent (sections 44 and 67). This does not necessarily mean that the notice is invalid.

If you have any doubts about whether this notice is valid, get advice immediately from a solicitor or a surveyor.

Further information

An explanation of the main points to consider when renewing or ending a business tenancy, "Renewing and Ending Business Leases: a Guide for Tenants and Landlords", can be found at *http://www.odpm.gov.uk/* Printed copies of the explanation, but not of this form, are available from 1st June 2004 from Free Literature, PO Box 236, Wetherby, West Yorkshire, LS23 7NB (0870 1226 236).

Completing the notice

14-07   The landlord must be careful to complete the s.25 notice correctly. If it is defective in any material respect, the court may hold it to be invalid (*Pearson v Alyo* [1990] 1 E.G.L.R. 114):

> " . . . it must be emphasised that the validity of a section 25 notice is to be judged, and judged objectively, at the date at which it is given. The question is not whether the inaccuracy actually prejudices the particular person to whom the notice is given but whether it is capable of

prejudicing a reasonable tenant in the position of that person"

Some general points are now made about the notices. Further points in relation to the main different types of notice are dealt with below (paras 14–14 and 14–15).

In completing the notice the landlord should have regard to the following points.

Name and address of tenant

As will be seen below under the heading "The competent **14–08** landlord; sub-tenants" on para.14–16, the tenant upon whom the notice is to be served will not necessarily be the immediate tenant of the person serving the notice. It is therefore generally essential to serve a notice under s.40(1) of the 1954 Act (which is a notice to the tenant requiring him to provide information about sub-tenants) before serving the s.25 notice (see Ch.16; para.16–02).

A business tenant whose lease has been forfeited for breach of covenant but whose application for relief has yet to be determined is a "tenant" for the purposes of Pt II of the 1954 Act and so may apply for a new tenancy under the Act (*Meadows v Clerical and General Life Assurance Society* [1980] 1 All E.R. 454). A s.25 notice may therefore be served upon a tenant whose lease has been forfeited but who has made an application for relief. An order for possession based on forfeiture, which has not yet been entered, does not destroy the sub-tenant's right to apply for relief and thus it is necessary to serve a s.25 notice on the sub-tenant in order to terminate the sub-tenancy (*Cadogan v Dimovic* [1984] 2 All E.R. 168).

Where there are joint tenants and the business is or has been run as a partnership, the s.25 notice may be given to "the business tenants" (s.41A(4) of the 1954 Act; see para.2–26). Subject to that provision, the notice should be served on all the joint tenants. If it is not, the notice will be defective unless the irregularity is waived (*Norton v Charles Deane Productions Ltd* (1969) 214 E.G. 559). As to waiver, see *Kammins Ballrooms* (para.24–12).

Service of a s.25 notice on an occupier who is a licensee rather than a tenant does not necessarily mean that the landlord is estopped from denying that the Act applies. (*Wroe v Exmos Cover Ltd* [2000] 1 E.G.L.R. 66 CA.

> "The appellant applied for a new tenancy because he wanted a new tenancy. The landlord's section 25 notice provided the opportunity to make the application, but it did not, in any sense, encourage the appellant to take that course. It was made clear to him in the notice itself that an application for a new tenancy would be opposed." (Chadwick LJ).)

Name and address of landlord/agent

14–09   It is important to note that the person to give the notice is not necessarily the tenant's immediate landlord. The proper person to give the notice is the person defined by s.44 of the 1954 Act as being "the landlord" and who is often referred to as the "competent landlord". This subject is dealt with in detail below (see para.14–16).

The correct person must be named as the landlord (*Morrow v Nadeem* [1987] 1 All E.R. 237). *Query*: what will happen if the name is not stated correctly or at all but any reasonable tenant would have known clearly what was intended? (See para.14–07; and compare *Lay v Ackerman* [2004] EWCA Civ 184 where a counter-notice served under s.45 of the Leasehold Reform, Housing and Urban Development Act 1993 was valid even though the notice wrongly identified the landlord. The landlord was named as "Portman Family Collateral Settlements" instead of "Portman Family Settled Estates". A reasonable person in the position of the tenant would know that the notice was sent by and with the authority of the landlord.)

Where two or more persons jointly own the landlord's interest, all such persons must join in the giving of the notice (*Pearson v Alyo* [1990] 1 E.G.L.R. 114).

Where there are a number of properties all subject to one tenancy but which are separately owned by different landlords, see para.14–22.

The expression "the landlord" in s.44 of the 1954 Act refers to the legal owner or owners and not to the equitable owner. Thus, a notice served by an equitable owner of the property will be

invalid even if he owns the whole of the equity (*Pearson v Alyo*).
A notice served by a limited liability company, whereas the
landlord is in fact that company's parent company, is invalid
(*Yamaha-Kemble Music (UK) Ltd v ARC Properties Ltd* [1990] 1
E.G.L.R. 261).

Where the landlord's interest is subject to a mortgage and the
mortgagee has entered into possession or a receiver has been
appointed and is in receipt of the rents, the mortgagee is the
person to serve the notice (s.67 of the 1954 Act). The notice
should be signed by the competent landlord or his duly
authorised agent (*Tennant v LCC* (1957) 121 J.P. 428).

Landlord and Tenant Act 1954 s.67

67.–Anything authorised or required by the provisions of this Act, other   **14–10**
than subsection (3) of section 40, to be done at any time by, to or with the
landlord, or a landlord of a specified description, shall, if at that time the
interest of the landlord in question is subject to a mortgage and the
mortgagee is in possession or a receiver appointed by the mortgagee or
by the courts is in receipt of the rents and profits, be deemed to be
authorised or required to be done by, to or with the mortgagee instead of
that landlord.

The property

Paragraph 1 of each form requires the landlord to specify the   **14–11**
property. The notice must relate to the whole of the property
comprised in the tenancy (*Southport Old Links Ltd v Naylor*
[1985] 1 E.G.L.R. 66 CA). Where the reversion is severed see
para.14–22. If the tenant holds different parts of the property
on different tenancies from the landlord, it will be necessary to
serve a separate s.25 notice in respect of each part. However,
it is possible for one document to create more than one
tenancy (*Moss v Mobil Oil Co Ltd* [1988] 1 E.G.L.R. 71).

Date of termination

The notice must specify the date at which the tenancy is to   **14–12**
come to an end ("the date of termination"): s.25(1). The notice
must be given not more than 12 and not less than six months
before the date of termination specified therein (s.25(2)).
Where the lease is for a fixed term, the date may not be earlier
than the expiry date in the lease (s.25(4)). In the case of a
periodic tenancy or where there is a break clause s.25(3)
specifies that where, apart from Pt II of the 1954 Act, the

tenancy could have been brought to an end by notice to quit, the date of termination specified in the notice must not be earlier than the date upon which it could have been brought to an end by a notice to quit served on the same date as the s.25 notice (s.25(3)(a)). Where, under the terms of the tenancy, more than six months' notice to quit would have been required to bring the tenancy to an end, the maximum period in which the s.25 notice may be given is the period specified in the lease plus six months (s.25(3)(b)). As to service of a s.25 notice see para.14–23. (Note that: if the tenant applies to the court for a new tenancy within the time limits prescribed (see para.24–08), the tenancy will not come to an end on the date specified in the notice but will continue for three months after final disposal of the case unless the notice date is later: ss.25(1), 64; see further para.27–02.) See also para.23–09 as to agreed extensions of time. Depending upon the wording of the break clause it is possible that service of a s.25 notice can double up as a notice operating the break clause (*Scholl Manufacturing Co Ltd v Clifton (Slim-Line) Ltd* [1967] Ch. 41; see further para.14–43). If it does not a break notice in addition to a s.25 notice will need to be served.

Date of notice

14–13   The form contains provision for the date of the notice to be stated. However, it must be remembered that it is the actual date of service that is relevant to any calculations as to time which may not be the same as the date stated on the notice (as to service of the notice see para.14–23).

Landlord not opposing new tenancy: Form 1

Landlord and Tenant Act 1954 s.25(8)

14–14   **25.**–(8) A notice under this section which states that the landlord is not opposed to the grant of a new tenancy to the tenant shall not have effect unless it sets out the landlord's proposals as to–

(a)   the property to be comprised in the new tenancy (being either the whole or part of the property comprised in the current tenancy);

(b)   the rent to be payable under the new tenancy; and

(c)   the other terms of the new tenancy.

A landlord who is not opposed to a new tenancy must, in his s.25 notice, set out his proposals as to:

- The property to be comprised in the new tenancy, being either the whole or part of the property comprised in the tenancy.
- The rent to be payable under the new tenancy.
- The other terms of the new tenancy.

This requirement is almost identical to the requirement on tenants to provide information in s.26 requests (see para.15-05). The reason for introducing a similar requirement in relation to s.25 notices was explained by the ODPM in its commentary on the changes:

> "This will help to speed up negotiations for the new lease and hence overall renewal procedures . . . However, there is a potential danger that the tenant may think that he or she is bound to accept the landlord's proposals. The new section 25 notice will therefore contain a 'health warning' explaining in plain English that the landlord's proposal are merely an opening bid in the negotiations and do not bind either party" (ODPM).

In order to avoid the possibility that a letter of acceptance by the tenant in response to the notice could give rise to a contract, para.3 of the notice states:

> "I am not opposed to granting you a new tenancy. You will find my proposals for the new tenancy, *which we can discuss*, in the Schedule to this notice." (emphasis added.)

The notes for the tenant in the notice also state that the proposals made by the landlord "are merely suggestions as a basis for negotiation".

The amount of detail required in relation to the proposals is not made clear in the section but something equivalent to heads of terms is no doubt sufficient.

Landlord opposed to a new tenancy: Form 2

Landlord and Tenant Act 1954 s.25(7)

25.–(7) A notice under this section which states that the landlord is opposed to the grant of a new tenancy to the tenant shall not have effect unless it also specifies one or more of the grounds specified in section 30(1) of this Act as the ground or grounds for his opposition.

14–15

As stated above, where a landlord opposes the grant of a new tenancy he must use Form 2, which states that the landlord is opposed to a new tenancy (para.3). The notice must also state the ground relied upon by reference to the relevant paragraph in s.30 (para.4). See Ch.17 for the various grounds. The notice contains a summary of all the grounds.

The notice cannot be amended at a subsequent date to insert a new ground. It is therefore important to insert the correct ground. The landlord must have an honest belief in the ground stated. If he does not have such a belief, the notice will be a nullity (*Betty's Cafes Ltd v Phillips Furnishing Stores Ltd* [1959] A.C. 20, dictum of Lord Denning at pp.51 and 52; *Rous, Earl of Stradbroke v Mitchell* [1991] 1 All E.R. 676—a case under the Agricultural Holdings Act 1986). But if the notice is given in good faith, the fact that the landlord is a different person at the date of the hearing does not matter. A s.25 notice is like a pleading (*British Waterways Board v Marks* [1963] 1 W.L.R. 1008).

The notice must be clear. In *Barclays Bank plc v Bee* [2001] EWCA Civ 1126; [2002] 1 W.L.R. 332 the landlord's solicitors served two inconsistent s.25 notices, both contained in the same envelope. The first said that the landlord would oppose under s.30(1) but did not specify a ground. The second said the landlord would not oppose! Neither notice was valid. A third notice served subsequently was therefore valid.

The "competent landlord": sub-tenants

14-16 As stated above, the "landlord" who is required to serve the s.25 notice is not necessarily the tenant's immediate landlord. The person who is required to serve the notice is "the landlord" as defined by s.44 of the 1954 Act and is generally known as "the competent landlord" (a term used in Sch.6 of the 1954 Act; see para.26–28). Depending upon the circumstances, he may be the immediate landlord or a superior landlord. Thus, a landlord will often find himself having to serve a s.25 notice on a sub-tenant.

Landlord and Tenant Act 1954 s.44

14-17 44.—(1) Subject to subsections (1A) and (2) below, in this Part of this Act the expression "the landlord" in relation to a tenancy (in this section referred to as "the relevant tenancy"), means the person (whether or not he is the immediate landlord) who is the owner of that interest in the property comprised in the relevant tenancy which for the time being fulfils the following conditions, that is to say—

(a) that it is an interest in reversion expectant (whether immediately or not) on the termination of the relevant tenancy, and

(b) that it is either the fee simple or a tenancy which will not come to an end within fourteen months by effluxion of time and, if it is such a tenancy, that no notice has been given by virtue of which it will come to an end within fourteen months or any further time by which it may be continued under section 36(2) or section 64 of this Act, and is not itself in reversion expectant (whether immediately or not) on an interest which fulfils those conditions.

(1A) The reference in subsection (1) above to a person who is the owner of an interest such as is mentioned in that subsection is to be construed, where different persons own such interests in different parts of the property, as a reference to all those persons collectively.

(2) References in this Part of this Act to a notice to quit given by the landlord are references to a notice to quit given by the immediate landlord.

(3) The provisions of the Sixth Schedule to this Act shall have effect for the application of this Part of this Act to cases where the immediate landlord of the tenant is not the owner of the fee simple in respect of the holding.

By virtue of s.44 the immediate landlord of any particular tenant is only the competent landlord and may serve a s.25 notice on him only if: **14–18**

(1) he is the freehold owner of the property; or

(2) he is a leasehold owner whose own tenancy will *not* come to an end by effluxion of time within 14 months or less of service of the notice; or

(3) he is a leasehold owner whose own tenancy would come to an end by effluxion of time within 14 months were it not for the continuation provisions of the Act (see para.1–02) but no notice has been served upon him (under s.25 or s.24(3); see para.14–27) and he has himself not served a s.26 request or any other notice that would bring his tenancy to an end within 14 months or any further time by which the tenancy might be continued whilst an application for a new tenancy was proceeding.

If the immediate landlord does not fall into any of these categories he will not be the competent landlord and may not serve a s.25 notice. That landlord's own immediate landlord may be the person who is the competent landlord. If so, he may serve the s.25 notice on the person whose contractual tenancy has expired or is due to expire. If not, the process of finding the correct person to serve the notice is continued on up the chain. There can be only one competent landlord at any one time in relation to any particular tenancy. He is the first person in the chain upwards from the tenancy in question who has either the freehold or the leasehold interest referred to above.

Any s.25 notice given by the competent landlord binds the interest of any mesne landlord (i.e. any landlord in the chain between the competent landlord and the tenant in question) notwithstanding that he has not consented to the giving of the notice (Sch.6 para.3(1); para.26-28) but the mesne landlord is entitled to compensation from the competent landlord for any loss arising in consequence of the giving of the notice if he has not been asked to consent or has reasonably refused (Sch.6 para.4(1)). If the competent landlord applies to any mesne landlord for his consent to the service of a s.25 notice, that consent may not be unreasonably withheld but may be given subject to any conditions that may be reasonable (including conditions as to the modification of the proposed notice or as to the payment of compensation by the competent landlord), any dispute being decided by the court (para.4(2)(3)).

14-19 Schedule 6 of the 1954 Act contains a procedure for ensuring that any superior landlords who have an interest in the proceedings are informed of notices that are served. If the competent landlord's interest in the property is a tenancy, which will come or can be brought to an end within 16 months (or any further time by which it may be continued under s.36(2) (see para.26-34) or s.64 (see para.27-02); i.e. in effect until after the application has been completed) and he serves a s.25 notice on the tenant or is himself served with a s.26 request (see Ch.15), the competent landlord must forthwith send a copy of the notice to his immediate landlord. Any superior landlord who is himself a tenant and has received such a notice must forthwith send a copy of any such notice that he has received to his immediate landlord (Sch.6 para.7; para.26-29).

The fact that the immediate landlord is not "the competent landlord" does not mean that he ceases to be entitled to the rent from the tenant. The concept of the competent landlord is only relevant to the right to renew under the Act. As long as the immediate landlord and the tenant continue in their relationship as such, the rent is payable and the covenants are enforceable between them.

Where the landlord wants the property back, he should serve the s.25 notice on the tenant first, and then a s.25 notice on the sub-tenant. This is because until the tenant receives a s.25 notice he remains "the landlord" within the meaning of s.44 as against the sub-tenant. When the tenant receives the s.25 notice, he ceases to be "the landlord".

If on the other hand the landlord does not want the property back but does want to sort out some new terms with the tenant, in order to avoid having two direct tenants in the future, he should serve one s.25 notice on the tenant; and inform the tenant that he intends to rely upon s.32(2). As a matter of general principle, the tenant is only entitled to a new tenancy of "the holding", i.e. the part he occupies (see para.26–05). However, under s.32(2) the landlord can require "any new tenancy ordered ... to be a tenancy of the whole of the property comprised in the current tenancy" (see further para.26–07). Part 56 of the CPR sets out the time at which the landlord is required to notify the tenant of his intention to rely upon s.32 during the course of the proceedings (see para.24–25 and 24–32) but it is suggested that the landlord should do this at the earliest opportunity, such as when the s.25 notice is served.

Change in person who is "competent landlord"

It will be apparent that the relationship between the parties **14–20** may change between the date upon which the s.25 notice is served and the final conclusion of the case. For example, a leasehold owner who was a competent landlord when he served the s.25 notice may not be so the day afterwards if he is then served with a s.25 notice in respect of his own tenancy. It will be seen that all further steps must be taken by or in relation to the "competent landlord". In particular, the proceedings for a new lease must be served on the competent landlord. If the identity of that person has changed, the person to be served with the proceedings will also have changed. Thus, a tenant applying for a new tenancy may be required to bring his proceedings against someone other than the person who served the s.25 notice (see further para.24–19). This is a point that needs to be borne in mind by all parties throughout the renewal procedure and is referred to again in the relevant parts of this book.

A landlord who serves a s.25 notice on his tenant and then serves a s.26 notice requesting a new tenancy on his own landlord (thus bringing to an end his tenancy within 14 months or within such further period that might occur prior to completion of proceedings for a new lease) so that he thereby ceases to be the "competent landlord" must inform the tenant of the change in circumstances. If he does not do so, he will be estopped from denying that he is the competent landlord in proceedings brought against him by the tenant. The estoppel will not, however, affect the true competent landlord (see *Shelley v United Artists Corp Ltd* [1990] 1 E.G.L.R. 103 and further at para.16–08 for the ability of the tenant to serve a notice upon the landlord requesting information as to his interest).

Where there is a change in the competent landlord, within two months of the giving of the s.25 notice, the new competent landlord may give to the tenant a notice in prescribed form (see para.A2–01) that he withdraws the notice previously given and the s.25 notice then ceases to have effect. However, the new competent landlord may serve a fresh notice of his own. (Sch.6 para.6; para.26–29.) He may wish to do so if he wishes to rely upon an objection to a new tenancy that was not stated in the original s.25 notice.

Finding out about the occupants

14–21 We have seen how the "competent landlord" is not necessarily the immediate landlord of any particular tenant. This will often present a problem because the various landlords/tenants will not necessarily know the existence of each other. In order to discover the relationship between the respective parties in the chain, s.40 of the Act provides for the service by a landlord of a notice in prescribed form requiring the recipient to give information relating to his tenancy. By service of such notices the landlord can discover whether or not he is the "competent landlord", i.e. whether he fulfils the definition of "landlord" within s.44 so that he may serve a s.25 notice. Notices under s.40 are dealt with in Ch.16.

(There are similar provisions permitting tenants to serve notices, requesting information, on their immediate and superior landlords: also dealt with in Ch.16.)

Divided reversions

Where there are a number of properties all subject to one tenancy but that are separately owned by different landlords, a difficult problem arises: should each landlord serve a separate s.25 notice in respect of his part; or should all the landlords join together to serve one notice? In *M&P Enterprises (London) Ltd v Norfolk Square Hotels Ltd* [1994] 1 E.G.L.R. 129 it was held that the landlords should join together in serving one notice. Although in theory a number of notices might be treated together as one notice, the service of a number of documents was more likely to mislead. In that case four separate notices served were, on the facts, not capable of being read as a single notice and were invalid because they did not make it clear to the tenant whether the tenancy was being treated as a single tenancy. He might have thought that he could apply for new tenancies in respect of such of the parts as he desired to retain.

14–22

On a complicated set of facts this case confirms that where the reversionary interest is severed then, in order to bring a tenancy to an end under Part II, all the reversioners must act together. Service of a s25 notice by one reversioner is defective. This is because even though the reversion is severed there still remains one tenancy (*EDF Energy Networks (EPN) Plc v BOH* Ltd [2009] EWHC 3193 (Ch D). This is now made clear in s44(1A) of the 1954 Act.

Service of the s.25 notice

Landlord and Tenant Act 1927 s.23

23.–(1) Any notice, request, demand or other instrument under this Act shall be in writing and may be served on the person on whom it is to be served either personally, or by leaving it for him at his last known place of abode in England or Wales, or by sending it through the post in a registered letter addressed to him there, or, in the case of a local or public authority of a statutory or a public utility company, to the secretary or other proper officer at the principal office or such authority or company . . .

14–23

Section 66(4) of the 1954 Act provides that "section 23 of the Landlord and Tenant Act 1927 (which relates to the service of notices) shall apply for the purposes of this Act". That section provides that notices may be served in writing:

(1) Personally on the intended recipient.

(2) By leaving it for him at his last known "place of abode" in England or Wales (which in the case of a business includes the business address: *Italica Holdings SA v Bayadea* [1985] 1 E.G.L.R. 70). It is sufficient if the document is left at a place that is the furthest that a member of the public or postman can go to communicate with the tenant (*Henry Smith's Charity Trustees v Kyriakou* [1989] 2 E.G.L.R. 110).

(3) By registered post to his last known place of abode. Section 1 of the Recorded Delivery Service Act 1962 provides that the notice may be served by recorded delivery rather than registered post. Service is deemed to be effected by properly addressing, pre-paying and posting the letter containing the notice. It is not sufficient for the tenant merely to deny having received the letter (*Lex Services plc v Johns* [1990] 1 E.G.L.R. 92—see Dillon LJ at 95A and Balcombe LJ at 95F). The notice is irrebuttably deemed to have been served on the date that the notice was put in the post and not its actual receipt (*CA Webber (Transport) Ltd v Railtrack plc* [2003] EWCA Civ 1167; [2004] 14 E.G. 142).

(4) In the case of a local or public authority or a statutory or a public utility company, to the secretary or other public officer of such authority or company.

Section 23 is permissive. Service may therefore be effected by any other method. If actual delivery is proved, service will be effective even if not served by one of the methods prescribed in s.23 (*Stylo Shoes Ltd v Prices Tailors Ltd* [1959] 3 All E.R. 901 Ch D). Further, service on a person who has actual or ostensible authority to receive the notice on behalf of the tenant, such as a solicitor, will be good service (*Galinski v McHugh* [1989] 1 E.G.L.R. 109).

However, if a person serves the notice by a method specified in s.23, he need only show that the method chosen was carried out. He does not need to show that the notice arrived (*Italica Holdings SA v Bayadea* [1985] 1 E.G.L.R. 70; *Lex Service plc v Johns* [1990] 1 E.G.L.R. 92).

Where the tenant is a limited company, the notice may be served by leaving it at or sending it to the company's registered office (Companies Act 1985 s.725(1); Companies Act 2006 s.1139). Personal delivery of a notice can be effected against a company by giving it to someone with authority to receive it (*Bottin (International) Investments Ltd v Venson Group PLC* [2004] EWCA Civ 1368)—delivery to a receptionist who expressly stated that she would make sure it was passed onto a director was sufficient, see para.77 of the judgment). A local authority may be served at an office that it designates for receiving notices (Local Government Act 1972 s.231(1)).

Where the tenant has died, see the provisions of ss.17 and 18 of the Law of Property (Miscellaneous) Provisions Act 1994 (para.14–39).

Tenant's action on receipt of notice

Service on landlord or request for information (s.40)

Reference has already been made to the fact that the person who has served the s.25 notice is not necessarily the tenant's immediate landlord but is the "competent landlord" (i.e. the landlord as defined by s.44 of the Act (para.14–16)) and to the fact that the identity of the competent landlord can change as the proceedings advance. It is therefore of assistance to the tenant to know whether or not the person who has served the s.25 notice is likely to remain the competent landlord. In order to ascertain this information, he may serve a request for information in prescribed form pursuant to s.40 or the 1954 Act. The recipient of the request must reply within one month after service. The reply to the notice may reveal that the person who has served the s.25 notice is the freehold or a leasehold owner with a term somewhat in excess of the minimum period of 14 months required to be a competent landlord, in which case the tenant will know that there is not likely to be any change in the course of the proceedings, unless there is an assignment of the reversion. If, however, the landlord is himself a tenant under a continuation tenancy, the tenant will have to be aware of the possibility that the landlord may cease to be the competent landlord during the course of the proceedings. If, within the period of six months beginning with the date of the service of the notice, the landlord becomes aware that any

14–24

information that has been given in pursuance of the notice is not, or is no longer correct, he must give the tenant the correct information. (See further on all these matters: Ch.16–para.16–07.)

Note also that the person who served the s.25 notice will be estopped from denying that he is the competent landlord where he ends his status as a competent landlord after serving a s.25 notice without telling the tenant (see para.14–20). (See also the response to the tenant's application, which must give certain information in relation to his interest; paras 24–32.)

Tenant's application to the court to renew

14-25   The tenant must make his application for a new tenancy by the date stated in the s.25 notice; unless there has been a valid agreement between the landlord and the tenant extending time for the making of the application (see para.24–09). If the tenant fails to make an application to the court, the landlord is entitled to possession on the date specified in the notice (*Smith v Draper* [1990] 2 E.G.L.R. 69 CA); or, if that date has been extended, the final date agreed upon (see para.24–09).

(Note that rather than waiting for the tenant to apply for a new tenancy, the landlord may do so (see Ch.24) or he may apply for the current tenancy to be terminated (Ch.22).)

Abolition of counter-notice

14-26   The requirement to serve a counter-notice (see the old s.25(5)) was abolished in relation to all s.25 notices served on or after June 1, 2004 (art.9 of the 2003 Reform Order). Where the s.25 notice was served before that date, the application to renew will only have been valid if a counter-notice was served within the two-month time period previously provided for.

The counter-notice was abolished because: (a) it was a potential trap for the tenant; and (b) it did not provide the landlord with any certainty. The tenant could serve the counter-notice stating that he was not willing to give up possession and still not make an application to renew. Under the regime that has been in force since June 1, 2004, a landlord who is not sure of what the tenant is likely to do and who would like matters to get underway has the right to apply for the lease to be terminated or, if he is content for the tenant to stay but on new terms, to apply for a new tenancy to be ordered (see Ch.24). If the landlord does apply for a new tenancy to be ordered but the tenant does not wish to have a new tenancy, the tenant should inform the court at which point the application will come to an end. The tenancy will then generally come to an end within three months of the court formally dismissing the application (s.64 (see para.27–02); see s.29(5)–para.24–05).

Continuation tenancies to which Pt II of the 1954 Act ceases to apply

Landlord and Tenant Act 1954 s.24(3)(a)

24.–(3) Notwithstanding anything in subsection (1) of this section–   **14–27**

(a)   where a tenancy to which this Part of this Act applies ceases to be such a tenancy, it shall not come to an end by reason only of the cesser, but if it was granted for a term of years certain and has been continued by subsection (1) of this section then (without prejudice to the termination thereof in accordance with any terms of the tenancy) it may be terminated by not less than three nor more than six months' notice in writing given by the landlord to the tenant;

(b)   where, at a time when a tenancy is not one to which this Part of this Act applies, the landlord gives notice to quit, the operation of the notice shall not be affected by reason that the tenancy becomes one to which this Part of this Act applies after the giving of the notice.

Circumstances may arise in which the 1954 Act ceases to apply to a continuation tenancy, for example if the tenant ceases to occupy the property for the purposes of a business (para.2–05). If this occurs, the tenancy does not automatically come to an end but if it was originally granted for a fixed term and has been continued by virtue of s.24 (see para.1–02) "it may be terminated by not less than three nor more than six month's notice in writing given by the landlord to the tenant", (s.24(3)(a) and see *Esselte v Pearl Assurance plc* [1997] 1 W.L.R. 891). So far as periodic tenancies or break clauses (see s.69), the tenancy can be determined by notice to quit; which will continue to have effect even if the tenancy once again becomes a tenancy to which Pt II applies (s.24(3)(b)).

Notice to quit

Introduction

14-28   As has been seen in Ch.1, it is not possible for a landlord to terminate a tenancy to which Pt II of the 1954 Act applies by notice to quit. However, if the Act does not apply and the tenancy is a periodic tenancy, it will be possible to bring it to an end by means of a notice to quit. As to whether a periodic tenancy, which has ceased to be subject to the 1954 Act, may also be terminated by a notice to quit of appropriate length, see above. As to break clauses in leases see para.14-43 below.

Where a landlord serves a notice to quit at a time when the tenancy is not protected by the 1954 Act, the operation of the notice is not affected by reason that the tenancy becomes one to which Pt II of the Act applies after the giving of the notice (s.24(3)(b); see para.14-27).

Unlike residential tenancies, there are no statutory rules that apply to notices to quit served in respect of business premises to which the 1954 Act does not apply. (Section 5(1) of the Protection from Eviction Act 1977 does not apply because the property is not "let as a dwelling".) The common law rules apply. This section is concerned with those common law rules.

Appropriate notice periods

14-29   The appropriate period of notice and the date upon which a notice to quit is to expire may be provided for in the tenancy agreement. If so, the notice should be served in accordance with the terms of the agreement.

Where there are no such terms, the rules in respect of different types of periodic tenancies apply. In calculating the minimum notice period required, include the day of service and exclude the day of expiry (*Schnabel v Allard* [1966] 3 All E.R. 816). The date of expiry must be at the end of a complete period of the tenancy or the first day of a new period (*Sidebotham v Holland* [1895] 1 Q.B. 378; *Crate v Miller* [1947] K.B. 946j; *Yeandle v Reigate and Banstead BC* [1996] 14 E.G. 90) unless the tenancy agreement provides otherwise (*Soames v Nicholson* [1902] 1 K.B. 157). Unless there is an indication in the lease to the contrary, a tenancy stated to be "from" a particular date commences immediately after midnight the following day (*Ladyman v Wirral Estates Ltd* [1968] 2 All E.R. 197). The notice should not give a particular time in the day before which the tenant must leave (*Bathavon RDC v Carlile* [1958] 1 Q.B. 461).

Yearly tenancy

If the rent is payable annually it is a yearly tenancy (eg *Erimus*   **14–30** *Housing Ltd v Barclays Wealth Trustees (Jersey) Ltd* [2014] EWCA Civ 303, para.10) and requires at least six months notice to quit. Usually this means 183 days but if the tenancy is to end on one of the quarter days (March 25, June 24, September 29 and December 25), then at least two quarters' notice must be given. For example, if a yearly tenancy is granted on May 1, 1982, the notice to quit must be given by October 29, 1982 to determine on April 30, 1983 or May 1, 1983 (i.e. 183 days). Whereas, if the tenancy is to end on December 25 (a quarter day), the notice must be served on or before June 23. The notice must expire on the last day of the year or the anniversary of the tenancy.

Monthly tenancy

Unless the lease expresses the contrary, a calendar month's   **14–31** notice is required ending on the last day of the month of the tenancy or the first day of the next month (*Dodds v Walker* [1981] 2 All E.R. 609 HL). For example, if a monthly tenancy commenced on 20th of a month, the notice to quit must be given by the 19th (or 20th) of any particular month to expire on the 19th (or 20th) of the next month. If the month in which the notice is due to expire has no corresponding date to the month in which the notice is served because it has less days, the notice should be dated to expire on the last day of that month (*Dodds v Walker*) or the first day of the next month.

Weekly tenancy

The provisions of the Protection from Eviction Act 1977 do not   **14–32** apply to premises let for business premises (s.5). There is therefore no minimum requirement for notices and a weekly tenancy may be determined by one week's notice. For example, if a weekly tenancy commenced on a Monday the notice to quit must expire on a Sunday (or a Monday) and must be given by the Sunday (or, if it is to expire on a Monday, by the Monday) one week beforehand.

In order to ensure that a notice to quit expires on the proper day the landlord may insert the following clause in the notice:

> "I hereby give you notice to quit on the — day of ———— 20–– or at the expiration of the period of your tenancy which shall expire next after the expiration of four weeks from the service upon you of this notice".

Unless the above requirements are strictly complied with, the notice will generally be ineffective. Only minor clerical errors will not invalidate a notice to quit, if the meaning would be clear to a reasonable tenant. The test is:

> "Is the notice quite clear to a reasonable tenant reading it? Is it plain that he cannot be misled by it?"

(*Carradine Properties Ltd v Aslam* [1976] 1 All E.R. 573; approved in *Mannai Investment Co Ltd v Eagle Star Life Assurance Co Ltd* [1997] 2 W.L.R. 945 HL–cases on break clauses but which it is submitted would apply to notices to quit). For example, a notice to quit dated in error 1890 when the landlord clearly meant 1990 will not invalidate the notice.

If proceedings for possession have been commenced on the basis of a defective notice to quit, they will be dismissed and the landlord will have to serve a valid notice before fresh proceedings can be commenced. The landlord should never commence proceedings until the notice to quit has expired. If he does so the proceedings are premature and will be dismissed pursuant to the rule that a party must have a cause of action at the date proceedings are commenced (as to which see *Eshelby v Federated European Bank Ltd* [1932] 1 K.B. 254–not a landlord and tenant case).

Who may give a notice?

14–33 The notice must be given by or on behalf of the tenant's immediate landlord at the time of the notice. Thus a prospective purchaser cannot serve a notice to quit but once a landlord has given a tenant notice, his successors in title may rely upon it (*Doe d. Earl of Egremont v Forwood* [1842] 3 Q.B.

627). A notice given by one of two or more joint landlords is valid if the tenancy is a periodic one (*Parsons v Parsons* [1983] 1 W.L.R. 1390; *Leckhampton Dairies Ltd v Artus Whitfield Ltd* (1986) 83 Law Soc. Gaz. 875j; see also *Hammersmith & Fulham LBC v Monk* [1992] 1 All E.R. 1 HL). However, if the tenancy is for a fixed term with a break clause providing for termination by a notice to quit, all of the joint owners must agree to service of the notice to quit unless the lease provides otherwise (see discussion in *Leek and Moorlands Building Society v Clark* [1952] 2 All E.R. 492 CA).

Notice given by agents

The purpose of the rules contained in this paragraph is to ensure that the tenant can rely upon the notice to quit: that he can be sure that it comes from the landlord. The first rule is that a person such as a managing agent, who has been given a general authority to deal with a property on behalf of a landlord, may give a tenant a notice to quit in his own name without having to show a specific authority to determine the tenancy. The notice is valid even if it is given by the agent as if he were the landlord and fails to disclose his own agency (*Doe d. Earl Manvers v Mizem* (1837) 2 Mood. & R. 56; *Harmond Properties Ltd v Gajdzis* [1968] 3 All E.R. 263; *Townsend Carriers Ltd v Pfizer Ltd* (1977) 33 P. & C.R. 361). **14–34**

The second rule is that all other persons (e.g. rent collectors, solicitors, spouses) may give a notice to quit on behalf of the landlord only if they have the landlord's actual authority to do so at the time the notice is given (*Jones v Phipps* (1868) L.R. 3 Q.B. 567). A landlord may not subsequently ratify the notice and thereby validate it. The fact of the agency should be expressed on the notice. The notice should state expressly that it is given on behalf of the landlord, who should be named or otherwise identified (*Lemon v Lardeur* [1946] 2 All E.R. 329). There is of course nothing to prevent a solicitor or spouse having a general authority to manage the property in which case the first rule set out above will apply.

Service upon whom?

The landlord must serve the notice to quit on his immediate tenant. He may not serve an assignor of the tenancy nor an under-tenant. An assignment of the tenancy in breach of covenant although unlawful is effective, and so even in these **14–35** circumstances the notice to quit should be served on the assignee (*Old Grovebury Manor Farm Ltd v W Seymour Plant Sales and Hire Ltd (No.2)* [1979] 1 W.L.R. 1397). If the tenancy is held by joint tenants but only one of them is in occupation, service on the occupying tenant is sufficient unless the lease provides that all must be served (*Doe d. Bradford (Lord) v Watkins* (1806) 7 East 551); although address it to both.

It sometimes occurs that the person in occupation is not the original tenant. If the tenancy was in writing, and contained a provision requiring a notice to quit to be served to terminate the tenancy, there should be no real problems about service because the provisions of s.196 of the Law of Property Act 1925 will be available (see below).

Mode of service for written tenancies

Law of Property Act 1925 s.196(5)

14–36   **196.**–(5) The provisions of this section shall extend to notices required to be served by any instrument affecting property executed or coming into operation after the commencement of this Act unless a contrary intention appears.

Where the tenancy is in writing, the provisions of s.196 of the Law of Property Act 1925, as extended by s.1 of the Recorded Delivery Service Act 1962 (see para.9–11) may apply. However, s.196(5) of the Law of Property Act 1925 will not apply unless the tenancy agreement makes express provision for service of a notice to quit (*Wandsworth LBC v Attwell* [1996] 01 E.G. 100 CA—weekly tenancy agreement contained in informal documents—the notice to quit was not "required" by the "instrument" but by the general law).

Further, s.196 will not apply if "a contrary intention appears" in the agreement.

The effect of s.196 taken together with s.1 of the Recorded Delivery Service Act 1962 where it does apply is as follows:

(1) A notice to quit is sufficiently served if it is sent by recorded delivery addressed to the tenant by name at the tenant's last known place of abode or business in the United Kingdom. If the letter is not returned through the post office undelivered, service is deemed to be made at the time at which the letter would in the ordinary course

of post be delivered (s.196(4)). To prove service the landlord need only show that the letter was prepaid, properly addressed and actually posted.

(2) The landlord may also serve the notice to quit by leaving it at the tenant's last know place of abode or business in the United Kingdom or affixing it or leaving it for him on the land or on any house or building comprised in the lease (s.196(3)). If this method is used it is sufficient if it is addressed to "the lessee" (s.196(2)).

In either of the above two cases the landlord will not need to show that the tenant actually received the notice to quit (*88 Berkley Road, London NW9, Re* [1971] Ch. 648).

Mode of service for oral tenancies and written tenancies to which s.196 does not apply

Where the tenancy is an oral one, the notice to quit must come to the tenant's attention before the notice period begins to run. Personal service is not required. The notice may be sent by post and in that case the court will as a matter of practice presume that the notice was delivered in the ordinary course of post. However, the presumption may be rebutted by evidence from the tenant that the notice was not in fact received. Simply leaving the notice to quit at the premises will not be sufficient unless the landlord can show (whether by the tenant's admission or otherwise) that it came to the tenant's attention prior to commencement of the notice period.   **14–37**

Where the notice is served by post, the landlord is probably best advised to serve the notice by recorded delivery. Whatever the method of service, it is also sensible to send the tenant a copy of the notice (in addition to the original) endorsed with a memorandum of service upon it. The tenant should be asked to sign, date and return the copy on the date of receipt. He may not always do so but if he does it should prevent arguments about service at a later date.

Service of notice to quit where the tenant has died

Where the tenant was an individual who has died service of the notice to quit will depend upon various factors: **14–38**

(1) If there are executors of the tenant's estate, the notice should be addressed and served on them. If the

provisions of s.196 of the Law of Property Act 1925 apply (see s.196(5); para.14–36) the notice to quit may be served by affixing it to the premises or leaving it for them there pursuant to s.196(3) (see para.9–12). Their names can be discovered by doing a probate search.

(2) If there are executors but no grant has been filed at the Principal Registry (so that the names of the executors are not known), the notice may be served on the Public Trustee (s.18(1),(2) of the Law of Property (Miscellaneous Provisions) Act 1994).

(3) If there are no executors or if the tenant died intestate and no administrators have yet been appointed, the property vests in the Public Trustee (see para.20–12) and (subject to anything in the agreement) the notice to quit should be addressed to "The Personal Representatives of" the deceased (naming him) and left at or sent by post to his last known place of residence or business in the United Kingdom and a copy of it, similarly addressed, should be served on the Public Trustee at PO Box 3010, London, WC2B 6JS (tel 0207 269 7196). (See s.18 of 1994 Act; *Practice Direction* [1995] 1 WLR 1120.) The Public Trustee keeps a register of all notices served on him. To enter a notice on the register it should be accompanied by Form NL(1) of The Public Trustee (Notices Affecting Land) (Title on Death) Regulations 1995 (SI 1995/1330). A search of the register may be made against the name of the deceased person by using Form NL(2). In the event that the search shows an entry, a copy of the document will be sent to the person requesting the search (reg.4 of the 1995 regulations). See further the Public Trustee website at *http://www.justice.gov.uk/about/ospt* [Accessed June 3rd, 2014].

(4) Once personal representatives have been appointed, any notice to quit should be served on them. In order to discover their names, the landlord can lodge an application for a standing search at the Probate Registry.

(5) Once the property is vested in beneficiaries, the notice to quit should be served upon them (s.36 of Administration of Estates Act 1925).

Where a person serving a notice to quit had no reason to believe that the tenant was dead and serves the notice as if he were alive, that service is valid even though he has in fact died (s.17 of the 1994 Act).

For the position generally on the death of a tenant see para.21-11.

Law of Property (Miscellaneous Provisions) Act 1994 ss.17 and 18

17.–(1) Service of a notice affecting land which would be effective but for the death of the intended recipient is effective despite his death if the person serving the notice has no reason to believe that he has died.

    (2) Where the person serving a notice affecting land has no reason to believe that the intended recipient has died, the proper address for the purposes of section 7 of the Interpretation Act 1978 (service of documents by post) shall be what would be the proper address apart from his death.

    (3) . . .

14–39

18.–(1) A notice affecting land which would have been authorised or required to be served on a person but for his death shall be sufficiently served before a grant of representation has been filed if—

    (a)   it is addressed to "The Personal Representatives of" the deceased (naming him) and left at or sent by post to his last known place of residence or business in the United Kingdom, and

    (b)   a copy of it, similarly addressed is served on the Public Trustee.

    (2) The reference in subsection (1) to the filing of a grant of representation is to the filing at the Principal Registry of the Family Division of the High Court of a copy of a grant of representation in respect of the deceased's estate or, as the case may be, the part of his estate which includes the land in question.

    (3) The method of service provided for by this section is not available where provision is made—

    (a)   by or under any enactment, or
    (b)   by an agreement in writing,

requiring a different method of service, or expressly prohibiting the method of service provided for by this section, in the circumstances.

Payment of rent after service of notice to quit

If the landlord accepts rent after expiry of the notice to quit, a new tenancy will not necessarily be implied and all the circumstances must be looked at to show the parties' true intentions (*Clarke v Grant* [1950] 1 K.B. 104; *Marcroft Wagons Ltd v Smith* [1951] 2 K.B. 496). In order to ensure that no intention to create a new tenancy is found, a landlord requiring

14–40

rent after service of a notice to quit should demand payment of damages for occupation (either equal to the rental sum or in some other sum, if appropriate) without prejudice to the effect of the notice to quit. In the circumstances, the court will probably hold that there has been no new tenancy created on the basis that there was no intention to create legal relations (see *Street v Mountford* [1985] 2 All E.R. 289; para.6–02).

Withdrawal of notice to quit

14–41 It is not possible to withdraw a notice to quit without the consent of the person upon whom it was served. If the parties do agree that the notice to quit should be withdrawn, the agreement operates as a grant of a new tenancy on the old terms (subject to any agreement to vary the terms) to take effect at the determination of the notice to quit (*Davies v Bristow* [1920] 3 K.B. 428, per Lush J at 438; *Lower v Sorrell* [1962] 3 All E.R. 1074).

Effect of notice to quit on sub-tenants

14–42 If the sub-tenancy is not a tenancy to which the 1954 Act applies "the branch falls with the tree", i.e. the sub-tenancy comes to an end on the termination of the head tenancy (*Moore Properties (Ilford) Ltd v McKeon* [1977] 1 All E.R. 262). If, however, the 1954 Act applies to the sub-tenancy, that tenancy continues by virtue of s.24 and the person with the next reversionary interest becomes the immediate landlord of the sub-tenant on the terms of the sub-tenancy (s.65 of the 1954 Act; see further para.17–04 in relation to position at the end of a fixed term).

Break clauses

14–43 A fixed-term tenancy may contain a provision for termination prior to the expiry of the term if a particular event should occur. For example, the landlord may be entitled to determine the tenancy by service of a notice in the event of his intending to redevelop the property. In these circumstances, the landlord should, if he wishes to determine the tenancy, serve such termination notice as is required by the terms of the lease (see further para.15–19). However, if the 1954 Act applies, the tenancy will not come to an end on the expiry date in the notice. It will continue pursuant to s.24 (see para.1–02) and in order to determine it the landlord will also have to serve a s.25 notice (see para.14–02).

It is not always necessary to serve a separate contractual notice in addition to the s.25 notice. There may be circumstances in which a s.25 notice will be sufficient to comply with the terms of the lease (*Scholl Manufacturing Co Ltd v Clifton (Slim-Line) Ltd* [1967] Ch. 41). For example, the terms of the lease may simply require the landlord to terminate the tenancy by service of a termination notice of not less than six months if he wishes to redevelop, without having to say in the notice the reason for its service. A s.25 notice terminating the tenancy, say, seven months from the date of the notice would therefore be sufficient. It is however advisable to state in an accompanying letter that the notice is served in accordance with both the relevant provisions of the lease and s.25 of the Act and to give the reason for service of the notice. If the lease requires the termination notice to be in a particular form or to be for a period of less than six months or more than 12 months, it will be necessary to serve such a notice in addition to that served pursuant to s.25. For errors in notices served pursuant to break clauses see *Mannai Investment Co Ltd v Eagle Star Life Assurance Co Ltd* [1997] 2 W.L.R. 945 HL; and see further para.15–19.

The provisions of s.196 of the Law of Property Act 1925 (see para.9–12) apply to service of notices terminating fixed terms (s.196(5), see para.14–36).

CHAPTER 15

TENANT'S NOTICES TO TERMINATE OR RENEW

15-01   The 1954 Act contains two sets of provisions for termination by the tenant. Section 26 is concerned with the "tenant's request for a new tenancy". Service of such a request brings the old tenancy to an end but it also starts the procedure whereby an application can be made for a new tenancy. Section 27 applies where the tenant wishes to terminate the present tenancy but does not wish to apply for a new tenancy. Common law notices to quit are also dealt with in this chapter.

Request for new tenancy: s.26 request

Introduction

15-02   Where a tenant of a tenancy to which Pt II of the 1954 Act applies wishes to set in motion the procedure for applying for a new tenancy, he may do so by serving a "request for a new tenancy" under s.26 of the 1954 Act. However, he may do so only if his original tenancy was granted for a fixed term exceeding one year or was granted for a term of years and thereafter from year to year (s.26(1) e.g. see *Manton Securites Ltd v Nazam* [2008] EWCA Civ 805).

Where the tenancy is held by joint tenants, all the tenants must be parties to the s.26 request unless some of the tenants are partners, in which case a request made by the tenants who are in occupation running the business will be sufficient (s.41A(3)(a); see further para.2-27).

Landlord and Tenant Act 1954 s.26(1), (4), (5)

15-03   26.—(1) A tenant's request for a new tenancy may be made where the current tenancy is a tenancy granted for a term of years certain exceeding

322

one year, whether or not continued by section 24 of this Act, or granted for a term of years certain and thereafter from year to year.

. . .

(4) A tenant's request for a new tenancy shall not be made if the landlord has already given notice under the last foregoing section to terminate the current tenancy, or if the tenant has already given notice to quit or notice under the next following section; and no such notice shall be given by the landlord or the tenant after the making by the tenant of a request for a new tenancy.

(5) Where the tenant makes a request for a new tenancy in accordance with the foregoing provisions of this section, the current tenancy shall, subject to the provisions of sections 29B(4) and 36(2) of this Act and the provisions of Part IV of this Act as to the interim continuation of tenancies, terminate immediately before the date specified in the request for the beginning of the new tenancy.

The tenant may not serve a s.26 request where the landlord has already served a termination notice pursuant to s.25 of the 1954 Act or the tenant has himself served a notice to quit or termination notice pursuant to s.27 (s.26(4)).

As will be seen below, the s.26 request contains a date upon which the tenant suggests that the new tenancy should commence. The effect of making the request is to bring the old tenancy to an end immediately before that date unless there is an application to the court for a new tenancy, in which case, the old tenancy continues until after the proceedings are complete (s.26(5); see above). As to the ability of the parties to agree an extension of the date, see Ch.24, para.24–09.

A tenant with a break clause in a fixed-term lease is not entitled to serve a s.26 request to expire at any time earlier than the expiry of the fixed term (*Garston v Scottish Widows* [1998] 2 E.G.L.R. 73 CA).

Deciding whether or not to serve a s.26 request

The tenant does not need to serve a s.26 request in order to apply for a new tenancy. He may instead wait for the landlord to serve a notice under s.25 (see Ch.14) and then apply for a new tenancy. However, this does not provide the business tenant with the security of tenure that he usually requires. Service of the s.26 request will get the procedure for a new tenancy under way. There used to be an advantage in serving a s.26 request with a long date where the market was rising. This meant that the tenant would continue to pay a low rent until an interim rent was ordered, which could only be backdated to the

15–04

date in the s.26 request or the date of the application whichever was the later. However, under the changes brought about by the 2003 Reform Order, interim rent is backdated to the earliest possible date that could have been specified in the notice served and, where the landlord does not oppose a new tenancy, the interim rent will usually be at the same rent as that determined for the new tenancy. This advantage has therefore been lost. (See further Ch.25 in relation to interim rent.)

Where the tenant is a "mesne landlord", that is where he is a person who is both landlord and tenant, because he has sublet part of the premises, he will have to decide whether or not to serve a s.25 notice terminating the sub-tenancy or a s.26 request first (see para.14–19). If he serves a s.25 notice on the sub-tenant and subsequently serves a s.26 request on his landlord, he must tell the sub-tenant that he has done so (*Shelley v United Artists Corp Ltd* [1990] 1 E.G.L.R. 103; see further para.14–20).

Prescribed form; contents of the request

Landlord and Tenant Act 1954 s.26(2), (3)

15–05   **26.**–(2) A tenant's request for a new tenancy shall be for a tenancy beginning with such date, not more than twelve nor less than six months after the making of the request, as may be specified therein;
     Provided that the said date shall not be earlier than the date on which apart from this Act the current tenancy would come to an end by effluxion of time or could be brought to an end by notice to quit given by the tenant.
     (3) A tenant's request for a new tenancy shall not have effect unless it is made by notice in the prescribed form given to the landlord and sets out the tenant's proposals as to the property to be comprised in the new tenancy (being either the whole or part of the property comprised in the current tenancy), as to the rent to be payable under the new tenancy and as to the other terms of the new tenancy.

The request must be made by notice in the form prescribed by The Landlord and Tenant Act 1954 Pt 2 (Notices) Regulations 2004 (Form 3) or in a form substantially to the like effect, (s.26(3); Landlord and Tenant Act 1954, see para.15–06, Form 19).

The request must specify a date for the new tenancy to begin that is not more than 12 nor less than six months after the making of the request (s.26(2)). The request is made when it is given to the landlord (s.26(3)). The date specified must also not be earlier than the date upon which, apart from the 1954 Act, the current tenancy would come to an end by effluxion of time or could be brought to an end by notice to quit given by the tenant (s.26(2)).

The request must set out the tenant's proposals as to the property to be comprised in the new tenancy (being either the whole or part of the property comprised in the current tenancy), as to the rent to be payable under the new tenancy and as to the other terms of the new tenancy (s.26(3)). When completing the request, the tenant should have regard to the terms that the court is likely to order, as to which see Ch.26.

A tenant is not required to have a genuine intention to take up a new tenancy when he serves his s.26 request. Nor do the proposals for a new term stated in the request need to be genuine. Service of the notice is a statutory formality; a "performative utterance"! (*Sun Life Assurance plc v Thales Tracs Ltd* [2001] EWCA Civ 704—tenants served a s.26 request. They did not actually wish to take a new lease—they had found alternative premises. They served the notice simply to preserve their compensation rights, knowing that the landlord wanted to redevelop the site. The notice was held to be valid and they were entitled to compensation.)

Form 19

Form 3

TENANT'S REQUEST FOR A NEW BUSINESS TENANCY

Section 26 of the Landlord and Tenant Act 1954

To:

....

....

....

(*insert name and address of landlord*)

From:

....

....

....

(*insert name and address of tenant*)

1. This notice applies to the following property: (*insert address or description of property*)

....

2. I am giving you notice under section 26 of the Landlord and Tenant Act 1954 that I request a new tenancy beginning on (*insert date*).

....

3. You will find my proposals for the new tenancy, which we can discuss, in the Schedule to this notice.

4. If we cannot agree on all the terms of a new tenancy, either you or I may ask the court to order the grant of a new tenancy and settle the terms on which we cannot agree.

5. If you wish to ask the court to order the grant of a new tenancy you must do so by the date in paragraph 2, unless we agree in writing to a later date and do so before the date in paragraph 2.

cont

---

cont

6. You may oppose my request for a new tenancy only on one or more of the grounds set out in section 30(1) of the Landlord and Tenant Act 1954. You must tell me what your grounds are within two months of receiving this notice. If you miss this deadline you will not be able to oppose renewal of my tenancy and you will have to grant me a new tenancy.

7. Please send all correspondence about this notice to:

Name:

....

Address:

....

....

Signed: .... Date: ....

*[Tenant] *[On behalf of the tenant]

*(*delete whichever is inapplicable)*

SCHEDULE

TENANT'S PROPOSALS FOR A NEW TENANCY

(attach or insert proposed terms of the new tenancy)

IMPORTANT NOTE FOR THE LANDLORD

This notice requests a new tenancy of your property or part of it. If you want to oppose this request you must act quickly.

Read the notice and all the Notes carefully. It would be wise to seek professional advice.

NOTES

The sections mentioned below are sections of the Landlord and Tenant Act 1954, as amended, (most recently by the Regulatory Reform (Business Tenancies) (England and Wales) Order 2003).

Tenant's request for a new tenancy

This request by your tenant for a new tenancy brings his or her current tenancy to an end on the day before the date mentioned in paragraph 2 of this notice. Section 26 contains rules about the date that the tenant can put in paragraph 2 of this notice.

cont

cont

Your tenant can apply to the court under section 24 for a new tenancy. You may apply for a new tenancy yourself, under the same section, but not if your tenant has already served an application. Once an application has been made to the court, your tenant's current tenancy will continue after the date mentioned in paragraph 2 while the application is being considered by the court. Either you or your tenant can ask the court to fix the rent which your tenant will have to pay whilst the tenancy continues (sections 24A to 24D). The court will settle any terms of a new tenancy on which you and your tenant disagree (sections 34 and 35).

Time limit for opposing your tenant's request

If you do not want to grant a new tenancy, you have two months from the making of your tenant's request in which to notify him or her that you will oppose any application made to the court for a new tenancy. You do not need a special form to do this, but the notice must be in writing and it must state on which of the grounds set out in section 30(1) you will oppose the application. If you do not use the same wording of the ground (or grounds), as set out below, your notice may be ineffective.

If there has been any delay in your seeing this notice, you may need to act very quickly. If you are in any doubt about what action you should take, get advice immediately from a solicitor or a surveyor.

Grounds for opposing tenant's application

If you wish to oppose the renewal of the tenancy, you can do so by opposing your tenant's application to the court, or by making your own application to the court for termination without renewal. However, you can only oppose your tenant's application, or apply for termination without renewal, on one or more of the grounds set out in section 30(1). These grounds are set out below. You will only be able to rely on the ground(s) of opposition that you have mentioned in your written notice to your tenant.

In this Table "the holding" means the property that is the subject of the tenancy.

Paragraph of section 30(1)	Grounds
(a)	Where under the current tenancy the tenant has any obligations as respects the repair and maintenance of the holding, that the tenant ought not to be granted a new tenancy in view of the state of repair of the holding, being a state resulting from the tenant's failure to comply with the said obligations.
(b)	That the tenant ought not to be granted a new tenancy in

cont

cont

view of his persistent delay in paying rent which has become due.

(c)   That the tenant ought not to be granted a new tenancy in view of other substantial breaches by him of his obligations under the current tenancy, or for any other reason connected with the tenant's use or management of the holding.

(d)   That the landlord has offered and is willing to provide or secure the provision of alternative accommodation for the tenant, that the terms on which the alternative accommodation is available are reasonable having regard to the terms of the current tenancy and to all other relevant circumstances, and that the accommodation and the time at which it will be available are suitable for the tenant's requirements (including the requirement to preserve goodwill) having regard to the nature and class of his business and to the situation and extent of, and facilities afforded by, the holding.

(e)   Where the current tenancy was created by the sub-letting of part only of the property comprised in a superior tenancy and the landlord is the owner of an interest in reversion expectant on the termination of that superior tenancy, that the aggregate of the rents reasonably obtainable on separate lettings of the holding and the remainder of that property would be substantially less than the rent reasonably obtainable on a letting of that property as a whole, that on the termination of the current tenancy the landlord requires possession of the holding for the purposes of letting or otherwise disposing of the said property as a whole, and that in view thereof the tenant ought not to be granted a new tenancy.

(f)   That on the termination of the current tenancy the landlord intends to demolish or reconstruct the premises comprised in the holding or a substantial part of those premises or to carry out substantial work of construction on the holding or part thereof and that he could not reasonably do so without obtaining possession of the holding.

(g)   On the termination of the current tenancy the landlord intends to occupy the holding for the purposes, or partly for the purposes, of a business to be carried on by him therein, or as his residence.

cont

cont

Compensation

If your tenant cannot get a new tenancy solely because one or more of grounds (e), (f) and (g) applies, he or she is entitled to compensation under section 37. If you have opposed your tenant's application on any of the other grounds mentioned in section 30(1), as well as on one or more of grounds (e), (f) and (g), your tenant can only get compensation if the court's refusal to grant a new tenancy is based solely on ground (e), (f) or (g). In other words, your tenant cannot get compensation under section 37 if the court has refused the tenancy on *other* grounds, even if one or more of grounds (e), (f) and (g) also applies.

If you are an authority possessing compulsory purchase powers (such as a local authority), your tenant may be entitled to a disturbance payment under Part 3 of the Land Compensation Act 1973.

Negotiating a new tenancy

Most tenancies are renewed by negotiation and your tenant has set out proposals for the new tenancy in paragraph 3 of this notice. You are not obliged to accept these proposals and may put forward your own. You and your tenant may agree in writing to extend the deadline for making an application to the court while negotiations continue. Your tenant may not apply to the court for a new tenancy until two months have passed from the date of the making of the request contained in this notice, unless you have already given notice opposing your tenant's request as mentioned in paragraph 6 of this notice (section 29A(3)).

If you try to agree a new tenancy with your tenant, remember:

- that one of you will need to apply to the court before the date in paragraph 2 of this notice, unless you both agree to extend the period for making an application.

- that any such agreement must be in writing and must be made before the date in paragraph 2 (sections 29A and 29B).

Validity of this notice

The tenant who has given you this notice may not be the person from whom you receive rent (sections 44 and 67). This does not necessarily mean that the notice is invalid.

If you have any doubts about whether this notice is valid, get advice immediately from a solicitor or a surveyor.

Further information

An explanation of the main points to consider when renewing or ending a business tenancy, "Renewing and Ending Business Leases: a Guide for Tenants

cont

cont
and Landlords", can be found at www.odpm.gov.uk. Printed copies of the explanation, but not of this form, are available from 1st June 2004 from Free Literature, PO Box 236, Wetherby, West Yorkshire, LS23 7NB (0870 1226 236).

Meaning of "the landlord": the competent landlord

Landlord and Tenant Act 1954 s.44

44.–(1) Subject to subsections (1A) and (2) below, in this Part of this Act the expression "the landlord" in relation to a tenancy (in this section referred to as "the relevant tenancy"), means the person (whether or not he is the immediate landlord) who is the owner of that interest in the property comprised in the relevant tenancy which for the time being fulfils the following conditions, that is to say— **15–07**

  (a) that it is an interest in reversion expectant (whether immediately or not) on the termination of the relevant tenancy, and

  (b) that it is either the fee simple or a tenancy which will not come to an end within fourteen months by effluxion of time and, if it is such a tenancy, that no notice has been given by virtue of which it will come to an end within fourteen months or any further time by which it may be continued under section 36(2) or section 64 of this Act, and is not itself in reversion expectant (whether immediately or not) on an interest which fulfils those conditions.

(1A) The reference in subsection (1) above to a person who is the owner of an interest such as is mentioned in that subsection is to be construed, where different persons own such interests in different parts of the property, as a reference to all those persons collectively.

(2) References in this Part of this Act to a notice to quit given by the landlord are references to a notice to quit given by the immediate landlord.

(3) The provisions of the Sixth Schedule to this Act shall have effect for the application of this Part of this Act to cases where the immediate landlord of the tenant is not the owner of the fee simple in respect of the holding.

The "landlord" who is required to be served with the s.26 notice is not necessarily the tenant's immediate landlord. The "landlord" is defined by s.44 of the 1954 Act and is frequently known as "the competent landlord" (a phrase used in Sch.6 of the Act; see para.26–28). By applying s.44, the immediate landlord of any particular tenant is only "the competent landlord" and may be served with a s.26 notice only if:

(1) he is the freehold owner of the property; or

(2) he is a leasehold owner whose own tenancy will *not* come to an end within 14 months of service of the notice; or

(3) he is a leasehold owner whose own tenancy would come to an end by effluxion of time within 14 months were it not for the continuation provisions of the Act (see para.1–02) but no notice has been served upon him (under s.25 or 24(3); see para.14–27) and he has himself not served a s.26 request or any other notice that would bring his tenancy to an end within 14 months or any further time by which the tenancy might be continued whilst an application for a new tenancy was proceeding.

If the immediate landlord does not fall into any of these categories, he will not be the competent landlord and may not be served with a s.26 notice. That landlord's own immediate landlord may be the person who is the competent landlord. If so, he may be served with a s.26 notice. If not, the process of finding the correct person to serve the notice is continued on up the chain (see the words "and is not itself" in s.44(1)(b)). There can be only one competent landlord at any one time in relation to any particular tenancy. He is the first person in the chain upwards from the tenancy in question who has either the freehold or one of the leasehold interests referred to above.

(See also s.23(2) of the Landlord and Tenant Act 1927 in relation to landlords who have assigned the reversion—dealt with in para.15–10 in relation to service.)

Discovering the competent landlord: s. 40

15–08 In order to discover the relationship between the respective parties in the chain, some of whom will probably not even be known to the tenant, s.40 of the Act provides for the service of notices requiring the recipients to give information relating to their interests in the property. The notices are in prescribed form. For full details, see Ch.16.

Divided reversions

15–09 In the rare case where more than one landlord owns the relevant reversionary interest, s.44(1A) applies (see para.14–17). This states that the reference in s.44(1) to "a person who is the owner of an interest" is to be construed "as a reference to all those persons collectively". The Office of the Deputy Prime Minister, in explaining the legislation, stated that this means that "a tenant would need to serve separate notices on all the landlords, taking proceedings against all of them either separately or naming them all as parties in a single set of proceedings". However, it seems to the authors that the requirement to treat them "collectively" means the service of one s.26 request containing a reference to all the properties and all the landlords, copies no doubt served on each, with one set of proceedings. This would seem to be supported by the fact that the Law Commission in proposing that this subsection was seeking to confirm the previous legal position. (See further discussion at para.14–22 in relation to service of s.25 notices where the reversion is divided.)

Service of the request

Landlord and Tenant Act 1927 s.23

23.–(1) Any notice, request, demand or other instrument under this Act **15–10** shall be in writing and may be served on the person on whom it is to be served either personally, or by leaving it for him at his last known place of abode in England or Wales, or by sending it through the post in a registered letter addressed to him there, or, in the case of a local or public authority or a statutory or a public utility company, to the secretary or other proper officer at the principal office of such authority or company, and in the case of a notice to a landlord, the person on whom it is to be served shall include any agent of the landlord duly authorised in that behalf.

(2) Unless or until a tenant of a holding shall have received notice that the person theretofore entitled to the rents and profits of the holding (hereinafter referred to as ("the original landlord") has ceased to be so entitled, and also notice of the name and address of the person who has become entitled to such rents and profits, any claim, notice, request, demand, or other instrument which the tenant shall serve upon or deliver to the original landlord shall be deemed to have been served upon or delivered to the landlord of such holding.

Section 66(4) of the 1954 Act provides that "section 23 of the **15–11** Landlord and Tenant Act 1927 (which relates to the service of notices) shall apply for the purposes of this Act". That section provides that notices may be served *in writing*:

(1) Personally on the intended recipient.
(2) By leaving it for him at his last known "place of abode" in England or Wales (which in the case of a business includes the business address: *Italica Holdings SA v Bayadea* [1985] 1 E.G.L.R. 70). It is sufficient if the

document is left at a place that is the furthest that a member of the public or postman can go to communicate with the intended recipient (*Henry Smith's Charity Trustees v Krakow* [1989] 2 E.G.L.R. 110).

(3) By registered post to his last known place of abode. Section 1 of the Recorded Delivery Service Act 1962 provides that the notice may be served by recorded delivery rather than registered post. Service is deemed to be effected by properly addressing, pre-paying and posting the letter containing the notice. It is not sufficient for the tenant merely to deny having received the letter (*Lex Services plc v Johns* [1990] 1 E.G.L.R. 92—see Dillon LJ at 95A and Buncombe LJ at 95F). The notice is irrefutably deemed to have been served on the date that the notice was put in the post and not its actual receipt (*CA Webber (Transport) Ltd v Rail track plc* [2003] EWCA Civ 1167).

(4) In the case of a local or public authority or a statutory or a public utility company, to the secretary or other public officer of such authority or company.

The request may be served on an agent of the landlord duly authorised to accept service (s.23(1)). Service on a person who has ostensible authority is also it seems sufficient (see *Galinski v McHugh* [1989] 1 E.G.L.R. 109).

15–12   Where the person who has been the tenant's landlord assigns the reversion, service of a s.26 request upon that person is sufficient unless and until the tenant has received notice of the assignment and of the name and address of the new landlord (s.23(2) of the Landlord and Tenant Act 1927).

Section 23 is permissive. Service may therefore be effected by any other method. If actual delivery is proved, service will be effective even if not served by one of the methods prescribed in s.23 (*Stylo Shoes Ltd v Prices Tailors Ltd* [1959] 3 All E.R. 901 Ch D). However, if a person serves the notice by a method specified in s.27, he need only show that the method chosen was carried out. He does not need to show that the notice arrived (*Italica Holdings SA v Bayadea* [1985] 1 E.G.L.R. 70; *Lex Services plc v Johns* [1990] 1 E.G.L.R. 92).

Where the landlord is a limited company, the notice may be served by leaving it at or sending it to the company's registered office (Companies Act 1985 s.725(1); Companies Act 2006 s.1139). A local authority may be served at an office that it designates for receiving notices (Local Government Act 1972 s.231(1)).

Where the landlord has died, see the provisions of ss.17 and 18 of the Law of Property (Miscellaneous Provisions) Act 1994 (see para.14–39).

Action by landlord on receipt of s.26 request

Landlord and Tenant Act 1954 s.26(6)

26.–(6) Within two months of the making of a tenant's request for a new tenancy the landlord may give notice to the tenant that he will oppose an application to the court for the grant of a new tenancy, and any such notice shall state on which of the grounds mentioned in section 30 of this Act the landlord will oppose the application. **15–13**

If the landlord wishes to oppose the tenant's proposed application to the court for a new tenancy, or to apply to terminate the tenancy (s.29(2)), he must give the tenant notice in writing (s.66(4) of the 1954 Act; s.23(1) of the Landlord and Tenant Act 1927, see para.15–10) that he will oppose the application and must state in the notice the ground(s) of opposition mentioned in s.30 (see Ch.17) that he will rely upon (s.26(6)). There is no prescribed form. If the landlord fails to serve a counter-notice within two months he will not be able to oppose the tenant's application for a new tenancy or to make his own application to the court to terminate the continuation tenancy (s.30(1)). Likewise, if he fails to specify a particular ground in his notice, he will not be able to oppose (or terminate) on that ground (s.30(1)–see para.17–02).

The landlord must have an honest belief in the ground stated. If he does not have such a belief, the notice will be a nullity (*Betty's Cafes Ltd v Phillips Furnishing Stores Ltd* [1959] A.C. 20, dictum of Lord Denning at pp.51 and 52; *Rous, Earl of Stradbroke v Mitchell* [1991] 1 All E.R. 676–a case under the Agricultural Holdings Act 1986). But if the notice is given in good faith, the fact that the landlord is a different person at the date of the hearing does not matter (cf. *Marks v BWB* [1963] 1 W.L.R. 1008–see also para.14–15 in relation to s.25 notices).

If the landlord's interest in the property is a tenancy that will come or can be brought to an end within 16 months (or any further time by which it may be continued under s.36(2) or 64; see paras 26–34 and 27–02), he must forthwith, upon receipt of the s.26 request, send a copy of the request to his immediate landlord; and any recipient of such a copy who is also himself a tenant, must forthwith send a copy of the notice to his immediate landlord (Sch.6 para.7; see para.26–29).

Application to the court for new tenancy

15–14 The application for a new tenancy must be made by the date immediately before the date specified in the request (s.29A(1)(2)(b)); or the date immediately before any other date agreed between the parties pursuant to s.29B (see in detail Ch.24). If the tenant fails to make his application in time, he cannot serve a fresh s.26 request. His tenancy will end immediately before the date specified in the request (or the agreed extension) and the tenant will have to leave the property (s.26(5)–para.15–03; *Polyviou v Seeley* [1979] 3 All E.R. 853).

Termination of the tenancy: s.27 notice

At expiry of fixed term

Landlord and Tenant Act 1954 s.27

15–15 **27.**–(1) Where the tenant under a tenancy to which this Part of this Act applies, being a tenancy granted for a term of years certain, gives to the immediate landlord, not later than three months before the date on which apart from this Act the tenancy would come to an end by effluxion of time, a notice in writing that the tenant does not desire the tenancy to be continued, section 24 of this Act shall not have effect in relation to the tenancy, unless the notice is given before the tenant has been in occupation in right of the tenancy for one month.

(1A) Section 24 of this Act shall not have effect in relation to a tenancy for a term of years certain where the tenant is not in occupation of the property comprised in the tenancy at the time when, apart from this Act, the tenancy would come to an end by effluxion of time.

If the tenant wishes to leave at the expiry of the fixed term he can do one of two things:

- he can serve a notice in accordance with s.27(1). This will inform the landlord that he will be leaving; or
- he can simply leave, making sure that he vacates prior to the expiry date stated in the lease. If he is not in occupation, no

continuation tenancy arises so there is nothing to terminate (s.24(1A)).

If the tenant is not in occupation, Pt II of the Act does not apply, there is no continuation tenancy and so nothing to terminate. As a consequence, the tenant who has gone does not have to pay any more rent after the expiry date in the lease. This has a disadvantage for the landlord who, if he is not served with a s.27(1) notice, does not know the position until the tenant actually leaves, resulting in possible void periods during which the property has no tenant. A landlord does have the ability to serve a s.25 notice to test the position.

However in *Single Horse Properties Ltd v Surrey County Council* [2002] EWCA Civ 367, the Court of Appeal held that where a landlord had served a s.25 notice and the tenant had made an application to the court for a new tenancy, the tenancy came to an end by effluxion of time when the tenant vacated before the expiry date in the lease.

If the tenant does serve a notice under s.27(1), it should be served on "the immediate landlord". There is no need to be concerned with the identity of "the competent landlord". Where the tenancy is held by joint tenants, all the tenants must be parties to the s.27 notice, unless some of the joint tenants are partners, in which case a notice served by the partners who are in occupation running the business will be sufficient (s.41A(3)(b); see further para.2–26).

The tenant may not serve a s.27 notice after he has made a request for a new tenancy (s.26(4)). Nor may he make a request for a new tenancy pursuant to s.26 once he has served a termination notice pursuant to s.27 (s.26(4)).

Section 27(1) does not apply to periodic tenancies.

If the tenant serves a s.27(1) notice but then remains in occupation, the tenancy will come to an end and the tenant will be a trespasser.

Termination after the tenant has held over

Landlord and Tenant Act 1954 s.27(2)

27.–(2) A tenancy granted for a term of years certain which is continuing by virtue of section 24 of this Act shall not come to an end by reason only **15–16**

of the tenant ceasing to occupy the property comprised in the tenancy but may be brought to an end on any day by not less than three months' notice in writing given by the tenant to the immediate landlord, whether the notice is given after the date on which apart from this Act the tenancy would have come to an end or before that date, but not before the tenant has been in occupation in right of the tenancy for one month.

(3) Where a tenancy is terminated under subsection (2) above, any rent payable in respect of a period which begins before, and ends after, the tenancy is terminated shall be apportioned, and any rent paid by the tenant in excess of the amount apportioned to the period before termination shall be recoverable by him.

The position is rather different if the tenant holds over after the expiry of the fixed term on a continuation tenancy by virtue of s.24 (para.1-02). In these circumstances, he must give the landlord notice of his intention to terminate the tenancy. It is not sufficient simply to give up occupation. This notice may be served before or after the contractual expiry date but not before the tenant has been in occupation under the tenancy for a month (s.27(2)). The restriction in the latter case, requiring the tenant to wait at least one month, is designed to prevent avoidance of the Act by the tenant being required to give notice under the section when he takes the tenancy.

The three month's notice required by s.27(2) can end on any day. Where necessary, rent is apportioned accordingly (new s.27(3)).

Note that the notice is served on "the immediate landlord". There is no need to be concerned with the identity of "the competent landlord". Where the tenancy is held by joint tenants, all the tenants must be parties to the s.27 notice unless some of the joint tenants are partners, in which case a notice served by the partners who are in occupation running the business will be sufficient (s.41A(3)(b); see further para.2-27).

If the tenant serves a s.27(2) notice but remains in occupation, the tenancy will come to an end and the tenant will be a trespasser.

Where a landlord has served a s.25 notice there would seem to be no reason why a tenant cannot determine the tenancy on an earlier date than that in the s.25 notice by serving a notice under s.27(2): see the comment of Dillon LJ at p.92 in *Long Acre Securities Ltd v Electro Acoustic Industries Ltd* [1990] 1 E.G.L.R. 91 (but note that the actual decision in the case was not followed in the later case of *Esselte AB* and in any event is overtaken by s.27(1A)—see generally above at para.15–15). However, it would seem pretty clear that the tenant cannot unilaterally *extend* the tenancy beyond the date in the s.25 notice (or any agreed extension; para.24–09) by service of a s.27(2) notice.

The tenant may not determine the tenancy under s.27 after he has made a request for a new tenancy. Nor may he make a request for a new tenancy pursuant to s.26 once he has served a termination notice pursuant to s.27 (s.26(4)). Section 27(2) does not apply to periodic tenancies.

Notice to quit

Landlord and Tenant Act 1954 s.24(2)

24.–(2) The last foregoing subsection shall not prevent the coming to an end of a tenancy by notice to quit given by the tenant, by surrender or forfeiture, or by the forfeiture of a superior tenancy unless— **15–17**

    (a)   in the case of a notice to quit, the notice was given before the tenant had been in occupation in right of the tenancy for one month;

Where the tenancy is a periodic tenancy, or is a tenancy for a fixed term containing a break clause entitling the tenant to terminate by notice to quit, the tenant may bring the tenancy to an end by service of a notice to quit, whether or not the 1954 Act applies to the tenancy. Where the Act does apply, the tenant may not serve a notice to quit until he has been in occupation under the tenancy for at least one month (s.24(2)(a)). Nor may he serve a notice to quit where he has previously served a s.26 request for a new tenancy (s.26(4)). If the tenant serves a notice to quit, he may not subsequently make a request for a new tenancy (s.26(4); para.15–03).

The rules governing the length of a notice to quit are the same as those that apply to common law notices to quit served by landlords. Thus, a monthly tenancy requires a calendar month's notice, a quarterly tenancy requires a quarter's notice and a yearly tenancy requires six months' notice. The notice should be made to expire on the last day of the tenancy or the anniversary of the tenancy unless the tenancy agreement provides otherwise (see further para.14–29). A notice served by a tenant to determine a tenancy of business premises does not need to be in any particular form. Section 5 of the Protection from Eviction Act 1977, which requires notices to be in prescribed form, applies only where premises are "let as a dwelling".

Unless the terms of the tenancy agreement otherwise provide, notice to quit given by one joint tenant without the concurrence of any other joint tenant is effective to determine a periodic tenancy (*Hammersmith and Fulham LBC v Monk* [1992] 1 All E.R. 1 HL); even if it has been served as a result of an agreement with the landlord. That agreement may expose the head tenant to a claim for damages for breach of covenant against derogation from grant but it does not invalidate the notice to quit (*Barrett v Morgan* [2000] L.&T.R. 209 HL). If the notice is served pursuant to an express term in a lease, the effectiveness of the notice will depend on whether the lease indicates that all joint tenants should give notice (*Violas Indenture of Lease, Re* [1909] 1 Ch. 244). A notice signed by only one of the joint tenants in these circumstances may also be effective if the tenant who served the notice had the authority of the others to give the notice (*Leek and Moorlands Building Society v Clark* [1952] 2 All E.R. 492 CA).

Service of a notice to quit by a tenant on his landlord destroys any sub-tenancy, whether lawful or not (*Pennell v Payne* [1995] 2 All E.R. 592 CA).

Break clauses

15–18 By virtue of s.69 of the 1954 Act, "notice to quit" includes a "notice to terminate a tenancy (whether a periodic tenancy or a tenancy for a term of years certain) given in accordance with the provisions (whether express or implied) of that tenancy". Thus, a notice served by a tenant pursuant to a break clause is permitted under s.24(2)(a) (above).

In *Friends Life v Siemens Hearing Instruments* [2014] EWCA Civ 382 the break clause stated that the break notice "***must*** be expressed to be given under section 24(2) of the Landlord and Tenant Act 1954" (emphasis added). The failure by the tenant to insert this phrase in the letter purporting to operate the break clause meant that the notice was ineffective to bring about the end of the lease. The following passage of Lord Hoffman in *Mannai Investment Co Ltd v Eagle Star Life Assurance Co Ltd* [1997] AC 749 was quoted by Lewison LJ:

> "If the clause has said that the notice had to be on blue paper, it would have been no good serving a notice on pink paper, however clear it might have been that the tenant wished to terminate the lease."

Lewison LJ went on to say:

> " . . . the word 'must' is an emphatic and imperative word. It is impossible in my judgment to interpret the clause as if it said that the notice 'must' be expressed in a certain way, but it does not matter if it is not."

Thus, a specific condition such as the one set out in *Friends Life v Siemens* must be followed for a notice to be valid. However, if the notice unambiguously conveys a decision to determine the tenancy, in accordance with the lease, the court may ignore immaterial errors that would not have misled a reasonable landlord receiving the notice. For example in *Manai*, the leading case in this area, the break clause entitled the tenant to terminate the lease on the third anniversary of the term commencement date. That date when calculated accurately was 13 January 1995 but the tenant gave a notice purporting to terminate the lease on January 12, 1995. The House of Lords held (by a majority of 3 to 2) that the notice was valid.

In *Prudential Assurance Co Ltd v Exel UK Ltd* [2009] EWHC 1350 (Ch) there were two joint tenants. Solicitors serving the notice had authority to serve on behalf of both tenants but in error only served on behalf of one of the two joint tenants. It was held that the break notice was invalid. It had clearly not been given on behalf of both tenants. On the facts a reasonable landlord receiving the notice would not unambiguously have understood the notice to be an effective notice.

Many break clauses set conditions that need to be complied with before the tenant can effect the break. These can sometimes be onerous and can effectively prevent the tenant from operating the break clause. For example, many leases will prevent the tenant from operating the break clause if he is in "material breach" of covenant. This was the situation in *Fitzroy House Epworth Street (No. 1) Ltd v The Financial Times Ltd*

[2006] EWCA Civ 329 where the Court of Appeal gave guidance as to how one determine materiality. The Chancellor of the High Court:

> "Materiality must be assessed by reference to the ability of the landlord to relet or sell the property without delay or additional expenditure. Where the provision is absolute then any breach will preclude an exercise of the break clause. But I see no justification for attributing to the parties an intention that the insertion of the word 'material' was intended to permit only breaches which were trivial or trifling. Those words are of uncertain meaning also and are not the words used by the parties. Nor is it, in my view, of any assistance to consider whether the word 'material' permits more or different breaches than the commonly used alternatives 'substantial' or 'reasonable'. The words 'substantial' and 'material' depending on the context, are interchangeable. The word 'reasonable' connotes a different test. The issue here is whether, notwithstanding the breaches found by the judge the Tenant had, nevertheless, 'materially complied' with its obligations. The application of an ordinary English word to a set of primary facts is itself a question of fact." (paras 35 and 36)

The expert evidence in the case was that a landlord seeking to relet the property might have to give credit for 75 per cent of the cost of the outstanding defects (£20,000—the tenant had already spent nearly £1 million pounds carrying out repairs) to an incoming tenant. When expressed as a rent free period that would be equivalent to nine days and in those circumstances it was likely that "the prospective tenant would not have raised the point in the first place for fear of creating the wrong impression". (para.31). As the outstanding defects were therefore likely only to have a limited effect on the ability to relet there was no "material" breach. A dramatic example of how a very minor breach can work to the tenant's detriment is supplied by *Avocet Industrial Estates v Merol Ltd* [2011] EWHC 3422 Ch D. One of the terms of the lease stated: "A break notice shall be of no effect if at the Break Date any payment under this lease due to have been paid on or before that date, has not been paid." The failure by the tenant to pay £130 default interest was sufficient to mean that the break clause had not been effectively operated.

Where the tenancy is a joint tenancy, all the joint tenants must be a party to the notice purporting to operate the break clause for it to be effective (*Hounslow LBC v Pilling* [1994] 1 All E.R. 432).

The provisions of s.196 of the Law of Property Act 1925 (see para.9–12) apply to service of notices terminating fixed terms unless a contrary intention appears (s.196(5); see para.14–36).

CHAPTER 16

OBTAINING INFORMATION

16-01   Where applications under Pt II of the 1954 Act are under consideration the landlord will want to have information relating to occupation of the premises and sub-tenancies so that he will know upon whom to serve s.25 notices; and whether or not the reversion is divided, requiring joint action with another person who is the landlord in relation to another part of the property (see para.14–22). The tenant will want information that will help him to decide who is "the landlord" for the purposes of s.44 (often referred to as "the competent landlord") so that he knows upon whom to serve a s.26 request (see para.15–07). The elements of the procedure are as follows:

- The landlord or the tenant may serve on the other a notice in prescribed form requiring certain relevant information. The prescribed forms are contained in Sch.1 to The Landlord and Tenant Act 1954, Pt 2 (Notices) (England and Wales) Regulations 2004, Forms 4 and 5 (Forms 20 and 21 of this book; paras 16–20 and 16–21).
- The notice may only be served within the period of two years ending on the expiry date in the lease. There are also provisions relating to periodic tenancies and break clauses.
- The information must be provided within one month of service of the notice.
- There is a duty on the recipient of the notice to notify the enquirer of any change that occurs within a period of six months of service of the notice.
- Provision is made for the situation where either the recipient of the notice or the server of the notice transfers his interest.
- Failure to comply with the requirements of s.40 gives rise to a breach of statutory duty, which may result in court orders enforcing the duty or damages for breach.

There are certain definitions that apply, in particular the term "*the appropriate person*" is used to describe the person who has served the notice requesting information (s.40(7), (8)—see further para.16-19).

Landlord's request

Landlord and Tenant Act 1954 s.40(1), (2), (5)

40.—(1) Where a person who is an owner of an interest in reversion expectant (whether immediately or not) on a tenancy of any business premises has *served on the tenant* a notice in the prescribed form requiring him to do so, it shall be the duty of the tenant to give the appropriate person in writing the information specified in subsection (2) below.

16-02

(2) That information is—

   (a)   whether the tenant *occupies* the premises or any part of them wholly or partly for the purposes of a business carried on by him;

   (b)   whether his tenancy has effect subject to any *sub-tenancy* on which his tenancy is immediately expectant and, if so—

     (i)   what premises are comprised in the sub-tenancy;

     (ii) for what term it has effect (or, if it is terminable by notice, by what notice it can be terminated);

     (iii) what is the rent payable under it;

     (iv) who is the sub-tenant;

     (v) (to the best of his knowledge and belief) whether the sub-tenant is in occupation of the premises or of part of the premises comprised in the sub-tenancy and, if not, what is the sub-tenant's address;

     (vi) whether an agreement is in force excluding in relation to the sub-tenancy the provisions of sections 24 to 28 of this Act; and

     (vii) whether a notice has been given under section 25 or 26(6) of this Act, or a request has been made under section 26 of this Act, in relation to the sub-tenancy and, if so, details of the notice or request; and

   (c)   (to the best of his knowledge and belief) the name and address of any other person who owns an interest in reversion in any part of the premises.

(5) A duty imposed on a person by this section is a duty—

   (a)   to give the information concerned within the period of *one month* beginning with the date of service of the notice; and

   (b)   if within the period of *six months* beginning with the date of service of the notice that person becomes aware that any information which has been given in pursuance of the notice is not, or is no longer, correct, to give the appropriate person correct information within the period of one month beginning with the date on which he becomes aware.

The notice

16-03 The landlord may serve a notice on the tenant in prescribed form requesting certain information. The relevant form is Form 4 (see para.16-20). The information that the tenant is required to provide is set out in the form and is derived from s.40(2). The information relates to:

- occupation;
- sub-tenancies;
- any other person who owns an interest in reversion in any part of the premises.

As stated in the introduction, these matters are relevant to the service of s.25 notices. The information in relation to occupation and sub-tenancies will assist the landlord in deciding upon whom the notices are to be served. Information regarding other persons who may own an interest in reversion in any part of the premises will assist the landlord if the reversion is divided (see para.14-22).

Who may serve the notice?

16-04 Any person "who is an owner of an interest in reversion expectant (whether immediately or not) on a tenancy of any business premises" may serve a notice on a tenant under s.40 (s.40(1)).

When may the notice be served?

Landlord and Tenant Act 1954 s.40(6)

16-05 40.—(6) This section shall not apply to a notice served by or on the tenant more than *two years* before the date on which apart from this Act his tenancy would come to an end by *effluxion of time* or could be brought to an end by *notice to quit* given by the *landlord*.

Fixed term: the landlord may not serve the notice more than two years before the expiry date stated in the lease.

> **Example**: 10-year lease expiring on July 10, 2012. The landlord cannot serve a s.40 notice prior to July 10, 2010.

Periodic tenancy: in the case of a periodic tenancy, the landlord may not serve the notice more than two years before the date on which (apart from Pt II of the 1954 Act) the tenancy could be brought to an end by notice to quit given by the landlord. This is unlikely to be an issue in any case but . . .

What about a break clause?: Section 69 provides that a "notice to quit" means "a notice to terminate a tenancy (whether a periodical tenancy or a tenancy for a term of years certain) given in accordance with the provisions (whether express or implied) of that tenancy". Thus, the notice may not be served more than two years before any termination date stated in a landlord's break clause in the lease.

> **Example**: 10-year lease expiring on December 10, 2017. The landlord has the option to break by serving not less than six months notice to quit expiring on December 10, 2012. The landlord cannot serve a s.40 notice prior to December 10, 2010.

If the notice is served prior to either of the permitted dates, there is no duty on the tenant to answer it (s.40(6)).

Providing the information

The tenant must give the landlord the information requested *in writing* (s.40(2)) within one month of receipt of the notice (s.40(5)). Response by e-mail is almost certainly in writing (see the definition of "writing" in the Interpretation Act 1978, s.5 and Sch.1; see para.24–10). However, even if not, if a tenant provides the information by e-mail it is difficult to see how a landlord will be able to complain and obtain a court order or damages for failure to comply with the statutory duty. **16–06**

Changes in the situation

If, within the period of six months beginning with the date of service of the notice, the tenant becomes aware that any information that has been given in pursuance of the notice is not, or is no longer, correct, he must give the landlord the correct information within the period of one month beginning with the date on which he becomes aware that the information is no longer correct (s.4(5)(b)). **16–07**

Tenant's request

Landlord and Tenant Act 1954 s.40(3)

16-08   **40.**–(3) Where the *tenant* of any business premises who is a tenant under such a tenancy as is mentioned in section 26(1) of this Act has served on a *reversioner* or a reversioner's *mortgagee in possession* a notice in the prescribed form requiring him to do so, it shall be the duty of the person on whom the notice is served to give the appropriate person in writing the information specified in subsection (4) below.

(4) That information is—

(a)   whether he is the *owner of the fee simple* in respect of the premises or any part of them or the mortgagee in possession of such an owner,

(b)   if he is not, then (to the best of his knowledge and belief)—

(i)   the name and address of the person who is his or, as the case may be, his mortgagor's immediate landlord in respect of those premises or of the part in respect of which he or his mortgagor is not the owner in fee simple;

(ii)   for what term his or his mortgagor's tenancy has effect and what is the earliest date (if any) at which that tenancy is terminable by notice to quit given by the landlord; and

(iii)   whether a notice has been given under section 25 or 26(6) of this Act, or a request has been made under section 26 of this Act, in relation to the tenancy and, if so, details of the notice or request;

(c)   (to the best of his knowledge and belief) the name and address of any other person who owns an interest in reversion in any part of the premises; and

(d)   if he is a reversioner, whether there is a mortgagee in possession of his interest in the premises and, if so, (to the best of his knowledge and belief) what is the name and address of the mortgagee.

(5) A duty imposed on a person by this section is a duty—

(a)   to give the information concerned within the period of *one month* beginning with the date of service of the notice; and

(b)   if within the period of *six months* beginning with the date of service of the notice that person becomes aware that any information which has been given in pursuance of the notice is not, or is no longer, correct, to give the appropriate person correct information within the period of one month beginning with the date on which he becomes aware.

The notice

16-09   The notice requesting the information must be in prescribed form (s.40(1)). The relevant form is Form 5 (see para.16-21).

The information required is stated on the prescribed form and is taken from s.40(4). It relates to:

- whether or not the recipient is the owner of the freehold, a mortgagee in possession of such an owner;
- the identity of any mortgagee in possession;
- superior interests;
- whether and s.25 notices or counter-notices to s.26 requests have been given or any s.26 requests made;
- any other person who owns an interest in reversion in any part of the premises.

As stated in the introduction, these matters are relevant to the service of s.26 requests. The information will assist the tenant in deciding upon whom the request is to be served (see para.16-01).

The tenant who may serve the notice

A s.40 notice requesting information may only be served by a **16-10** "tenant of business premises who is a tenant under such a tenancy as is mentioned in s.26(1)", i.e. "a tenancy granted for a term of years certain exceeding one, whether or not continued by section 24 of this Act, or granted for a term of years certain and thereafter from year to year" (see s.40(3)).

Service upon whom?

The tenant may serve the notice on any reversioner (i.e. "any **16-11** person having an interest in the premises, being an interest in reversion expectant (whether immediately or not) on the tenancy" (ss.40(3); 40(8)). The notice may also be served on any such reversioner's mortgagee in possession (s.40(3)). The term "mortgagee in possession" includes a receiver appointed by the mortgagee or by the court that is in receipt of the rents and profits (s.40(8)).

When may the notice be served?

Landlord and Tenant Act 1954 s.40(6)

40.–(6) This section shall not apply to a notice served by or on the tenant **16-12** more than two years before the date on which apart from this Act his tenancy would come to an end by effluxion of time or could be brought to an end by notice to quit given by the *landlord.*

The tenant should not serve the s.40 notice more than two years before the expiry date stated in the lease. If it is served before that time, there is no duty on the landlord to provide the information requested in the notice (s.40(6)).

Example: 10-year lease expiring on July 10, 2012. The tenant cannot serve a s.40 notice prior to July 10, 2010.

The reference in s.40(6) to "notice to quit given by the landlord" will not assist the tenant and there is no equivalent in relation to a tenant's notice to quit (which includes break clauses: s.69). This is because if the tenant serves a notice to quit either in respect of a periodic tenancy or pursuant to a break clause he cannot also serve a s.26 request and seek a new tenancy (see para.15–03).

Providing the information

16–13 Where a reversioner or a reversioner's mortgagee in possession has been served with a notice in prescribed form, the recipient of the notice must give the tenant the information requested (s.40(4)) within month of receipt of the notice (s.40(5)). The information must be provided in writing. As to e-mail, see para.16–06 above.

Changes in the situation

16–14 If, within the period of six months beginning with the date of service of the notice, the landlord becomes aware that any information that has been given in pursuance of the notice is not, or is no longer, correct, he must give the tenant the correct information within the period of one month beginning with the date on which he becomes aware that the information is no longer correct (s.40(5)(b)).

Transfer

16–15 Section 40A deals with the situations where one of the parties transfers his interest in the property after receipt or service of a s.40 notice requesting information.

Person who received the notice

Landlord and Tenant Act 1954 s.40A(1)

40A.–(1) If a *person on whom* a notice under section 40(1) or (3) of this   **16–16**
Act has been served has *transferred his interest* in the premises or any
part of them to some other person and gives the appropriate person
notice in writing–

(a)   of the transfer of his interest; and
(b)   of the name and address of the person to whom he transferred
      it,

on giving the notice *he ceases* in relation to the premises or (as the case
may be) to that part to be under any duty imposed by section 40 of this
Act.

A person who has received a request for information under s.40
(landlord or tenant) and who transfers his interest is no longer
under a duty to provide information or to update that
information within the six-month period provided for in
s.40(5)(b), if he notifies the person who served the notice that
he has done so and has in writing given the person who served
the s.40 notice the name and address of the person to whom
he has transferred the interest. The person requiring the
information is then free to serve a fresh notice on the
transferee.

> **Example**: T serves a s.40 notice on L requesting
> information. Before he provides the information, L assigns
> his interest in the property. Until he or the new landlord
> informs T of the name and address of the new landlord, the
> original landlord is under a duty to provide the information
> requested. In fact of course in answering the questions he
> will need to inform the tenant of the fact of the assignment
> and the details of the new landlord.

Person who gave the notice

Landlord and Tenant Act 1954 s.40A(2), (3)

40A.–(2) If–   **16–17**

(a)   the *person who served the notice* under section 40(1) or (3) of
      this Act ("the transferor") has *transferred his interest* in the
      premises to some other person ("the transferee"); and
(b)   *the transferor or the transferee* has given the person required
      to give the information *notice in writing*–

(i) of the transfer; and

(ii) of the transferee's name and address,

the appropriate person for the purposes of section 40 of this Act and subsection (1) above is the transferee.

(3) If—

(a) a transfer such as is mentioned in paragraph (a) of subsection (2) above has taken place; but

(b) neither the transferor nor the transferee has given a notice such as is mentioned in paragraph (b) of that subsection,

any duty imposed by section 40 of this Act may be performed by giving the information either to the transferor or to the transferee.

If a person who has served a s.40 notice requesting information (whether landlord or tenant) transfers his interest in the property he, or the transferee of the interest, may give notice of the transfer in writing to the person upon whom he served the s.40 notice giving details of the transfer and the name and address of the transferee. If such a notice is given the person required to provide the information must give it to the transferee (s.40A(2)).

> **Example**: L serves a s.40 notice on T requesting information. T provides that information within the one month period required by s.40(5)(a). Two months later L transfers his interest in the property and informs T. He gives T the name and address of the new landlord. Another two months pass and T enters into a sub-tenancy. T is required to provide details of the sub-tenancy to the new landlord.

If neither the transferor nor the transferee provides the recipient of the s.40 notice with the details required (i.e. details of the transfer and the name and address of the transferee), the obligation to provide information may be fulfilled by giving the information to the transferor or, if he happens to know the details, to the transferee (s.40A(3)).

> **Example**: if in the above example both the old landlord and the new had failed to provide T with notice in writing of the transfer, together with the new landlord's name and address, but T was nonetheless aware of the transfer and those details, he would be entitled to inform either the old landlord or the new landlord of the details relating to the sub-tenancy.

Breach of statutory duty

Landlord and Tenant Act 1954 s.40B

40B.—A claim that a person has broken any duty imposed by section 40 of this Act may be made the subject of civil proceedings for breach of statutory duty; and in any such proceedings a court may order that person to comply with that duty and may make an award of damages.

16–18

There were many defects with the old s.40. One of the major problems was that there was no sanction for failing to provide the information requested or if the wrong information was given. This defect has been remedied by the new s.40B. This makes breach of any duty imposed by s.40 the subject of civil proceedings. The court can make an order that the recipient of the notice complies with his obligations. The court can also make an award of damages if some loss is suffered.

> **Example**: L serves a notice on T requesting information. T replies to the request for information but fails to inform L that he has sublet part of the property. Furthermore, he fails to inform L that the sub-tenant has served a s.26 request on T, making L the competent landlord as against the sub-tenant. L brings proceedings for termination of the tenancy relying upon ground (f) in s.30 (redevelopment) but, unaware of the sub-tenancy, takes no steps in relation to it. Some time later he finds out about the sub-tenant and serves a s.25 notice upon him. This delays his ability to get back the property and in the meantime L loses a lucrative opportunity to assign the reversion. L might consider bringing a claim for damages against T.

Definitions

Landlord and Tenant Act 1954 s.40(7), (8)

40.—(7) Except as provided by section 40A of this Act, the appropriate person for the purposes of this section and section 40A(1) of this Act is the person who served the notice under subsection (1) or (3) above.

(8) In this section—

"business premises" means premises used wholly or partly for the purposes of a business;

"mortgagee in possession" includes a receiver appointed by the mortgagee or by the court who is in receipt of the rents and profits, and "his mortgagor" shall be construed accordingly;

16–19

"reversioner" means any person having an interest in the premises, being an interest in reversion expectant (whether immediately or not) on the tenancy;

"reversioner's mortgagee in possession" means any person being a mortgagee in possession in respect of such an interest; and

"sub-tenant" includes a person retaining possession of any premises by virtue of the Rent (Agriculture) Act 1976 or the Rent Act 1977 after the coming to an end of a sub-tenancy, and "sub-tenancy" includes a right so to retain possession.

16–20   **Form 20**

Form 4

LANDLORD'S REQUEST FOR INFORMATION ABOUT OCCUPATION AND SUB-TENANCIES

Section 40(1) of the Landlord and Tenant Act 1954

To:

....

....

....

(*insert name and address of tenant*)

From:

....

....

....

(*insert name and address of landlord*)

1. This notice relates to the following premises: (*insert address or description of premises*)

....

cont

---

cont

2. I give you notice under section 40(1) of the Landlord and Tenant Act 1954 that I require you to provide information—

(a) by answering questions (1) to (3) in the Table below;

(b) if you answer "yes" to question (2), by giving me the name and address of the person or persons concerned;

(c) if you answer "yes" to question (3), by also answering questions (4) to (10) in the Table below;

(d) if you answer "no" to question (8), by giving me the name and address of the sub-tenant; and

(e) if you answer "yes" to question (10), by giving me details of the notice or request.

TABLE

(1) Do you occupy the premises or any part of them wholly or partly for the purposes of a business that is carried on by you?

(2) To the best of your knowledge and belief, does any other person own an interest in reversion in any part of the premises?

(3) Does your tenancy have effect subject to any sub-tenancy on which your tenancy is immediately expectant?

(4) What premises are comprised in the sub-tenancy?

(5) For what term does it have effect or, if it is terminable by notice, by what notice can it be terminated?

(6) What is the rent payable under it?

(7) Who is sub-tenant?

(8) To the best of your knowledge and belief, is the sub-tenant in occupation of the premises or of part of the premises comprised in the sub-tenancy?

(9) Is an agreement in force excluding, in relation to the sub-tenancy, the provisions of sections 24 to 28 of the Landlord and Tenant Act 1954?

(10) Has a notice been given under section 25 or 26(6) of that Act, or has a request been made under section 26 of that Act, in relation to the sub-tenancy?

---

cont

cont

3. You must give the information concerned in writing and within the period of one month beginning with the date of service of this notice.

4. Please send all correspondence about this notice to:

Name:

....

Address:

....

....

Signed: .... Date: ....

*[Landlord] *[On behalf of the landlord]

*(*delete whichever is inapplicable)*

IMPORTANT NOTE FOR THE TENANT

This notice contains some words and phrases that you may not understand. The Notes below should help you, but it would be wise to seek professional advice, for example, from a solicitor or surveyor, before responding to this notice.

Once you have provided the information required by this notice, you must correct it if you realise that it is not, or is no longer, correct. This obligation lasts for six months from the date of service of this notice, but an exception is explained in the next paragraph. If you need to correct information already given, you must do so within one month of becoming aware that the information is incorrect.

The obligation will cease if, after transferring your tenancy, you notify the landlord of the transfer and of the name and address of the person to whom your tenancy has been transferred.

If you fail to comply with the requirements of this notice, or the obligation mentioned above, you may face civil proceedings for breach of the statutory duty that arises under section 40 of the Landlord and Tenant Act 1954. In any such proceedings a court may order you to comply with that duty and may make an award of damages.

NOTES

The sections mentioned below are sections of the Landlord and Tenant Act

cont

cont

1954, as amended, (most recently by the Regulatory Reform (Business Tenancies) (England and Wales) Order 2003).

Purpose of this notice

Your landlord (or, if he or she is a tenant, possibly your landlord's landlord) has sent you this notice in order to obtain information about your occupation and that of any sub-tenants. This information may be relevant to the taking of steps to end or renew your business tenancy.

Time limit for replying

You must provide the relevant information within one month of the date of service of this notice (section 40(1), (2) and (5)).

Information required

You do not have to give your answers on this form; you may use a separate sheet for this purpose. The notice requires you to provide, in writing, information in the form of answers to questions (1) to (3) in the Table above and, if you answer "yes" to question (3), also to provide information in the form of answers to questions (4) to (10) in that Table. Depending on your answer to question (2) and, if applicable in your case, questions (8) and (10), you must also provide the information referred to in paragraph 2(b), (d) and (e) of this notice. Question (2) refers to a person who owns an interest in reversion. You should answer "yes" to this question if you know or believe that there is a person who receives, or is entitled to receive, rent in respect of any part of the premises (other than the landlord who served this notice).

When you answer questions about sub-tenants, please bear in mind that, for these purposes, a sub-tenant includes a person retaining possession of premises by virtue of the Rent (Agriculture) Act 1976 or the Rent Act 1977 after the coming to an end of a sub-tenancy, and "sub-tenancy" includes a right so to retain possession (section 40(8)).

You should keep a copy of your answers and of any other information provided in response to questions (2), (8) or (10) above.

If, once you have given this information, you realise that it is not, or is no longer, correct, you must give the correct information within one month of becoming aware that the previous information is incorrect. Subject to the next paragraph, your duty to correct any information that you have already given continues for six months after you receive this notice (section 40(5)). You should give the correct information to the landlord who gave you this notice unless you receive notice of the transfer of his or her interest, and of the name and address of the person to whom that interest has been transferred. In that case, the correct information must be given to that person.

If you transfer your tenancy within the period of six months referred to above, your duty to correct information already given will cease if you notify the

cont

cont

landlord of the transfer and of the name and address of the person to whom your tenancy has been transferred.

If you do not provide the information requested, or fail to correct information that you have provided earlier, after realising that it is not, or is no longer, correct, proceedings may be taken against you and you may have to pay damages (section 40B).

If you are in any doubt about the information that you should give, get immediate advice from a solicitor or a surveyor.

Validity of this notice

The landlord who has given you this notice may not be the landlord to whom you pay your rent (sections 44 and 67). This does not necessarily mean that the notice is invalid.

If you have any doubts about whether this notice is valid, get advice immediately from a solicitor or a surveyor.

Further information

An explanation of the main points to consider when renewing or ending a business tenancy, "Renewing and Ending Business Leases: a Guide for Tenants and Landlords", can be found at http://www.odpm.gov.uk/ Printed copies of the explanation, but not of this form, are available from 1st June 2004 from Free Literature, PO Box 236, Wetherby, West Yorkshire, LS23 7NB (0870 1226 236).

16–21

Form 21

Form 5

TENANT'S REQUEST FOR INFORMATION FROM LANDLORD OR LANDLORD'S MORTGAGEE ABOUT LANDLORD'S INTEREST

Section 40(3) of the Landlord and Tenant Act 1954

To:

....

....

....

(insert name and address of reversioner or reversioner's mortgagee in possession [see the first note below])

cont

cont

From:

....

....

....

(*insert name and address of tenant*)

1. This notice relates to the following premises: (*insert address or description of premises*).

....

2. In accordance with section 40(3) of the Landlord and Tenant Act 1954 I require you—

   (a) to state in writing whether you are the owner of the fee simple in respect of the premises or any part of them or the mortgagee in possession of such an owner,

   (b) if you answer "no", to (a), to state in writing, to the best of your knowledge and belief—

      (i) the name and address of the person who is your or, as the case may be, your mortgagor's immediate landlord in respect of the premises or of the part in respect of which you are not, or your mortgagor is not, the owner in fee simple;

      (ii) for what term your or your mortgagor's tenancy has effect and what is the earliest date (if any) at which that tenancy is terminable by notice to quit given by the landlord; and

      (iii) whether a notice has been given under section 25 or 26(6) of the Landlord and Tenant Act 1954, or a request has been made under section 26 of that Act, in relation to the tenancy and, if so, details of the notice or request;

   (c) to state in writing, to the best of your knowledge and belief, the name and address of any other person who owns an interest in reversion in any part of the premises;

   (d) if you are a reversioner, to state in writing whether there is a mortgagee in possession of your interest in the premises; and

   (e) if you answer "yes" to (d), to state in writing, to the best of your knowledge and belief, the name and address of the mortgagee in possession.

3. You must give the information concerned within the period of one month beginning with the date of service of this notice.

cont

cont

4. Please send all correspondence about this notice to:

Name:

....

Address:

....

....

Signed: .... Date: ....

*[Tenant] *[On behalf of the tenant]

*(*delete whichever is inapplicable)*

IMPORTANT NOTE FOR LANDLORD OR LANDLORD'S MORTGAGEE

This notice contains some words and phrases that you may not understand. The Notes below should help you, but it would be wise to seek professional advice, for example, from a solicitor or surveyor, before responding to this notice.

Once you have provided the information required by this notice, you must correct it if you realise that it is not, or is no longer, correct. This obligation lasts for six months from the date of service of this notice, but an exception is explained in the next paragraph. If you need to correct information already given, you must do so within one month of becoming aware that the information is incorrect.

The obligation will cease if, after transferring your interest, you notify the tenant of the transfer and of the name and address of the person to whom your interest has been transferred.

If you fail to comply with the requirements of this notice, or the obligation mentioned above, you may face civil proceedings for breach of the statutory duty that arises under section 40 of the Landlord and Tenant Act 1954. In any such proceedings a court may order you to comply with that duty and may make an award of damages.

NOTES

The sections mentioned below are sections of the Landlord and Tenant Act 1954, as amended, (most recently by the Regulatory Reform (Business Tenancies) (England and Wales) Order 2003).

Terms used in this notice

The following terms, which are used in paragraph 2 of this notice, are defined in section 40(8):

cont

cont

> "mortgagee in possession" includes a receiver appointed by the mortgagee or by the court who is in receipt of the rents and profits;
>
> "reversioner" means any person having an interest in the premises, being an interest in reversion expectant (whether immediately or not) on the tenancy; and
>
> "reversioner's mortgagee in possession" means any person being a mortgagee in possession in respect of such an interest.

Section 40(8) requires the reference in paragraph 2(b) of this notice to your mortgagor to be read in the light of the definition of "mortgagee in possession".

A mortgagee (mortgage lender) will be "in possession" if the mortgagor (the person who owes money to the mortgage lender) has failed to comply with the terms of the mortgage. The mortgagee may then be entitled to receive rent that would normally have been paid to the mortgagor.

The term "the owner of the fee simple" means the freehold owner.

The term "reversioner" includes the freehold owner and any intermediate landlord as well as the immediate landlord of the tenant who served this notice.

Purpose of this notice and information required

This notice requires you to provide, in writing, the information requested in paragraph 2(a) and (c) of the notice and, if applicable in your case, in paragraph 2(b), (d) and (e). You do not need to use a special form for this purpose.

If, once you have given this information, you realise that it is not, or is no longer, correct, you must give the correct information within one month of becoming aware that the previous information is incorrect. Subject to the last paragraph in this section of these Notes, your duty to correct any information that you have already given continues for six months after you receive this notice (section 40(5)).

You should give the correct information to the tenant who gave you this notice unless you receive notice of the transfer of his or her interest, and of the name and address of the person to whom that interest has been transferred. In that case, the correct information must be given to that person.

If you do not provide the information requested, or fail to correct information that you have provided earlier, after realising that it is not, or is no longer, correct, proceedings may be taken against you and you may have to pay damages (section 40B).

If you are in any doubt as to the information that you should give, get advice immediately from a solicitor or a surveyor.

cont

cont

If you transfer your interest within the period of six months referred to above, your duty to correct information already given will cease if you notify the tenant of that transfer and of the name and address of the person to whom your interest has been transferred.

Time limit for replying

You must provide the relevant information within one month of the date of service of this notice (section 40(3), (4) and (5)).

Validity of this notice

The tenant who has given you this notice may not be the person from whom you receive rent (sections 44 and 67). This does not necessarily mean that the notice is invalid.

If you have any doubts about the validity of the notice, get advice immediately from a solicitor or a surveyor.

Further information

An explanation of the main points to consider when renewing or ending a business tenancy, "Renewing and Ending Business Leases: a Guide for Tenants and Landlords", can be found at http://www.odpm.gov.uk/ Printed copies of the explanation, but not of this form, are available from 1st June 2004 from Free Literature, PO Box 236, Wetherby, West Yorkshire, LS23 7NB (0870 1226 236).

CHAPTER 17

LANDLORD'S GROUNDS

. . . .

The grounds upon which the landlord may apply for termination **17-01**
of the continuation tenancy or oppose the order for a grant of
a new tenancy are set out in s.30 of the 1954 Act. When
considering this section, readers should note the references to
"the holding" in a number of the grounds. The "holding" is
defined by s.23(3) as:

"... the property comprised in the tenancy, there being
excluded any part thereof which is occupied neither by the
tenant nor by a person employed by the tenant and so
employed for the purposes of a business by reason of
which the tenancy is one to which this Part of this Act
applies".

The grounds

Landlord and Tenant Act 1954 s.30

30.–(1) The grounds on which a landlord may oppose an application **17-02**
under section 24(1) of this Act, or make an application under section
29(2) of this Act, are such of the following grounds as may be stated in
the landlord's notice under section 25 of this Act or, as the case may be,
under subsection (6) of section 26 thereof, that is to say—

    (a)   where under the current tenancy the tenant has any
obligations as respects the repair and maintenance of the
holding, that the tenant ought not to be granted a new tenancy
in view of the state of repair of the holding, being a state
resulting from the tenant's failure to comply with the said
obligations;

    (b)   that the tenant ought not to be granted a new tenancy in view
of his persistent delay in paying rent which has become due;

    (c)   that the tenant ought not to be granted a new tenancy in view
of other substantial breaches by him of his obligations under
the current tenancy, or for any other reason connected with
the tenant's use or management of the holding;

    (d)   that the landlord has offered and is willing to provide or secure
the provision of alternative accommodation for the tenant, that
the terms on which the alternative accommodation is available

are reasonable having regard to the terms of the current tenancy and to all other relevant circumstances, and that the accommodation and the time at which it will be available are suitable for the tenant's requirements (including the requirement to preserve goodwill) having regard to the nature and class of his business and to the situation and extent of, and facilities afforded by, the holding;

(e) where the current tenancy was created by the sub-letting of part only of the property comprised in a superior tenancy and the landlord is the owner of an interest in reversion expectant on the termination of that superior tenancy, that the aggregate of the rents reasonably obtainable on separate lettings of the holding and the remainder of that property would be substantially less than the rent reasonably obtainable on a letting of that property as a whole, that on the termination of the current tenancy the landlord requires possession of the holding for the purpose of letting or otherwise disposing of the said property as a whole, and that in view thereof the tenant ought not to be granted a new tenancy;

(f) that on the termination of the current tenancy the landlord intends to demolish or reconstruct the premises comprised in the holding or a substantial part of those premises or to carry out substantial work of construction on the holding or part thereof and that he could not reasonably do so without obtaining possession of the holding;

(g) subject as hereinafter provided, that on the termination of the current tenancy the landlord intends to occupy the holding for the purposes, or partly for the purposes, of a business to be carried on by him therein, or as his residence.

Introduction

17–03 The landlord may rely upon any particular ground only if that ground was stated in the s.25 notice or, as the case may be, in the counter-notice served in answer to the tenant's s.26 request for a new tenancy (s.30(1)).

It can be seen that there are two sorts of grounds in this list:

- Those that imply fault on the part of the tenant—where the phrase the tenant "ought to be granted a new tenancy" is used: (a), (b), (c).
- Those that do not imply any fault on the tenant's part and involve a desire on the part of the landlord to obtain possession for some other reason: (d), (e), (f), (g).

In the fault grounds, where the phrase "ought not" is used, the court has a discretion when deciding whether or not terminate the current tenancy or to refuse to order the grant of a new tenancy even if the substance of the ground is established (*Lyons v Central Commercial Properties Ltd* [1958] 2 All E.R. 767).

Landlord's tactics

The landlord needs to think very carefully before deciding whether or not to oppose a new tenancy and on what grounds. In the past, landlords have served s.25 notices containing a number of grounds as part of the tactics for getting the tenant out or otherwise seeking to negotiate a favourable deal. There are, however, a number of factors to consider when deciding how to proceed, including the following:

17-04

- The increasing use by the courts of their ability to penalise parties in costs, even where they win the case, if they rely on grounds that are not subsequently established (see para.27-28).
- Interim rent. As can been seen in Ch.25, the landlord will only be entitled to the more favourable basis for assessing interim rent if he does *not* oppose a new tenancy (para.25-12).
- Compensation under s.37. A landlord will be able to avoid compensation if he succeeds on one of the fault grounds and this may lead him to rely upon it. However, unless his case is a good one, the costs penalties referred to above may have effect. See further para.27-15.

We now turn to each of the grounds in s.30.

(a) Failure to comply with repairing covenants

Note that this ground is discretionary. The landlord seeks to show that the tenant "ought not to be granted a new tenancy" in view of the state of repair of the holding. See para.11-13 in relation to damages for disrepair at the end of the term.

17-05

(b) Persistent delay in paying rent

Note that this ground is discretionary. The landlord seeks to show that the tenant "ought not to be granted a new tenancy" in view of the persistent delay in paying rent which has become due.

17-06

> **Example**: T was in arrears on 11 consecutive quarter days but began to pay promptly from the date of service of the

s.25 notice. The judge was satisfied there would be no repetition and made an order for a new tenancy (*Hurstfell v Leicester Square Property Co Ltd* [1988] 2 E.G.L.R. 105).

Example: L opposed T's application for a new lease on grounds (a) and (b) of s.30; i.e. disrepair and persistent delay in paying rent. The rent was payable quarterly in advance. T had paid the rent a few days in arrears throughout the whole period of the lease. This practice had been acceptable to L, and there had been no complaint about it, until new agents were appointed. The judge had refused the claim for a new lease, having regard to the whole history of delay in paying rent. However, the Court of Appeal said that he was wrong to do so. The Court of Appeal did not merely state that the judge had wrongly exercised his discretion but went so far as to hold that the landlord was estopped from insisting upon the strict terms of the lease until clear notice had been given to the tenant. Having regard to both the rent and disrepair issues, the Court of Appeal considered that the decision of the judge was "unduly harsh" and ordered a new lease. The estoppel point is perhaps a bit doubtful. There was no clear representation/reliance/detriment analysis in the judgment and counsel for the tenant had not put the argument quite as high. However, the case does give some indication of the sort of case in which the landlord will be unsuccessful (*Hazel v Akhtar* [2001] EWCA Civ 1883).

(c) Other substantial breaches by him of his obligations under the tenancy or for any other reason connected with the use or management of the holding

17–07   "The word 'or' separating [the two] parts of the subsection make it clear that it is not necessary to find a breach of obligation for the reason to come within the subsection . . . the reasons need not be directly concerned with the relationship between the parties qua landlord and tenant . . . and . . . the word [are] broad and [enable] the court to look at everything it regards as relevant in connection with the tenants use and management of the holding." Per Lewison LJ in *Horne and Meredith Properties v. Cox* [2014] EWCA Civ 423. In which it was stated that the ground could be made out from the existence of extensive litigation between landlord and tenant, however, whether that would be sufficient to refuse renewal would depend on each case.

Activities that take place off the land may, if there is a sufficient nexus to the business that is carried on on the holding, be "connected with the tenant's use or management of the holding" and in those circumstances may be relied upon by the landlord under this ground (*Beard v Williams* [1986] 1 E.G.L.R. 148 CA).

Note that this ground is discretionary. The landlord seeks to show that the tenant "ought not to be granted a new tenancy" in view of the state of the breaches or the mismanagement of the holding. In exercising its discretion, the court should ask itself whether the landlord's interest, as landlord, is likely to be prejudiced by the matters complained of (*Beard v Williams*).

The final phrase of para.(c) includes the tenant's use of the holding for an unlawful purpose (*Turner & Bell v Searles (Stanford-le-Hope) Ltd* [1977] 33 P. & C.R. 208). In *Fowles v Heathrow Airport Ltd* [2008] EWCA Civ 1270 the trial judge found that the tenant had been in flagrant and persistent breaches of planning control some of which at least amounted to the commission of criminal offences and refused to order the grant of a new lease. On appeal the tenant submitted that it was "only if the renewal of the tenancy *necessarily* involves a criminal offence in the use of the land that such a prospect becomes a relevant consideration." The submission was rejected as "virtually unarguable". It was contrary to common sense and the broad language of para.(c). The judge was entitled to exercise the discretion in the way that he did. Indeed "it would have been perverse for the court to have ordered the respondent to grant the new tenancy to the appellant" (per Lawrence Collins LJ).

(d) Suitable alternative accommodation

17–08 This is not a discretionary ground. If the landlord proves the facts stated in para.(d) the court must refuse to order the granting of a new lease. The use of the present tense ("is willing") in the sub-para.(d) makes it clear that the landlord must be willing at the date of the hearing to provide or secure the provision of alternative accommodation (*Betty's Café Ltd v Phillips Furnishing Stores Ltd* [1958] 1 All E.R. 607, per Viscount Simonds at 613I HL). The accommodation must be made available at a time that is suitable to the tenant's requirements. It is suggested that the tenant should ask the court to seek an undertaking from the landlord to provide or secure the provision of the suitable alternative accommodation prior to the making of an order refusing the grant of a new tenancy on this ground.

Where the landlord is unable to establish that this ground applies at the date of the hearing but does satisfy the court that the ground will be established at some future date, not later than one year after the termination date specified in the s.25 notice or s.26 request, the court may not make an order for a new tenancy but may, if the tenant wishes, extend the date for termination specified in the s.25 notice or s.26 request (s.31(2); see further para.27–05).

It has been held in the county court that the words "has offered" in s.30(1)(d) do not require the landlord to have made an offer of suitable alternative accommodation prior to service of the s.25 notice. It is sufficient if the offer is made before the issue is joined in the pleadings. The requirement of reasonableness in respect of the terms on which the alternative accommodation is offered is established at the date of the hearing and need not necessarily have been reasonable at the time of the offer. The requirement of suitability is also determined at the time of the hearing (*M Chaplin Ltd v Regent Capital Holdings Ltd* [1994] 1 E.G.L.R. 249–Judge Aron Owen, Clerkenwell County Court).

(e) Property uneconomically sublet

17–09   Note that this is a discretionary ground (". . . and that in view thereof the tenant ought not to be granted a new tenancy").

Where the landlord is unable to establish this ground at the date of the hearing but does satisfy the court that the ground will be established at some future date, not later than one year after the termination date specified in the s.25 notice or s.26 request, the court may not make an order for a new tenancy but it may, if the tenant wishes, extend the date for termination specified in the s.25 notice or s.26 request (s.31(2); see further para.27–05).

(f) Demolition, reconstruction or substantial works of construction

Introduction

The tenant will not be entitled to a new tenancy if the landlord **17–10** can show that:

(a)   he "intends" to demolish or reconstruct the premises comprised in the *holding* (see introduction to this chapter) or a substantial part of those premises; or

(b)   he "intends" to carry out substantial works of construction on the *holding* or part thereof.

In either case he must also show that he cannot reasonably do so without obtaining possession of the holding (*Barth v Pritchard* [1990] 1 E.G.L.R. 109 at 110D). The word "possession" in para.(f) means legal possession and the whole phrase "without obtaining possession of the holding" means without putting an end to the tenant's right to possession of the holding. Thus, if the tenant's lease contains a term entitling the landlord to enter upon the premises to carry out the necessary work, the landlord does not require "possession" and the tenant is entitled to a new tenancy (*Heath v Drown* [1972] 2 All E.R. 561 HL; *Mularczyk v Azralnove Investments* [1985] 2 E.G.L.R. 141 CA).

Intention

Provided that the landlord has a genuine intention to demolish or reconstruct the premises, his motive is irrelevant. Nor is it necessary for the landlord to carry out the work himself. It may be done by an agent or a tenant on his behalf. In *Turner v Wandsworth LBC* [1994] 1 E.G.L.R. 134 CA the landlord had agreed to enter into a four-year tenancy with a company on condition that the company demolish the buildings on the land and convert the area into a car park with a landscaped surrounding. The fact that the landlord's motive was to sell the freehold of the land was irrelevant. For a full discussion dealing with the date upon which it is necessary for the landlord to have the requisite intention and the nature of the intention required see below (for a more detailed discussion on intention see para.17–21).

Demolition, Reconstruction or substantial works of construction

17-11 Whether or not the landlord can establish that the work proposed amounts to demolition, reconstruction or substantial works of construction is a question of fact to be determined by the judge in each case. In determining whether or not the works proposed will amount to "reconstruction", it is necessary:

> "to look at the position as a whole and to compare the results on the premises of carrying out the proposed work with the condition and state of the premises before the work [is] done; in other words, you want to regard the whole position as one total or entire picture" (*Joel v Swaddle* [1957] 1 W.L.R. 1094, per Romer LJ at 1101).

However, the proposed works considered as a whole cannot amount to construction works if none of the individual items involved considered separately could be so regarded.

> "It is only in the context of works which are, or might be, properly regarded as construction works that other works which are not themselves construction fall to be considered when the works are regarded as a whole" (*Barth v Pritchard* [1990] 1 E.G.L.R. 109, per Stocker LJ at p.111E).

It is necessary to distinguish works of construction from works of refurbishment or improvements. For there to be construction:

> "some form of building upon the premises which involves the structure is required. I would not consider wooden partitions, however extensive, as falling within the definition of construction, but such a situation would have to be reviewed in accordance with the facts of any given case" (per Stocker LJ at p.111K).

In *Marazzi v Globalrange Ltd* [2002] EWHC 3010 Ch a hotel was to be upgraded. It was held by the county court judge that the installation of a new lift, new partition walls and improved bedroom facilities were not sufficient to establish L's ground of opposition even though the works were going to take 12 months and cost over £2m. The internal structure would remain virtually untouched. On appeal, the High Court judge held that the county court judge's decision was within the range available to him. However, in *Ivory Grove Ltd v Global Range Ltd* [2003] EWHC 1409 Ch, on fairly similar facts in relation to a neighbouring property, Lawrence Collins J. upheld a different county court judge's finding (in a case in which there was additional expert evidence) that s.30(1)(f) was satisfied.

> "There is plainly nothing in the wording of section 30(1)(f) which requires the demolition or construction of structural or load-bearing features as a condition of its applicability . . . It follows that whether the relevant parts of the premises are load-bearing is simply one of the factors to be taken into account in determining the jury question of whether there is a demolition or reconstruction, or demolition or construction of a substantial part, or substantial work of construction on the holding or part of it, and not a pre-condition of the applicability of section 30(1)(f)). It also follows that, where partitioning is concerned, it will be a matter of fact and degree whether their replacement and reconfiguration will be within either limb of section 30(1)(f). . . . It was also open to him to find that view confirmed when there was taken into account the construction of a larger lift, the excavations and underpinning required, the construction of two steel beams, the openings made in some load-bearing internal walls, and the amount of strengthening to the floors and laying of the new drains. . . . In any event it was plainly open to him on the agreed evidence to find that there was a bedrock of work to the structure totalling over £450,000, which on any view was a 'substantial work or construction'." (paras 66–70).

In *Pumperninks of Piccadilly Ltd v Land Securities plc* [2002] EWCA Civ 621 the tenancy related to a ground floor shop. It was an "eggshell tenancy", i.e. the demise was confined to the internal skin of the shop and excluded any part of the structure of the building. L wanted to carry out substantial works so that "every physical thing in the demise will be removed". T argued that as there were no structural parts to the demise it was impossible to demolish "the premises". The argument was rejected. The word "premises" can include an eggshell within a building. The property comprised in the tenancy was something that was capable of being demolished and reconstructed. The following words of the judge at first instance were approved:

> "The structure is the fabric which encloses the demise in so far as it is itself demised. . . . The physical boundaries of the demise, be they constituted by walls, ceiling or floor, or only their surfaces, are premises within the meaning of the paragraph at least if they are of such physical quality as to be sensibly capable in ordinary language of being constructed or part of the construction, or of being demolished."

In *Wessex Reserve Forces & Cadets Association v White* [2005] EWHC 983 QB the landlord relied upon s.30(1)(f) as a ground of opposition, stating that it intended to demolish some huts on the land. However, the huts were tenants' fixtures. These were the most substantial structures on the land and the evidence was that the tenant would remove them if a new lease was not granted. The landlord was therefore unable to establish that it was going to demolish them.

Tenant willing to give access or take smaller part etc.

17-12 Section 31A of the 1954 Act provides that the court must not hold that the landlord cannot reasonably carry out the relevant works without obtaining possession if the tenant agrees:

(a) to a term in the new tenancy giving the landlord access and other facilities that will allow him reasonably to carry out the works without obtaining possession and without substantially interfering with the tenant's business; or

(b) to accept a tenancy of an economically separable part of the holding in circumstances set out in the Act that will permit the works to be carried out. (As to whether part of the holding is economically separable, see s.31A(2).)

The tenant is not required to elect one of these options prior to the hearing. He may rely upon them in the alternative. If (a) is satisfied, the tenant will be entitled to a new tenancy of the whole holding. If (a) is not satisfied, the tenant may still, under (b), succeed in obtaining a tenancy of part. (See *Romulus Trading Co Ltd v Henry Smith's Charity Trustees (No.2)* [1991] 1 E.G.L.R. 95; see also s.32(1A), para.26-05.)

Landlord and Tenant Act 1954 s.31A

31A.—(1) Where the landlord opposes an application under section 24(1)
of this Act on the ground specified in paragraph (f) of section 30(1) of this
Act, or makes an application under section 29(2) of this Act on that
ground, the court shall not hold that the landlord could not reasonably
carry out the demolition, reconstruction or work of construction intended
without obtaining possession of the holding if—

    (a)   the tenant agrees to the inclusion in the terms of the new
tenancy of terms giving the landlord access and other facilities
for carrying out the work intended and, given that access and
those facilities, the landlord could reasonably carry out the
work without obtaining possession of the holding and without
interfering to a substantial extent or for a substantial time with
the use of the holding for the purposes of the business carried
on by the tenant; or

    (b)   the tenant is willing to accept a tenancy of an economically
separable part of the holding and either paragraph (a) of this
section is satisfied with respect to that part or possession of
the remainder of the holding would be reasonably sufficient to
enable the landlord to carry out the intended work.

(2) For the purposes of subsection (1) (b) of this section a part of a
holding shall be deemed to be an economically separate part if, and only
if, the aggregate of the rents which, after the completion of the intended
work, would be reasonably obtainable on separate lettings of that part
and the remainder of the premises affected by or resulting from the work
would not be substantially less than the rent which would then be
reasonably obtainable on a letting of those premises as a whole.

Works to be done at a future date

Where the landlord is unable to establish ground (f) at the date
of the hearing but does satisfy the court that the ground will be
established at some future date, not later than one year after
the termination date specified in the s.25 notice or s.26
request, the court may not make an order for a new tenancy but
it may, if the tenant wishes, extend the date for termination
specified in the s.25 notice or s.26 request (s.31(2); see further
para.27-05).

(g) Landlord intends to occupy the holding for own business or as his residence

Introduction

The final ground set out in s.30 is that the landlord intends to
occupy the *holding* (see introduction to this chapter) for the
purposes, or partly for the purposes, of a business carried on by
him therein or as his residence. The landlord is not intending to

17-13

17-14

"occupy" the holding when it consists of residential premises that he intends to let (*Jones v Jenkins* [1986] 1 E.G.L.R. 113).

The court can properly conclude that the landlord has not shown the requisite intention to occupy where it is found that a sale of the property is likely in the short term (*Patel v Keles* [2009] EWCA Civ 1187). The trial judge came to the conclusion that it was "highly likely that at the expiry of the two-year period there will either be a sale or the grant of a lease of some kind". He therefore made an order that the tenant be granted a new lease. The landlord's appeal was refused. Arden LJ:

> "Section 30(1)(g) does not require that the landlord should intend to occupy the premises for any particular length of time. Clearly . . . his intended occupation must not be fleeting or illusory, but this is a minimum requirement, which might be an appropriate test to apply where the business is to be continued through successors in title. In other circumstances, in my judgment there must be some substance in the intended occupation for the purpose of carrying on the landlord's business and thus I agree with the judge that the occupation must be more than short-term. Parliament could hardly have intended that the landlord should be able to prevent the renewal of a business tenancy if that were not so. What is short-term must depend on the facts of the particular case."

It is sufficient if the landlord intends to occupy and carry on the business through an agent or manager (*Skeet v Powell-Sheddon* [1988] 2 E.G.L.R. 113—premises to be run as a hotel by way of family enterprise with husband of the landlord to be in day-to-day control). For a case in which a local authority was to run a bowling club through a management company, see *Teeside Indoor Bowls Ltd v Stockton on Tees BC* [1990] 2 E.G.L.R. 87.

There are a number of cases dealing with the nature of the intention required of the landlord. For a full discussion, see para.17–22, where the date upon which the intention should exist is also dealt with.

Companies

17–15 Prior to the 2003 Reform Order s.30(3) of the 1954 Act provided that an *individual* in control of a company could rely upon the ground (e.g. see *Ambrose v Kaye* [2002] EWCA Civ 91). However, a *company landlord* was unable to recover the property relying on the ground so as to allow the controlling shareholder to trade on the premises. This defect was remedied on June 1, 2004 (in respect of cases where a notice was served on or after that date; art.29(1) of the 2003 Reform Order) by the provisions of subss.(1A) and (1B) of s.30; subject to the five-year rule (see below, para.17–19).

Landlord and Tenant Act 1954 s.30(1A), (1B)

30.–(1A) Where the landlord has a controlling interest in a company, the reference in subsection (1)(g) above to the landlord shall be construed as a reference to the landlord or that company.

(1B) Subject to subsection (2A) below, where the landlord is a company and a person has a controlling interest in the company, the reference in subsection (1)(g) above to the landlord shall be construed as a reference to the landlord or that person.

Where the company is part of a group of companies, see s.42(3); para.2–22.

17–16

Trusts

Where the landlord's interest is held on trust, the intention of either the landlord or any of the beneficiaries to occupy the holding for business or residential purposes may be relied upon (s.41(2); *Morar v Chauhan* [1985] 3 All E.R. 493) but the beneficiary must establish that he is entitled to occupy the property by virtue of his interest under the trust and not otherwise (*Meyer v Riddick* [1990] 1 E.G.L.R. 107 CA). Similar rules apply in relation to a company that is part of a group of companies (s.42(3); para.2–22).

17–17

Landlord and Tenant Act 1954 s.41(2)

41.–(2) Where the landlord's interest is held on trust the references in paragraph (g) of subsection (1) of section 30 of this Act to the landlord shall be construed as including references to the beneficiaries under the trust or any of them; but, except in the case of a trust arising under a will or on the intestacy of any person, the reference in subsection (2) of that section to the creation of the interest therein mentioned shall be construed as including the creation of the trust.

17–18

The "five-year rule"

Landlord and Tenant Act 1954 s.30(2), (3)

17–19

30.–(2) The landlord shall not be entitled to oppose an application under section 24(1) of this Act, or make an application under section 29(2) of this Act, on the ground specified in paragraph (g) of the last foregoing subsection if the interest of the landlord, or an interest which has merged in that interest and but for the merger would be the interest of the landlord, was purchased or created after the beginning of the period of *five years which ends with the termination of the current tenancy*, and at all times since the purchase or creation thereof the holding has been comprised in a tenancy or successive tenancies of the description specified in subsection (1) of section 23 of this Act.

(2A) *Subsection (1B)* above shall not apply if the controlling interest was acquired after the beginning of the period of five years which ends with the termination of the current tenancy, and at all times since the acquisition of the controlling interest the holding has been comprised in a tenancy or successive tenancies of the description specified in section 23(1) of this Act.

The landlord is not entitled to rely upon ground (g) if:

(1) His interest (or an interest which has merged in that interest and but for the merger would be the interest of the landlord) was *purchased* or *created* after the beginning of the period of five years which ends with the termination of the current tenancy.

(2) Throughout that period the property has been let on one or a number of tenancies protected by Pt II of the 1954 Act (s.30(2)).

"The object of subsection (2) is to prevent an incoming landlord, within the last year or two of a tenancy, from buying up the premises over the head of the tenant and then ejecting the tenant on the ground that he requires it for his own purposes. In order to prevent this, the Act says that the landlord cannot rely on sub-para.(g) unless he has bought the relevant interest more than five years before the end of the tenancy" (*HL Bolton (Engineering) Co Ltd v TJ Graham & Sons Ltd* [1956] 3 All E.R. 624, per Denning LJ at 627E).

The word "purchased" is "not used in its technical legal sense, but is used in its popular sense of buying for money" (per Denning LJ at 627I).

The word "created" is intended to prevent an incoming landlord from avoiding the effect of the subsection "by taking a long lease in his own favour instead of buying the premises" (*HL Bolton (Engineering) Co Ltd*, per Denning LJ at 628E). Where the landlord's interest in the property is a leasehold one, his lease is "created" on the date of execution and not, if different, on the date of commencement (*Northcote Laundry v Frederick Donnelly Ltd* [1968] 2 All E.R. 50 CA). Where the landlord's interest is held on trust, the reference in subs.(2) to the creation of an interest is (except in the case of a trust arising under a will or on intestacy) construed as including the creation of the trust (s.41(2); para.2–25) so that the intention of the beneficiaries cannot be relied upon if the trust was created within the five-year period (*Morar v Chauhan* [1985] 3 All E.R. 493).

> "In my opinion the intent and proper construction of the subsection (s.40(2)) is clear. Where the landlord of business premises is a trustee for one or more beneficiaries, then the subsection *prima facie* entitles those beneficiaries as well as the landlord to oppose the grant of a new tenancy on the ground contained in para.(g). For instance, if the beneficiary or beneficiaries *bona fide* intend, on the termination of the relevant tenancy, to use the premises as a residence for themselves, then they can oppose the grant of a new tenancy on this ground. But the second part of s.41(2) places such beneficiaries under a similar 'limitation' as there would be on the landlord were he alone beneficially entitled to the reversion: if the trust under which the beneficiaries acquired their beneficial interest was created within the preceding five years, then they too are barred from relying on para.(g)." (*Morar v Chauhan* [1985] 3 All E.R. 493, per May LJ at 496g.)

Where the landlord's interest is held by a member of a group of companies, the five-year rule does not apply if the interest was purchased from or created by another member of the group (s.42(3)(b); para.2–23).

The landlord must be the "competent landlord" (see para 14-16) for the whole 5-year period (*Frozen Value Ltd v Heron Foods Ltd* [2012] EWCA Civ 473).

In calculating the period of five years, one starts with the date of "termination of the current tenancy". That date is the date contained in the s.25 notice or the s.26 request (*F Lawrence Ltd v Freeman Hardy & Willis Ltd* [1959] 3 All E.R. 77—it is not the date that occurs three months after the case is finally disposed of; i.e. the provisions of s.64 (see para.27–02) do not apply to s.30(2)).

If the landlord is unable to rely upon para.(g) because of the five-year rule, the court may, if it is satisfied as to the landlord's intention, reduce the length of the tenancy granted to the tenant (see further para.27–05).

The landlord's "intention" in cases under s.30(1)(f) and (g)

17–20   As has been seen above, paras (f) and (g) require proof of a particular intention on the part of the landlord in relation to the holding. Under (f), he must show that he intends to demolish, reconstruct or carry out substantial works of reconstruction. Under (g), the landlord must show that he intends to occupy the holding for business or residential purposes.

Date upon which intention is required

17–21   The landlord must intend to do the works or occupy the holding on "the termination of the current tenancy" (i.e. three months after final disposal of the case; see s.64, para.27–02) or within a reasonable time thereof (*London Hilton Jewellers v Hilton International Hotels* [1990] 1 E.G.L.R. 112 CA). But the intention itself must exist at the date of the hearing (*Betty's Café Ltd v Phillips Furnishings Stores Ltd* [1958] 1 All E.R. 607 HL). The person who is required to have the requisite intention is the "competent landlord" (*Marks v British Waterways Board* [1963] 1 W.L.R. 1008). Thus, at the date of the hearing, the competent landlord must have the intention to do the works or, as the case may be, to occupy the holding three months after the hearing or within a reasonable time thereof.

Where there has been a change in the identity of the competent landlord since the s.25 notice (or counter-notice to s.26 request) was served, the new competent landlord may rely on the ground stated in the s.25 notice (counter-notice) but it is obviously the new landlord's intention that is relevant (*AD Wimbush & Son Ltd v Franmills Properties Ltd* [1961] 2 All E.R. 197).

Where the landlord cannot show that he intends to carry out the works or occupy at the termination of the current tenancy but can show that he intends to do so at some future time, the court will have regard to that intention when considering the duration of the tenancy to be granted to the tenant (see further, para.27–05).

Nature of intention required

Perhaps the most famous statement dealing with the nature of   **17–22**
the intention required by the landlord is that of Lord Denning in
Fisher v Taylors Furnishing Stores Ltd [1956] 2 All E.R. 78
where he said that the landlord is required to show that he has
"a firm and settled intention, not likely to be changed".

A landlord cannot satisfy para.(f) where his intention is to sell
outright to a person who intends to carry out the works but he
does have a sufficient intention if he intends that the work
should be carried out pursuant to a building lease granted by
him after he recovers possession (*Gilmour Caterers Ltd v St
Bartholomew's Hospital Governors* [1956] 1 All E.R. 314; *Spook
Erection Ltd v British Railways Board* [1988] 1 E.G.L.R. 76).

> "It is plain law that the necessary intent for the purposes
> of section 30(1)(f) must be an intent extant at the time of
> the hearing of the application. The intent is not necessarily
> an intent to reconstruct or rebuild with one's own hands.
> It is sufficient that, for example, the intention should be to
> effect the rebuilding or the reconstruction by the
> mechanism of a building lease. That has been clear for
> upwards of 30 years. It was established in *Gilmour
> Caterers Ltd v St Bartholomew's Hospital Governors* where
> Denning L.J. said: 'The landlord intends to demolish or
> reconstruct the premises even though he does it through
> the hands of a building lessee. In a way, the grant of a
> building lease is a means for paying for the work. Just as
> when you employ a building contractor you pay him in
> money, so you pay the building lessee by granting him a
> period of years of occupation. It seems to me that,
> whether the work is done directly by a building contractor
> or less directly through a building lessee, the landlord
> intends to demolish or reconstruct the premises. He
> intends to have it demolished and reconstructed, and that
> is sufficient.' " (*Spook Erection Ltd v British Railways
> Board* [1988] 1 E.G.L.R. 76, per Hann LJ at 76L.)

A further example of how the section can operate is *Edwards v
Thompson* [1990] 2 E.G.L.R. 71 where the landlord wished to
convert a smithy to a dwelling-house. He had received planning

permission for the conversion and was able to show that the work could be carried out. If the case had been as simple as that the landlord, on the facts, would have had little difficulty in persuading the court that he had the necessary intention.

> "An 'intention' . . . connotes a state of affairs which the party 'intending'—I will call him X—does more than merely contemplate. It connotes a state of affairs which, on the contrary, he decided so far as in him lies, to bring about, and which, in point of possibility, he has a reasonable prospect of being able to bring about by his own act of volition. X cannot, with any due regard for the English language, be said to 'intend' a result which is wholly beyond the control of his will. He cannot 'intend' that it shall be a fine day tomorrow; at most he can hope or desire or pray that it will. Nor, short of this, can X be said to 'intend' a particular result if its occurrence, though it may not be wholly uninfluenced by X's will, is dependent on so many other influences, accidents and cross-currents of circumstance that, nor merely is it quite likely not to be achieved at all, but if it is achieved, X's volition will have been no more than minor agency collaborating with, or not thwarted by, the factors which predominantly determine its occurrence. If there is a sufficiently formidable succession of fences to be surmounted before the result at which X aims can be achieved, it may well be unmeaning to say that X 'intended' that result . . . This leads me to the second point bearing on the existence . . . of 'intention' as opposed to mere contemplation. Not merely is the term 'intention' unsatisfied if the person professing it has too many hurdles to overcome, or too little control of events; it is equally inappropriate if at the material date that person is in effect not deciding to proceed but feeling his way and reserving his decision until he shall be in possession of financial data sufficient to enable him to determine whether the project will be commercially worthwhile. (*Cunliffe v Goodman* [1950] 1 All E.R. 720, per Asquith LJ at 724.)

> . . .

The court must be satisfied that the intention to reconstruct is genuine and not colourable; that it is a firm and settled intention, not likely to be changed; that the reconstruction is of a substantial part of the premises, indeed so substantial that it cannot be thought to be a device to get possession of the holding in order to do it; and that it is intended to do the work at once and not after a time. (*Fisher v Taylors Furnishing Stores Ltd* [1956] 2 All E.R. 78, per Lord Denning 80.)

In the present case, the premises are ripe for development and the proposed work is obviously desirable; but the difficulty is to be satisfied that the corporation have the present means and ability to carry out the work. 'Intention' connotes an ability to carry it into effect. A man cannot properly be said to 'intend' to do a work of reconstruction when he has not got the means to carry it out. He may *hope* to do so; he will not have the *intention* to do so. In this case the corporation contemplate turning this land into a splendid estate by the sea. They are exploring the possibilities of it; they are discussing the ways and means, in the shape of a building lease; but that is as far as they have got. Their ability to do the work, or to cause it to be done, is I think, open to question" (*Roehorn v Barry Corp* [1956] 2 All E.R. 742, per Lord Denning at 744g.)

However, the planning permission that related to the smithy also related to the construction of a number of dwellings on neighbouring land and only permitted development of each piece of land to proceed together. In respect of the remainder of the development, no specific developer had been selected, no estimates had been obtained in regard to the costs and no advice had been received about what a developer would be likely to pay for it. There was also evidence that if a good offer had been received for the whole of the land the landlord and the owner of the neighbouring land might have accepted. The Court of Appeal therefore held that there was no firm and settled intention to carry out the works at the termination of the current tenancy.

Section 30(1)(g) also states quite simply " . . . that on termination of the current tenancy the landlord intends to occupy the holding for the purposes . . . of a business carried on by him". However, the courts have added a "judicial gloss" to that section. For example:

17–23

"The question whether the landlords intend to occupy the premises is primarily one of fact, but the authorities establish that, to prove such an intention, the landlord

> must prove two things. First, a genuine *bona fide* intention on the part of the landlords that they intend to occupy the premise for their own purposes. Second, the landlords must prove that, in point of possibility, they have a reasonable prospect of being able to bring this occupation by their own act of volition" (*Gregson v Cyril Lord Ltd* [1962] 3 All E.R. 907).

The issue of whether or not the landlord has the requisite intention is a matter for the judge to decide on the evidence before him. He may come to the conclusion that the landlord has the requisite intention merely on the oral evidence that the landlord gives in the witness box. There is no requirement for corroboration and there is no legal requirement to show that particular things have been done (*Mirza v Nicola* [1990] 2 E.G.L.R. 73 CA).

> "What is said on behalf of the appellant tenants is that in a case such as this the judge should look for corroboration of the landlord's assertion that he desires to occupy the premises for the purposes of a business. That may very well be a desirable state of affairs, and in this case the judge did look for and find such corroboration in the letters to which I have referred. But, for my part, I am quite unable to accept the submission made . . . on behalf of the tenants that there is in some way an obligation on the judge not to accept resistance to an application for a new lease on the grounds disclosed in section 30(1)(g) unless there is in existence some corroborative material of the landlord's assertions.
>
> In my judgment, provided that the judge asks himself the right question—which is whether it is established that there is in fact at the date of the hearing a fixed and firm intention on the part of the landlord to occupy the premises for business purposes—he is entitled, on the sworn testimony of the landlord alone, to come to the conclusion that the burden of proof has been discharged." (*Mirza v Nicola* [1990] 2 E.G.L.R. 73 CA, per Russell LJ at p.74J.)

It is important to remember that the purpose of the judicial gloss is only to ensure that landlord satisfies the court as to intention and that the burden is not a particularly heavy one:

" . . . the function of the judicial gloss on the statutory test of intention is to determine the reality of a landlord's intention to start a business, not the probability of his achieving its start or, even less, its ultimate success. . . . The test is whether the landlord has a reasonable prospect of achieving his genuine intention of occupying the demised property for the purpose of conducting a business there within a short or reasonable time after termination of the tenancy . . . The wisdom or long-term viability of the project are not, in my judgment, candidates for further judicial gloss on that provision." (*Dolgellau Golf Club v Hett* [1998] 2 E.G.L.R. 76 Auld LJ at 79E.)

> **Example**: The landlord intended to take over and run a golf course. He had no schemes, gave no evidence of the of likely cost and had no real idea of finances. Yet the judge believed him and application for a new tenancy refused (*Dolgellau Golf Club v Hett* [1998] 2 E.G.L.R. 76).

> **Example**: Don't overdo the planning requirement. A collateral mother of all battles over planning did not stop the landlord from successfully relying upon s.30(1)(g). (*Gatwick Parking Services Ltd v Sargent* [2000] 2 E.G.L.R. 45; *Dogan v Semali Investments Ltd* [2005] EWCA Civ 1036—L does not have to demonstrate that on the balance of probability permission will be granted. He only has to show that there is a real, not merely a fanciful, chance.)

However, a landlord is usually best advised to go as far as possible in preparing his plans for the demolition, reconstruction etc. and to be in a position to show the court that he has done so. This will include:

- the obtaining of any necessary planning permission—see *Cadogan & McCarthy v Stone Developments Ltd* [1996] E.G.C.S. 94—showing a reasonable prospect of obtaining permission;
- the arrangement of finance;
- if the landlord is a company, the passing of any necessary resolutions;
- the preparation of plans and the obtaining of tenders from building contractors; and

- in a case where the landlord is relying upon para.(g), evidence relating to any arrangements that he has made with suppliers, customers etc.

The tenant will wish to challenge the landlord as to his preparations and, if the landlord has failed to take the necessary steps, the tenant will seek to persuade the court that the landlord does not have a firm and settled intention. The problem from the tenant's point of view is that all the information that shows whether or not the landlord has a genuine and sufficient intention is in the landlord's possession. If the landlord has taken the steps referred to above, there will be documentation that will be disclosed but the key evidence in any case may not become apparent until later. Service of questions is a way of finding out details of this evidence.

It is often difficult to know how to approach the case tactically from the tenant's point of view. Does he insist upon full disclosure of as much information as possible? If he does so, he may simply push the landlord into preparing his case. (Cases are often lost because of bad preparation.) On the other hand, if he fails to do so, the tenant may find that he is taken by surprise at some late point in the case, possibly even by oral evidence at the trial. In theory of course there should be no surprises. Everything that the landlord wishes to say should be contained in witness statements served prior to the trial. However, things don't always work like that!

A step that is sometimes taken, particularly by the tenant who wishes to avoid playing litigation games, is to write to the landlord at an early stage (perhaps immediately after service of the s.25 notice) requesting full details of the landlord's plans and preparations together with all relevant documentation. The tenant's letter will state that, if he is persuaded as to the landlord's intention by the early disclosure of evidence, he will not pursue a claim for a new tenancy. This will put him in a very good position when it comes to costs.

Similarly a landlord who wishes to maximise his chances of persuading the tenant to go without a fight, and of recovering costs should the tenant dispute the matter to trial, should give the tenant as much information as possible at the earliest possible stage (see also para.22–02).

Part 4

Other Cases of Termination

Chapter 18

EXPIRY OF FIXED TERM

Expiry of fixed term

When does the fixed term expire?

It is sometimes important to know the precise date upon which   **18–01**
the fixed term is due to come to an end. For example, a s.25
notice may not be served so as to expire prior to the date of
expiry of the lease. Normally, there is no difficulty in calculating
that date but there can sometimes be ambiguity. For example,
the use of the word "from" in a lease has caused difficulty in
the past. It has now been held that, unless the lease indicates
to the contrary, a term that is expressed to commence "from"
a particular date, commences on the first moment of the day
following that named (*Ladyman v Wirral Estates Ltd* [1968] 2 All
E.R. 197; compare *Meadfield Properties Ltd v Secretary of
State for Environment* [1995] 1 E.G.L.R. 39 where the lease
specified a beginning date and an expiry date. See further in
relation to break clauses para.15–19).

Status of tenancy after expiry: 1954 Act applies

As has been explained in Ch.1, if the 1954 Act applies to the   **18–02**
tenancy, the effect of s.24 is to continue the tenancy beyond
the expiry date stated in the lease unless and until it is
terminated in accordance with the provisions of the Act
(para.1–02). If an application to the court is made for a new
tenancy, the current tenancy is generally continued until three
months after the proceedings are finally disposed of (s.64;
para.27–02). However, if the court awards a tenancy that the
tenant decides not to accept, the current tenancy comes to an
end three months after an order is made revoking the order for
the grant of a new tenancy *unless* the parties agree or the court
determines that it should continue beyond that date. If so, the
tenancy will continue for such period as is agreed or

determined by the court "to be necessary to afford to the landlord a reasonable opportunity for reletting or otherwise disposing of the premises which would have been comprised in the new tenancy" (s.36(2); para.26–34).

Status of tenancy after expiry: 1954 Act has never applied

18–03   Unless the lease provides otherwise, it is not necessary for the landlord or the tenant to serve the other party with a notice to quit at the end of the fixed term. The tenant has until midnight on the last day before he need leave (*Crowhurst Park, Re* [1974] 1 W.L.R. 583 at 588).

A tenant who remains in occupation without the landlord's consent does so as a tenant at sufferance and is liable to the landlord for damages for use and occupation (*Bayley v Bradley* (1848) 5 CB 396 at 406). It is not necessary to serve a notice to terminate a tenancy at sufferance. Once consent is granted the former tenant is likely to become a tenant at will and can in some circumstances become a periodic tenant (*Erimus Housing Ltd v Barclays Wealth Trustees (Jersey) Ltd* [2014] EWCA Civ 303). Patten LJ:

> "When a party holds over after the end of the lease he does so, without more, as a tenant on sufferance until his possession is consented to by the landlord. With such consent he becomes at the very least a tenant at will and his continued payment of the rent is not inconsistent with his remaining a tenant at will even though the rent reserved by the former lease was an annual rent. The payment of rent gives rise to no presumption of a periodic tenancy. Rather, the parties' contractual intentions fall to be determined by looking objectively at all relevant circumstances."

In *Erimus* the tenant held over after the end of a contracted out lease paying the rent and service charges. Negotiations for a lease started before the end of the term. They continued at a "leisurely pace" for two years afterwards. There was nothing to indicate that they ceased or that the parties intended to enter into a new lease except upon terms which were to be agreed. Applying *Javad v Aqil* [1991] 1 WLR 1007 (see further para.4–11) the Court of Appeal held that the tenant remained in occupation under a tenancy at will—not under a periodic tenancy. Patten LJ:

> "The most obvious and significant circumstance in the present case, as in *Javid v Aqil*, was the fact that the parties were in negotiation for the grant of a formal lease. In these circumstances, as in any other subject to contract negotiations, the obvious and almost overwhelming inference will be that the parties did not intend to enter into any intermediate contractual arrangement inconsistent with remaining parties to ongoing negotiations. In the landlord and tenant context that will in most cases lead to the conclusion that the occupier remained a tenant at will pending the execution of the new lease. The inference is likely to be even stronger when any periodic tenancy would carry with it statutory protection under the 1954 Act which could be terminated by the tenant agreeing to surrender or terminating the tenancy by notice to quit: *Cardiothoracic Institute Shrewdcrest Ltd* [1986] 1 WLR 368. This point is given additional force in the present case by the fact that the intended new lease, like the old lease, was to be contracted out."

After negotiations stalled the tenant served a notice on the landlord to terminate the tenancy. If the tenant had held over under a periodic tenancy it would have been an annual tenancy, not contracted out of the 1954 Act, and would have required six months' notice to quit by virtue of s.24(2) of the 1954 (see para.14–30 in respect of annual tenancies and para.15–18 in respect of s.24(2)); the tenant's notice would have been invalid, thus entitling the landlord to continuing rent. However, as the occupier remained a tenant at will pending the execution of the new lease, the tenancy was a tenancy at will, the tenant's notice was valid and no more rent was payable.

By contrast in *Walji v Mount Cook Land Ltd* [2002] 1 P. & C.R. 13 the parties reached agreement on the terms of a new lease but then did nothing further for years in terms of executing such a lease. The court held that a periodic tenancy had come into existence. (Referred to by Patten LJ at para 24 in *Erimus*.) See also para.4–08 for the arising of a periodic tenancy at the end of a fixed term.

A tenancy at will may be determined by simply asking the tenant to leave, or by the service of proceedings for possession (*Martinali v Ramuz* [1953] 2 All E.R. 892). No special form of notice is required. If the tenant remains in occupation as a tenant at will, the damages for use and occupation will be assessed in the same way as mesne profits (see para.7-46); *Dean and Chapter of the Cathedral and Metropolitan Church of Christ Canterbury v Whitbread plc* [1995] 1 E.G.L.R. 82 Ch D—tenant remained in occupation for a year after expiry of a s.26 request with no application to court during negotiations for a new lease which came to nothing).

Where the circumstances are such that a new periodic tenancy is to be inferred, the terms of the tenancy are (subject to any contrary agreement) the same as the terms that applied to the fixed term so far as they are consistent with a periodic tenancy. In particular, this means that any forfeiture clause in the fixed term carries over into the periodic term (*Thomas v Packer* (1857) 1 H. & N. 669) but the tenancy may also be determined by giving notice appropriate to the period of the tenancy as to which see para.14-29.

Vacant Possession

Where a fixed term has expired and the tenant has no statutory or other right to remain in occupation, the tenant must give vacant possession. If vacant possession is not given the tenant will be liable to pay the landlord damages for use and occupation. A useful definition of "vacant possession" was given in *NYK Logistics (UK) Ltd v Ibrend Estates BV* [2011] EWCA Civ 683. Rimer LJ at para.44:

> "The concept of 'vacant possession' in the present context is not, I consider, complicated. It means what it does in every domestic and commercial sale in which there is an obligation to give 'vacant possession' is required to be given, the property is empty of people and that the purchaser is able to assume and enjoy immediate and exclusive possession, occupation and control of it. It must also be empty of chattels, although the obligation in this respect is likely only to be breached if any chattels left in the property substantially prevent or interfere with the enjoyment of the right of possession of a substantial part of the property."

Effect on sub-tenants

Landlord and Tenant Act 1954 s.65

65.–(1) Where by virtue of any provision of this Act a tenancy (in this subsection referred to as "the inferior tenancy") is continued for a period such as to extend to or beyond the end of the term of a superior tenancy, the superior tenancy shall, for the purposes of this Act and of any other enactment and of any rule of law, be deemed so long as it subsists to be an interest in reversion expectant on the termination of the inferior tenancy and, if there is no intermediate tenancy, to be the interest in reversion immediately expectant on the termination thereof.

(2) In the case of a tenancy continuing by virtue of any provision of this Act after the coming to an end of the interest in reversion immediately expectant upon the termination thereof, subsection (1) of section 139 of the Law of Property Act 1925 (which relates to the effect of the extinguishment of a reversion) shall apply as if references in the said subsection (1) to the surrender or merger of the reversion included references to the coming to an end of the reversion for any reason other than surrender or merger.

(3) Where by virtue of any provision of this Act a tenancy (in this subsection referred to as "the continuing tenancy") is continued beyond the beginning of a reversionary tenancy which was granted (whether before or after the commencement of this Act) so as to begin on or after the date on which apart from this Act the continuing tenancy would have come to an end, the reversionary tenancy shall have effect as if it had been granted subject to the continuing tenancy.

(4) Where by virtue of any provision of this Act a tenancy (in this subsection referred to as "the new tenancy") is granted for a period beginning on the same date as a reversionary tenancy or for a period such as to extend beyond the beginning of the term of a reversionary tenancy, whether the reversionary tenancy in question was granted before or after the commencement of this Act, the reversionary tenancy shall have effect as if it had been granted subject to the new tenancy.

18–04

Where the 1954 Act applies neither to the tenancy nor the sub-tenancy "the branch falls with the tree", i.e. the sub-tenancy automatically comes to an end on the termination of the tenancy. Where the 1954 Act does not apply to the tenancy but does apply to the sub-tenancy, the latter continues by virtue of s.24(1) of the 1954 Act and the position is governed by the provisions of s.65 of the 1954 Act (see above) and s.139 of the Law of Property Act 1925 (para.19–09). In effect, the sub-tenancy continues with the landlord becoming the immediate landlord of the sub-tenant.

A sub-tenant of a residential part of the premises is not entitled to the protection of the Rent Act 1977 upon the coming to an end of a head tenancy of a building that was let as a whole for business purposes (*Pittalis v Grant* [1989] 2 All E.R. 622;

Bromley Park Garden Estates Ltd v George [1991] 2 E.G.L.R. 95). Compare the position of a lawful assured tenant (para.27-08).

Failure by tenant to remove sub-tenant

18-05   Where a tenancy comes to an end, the tenant must give up complete possession. If a sub-tenant or other person who originally entered into occupation under the tenant remains in occupation, the tenant remains liable to pay for use and occupation until possession is delivered up, unless the landlord accepts that person as a new tenant (*Harding v Crethorn* (1793) 1 Esp. 56); even if the occupier remains in occupation against the wishes of the tenant (*Ibbs v Richardson* (1839) 9 A. & E. 849).

> "When a lease is expired, the tenant's responsibility is not at an end; for if the premises are in possession of an undertenant, the landlord may refuse to accept possession, and hold the original lessee liable; for the lessor is entitled to receive the absolute possession at the end of the term. But it may be proved, that the lessor had accepted the undertenant as his tenant, as by his having accepted the key from the original lessee, while the undertenant was in possession, by his acceptance of rent from him, or by some act tantamount to it." (*Harding v Crethorn*, per Lord Kenyon.)

Where the sub-tenant has statutory protection the tenant may have a defence if he has done his best to get the sub-tenant out (see further *Reynolds v Bannerman* [1922] 1 K.B. 719 and *Walton v Saunders-Roe* [1947] K.B. 437 discussed in *Woodfall* at 19.006).

CHAPTER 19

SURRENDER, MERGER, FRUSTRATION AND REPUDIATION

. . . .

Actual surrender

When considering surrender it is necessary to make a clear distinction between (i) actual surrender and (ii) an agreement to surrender. An actual surrender is always possible but, where Pt II of the 1954 Act applies, an agreement to surrender is only permitted if the procedures set out in s.38A are complied with. See para.19–11.

19–01

The fact that an actual surrender is permitted by Pt II of the Act in all circumstances is made clear by s.24(2).

19–02

Landlord and Tenant Act 1954 s.24

24.–(2) The last foregoing subsection shall not prevent the coming to an end of a tenancy . . . by surrender . . .

Example: Lease of a pub for three years from December 1, 1992. When the contractual term expired the tenancy continued under s.24. L wrote offering a new temporary tenancy at a lower rent. This was a tenancy at will. T accepted the offer in February 1996. Arrears of rent subsequently accrued and in October 1996 L terminated tenancy at will and brought possession proceedings. L argued that the continuation tenancy had been surrendered when T entered into the tenancy at will. T argued that any surrender was void under s.38. *Held*: the tenancy at will "was plainly intended by L and T to replace the tenancy arising out of the 1994 lease with which it was inconsistent". T was estopped from denying that he had surrendered the tenancy. Section 38(1) does not preclude an actual surrender. (*Gibbs Mew plc v Gemmell* [1999] 1 E.G.L.R. 43 CA.)

If the tenancy is a joint tenancy, all the joint tenants must agree to the surrender for it to be effective (*Leek and Moorlands Building Society v Clark* [1952] 2 Q.B. 788; *Hounslow LBC v Pilling* [1994] 1 All E.R. 433—compare periodic tenancies where one of them may terminate the tenancy by notice; para.15–18).

The surrender may be express or by operation of law.

Express surrender

19–03   An express surrender must be made by deed unless the lease is granted for a term of three years or less at the best rent that could reasonably be obtained without taking a fine in which case the lease may be surrendered in writing (Law of Property Act 1925 ss.52(1), 52(2), (2)(d) and 54(2)).

Surrender by operation of law

Intention

19–04   The essence of a surrender by operation of law is the consensual giving up of possession of the property to the landlord by the tenant. Thus, where the tenant returns the keys to the landlord with the intention of giving up possession of the property and the landlord accepts them with the intention of accepting possession, there is a surrender by operation of law. Simply leaving the keys at the landlord's office or abandoning the premises will not however operate as a surrender. Peter Gibson LJ in *Belcourt Estates Ltd v Adesina* [2005] EWCA Civ 208:

> "30. The doctrine of surrender by operation of law is founded on the principle of estoppel, in that the parties must have acted towards each other in a way which is inconsistent with the continuation of the tenancy. That imposes a high threshold which must be crossed if the tenant is to be held to have surrendered and the landlord is to be held to have accepted the surrender.
>
> 31. The effective re-delivery of possession by the tenant and its acceptance by the landlord are vital. Thus there will be a surrender when the tenant returns the keys of the premises and the landlord accepts them in circumstances which indicate that the tenancy thereafter no longer

exists. The landlord must take possession in such a manner as to estop him from denying that the tenancy is at an end."

In determining the intention of the parties it is necessary to look at their actions. See Dyson LJ at para.18 in *Artworld Financial Corp v Safaryan* [2009] EWCA Civ 303:

" . . . whether there has been a deemed surrender by operation of law does not depend on the landlord's stated intention, but on the intention demonstrated on an objective basis by its conduct as a whole . . . this includes both what it says and what it does, and what it says may assist in interpreting the true effect of acts which might otherwise be equivocal, but it is not open to the landlord to turn black into white merely by assertion. . . . where aspects of the landlord's conduct are contradictory the court must look at that conduct as a whole, and decide what is its real effect."

Abandonment

Many disputes arise where the tenant has unilaterally left the premises and thereafter states that the landlord has done something which amounts to an acceptance of the surrender. **19–05**

In *Belcourt Estates Ltd v Adesina* [2005] EWCA Civ 208 the property had been let to the tenant in August 2000. The tenant never paid any rent and left in November 2000. The landlord knew this and made no claim for rent at the next quarter day. The property was then left empty for many months because the "landlord was too busy" to deal with it. *Held*: There was no surrender. Peter Gibson LJ:

"32. . . . the facts relied on [in this case], being omissions on the part of the landlord, do not amount to unequivocal conduct by the landlord accepting any surrender. No authority has been shown to us in which mere inaction is enough. Griffiths LJ in *Preston BC v Fairclough* (1982) 8 H.L.R. 70, at p.73, does say that:

'If it could be shown that a tenant had left owing a very substantial sum of money and had been absent for a substantial time, then an application by the landlord under Order 24 might well be sufficient for a court to

> regard the tenancy as surrendered by operation of
> law . . . '

> 33. To the extent that that tentative suggestion is based on
> the failure by the landlord to assert his rights for a
> substantial time, it is one about which, with all respect to
> Griffiths LJ, I would have serious reservations. In my
> judgment mere inaction would not be unequivocal conduct
> by the landlord. However, every case must turn on its own
> particular facts. It is sufficient to say that in the present
> case . . . it has not been shown that any surrender has
> been accepted by the claimant."

It is to be noted that this is a case where the tenant was
seeking to assert that there had been a surrender so as to avoid
continuing liability to pay rent. Where the landlord asserts that
there has been a surrender it will usually be much easier for him
to establish that he has done an act accepting the tenant's
giving up of the property.

The most recent comprehensive statement of the law in this
area is to be found in the judgment of Dyson LJ in *Artworld
Financial Corp v Safaryan* [2009] EWCA Civ 303. In para.29 of
his judgment he approved the following passage from the
judgment of the trial judge (HH Judge Marshall Q.C.):

> "(1) The issue of whether there has been a surrender by
> operation of law after a tenant's abandonment of the
> leased premises must be determined by evaluating the
> effect of the landlord's conduct as a whole (cf. *Brent LBC
> v Sharma* (1992) 25 H.L.R. 257 at 259) . . . the totality of
> such acts can amount to a resumption of possession even
> though individual acts might each be only equivocal. With
> this in mind—

> (2) The test is whether the landlord's conduct is 'so'
> inconsistent (*Oastler v Henderson* [1877] 2 Q.B.D. 575 at
> 577) with the continuation of the tenant's lease that it
> could only be justified as being lawful on the basis that the
> landlord has accepted the tenant's implied offer to give
> back possession, and has taken possession of the
> premises beneficially for himself.

> (3) Accepting back the keys without more will always be
> equivocal. As a matter of practicality and common sense,
> one party has to hold the keys to prevent an absurd

situation in which they are passed back and forth because neither party wants to risk it being suggested that it has made an admission by holding them.

(4) Any act of the landlord which is consistent with its rights under the lease, such as entering the premises to inspect or to repair them, will not in itself give rise to a surrender because, by definition, it is not inconsistent with the lease continuing.

(5) Any further act of the landlord which amounts to protecting or preserving the property, such as taking security measures or doing necessary repairs, will not in itself give rise to a surrender because such self-help, necessary to preserve the landlord's interest in the value of his property, is a reasonable response to the tenant's evinced intention not to perform the obligations of the tenancy: cf. *McDougall's Catering Foods Ltd v BSE Trading Ltd* (1998) 76 P. & C.R. 312; *Relvok Properties Ltd v Dixon* (1972) 25 P. & C.R.1, at p 7.

(6) Similarly, any act of the landlord which amounts to the landlord's performing the tenant's covenants under the lease, such as keeping the garden tidy, would not necessarily amount to a resumption of possession as it is not inconsistent with holding the defaulting tenant to performing the lease.

(7) Any further act of the landlord referable to the landlord's seeking to re-let the premises will not necessarily give rise to a surrender by operation of law, as it is no more than what the landlord might reasonably be expected to do in the circumstance for the potential benefit of all parties: *Oastler v Henderson* [1877] 2 Q.B.D. 575. The landlord must be entitled to seek to mitigate the damage caused in reality (even if not yet technically in law so long as the lease remains extant) by the tenant's abandoning the lease, by seeking to obtain another tenant, without thereby losing his rights against the original tenant if he is unable to do so.

(8) However, if the landlord goes further and uses the premises for his own benefit beyond the totally trivial—and certainly, in my judgment, if such use amounts to occupation of the premises—then he re-takes possession of the premises inconsistently with the continuance of the lease. This will give rise to a surrender by operation of law,

since it is only on the basis of having accepted such a surrender that the landlord's acts would be lawful."

See also the reference to *QFS Scaffolding* (2010) below at para.19–06.

New tenancy to existing tenant

19–06 Where the parties enter into a new tenancy during the currency of an existing tenancy a surrender of the old tenancy comes about; but only where the parties intend that the tenancy should have a new tenant on different terms from those of the former tenancy (*Jenkin R Lewis & Son Ltd v Kerman* [1970] 3 All E.R. 414 at 419; *Take Harvest Ltd v Liu* [1993] 2 All E.R. 459 PC).

> "If a tenant holding land under a lease accepts a new lease of the same land from his landlord, he is taken to have surrendered his original lease immediately before he accepts the new one. The landlord has no power to grant the new lease except on the footing that the old lease is surrendered and the tenant by accepting the new lease is estopped from denying the surrender of the old one. This surrender by operation of law takes effect whether or not the parties to the new lease intend it to take effect. Moreover, even if there is no express grant of a new lease the old lease will be surrendered by operation of law if the arrangements made between the landlord and the tenant are such as can only be carried out so as to achieve the result which they have in mind if a new tenancy is in fact created." (*Jenkin R Lewis & Son Ltd v Kerman*, per Russell LJ at 419.)

> "The substantial result which the landlord and tenant have in mind in making their arrangements in the hypothetical case postulated by Russell L.J. is that *the tenant shall have a new tenancy of the premises on different terms from those of his former tenancy,* whether or not they realise that the law would analyse their agreement as having the effect of the grant of a new tenancy and a surrender of the former tenancy. In cases where the parties do not have this substantial result in mind, the grant of a new tenancy (with a consequent surrender by operation of law) will not be inferred." (*Take Harvest Ltd v Liu*, per Sir Christopher Slade at 468d.)

Negotiations between a landlord and a prospective tenant for the grant of a new lease of premises, which are ultimately **unsuccessful**, are **not** an unequivocal acceptance by the parties to the existing lease that it has come to an end by surrender. The fact that the tenant had stopped using the property did not amount to an unequivocal acceptance that the lease had come to an end. (*QFS Scaffolding Ltd v Sable* [2010] EWCA Civ 682).

Variation

A variation of the terms of the lease that affect the legal estate **19–07** either by increasing the extent of the premises demised or the term for which they are held, operates as a surrender of the old tenancy and the grant of a new one. Other changes, however substantial, do not have this effect (*Friends Provident Life Office v British Railways Board* [1996] 1 All E.R. 336—deed of variation substantially increasing the rent and making it payable in advance instead of arrears, and alterations to the alienation and user clauses did not effect a surrender and re-grant). In particular, an increase in rent will not be sufficient to give rise to a new tenancy and a surrender of the old (*Jenkin R Lewis & Son v Kerman* [1970] 3 All E.R. 414 CA applied in *Friends Provident*).

> "Viewing the matter apart from authority it is difficult to see why the fiction of a new lease and a surrender by operation of law should be necessary in this case; for by simply increasing the amount of rent and providing that the additional rent shall be annexed to the reversion, one is not altering the nature of the pre-existing item of property." (*Jenkin R Lewis & Son v Kerman* [1970] 3 All E.R. 414 CA per Russell LJ at 420b.)

An agreement adding a new person as a joint tenant constitutes an agreement to vary the existing contract and does not operate as a surrender and re-grant (*Francis Perceval Saunders Dec'd Trustees v Ralph* (1993) 28 E.G. 129 QBD).

There is a surrender where the landlord and tenant agree that the tenant is to occupy the premises in the future as a licensee (*Foster v Robinson* [1951] 1 K.B. 149) assuming of course that the new agreement is truly a licence (see Ch.6).

Rent

19–08   If the tenant abandons the premises, his liability for rent continues until the landlord accepts the surrender. The onus is on the tenant to show that the landlord's act amounts to an unequivocal acceptance of the surrender if he wishes to avoid paying rent for the period after he left (*Relvock Properties Ltd v Dixon* (1973) 25 P. & C.R. 1).

Effect on sub-tenants

Law of Property Act 1925 s.139

19–09   **139.**–(1) Where a reversion expectant on a lease of land is surrendered or merged, the estate or interest which as against the lessee for the time being confers the next vested right to the land, shall be deemed the reversion for the purpose of preserving the same incidents and obligations as would have affected the original reversion had there been no surrender or merger thereof.

A tenant, by voluntarily surrendering his term, does not destroy the sub-tenancy that he has created (*Parker v Jones* [1910] 2 K.B. 32; *Cow v Casey* [1949] 1 K.B. 474 at 478). Instead the sub-tenant in effect becomes the tenant of the landlord on the terms of the sub-lease (s.139 of the Law of Property Act 1925). However, the sub-tenancy is preserved only for the period that it would have been preserved had there been no surrender. If the sub-tenant was a residential tenant with the protection of the Rent Act 1977 that protection comes to an end on the contractual expiry date of the sub-tenancy (*Pittalis v Grant* [1989] 2 All E.R. 622; *Bromley Park Garden Estates Ltd v George* [1991] 2 E.G.L.R. 95). Compare the position of a lawful assured tenant (para.27–08) and a secure tenant (*Basingstoke and Dean BC v Paice* [1995] 2 E.G.L.R. 9 CA).

Agreement to surrender a Pt II tenancy

Introduction

Landlord and Tenant Act 1954 s.38

19–10   **38.**–(1) Any agreement relating to a tenancy to which this Part of this Act applies (whether contained in the instrument creating the tenancy or not) shall be void (except as provided by section 38A of this Act) *in so far as it purports to preclude the tenant from making an application or request under this Part of this Act* or provides for the termination or the *surrender* *of the tenancy in the event of his making such an application* or request or for the imposition of any penalty or disability on the tenant in that event.

Although the tenant is not prevented from actually surrendering a tenancy to which Pt II applies (see above), s.38 of the 1954 Act makes void any agreement for the surrender of a tenancy that will take effect *if the tenant makes an application or request for a new tenancy*. Note that the section does not explicitly refer to surrender in any other set of circumstances. However, a straightforward agreement to surrender a tenancy at some future date is also void because *"it purports to preclude"*, that is it has the effect of precluding, the tenant from making such an application, and so is caught under the first limb (*Joseph v Joseph* [1967] Ch. 78):

> "What happens when the tenant of business premises on a long lease agrees to surrender them on a named date before the end of the term but afterwards changes his mind and declines to surrender on the named date? I think the tenancy does not come to an end. It can come to an end by 'surrender' proper: see s.24(2) of the Act. But I do not think it comes to an end by a mere agreement to surrender. The very agreement to surrender is 'void in so far as it purports to preclude the tenant from making an application or request' for a new tenancy: see s.38(1) of the Act. The word 'purports', as used in subsections (1) and (2) of this section, does not mean 'professes'. It means 'has the effect of'. The agreement to surrender is void, therefore, in so far as it has the effect of precluding the tenant from applying for a new lease". (*Joseph v Joseph*, per Lord Denning M.R. at p.87.)

> "In my judgment this subsection does render void any provision of an agreement between landlord and tenant whereby the tenant undertakes to do in the future any act which will have the effect under the statute of disqualifying him from applying for a new tenancy under sections 24(1) and 29." (*Joseph v Joseph*, per Diplock LJ at p.90.)

(Applied in *Allnatt London Properties Ltd v Newton* [1984] 1 All E.R. 423.)

It is also clear that the Law Commission considered that all agreements to surrender should require a procedure to be adopted:

> "We recommend that the provision in s.24(2)(b) be repealed. The position will then be clear: all surrenders will be effective, but *no agreement for surrender* will be valid unless the requirements for such agreements are complied with" (Law Com. 208 para.2.21).

Section 38A(4) is now explicit on the point—see below.

Note that the restriction in s.38 only applies to tenancies to which the 1954 Act applies. Thus, if the Act does not apply there are no restrictions on agreements to surrender.

Permitted agreements

Landlord and Tenant Act 1954 s.38A

19–11

38A.—(2) The persons who are the landlord and the tenant in relation to a tenancy to which this Part of this Act applies may agree that the tenancy shall be surrendered on such date or in such circumstances as may be specified in the agreement and on such terms (if any) as may be so specified.
. . .
(4) An agreement under subsection (2) above shall be void unless—

(a) the landlord has served on the tenant a notice in the form, or substantially in the form, set out in Schedule 3 to the 2003 Order; and

(b) the requirements specified in Schedule 4 to that Order are met.

Prior to the changes made by the 2003 Reform Order, parties to a tenancy to which Pt II applied who wished to enter into an agreement to surrender the tenancy were required to apply to the court for approval. That procedure has now disappeared. (The changes made by the 2003 Reform Order do not affect any agreement to surrender authorised by the court under the old s.38(4) prior to June 1, 2004: art.29(2).) There is now a new procedure based on notice that is substantially the same as the procedure that applies to contracting out (Ch.3). The procedure is set out in Schs 3 and 4 of the 2003 Order. As with contracting out, there are differences in the procedure depending upon whether or not 14 days' notice is given. There are three elements to the procedure:

- A notice informing the tenant of the consequences of entering into the agreement to surrender and advising him to obtain professional advice. The notice is in a prescribed form (Sch.3 to the Order; see Form 22, para.19–14).

- A declaration that the notice has been received—a "simple declaration" where the full 14 days' notice or more is given. A statutory declaration where less than 14 days' notice is given.
- A reference to the notice and the declaration in the agreement to surrender.

More precise details are as follows:

14 days—"Simple declaration"

- The general rule is that the landlord must serve a notice on **19-12** the tenant not less than 14 days before the tenant enters into the surrender agreement, or (if earlier) becomes contractually bound to do so, informing him of the consequences of so doing. The notice must be in the form, or substantially in the form set out in Sch.3 of the 2003 Order (Sch.4 para.2). See para.19-14 for the form.
- The tenant or a person duly authorised by him to do so must, before the tenant enters into the agreement to surrender, or (if earlier) becomes contractually bound to do so, make a "simple declaration" that the required notice was served on him not less than 14 days before he enters into the agreement; that he has read the notice and accepted the consequences of entering into the agreement. The declaration must be in the form, or substantially in the form, set out in para.6 of Sch.4 to the 2003 Order. (para.3.) (See para.19-15.)
- A reference to the notice and declaration must be contained in or endorsed on the agreement to surrender. (para.5.)

More than 14 days—statutory declaration

- There will be many cases where it will not be possible for the **19-13** landlord to serve the notice at least 14 days before the agreement to surrender (or, if earlier, becomes contractually bound to do so).
- If it is not possible to do so, 14 days' notice is not required but the notice must still be served on the tenant before the tenant enters into the agreement to surrender, or (if earlier) becomes contractually bound to do so.
- The tenant or a person duly authorised by him to do so must, before that time, make a *statutory declaration* in the form, or substantially in the form, set out in para.7 of Sch.4 (see para.4; and see para.19-15).

- Once again a reference to the notice and (in this case) the statutory declaration must be contained in, or endorsed on, the instrument creating the agreement to surrender. (para.5.)

19–14   **Form 22**

**FORM OF NOTICE THAT AN AGREEMENT TO SURRENDER
A BUSINESS TENANCY IS TO BE MADE**

To:

....

....

....

[Name and address of tenant]

From:

....

....

....

[Name and address of landlord]

IMPORTANT NOTICE FOR TENANT

Do not commit yourself to any agreement to surrender your lease unless you have read this message carefully and discussed it with a professional adviser.

Normally, you have the right to renew your lease when it expires. By committing yourself to an agreement to surrender, **you will be giving up this important statutory right.**

- You will **not** be able to continue occupying the premises beyond the date provided for under the agreement for surrender, **unless** the landlord chooses to offer you a further term (in which case you would lose the right to ask the court to determine the new rent). You will need to leave the premises.

cont

---

cont

- You will be unable to claim compensation for the loss of your premises, unless the lease or agreement for surrender gives you this right.

A qualified surveyor, lawyer or accountant would be able to offer you professional advice on your options.

You do not have to commit yourself to the agreement to surrender your lease unless you want to.

If you receive this notice at least 14 days before committing yourself to the agreement to surrender, you will need to sign a simple declaration that you have received this notice and have accepted its consequences, before signing the agreement to surrender.

But if you do not receive at least 14 days' notice, you will need to sign a "statutory" declaration. To do so, you will need to visit an independent solicitor (or someone else empowered to administer oaths).

Unless there is a special reason for committing yourself to the agreement to surrender sooner, you may want to ask the landlord to let you have at least 14 days to consider whether you wish to give up your statutory rights. If you then decided to go ahead with the agreement to end your lease, you would only need to make a simple declaration, and so you would not need to make a separate visit to an independent solicitor.

19–15

SCHEDULE 4

REQUIREMENTS FOR A VALID AGREEMENT TO SURRENDER A BUSINESS TENANCY

1. The following are the requirements referred to in section 38A(4)(b) of the Act.

2. Subject to paragraph 4, the notice referred to in section 38A(4)(a) of the Act must be served on the tenant not less than 14 days before the tenant enters into the agreement under section 38A(2) of the Act, or (if earlier) becomes contractually bound to do so.

3. If the requirement in paragraph 2 is met, the tenant or a person duly authorised by him to do so, must, before the tenant enters into agreement under section 38A(2) of the Act, or (if earlier) becomes contractually bound to do so, make a declaration in the form, or substantially in the form, set out in paragraph 6.

cont

cont

4. If the requirement in paragraph 2 is not met, the notice referred to in section 38A(4)(a) of the Act must be served on the tenant before the tenant enters into the agreement under section 38A(2) of the Act, or (if earlier) becomes contractually bound to do so, and the tenant, or a person duly authorised by him to do so, must before that time make a statutory declaration in the form, or substantially in the form, set out in paragraph 7.

5. A reference to the notice and, where paragraph 3 applies, the declaration or, where paragraph 4 applies, the statutory declaration must be contained in or endorsed on the instrument creating the agreement under section 38A(2).

6. The form of declaration referred to in paragraph 3 is as follows:

I

....

(*name of declarant*) of

....

(*address*) declare that—

1. I have/

....

(*name of tenant*) has a tenancy of premises at

....

(*address of premises*) for a term commencing on

....

2. I/The tenant propose(s) to enter into an agreement with

....

(*name of landlord*) to surrender the tenancy on a date or in circumstances specified in the agreement.

3. The landlord has not less than 14 days before I/the tenant enter(s) into the agreement referred to in paragraph 2 above, or (if earlier) become(s) contractually bound to do so, served on me/the tenant a notice in the form, or substantially in the form, set out in Schedule 3 to Regulatory Reform (Business Tenancies) (England and Wales) Order 2003. The form of notice set out in that Schedule is reproduced below.

4. I have/The tenant has read the notice referred to in paragraph 3 above and accept(s) the consequences of entering into the agreement referred to in paragraph 2 above.

5. (*as appropriate*) I am duly authorised by the tenant to make this declaration.

cont

cont

DECLARED this

....

day of

....

To:

....

....

....

[*Name and address of tenant*]

From:

....

....

....

[*name and address of landlord*]

IMPORTANT NOTICE FOR TENANT

Do not commit yourself to any agreement to surrender your lease unless you have read this message carefully and discussed it with a professional adviser.

Normally, you have the right to renew your lease when it expires. By committing yourself to an agreement to surrender, **you will be giving up this important statutory right.**

- You will **not** be able to continue occupying the premises beyond the date provided for under the agreement for surrender, **unless** the landlord chooses to offer you a further term (in which case you would lose the right to ask the court to determine the new rent). You will need to leave the premises.

- You will be unable to claim compensation for the loss of your premises, unless the lease or agreement for surrender gives you this right.

A qualified surveyor, lawyer or accountant would be able to offer you professional advice on your options.

cont

cont

You do not have to commit yourself to the agreement to surrender your lease unless you want to.

If you receive this notice at least 14 days before committing yourself to the agreement to surrender, you will need to sign a simple declaration that you have received this notice and have accepted its consequences, before signing the agreement to surrender.

But if you do not receive at least 14 days notice, you will need to sign a "statutory" declaration. To do so, you will need to visit an independent solicitor (or someone else empowered to administer oaths).

Unless there is a special reason for committing yourself to the agreement to surrender sooner, you may want to ask the landlord to let you have at least 14 days to consider whether you wish to give up your statutory rights. If you then decided to go ahead with the agreement to end your lease, you would only need to make a simple declaration, and so you would not need to make a separate visit to an independent solicitor.

7. The form of statutory declaration referred to in paragraph 4 is as follows:

I
....
(*name of declarant*) of

....
(*address*) do solemnly and sincerely declare that—

1. I have/
....
(*name of tenant*) has a tenancy of premises at

....
(*address of premises*) for a term commencing on

....

2. I/The tenant propose(s) to enter into an agreement with

....
(*name of landlord*) to surrender the tenancy on a date or in circumstances specified in the agreement.

3. The landlord has served on me/the tenant a notice in the form, or substantially in the form, set out in Schedule 3 to the Regulatory Reform (Business Tenancies) (England and Wales) Order 2003. The form of notice set out in that Schedule is reproduced below.

cont

cont

4. I have/The tenant has read the notice referred to in paragraph 3 above and accept(s) the consequences of entering into the agreement referred to in paragraph 2 above.

5. (*as appropriate*) I am duly authorised by the tenant to make this declaration.

To:

....

....

....

[*Name and address of tenant*]

From:

....

....

....

[*name and address of landlord*]

IMPORTANT NOTICE FOR TENANT

Do not commit yourself to any agreement to surrender your lease unless you have read this message carefully and discussed it with a professional adviser.

Normally, you have the right to renew your lease when it expires. By committing yourself to an agreement to surrender, **you will be giving up this important statutory right.**

- You will **not** be able to continue occupying the premises beyond the date provided for under the agreement for surrender, **unless** the landlord chooses to offer you a further term (in which case you would lose the right to ask the court to determine the new rent). You will need to leave the premises.

- You will be unable to claim compensation for the loss of your premises, unless the lease or agreement for surrender gives you this right.

A qualified surveyor, lawyer or accountant would be able to offer you professional advice on your options.

cont

---

cont

You do not have to commit yourself to the agreement to surrender your lease unless you want to.

If you receive this notice at least 14 days before committing yourself to the agreement to surrender, you will need to sign a simple declaration that you have received this notice and have accepted its consequences, before signing the agreement to surrender.

But if you do not receive at least 14 days' notice, you will need to sign a "statutory" declaration. To do so, you will need to visit an independent solicitor (or someone else empowered to administer oaths).

Unless there is a special reason for committing yourself to the agreement to surrender sooner, you may want to ask the landlord to let you have at least 14 days to consider whether you wish to give up your statutory rights. If you then decided to go ahead with the agreement to end your lease, you would only need to make a simple declaration, and so you would not need to make a separate visit to an independent solicitor.

AND I make this solemn declaration conscientiously believing the same to be true and by virtue of the Statutory Declarations Act 1835

DECLARED at

....
this

....
day of

....

Before me (*signature of person before whom declaration is made*)

A commissioner for oaths or A solicitor empowered to administer oaths *or* (*as appropriate*)

Merger

19–16   Whereas a surrender takes place when the owner of the lesser interest gives it up to the greater interest, a merger takes place where the owner of the lesser interest acquires the greater interest.

Where the ownership of the reversion and the tenancy are in the same hands, the two interests merge and the person concerned remains in possession pursuant to the greater interest (*Rye v Rye* [1962] A.C. 496). Thus, if the owner of an underlease purchases his immediate lessor's lease he thereafter remains in possession pursuant to the lease rather than the underlease.

> "A person cannot be, at the same time, both landlord and tenant of the same premises; for as soon as the tenancy and the reversion are in the same hands the tenancy is merged, that is, sunk or drowned, in the reversion" (*Rye v Rye* [1962] A.C. 496 per Lord Denning at 513).

The above rule does not apply where the person concerned holds each interest in a different capacity. At common law, the interests would have merged but equity intervened so as to prevent the merger of the beneficial interest. And since 1925, statute has prevented the legal interests merging where the beneficial interests remain separate (s.185 of the Law of Property Act 1925).

There may be an express intention to merge or a presumed intention. When deciding whether or not to presume an intention the court must look at the interests of the party holding the two estates. If it is against his interests, it will be presumed that there was no intention to merge the two estates (*BOH Ltd v Eastern Power Networks plc* [2011] EWCA Civ 19).

Law of Property Act 1925 s.185

185. There is no merger by operation of law only of any estate the beneficial interest in which would not be deemed to be merged or extinguished in equity.

19-17

For example, if the tenant of a property becomes the executor of the estate of his landlord's interest and thus the owner of both interests in different capacities the reversion and the leasehold will not merge. In *Sargeant v National Westminster Bank* (1989) 59 P. & C.R. 182 Ch D an argument to the effect that in these circumstances the person concerned was under a duty as executor to obtain vacant possession from himself so that the property could be sold with vacant possession for the benefit of the estate was rejected.

Frustration

Leases can be terminated through the contractual doctrine of frustration, although rarely (*National Carriers Ltd v Panalpina (Northern) Ltd* [1981] AC 675).

> " . . . though such cases may be rare, the doctrine of frustration is capable of application to leases of land. It must be so applied with proper regard to the fact that a lease, that is, a grant of a legal estate, is involved. The court must consider whether any term is to be implied which would determine the lease in the event which has happened and/or ascertain the foundation of the agreement and decide whether this still exists in the light of the terms of the lease, the surrounding circumstances and any special rules which apply to leases or to the particular lease in question. If the "frustrating event" occurs during the currency of the lease it will be appropriate to consider the Law Reform (Frustrated Contracts) Act 1943." (per Lord Wilberforce at pp.697A–C)

Repudiation

Breach of the terms of a lease, can in extreme cases, amount to a repudiatory breach, entitling the innocent party to bring the lease to an end.

A landlord has been held have committed repudiatory breaches entitling the tenant to determine the lease where he refused to repair defects which made the premises unfit for habitation (*Hussein v Mehlman* [1992] 32 E.G. 59) and where the landlord made the tenant's unit dark and virtually unusable as a result of having leased adjoining premises to a pawnbroker (*Chartered Trust plc v Davies* [1997] 2 E.G.L.R. 83).

A landlord's derogation from grant in failing to stop other tenants from parking on a forecourt in breach of the tenant's exclusive right so to do, will not constitute a repudiatory breach (*Nynehead Developments Ltd v R.H. Fibreboard Containers Ltd* [1999] 1 E.G.L.R. 7). Nor will a tenant's refusal to pay rent entitle the landlord to determine, as distinct from forfeit, the lease.

Chapter 20

DISCLAIMER

. . . .

Disclaimer of leases generally arises in the context of insolvency. In broad terms, an insolvency practitioner, faced with a lease that is onerous, seeks to avoid further liabilities arising under its terms. They are able to do so by disclaiming it.

20–01

Where the tenant is a bankrupt individual, his interest in the property vests as part of his estate in his trustee in bankruptcy immediately on the trustee's appointment taking effect (ss.283 and 306 of the Insolvency Act 1986). The trustee is required "to get in, realise and distribute the bankrupt's estate" in accordance with the Act (s.305).

Where the tenant is an insolvent company, a liquidator acts asthe agent of the company he is winding up and unlike a trustee in bankruptcy the property of the company does not automatically vest in him. He is under a duty "to secure that the assets of the company are got in, realised and distributed to the company's creditors and, if there is a surplus, to the persons entitled to it" (s.143 of the Insolvency Act 1986). As part of the exercise, he is required "to take into his custody or under his control all the property and things in action to which the company is or appears to be entitled" (s.144). He may apply for any property to be vested in his official name (s.145) but this rarely occurs.

The right to disclaim

If the liquidator or trustee considers a lease held by the company or individual to be a burden rather than an asset to be realised he is not required to retain it. He may, by giving the prescribed notice, disclaim the tenancy (ss.178, 179, 315 and 317). He may do so notwithstanding that he has taken possession, endeavoured to sell the lease or otherwise

20–02

exercised rights of ownership in relation to it (s.178(2); s.315(1)).

Insolvency Act 1986 s.178 (Company)

20-03   **178.**—(1) This and the next two sections apply to a company that is being wound up in England and Wales.

(2) Subject as follows, the liquidator may, by the giving of the prescribed notice, disclaim any onerous property and may do so notwithstanding that he has taken possession of it, endeavoured to sell it, or otherwise exercised rights of ownership in relation to it.

(3) The following is onerous property for the purposes of this section—

(a)   any unprofitable contract, and
(b)   any other property of the company which is unsaleable or not readily saleable or is such that it may give rise to a liability to pay money or perform any other onerous act.

Insolvency Act 1986 s.315 (Individual)

20-04   **315.**—(1) Subject as follows, the trustee may, by the giving of the prescribed notice, disclaim any onerous property and may do so notwithstanding that he has taken possession of it, endeavoured to sell it or otherwise exercised rights of ownership in relation to it.

(2) The following is onerous property for the purposes of this section—

(a)   any unprofitable contract, and
(b)   any other property comprised in the bankrupt's estate which is unsaleable or not readily saleable or is such that it may give rise to a liability to pay money or perform any other onerous act.

Loss of right to disclaim

20-05   The liquidator or trustee may not disclaim where a "person interested in the property" (for example, the landlord) has applied in writing to the liquidator (trustee) to ask him whether he will disclaim or not and the liquidator (trustee) has not served a notice of disclaimer within the period of 28 days beginning with the date of that application (ss.178(5), 316). This period can be extended by making an application to the court for an extension of time (see para.20-30).

Insolvency Act 1986 s.178(5) (Company)

20-06   **178.**—(5) A notice of disclaimer shall not be given under this section in respect of any property if—

(a) a person interested in the property has applied in writing to the liquidator or one of his predecessors as liquidator requiring the liquidator or that predecessor to decide whether he will disclaim or not, and

(b) the period of 28 days beginning with the day on which that application was made, or such longer period as the court may allow, has expired without a notice of disclaimer having been given under this section in respect of that property.

Insolvency Act s.316(1) (Individual)

316.–(1) Notice of disclaimer shall not be given under section 315 in respect of any property if– **20–07**

(a) a person interested in the property has applied in writing to the trustee or one of his predecessors as trustee requiring the trustee or that predecessor to decide whether he will disclaim or not, and

(b) the period of 28 days beginning with the day on which that application was made has expired without a notice of disclaimer having been given under section 315 in respect of that property.

(2) The trustee is deemed to have adopted any contract which by virtue of this section he is not entitled to disclaim.

Insolvency Rules 1986 r.4.191A (Company)

4.191A.–(1) The following applies where, in the case of any property, application is made to the liquidator by an interested party under section 178(5). **20–08**
(2) The application must be delivered to the liquidator–

(a) personally;
(b) by electronic means in accordance with Part 12A; or
(c) by any other means of delivery which enables proof of receipt of the application by the liquidator to be provided, if requested.

Insolvency Rules 1986 r.6.183 (Individual)

6.183.–(1) The following applies where, in the case of any property, application is made to the trustee by an interested party under section 316. **20–09**
(2) The application must be delivered to the trustee–

(a) personally;
(b) by electronic means in accordance with Part 12A; or
(c) by any other means of delivery which enables proof of receipt of the application by the trustee to be provided, if requested.

(3) This paragraph applies in a case where the property concerned cannot be disclaimed by the trustee without the permission of the court.

> If within the period of 28 days mentioned in section 316(1) the trustee applies to the court for permission to disclaim, the court shall extend the time allowed by that section for giving notice of disclaimer to a date not earlier than the date fixed for the hearing of the application.

After acquired property: permission to disclaim

20-10   A notice of disclaimer may not be given under s.315 in respect of any property that has been acquired by, or has devolved upon, a bankrupt since the commencement of the bankruptcy and which the trustee has claimed for the estate under s.307, except with the permission of the court (s.315(4)). An application for permission to disclaim is made pursuant to r.6.182.

The notice of disclaimer: service

20-11   In order to disclaim a lease the liquidator or trustee must give a notice in prescribed form (s.178(2)). The prescribed notices are to be found in Sch.4 to the Insolvency Rules 1986. They are Form 4.53A in relation to disclaimer by a liquidator and Form 6.61A in relation to a disclaimer by a trustee.

A copy of the notice must be authenticated and dated by the trustee and in the case of companies sent to the registrar of companies and in the case of individuals filed with court and in both cases a copy sent to the Chief Land Registrar (rr.4.187, 6.178). The 1986 Act does not provide for service of disclaimer on the landlord; nor do the rules do so expressly. However, it is generally considered that service on the landlord is required by virtue of r.4.188(3) (companies) and r.6.179(4) (individuals) as a person with an interest in the property. The liquidator or trustee must also (so far as he is aware of their addresses) serve a copy of the disclaimer on every person claiming under the tenant as a sub-tenant or mortgagee (rr.4.188(2), 6.179(2)).

Insolvency Rules 1986 rr.4.187–4.189, 4.192, 4.193
(Company)

20-12   **4.187.**—(1) Where the liquidator disclaims property under section 178, the notice of disclaimer shall contain such particulars of the property disclaimed as enable it to be easily identified.
   (2) The notice of disclaimer must be authenticated and dated by the liquidator.

(3A) As soon as reasonably practicable after authenticating the notice of disclaimer, the liquidator must—

(a) send a copy of the notice to the registrar of companies; and

(b) in any case where the disclaimer is of registered land as defined in section 132(1) of the Land Registration Act 2002, send a copy of the notice to the Chief Land Registrar.

(4) For the purposes of section 178, the date of the prescribed notice is that on which the liquidator authenticated it.

4.188.—(1) Within 7 business days after the date of the notice of disclaimer, the liquidator shall send or give copies of the notice to the persons mentioned in paragraphs (2) to (4).

(2) Where the property disclaimed is of a leasehold nature, he shall send or give a copy to every person who (to his knowledge) claims under the company as underlessee or mortgagee.

(3) He shall in any case send or give a copy of the notice to every person who (to his knowledge)—

(a) claims an interest in the disclaimed property, or

(b) is under any liability in respect of the property, not being a liability discharged by the disclaimer.

. . .

(5) If subsequently it comes to the liquidator's knowledge, in the case of any person, that he has such an interest in the disclaimed property as would have entitled him to receive a copy of the notice of disclaimer in pursuance of paragraphs (2) to (4), the liquidator shall then as soon as reasonably practicable send or give to that person a copy of the notice.

But compliance with this paragraph is not required if—

(a) the liquidator is satisfied that the person has already been made aware of the disclaimer and its date, or

(b) the court, on the liquidator's application, orders that compliance is not required in that particular case.

4.189.—The liquidator disclaiming property may, without prejudice to his obligations under sections 178 to 180 and Rules 4.187 and 4.188 , at any time send or give copies of the notice of the disclaimer to any persons who in his opinion ought, in the public interest or otherwise, to be informed of the disclaimer.

4.192.—(1) If, in the case of property which the liquidator has the right to disclaim, it appears to him that there is some person who claims, or may claim, to have an interest in the property, he may give notice to that person calling on him to declare within 14 days whether he claims any such interest and, if so, the nature and extent of it.

(2) Failing compliance with the notice, the trustee is entitled to assume that the person concerned has no such interest in the property as will prevent or impede its disclaimer.

4.193. Any disclaimer of property by the liquidator is presumed valid and effective, unless it is proved that he has been in breach of his duty with respect to the giving of notice of disclaimer, or otherwise under section 178 to 180, or under this Chapter of the Rules.

Insolvency Rules 1986 rr.6.178–180, 6.184 and 6.185 (Individual)

20–13

6.178.–(1) Where the trustee disclaims property under section 315, the notice of disclaimer shall contain such particulars of the property disclaimed as enable it to be easily identified.

(2) The notice of disclaimer must be authenticated and dated by the trustee.

(3) As soon as reasonably practicable after authenticating the notice of disclaimer, the trustee must—

(a)　file a copy of the notice with the court; and

(b)　in any case where the disclaimer is of registered land as defined in section 132(1) of the Land Registration Act 2002, send a copy of the notice to the Chief Land Registrar.

(4) For the purposes of section 315, the date of the prescribed notice is that on which the trustee authenticates it.

6.179.–(1) Within 7 business days after the date of the notice of disclaimer, the trustee shall send or give copies of the notice to the persons mentioned in paragraphs (2) to (5).

(2) Where the property disclaimed is of a leasehold nature, he shall send or give a copy to every person who (to his knowledge) claims under the bankrupt as underlessee or mortgagee.

. . .

(4) He shall in any case send or give a copy of the notice to every person who (to his knowledge)—

(a)　claims an interest in the disclaimed property, or

(b)　is under any liability in respect of the property, not being a liability discharged by the disclaimer.

. . .

(6) If subsequently it comes to the trustee's knowledge, in the case of any person, that he has such an interest in the disclaimed property as would have entitled him to receive a copy of the notice of disclaimer in pursuance of paragraphs (2) to (5), the trustee shall then as soon as reasonably practicable send or give to that person a copy of the notice.

But compliance with this paragraph is not required if—

(a)　the trustee is satisfied that the person has already been made aware of the disclaimer and its date, or

(b)　the court, on the trustee's application, orders that compliance is not required in that particular case.

(7) A notice or copy notice to be served on any person under the age of 18 in relation to the disclaimer of property in a dwelling-house is sufficiently served if sent or given to the parent or guardian of that person.

6.180. The trustee disclaiming property may, without prejudice to his obligations under sections 315 to 319 and Rules 6.178 and 6.179, at any time send or give copies of thenotice of the disclaimer to any persons who in his opinion ought, in the public interest or otherwise, to be informed of the disclaimer.

6.184.—(1) If, in the case of property which the trustee has the right to disclaim, it appears to him that there is some person who claims, or may claim, to have an interest in the property, he may give notice to that person calling on him to declare within 14 days whether he claims any such interest and, if so, the nature and extent of it.

(2) Failing compliance with the notice, the trustee is entitled to assume that the person concerned has no such interest in the property as will prevent or impede its disclaimer.

6.185. Any disclaimer of property by the trustee is presumed valid and effective, unless it is proved that he has been in breach of his duty with respect to the giving of notice of disclaimer, or otherwise under sections 315 to 319, or under this Chapter of the Rules.

Date upon which disclaimer takes effect

The disclaimer will take effect if there is no application made for a vesting order (see below) within a period of 14 days beginning with the day on which the last notice was served on every sub-tenant or mortgagee of the company or, if there is such an application, the court directs that the disclaimer is to take effect (ss.179, 317).   **20–14**

Insolvency Act 1986 s.179 (Company)

179.—(1) The disclaimer under s.178 of any property of a leasehold nature does not take effect unless a copy of the disclaimer has been served (so far as the liquidator is aware of their addresses) on every person claiming under the company as underlessee or mortgagee and either—   **20–15**

    (a)   no application under section 181 below is made with respect to that property before the end of the period of 14 days beginning with the day on which the last notice served under this subsection was served; or

    (b)   where such an application has been made, the court directs that the disclaimer shall take effect.

(2) Where the court gives a direction under subsection (1)(b) it may also, instead of or in addition to any order it makes under section 181, make such orders with respect to fixtures, tenant's improvements and other matters arising out of the lease as it thinks fit.

Insolvency Act 1986 s.317 (Individual)

317.—(1) The disclaimer under any property of a leasehold nature does not take effect unless a copy of the disclaimer has been served (so far as the trustee is aware of their addresses) on every person claiming under the bankrupt as underlessee or mortgagee and either—   **20–16**

    (a)   no application under section 320 below is made with respect to the property before the end of the period of 14 days beginning with the day on which the last notice served under this subsection was served; or

(b) where such an application has been made, the court directs that the disclaimer is to take effect.

(2) Where the court gives a direction under subsection (1)(b) it may also, instead of or in addition to any order it makes under section 320, make such orders with respect to fixtures, tenant's improvements and other matters arising out of the lease as it thinks fit.

Effect of disclaimer on tenant

Insolvency Act 1986 s.178(4) (Company)

20-17   **178.**–(4) A disclaimer under this section–

(a) operates so as to determine, as from the date of the disclaimer, the rights, interest and liabilities of the company in or in respect of the property disclaimed;

. . .

[See para.20-20 for subsection (4)(b) in relation to third parties].

Insolvency Act 1986 s.315(3) (Individual)

20-18   **315.**– . . .

(3) A disclaimer under this section–

(a) operates so as to determine, as from the date of the disclaimer, the rights, interest and liabilities of the bankrupt and his estate in or in respect of the property disclaimed, and

(b) discharges the trustee from all personal liability in respect of that property as from the commencement of his trusteeship.

[See para.20-21 for the rest of the section in relation to third parties].

Where the lease is disclaimed the disclaimer operates "so as to determine, as from the date of the disclaimer, the rights, interest and liabilities of the bankrupt and his estate in or in respect of the property disclaimed" (ss.178(4)(a), 315(3)(a)).

"Disclaimer operates to determine all the tenant's obligations under the tenant's covenants, and all his rights under the landlord's covenants. In order to determine these rights and obligations it is necessary, in the nature of things, that the landlord's obligations and rights, which are the reverse side of the tenant's rights and obligations must also be determined. If the tenant's liabilities to the landlord are to be extinguished, of necessity so also must be the landlord's rights against the tenant. The one cannot be achieved without the other.

Disclaimer also operates to determine the tenant's interest in the property, namely the lease. Determination of a leasehold estate has the effect of accelerating the reversion expectant upon the determination of that estate. The leasehold estate ceases to exist. I can see no reason to question that this is the effect of disclaimer when the only parties involved are the landlord and the tenant." (*Hindcastle Ltd v Barbara Attenborough Associates Ltd* [1997] AC 70, per Lord Nicholls at p87)

Upon disclaimer the original tenant becomes a trespasser and has no right to remain on the premises; and if he continues to do so without the consent of the landlord proceedings for possession can be issued. The landlord can use the procedure that applies to trespassers because the former tenant was not a tenant when the claim is made (*Smalley v Quarrier* [1975] 1 WLR 938; see para.22–53).

Sub-tenants

The disclaimer does not affect any sub-tenant's right to possession. This is a consequence of ss.178(4)(b) and 315(3) each of which states that the disclaimer "does not, except so far as is necessary for the purposes of releasing the company from any liability, affect the rights of any other person" (see further below in relation to other third parties). The determination of the sub-tenant's interest in the property is not necessary to free the tenant company from liability. The landlord may not therefore recover possession from the sub-tenant of a tenant where the liquidator (trustee) has disclaimed (*Smalley v Hardinge* (1881) 7 Q.B.D. 524). However, the sub-tenant is effectively obliged to perform the tenant's obligations in the lease. He is not under any direct obligation to the landlord to do so but if he does not do so and there is a proviso for re-entry the landlord may forfeit the lease (*Finley, Ex p. Clothworkers Co, Re* (1888) 21 Q.B.D. 475 at 486; *Levy, Ex p. Walton, Re* (1881) 17 Ch D 746).

20–19

If the landlord does forfeit the lease the sub-tenant can apply for relief from forfeiture (*Hill v Griffin* [1987] 1 E.G.L.R. 81).

> "Determination of the sub-tenant's interest in the property is not necessary to free the tenant from liability. Hence the sub-tenant's interest continues. No deeming is necessary to produce this result. Here the deeming relates to the terms on which the sub-tenant's proprietary interest continues. His interest continues unaffected by the determination of the tenant's interest. Accordingly the sub-tenant holds his estate on the same terms, and subject to the same rights and obligations, as *would* be applicable *if* the tenant's interest had continued. If he pays the rent and performs the tenant covenants in the disclaimed lease, the landlord cannot eject him. If he does not, the landlord can distrain upon his goods for the rent reserved by the disclaimed lease or bring forfeiture proceedings. In practice, matters are likely to be brought to a head by one of the parties making an application for a vesting order." (*Hindcastle Ltd v Barbara Attenborough Ltd* [1996] 1 All E.R. 737, per Lord Nicholls at 749b–d.)

Either the landlord or the tenant may apply for a vesting order (see below) in order to regularise the position. The effect of the order will be to put the landlord and sub-tenant into a direct relationship of landlord and tenant.

As seen above the liquidator or trustee is required to serve the notice of disclaimer on sub-tenants and mortgagees so far as he is aware of their addresses (ss.179(1), 317(1); see para.20–11).

Effect on other third parties

Insolvency Act 1986 s.178(4), (6) (Company)

20–20   178.–(4) A disclaimer under this section–
    (a)   [see para.20–17]
    (b)   does not, except so far as is necessary for the purposes of releasing the company from any liability, affect the rights and liabilities of any other person.

. . .

    (6) Any person sustaining loss or damage in consequence of the operation of a disclaimer under this section is deemed a creditor of the

company to the extent of the loss or damage and accordingly may prove for the loss or damage in the winding up.

Insolvency Act 1986 s.315(3), (5)

315.–   **20–21**

. . .

(3) A disclaimer under this section . . . does not, except so far as is necessary for the purpose of releasing the bankrupt, the bankrupt's estate and the trustee from any liability, affect the rights or liabilities of any other person.

. . .

(5) Any person sustaining loss or damage in consequence of the operation of a disclaimer under this section is deemed to be a creditor of the bankrupt to the extent of the loss or damage and accordingly may prove for the loss or damage as a bankruptcy debt.

The disclaimer does not affect third party rights and liabilities   **20–22** "except so far as is necessary for the purpose of releasing the company in liquidation (bankrupt) from any liability" (ss.178(4), 315(3)). Thus, a range of persons may continue to be liable to the landlord in respect of the lease notwithstanding the disclaimer. They remain liable because it is not necessary to release any of them for the purpose of releasing the company in liquidation or the bankrupt from his or its liability to the landlord. See the House of Lords in *Hindcastle Ltd v Barbara Attenborough Associates Ltd* [1996] 1 All E.R. 737

> " . . . where the landlord has the benefit of covenants from a guarantor . . . the liabilities of the insolvent tenant to the landlord are ended, but not so as to affect the obligations of the guarantor to the landlord. That is the effect of para.(b) of s.178(4). Similarly where the insolvent tenant is an assignee and the landlord has the benefit of the covenants of the original tenant: the original tenant's obligations to the landlord are not affected.
>
> Also ended is the obligation of the insolvent tenant to indemnify the guarantor but, here again, not so as to affect the mutual rights and obligations of the landlord and the guarantor. Termination of the liabilities of the insolvent does not carry with it any legal necessity to determine the guarantor's obligations to the landlord. The right recourse of the guarantor against the insolvent can be effectually determined without, at the same time, releasing the guarantor from his liability to the landlord. His liability to the landlord can survive extinguishment of his right of

recourse. Similar considerations apply to the liabilities of the original tenant where the insolvent is an assignee." (Lord Nicholls at 747g–j.)

The position in relation to various parties is therefore as follows:

(1) If the insolvent tenant was the *original tenant*, any *surety* of that tenant remains liable notwithstanding the termination of the tenancy by virtue of the disclaimer. In this respect *Hindcastle* overrules the Court of Appeal decision in *Stacey v Hill* [1901] 1 K.B. 660. Thus, the surety of the original tenant will be held "liable in the very circumstance at which the guarantee is primarily aired: the insolvency of the person whose obligations are being guaranteed" (per Lord Nicholls at 754d).

(2) If the tenancy is an "old" tenancy and the insolvent tenant was an *assignee* the *original tenant* and his surety remain liable after the disclaimer. If the tenancy is a "new tenancy" under the Landlord and Tenant (Covenants) Act 1995 (para.13–02), the original tenant will remain liable if he has entered into an authorised guarantee agreement ("AGA") for the period of that agreement, as will any surety of his obligations under that agreement (para.13–21); *Shaw v Doleman* [2009] EWCA Civ 279—held liable even though the AGA was expressed to be limited to the "the period during which [the company] is bound by the tenant covenants in the Lease". A surety of the assignee (i.e. of the insolvent assignee) in either situation will also remain liable after the disclaimer.

(3) Any intermediate assignees who have entered into direct covenants with the landlord (see para.13–23) and their respective sureties remain liable on those covenants after disclaimer by the liquidator or trustee of the final assignee.

20–23 A consequence of a disclaimer is that a number of parties remain liable to the landlord but no one is entitled to possession of the premises.

"The disclaimed lease in this situation has been described as 'being something like a dormant volcano. It may break out into active operation at any time.' The activating event is the making of a vesting order."

(Megarry V.C. in *Warnford* quoting Uthwatt J. in *Thompson and Cottrell's Contract, Re* [1943] Ch. 97). This is a concept that many find difficult to grasp. However, that is the effect of the statute. It was explained by Lord Nicholls thus:

> "If . . . disclaimer does not end the lease, so that rent continues to accrue what happens to the lease, bearing in mind that the insolvent's interest in the property has been ended? . . .
>
> The starting point for attempting to solve this puzzling conundrum is to note that the Act clearly envisages that a person may be liable to perform the tenant's covenants even after the lease has been disclaimed. A vesting order may be made in favour of such a person: see s.182(3) and see also s.181(2)(b). The proper legal analysis has to be able to accommodate this conclusion. The search, therefore, is for an interpretation of the legislation which will enable this to be achieved as well as fulfilling the primary purpose of freeing the insolvent from all liability while, overall, doing the minimum violence to accepted property law principles.
>
> If the problem is approached in this way, the best answer seems to be that the statute takes effect as a deeming provision so far as other persons' preserved rights and obligations are concerned. A deeming provision is a commonplace statutory technique. The statute provides that a disclaimer operates to determine the interest of the tenant in the disclaimed property but not so as to affect the rights or liabilities of any other person. Thus, when the lease is disclaimed it is determined and the reversion accelerated but the rights and liabilities of others such as guarantors and original tenants, are to remain as *though* the lease had continued and not been determined. In this way the determination of the lease is not permitted to affect the rights or liabilities of other persons. Statute has so provided" (per Lord Nicholls at p.748a–f).

However, a landlord will lose his right to recover from third parties if he takes back possession of the property. This will bring the lease to an end and all liability in respect of it. He should not therefore take any steps that might be construed as a forfeiture of the lease although it should be noted that there are circumstances in which the securing of the property, or the acceptance of keys, by the landlord will not be construed as taking back possession (see para.7–11).

> "If no vesting order is made and the landlord takes back possession, the liabilities of other persons to pay the rent and perform the tenant's covenants will come to an end as far as the future is concerned. If the landlord acts in this way, he is no longer merely the involuntary recipient of a disclaimed lease. By his own act of taking possession he has demonstrated that he regards the lease as ended for all purposes. His conduct is inconsistent with there being a continuing liability on others to perform the tenant covenants in the lease. He cannot have possession of the property and, at the same time, claim rent for the property from others" (per Lord Nicholls, p.749g–h).

Vesting orders

20–24 Any person who claims an interest in the disclaimed property and any person who is under a liability in respect of it may seek a vesting order in respect of it (ss.181–182, ss.320–321). Persons who may apply pursuant to these sections include:

(1) The landlord (*In re Cock, Ex p. Shilson* (1888) 20 Q.B.D. 343).
(2) Any original tenants, intermediate assignees who remain liable under covenants in a licence to assign or authorised guarantee agreement.
(3) Sureties of any of the above persons.
(4) Sub-tenants and mortgagees (*Finlay, Ex p. Clothworkers Co, Re* (1888) 21 Q.B.D. 475).

The application must be made within three months of the applicant becoming aware of the disclaimer or of his receiving a copy of the notice of disclaimer, whichever is the earlier (rr.4.194(2), 6.186(2)). However, the court has power to extend time in an appropriate case (see para.20–30).

A person making an application for a vesting order will usually be applying to have the lease vested in himself. For example, a sub-tenant may be applying for the lease to be vested in himself so that he can enforce the repairing covenants against the landlord. However, an applicant can apply for the property to be vested in another person. For example, an original tenant might seek an order vesting the property in a sub-tenant or mortgagee (*Finlay, Ex p. Clothworker's Co, Re* (1888) 21 Q.B.D. 475 CA) or the landlord may apply to have it vested in a mortgagee (*In re Baker, Ex p. Lupton* [1901] 2 K.B. 628 CA). (Where a number of persons are applying for a vesting order see *AE Realisations (1985) Ltd, Re* [1987] 3 All E.R. 83 Ch D but note that much of what is said in that case is now incorrect in the light of *Hindcastle Ltd v Barbara Attenborough Ltd*).

The procedure on an application for a vesting is dealt with in rr.4.194 (companies) and 6.186 (individuals).

The court may not make an order vesting the lease in a sub-tenant or mortgagee except on terms making that person subject to the same liabilities and obligations the insolvent tenant was under or subject to the same liabilities and obligations that person would have been subject to if the lease has been assigned to him just before the winding up or bankruptcy (ss.182(1), 321(1)).

A sub-tenant or mortgagee is not obliged to accept a vesting order but if he refuses to do so he is excluded from all interest in the property (ss.182(4), 321(4); *AE Realisations Ltd (1985) Ltd, Re* [1987] 3 All E.R. 83 Ch D). Where there is no sub-tenant or mortgagee willing to accept a vesting order, the court may vest the property in any person who is liable to perform the lessee's covenants in the lease (ss.182(3), 321(3)). It would seem that other persons have no choice. If the court orders them to take the property it will vest in them on the making of the order. A landlord could therefore apply for the tenancy to be vested in the original tenant and he would have no choice but to accept it; although as his liabilities continue he would probably be willing to accept it.

The vesting order of itself vests the lease in the person in whose favour the order is made. No conveyance is required (ss.181, 320). Where the land is registered the disposition needs to be registered (see r.161 of the Land Registration Rules 2003).

Insolvency Act 1986 ss.181–2 (Company)

181.—(1) This section and the next apply where the liquidator has disclaimed property under section 178.   **20–25**

427

(2) An application for a vesting order may be made to the court by—

(a) any person who claims an interest in the disclaimed property, or

(b) person who is under any liability in respect of the disclaimed property, not being a liability discharged by the disclaimer.

(3) Subject as follows, the court may on the application make an order, on such terms as it thinks fit, for the vesting of the disclaimed property in, or for its delivery to—

(a) a person entitled to or a trustee for such a person, or

(b) a person subject to such a liability as is mentioned in subsection (2)(b) or a trustee for such a person.

(4) The court shall not make an order under subsection (3)(b) except where it appears to the court that it would be just to do so for the purpose of compensating the person subject to the liability in respect of the disclaimer.

(5) The effect of any order under this section shall be taken into account in assessing for the purpose of section 178(6) the extent of any loss or damage sustained by any person in consequence of the disclaimer.

(6) An order under this section vesting property in any person need not be completed by conveyance, assignment or transfer.

182.—(1) The court shall not make an order under section 181 vesting property of a leasehold nature in any person claiming under the company as underlessee or mortgagee except on terms making that person—

(a) subject to the same liabilities and obligations as the company was subject to under the lease at the commencement of the winding up, or

(b) if the court thinks fit, subject to the same liabilities and obligations as that person would be subject to if the lease had been assigned to him at the commencement of the winding up.

(2) For the purpose of an order under section 181 relating to only part of any property comprised in a lease, the requirements of subsection (1) apply as if the lease comprised only the property to which the order relates.

(3) Where subsection (1) applies and no person claiming under the company as underlessee or mortgagee is willing to accept an order under section 181 on the terms required by virtue of that subsection, the court may, by order under that section, vest the company's estate or interest in the property in any person who is liable (whether personally or in a representative capacity, and whether alone or jointly with the company) to perform the lessee's covenants in the lease.

The court may vest that estate and interest in such a person freed and discharged from all estates, incumbrances and interest created by the company.

(4) Where subsection (1) applies and a person claiming under the company as underlessee or mortgagee declines to accept an order under section 181, that person is excluded from all interest in the property.

Insolvency Rules 1986 r.4.194 (Company)

4.194.–(1) This Rule applies with respect to an application by any person under section 181 for an order of the court to vest or deliver disclaimed property.

20-26

(2) The application must be made within 3 months of the applicant becoming aware of the disclaimer, or of his receiving a copy of the liquidator's notice of disclaimer sent under Rule 4.188, whichever is the earlier.

(3) The applicant shall with his application file in court a witness statement affidavit–

    (a)   stating whether he applies under paragraph (a) of section 181(2) (claim of interest in the property) or under paragraph (b) (liability not discharged);

    (b)   specifying the date on which he received a copy of the liquidator's notice of disclaimer, or otherwise became aware of the disclaimer; and

    (c)   specifying the grounds of his application and the order which he desires the court to make under section 181.

(4) The court shall fix a venue for the hearing of the application; and the applicant shall, not later than 5 business days before the date fixed, give to the liquidator notice of the venue, accompanied by copies of the application and the witness statement required by paragraph (3).

(5) On the hearing of the application, the court may give directions as to other persons (if any) who should be sent or given notice of the application and the grounds on which it is made.

(6) Sealed copies of any order made on the application shall be sent by the court to the applicant and the liquidator.

(7) In a case where the property disclaimed is of a leasehold nature, and section 179 applies to suspend the effect of the disclaimer, there shall be included in the court's order a direction giving effect to the disclaimer.

This paragraph does not apply if, at the time when the order is issued, other applications under section 181 are pending in respect of the same property.

Insolvency Act 1986 ss.320–321 (Individual)

320.–(1) This section and the next apply where the liquidator has disclaimed property under section 315.

20-27

(2) An application for a vesting order may be made to the court by–

    (a)   any person who claims an interest in the disclaimed property, or

    (b)   person who is under any liability in respect of the disclaimed property, not being a liability discharged by the disclaimer, . . .

(3) Subject as follows, the court may on the application make an order, on such terms as it thinks fit, for the vesting of the disclaimed property in, or for its delivery to–

    (a)   a person entitled to or a trustee for such a person, or

(b)   a person subject to such a liability as is mentioned in subs.(2)(b) or a trustee for such a person . . .

(4) The court shall not make an order under subsection (3)(b) except where it appears to the court that it would be just to do so for the purpose of compensating the person subject to the liability in respect of the disclaimer.

(5) The effect of any order under this section shall be taken into account in assessing for the purpose of section 315(5) the extent of any loss or damage sustained by any person in consequence of the disclaimer.

(6) An order under this section vesting property in any person need not be completed by conveyance, assignment or transfer.

321.–(1) The court shall not make an order under section 320 vesting property of a leasehold nature in any person claiming under the company as underlessee or mortgagee except on terms making that person–

(a)   subject to the same liabilities and obligations as the bankrupt was subject to under the lease on the day the bankruptcy petition was presented, or

(b)   if the court thinks fit, subject to the same liabilities and obligations as that person would be subject to if the lease had been assigned to him on that day.

(2) For the purpose of an order under section 320 relating to only part of any property comprised in a lease, the requirement of subsection (1) applies as if the lease comprised only the property to which the order relates.

(3) Where subsection (1) applies and no person claiming under the company as underlessee or mortgagee is willing to accept an order under section 320 on the terms required by virtue of that subsection, the court may, by order under section 320, vest the company's estate or interest in the property in any person who is liable (whether personally or in a representative capacity, and whether alone or jointly with the bankrupt) to perform the lessee's covenants in the lease.

The court may by virtue of this subsection vest that estate and interest in such a person freed and discharged from all estates, incumbrances and interest created by the company.

(4) Where subsection (1) applies and a person claiming under the company as underlessee or mortgagee declines to accept an order under section 320, that person is excluded from all interest in the property.

Insolvency Rules 1986 r.6.186 (Individual)

20–28

6.186–(1) This Rule applies with respect to an application by any person under section 320 for an order of the court to vest or deliver disclaimed property.

(2) The application must be made within 3 months of the applicant becoming aware of the disclaimer, or of his receiving a copy of the trustee's notice of disclaimer sent under Rule 6.179, whichever is the earlier.

(3) The applicant shall with his application file in court a witness statement–

(a) stating whether he applies under paragraph (a) of section 320(2) (claim of interest in the property) or under paragraph (b) (liability not discharged) or under paragraph (c) (occupation of dwelling-house);

(b) specifying the date on which he received a copy of the trustee's notice of disclaimer, or otherwise became aware of the disclaimer; and

(c) specifying grounds of his application and the order which he desires the court to make under section 320.

(4) The court shall fix a venue for the hearing of the application; and the applicant shall, not later than 5 business days before the date fixed, give to the trustee notice of the venue, accompanied by copies of the application and the witness statement required by paragraph (3).

(5) On the hearing of the application, the court may give directions as to other persons (if any) who should be sent or given notice of the application and the grounds on which it is made.

(6) Sealed copies of any order made on the application shall be sent by the court to the applicant and the liquidator.

(7) In a case where the property disclaimed is of a leasehold nature, or is property in a dwelling-house, and section 317 or (as the case may be) section 318 applies to suspend the effect of the disclaimer, there shall be included in the court's order a direction giving effect to the disclaimer.

This paragraph does not apply if, at the time when the order is issued, other applications under section 320 are pending in respect of the same property.

Overriding lease under Landlord and Tenant (Covenants) Act 1995

It should be remembered that any person who pays makes full payment of an amount which he has been required to pay under s.17 of the 1995 Act is also entitled to apply for an overriding lease under s.19 of the 1995 Act (see para.13-54). Section 19 applies to leases created before the 1995 Act came into force (s.1(2)).   **20-29**

Time limits

The provisions in relation to time limits are a little confusing. Section 376 of the 1986 Act provides that where any provision in the parts or rules relating to bankruptcy limit the time for doing something the court may extend time, either before or after it has expired, on such terms, if any, as it thinks fit. There is no such provision in the Act relating to companies being wound up. However, there is a similar provision in the 1986 Rules to that effect (r.4.3). Furthermore, r.7.51 of the 1986 Rules provides that the usual High Court and the County Court   **20-30** rules apply to insolvency proceedings except insofar as they are inconsistent with the 1986 Rules. Thus, under one provision or another it is possible to apply for an extension of time, for example, to apply for a vesting order.

Insolvency Act 1986 s.376

20-31 Where by any provision in this Group of Parts or by the rules the time for doing anything limited, the court may extend time, either before or after it has expired, on such terms, if any, as it thinks fit.

Insolvency Rules 1986 r.4.3

20-32 Where by any provision of the Act or the Rules about winding up, the time for doing anything is limited, the court may extend the time, either before or after it has expired on such terms, if any, as it thinks just.

Insolvency Rules 1986 r.7.51A

20-33 **7.51A.**–(1) The provisions of the CPR in the first column of the table in this Rule (including any related practice direction) apply to insolvency proceedings by virtue of the provisions of these Rules set out in the second column with any necessary modifications, except so far as inconsistent with these Rules.

Provisions of CPR	*Provisions of these Rules*
CPR Part 6 (except 6.30 to 6.51) (service of documents)	Chapter 3 of Part 12A
CPR Part 18 (further information)	Rules 7.60 and 9.2(3)(b)
CPR Part 31 (disclosure and inspection of documents)	Rules 7.60 and 9.2
CPR Part 37 (miscellaneous provisions about payments into court)	Rule 7.59
CPR Parts 44 and 47 (costs)	Chapter 6 of Part 7
CPR Part 52 (appeals)	Rule 7.49

(2) Subject to paragraph (3), the provisions of the CPR (including any related practice direction) not referred to in the table apply to proceedings under the Act and Rules with any necessary modifications, except so far as inconsistent with these Rules.

(3) All insolvency proceedings must be allocated to the multi-track for which CPR Part 29 make provision, and accordingly those provisions of the CPR which provide for allocation questionnaires and track allocation do not apply.

(4) CPR Part 32 applies to a false statement in a document verified by a statement of truth made under these Rules as it applies to a false statement in a document verified by a statement of truth made under CPR Part 22.

CHAPTER 21

DISSOLVED AND STRUCK-OFF COMPANIES AND DEATH

. . . .

Dissolved companies

Effect of the dissolution

Companies Act 2006 s.1012

1012.—(1) When a company is dissolved, all property and rights **21–01** whatsoever vested in or held on trust for the company immediately before its dissolution (including leasehold property, but not including property held by the company on trust for any other person) are deemed to be *bona vacantia* and—

    (a)   accordingly belong to the Crown, or to the Duchy of Lancaster or to the Duke of Cornwall for the time being (as the case may be), and

    (b)   vest and may be dealt with in the same manner as other *bona vacantia* accruing to the Crown, to the Duchy of Lancaster or to the Duke of Cornwall.

(2) Subsection (1) has effect subject to the possible restoration of the company to the register under Chapter 3 (see s.1034).

Where a company is being wound up, the liquidator will often disclaim the lease (see Ch.20). However, if he does not do so the tenancy will vest in the Crown at the date of the dissolution, unless it was held by the company on trust for any other person (s.1012 of the Companies Act 2006). Where the company did hold the property on trust, an application to vest it in some other suitable person may be made under s.44 of the Trustee Act 1925 (see "vesting orders" below).

Restoration

Where a company has been dissolved an application can be **21–02** made, in certain circumstances, to restore the company to the register (see s.1029 of the Companies Act 2006 Act). The persons who may make such an application include:

- Any person having an interest in land in which the company had a superior or derivative interest;
- Any person having an interest in land or other property (i) that was subject to rights vested in the company, or (ii) that was benefited by obligations owed by the company (s.1029(2)).

The general rule is that an application to the court for restoration of a company to the register may not be made after the end of the period of six years from the date of the dissolution of the company (see more fully s.1030).

Struck-off companies

Companies Act 2006 s.1000

21–03   **1000.**—(1) If the registrar has reasonable cause to believe that a company is not carrying on business or in operation, the registrar may send to the company a communication inquiring whether the company is carrying on business or in operation.

(2) If the registrar does not within one month of sending the communication receive any answer to it, the registrar must within 14 days after the expiration of that month send to the company a second communication referring to the first communication, and stating—

(a)   that no answer to it has been received, and
(b)   that if an answer is not received to the second communication within one month from its date, a notice will be published in the Gazette with a view to striking the company's name off the register.

(3) If the registrar—

(a)   receives an answer to the effect that the company is not carrying on business or in operation, or
(b)   does not within one month after sending the second communication receive any answer,

the registrar may publish in the Gazette, and send to the company, a notice that at the expiration of three months from the date of the notice the name of the company mentioned in it will, unless cause is shown to the contrary, be struck off the register and the company will be dissolved.

(4) At the expiration of the time mentioned in the notice the registrar may, unless cause to the contrary is previously shown by the company, strike its name off the register.

(5) The registrar must publish notice in the Gazette of the company's name having been struck off the register.

(6) On the publication of the notice in the Gazette the company is dissolved.

(7) However—

    (a)   the liability (if any) of every director, managing officer and member of the company continues and may be enforced as if the company had not been dissolved, and

    (b)   nothing in this section affects the power of the court to wind up a company the name of which has been struck off the register.

The companies registrar has power (after following the statutory procedure) to strike a company off the register where he has reasonable cause to believe that the company is no longer carrying on business or is no longer in operation (s.1000 of the 2006 Act). The striking off dissolves the company (s.1000(3)). As with any other dissolved company, its property (including leases but excluding any property held on trust) will vest in the Crown (s.1002; para.21–01).   **21–04**

Where a company or any member or creditor of a company feels aggrieved by the company having been struck off the register, he may apply to have the company restored under s.1029 of the 2006 Act. A landlord creditor may therefore apply to restore the company if he thinks that it is in his interests to do so.

Disclaimer by the Crown

Companies Act 2006 ss.1013 and 1014

1013.—(1) Where property vests in the Crown under section 1012, the Crown's title to it under that section may be disclaimed by a notice signed by the Crown representative, that is to say the Treasury Solicitor, or, in relation to property in Scotland, the Queen's and Lord Treasurer's Remembrancer.   **21–05**

(2) The right to execute a notice of disclaimer under this section may be waived by or on behalf of the Crown either expressly or by taking possession.

(3) A notice of disclaimer must be executed within three years after—

    (a)   the date on which the fact that the property may have vested in the Crown under s.1012 first comes to the notice of the Crown representative, or

    (b)   if ownership of the property is not established at that date, the end of the period reasonably necessary for the Crown representative to establish the ownership of the property.

(4) If an application in writing is made to the Crown representative by a person interested in the property requiring him to decide whether he will

or will not disclaim, any notice of disclaimer must be executed within twelve months after the making of the application or such further period as may be allowed by the court.

(5) A notice of disclaimer under this section is of no effect if it is shown to have been executed after the end of the period specified by subsection (3) or (4).

(6) A notice of disclaimer under this section must be delivered to the registrar and retained and registered by him.

(7) Copies of it must be published in the Gazette and sent to any persons who have given the Crown representative notice that they claim to be interested in the property.

(8) This section applies to property vested in the Duchy of Lancaster or the Duke of Cornwall under section 1012 as if for references to the Crown and the Crown representative there were respectively substituted references to the Duchy of Lancaster and to the Solicitor to that Duchy, or to the Duke of Cornwall and to the Solicitor to the Duchy of Cornwall, as the case may be.

1014.–(1) Where notice of disclaimer is executed under section 1013 as respects any property, that property is deemed not to have vested in the Crown under section 1012.

(2) The following sections contain provisions as to the effect of the Crown disclaimer—

sections 1015 to 1019 apply in relation to property in England and Wales or Northern Ireland;
sections 1020 to 1022 apply in relation to property in Scotland.

1015. General effect of disclaimer

(1) The Crown's disclaimer operates so as to terminate, as from the date of the disclaimer, the rights, interests and liabilities of the company in or in respect of the property disclaimed.

(2) It does not, except so far as is necessary for the purpose of releasing the company from any liability, affect the rights or liabilities of any other person.

1016. Disclaimer of leaseholds

(1) The disclaimer of any property of a leasehold character does not take effect unless a copy of the disclaimer has been served (so far as the Crown representative is aware of their addresses) on every person claiming under the company as underlessee or mortgagee, and either—

(a) no application under section 1017 (power of court to make vesting order) is made with respect to that property before the end of the period of 14 days beginning with the day on which the last notice under this paragraph was served, or
(b) where such an application has been made, the court directs that the disclaimer shall take effect.

(2) Where the court gives a direction under subsection (1)(b) it may also, instead of or in addition to any order it makes under section 1017, make such order as it thinks fit with respect to fixtures, tenant's improvements and other matters arising out of the lease.

(3) In this section the "Crown representative" means—

(a) in relation to property vested in the Duchy of Lancaster, the Solicitor to that Duchy;

(b) in relation to property vested in the Duke of Cornwall, the Solicitor to the Duchy of Cornwall;

(c) in relation to property in Scotland, the Queen's and Lord Treasurer's Remembrancer;

(d) in relation to other property, the Treasury Solicitor.

1017. Power of court to make vesting order

(1) The court may on application by a person who—

(a) claims an interest in the disclaimed property, or

(b) is under a liability in respect of the disclaimed property that is not discharged by the disclaimer,

make an order under this section in respect of the property.

(2) An order under this section is an order for the vesting of the disclaimed property in, or its delivery to—

(a) a person entitled to it (or a trustee for such a person), or

(b) a person subject to such a liability as is mentioned in subsection (1)(b) (or a trustee for such a person).

(3) An order under subsection (2)(b) may only be made where it appears to the court that it would be just to do so for the purpose of compensating the person subject to the liability in respect of the disclaimer.

(4) An order under this section may be made on such terms as the court thinks fit.

(5) On a vesting order being made under this section, the property comprised in it vests in the person named in that behalf in the order without conveyance, assignment or transfer.

1018. Protection of persons holding under a lease

(1) The court must not make an order under section 1017 vesting property of a leasehold nature in a person claiming under the company as underlessee or mortgagee except on terms making that person—

(a) subject to the same liabilities and obligations as those to which the company was subject under the lease, or

(b) if the court thinks fit, subject to the same liabilities and obligations as if the lease had been assigned to him.

(2) Where the order relates to only part of the property comprised in the lease, subsection (1) applies as if the lease had comprised only the property comprised in the vesting order.

(3) A person claiming under the company as underlessee or mortgagee who declines to accept a vesting order on such terms is excluded from all interest in the property.

(4) If there is no person claiming under the company who is willing to accept an order on such terms, the court has power to vest the company's estate and interest in the property in any person who is liable (whether personally or in a representative character, and whether alone or jointly with the company) to perform the lessee's covenants in the lease.

(5) The court may vest that estate and interest in such a person freed and discharged from all estates, incumbrances and interests created by the company.

1019. Land subject to rentcharge

Where in consequence of the disclaimer land that is subject to a rentcharge vests in any person, neither he nor his successors in title are subject to any personal liability in respect of sums becoming due under the rentcharge, except sums becoming due after he, or some person claiming under or through him, has taken possession or control of the land or has entered into occupation of it.

21-06 Where property vests in the Crown on the dissolution of a company, the Crown's title to it may be disclaimed. Where the Crown does disclaim, the property is deemed not to have vested in the Crown (s.1015).

Disclaimer by the Crown operates to determine the liabilities of the company in the property disclaimed "but it does not except so far as is necessary for the purposes of releasing the company and its property from liability affect the rights or liabilities of any other person" (s.1015(2)). For the effect of these words on assignees and sureties of original tenants and assignees etc, see the discussion of *Hindcastle Ltd v Barbara Attenborough Ltd* [1996] 1 All E.R. 737 on para.20-22—which is concerned with the position where a liquidator disclaims).

Vesting orders and reversionary leases

After disclaimer by the Crown

21-07 Where the Crown disclaims, any person who claims an interest in the disclaimed property and any person who is under any liability in respect of the disclaimed property may apply for a vesting order (s.1017; see above).

Reversionary leases: 1995 Act

21-08 Where a person other than the tenant is required to pay the landlord the rent for the property, he may, if the requisite conditions are satisfied, apply to him for a reversionary lease under s.19 of the Landlord and Tenant (Covenants) Act 1995 (see para.13-54). This provision applies to leases granted before as well as after January 1, 1996 when the Act came into force (s.1(2) of the 1995 Act). Thus, if (for example) a surety of a dissolved company, which was the original tenant, pays the landlord arrears of rent that the company in dissolution has not paid, he may, instead of applying for a vesting order under s.1017 of the Companies Act 2006 apply to the landlord for a reversionary lease.

Where the company was a trustee

As stated above, property held on trust by a company does not vest in the Crown on the dissolution. Where a company that has been dissolved was a trustee of property, the court may make a vesting order under s.44 of the Trustee Act 1925. The property is vested "in any such person in any such manner and for any such estate or interest as the court may direct" (s.44(1)(ii)(c)).

21–09

Other provisions to note are s.36(3) of the Trustee Act 1925 (a company that is dissolved cannot, from the date of the dissolution, act as trustee) and s.41(1) of that Act (the court may appoint new trustees).

Trustee Act 1925 s.44(ii), (c)

44. In any of the following cases, namely:

21–10

. . .

(ii) Where a trustee entitled to or possessed of any land or interest therein, whether by way of mortgage or otherwise, or entitled to a contingent right therein, either solely or jointly with any other person—

. . .

(c) cannot be found, or being a corporation has been dissolved.

. . .

the court may make an order (in this Act called a vesting order) vesting the land or interest therein in any such person in any such manner and for any such estate or interest as the court may direct, or releasing or disposing of the contingent right to such person as the court may direct:
Provided that—

. . .

(b) Where the order relates to a trustee entitled or formerly entitled jointly with another person, and such trustee . . . being a corporation has been dissolved, the land interest or right shall be vested in such other person who remains entitled, either alone or with any other person the court may appoint.

Death of the tenant

The death of the tenant does not terminate the tenancy (ss.1 and 3(1) of the Administration of Estates Act 1925). The

21–11

tenant's interest whether it be for a fixed or periodic term vests in the personal representatives who are liable to pay the rent from the estate (*Youngmin v Heath* [1974] 1 All E.R. 461).

Where the tenant has left a will and the named executors are alive and prepared to administer the estate the tenancy will vest in them from the date of death if they have obtained a grant of probate (*Crowhurst Park, Re* [1974] 1 W.L.R. 583). Where there is a will but no executor with power to obtain a grant the estate vests in the Public Trustee (s.9 of the Administration of Estates Act 1925, as amended). Where the tenant has died intestate the estate vests in the Public Trustee until administrators are appointed (s.9 of the Administration of Estates Act 1925, as amended).

Administration of Estates Act 1925 s.9

21–12

9.–(1) Where a person dies intestate, his real and personal estate shall vest in the Public Trustee until the grant of administration.
  (2) Where a testator dies and—

  (a) at the time of his death there is no executor with power to obtain probate of the will, or
  (b) at any time before probate of the will is granted there ceases to be any executor with power to obtain probate,

the real and personal estate of which he disposes by the will shall vest in the Public Trustee until the grant of representation.
  (3) The vesting of real or personal estate in the Public Trustee by virtue of this section does not confer on him any beneficial interest in, or impose on him any duty, obligation or liability in respect of the property.

Once letters of administration have been granted, the estate vests in the administrators from the date of the grant. Their title to the property does not relate back to the date of death as with executors (*Fred Long and Sons Ltd v Burgess* [1950] K.B. 115).

The beneficiaries become entitled to hold the tenancy when it has been vested in them by an assent (s.36 of the Administration of Estates Act 1925). If the title is registered, the beneficiary should register as proprietor (see rr.162 and 163 of the Land Registration Rules 2003).

As a periodic tenancy continues notwithstanding the death of the tenant failure to terminate the tenancy by notice to quit will leave the tenancy in being (*Wirral BC v Smith and Cooper*

(1982) 43 P. & C.R. 312—landlord unable to bring possession proceedings against squatters because of failure to determine the periodic tenancy).

As to service of a notice to quit after the death of a tenant, see para. 14–38.

Part 5

Proceedings for Possession

CHAPTER 22

LANDLORD'S APPLICATION TO TERMINATE CONTINUATION TENANCY

. . . .

One of the major changes brought about by the Regulatory **22–01**
Reform (Business Tenancies) (England and Wales) Order 2003
SI 2003/3096 was the right given to the landlord to apply to
terminate the current tenancy by relying upon one of the
grounds in s.30 (see Ch.17). He does not have to wait for the
tenant to apply for a new tenancy and then oppose. He can, for
example, serve a short s.25 notice and start the proceedings at
any time up to the date specified in the notice. The tenancy will
then generally come to an end three months after the matter is
finally disposed of by the court; in accordance with s.64 of the
Act (s.29(4)(a); para.27–02). He will then be entitled to
possession.

Notice first

Landlord and Tenant Act 1954 s.29(2)

29.–(2) Subject to the following provisions of this Act, a landlord may **22–02**
apply to the court for an order for the termination of a tenancy to which
this Part of this Act applies without the grant of a new tenancy—

    (a)   if he has given notice under section 25 of this Act that he is
            opposed to the grant of a new tenancy to the tenant; or
    (b)   if the tenant has made a request for a new tenancy in
            accordance with section 26 of this Act and the landlord has
            given notice under subsection (6) of that section.

The landlord may not apply for termination unless:

- he has given a notice under s.25 that he is opposed to the
  grant of a new tenancy (see para.14–02); or
- the tenant has made a s.26 request and the landlord has
  given a counter-notice under s.26(6) (see para.15–02).

445

Putting it the other way round, the landlord may apply to the court for termination as soon as he has served a s.25 notice (or counter-notice to a s.26 request). He does not to have to wait for any period to pass before he can do so (as used to be required of a tenant before he could apply to renew). Thus, a landlord who wishes to redevelop quickly can serve a s.25 notice relying upon ground (f) (see para. 17–02) and the very next day apply to the court for termination. However, any such landlord should be aware that there may be costs consequences if he has not previously given the tenant some advance warning together with any available information that the landlord might have as to his plans. See also para. 17–23.

Time limits

Landlord and Tenant Act 1954 s.29A

22–03   **29A.**–(1) Subject to section 29B of this Act, the court shall not entertain an application—

(a)   . . .
(b)   by the landlord under section 29(2) of this Act,

if it is made after the end of the statutory period.
   (2) In this section and section 29B of this Act "the statutory period" means a period ending—

(a)   where the landlord gave a notice under section 25 of this Act, on the date specified in his notice; and
(b)   where the tenant made a request for a new tenancy under section 26 of this Act, immediately before the date specified in his request.

   . . .

The landlord must make his application to terminate prior to the date specified in the s.25 notice or the date immediately before the date specified in the s.26 request. However, as will be seen immediately below it is possible, by written agreement, to extend the time limits and failure by a landlord to apply to terminate within that period is unlikely to have serious consequence for him—although it may have for the tenant.

Agreements extending time limits

Landlord and Tenant Act 1954 s.29B

22–04   **29B.**–(1) After the landlord has given a notice under section 25 of this Act, or the tenant has made a request under section 26 of this Act, but before the end of the statutory period, the landlord and tenant may agree that an application such as is mentioned in section 29A(1) [i.e. *which includes an application to terminate*] of this Act may be made before the end of a period specified in the agreement which will expire after the end of the statutory period.

(2) The landlord and tenant may from time to time by agreement further extend the period for making such an application, but any such agreement must be made before the end of the period specified in the current agreement.

(3) Where an agreement is made under this section, the court may entertain an application such as is mentioned in section 29A(1) of this Act if it is made before the end of the period specified in the agreement.

(4) Where an agreement is made under this section, or two or more agreements are made under this section, the landlord's notice under section 25 of this Act or tenant's request under section 26 of this Act shall be treated as terminating the tenancy at the end of the period specified in the agreement or, as the case may be, at the end of the period specified in the last of those agreements.

As will be seen in Ch.24, the parties may agree to extend the time for issuing an application for a new tenancy. Those provisions also apply to applications by landlords to terminate (s.29B); i.e. the landlord and tenant can agree that the landlord shall have more time to issue his application to terminate. In Ch.24 we discuss the problems that a tenant in particular may suffer if the procedure is not correctly followed. However, the danger for landlords is far less great, if not non-existent. If the landlord misses the time limit and the tenant has not made an application to renew in the meantime, the tenancy will come to an end and the tenant will lose his right to renew.

No application for termination if already an application to renew

Landlord and Tenant Act 1954 s.29(3)

29.–(3) The landlord may not make an application under subsection (2) above if either the tenant or the landlord has made an application under section 24(1) of this Act.

22–05

The landlord may not apply to terminate the continuation tenancy if either he or the tenant has applied to renew. The issues between the parties will be determined on the application to renew and, if the tenant is unsuccessful, his current tenancy will generally come to an end three months hence in accordance with s.64; para.27–02.

If the landlord does apply to terminate in ignorance of an application by the tenant to renew because the application to renew has not yet been served—see CPR 56 PD para.3.2 (para.24–07)—the position is as follows:

- If the application to renew has been served, the landlord cannot serve his application to terminate without permission (56 PD 3.2(1)).
- If the landlord's application to terminate and the tenant's application to renew are served on the same day, the tenant's application to renew is stayed until further order (56 PD 3.2(3)).
- If the tenant issues but does not serve his application to renew and the landlord issues afterwards and serves, the landlord's service of his application is deemed to be a notice under CPR 7.7 requiring service or discontinuance of the tenant's application to renew within a period of 14 days after service of the application to terminate. If the tenant fails to comply with the deemed notice, the court may on the application of the landlord: (a) dismiss the tenant's claim; or (b) make any other order it thinks just (CPR, 7.7). If the tenant's claim is dismissed, it will then be possible for the landlord's claim for termination to proceed.

If the landlord fails in his application to terminate the tenancy, the tenant does not have to start his own claim for a new tenancy. The court is required at the end of the case to make an order for the grant of a new tenancy (s.29(4)(b)—see below). It is not necessary for the tenant to cross-apply for a new tenancy. Indeed the tenant is not allowed to make an application for a new tenancy if the landlord has made *and served* an application to terminate (s.24(2B)—see para.24–06).

See further paras 24–06 and 24–07.

Civil Procedure Rules

Introduction

22–06 The rules governing applications to terminate are primarily set out in CPR 56 and CPR 56 PD as amended. The application to terminate is dealt with under CPR 7 (CPR 56.3(2)(c)(ii); 56.3(4)(b); CPR 56 PD paras 2.1A, 3.1(2)(b)).

High Court or County Court

Ideally the claim should be started in the County Court hearing **22–07** centre which serves the address of the property otherwise there is likely to be a delay whilst the claim is transferred to that hearing centre (CPR 56.2(1)). Only exceptional circumstances justify starting the claim in the High Court. (CPR 56.2 (2)) If the claim is started in the High Court and the court decides that it should have been started in the County Court, the court will normally either strike out the claim or transfer it to the County Court on its own initiative. "This is likely to result in delay and the court will normally disallow the costs of starting the claim in the High Court and of any transfer." Circumstances that may, in an appropriate case, justify starting a claim in the High Court are if there are complicated disputes of fact or there are points of law of general importance. The value of the property and the amount of any financial claim may be relevant circumstances but these factors alone will not normally justify starting the claim in the High Court. (CPR 56 PD para 2) The best policy is therefore almost invariably to start the claim in the County Court and, if it is thought appropriate, ask that court to transfer to the High Court.

If the claim is begun in the High Court it must be brought in the Chancery Division. (CPR 56 PD para.2.6.)

Claim form

The details required in the claim form are set out in CPR 56 PD **22–08** 3.4 and 3.9 and consist of the following:

- the property to which the claim relates;
- the particulars of the current tenant (including date, parties and duration), the current rent (if not the original rent) and the date and method of termination;
- every notice or request given or made under s.25 or 26 of the 1954 Act; and
- the expiry date of (a) the statutory period under s.29A(2)—see para.22–03, or (b) any agreed extended period under s.29B(1) or (2)—see para.22–04;
- the claimant's grounds of opposition (see Ch.17);
- full details of those grounds of opposition;
- the terms of a new tenancy that the claimant proposes in the event that his claim fails.

Service

22–09 The claim must be served within four months after the date of issue. CPR 7.5 (general rule for service) and 7.6 (extensions of time for service).

Acknowledgment of service

22–10 The appropriate acknowledgment of claim form is Form N9, the standard acknowledgment for Pt 7 claims. (CPR 56 PD 3.13.)

Defence

22–11 CPR 56 PD 3.13 requires that in his defence the tenant must state *with particulars*:

- Whether the tenant relies on s.23(1A) (relating to companies; see para.2–21); s.41 (trusts; para.2–22) or s.42 (groups of companies; para.2–21) and if so, the basis on which he does so. There is no reference in the PD to s.41A (partnerships—para.2–26) but, if relevant, it is suggested that appropriate details are included.
- Whether the tenant relies on s.31A (relevant to ground (f) claims; para.17–13) and, if so, the basis on which he does so.
- The terms of the new tenancy that the defendant would propose in the event that the claimant's claim to terminate the tenancy fails.

The tenant should also, as a matter of good practice, include any matters relating to the grounds of the claim that the tenant wishes to assert.

Allocation and directions

22–12 A claim to terminate under s.29 is not suitable for the small claims track (CPR 26 PD para.8.1(c)).

Unless in the circumstances of the case it is unreasonable to do so, the court will order that any grounds specified in s.30 upon which the landlord or any other basis on which the landlord asserts that a new tenancy ought not to be granted shall be tried as a preliminary issue (CPR 56 PD para 3.1(3)(b) and 3.16).

Evidence, including expert evidence, must be filed by the parties as the court directs. The landlord will be required to file his evidence first (56 PD 3.15). As with all other Pt 7 claims the parties should make suggested directions when they complete their allocation questionnaires.

In the Chancery Division, a Master or District Judge may not deal with the claim without the consent of the Chancellor except by consent of the parties (CPR 2B PD para 5.1(j)). In the County Court, the District Judge may not hear the claim, except with the consent of the parties and the permission of the Designated Civil Judge in respect of that case (CPR 2B PD para.11.1(d)).

See also para.23–43.

Judgment in default

If the tenant fails to acknowledge service or file a defence within time and the landlord wishes to obtain a default judgment, he must make an application in accordance with Pt 23 (CPR 12.4(2)(a)).

22–13

However, it has been suggested that in the light of s.29(4)(a), which states: "If he [the landlord] establishes, to the satisfaction of the court, any of the grounds . . . [for termination], the court shall make an order for termination of the current tenancy" it is not possible for the court to make an order without considering the merits of the landlord's claim that a ground applies. (See "In default of a defence" by David Stevens *Estates Gazette*, September 24, 2005, p.137—the author of the article suggests that landlords would be prudent to combine an application for default judgment with an application for summary judgment.).

Withdrawal by landlord

Landlord and Tenant Act 1954 s.29(6)

29.–(6) The landlord may not withdraw an application under subsection (2) above unless the tenant consents to its withdrawal.

22–14

The landlord may not withdraw an application to terminate unless the tenant consents (s.29(6)). The reason for this is that if the landlord withdraws his application the current tenancy will automatically come to an end and the tenant will not be able to apply for a new tenancy.

The order

Landlord and Tenant Act 1954 s.29(4)

22-15   **29.**—(4) Subject to the provisions of this Act, where the landlord makes an application under subsection (2) above—

(a)   if he establishes, to the satisfaction of the court, any of the grounds on which he is entitled to make the application in accordance with section 30 of this Act, the court shall make an order for the termination of the current tenancy in accordance with section 64 of this Act without the grant of a new tenancy; and

(b)   if not, it shall make an order for the grant of a new tenancy and accordingly for the termination of the current tenancy immediately before the commencement of the new tenancy.

Where the landlord's application to terminate is successful, s.29(4)(a) provides that the court shall make an order for the termination of the current tenancy without the grant of a new tenancy. The section does not provide detailed guidance on the contents of the court order, but it does make it clear that the order for termination of the current tenancy without renewal, will be in accordance with s.64 of the Act (para.27–02).

If the landlord fails in his application to terminate the tenancy, the tenant does not have to start his own claim for a new tenancy. The court is required at the end of the case to make an order for the grant of a new tenancy (s.29(4)(b)). As the landlord's grounds will almost invariably have been tried as a preliminary issue (see para.22–12), the court will no doubt give directions as to the further conduct of the case if the parties are not able to agree the terms of the new tenancy.

(Note that the provisions of s.31 will also apply—i.e. the landlord would have been satisfied on any of the grounds (d), (e) or (f) on any date within one year of the date specified in the s.25 notice or s.25 request; see para.27–05.)

CHAPTER 23

POSSESSION CLAIMS AND PEACEABLE RE-ENTRY

. . . .

Peaceable re-entry

After the lease has ended a landlord of business premises is not **23–01**
precluded from obtaining possession by peaceable re-entry. The
prohibitions against reliance on self-help, contained in ss.2 and
3 of the Protection from Eviction Act 1977 (see below), apply
only where the property was "let as a dwelling".

However, premises that have a mixed commercial residential
use such as a property with a shop on the ground floor with a
flat above let to the tenant for the purposes of a business are
for the purposes of s.2 (and presumably s.3) treated as
premises "let as a dwelling" even where the residential part has
its own separate entrance (*Pirabakaran v Patel* [2006] EWCA
Civ 685—the words "let as a dwelling" in s.2 mean "let wholly
or partly as a dwelling". They do not mean "let exclusively as a
dwelling". See in particular Wilson LJ at paras 5 and 34). The
lease in *Pirabakaran v Patel* contained a forfeiture clause in
standard form, permitting the landlord to forfeit by re-entering
the premises "or any part thereof". The tenant ran a retail
business on the ground floor and resided on the first floor,
which was self-contained with its own separate entrance. When
the tenant got into arrears of rent the landlord purported to
forfeit by causing bailiffs to change the locks of the shop but
took no steps to take possession of the flat; and the tenant
remained in occupation of the flat. In subsequent possession
proceedings relating to the flat the Court of Appeal held that as
s.2 applied to the premises the original forfeiture was invalid.
The lease of the whole was therefore still in existence!

Where the sub-tenant of the residential part is an *assured*
tenant in occupation pursuant to a *lawful* tenancy, s.18 of the
Housing Act 1988 provides that the assured tenant becomes a
direct tenant of the head landlord on termination of the head

tenancy (see para.27-08). It is not therefore possible to obtain possession from him at all. Where the assured tenancy is an unlawful one, that is granted in breach of a covenant against subletting s.18 does not apply.

For the position in relation to residential occupiers see further *Residential Possession Proceedings*, 9th edn (Sweet & Maxwell), Ch.22.

Protection from Eviction Act 1977 ss.2, 3, 3A and 8

23-02

2. Where any premises are let as a dwelling on a lease which is subject to a right of re-entry or forfeiture it shall not be lawful to enforce *that right* otherwise than by proceedings in the court while any person is lawfully residing in the premises or part of them.

3.—(1) Where any premises have been let as a dwelling under a tenancy which is neither a statutorily protected tenancy nor an excluded tenancy and—

    (a)   the tenancy (in this section referred to as the former tenancy) has come to an end, but

    (b)   the occupier continues to reside in the premises or part of them,

it shall not be lawful for *the owner* to enforce against the occupier, otherwise than by proceedings in the court, his right to recover possession of the premises.

(2) In this section "the occupier", in relation to any premises, means any person lawfully residing in the premises or part of them at the termination of the former tenancy.

(2A) Subsections (1) and (2) above apply in relation to any restricted contract (within the meaning of the Rent Act 1977) which—

    (a)   creates a licence; and

    (b)   is entered into after the commencement of section 69 of the Housing Act 1980;

as they apply in relation to a restricted contract which creates a tenancy

(2B) Subsections (1) and (2) above apply in relation to any premises occupied as a dwelling under a licence, other than an excluded licence, as they apply in relation to premises let as a dwelling under a tenancy, and in those subsections the expressions "let" and "tenancy" shall be construed accordingly.

(2C) References in the preceding provisions of this section and section 4(2A) below to an excluded tenancy do not apply to—

    (a)   a tenancy entered into before the date on which the Housing Act 1988 came into force, or

    (b)   a tenancy entered into on or after that date but pursuant to a contract made before that date,

but, subject to that, "excluded tenancy" and "excluded licence" shall be construed in accordance with section 3A below.

(3) This section shall, with the necessary modifications, apply where the owner's right to recover possession arises on the death of the tenant under a statutory tenancy within the meaning of the Rent Act 1977 or the Rent (Agriculture) Act 1976.

3A.–(1) Any reference in this Act to an excluded tenancy or an excluded licence is a reference to a tenancy or licence which is excluded by virtue of any of the following provisions of this section.

23-03

(2) A tenancy or licence is excluded if—

(a) under its terms the occupier shares any accommodation with the landlord or licensor; and

(b) immediately before the tenancy or licence was granted and also at the time it comes to an end, the landlord or licensor occupied as his only or principal home premises of which the whole or part of the shared accommodation formed part.

(3) A tenancy or licence is also excluded if—

(a) under its terms the occupier shares any accommodation with a member of the family of the landlord or licensor;

(b) immediately before the tenancy or licence was granted and also at the time it comes to an end, the member of the family of the landlord or licensor occupied as his only or principal home premises of which the whole or part of the shared accommodation formed part; and

(c) immediately before the tenancy or licence was granted and also at the time it comes to an end, the landlord or licensor occupied as his only or principal home premises in the same building as the shared accommodation and that building is not a purpose-built block of flats.

(4) For the purposes of subsections (2) and (3) above, an occupier shares accommodation with another person if he has the use of it in common with that person (whether or not also in common with others) and any reference in those subsections to shared accommodation shall be construed accordingly, and if, in relation to any tenancy or licence, there is at any time more than one person who is the landlord or licensor, any reference in those subsections to the landlord or licensor shall be construed as a reference to any one of those persons.

(5) In subsections (2) to (4) above—

(a) "accommodation" includes neither an area used for storage nor a staircase, passage, corridor or other means of access;

(b) "occupier" means, in relation to a tenancy, the tenant and, in relation to a licence, the licensee; and

(c) "purpose-built block of flats" has the same meaning as in Part III of Schedule 1 to the Housing Act 1988;

and section 113 of the Housing Act 1985 shall apply to determine whether a person is for the purposes of subsection (3) above a member of another's family as it applies for the purposes of Part IV of that Act.

(6) A tenancy or licence is excluded if it was granted as a temporary expedient to a person who entered the premises in question or any other premises as a trespasser (whether or not, before the beginning of that tenancy or licence, another tenancy or licence to occupy the premises or any other premises had been granted to him).

(7) A tenancy or licence is excluded if—

(a)   it confers on the tenant or licensee the right to occupy the premises for a holiday only; or

(b)   it is granted otherwise than for money or money's worth.

(7A) . . .

(7B) . . .

(8) A licence is excluded if it confers rights of occupation in a hostel, within the meaning of the Housing Act 1985, which is provided by—

(a)   the council of a county, county borough, district or London Borough, the Common Council of the City of London, the Council of the Isle of Scilly, the Inner London Education Authority, the London Fire and Emergency Planning Authority, a joint authority within the meaning of the Local Government Act 1985 or a residuary body within the meaning of that Act;

(b)   a development corporation within the meaning of the New Towns Act 1981;

(c)   the Commission for the New Towns;

(d)   an urban development corporation established by an order under section 135 of the Local Government, Planning and Land Act 1980;

(e)   a housing action trust established under Part III of the Housing Act 1988;

(f)   . . . ;

(g)   the Housing Corporation . . . ;

(ga)   the Secretary of State under s.89 of the Housing Association Act 1985;

(h)   a housing trust which is a charity or a registered housing association, within the meaning of the Housing Association Act 1985; or

(i)   any other person who is, or who belongs to a class of person which is, specified in an order made by the Secretary of State.

(9) The power to make an order under subsection (8)(i) above shall be exercisable by statutory instrument which shall be subject to annulment in pursuance of a resolution of either House of Parliament.

. . .

23-04   **8.**—(1) In this Act "statutorily protected tenancy" means—

(a)   a protected tenancy within the meaning of the Rent Act 1977 or a tenancy to which Part I of the Landlord and Tenant Act 1954 applies;

(b)   a protected occupancy or statutory tenancy as defined in the Rent (Agriculture) Act 1976;

(c)   a tenancy to which Part II of the Landlord and Tenant Act 1954 applies;

(d)   a tenancy of an agricultural holding within the meaning of the [Agricultural Holdings Act 1986] [which is a tenancy in relation to which that Act applies];

(e)   an assured tenancy or assured agricultural occupancy under Part I of the Housing Act 1988;

(f)   a tenancy to which Schedule 10 to the Local Government and Housing Act 1989 applies;

(g)   a farm business tenancy within the meaning of the Agricultural Tenancies Act 1995.

(2) For the purposes of Part I of this Act a person who, under the terms of his employment, had exclusive possession of any premises other than as a tenant shall be deemed to have been a tenant and the expressions "let" and "tenancy" shall be construed accordingly.

(3) In Part I of this Act "the owner", in relation to any premises, means the person who, as against the occupier, is entitled to possession thereof.

(4) In this Act "excluded tenancy" and "excluded licence" have the meaning assigned by section 3A of this Act.

(5) If, on or after the date on which the Housing Act 1988 came into force, the terms of an excluded tenancy or excluded licence entered into before that date are varied, then—

(a)   if the variation affects the amount of the rent which is payable under the tenancy or licence, the tenancy or licence shall be treated for the purposes of sections 3(2C) and 5(1B) above as a new tenancy or licence entered into at the time of the variation; and

(b)   if the variation does not affect the amount of the rent which is so payable, nothing in this Act shall affect the determination of the question whether the variation is such as to give rise to a new tenancy or licence.

(6) Any reference in subsection (5) above to a variation affecting the amount of the rent which is payable under a tenancy or licence does not include a reference to—

(a)   a reduction or increase effected under Part III or Part VI of the Rent Act 1977 (rents under regulated tenancies and housing association tenancies), section 78 of that Act (power to rent tribunal in relation to restricted contracts) or sections 11 to 14 of the Rent (Agriculture) Act 1976; or

(b)   a variation which is made by the parties and has the effect of making the rent expressed to be payable under the tenancy or licence the same as a rent for the dwelling which is entered in the register under Part IV or section 79 of the Rent Act 1977.

23–05   Although in purely commercial cases in theory it is possible to obtain possession without a court order it should always be remembered that any resort to self-help must be peaceful. Section 6 of the Criminal Law Act 1977 makes it illegal to use force or violence against person or property to recover possession when there is someone present on the premises (whether living there or not) who opposes the entry.

It is recommended that proceedings be taken whenever someone is or may be on the premises or part of them. If there clearly is no one on the premises and a decision is taken to re-enter peaceably certificated bailiffs should be used if the property is occupied albeit for business purposes.

Criminal Law Act 1977 s.6

6.–(1) Subject to the following provisions of this section, any person who, without lawful authority, uses or threatens violence for the purpose of securing entry into any premises for himself or for any other person is guilty of an offence, provided that–

   (a)   there is someone present on those premises at the time who is opposed to the entry which the violence is intended to secure; and

   (b)   the person using or threatening the violence knows that that is the case.

   (2) . . . the fact that a person has any interest in or right to possession or occupation of any premises shall not for the purposes of subsection (1) above constitute lawful authority for the use or threat of violence by him or anyone else for the purpose of securing his entry into those premises.

   . . .

   (4) It is immaterial for the purposes of this section–

   (a)   whether the violence in question is directed against the person or against property; and

   (b)   whether the entry which the violence is intended to secure is for the purpose of acquiring possession of the premises in question or for any other purpose.

Damages for unlawful eviction

"Unlawful eviction of a tenant by a landlord is not a tort. It is a breach of contract for which the tenant is entitled to claim damages" (per Jackson LJ in *Grange v Quinn* [2013] EWCA Civ 24). In that case the landlord unlawfully evicted a business tenant from his premises after only six months of a six-year lease. The Court of Appeal held (2-1) that the tenant was entitled to damages equivalent to a premium the tenant had paid on the granting of the lease, less a small sum to represent the period that the tenant was in occupation running her business. Jackson LJ at para.85:

> "The starting point for assessing damages is the purchase price which the claimant paid, namely £9,950. It would be manifestly unjust if [L] could evict [T] after only six months and still keep the purchase price."

In another case, a businessman was awarded damages for unlawful eviction based upon loss of profit from sublettings but was refused a sum in respect of the capital value of the lease, as this would have amounted to double recovery. He was also awarded interest at a rate that reflected the cost to him, as a small businessman of being kept out of his money, rather than the lower conventional sums awarded in commercial cases. He received 3% over base prevailing from time to time (*Jaura v Ahmed*[2002] EWCA Civ 210).

Parties

The claimant/landlord

In most claims the position will be straightforward. The claimant **23–06** will be the owner of the property and the landlord or licensor of the defendant. However, the claimant is not necessarily the absolute owner of the property. He need only show that he has a better right to possession than the defendant. Whenever the claimant has let the defendant into possession as a tenant or licensee, the tenant/licensee is estopped from denying the claimant's title (see paras 4–09 and 6–12). He is also estopped from denying his title where the claimant is an assignee of the original landlord (see *Cuthbertson v Irving* (1859) 4 H.&N. 742).

Where a person has a licence to enter premises for certain purposes (e.g. to carry out building works), he may have sufficient interest to permit him to bring a possession claim against trespassers. Whether or not he has such a right will depend upon the agreement between the owner and the licensee (*Dutton v Manchester Airport* [2001] 1 Q.B. 133; *Countryside Residential (North Thames) Ltd v T (a Child)* (2001) 81 P.&C.R. 10; *Alamo Housing Co-operative Ltd v Meredith* [2003] EWCA Civ 495 and *Mayor of London v Hall* [2010] EWHC 1613, (QB) (reversed in part, but not on this point).

Somewhat surprisingly, the Court of Appeal in *Dearman v Simpletest* [1999] P.L.S.C.S. 280; [1999] All E.R. (D) 1365 even upheld a possession order where the claimant held only one half of the equitable interest in the property at the date of the hearing. However, it should be noted that the legal owners were in court, one of them gave evidence on behalf of the claimant and they agreed to be bound by the order of the court. The defendants also had no defence on the merits and were merely taking the technical point.

Joint owners

23-07 Where there are two or more persons who are jointly entitled to possession as against the defendant(s), e.g. two joint landlords, they should generally both be joined as claimants (CPR 19.3):

> **19.3**–(1) Where a claimant claims a remedy to which some other person is jointly entitled with him, all persons jointly entitled to the remedy must be parties unless the court orders otherwise.
>
> (2) If any person does not agree to be a claimant, he must be made a defendant, unless the court orders otherwise.

However, following the principle stated above of estoppel where only one or some of the owners of the property are actually in the position of the landlord, only that (those) person(s) need bring the claim.

> **Example**: If a husband and wife own a property that was let to tenants but the tenancy agreement was signed by the husband, only he needs to be named as the claimant.

The position of particular landlords is now considered before turning to the question of who should be made a defendant to the action.

Companies, partners and sole traders

23-08 A company or other corporation may be represented at trial by an employee if the employee has been authorised by the company or corporation to appear at trial on its behalf and the court gives permission. Permission will normally be granted (CPR 39.6 and 39 PD para.5.3; see further 39 PD para.5.2–for the written statement that should be given to the court about the representation).

Where a claim is brought by a partnership see CPR 7 PD paras 5A and 5B. Generally speaking partners should sue or be sued in the partnership name at the time the cause of action accrued; but if requested to do so the partners must provide a written statement of the names and last known residence of all the partners.

Proceedings may be brought against an individual using that person's trading name if only the trading name is known (CPR 7 PD para.5C).

Executors and administrators

If the landlord dies leaving a will, the property vests in his **23-09** executors from the date of his death. The executors may therefore commence proceedings for possession prior to the grant of probate. Their title however is proved by the grant and so if their title is in dispute the executors will not be able to proceed with the possession action until the grant of probate. The position of an administrator however is rather different. He derives title entirely from the grant of letters of administration and the deceased's estate does not vest in him until that time. An administrator may thus *commence* and continue proceedings for possession only once he has obtained the grant. As to the right of the personal representative to costs out of the estate where they are not fully recovered from the Defendant, see CPR 46.3.

LPA receivers

A receiver appointed under the powers that used to be **23-10** conferred by the Law of Property Act 1925 is deemed to be the agent of the mortgagor (s.109(2)). A receiver wishing to obtain possession should therefore do so in the name of the mortgagor. However, in some cases it may be more advantageous for the mortgagor to take mortgage possession proceedings, for example, where the tenancy was created after the mortgage and is not binding on the mortgagee (if the powers of leasing implied by s.99 of the 1925 Act have been excluded); unless the mortgagee does not wish to be a mortgagee in possession with all the responsibilities that that entails (see generally Fisher & Lightwood, *Law of Mortgages*, 13th edn (Butterworths, 1988), para.29-54).

Change of landlord by reason of assignment

Where the landlord assigns or dies during the course of the **23-11** proceedings, the claim does not cease. The assignee or personal representatives may apply without notice for an order to carry on the proceedings (CPR 19.2 and 19.4).

In the case of an assignment where the land is registered the assignment takes place on the date the transfer is registered (s.27 Land Registration Act 2002).

If the landlord dies and there are no personal representatives, the court may proceed in his absence or appoint someone to represent the estate (CPR 19.8). If one of two or more claimants who are suing jointly in respect of a joint cause of action dies the other(s) continue the claim without appointing a personal representative. Service of a statement of case in the name of the deceased after he has in fact died is an irregularity but it does not render the proceedings a nullity. The irregularity can be rectified by an amendment (*Fielding v Rigby* [1993] 4 All E.R. 294).

As to bankruptcy see s.49 of the County Courts Act 1984.

County Courts Act 1984 s.49

23-12   **49.**—(1) The bankruptcy of the plaintiff in any action in a County Court which the trustee might maintain for the benefit of the creditors shall not cause the action to abate if, within such reasonable time as the court orders, the trustee elects to continue the action and to give security for the costs of the action.
    (2) The hearing of the action may be adjourned until such an election is made.
    (3) Where the trustee does not elect to continue the action and to give such security as mentioned in subsection (1) within the time limited by the order, the defendant may avail himself of the bankruptcy as a defence to the action.

The defendant/tenant

23-13   The defendant will be the person in possession against whom the landlord has an immediate right to possession, i.e. the claimant's immediate tenant or licensee whose contractual tenancy or licence has been determined. The phrase "in possession" includes persons who are in receipt of rents. A tenant who has sublet the whole of the premises should therefore be made a defendant even though he may not be in actual occupation. If any person in possession has not been joined as a defendant he may apply, without notice, to be joined in the proceedings. The application may be made at any stage, even after judgment and execution of the order for possession and should be made pursuant to CPR 19.4(2)—see para.23-66. The order for possession operates against any person on the land (*R. v Wandsworth County Court, Ex p. Wandsworth LBC* [1975] 1 W.L.R. 1314) so it is not strictly necessary to join any of the tenant's licensees or sub-tenants but for forfeiture cases see para.7-33. However, it is suggested that if the names of any such persons are known or can be ascertained, it is usually advisable to join them so as to avoid any possible application by such persons for the order for possession to be set aside. Alternatively, the landlord might serve a copy of the claim on persons in occupation together with a letter informing them of their right to be joined in the proceedings. For safe measure, a further copy can be put through the letter box or affixed to the front door in an envelope addressed to "the occupiers". For service on sub-tenants and mortgagees in a forfeiture claim, see para.7–33.

Insolvency of the defendant: restrictions on proceedings

Where a potential defendant is insolvent or facing insolvency, reference must be made to the Insolvency Act 1986. See paras 7–41 onwards.

23–14

Company: winding up

At any time between the presentation of a winding-up petition and the making of a winding-up order, a creditor or a contributor may where any action is being brought in the High Court or Court of Appeal, apply to the court in which the proceedings are pending for a stay of proceedings on application by the company. Where any other action or proceedings is pending, an application may be made to the court having jurisdiction in relation to the winding up (s.126 of the 1986 Act).

23–15

When a winding-up order has been made or a provisional liquidator appointed no action or proceedings may be proceeded with or commenced against the company or its property except with the leave of the court (s.130). (See also the reference to *Blue Jeans* in para.7–37.)

Insolvency Act 1986 ss.126 and 130

126.–(1) At any time after the presentation of a winding up petition, and before a winding up order has been made, the company, or any creditor or contributory, may—

23–16

    (a)   where any action or proceeding against the company is pending in the High Court or Court of Appeal in England and Wales or Northern Ireland, apply to the court in which the action or proceeding is pending for a stay of proceedings therein, and

(b) where any other action or proceeding is pending against the company, apply to the court having jurisdiction to wind up the company to restrain further proceedings in the action or proceeding;

and the court to which application is so made may (as the case may be) stay, sist or restrain the proceedings accordingly on such terms as it thinks fit.

(2) In the case of a company registered but not formed under the Companies Act 2006, where the application to stay, sist or restrain is by a creditor, this section extends to actions and proceedings against any contributory of the company.

130.–(1) On the making of a winding up order, a copy of the order must forthwith be forwarded by the company (or otherwise as may be prescribed) to the registrar of companies, who shall enter it in his records relating to the company.

(2) When a winding up order has been made or a provisional liquidator has been appointed, no action or proceeding shall be proceeded with or commenced against the company or its property, except by leave of the court and subject to such terms as the court may impose.

(3) When an order has been made for winding up a company registered but not formed under the Companies Act 2006, no action or proceeding shall be commenced or proceeded with against the company or its property or any contributory of the company, in respect of any debt of the company, except by leave of the court, and subject to such terms as the court may impose.

(4) An order for winding up a company operates in favour of all the creditors and of all contributories of the company as if made on the joint petition of a creditor and of a contributory.

Individual: interim order

23-17 It is not possible to commence proceedings for forfeiture when an interim order is in place or has been applied for (s.252; see para.7–51. It should also be noted that a subsequent voluntary arrangement will not prevent forfeiture (para.7–47).

Individuals: bankruptcy

23-18 The restrictions that apply in relation to bankruptcy proceedings are set out in ss.285 and 346 of the Insolvency Act 1986. However, see the decision of *Ezekiel v Orakpo* [1977] Q.B. 260 and *Sharples v Places for People Homes Ltd* [2011] EWCA Civ 813 in relation to the meaning of the words "property or person of the debtor" (see para.7–52).

Insolvency Act 1986 ss.285 and 346

285.–(1) At any time when proceedings on a bankruptcy petition are pending or an individual has been adjudged bankrupt the court may stay any action, execution or other legal process against the property or person of the debtor or, as the case may be, of the bankrupt.

(2) Any court in which proceedings are pending against any individual may, on proof that a bankruptcy petition has been presented in respect of that individual or that he is an undischarged bankrupt, either stay the proceedings or allow them to continue on such terms as it thinks fit.

(3) After the making of a bankruptcy order no person who is a creditor of the bankrupt in respect of a debt provable in the bankruptcy shall—

(a) have any remedy against the property or person of the bankrupt in respect of that debt, or

(b) before the discharge of the bankrupt, commence any action or other legal proceedings against the bankrupt except with the leave of the court and on such terms as the court may impose.

This is subject to sections 346 (enforcement procedures) and 347 (limited right to distress).

(4) Subject as follows, subsection (3) does not affect the right of a secured creditor of the bankrupt to enforce his security.

. . .

346.–(1) Subject to section 285 in Chapter II (restrictions on proceedings and remedies) and to the following provisions of this section, where the creditor of any person who is adjudged bankrupt has, before commencement of the bankruptcy—

(a) issued execution against the goods or land of that person,

. . .

that creditor is not entitled, as against the official receiver or trustee of the bankrupt's estate, to retain the benefit of the execution or attachment, or any sums paid to avoid it, unless the execution or attachment was completed, or the sums were paid, before the commencement of the bankruptcy.

. . .

23–19

Court proceedings

Introduction

Part 55 of the Civil Procedure Rules and the Practice Direction made under that Part largely govern claims for possession—see para.23-75 onwards.

Part 55 must be used where the claim *includes* a "possession claim" brought by a:

23–20

- landlord (or former landlord), or
- licensor (or former licensor).

A "possession claim" means a claim for recovery of possession of land (including buildings or parts of buildings) (CPR 55.1(a)). When the court issues the claim form, it will fix a date for the hearing (see further below).

Part 55 also applies to claims against trespassers and where the claim is brought by a mortgagee but subject to certain variations. (Trespassers are dealt with below—para.23–53. The differences that apply to mortgage claims can be seen in CPR 55.10 at para.23–84 and PD 55 2.5 at para.23–95.)

High Court or County Court

23–21 The County Court now has jurisdiction to hear all claims for possession of land, whatever the rateable value of the premises (s.21(1) of the County Courts Act 1984; as amended by the High Court and County Courts Jurisdiction Order 1991). Therefore, both the High Court and the County Court, in theory, have jurisdiction to hear all claims for possession of business premises.

County Courts Act 1984 s.21

21.—(1) The County Court shall have jurisdiction to hear and determine any action for the recovery of land.

However, the Civil Procedure Rules provide that possession claims should only rarely be started in the High Court; see immediately below.

County Court

23–22 Claims for possession should generally be issued:

- in the County Court;
- at the hearing centre which serves the address;

If the claimant starts in a different hearing centre, the claim will be transferred to the hearing centre which serves the address with consequential delays (CPR 55.3, CPR 55A PD, para.1.1(2))

High Court

It will sometimes be possible to issue in the High Court but only **23-23** in "exceptional circumstances" (CPR 55 PD, para.1.1). Circumstances that may provide justification for starting in the High Court will be if there are:

- complicated disputes of fact; or
- points of law of general importance;
- in certain trespasser cases (CPR 55 PD para 1.3).

The value of the property and the amount of any financial claim may be relevant circumstances but "these factors alone will not normally justify starting the claim in the High Court" (55 PD 1.4).

The PD also provides that the claim may be begun in the High Court if the County Court does not have jurisdiction. However, as stated above, s.21 of the County Courts Act 1984 states: "The County Court shall have jurisdiction to hear and determine any action for the recovery of land" (para.23-21).

If the claimant does start in the High Court, he will have to file, with his claim form, a certificate stating the reasons for doing so. The certificate will need to be verified with a statement of truth under CPR 22.1(d) (CPR 55.3(2)).

A claim wrongly started in the High Court will normally be struck out or transferred to the County Court by the court on its own initiative. This is likely to result in delay and the court will normally disallow the costs of starting the claim in the High Court and of any transfer (CPR 55 PD, para.1.2).

Starting the claim

The online system for bringing possession claims does not **23-24** apply to commercial premises (CPR 55 PD 55B, para.5.1(2)).

Documents required

Two forms are required to issue the claim: **23-25**

- A claim form—Form N5.

- Particulars of claim (see below)—which must be filed and served with the claim form (CPR 55.4).

The various forms used in the proceedings can also be found on the Court Service website: http://hmctsformfinder.justice .gov.uk/HMCTS/FormFinder.do [Accessed November 24, 2014]

Claim form

23-26   The claim form (N5) is a simple document and, after completion and issue, will tell the court immediately whether or not the property is residential and the basic ground for the claim. It refers to the particulars of claim that need to be served with it and contains a statement of truth. It must be used in all possession claims, whatever the nature of the property (CPR 55.3(5); 55 PD, para.1.5). However, the claim is not a nullity simply because the wrong form has been used (CPR 3.10).

The claim form must include the full name of each party. "The full name means, in each case where it is known in the case of an individual, his full unabbreviated name and title by which he is known" (CPR 16 PD, para.2.6). The claim form must identify the land to which the claim relates (CPR 55 PD, para.2.1). The addresses of the claimants and defendants must include postcodes unless the court orders otherwise. Postcodes can be obtained from *http://www.royalmail.com* [Accessed November 24, 2014] (CPR 16 PD, para.2.4).

Particulars of claim

All cases

23-27   A note to CPR 55.4 states that the relevant practice direction (meaning CPR 55 PD, para.2.1) and CPR 16 provide details about the contents of the particulars of claim. The combined effect of the PDs is that particulars of claim must:

- Identify the land to which the claim relates.
- State whether the claim relates to residential property.
- Give full details about any tenancy agreement.
- State the ground on which possession is claimed.
- Give details of every person who, to the best of the claimant's knowledge, is "in possession" of the property (see note below).

- Give the name of any person known to be entitled to apply for relief from forfeiture—a copy of the particulars of claim must be filed for service upon the named persons (CPR 55 PD, para.2.4).
- Give details of interest claimed (CPR 16.4).

Notes/suggestions

- The term "possession" usually has a technical meaning, referring only to the tenant. However, it is probably wise to give details of all persons who, to the knowledge of the claimant, are in "occupation" including e.g. minors in a residential part of the property. The person "in possession" will be the defendant.
- A person with a charging order is entitled to claim relief "indirectly" (*Bland v Ingram's Estates Ltd* [2001] 24 E.G. 163) (see para.12–41). His name and address, if known, should therefore also be given and he should be served.

23–28

CPR 16 PD states that particulars of claim should contain a concise statement of the facts upon which the claimant intends to rely. However, as will be seen below CPR 55 PD also permits and encourages claimants to put all their intended evidence into the particulars of claim. It is necessary to achieve a sensible balance. In simple claims it will normally be appropriate to include all the relevant information in the particulars of claim.

Property with a residential element—rent cases

Where the claim *"relates to residential property* let on a tenancy" and the claim *includes* a claim for non-payment of *rent*, it is also necessary (CPR 55 PD, para.2.3) to set out:

23–29

- the amount due at the start of the proceedings;
- in schedule form, the dates when the arrears of rent arose, all amounts of rent due, the dates and amounts of all payments made and a running total of the arrears;
- the daily rate of any rent and interest;
- any previous steps taken to recover the arrears of rent with full details of any court proceedings; and
- any relevant information about the defendant's circumstances, in particular—

1. whether the defendant is in receipt of social security benefits; and
2. whether any payments are made on his behalf directly to the claimant under the Social Security Contributions and Benefits Act 1992.

23–30   The requirements relate not only to claims where the ground for possession is non-payment of rent but any case where rent is claimed in addition to possession.

Further, the form that must be used in such residential rent cases is Form N119 (CPR 55 PD, paras 1.5 and Table 1 (forms)–para.4). Although mixed use premises are treated as being "let as a dwelling" for the purposes of s.2 of the Protection from Eviction Act 1977 (para.23–01) it would seem that a claim for premises let under a business tenancy is not a claim "relating to residential property let on a tenancy" even if part of the property is used for residential purposes, so that it is not necessary to use Form N119 where the claim includes a claim for non-payment of rent. Form N119 seeks much information which is not really relevant to a commercial lease and it will invariably more helpful to the court to draft an appropriate particulars of claim. However, the first three items above would obviously be required in a commercial claim and the other two items might be relevant.

Documents to attach

23–31   The Practice Direction relating to statements of case states that, where a claim is based upon a written agreement, "a copy of the contract . . . should be attached to or served with the particulars of claim and the original should be available at the hearing" (CPR 16 PD, para.7.3(1)). It also states that a party may "attach to or serve with this statement of case a copy of any document which he considers to be necessary to his claim or defence" (CPR 16 PD, para.13.3(3)). It should also be noted that CPR 55 PD permits and encourages all the evidence in the case to be in the particulars of claim (see CPR 55 PD, para.5.1 at para.23–98).

The authors suggest that the practice of attaching documents to particulars of claim should be adopted in possession claims. However, the documentation should be kept to a minimum. If the tenancy agreement is more than, say, three or four pages only the relevant parts should be attached. Perhaps, the front page showing the term and the rent etc, any page containing a relevant clause and the final page showing the signatures. Any relevant notice or other key document should also be attached. Careful annexation of the relevant documents will limit the need for further evidence at the hearing in very many standard cases.

See further paras 23-41 and 23-42.

Statement of truth

The particulars of claim (as well as the claim form) must be verified by a statement of truth (CPR 22.1(1)(a)). If the statement is in a separate document, it must clearly identify the document that it is verifying (CPR 22.1(7)). The format of the statement should be as described in CPR 22 PD, para.2.3. If the claimant fails to verify his statement of case by a statement of truth, he may not rely upon it as evidence of any of the matters set out in it; and the court may even strike out the statement of case (CPR 22.2).   **23-32**

The hearing date

General rule

A stated above the court will give the claimant a hearing date when the claim is issued. In most cases: **23-33**

- The hearing date will be not less than 28 days from the date of issue of the claim form—although it may be possible to have this period varied under CPR 3.1(2)(a), (b) (see below—urgent cases).
- The *standard period* between the issue of the claim form and the hearing will be not more than eight weeks (CPR 55.5(3)).

Urgent cases

The Practice Direction (CPR 55 PD, para.3.2) states that particular consideration should be given to the exercise of the power to shorten time periods if: **23-34**

- the defendant, or a person for whom the defendant is responsible, has assaulted or threatened to assault—

1. the claimant;
2. a member of the claimant's staff; or
3. another resident in the locality;

- there are reasonable grounds for fearing such an assault; or
- the defendant or a person, for whom the defendant is responsible, has caused serious damage or threatened to cause serious damage to the property or to the home or property of another resident in the locality.

Service

23-35   The defendant must be served with the claim form and the particulars of claim not less than 21 days before the hearing date (CPR 55.5(3)). However, the court may extend or shorten the time for compliance under (CPR r.3.1(2)(a), (b)).

The normal rules of service in Pt 6 will generally apply to standard claims. However, where the claimant serves the claim form and particulars of claim, he must produce a certificate of service of those documents *at the hearing* (CPR 6.17(2)(a), which provides for filing of a certificate within 21 days, does not apply: CPR 55.8(6)).

Action by the defendant

Defence and evidence

23-36   There is no requirement on the defendant to file an acknowledgment of service. However, he must file a defence. If he fails to do so within 14 days of service of the particulars of claim, he may take part in the hearing but his failure to do so may be taken into account when deciding what order to make about costs (CPR 55.7(3)). It is not possible for the claimant to obtain judgment in default (CPR 55.7(4)).

The defence filed must be in the form set out in the relevant practice direction (CPR 55.3(5)), i.e. revised Form N11. This is basically a blank sheet of paper with a statement of truth on it. The provisions, which allow and encourage all parties to rely upon written evidence verified by a statement of truth, in particular in the statements of case (para.23-98), apply to defendants as much as to claimants. Completion of Form N11 is therefore an important matter.

If the defendant wishes to put in written evidence, in addition to matters set out in his defence (N11), he must serve the witness statements at least two days prior to the hearing.

None of the above prevents the defendant from giving oral evidence at the hearing.

The hearing

The judge

In the County Court, the claim may be heard by a judge or a district judge (CPR 2.4; PD 2B, para.11.1(b)). **23–37**

Open court?

CPR 39.2(3)(c) provides that a hearing may be in private if "it involves confidential information (including relating to personal financial matters) and publicity would damage that confidentiality". The Practice Direction relating to this rule states that: "A claim by a landlord against one or more tenants or former tenants for the repossession of a *dwelling house* based on the non-payment of *rent*" ... "shall in the first instance be listed by the court ... *in private* under rule 39.2(3)(c)" (CPR 39 PD, para.1.5(2)). Thus claims in respect of commercial premises should be in open court. **23–38**

Urgent cases

Where the claim is an appropriate one for shortening the time between issue and the hearing of the claim but the case cannot be determined at the first hearing "the court will consider what steps are needed finally to determine the case as quickly as reasonably practicable" (CPR 55 PD, para.3.3). **23–39**

Case management

At the initial hearing, or at any adjournment of that hearing, the court may decide the claim or give case management directions (CPR 55.8(1)). Where the claim is "*genuinely disputed* on grounds which *appear to be substantial*", case management directions will include the allocation of the claim to a track or **23–40** directions to enable it to be allocated (CPR 55.8(1)(2))—see further below. It should be noted that the court may give case management directions in relation to a claim without allocating to a specific track.

Evidence

23-41   If the case is allocated to the fast track or the multi-track or if the court so orders the normal rules about evidence in, CPR 32 will apply (CPR 55.8(1)). However, in any other case it is possible to prove the case by written evidence: CPR 55.8(3) expressly provides that any fact that needs to be proved by the evidence of witnesses at a hearing (or adjourned hearing) may be proved by evidence in writing. Indeed, evidence in written form is encouraged: "*Each party* should wherever possible include all the evidence he wishes to present in his statement of case, verified by a statement of truth" (CPR 55 PD, para.5.1: see para.23-98).

Where a party wishes to rely upon further written evidence, the witness statements must be filed and served at least two days before the hearing (CPR 55.8(4)).

Rent cases

23-42   In a rent case, the details contained in the particulars of claim or any witness statement that has been served may be out of date by the date of the hearing, even if served only two days beforehand. If so, the claimant may give evidence orally or in writing on the day of the hearing if necessary (CPR 55 PD, para.5.2).

Disputing written evidence

23-43   Although written evidence is encouraged, if material evidence is disputed and the witness is not at court, the court will normally adjourn the hearing so that oral evidence can be given (CPR 55 PD, para.5.4).

Track allocation

Generally

23-44   As stated above, where the claim is "genuinely disputed on grounds which appear to be substantial", case management directions will include the allocation of the claim to a track or directions to enable it to be allocated. The general criteria for allocation set out in CPR 26.8 are not really appropriate to possession claims. CPR 55.9 therefore provides that the matters to which regard should be had include:

- the matters set out in CPR 26.8 as modified by the relevant practice direction (see below);
- the amount of the arrears in a rent case;
- the importance to the defendant of retaining possession;
- the importance of vacant possession to the claimant.

Small claims track

It is only possible to allocate the case to the small claims track **23–45** if the parties agree (CPR 55.9(2)). In that case, special provisions apply in relation to costs, allowing recovery under a modified form of the fast track rules unless all parties want the small claims costs rules to apply. The claim will be treated, for the purpose of costs, as if it were proceedings on the fast track except that the trial costs "shall be in the discretion of the court and shall not exceed the amount that would be recoverable under CPR 45.38 (amount of fast track costs) if the value of the claim were up to £3,000"—currently £485. If the parties do agree otherwise, the court may when it allocates the claim order that CPR 27.14 (costs on the small claims track) applies (CPR 55.9(3)(4)).

Summary judgment

It is possible for a claimant to apply for summary judgment in **23–46** commercial possession claims. (It is not possible where the claim is in respect of residential premises "against a tenant or person holding over after the end of his tenancy, whose occupancy is protected within the meaning of the Rent Act 1977 or the Housing Act 1988": CPR 24.3(2)(a) as amended.)

Although permitted, it is perhaps unlikely that the claimant will apply for summary judgment. This is because the court will only have allocated the case to a track where the claim is "genuinely disputed on grounds which appear to be substantial". However, as the case proceeds, it may become apparent that the defendant has no real prospects of success. Defendants may also consider it appropriate to apply in some cases.

See also para.7-32 relating to forfeiture claims.

The order for possession

23-47 Where the claimant succeeds in obtaining an order for possession, the court has only a limited power to postpone the order for possession. Except in forfeiture cases, the court may not make any order postponing the date for possession for more than 14 days, or six weeks in cases of exceptional hardship (s.89 of the Housing Act 1988).

Housing Act 1980 s.89

23-48   **89.**–(1) Where a court makes an order for possession of any land in a case not falling within the exceptions mentioned in subsection (2) below, the giving up of possession shall not be postponed (whether by the order or any variation, suspension or stay of execution) to a date later than fourteen days after the making of the order, unless it appears to the court that exceptional hardship would be caused by requiring possession to be given up by that date; and shall not in any event be postponed to a date later than six weeks after the making of the order.
    (2) The restrictions in subsection (1) above do not apply if—

    (a)   the order for possession is made in an action by a mortgagee for possession; or
    (b)   the order is made in an action for forfeiture or a lease;

    . . .

These provisions apply whether the premises are residential or commercial. The limitations imposed on the court's discretion by s.89 apply when proceedings are in the High Court as well as the County Court (*Boyland and Son Ltd v Rand* [2006] EWCA Civ 1860 but do not apply to a court exercising appellate jurisdiction during the appeal process so that a warrant can be stayed pending appeal (*Admiral Taverns (Cygnet) Ltd v Daniel* [2008] EWHC 1688).

Where the defendant entered onto the land unlawfully the court has no power to postpone the order for possession without the consent of the claimant; s.89 does not apply (*Boyland*).

Costs

Summary assessment

CPR 44 PD para.9 states: "The general rule is that the court **23–49** should make a summary assessment of costs − (a) at the conclusion of the trial of a case which has been dealt with on the fast track, and 9 (b) at the conclusion of any other hearing, which has lasted not more than one day . . . ".

CPR 44 PD Para.9 requires that a written statement of costs should be prepared following as closely as possible Form N260. In principle, there is no reason why a defeated party to a possession claim should not pay the other party's reasonable costs. The principle of proportionality will of course apply (CPR 44.3 and 44.4) but recovery of possession of a property or the defeat of a claim for possession is very often a matter of great concern to the parties involved.

Indemnity costs; contractual terms

Where a party has a contractual right to costs on a particular **23–50** basis, he is not to be deprived of that right unless there is a good reason. The fact that the claim is a straightforward possession claim is no such reason (*Gomba Holdings (UK) Ltd v Minories Finance Ltd (No.2)* [1992] 4 All E.R. 588 CA; *Church Commissioners for England v Ibrahim* [1997] 1 E.G.L.R. 13 CA—the lease required the tenant "to pay and compensate the landlords fully for any costs expense loss or damage incurred or suffered by the landlords as a consequence of any breach of the agreements on the part of the tenant"—the judge was wrong not to order costs on an indemnity basis). Thus, where the tenancy agreement provides for costs on an indemnity basis, the landlord is entitled to the costs on that basis, whether on a summary or detailed assessment.

See further CPR 44.5.

Fixed costs

Unless the court otherwise orders the amount to be allowed in **23–51** respect of solicitor's charges is fixed where the claim is for the recovery of land, including a possession claim under CPR 55, where one of the grounds for possession is arrears of rent, for which the court gave a fixed date for the hearing when it issued the claim and judgment is given for the possession of land (whether or not the order for possession is suspended on terms) and the defendant—has neither delivered a defence, or counterclaim, nor otherwise denied liability; or has delivered a defence which is limited to specifying his proposals for the payment of arrears of rent (CPR 45.1(2)(d)).

Where the claimant obtains judgment in these circumstances the amount to be included in the judgment for the claimant's solicitor's charges is the total of the fixed commencement costs and (at the time of writing) the sum of £57.25 (CPR 45.6). In addition the claimant is entitled to the court fee (CPR 45.1(4)). Note that these provisions are not confined to residential cases.

As stated, above the court can "*otherwise order*"; i.e. award costs greater than the fixed costs. The sort of circumstances in which it might do so are:

- Where there has been one or more adjournments at the request of the defendant;
- Where there is a complication in the case; or
- Where the tenancy agreement makes specific provisions as to costs (see para.23–50).

Appeals

23–52 CPR Part 52 and the Practice Direction to that part, to which readers are referred, govern appeals. However, the main points that are relevant to possession claims are probably as follows:

- It is necessary to obtain permission to appeal. The application may be made to the lower court at the hearing or to the appeal court in an appeal notice. Where the lower court refuses the application for permission, a further application may be made to the appeal court (CPR 52.3).
- Permission to appeal will only be given where the court considers that the appeal would have "a real prospect of success or there is some other compelling reason why the appeal should be heard" (52.3(6)).
- The notice of appeal must be filed "at the appeal court within such period as may be directed by the lower court or where

the court makes no such direction" within 21 days of the decision of the lower court (CPR 52.4). If more time is required it must therefore be expressly requested.

- Unless the appeal court or the lower court orders otherwise, an appeal does not operate as a stay of any order or decision of the lower court (CPR 52.7). It is thus very important for a losing defendant specifically to apply for a stay if he is contemplating an appeal. Section 89 of the Housing Act 1980 does not prevent the court from staying the order for possession pending the appeal (see para.23–48).
- Where the case was not allocated or was allocated to the fast track, an appeal (i) from a district judge is made to the circuit judge and (ii) an appeal from a circuit judge in the County Court is made to a High Court Judge (CPR 52 PD, para.2A.1). If the case was allocated to the multi-track an appeal is to the Court of Appeal for a final decision.
- It is necessary for the advocate to make a note of the judgment. It is no good waiting for a transcript (CPR 52 PD, paras 5.12 and 5.14).
- In very limited circumstances, the appeal can be referred to the Court of Appeal even though that would not be the usual court to hear the appeal (CPR 52.14(a)).

One of the categories of appeal in which the Court of Appeal will consider favourably an application for an expedited hearing of an appeal is cases in which the execution of a possession order is imminent and which appears to have some merit (*Unilver plc v Chefaro Proprietaries Ltd* [1995] 1 All E.R. 587).

Trespassers

CPR 55 and its practice direction must be used where "the claim *includes* a possession claim against trespassers" (CPR 55.2). However, there are certain modifications that apply where the claim is against trespassers. These are dealt with in this section. The term "a possession claim against trespassers" is defined in CPR 55.1(b). It means:

23–53

> " . . . a claim for the recovery of land which the claimant alleges is occupied only by a person or persons who entered or remained on the land without the consent of a person entitled to possession of that land but does not

479

include a claim against a tenant or sub-tenant whether his tenancy has been terminated or not".

The modifications of the normal CPR 55 procedure relate to:

- issue in the High Court;
- claims against persons whose names are not known;
- the particulars of claim;
- the date of the hearing;
- service of the claim and other evidence;
- the lack of a requirement on the defendants to file a defence.

High Court

23-54 CPR 55A PD, para.1.1 states: "Except where the County Court does not have jurisdiction, possession claims should normally be brought in the County Court. *Only exceptional circumstances* justify starting a claim in the High Court" (see generally above para.23–23). However, the PD specifically states that circumstances that may, in an appropriate case, justify starting a claim in the High Court include where "the claim is against trespassers and there is a substantial risk of public disturbance or of serious harm to persons or property which properly require immediate determination".

Defendants whose names are not known

23-55 Where the claimant does not know the name of a person in occupation, the claim must be brought against "persons unknown" in addition to any named defendants.

Particulars of claim

23-56 As with all possession claims, it is necessary to use two documents: (i) a claim form (Form N5); and (ii) particulars of claim. The forms can be found on the Court Service website (http://hmctsformfinder.justice.gov.uk/HMCTS/Form Finder.do [Accessed November 24, 2014]). The claim form has a specific question, which indicates immediately to the court that the claim is against trespassers. There is a form of Particulars of Claim that has been drafted that relates specifically to trespassers (Form N121). In addition to any other relevant matters, the particulars of claim must state:

- The identity of the land to which the claim relates.
- Whether the claim relates to residential property.
- The claimant's interest in the land or the basis of his right to claim possession.
- The circumstances in which it has been occupied without licence or consent (CPR 55A PD, para.2.6).

Hearing date

As with all possession claims, the court fixes a date for the hearing when it issues the claim form. Presumably, the hearing date will be much closer to the issue date in trespasser claims than in other cases. However, there is no specific statement within CPR 55 or the PD to the effect that the case will be listed within a specific period. The rules merely refer to the date of service. In the case of residential property, the defendant must be served with the claim form, particulars of claim and any witness statements not less than five days before the hearing date. In all other cases, these documents must be served not less than two days before the hearing date (55.5). In a particularly urgent case, an application can be made to shorten time under CPR 3.1(2)(a). All the witness statements on which the claimant intends to rely must be filed and served with the claim form (CPR 55.8(5)).

23-57

Service of the documents

Where the claim is issued against "persons unknown", there are specific rules for service by attaching the documents to the main door or some other part of the land so that they are clearly visible and if practicable, inserting them in a sealed transparent envelope to the occupiers through the letter box. As an alternative, service may be effected by placing stakes in the land where they are clearly visible with the documents attached (CPR 55.6). The court will effect service if the claimant wishes but it will be necessary to provide the court with sufficient stakes and transparent envelopes (CPR 55A PD, para.4.1).

23-58

The defendant

The defendant does not need to respond. There is no requirement to serve an acknowledgment or a defence. He may just turn up and defend the claim (CPR 55.8). However, if he has time, a defendant with a substantive defence will be well

23-59

advised to file a defence or witness statement, verified by a statement of truth, setting out his or her position.

Order for possession

23-60 The court has no power to postpone an order for possession made against a trespasser without the consent of the claimant; s.89 of the Housing Act 1980 does not apply (see para.23-47).

Where there is a fear that trespassers will move onto land and occupy it, the proper route is for an application for an injunction, not an order for possession. An order for possession of land not actually occupied is too wide (*Secretary of State for the Environment Food & Rural Affairs v Meier* [2009] UKSC 11).

Interim possession orders

23-61 There is also a procedure whereby a land owner may apply for an "interim possession order" under CPR 55 section.III; (para.23-84). If made, the interim order requires the respondent to vacate within 24 hours of service of the order. It can also be an offence to be present on the premises as a trespasser at any time during the currency of the order (s.76 of the Criminal Justice and Public Order Act 1994). On the making of the order, the court fixes a hearing date "which will be not less than seven days after the date on which the IPO is made" (CPR 55.25(4)). There are a number of County Court forms to be used from the application to the order; see Forms N130 to 136 (not in this book).

On the face of it, the "interim possession order" provides the property owner with a powerful weapon. However, the conditions to be satisfied before an interim order can be made are stringent. They include a requirement that the claimant has had an immediate right to possession "throughout the period of unlawful occupation alleged" (CPR 55.21(1)(b)), and that "the claim is made within 28 days of the date on which the claimant first knew, or ought reasonably to have known, that the defendant, or any of the defendants, was in occupation" (CPR 55.21(1)(c)). The procedure and the rules governing it are also complicated and, being of an interim nature, provide no certainty. It would, for example, not help in evicting a person who claims some sort of right to possession, however spurious, just before exchange of contracts for the sale of premises. The claimant may obtain his interim order and then exchange contracts only to find that the order is not converted into a final order on the hearing date. This procedure is therefore unlikely to be of any use except in the simplest of squatter cases; and even there the extra costs and time likely to be expended in using the procedure will deter many property owners.

Setting aside orders for possession

Although the hearing of a possession claim on the first date is not a trial for the purposes of CPR 39.3, in most cases that part should be used to determine whether or not an order should be set aside for failure to attend that hearing (*Hackney LBC v Findlay* [2011] EWCA Civ 8, see also *Forcelux v Binnie* [2009] EWCA Civ 854 for an example of an exceptional case where failure to attend a hearing meant that it was appropriate for the court to have recourse to the wider provisions for setting aside an order under CPR 3.1: a case of forfeiture of a long lease). **23–62**

Therefore, where a party does not attend the hearing and the court gives judgment or makes an order against him the party who failed to attend may apply for the judgment or order to be set aside, applying CPR 39.3(3), the court may grant the application only if the applicant—

(a) acted promptly when he found out that the court had exercised its power to make the order against him;
(b) had a good reason for not attending trial; and
(c) has a reasonable prospect of success at the trial (CPR 39.3(5), see *Bank of Scotland v Pereira* [2011] EWCA Civ 241 where Neuberger MR sets out in detail the considerations to be made on such an application).

It is not necessary for a defendant to have a system in place to make sure that litigation comes to his attention. If a person fails to attend a hearing of which he is unaware he has a "good reason" for failing to attend (*Estate Acquisition and Development Ltd v Wiltshire* [2006] EWCA Civ 533, see Dyson LJ at [24]).

An application to set aside by someone who was not a party to the proceedings should be made (CPR 40.9) together with an application to be joined in the proceedings (CPR 19.4(2)(b)).

An application to set aside an order for possession may be made after the order has been executed (*Minet v Johnson* (1890) 63 L.T. 507). If a judgment or order for possession is set aside, any execution issued on the judgment or order for possession ceases to have effect, even if the order for possession has actually been executed; see further "setting aside warrant of execution" below at para.23–66.

Where a party is dissatisfied with judgment at a hearing at which they failed to attend and their main cause for complaint arises out of the failure to adjourn the matter, the proper route is an application to set the judgment aside under CPR 39.3(3) rather than appeal (*Williams v Hinton* [2011] EWCA Civ 1123).

Once a warrant is executed the court no longer has any power to suspend the order for possession. The defendant will only have a remedy if he is entitled to have the order for possession set aside (*Governors of the Peabody Donation Fund v Hay* (1986) 19 H.L.R. 145) or if the warrant has been obtained by fraud, abuse of process or oppression (*Hammersmith and Fulham LBC v Hill* [1994] 2 E.G.L.R. 51 at 52H; *Circle 33 Housing Trust Ltd v Ellis* [2005] EWCA Civ 1233–see below).

The authors consider that the Jackson reforms brought in in 2013 do not directly impact on these provisions in that those reforms concentrated on relief from sanctions and not the specific parts outlined above.

Enforcement

County Court

Warrant of possession

23–63 An order for possession is enforced in the County Court by a "warrant of possession" (CPR 83.26). In order to obtain the warrant for possession the landlord must make an application to the court (on Form N325) plus a fee within 6 years of the date of the order of possession (CPR 83.2 (3): if required after that time an application for permission must be made). The warrant should not be requested before the day after the day on which the court has ordered the tenant to give up possession (*Tuohy v Bell* [2002] EWCA Civ 423). The application must be accompanied by a certificate that the land which is subject of the judgment or order has not been vacated. Where a money judgment was made in addition to the order for possession, the landlord may also apply for execution against the tenant's goods (CPR 83.26(6)).

The warrant remains in force for one year (CPR 83.3(3)). After that time it may be renewed but only with the permission of the court. The application for renewal may be made without notice and in Form N244 setting out the circumstances and reason for the delay.

Where a claimant is seeking to enforce the order for possession by writ or warrant for possession there is no requirement to give notice to an occupier of the date for eviction (*Pritchard v Teitlebaum* [2011] EWHC 1063—a case under RSC Ord.45 in relation to the High Court but which seem to apply in both the High Court and the County Court under the new CPR 83.13 and 83.26 respectively).

Order for possession suspended on terms

Where an order for possession has been suspended on terms as to payment of a sum of money by instalments the landlord in his request must certify:

23-64

(a) the amount of money remaining due under the judgment or order, and
(b) that the whole or part of any instalment remains unpaid (CPR 83.26 (7)).

Execution of the warrant

In order to enforce the warrant, the bailiff need not remove any goods or chattels from the premises (County Courts Act 1984 s.111(1)). See further below. The bailiff is entitled to evict anyone he finds on the premises even though that person was not a party to the proceedings (*R. v Wandsworth County Court, Ex p. Wandsworth LBC* [1975] 3 All E.R. 390). If a person on the

23-65

premises claims to have some right as against the landlord to remain there, he should apply to the court to be joined in the proceedings pursuant to CPR 19.4(2)(b) and for the order for possession to be set aside (see para.23–66). If he fails to do so within a reasonable time, the bailiff may evict him.

Setting aside warrant of execution

23-66 In *Circle 33 Housing Trust Ltd v Ellis* [2005] EWCA Civ 1233 the Court of Appeal re-affirmed the principles to be applied when setting aside a warrant *after execution*. This will only occur where (1) the order on which it is issued is itself set aside, (2) the warrant has been obtained by fraud, or (3) there has been an abuse of process or oppression in its execution (*Jephson Homes v Moisejevs* [2000] EWCA Civ 271 applied).

The court will rarely be willing to find "oppression" but "the categories of oppression are not closed and the court must have the power to intervene in the interests of justice in an appropriate case to correct the position where its procedures have been used unfairly to the oppression of a party" (*Barking & Dagenham LBC v Saint* (1998) 31 H.L.R. 620 CA per Gibson LJ at 626). "Oppression includes oppressive conduct which effectively deprives a tenant of his opportunity to apply for a stay" (*Lambeth LBC v Hughes* (2001) 33 H.L.R. 350 CA per Arden LJ; and see *Circle 33 Housing Trust*). However, "a possession warrant obtained and executed without fault on anyone's part cannot properly be set aside as oppressive" (*Jephson Homes v Moisejevs*, per Simon Brown LJ at para.37). Oppression can include oppression caused by misleading information given by the court office (*Hammersmith & Fulham LBC v Lemeh* (2001) 33 H.L.R. 23—tenant wrongly told by member of court staff that there appeared to be no case on the court system—warrant then executed; *Lambeth LBC v Hughes*—tenant told inaccurately that no warrant had been issued and given other inaccurate information).

If a judgment or order for possession is set aside "any execution issued on the judgment or order shall cease to have effect unless the Court otherwise orders" (CPR 70.6); even if the order for possession has been executed (*Governor of Peabody Donation Fund v Hay* (1986) 19 H.L.R. 45). However, so long as the order is in force the claimant is entitled to enforce it. Execution of the order for possession does not make the landlord liable for breach of the covenant for quiet enjoyment if it is subsequently set aside (*Brent LBC v Botu* (2001) 33 H.L.R. 14 CA). A warrant obtained without the court's permission in breach of CPR 83.2 (3) in a case where six years or more have elapsed since the date of the order for possession is an abuse of the process of the court (*Governors of the Peabody Donation Fund v Hey* (1986) 19 H.L.R. 145).

Warrant of restitution

If the tenant unlawfully re-enters the premises after the warrant for possession has been executed, the landlord should apply for a warrant of restitution (CPR 83.26(8)). Permission to issue the warrant is required and may be applied for without notice. The application should be supported by an evidence of the wrongful re-entry and such further facts as would, in the High Court, enable the judgment creditor to have writ of restitution issued (CPR 83.26 (9)).   **23-67**

The warrant may be issued in order to evict any persons on the land, whether they were parties to the original possession proceedings or not, provided there is a sufficient nexus between the acts of trespass concerned. The question to ask is, "were the acts or episodes of trespass complained of during the overall period properly to be regarded as essentially one transaction?" (*Wiltshire County Council v Frazer* [1986] 1 All E.R. 65).

High Court

A judgment for possession of land may be enforced by one or more of the following methods: **23-68**

(1) writ of possession;
(2) committal (in certain cases); or
(3) writ of sequestration (in certain cases) (CPR 83.13 (1)).

The normal method of enforcing an order for possession is by writ of possession. Such a writ may include provision for the payment of any money adjudged or ordered to be paid by the judgment or order to be enforced by the writ (CPR 83.13 (9))

Writ of possession—application for permission

A writ of possession will not be issued without the permission of the court (CPR 83.13 (2)) and such permission will not be   **23-69** granted except in certain mortgage cases unless it is shown that every person in actual possession of the whole or any part of the land has received such notice of the proceedings as appears to the court sufficient to enable him to apply to the court for any relief to which he may be entitled (CPR 83.13 (8)).

Where the claimant is seeking to enforce a suspended order for possession on the basis that the condition for the suspension has not been complied with, the application for permission must be made on notice so that the defendant has an opportunity of being heard (*Fleet Mortgage and Investment Co Ltd v Lower Maisonette 46 Eaton Place Ltd* [1972] 2 All E.R. 737).

Issue of writ

23-70 A request signed by the landlord's solicitor is filed with the court (CPR 83.9). The writ will not be issued unless the Claimant also produces the judgment or order on which the writ is to issue or an office copy thereof and the order granting permission (if necessary) or evidence that it was granted (CPR 83.9(5)). The writ is valid for 12 months from the date of issue (CPR 83.3(3)) although if it is not executed within that time an application for extension can me made (CPR 83.3(4)).

Execution of the writ

23-71 Enforcement of High Court writs of execution are carried out by High Court Enforcement Officers or Agents who are directly instructed by the claimant. The writ of possession is Form No.66.

Where a claimant is seeking to enforce the order for possession by writ for possession there is no requirement to give notice to an occupier of the date for eviction (*Pritchard v Teitlebaum* [2011] EWHC 1063—a case under RSC Ord.45 in relation to the High Court, now CPR 83.13).

Writ of restitution

23-72 If, after the Enforcement Officer has completed execution the tenant unlawfully re-enters the property, the landlord may apply for a writ of restitution to be issued (CPR 83.13(5)).

Enforcement against Trespassers

The provisions for enforcement contained in CPR 83.13 and **23-73** 83.26 stream line the rules relating to writs and warrants for possession where an order for possession has been obtained against trespassers. In the High Court, the court's permission is not required if the request is made within three months of the date of the order (CPR 83.13(3)). A warrant for possession can be obtained in the County Court any time after the order is made (CPR 83.26(10), but must be requested within three months of the order or permission will then be needed (CPR 83.26(11)).

Goods left on the premises

When the matter is in the County Court and the order for **23-74** possession is being enforced by a warrant the bailiff is not required to remove any goods or chattels from the premises (County Courts Act 1984 s.111(1)). In the High Court there is no statutory position dealing with the situation. In practice the High Court Enforcement Officer is also only likely to secure the premises; and will not remove any goods found there.

Where goods are left on the premises by a former tenant, whether following an eviction or a voluntary departure, the land owner is left with the problem of knowing what to do with them. Very often they will look like unwanted rubbish and the landlord will simply dispose of them. However, the landlord may be wary of such a course and will want to avoid any potential claim from the former tenant in respect of the goods. If practicable, the best solution is often for the landlord simply to store them safely until they are collected by the tenant.

In strict legal terms the landlord is (it is submitted) between himself and the tenant usually entitled at common law to put the goods out on the street (see a combination of *Jones v Foley* [1891] 1 Q.B. 730; *Hemmings v The Stoke Poges Golf* Club [1920] 1 K.B. 720 CA; *Aglionby v Cohen* [1955] 1 Q.B. 558 QBD). In many cases he will obviously not want, or be able, to do so; not least because the local authority will not exactly be delighted.

In some cases what should happen to goods left on the premises is dealt with by a provision in the lease. If not, another option might be to sell the goods in accordance with the procedures set out in ss.12 and 13 of the Torts (Interference with Goods) Act 1977; and see Sch.1. Note that the Act does not allow the landlord to deduct rent arrears from the proceeds of sale—only the costs of sale (s.12(5)). However, if the landlord proceeds under s.12 and the tenant turns up claiming some money the landlord can no doubt counterclaim/set-off the arrears due. The landlord has no right to sell the goods other than pursuant to the provisions of the 1977 Act; or possibly under the terms of the lease.

CIVIL PROCEDURE RULES Part 55

Possession Claims

Interpretation

23–75   **55.1.** In this Part—

(a)   "a possession claim" means a claim for the recovery of possession of land (including buildings or parts of buildings);

(b)   "a possession claim against trespassers" means a claim for the recovery of land which the claimant alleges is occupied only by a person or persons who entered or remained on the land without the consent of a person entitled to possession of that land but does not include a claim against a tenant or sub-tenant whether his tenancy has been terminated or not;

(c)   "mortgage" includes a legal or equitable mortgage and a legal or equitable charge and "mortgagee" is to be interpreted accordingly;

Scope

23–76   **55.2.**—(1) The procedure set out in this Section of this Part must be used where the claim includes—

(a)   a possession claim brought by a—
  (i) landlord (or former landlord);
  (ii) mortgagee; or
  (iii) licensor (or former licensor);

(b)   a possession claim against trespassers; or

(c)   a claim by a tenant seeking relief from forfeiture.

(Where a demotion claim is made in the same claim form in which a possession claim is started, this Section of this Part applies as modified by rule 65.12. Where the claim is a demotion claim only, Section III of Part 65 applies).

(2) This Section of this Part—

(a)   is subject to any enactment or practice direction which sets out special provisions with regard to any particular category of claim;

(b)   does not apply where the claimant uses the procedure set out in Section II of this Part; and

(c)   does not apply where the claimant seeks an interim possession order under Section III of this Part except where the court orders otherwise or that Section so provides.

Starting the claim

55.3.—(1) In the County Court-   **23–77**

(a)   the claimant may make the claim at any County Court hearing centre, unless paragraph (2) applies or an enactment provides otherwise;

(b)   the claim will be issued by the hearing centre where the claim is made; and

(c)   if the claim is not made at the County Court hearing centre which serves the address where the land is situated, the claim will be sent to the hearing centre serving that address when it is issued.

(Practice Direction 55A includes further direction in respect of claims which are not made at the County Court hearing centre which serves the address where the land is situated.)

(2) The claim may be started in the High Court if the claimant files with his claim form a certificate stating the reasons for bringing the claim in that court verified by a statement of truth in accordance with rule 22.1(1).

(3) Practice Direction 55A refers to circumstances which may justify starting the claim in the High Court.

(4) Where, in a possession claim against trespassers, the claimant does not know the name of a person in occupation or possession of the land, the claim must be brought against "persons unknown" in addition to any named defendants.

(5) The claim form and form of defence sent with it must be in the forms set out in the Practice Direction 55A.

Particulars of claim

55.4. The particulars of claim must be filed and served with the claim   **23–78**
form.

(Part 16 and Practice Direction 55A provide details about the contents of the particulars of claim.)

Hearing date

55.5.—(1) Subject to paragraph (1A), the court will fix a date for the   **23–79**
hearing when it issues the claim form.

(1A) If the claim is not made at the County Court hearing centre which serves the address where the land is situated, a date will be fixed for hearing when the claim is received by that hearing centre.

(2) In a possession claim against trespassers the defendant must be served with the claim form, particulars of claim and any witness statements—

(a)   in the case of residential property, not less than 5 days; and

(b)   in the case of other land, not less than 2 days,

before the hearing date.

(3) In all other possession claims—

(a)   the hearing date will be not less than 28 days from the date of issue of the claim form;

(b)   the standard period between the issue of the claim form and the hearing will be not more than 8 weeks; and

(c)   the defendant must be served with the claim form and particulars of claim not less than 21 days before the hearing date.

(Rule 3.1(2)(a) provides that the court may extend or shorten the time for compliance with any rule)

Service of claims against trespassers

23-80   **55.6.** Where, in a possession claim against trespassers, the claim has been issued against "persons unknown", the claim form, particulars of claim and any witness statements must be served on those persons by—

(a)   (i) attaching copies of the claim form, particulars of claim and any witness statements to the main door or some other part of the land so that they are clearly visible; and

(ii) if practicable, inserting copies of those documents in a sealed transparent envelope addressed to "the occupiers" through the letter box; or

(b)   placing stakes in the land in places where they are clearly visible and attaching to each stake copies of the claim form, particulars of claim and any witness statements in a sealed transparent envelope addressed to "the occupiers".

Defendant's response

23-81   **55.7.**—(1) An acknowledgment of service is not required and Part 10 does not apply.

(2) In a possession claim against trespassers rule 15.2 does not apply and the defendant need not file a defence.

(3) Where, in any other possession claim, the defendant does not file a defence within the time specified in rule 15.4, he may take part in any hearing but the court may take his failure to do so into account when deciding what order to make about costs.

(4) Part 12 (default judgment) does not apply in a claim to which this Part applies.

The hearing

55.8.–(1) At the hearing fixed in accordance with rule 55.5(1) or at any adjournment of that hearing, the court may–   **23–82**

(a) decide the claim; or
(b) give case management directions.

(2) Where the claim is genuinely disputed on grounds which appear to be substantial, case management directions given under paragraph (1)(b) will include the allocation of the claim to a track or directions to enable it to be allocated.

(3) Except where–

(a) the claim is allocated to the fast track or the multi-track; or
(b) the court orders otherwise,

any fact that needs to be proved by the evidence of witnesses at a hearing referred to in paragraph (1) may be proved by evidence in writing.

(Rule 32.2(1) sets out the general rule about evidence. Rule 32.2(2) provides that rule 32.2(1) is subject to any provision to the contrary.)

(4) Subject to paragraph (5), all witness statements must be filed and served at least 2 days before the hearing.

(5) In a possession claim against trespassers all witness statements on which the claimant intends to rely must be filed and served with the claim form.

(6) Where the claimant serves the claim form and particulars of claim, the claimant must produce at the hearing a certificate of service of those documents and rule 6.17(2)(a) does not apply.

Allocation

55.9.–(1) When the court decides the track for a possession claim, the matters to which it shall have regard include–   **23–83**

(a) the matters set out in rule 26.8 as modified by the relevant practice direction;
(b) the amount of any arrears of rent or mortgage instalments;
(c) the importance to the defendant of retaining possession of the land;
(d) the importance of vacant possession to the claimant; and
(e) if applicable, the alleged conduct of the defendant.

(2) The court will only allocate possession claims to the small claims track if all the parties agree.

(3) Where a possession claim has been allocated to the small claims track the claim shall be treated, for the purposes of costs, as if it were proceeding on the fast track except that trial costs shall be in the discretion of the court and shall not exceed the amount that would be recoverable under rule 45.38 (amount of fast track costs) if the value of the claim were up to £3,000.

(4) Where all the parties agree the court may, when it allocates the claim, order that rule 27.14 (costs on the small claims track) applies and, where it does so, paragraph (3) does not apply.

III INTERIM POSSESSION ORDERS

When this section may be used

23-84   **55.20.**—(1) This Section of this Part applies where the claimant seeks an Interim Possession Order.

(2) In this section—

    (a)   "IPO" means Interim Possession Order; and

    (b)   "premises" has the same meaning as in section 12 of the Criminal Law Act 1977.

(3) Where this Section requires an act to be done within a specified number of hours, rule 2.8(4) does not apply.

Conditions for IPO application

23-85   **55.21.**—(1) An application for an IPO may be made where the following conditions are satisfied—

    (a)   the only claim made is a possession claim against trespassers for the recovery of premises;

    (b)   the claimant—

        (i)   has an immediate right to possession of the premises; and

        (ii)   has had such a right throughout the period of alleged unlawful occupation; and

    (c)   the claim is made within 28 days of the date on which the claimant first knew, or ought reasonably to have known, that the defendant (or any of the defendants), was in occupation.

(2) An application for an IPO may not be made against a defendant who entered or remained on the premises with the consent of a person who, at the time consent was given, had an immediate right to possession of the premises.

The application

23-86   **55.22.**—(1) Rules 55.3(1) and (4) apply to the claim.

(2) The claim form and the defendant's form of witness statement must be in the form set out in the relevant practice direction.

(3) When he files his claim form, the claimant must also file—

    (a)   an application notice in the form set out in Practice Direction 55A; and

    (b)   written evidence.

(4) The written evidence must be given—

    (a)   by the claimant personally; or

    (b)   where the claimant is a body corporate, by a duly authorised officer.

(Rule 22.1(6)(b) provides that the statement of truth must be signed by the maker of the witness statement.)

(5) The court will—

    (a)   issue—
        (i) the claim form; and
        (ii) the application for the IPO; and

    (b)   set a date for the hearing of the application.

(6) The hearing of the application will be as soon as practicable but not less than 3 days after the date of issue.

Service

55.23.—(1) Within 24 hours of the issue of the application, the claimant must serve on the defendant—   **23–87**

    (a)   the claim form;
    (b)   the application notice together with the written evidence in support; and
    (c)   a blank form for the defendant's witness statement (as set out in Practice Direction 55A) which must be attached to the application notice.

(2) The claimant must serve the documents listed in paragraph (1) in accordance with rule 55.6(a).

(3) At or before the hearing the claimant must file a certificate of service in relation to the documents listed in paragraph (1) and rule 6.17(2)(a) does not apply.

Defendant's response

55.24.—(1) At any time before the hearing the defendant may file a witness statement in response to the application.   **23–88**

(2) The witness statement should be in the form set out in Practice Direction 55A.

Hearing of the application

55.25.—(1) In deciding whether to grant an IPO, the court will have regard to whether the claimant has given, or is prepared to give, the following undertakings in support of his application—   **23–89**

    (a)   if, after an IPO is made, the court decides that the claimant was not entitled to the order to—
        (i) reinstate the defendant if so ordered by the court; and
        (ii) pay such damages as the court may order; and
    (b)   before the claim for possession is finally decided, not to—
        (i) damage the premises;
        (ii) grant a right of occupation to any other person; and
        (iii) damage or dispose of any of the defendant's property.

(2) The court will make an IPO if—

    (a)   the claimant has—
        (i) filed a certificate of service of the documents referred to in rule 55.23(1); or

  (ii) proved service of those documents to the satisfaction of the court; and

 (b) the court considers that—

  (i) the conditions set out in rule 55.21(1) are satisfied; and

  (ii) any undertakings given by the claimant as a condition of making the order are adequate.

(3) An IPO will be in the form set out in Practice Direction 55A and will require the defendant to vacate the premises specified in the claim form within 24 hours of the service of the order.

(4) On making an IPO the court will set a date for the hearing of the claim for possession which will be not less than 7 days after the date on which the IPO is made.

(5) Where the court does not make an IPO—

 (a) the court will set a date for the hearing of the claim;

 (b) the court may give directions for the future conduct of the claim; and

 (c) subject to such directions, the claim shall proceed in accordance with Section I of this Part.

Service and enforcement of the IPO

23–90 **55.26.**—(1) An IPO must be served within 48 hours after it is sealed.

(2) The claimant must serve the IPO on the defendant together with copies of—

 (a) the claim form; and

 (b) the written evidence in support, in accordance with rule 55.6(a).

(3) CCR Order 26, rule 17 does not apply to the enforcement of an IPO.

(4) If an IPO is not served within the time limit specified by this rule, the claimant may apply to the court for directions for the claim for possession to continue under Section I of this Part.

After IPO made

23–91 **55.27.**—(1) Before the date for the hearing of the claim, the claimant must file a certificate of service in relation to the documents specified in rule 55.26(2).

(2) The IPO will expire on the date of the hearing of the claim.

(3) At the hearing the court may make any order it considers appropriate and may, in particular—

 (a) make a final order for possession;

 (b) dismiss the claim for possession;

 (c) give directions for the claim for possession to continue under Section I of this Part; or

 (d) enforce any of the claimant's undertakings.

(4) Unless the court directs otherwise, the claimant must serve any order or directions in accordance with rule 55.6(a).

(5) CCR Order 24, rule 6 applies to the enforcement of a final order for possession.

Application to set aside IPO

55.28.–(1) If the defendant has left the premises, he may apply on grounds **23–92** of urgency for the IPO to be set aside before the date of the hearing of the claim.

(2) An application under paragraph (1) must be supported by a witness statement.

(3) On receipt of the application, the court will give directions as to—

    (a)   the date for the hearing; and
    (b)   the period of notice, if any, to be given to the claimant and the method of service of any such notice.

(4) No application to set aside an IPO may be made under rule 39.3.

(5) Where no notice is required under paragraph (3)(b), the only matters to be dealt with at the hearing of the application to set aside are whether—

    (a)   the IPO should be set aside; and
    (b)   any undertaking to re-instate the defendant should be enforced, and all other matters will be dealt with at the hearing of the claim.

(6) The court will serve on all the parties—

    (a)   a copy of the order made under paragraph (5); and
    (b)   where no notice was required under paragraph (3)(b), a copy of the defendant's application to set aside and the witness statement in support.

(7) Where notice is required under paragraph (3)(b), the court may treat the hearing of the application to set aside as the hearing of the claim.

Practice Direction 55A—Possession Claims

Section I—General rules

55.3—Starting the claim

1.1 (1) Except where the County Court does not have jurisdiction, **23–93** possession claims should normally be brought in the County Court. Only exceptional circumstances justify starting a claim in the High Court.

(2) In the County Court, the claim will be issued by the County Court hearing centre where the claim is made, but will then be sent to the County Court hearing centre which serves the address where the land is situated. A claimant should consider the potential delay which may result if a claim is not made at the appropriate hearing centre in the first instance.

1.2 If a claimant starts a claim in the High Court and the court decides that it should have been started in the County Court, the court will normally either strike the claim out or transfer it to the County Court on its own initiative. This is likely to result in delay and the court will normally disallow the costs of starting the claim in the High Court and of any transfer.

1.3 Circumstances which may, in an appropriate case, justify starting a claim in the High Court are if –

    (1) there are complicated disputes of fact;
    (2) there are points of law of general importance; or
    (3) the claim is against trespassers and there is a substantial risk of public disturbance or of serious harm to persons or property which properly require immediate determination.

1.4 The value of the property and the amount of any financial claim may be relevant circumstances, but these factors alone will not normally justify starting the claim in the High Court.

1.5 The claimant must use the appropriate claim form and particulars of claim form set out in Table 1 to Practice Direction 4. The defence must be in form N11, N11B, N11M or N11R, as appropriate.

1.6 High Court claims for the possession of land subject to a mortgage will be assigned to the Chancery Division.

1.7 A claim which is not a possession claim may be brought under the procedure set out in Section I of Part 55 if it is started in the same claim form as a possession claim which, by virtue of rule 55.2(1) must be brought in accordance with that Section.

(Rule 7.3 provides that a claimant may use a single claim form to start all claims which can be conveniently disposed of in the same proceedings)

1.8 For example a claim under paragraphs 4, 5 or 6 of Part I of Schedule 1 to the Mobile Homes Act 1983 may be brought using the procedure set out in Section I of Part 55 if the claim is started in the same claim form as a claim enforcing the rights referred to in section 3(1)(b) of the Caravan Sites Act 1968 (which, by virtue of rule 55.2(1) must be brought under Section I of Part 55).

1.9 Where the claim form includes a demotion claim, the claim must be started in the County Court for the district in which the land is situated.

55.4–PARTICULARS OF CLAIM

2.1 In a possession claim the particulars of claim must:

    (1) identify the land to which the claim relates;
    (2) state whether the claim relates to residential property;
    (3) state the ground on which possession is claimed;
    (4) give full details about any mortgage or tenancy agreement; and
    (5) give details of every person who, to the best of the claimant's knowledge, is in possession of the property.

Residential property let on a tenancy

2.2 Paragraphs 2.3 to 2.4B apply if the claim relates to residential property let on a tenancy.

2.3 If the claim includes a claim for non-payment of rent the particulars of claim must set out:

(1) the amount due at the start of the proceedings;
(2) in schedule form, the dates and amounts of all payments due and payments made under the tenancy agreement for a period of two years immediately preceding the date of issue, or if the first date of default occurred less than two years before the date of issue from the first date of default and a running total of the arrears;
(3) the daily rate of any rent and interest;
(4) any previous steps taken to recover the arrears of rent with full details of any court proceedings; and
(5) any relevant information about the defendant's circumstances, in particular:

 (a) whether the defendant is in receipt of social security benefits; and
 (b) whether any payments are made on his behalf directly to the claimant under the Social Security Contributions and Benefits Act 1992.

2.3A If the claimant wishes to rely on a history of arrears which is longer than two years, he should state this in his particulars and exhibit a full (or longer) schedule to a witness statement.

2.4 If the claimant knows of any person (including a mortgagee) entitled to claim relief against forfeiture as underlessee under section 146(4) of the Law of Property Act 1925 (or in accordance with section 38 of the Senior Courts Act 1981, or section 138(9C) of the County Courts Act 1984):

(1) the particulars of claim must state the name and address of that person; and
(2) the claimant must file a copy of the particulars of claim for service on him.

2.4A If the claim for possession relates to the conduct of the tenant, the particulars of claim must state details of the conduct alleged.

2.4B If the possession claim relies on a statutory ground or grounds for possession, the particulars of claim must specify the ground or grounds relied on.

2.5A If the claimant wishes to rely on a history of arrears which is longer than two years, he should state this in his particulars and exhibit a full (or longer) schedule to a witness statement.

Possession claim against trespassers

2.6 If the claim is a possession claim against trespassers, the particulars of claim must state the claimant's interest in the land or the basis of his right to claim possession and the circumstances in which it has been occupied without licence or consent.

55.5—HEARING DATE

3.1 The court may exercise its powers under rules 3.1(2)(a) and (b) to shorten the time periods set out in rules 55.5(2) and (3).

3.2 Particular consideration should be given to the exercise of this power if:

(1) the defendant, or a person for whom the defendant is responsible, has assaulted or threatened to assault:

    (a) the claimant;
    (b) a member of the claimant's staff; or
    (c) another resident in the locality;

(2) there are reasonable grounds for fearing such an assault; or
(3) the defendant, or a person for whom the defendant is responsible, has caused serious damage or threatened to cause serious damage to the property or to the home or property of another resident in the locality.

3.3 Where paragraph 3.2 applies but the case cannot be determined at the first hearing fixed under rule 55.5, the court will consider what steps are needed to finally determine the case as quickly as reasonably practicable.

55.6—SERVICE IN CLAIMS AGAINST TRESPASSERS

4.1 If the claim form is to be served by the court and in accordance with rule 55.6(b) the claimant must provide sufficient stakes and transparent envelopes.

55.8—THE HEARING

5.1 Attention is drawn to rule 55.8(3). Each party should wherever possible include all the evidence he wishes to present in his statement of case, verified by a statement of truth.

5.2 If relevant the claimant's evidence should include the amount of any rent or mortgage arrears and interest on those arrears. These amounts should, if possible, be up to date to the date of the hearing (if necessary by specifying a daily rate of arrears and interest). However, rule 55.8(4) does not prevent such evidence being brought up to date orally or in writing on the day of the hearing if necessary.

5.3 If relevant the defendant should give evidence of:

(1) the amount of any outstanding social security or housing benefit payments relevant to rent or mortgage arrears; and
(2) the status of:

    (a) any claims for social security or housing benefit about which a decision has not yet been made; and
    (b) any applications to appeal or review a social security or housing benefit decision where that appeal or review has not yet concluded.

5.4 If:

(1) the maker of a witness statement does not attend a hearing; and
(2) the other party disputes material evidence contained in his statement,

the court will normally adjourn the hearing so that oral evidence can be given.

5.5 The claimant must bring 2 completed copies of Form N123 to the hearing.

SECTION III—INTERIM POSSESSION ORDERS

9.1 The claim form must be in form N5, the application notice seeking the interim possession order must be in form N130 and the defendant's witness statement must be in form N133.

9.2 The IPO will be in form N134 (annexed to this practice direction).

Part 6

Application for a New Tenancy

Chapter 24

APPLICATIONS FOR RENEWAL: LANDLORD OR TENANT

. . . .

The following key points should be noted and are dealt with in this chapter:

24-01

- Either the landlord or the tenant can apply for an order that the tenant be granted a new tenancy.
- There are time limits for applying.
- The parties are able to apply as soon as a s.25 or s.26 notice has been served.
- The final date for applying is, in the first instance, the date stated as the termination date in the s.25 notice (or the date immediately before a s.26 request).
- The parties can agree unlimited extensions of time without reference to the court.

Right to apply: Pt II of the Act must apply

An application can only be made for a new tenancy if Pt II of the Act applies (s.24). The Act must apply at all times throughout the application (*I & H Caplan Ltd v Caplan (No.2)* [1963] 1 W.L.R. 1247). If the tenant ceases to occupy the property for the purposes of a business (see para.2-04) so that Pt II of the Act ceases to apply, an application may be made to have the application struck out.

24-02

> "As I see it, it really is a continuing condition of the tenant's right to a new tenancy that he should be throughout the proceedings a tenant under a tenancy to which the Act applies. If this condition ceases to be fulfilled at any time, then I think that the landlord can apply to have the tenant's summons dismissed just as he could if the tenancy was not protected by the Act when the

24-03

application was made." (*I & H Caplan Ltd v Caplan (No.2)* [1963 1 W.L.R. 1247, per Cross J. at 1255.)

Landlords and tenants may apply to renew

Earliest date for application

Landlord and Tenant Act 1954 ss.24, 29(5)

24–04

24.–(1) A tenancy to which this Part of this Act applies shall not come to an end unless terminated in accordance with the provisions of this Part of this Act; and, subject to the following provisions of this Act *either the tenant or the landlord* under such a tenancy may apply to the court for an order for the grant of a new tenancy—

(a)　if the landlord has given notice under section 25 of this Act to terminate the tenancy, or

(b)　if the tenant has made a request for a new tenancy in accordance with section 26 of this Act.

As stated in the introduction, either the landlord or the tenant may apply to the court to renew the tenancy (s.24(1)). The pre-conditions for such an application are that: (a) the landlord has served a s.25 notice; or (b) the tenant has served a s.26 request. In respect of s.26 notices see also s.29A(3) which provides that the application may not be made until the landlord has served a counter-notice or the time for doing so has passed (see para.24–08).

Tenant does not want new a tenancy

Landlord and Tenant Act 1954 ss.24, 29(5)

24–05

29.–(5) The court shall dismiss an application by the landlord under section 24(1) of this Act if the tenant informs the court that he does not want a new tenancy.

Although the landlord may apply for a new tenancy, there is obviously no point in the application continuing if the tenant does not want a new tenancy. Thus, the Act provides for dismissal of the application if the tenant *informs the court* (not the landlord) that he or she does not want a new tenancy (s.29(5)). The effect will be generally to bring the tenancy to an end three months from the final disposal of the case in accordance with the provisions of s.64 (see para.27–02). A simple letter to the court from the tenant will no doubt suffice.

Costs: Where a tenant serves a notice under s.29(5), having first filed an acknowledgement of service agreeing to the grant of a new lease but disputing the terms, service of the notice is equivalent to discontinuance and the landlord is entitled to an order for costs of the action against the tenant (*Trustees of the Portman Estate v Drexler* [2007] EWCA Civ 464). Evans-Lombe J. at paras 20 (ii) and (ii):

> " . . . by entering an acknowledgement of service assenting to such grant, the defendants were, in effect, themselves launching proceedings for the granting of a new tenancy but upon terms more favourable to them than the Claimants were prepared to offer . . . It seems to me that the service on the court by the Defendants of notice under s.29(5) was the equivalent of a notice to discontinue proceedings in which they had been seeking an order from the court awarding them a new tenancy upon terms settled by the court. It follows that the judge should have placed the burden of proof on the Defendants to establish facts which would justify his departure from the normal order in these circumstances."

No application by one party if the other has already applied

Landlord and Tenant Act 1954 s.24(2A), (2B)

24.–(2A) Neither the tenant nor the landlord may make an application under subsection (1) above if the other has made such an application and the application has been *served*.

   (2B) Neither the tenant nor the landlord may make such an application if the landlord has made an application *under section 29(2)* of this Act and the application has been served.

24–06

In order to avoid a multiplicity of actions, once either the tenant or the landlord has applied for renewal *and the application has been served*, the other may not apply for renewal (s.24(2A)). Nor may application for renewal be made if the landlord has issued *and served* an application for termination of the current tenancy under s.29(2) (see Ch.22) (s.24(2B)).

The reason for providing that the application must be served, and not just issued, is to prevent abuse by landlords. There was some fear that a landlord might issue the application (which would prevent the tenant from applying) and then fail to serve the application within the period for service provided for by the Civil Procedure Rules (56.3(4), see para.24–16). The landlord's application would fall and because the landlord had already made an application, the tenant would be unable to do so and so would lose the right to renew.

This requirement, that the application be served before the other party is prevented from making his or her own application, does give rise to " . . . a slight risk that the other party could make an application during a period in which normal service of the first application was taking place . . . " (Office of the Deputy Prime Minister). PD 56 3.2 therefore contains specific provisions to deal with such situations.

PD 56 para.3.2

Precedence of claim forms where there is more than one application to the court under s.24(1) or s.29(2) of the 1954 Act

24–07   3.2 Where more than one application to the court under section 24(1) or section 29(2) of the 1954 Act is made, the following provisions shall apply—

(1) once an application to the court under section 24(1) of the 1954 Act has been served on a defendant, no further application to the court in respect of the same tenancy whether under section 24(1) or section 29(2) of the 1954 Act may be served by that defendant without the permission of the court;

(2) if more than one application to the court *under section 24(1)* of the 1954 Act in respect of the same tenancy is served on the *same day,* any *landlord's* application shall stand stayed until further order of the court;

(3) if applications to the court under both *section 24(1) and section 29(2)* of the 1954 Act in respect of the same tenancy are served on the *same day,* any *tenant's* application shall stand stayed until further order of the court; and

(4) if a defendant is served with an application under section 29(2) of the 1954 Act ("the section 29(2) application") which was issued at a time when an application to the court had already been made by that defendant in

respect of the same tenancy under section 24(1) of the 1954 Act ("the section 24(1) application") the service of the section 29(2) application shall be deemed to be a notice under rule 7.7 requiring service or discontinuance of the section 24(1) application within a period of 14 days after service of the section 29(2) application.

Situations can be envisaged that are not covered by any of the above provisions. For example, the landlord may issue but not serve his application to terminate. The tenant may then issue his application to renew without knowledge of the application to terminate. This is not invalid because the landlord's application to terminate was not served—i.e. s.24(2B) does not apply. Nor is the situation dealt with in PD 56 para.3.2(4). In a situation such as this the court will probably stay the tenant's application and proceed on the basis of the landlord's application to terminate (being first in time). Either way it does not matter very much because if the landlord is unsuccessful in the application to terminate the court will order the grant of a new tenancy (s.29(4)(b)).

Time limits for applications to court

Basic limits

Landlord and Tenant Act 1954 ss.29A, 29B

29A.—(1) Subject to section 29B of this Act, the court shall not entertain an application—   **24–08**

(a) by the tenant or the landlord under section 24(1) of this Act; or
(b) by the landlord under section 29(2) of this Act,

if it is made *after the end of the statutory period*.
(2) In this section and section 29B of this Act *"the statutory period" means* a period ending—

(a) where the landlord gave a notice under section 25 of this Act, on the date specified in his notice; and
(b) where the tenant made a request for a new tenancy under section 26 of this Act, immediately before the date specified in his request.

The initial deadline for the application for a new tenancy is (i) the date specified in the s.25 notice or (ii) where a s.26 request is given, the date immediately before the date specified in the s.26 request. However, it should be noted (by tenants in particular) that, where a s.26 request has been made by the tenant, an application for a new tenancy cannot be made until the landlord has served a counter-notice or the time for so doing has passed. Thus, there still remains a potential trap that could invalidate applications (see further para.24–11).

Landlord and Tenant Act 1954 s.29A(3)

(3) Where the tenant has made a request for a new tenancy under section 26 of this Act, the court shall not entertain an application under section 24(1) of this Act which is made before the end of the period of *two months* beginning with the date of the making of the request, *unless* the application is made after the landlord has given a notice under section 26(6) of this Act.

Agreements to extend time

Landlord and Tenant Act 1954 s.29B

24–09

29B.–(1) After the landlord has given a notice under section 25 of this Act, or the tenant has made a request under section 26 of this Act, but *before the end of the statutory period*, the landlord and tenant may *agree* that an application such as is mentioned in section 29A(1) of this Act may be made before the end of a period specified in the agreement which will expire after the end of the statutory period.

(2) The landlord and tenant may from time to time by agreement *further extend* the period for making such an application, but any such agreement must be made before the end of the period specified in the current agreement.

(3) Where an agreement is made under this section, the court may entertain an application such as is mentioned in section 29A(1) of this Act if it is made before the end of the period specified in the agreement.

(4) Where an agreement is made under this section, or two or more agreements are made under this section, the landlord's notice under section 25 of this Act or tenant's request under section 26 of this Act shall be treated as terminating the tenancy at the end of the period specified in the agreement or, as the case may be, at the end of the period specified in the last of those agreements.

The parties can *extend the deadline* by written agreement (s.69(2)—see further para.24–10) *provided that they do so before the deadline expires*. Further extensions are also possible, once again provided that they are made before the then current deadline expires.

It is unlikely that one party will be able unilaterally to withdraw the agreement to extend time, perhaps because he believes that the other is being unco-operative in the negotiations. The agreement is contractually binding but more importantly s.29B(4) expressly states that the effect of the agreement is to change the termination date in the s.25 request or, as the case may be, s.26 request. However, that does not matter. The party that wants to get on with the action can simply do so. The effect of the agreement is not to prevent a party from applying before a certain date. Rather, it extends the time for applying to a later date.

The ability to extend time means that parties can negotiate for as long as they like without interference from the court. Indeed, they do not even need to apply to the court so long as they continue to enter into extensions permitted by the Act.   **24–10**

It is very important to note that that the agreement must be in writing. This is not required by the sections set out above but by s.69(2), which states that any agreement between landlord and tenant under Pt II must be in writing (para.26–02). Is an agreement by e-mail in writing? Almost certainly, yes. Section 5 of and Sch.1 to the Interpretation Act 1978 provides that "writing" includes "typing, printing, lithography, photography and other modes of representing or reproducing words in a visible form, and expressions referring to writing are construed accordingly". However, any practitioner who has any doubt about this should insist upon an agreement by an old fashioned correspondence. If the agreement is not forthcoming, the application should be made before the time limit expires.

Tenants beware

The requirements set out above apply to applications whether made by the landlord or the tenant. However, it is the tenant who needs to take particular care to ensure that nothing goes wrong. If a deadline expires, the tenancy comes to an end and it is the tenant who loses out. The landlord may have been willing to grant a new tenancy and even have contemplated applying to the court. However, now that the tenancy has come to an end he is in a much stronger bargaining position. Tenants in particular should therefore be aware of seven particular points if they wish to avoid losing the right to apply for a new tenancy: **24–11**

- If no application to the court is made before the expiry of the deadline or any agreed extension, *the right to renew will be lost* (ss.29A; 29B(3)).

- Any agreement to extend must be in writing (s.69(2)).
- The agreement to extend must be made before the current deadline expires (s.29B(2)).
- When agreeing a new deadline, the parties should use whole days not specific moments (e.g. 3.30pm on . . . .). Although the statute does not expressly forbid times, it does seem to follow from the definition of "the statutory period" in s.29A(2) that only whole days are allowed. Indeed, generally speaking, the law does not recognise parts of days when dealing with notices.
- It is sensible to choose an expiry date when the court office is open. This will avoid arguments and problems where it is on a date on which the court office is closed. Where the time limit imposed for filing a claim under the old s.29 expires on a day upon which the court office is closed, the period is extended to the next day upon which the court office is open (*Hodgson v Armstrong* [1967] 1 All E.R. 307). If the last day is a day upon which the court office is open but the tenant posts the claim form through the door after office hours, the claim will be deemed to be filed in time. A document is filed within the meaning of CPR 2.3(1) when it is delivered to the court office, whether or not the office is open (*Van Aken v Camden LBC* [2003] 1 WLR 684).
- Where a tenant has made a request for a new tenancy under s.26, no application may be made to the court for a new tenancy until the landlord has either served a counter-notice under s.26(6) (see para.15–13) or the two-month opportunity for doing has expired (s.29B(3); para.24–08).
- Note the slight difference between the position where a s.25 notice is given and a s.26 request is made (s.29A(2)(a)). In the latter case, the deadline for applying to the court is one day earlier (s.29A(2)(b)).

> **Example**: L serves a s.25 notice with an expiration date of June 17, 2005. The last date for applying to the court for a new tenancy is June 17. However, if the tenant had made a request for a new tenancy containing the same termination date, the last date for applying to the court for a new tenancy is June 16.

Application made out of time

24–12 Under the law prior to June 2004, the time limits set out in s.29(3) were fixed and the court had no power to extend them (*Hodgson v Armstrong* [1967] 1 All E.R. 307). However, in certain circumstances, the landlord could be regarded as having "waived" the failure to comply with the limits. The established principles as to estoppel and "quasi-estoppel by acquiescence" apply (*Kammins Ballrooms Co Ltd v Zenith Investments (Torquay) Ltd* [1970] 2 All E.R. 871 HL). No doubt they also apply to failure to comply with a time limit under the current provisions.

In the case of estoppel, the tenant must show that the landlord has made a promise intending that his existing legal relationship with the tenant should be affected and that he (the tenant) has acted in reliance of that promise.

Where the tenant relies on the principle of acquiescence, he must show that:

1. he had a mistaken view as to legal rights; and
2. he did some act on the faith of his mistaken belief;
3. the landlord encouraged him to act in that way either actively or passively by refraining from asserting his own legal right;
4. at the time of his active or passive encouragement, the landlord knew of the existence of his legal right and of the tenant's mistaken belief in his own inconsistent legal right.

It is not enough that the landlord should know of the facts that gave rise to his legal right to object to the application being out of time. He must also have known that he was entitled to the legal right to which those facts give rise.

Merely serving a defence and taking other steps in the proceedings will be insufficient to prevent the landlord, either on the basis of estoppel or acquiescence, from objecting to the tenant's application on the ground that it is out of time (see *Kammins Ballrooms Co Ltd v Zenith Investments (Torquay) Ltd* [1970] 2 All E.R. 871 HL; in particular, Lord Diplock at 894c to 895j upon which this section is based). For another case in which the tenant failed to establish waiver of estoppel, see *Stevens & Cutting Ltd v Anderson* [1990] 1 E.G.L.R. 95.

The danger of not applying to the court in time where it looks like the parties might well agree a new lease, is demonstrated by the case of *Akiens v Salomon* [1993] 1 E.G.L.R. 101 CA. The landlord and tenant agreed to the grant of a new lease in letters that were marked "subject to lease". However, the landlord subsequently changed his mind and obtained an order for possession because the tenant had not applied for a lease within the statutory period. The tenant's arguments, based on estoppel and on an agreement to grant a new lease in return for the tenant's forbearance to apply for a new tenancy, were rejected. The usual rule, that either party may withdraw before exchange of lease and counterpart where the term "subject to lease" was used, applied.

Application made in time but defective

24-13 Where the application is made in time but is defective, the court has power to permit an amendment, applied for after the time limit has expired, to cure the defect (*G Orlik (Meat Products) Ltd v Hastings & Thanet Building Society* (1974) P. & C.R. 126—amendment to proposals for new lease). In *Teltscher Brothers Ltd v London & India Dock Investments Ltd* [1989] 2 E.G.L.R. 261 Ch D the proceedings were defective in that the landlord was named as plaintiff and the names of the plaintiff and the defendant in the body of the summons were transposed. The mistake was a genuine one and no-one was misled. The court permitted the tenant to amend the summons pursuant to RSC Ord 20 r.5(3), which provided for amendment to correct the name of a party; see also para.24-19. In *Nurit Bar v Pathwood Investments Ltd* [1987] 1 E.G.L.R. 90 the tenant's originating application was within time but referred to only part of the premises. After the time limit expired, the tenant sought to amend the application so as to add the rest of the premises. The Court of Appeal held that the county court had the power to make the amendment and rejected the landlord's submission that he was being deprived of a vested right acquired as a result of the expiry of the time limit.

Presumably the position would be similar under the Civil Procedure Rules.

Application after forfeiture

24-14 A tenant whose tenancy has been forfeited for breach of covenant but whose application for relief has yet to be determined is a "tenant" for the purposes of Pt II of the 1954 Act and so may apply to the court for a new tenancy (*Meadows v Clerical Medical and General Life Assurance Society* [1980] 1

All E.R. 454; see para.7–34). A sub-tenant may also apply for a new tenancy notwithstanding that the immediate landlord's tenancy has been forfeited (*Cadogan v Dimovic* [1984] 2 All E.R. 168–but presumably only if the sub-tenant has not lost his right to relief, as to which see para.12–32).

Civil Procedure Rules: Pt 56

Introduction

The rules governing applications to renew are primarily set out in CPR Pt 56 and PD 56 as amended. Part 56 divides claims into opposed claims and unopposed claims. Opposed claims are dealt with under Pt 7; and unopposed claims are dealt with under Pt 8. (CPR 56.3; PD 56 paras 2.1A and 3.1.)

24–15

CPR Part 56.3

56.3.–(1) This rule applies to a claim for a new tenancy under s.24 and to a claim for the termination of a tenancy under s.29(2) of the 1954 Act.

24–16

(2) In this rule—

(a) "the 1954 Act" means the Landlord and Tenant Act 1954;

(b) "an unopposed claim" means a claim for a new tenancy under s.24 in circumstances where the grant of a new tenancy is not opposed;

(c) "an opposed claim"—

(i) a new tenancy under section 24 of the 1954 Act in circumstances where the grant of a new tenancy is opposed; or

(ii) the termination of a tenancy under s.29(2) of the 1954 Act.

(3) Where the claim is an unopposed claim—

(a) the claimant must use the Part 8 procedure, but the following rules do not apply—

(i) rule 8.5; and

(ii) rule 8.6;

(b) [. . .]

(c) the court will give directions about the future management of the claim following receipt of the acknowledgment of service.

(4) Where the claim is an opposed claim the claimant must use the Part 7 procedure.

(Practice Direction 56 contains provisions about evidence, including expert evidence in opposed claims.)

PD 56 paras 2.1, 2.1A, 3.1

24–17   2.1 Subject to paragraph 2.1A, the claimant in a landlord and tenant claim must use the Part 8 procedure as modified by Part 56 and this practice direction.

2.1A Where the landlord and tenant claim is a claim for—

(1) a new tenancy under section 24 of the 1954 Act in circumstances where the grant of a new tenancy is opposed; or
(2) the termination of a tenancy under s.29(2) of the 1954 Act,

the claimant must use the Part 7 procedure as modified by Part 56 and this practice direction.

3.1 This paragraph applies to a claim for a new tenancy under section 24 and termination of a tenancy under section 29(2) of the 1954 Act where rule 56.3 applies and in this paragraph—

(1) "an unopposed claim" means a claim for a new tenancy under section 24 of the 1954 Act in circumstances where the grant of a new tenancy is not opposed;
(2) "an opposed claim" means a claim for—

  (a) a new tenancy under section 24 of the 1954 Act in circumstances where the grant of a new tenancy is opposed; or
  (b) the termination of a tenancy under section 29(2) of the 1954 Act; and

(3) "grounds of opposition" means—

  (a) the grounds specified in section 30(1) of the 1954 Act on which a landlord may oppose an application for a new tenancy under section 24(1) of the 1954 Act or make an application under section 29(2) of the 1954 Act; or
  (b) any other basis on which the landlord asserts that a new tenancy ought not to be granted.

Which court?

24–18   Both the High Court and the County Court have jurisdiction to hear a claim for a new tenancy (Landlord and Tenant Act 1954 s.63).

The claim should be started in the County Court hearing centre which serves the address. If it is not, then there is likely to be a delay in proceedings whilst the matter is transferred to the appropriate hearing centre (CPR 56.2(1) and CPR 56 PD, para.2.2(2)). Only exceptional circumstances justify starting the claim in the High Court. (CPR 56 PD, para.2.2.) If the claim is started in the High Court and the court decides that it should have been started in the County Court, the court will normally either strike out the claim or transfer it to the county court on its own initiative. Circumstances that may, in an appropriate case, justify starting a claim in the High Court are if there are complicated disputes of fact or there are points of law of general importance. The value of the property and the amount of any financial claim may be relevant circumstances but these factors alone will not normally justify starting the claim in the High Court. (PD 56.2.) The best policy is therefore almost invariably to start the claim in the County Court and if it is thought appropriate to ask that court to transfer the claim to the High Court.

If the claim is begun in the High Court, it must be brought in the Chancery Division. (PD 56, para.2.6.)

The defendant

PD 56 3.3

3.3 Where a claim for a new tenancy under s.24 of the 1954 Act is made by a tenant, the person who, in relation to the claimant's current tenancy, is the landlord as defined in s.44 of the 1954 Act must be a defendant. **24-19**

It is the "competent landlord" (more accurately "the landlord" as defined by s.44; see para.14-17) who must be made a defendant to the tenant's application for a new tenancy. This is not necessarily the tenant's immediate landlord. If a mistake is made it may be possible to have the claim amended to name the correct party under CPR 19.5 even after the time for applying for a new lease has passed (*Parsons v George* [2004] EWCA Civ 912).

If the identity of the competent landlord changes before the hearing the new competent landlord must be joined as a party to the proceedings. It is not good enough merely to serve him with notice of them. Where the landlord's interest is subject to a mortgage and a receiver has been appointed the mortgagee must be joined (*Meah v Mouskos* [1963] 3 All E.R. 908).

Landlord in administration

An application by a tenant for a new lease under Part II is a "legal process" within para.43, Sch.B1 of the Insolvency Act **24-20**

1986 (para.7-41). This means that if the landlord goes into administration the tenant cannot proceed with the claim without the consent of the administrator or the permission of the court. In *Somerfield Stores Ltd v Spring (Sutton Coldfield Ltd* [2009] EWHC 2384 (Ch) and the landlord went into administration the administrator refused to consent to the claim. It wanted to explore the possibility of a scheme that would allow it to redevelop and thereby increase the sums available for the creditors. The landlord had previously served a notice under s.30(1)(f) objecting to a new lease. The tenant was given to permission with the claim for a new lease (*Atlantic Computer Systems* [1992] Ch. 505 applied—see para.7-41). In striking a balance between the rights of the administrators in accordance with the administration objective, and the right of the tenant to have its claim heard, and to be granted a new lease to which it was entitled as things stood, the court considered that the interests of the tenant prevailed. Perle J at para.17:

> "The claimant is presently in a state of continuing uncertainty in relation to a store that it wishes to refurbish. It is wrong for that uncertainty to continue indefinitely. It is possible, when the matter comes before the court on the 1954 Act application, that either a short tenancy will be granted or a tenancy with a break clause. This might itself create some uncertainty, but that is a matter which can be considered upon all the evidence before the appropriate court, which both sides accept must eventually come to adjudicate upon this issue. Given that acceptance, it seems to me right that the matter should proceed with proper expedition. It would be wrong of this court to improve the position of the defendant or the bank to the prejudice of the claimant, which has a right to have its proceedings heard without undue delay, and (on the evidence as it stands) the terms of a new tenancy determined."

Contents of the claim form

24-21 There are certain particulars that are required in all claims, whether it is the landlord or the tenant applying for the new lease. These are set out in PD 56 para.3.4. There are then further, different, particulars that are required depending upon whether or not the claim is being brought by the tenant (para.3.5) or the landlord (para.3.7).

PD 56 paras 3.4, 3.5 and 3.7

3.4 The claim form must contain details of—　　　　　　　　　　**24–22**

(1)　the property to which the claim relates;

(2)　the particulars of the current tenancy (including date, parties and duration), the current rent (if not the original rent) and the date and method of termination;

(3)　every notice or request given or made under sections 25 or 26 of the 1954 Act; and

(4)　the expiry date of—

　　(a)　the statutory period under section 29A(2) of the 1954 Act; or

　　(b)　any agreed extended period made under section 29B(1) or 29B(2) of the 1954 Act.

Claim form where the claimant is the tenant making a claim for a new tenancy under s.24 of the 1954 Act

3.5 Where the claimant is the tenant making a claim for a new tenancy　　**24–23** under section 24 of the 1954 Act, in addition to the details specified in paragraph 3.4, the claim form must contain details of—

(1)　the nature of the business carried on at the property;

(2)　whether the claimant relies on section 23(1A), 41 or 42 of the 1954 Act and, if so, the basis on which he does so;

(3)　whether the claimant relies on section 31A of the 1954 Act and, if so, the basis on which he does so;

(4)　whether any, and if so what part, of the property comprised in the tenancy is occupied neither by the claimant nor by a person employed by the claimant for the purpose of the claimant's business;

(5)　the claimant's proposed terms of the new tenancy; and

(6)　the name and address of—

　　(a)　anyone known to the claimant who has an interest in the reversion in the property (whether immediate or in not more than 15 years) on the termination of the claimant's current tenancy and who is likely to be affected by the grant of a new tenancy; or

　　(b)　if the claimant does not know of anyone specified by sub-paragraph (6)(a), anyone who has a freehold interest in the property.

3.6 The claim form must be served on the persons referred to in paragraph　　**24–24** 3.5(6)(a) or (b) as appropriate.

Claim form where the claimant is the landlord making a claim for a new tenancy under s.24 of the 1954 Act

24-25 3.7 Where the claimant is the landlord making a claim for a new tenancy under section 24 of the 1954 Act, in addition to the details specified in paragraph 3.4, the claim form must contain details of—

    (1) the claimant's proposed terms of the new tenancy;

    (2) whether the claimant is aware that the defendant's tenancy is one to which section 32(2) of the 1954 Act applies and, if so, whether the claimant requires that any new tenancy shall be a tenancy of the whole of the property comprised in the defendant's current tenancy or just of the holding as defined by section 23(3) of the 1954 Act; and

    (3) the name and address of—

        (a) anyone known to the claimant who has an interest in the reversion in the property (whether immediate or in not more than 15 years) on the termination of the claimant's current tenancy and who is likely to be affected by the grant of a new tenancy; or

        (b) if the claimant does not know of anyone specified by sub-paragraph (3)(a), anyone who has a freehold interest in the property.

24-26 3.8 The claim form must be served on the persons referred to in paragraph 3.7(3)(a) or (b) as appropriate.

Service of the claim form

24-27 The period for service of a claim form in a lease renewal claim is four months (see CPR r.7.5).

The court's power to extend time for service is severely limited (CPR 7.6(3)).

In addition to service on the defendant, the claim form must also be served on any person named in the claim form in accordance with PD 56 3.5(6) or 3.7 (3)—see paras 24–22 and 24–24. (PD 56, 3.6 and 3.8.)

Acknowledgment of service

24-28 Where the *claimant is the tenant* and the claim is *unopposed* the landlord must use form N210 for his acknowledgment of service and state with particulars the matters set out in para.3.10 of PD 56.

PD 56 3.10

Acknowledgment of service where the claim is an unopposed claim and where the claimant is the tenant

3.10 Where the claim is an unopposed claim and the claimant is the tenant, **24–29**
the acknowledgment of service is to be in form N210 and must state with
particulars—

(1) whether, if a new tenancy is granted, the defendant objects to any of
the terms proposed by the claimant and if so—

    (a) the terms to which he objects; and
    (b) the terms that he proposes in so far as they differ from those
        proposed by the claimant;

(2) whether the defendant is a tenant under a lease having less than 15
years unexpired at the date of the termination of the claimant's
current tenancy and, if so, the name and address of any person who,
to the knowledge of the defendant, has an interest in the reversion in
the property expectant (whether immediate or in not more than 15
years from that date) on the termination of the defendant's
tenancy;

(3) the name and address of any person having an interest in the
property who is likely to be affected by the grant of a new tenancy;
and

(4) if the claimant's current tenancy is one to which section 32(2) of the
1954 Act applies, whether the defendant requires that any new
tenancy shall be a tenancy of the whole of the property comprised in
the claimant's current tenancy.

Where the claim is brought *by the landlord* and is *unopposed*,
the acknowledgment of service must be in form N210 and must
state the particulars required by PD 56 3.11.

PD 56 para.3.11

Acknowledgment of service where the claim is an unopposed claim and the claimant is the landlord

3.11 Where the claim is an unopposed claim and the claimant is the **24–30**
landlord, the acknowledgment of service is to be in form N210 and must
state with particulars—

(1) the nature of the business carried on at the property;
(2) if the defendant relies on section 23(1A), 41 or 42 of the 1954 Act,
the basis on which he does so;
(3) whether any, and if so what part, of the property comprised in the
tenancy is occupied neither by the defendant nor by a person
employed by the defendant for the purpose of the defendant's
business;

(4) the name and address of—

(a) anyone known to the defendant who has an interest in the reversion in the property (whether immediate or in not more than 15 years) on the termination of the defendant's current tenancy and who is likely to be affected by the grant of a new tenancy; or

(b) if the defendant does not know of anyone specified by sub-paragraph (4)(a), anyone who has a freehold interest in the property; and

(5) whether, if a new tenancy is granted, the defendant objects to any of the terms proposed by the claimant and, if so—

(a) the terms to which he objects; and

(b) the terms that he proposes in so far as they differ from those proposed by the claimant.

Where the claim is *an opposed claim* for a new lease *brought by the tenant* the acknowledgment of service must be in form N9 (PD 3.12(1)). (If a landlord brings a claim for a new lease that the tenant does not want, see para.24–05 above.) As to the contents of the defence, see immediately below.

Defence in opposed claims for renewal brought be tenant

24–31 The contents of the defence required of the landlord are set out in PD 56, para.3.12:

Acknowledgment of service and defence where the claim is an opposed claim and where the claimant is the tenant

24–32 3.12 Where the claim is an opposed claim and the claimant is the tenant—

(1) the acknowledgment of service is to be in form N9; and

(2) in his defence the defendant must state with particulars—

(a) the defendant's grounds of opposition;

(b) full details of those grounds of opposition;

(c) whether, if a new tenancy is granted, the defendant objects to any of the terms proposed by the claimant and if so—

(i) the terms to which he objects; and

(ii) the terms that he proposes in so far as they differ from those proposed by the claimant;

(d) whether the defendant is a tenant under a lease having less than 15 years unexpired at the date of the termination of the claimant's current tenancy and, if so, the name and address of any person who, to the knowledge of the defendant, has an interest in the reversion in the property expectant (whether immediately or in not more than 15 years from that date) on the termination of the defendant's tenancy;

(e) the name and address of any person having an interest in the property who is likely to be affected by the grant of a new tenancy; and

(f) if the claimant's current tenancy is one to which section 32(2) of the 1954 Act applies, whether the defendant requires that any new tenancy shall be a tenancy of the whole of the property comprised in the claimant's current tenancy.

Amending acknowledgement to include new clause

In *Benchmark Group plc v Davies Attbrook (Chemists) Ltd* **24–33** [2005] EWHC 3413 (Ch) Lewison J held that the trial judge should have allowed the landlord to amend the acknowledgement of service the day before the trial so as to seek a landlord's redevelopment clause. It is not uncommon for things to change in the course of an application for the grant of a new tenancy, which is concerned with the future relationship of the parties. (See also the discussion of the case in Kate Andrews, "Making up your mind" (2006) *Property Law Journal*, p.23).

Allocation; directions; evidence

An *unopposed* claim is brought under Pt 8 and so is **24–34** automatically treated as allocated to the multi-track "and therefore Pt 26 does not apply" (CPR Pt 8.9(c)). The words in quotes would seem to suggest that the court may not use Pt 26.10 to re-allocate a case that has automatically been allocated to the multi-track to a different track.

An *opposed* claim is brought under Pt 7 so needs to be assigned to a track. There are no specific rules in Pt 56 relating to allocation. Thus, the usual rules in Pt 56 apply—although opposed claims under Pt 56 may not be allocated to the small claims track (PD 26 8.1). Thus, one has the odd position that an *unopposed* claim must be allocated to the multi-track but an *opposed* claim could be allocated to the fast track. In deciding the track, the court should have regard to the factors set out in CPR 26.8 (see CPR 26.7).

CPR 26.8

(1) When deciding the track for a claim, the matters to which the court **24–35** shall have regard include:

(a) the financial value, if any, of the claim;
(b) the nature of the remedy sought;
(c) the likely complexity of the facts, law or evidence;
(d) the number of parties or likely parties;
(e) the value of any counterclaim or other Part 20 claim and the complexity of any matters relating to it;
(f) the amount of oral evidence which may be required;
(g) the importance of the claim to persons who are not parties to the proceedings;
(h) the views expressed by the parties; and
(i) the circumstances of the parties.

Evidence in an unopposed claim

24-36 PD56, 3.14 Where the claim is an unopposed claim, no evidence need be filed unless and until the court directs it to be filed.

Evidence in an opposed claim

24-37 PD56, 3.15 Where the claim is an opposed claim, evidence (including expert evidence) must be filed by the parties as the court directs and the landlord shall be required to file his evidence first.

Grounds of opposition to be tried as a preliminary issue

24-38 PD56, 3.16 Unless in the circumstances of the cases it is unreasonable to do so, any grounds of opposition shall be tried as a preliminary issue.

Unless in the circumstances of the case it is unreasonable to do so, the court will order that any grounds specified in s.30 upon which the landlord relies or any other basis on which the landlord asserts that a new tenancy ought not to be granted shall be tried as a preliminary issue (PD 56, 3.1(3) (para.24-17) and 3.16).

Directions

24-39 Where the claim is an *unopposed* claim (para.24-17) the court will, upon receipt of the acknowledgement of service, give directions about the future management of the claim (CPR 56.3(3)(c)). If the parties have not already written to the court with suggested directions the district judge will usually make a direction that the parties file suggested directions, to be agreed if possible. In practice the parties do often file agreed suggested directions, often based on the directions suggested by the Property Litigation Association on its website (*http://www.pla.org.uk* [Accessed November 24, 2014]). The court will invariably then make the order as part of the "box work"; unless there is some particular point that needs to be discussed in which case the court usually directs a telephone hearing. Full case management conferences with an oral hearing are rare in lease renewal claims.

Where the claim is an *opposed claim* the normal Pt 7 procedure applies (CPR 56.3). The parties must file completed direction questionnaires (CPR 26.3) with suggested directions in the usual way. (Once again the PLA website has suggested directions, although care must be taken in that compliance with the need for cost budgeting (CPR 3.12 et seq), expert evidence consideration (CPR 35.4) and disclosure (CPR 31.5) should be adhered to as well as the general exhortation in CPR 26 PD para 2.3(1) to base the directions on those found on the website www.justice.gov.uk/courts/procedure-rules/civil [Accessed November 24, 2014] in the case of cases allocated to the multi-track and those contained in CPR 28 for cases allocated to the fast-track).

Particular comments on directions relating to preliminary issues, expert evidence and other matters are dealt with below.

Evidence; general

Whether the claim is opposed or unopposed the evidence, **24–40** including expert evidence, is filed in accordance with court directions (CPR 56 PD paras 3.14 and 3.15—the slightly different wording of each would seem to make no practical difference). In an opposed claim, the landlord must file his evidence first (CPR 56 PD para 3.15). For example, if the landlord is seeking to terminate the tenancy or oppose a claim for a new lease by relying upon the development ground in s.30(1)(f) he will be required to file evidence supporting the ground before the tenant will be required to reply to it.

Expert evidence; experts

See CPR Pt 35 and its practice direction generally on experts; **24–41** and in particular CPR 35.4 on the court's power to restrict expert evidence. See also in particular para.4 of the *Protocol for the Instruction of Experts to give evidence in civil claims* (appended to PD 35), which sets out the duties of experts—primarily to assist the court by giving independent opinion evidence. Paragraph 4.3 of the guidance states as follows:

"Experts should provide opinions which are independent, regardless of the pressures of litigation. In this context a useful test of 'independence' is that the expert would express the same opinion if given the same instructions by an opposing party. Experts should not take it upon themselves to promote the point of view of the party instructing them or engage in the role of advocates."

CPR 35.7 gives the court a discretion to appoint a *single joint expert*. Paragraph 7 of PD 35 gives guidance on the appointment of experts in general and single joint experts in particular:

PD 35, para 7

24–42   When considering whether to give permission for the parties to rely on expert evidence and whether that evidence should be from a single joint expert the court will take into account all the circumstances in particular, whether:

(a) it is proportionate to have separate experts for each party on a particular issue with reference to—
   (i)   the amount in dispute;
   (ii) the importance to the parties; and
   (iii) the complexity of the issue;
(b) the instruction of a single joint expert is likely to assist the parties and the court to resolve the issue more speedily and in a more cost-effective way than separately instructed experts;
(c) expert evidence is to be given on the issue of liability, causation or quantum;
(d) the expert evidence falls within a substantially established area of knowledge which is unlikely to be in dispute or there is likely to be a range of expert opinion;
(e) a party has already instructed an expert on the issue in question and whether or not that was done in compliance with any practice direction or relevant pre-action protocol;
(f) questions put in accordance with rule 35.6 are likely to remove the need for the other party to instruct an expert if one party has already instructed an expert;
(g) questions put to a single joint expert may not conclusively deal with all issues that may require testing prior to trial;
(h) a conference may be required with the legal representatives, experts and other witnesses which may make instruction of a single joint expert impractical; and
(i) a claim to privilege makes the instruction of any expert as a single joint expert inappropriate.

The Pre-action protocol on pre-action conduct that applies when there is no specific protocol (which is the case in claims under Pt 2 of the 1954 Act) contains (in Annex C) guidance on instructing experts. The following provisions are particularly relevant:

Pre-Action Protocol—Practice Direction—Pre-Action Conduct (i.e. the general protocol)—Annex C (Guidance on instructing experts)

2. Parties should be aware that once proceedings have been started: **24–43**

    (1) expert evidence may not be used in court without the permission of the court;

    (2) a party who instructs an expert will not necessarily be able to recover the cost from another party; and

    (3) it is the duty of an expert to help the court on matters within the expert's scope of expertise and this duty overrides any obligation to the person instructing or paying the expert.

3. Many matters can and should be resolved without the need for advice or evidence from an expert. If an expert is needed, the parties should consider how best to minimise the expense for example by agreeing to instruct-

    (1) a single joint expert (i.e. engaged and paid jointly by the parties whether instructed jointly or separately); or

    (2) an agreed expert (i.e. the parties agree the identity of the expert, but only one party instructs the expert and pays the expert's costs).

4. If the parties do not agree that the nomination of a single joint expert is appropriate, then the party seeking the expert evidence (the first party) should give the other party (the second party) a list of one or more experts in the relevant field of expertise who the first party would like to instruct.

5. Within 14 days of receipt of the list of experts, the second party may indicate in writing an objection to one or more of the experts listed. If there remains on the list one or more experts who are acceptable, then the first party should instruct an expert from the list.

6. If the second party objects to all the listed experts, the first party may then instruct an expert of the first party's own choice. Both parties should bear in mind that if proceedings are started the court will consider whether a party has acted reasonably when instructing (or rejecting) an expert.

It can be seen that the pre-action protocol encourages the parties to consider how best to minimise the expense of litigation, for example by agreeing to instruct a "single joint expert" or an "an agreed expert".

How do these provisions relate to lease renewal claims? The following points may be noted:

    (1) In many standard cases, particularly where the rental value is low, the appointment of a single joint expert or an

"agreed" expert in relation to rent will be appropriate. It may also be appropriate on one or more issues even in the bigger or more complicated cases. In practice, it is more common for a direction to be given that each party has its own expert, at least on the question of rent. Agreed directions, providing for two experts, are submitted and approved, sometimes without a great deal of scrutiny by the district judge who may not have much if any experience of lease renewal claims. However, generally speaking the parties then negotiate a settlement and the matter never in fact goes to a hearing. Thus, in most cases the debate about whether or not there should be a single joint expert is somewhat sterile.

(2) If the court orders a single joint expert, over the objection of the parties, there is a risk that each party will employ his own expert to check on the report of the joint expert. However, that risk is no greater in lease renewal claims than in other cases; and it is not a matter specifically listed in paragraph 7 of the PD 35. However, para.7(h) does state that the court will take into account the requirement for a conference "with the legal representatives, experts and other witnesses which may make instruction of a single joint expert impractical". This can often be the position in more complicated lease renewal claims. Where a party is unhappy with the single joint expert's report he will be allowed to have an expert of his own in an appropriate case (*Daniels v Walker* [2000] 1 WLR 1382 —where the reasons given are not fanciful and a large sum is involved; *Peet v Mid-Kent Healthcare* [2002] 1 WLR 210—where good reasons are given).

(3) If one party instructs an expert prior to an order of the court he will not necessarily be able to use that expert and will not necessarily be able to recover the costs.

(4) It is the duty of an expert to help the court and this duty overrides any obligation to the person instructing or paying the expert. The old practice, whereby the landlord's expert always specified a high rent and the tenant's expert low rent (each backed up by different comparables), is contrary to the experts' duty to give independent evidence to the court.

(5) Where an expert has been negotiating on behalf of a party, on e.g. the amount of rent to be paid under the

lease, it is difficult to see (in the view of the author) how that person can be an appropriate person to be an expert in the case if the negotiations break down.

(6) If the court allows separate experts for each party, they will be required to discuss the issues, reach agreement where possible and list the remaining unresolved items (CPR 35.12). See more fully PD 35, para.9.

(7) Perhaps if landlords follow the procedure in paras 4 and 5 of the pre-action protocol for the appointment of an "agreed expert" this might lead to more settlements at an earlier stage.

(8) In *Capita Alternative Fund Services (Gurnsey) Ltd v Driver Jonas* [2012] EWCA Civ 1417 Gross LJ pointed out that a judge is never bound by expert evidence, even undisputed expert evidence. In a typical valuation case the figure arrived at by the judge may well be somewhere between those advanced by the rival experts. A judge may simply have to do "the best he can".

(9) See further "Valuers' reports; rent and other terms" below.

Valuers' reports

Rent

The most common type of expert evidence in a lease renewal claim relates to the amount of rent that should be payable under the new lease. As a matter of principle, if there is a dispute as to the rent and as to some of the terms of the lease, the dispute over the terms should be dealt with first. This follows from the requirement of s.34(1) of the 1954 Act that the rent payable shall be such sum at which having regard to the terms of the tenancy (other than relating to rent) the holding might reasonably be expected to be let in the open market (see para.26–21). The parties should therefore do their best to negotiate the terms of the lease, other than rent, as far as possible in advance so that a direction can be given that the surveyor(s) simply prepare a report dealing with that issue, and possibly interim rent (see Ch.25).

24–44

If it is not possible to agree all the terms by the directions stage the valuer will either have to give alternative views on the amount of rent payable depending on the possible outcomes or will have to give a final view once those other issues have been resolved; or, if necessary, after the judge has decided between the parties on the other terms. This may have to be done by supplementary report.

In practice, valuers advising the parties during negotiations will often say that the difference over the terms will in fact have no or very little impact on the correct level of rent. If that is the case then the report should state as much—and it is unlikely that there will need to be a supplementary report.
See further, paras 26–22 to 26–26.

Disputes about terms

24–45 Where there is a dispute as to the terms of the new lease, in theory the person who is seeking to change the terms of the lease should be required to specify his suggested amendments first. This follows from the legal principle that the burden is upon the person seeking to change the terms to show that the changes are justified (see further para.26–14). In practice, orders for directions tend to direct that the landlord should serve on the tenant a draft lease first. The tenant is then required to serve on the landlord his proposed amendments marked in red on the draft, or by schedule, by a certain date. This follows the usual conveyancing practice on the grant of a lease; and will usually be regarded as more convenient and appropriate (at least by the landlord's solicitors) in lease renewal claims, particularly where the original lease is somewhat ancient and the landlord is seeking to use a new modern format. Whichever practice is adopted the principle that it is for the party seeking to change the lease to justify the change should not be forgotten.

Where there is a dispute about the terms, the valuer should (if appropriate) deal expressly with those matters in their reports. For example, if the landlord states that there should be three-yearly rent reviews and the tenant says that there should be five-yearly rent reviews the valuer should give their views as to market conditions in relation to this issue. In other cases the expert evidence of a conveyancer may be required (perhaps on the modern format of leases) but this is rare. If allowed by the court it is important to get the right sort of conveyancer. There is no point in using a lawyer from a big city firm who specialises in industrial estates if the case is about a lock up shop.

Which level of judge?

In order to understand the following paragraphs it will be **24-46** necessary to have CPR PD 2B open in front of the reader.

High Court

Where the proceedings are in the Chancery Division **24-47** (para.24-18) a Master or District Judge may *not* make a final order in any claim under Pt II of the 1954 Act without the consent of the Chancellor of the High Court except by consent; except for one relating to interim rent (PD 2B para.5.1(j)).

County Court; unopposed claims

In the County Court the District Judge may hear an *unopposed* **24-48** claim (the author believes) if the Designated Civil Judge (DCJ) gives permission. This follows from PD 2B para.11.1(d):

- The basic principle is that a district judge has jurisdiction to hear claims automatically allocated to the multi-track (para.11.1(a)) unless one of the exceptions in that paragraph applies. (An unopposed claim is deemed to be allocated to the multi-track; para.24-31)
- The items in (i) to (vii) in paragraph (a) of para.11.1 are the exceptions to the deemed multi-track cases in (a).
- The "other proceedings" in (d) refer to proceedings other than those in (a), (b) and (c) of para.11.1.
- As the exceptions listed in (a) are not part of (a)—having been excepted from (a)—they are therefore part of the "other proceedings".
- As these are "other proceedings" the DCJ can give permission for a district judge to hear the claim.

Although district judges have jurisdiction if the DCJ gives permission, it does seem that at case management stage the *unopposed* claims are usually listed before circuit judges.

Opposed claims

However, if the claim is deliberately allocated to the multi-track **24-49** in an *opposed* claim (para.24-31)—as opposed to there being a deemed allocation in an unopposed claim (para.24-21) —para.11.1(a) of PD 2B has no relevance and a district judge in the County Court can clearly only hear the claim if the DCJ gives permission (2B para.11.1(d)).

If (which is unlikely) the claim is allocated to the fast track the district judge can only hear the claim with the permission of the DCJ (see PD 2B 11.1(a) and the arguments referred to above in relation to unopposed claims).

Judgment in default

24–50   Where the claim is an opposed claim, it is brought under Pt 7. Thus, it would seem that the normal default judgment provisions apply. If the landlord fails to acknowledge service or file a defence within time and the tenant wishes to obtain a default judgment, he must make an application in accordance with Pt 23 (CPR 12.4(2)(a)) Compare para.22–13 where the landlord is seeking a default judgment.

Summary judgment

24–51   In a claim where the landlord was opposing the tenant's application for a new lease under ground s.30(1)(f) the tenant applied for summary judgment. The judge concluded that "the date of the hearing at which the necessary intention must be shown to exist is always the date of the substantive trial of the landlord's ground of objection." It was not therefore possible to apply for summary judgment (*Somerfield Stores Ltd v Spring* [2010] EWHC 2084 (Ch)). Query, whether it would work the other way round? Could a landlord which considers that it has overwhelming evidence to show that it has a clear intention to redevelop (or indeed of any other ground) apply for summary judgment dismissing the tenant's application for a new lease?

Protecting the application to renew: relationship with the Land Registration Act 2002

24–52   There has been some debate as to whether or not it is necessary for a tenant to protect a claim for a new lease by notice or restriction where the lease was entered into on or after October 13, 2003 (when the Land Registration Act 2002 came into force). The author's view is that it is not necessary for the following reasons:

● If the original fixed-term tenancy was for a term of *more than seven years* (and thus registered), the continuation tenancy will continue to be protected by the original registration.

- If the tenancy is protected by a notice (which is permitted where the tenancy is for *more than three years but seven years or less*), the continuation ten- ancy will continue to be protected so long as the notice remains on the register.
- If the tenancy is overriding (*seven years or less*), it will continue to be an overriding interest under the continuation tenancy even if more than seven years has passed because it was (and is) a lease that was "granted for a term not exceeding seven years" (LRA, Schs 1 and 3 para.1); i.e. it was originally granted for seven years or less and by operation of the 1954 Act it is still the same tenancy.
- The continuation tenancy continues until three months after the court order: s.64 of the 1954 Act.
- Whoever is the landlord at the date of the order or indeed afterwards is required under the 1954 Act to give effect to the order by the grant of the new tenancy (s.44 of and Sch.6 to the 1954 Act).

However, there is an alternative view. See the article: "Get in on the action—and get registered" by Malcolm Dowden, Charles Russell. He suggests that a tenant applying for a new tenancy under the 1954 Act should protect the claim by entering a notice of the claim on the landlord's title. (*Estates Gazette*, October 4, 2003).

Withdrawal of application by landlord

Landlord and Tenant Act 1954 s.24(2C)

24.–(2C) The landlord may not withdraw an application under subsection (1) above unless the tenant consents to its withdrawal.   **24–53**

If the landlord issues an application for a new tenancy under s.24 and then withdraws it, the effect generally will be to bring the continuation tenancy to an end three months from the final disposal of the case in accordance with s.64 (see para.27–02). In order to prevent a landlord from using such a device to deprive the tenant of his right to a new tenancy under the Act, s.24(2C) provides that the landlord may not withdraw the application to renew unless the tenant consents. The court will obviously want to have the tenant present when the consent is given or to see clear written evidence of the consent before permitting the landlord to withdraw the application.

Discontinuance by tenant

24-54 If the tenant moves out of the property after making an application to the court but before the termination date stated in the lease (presuming it was a fixed term) the tenancy will automatically come to an end (as will the right to proceed with the claim) on the expiry date stated in the lease; and the tenant will not be required to pay any more rent thereafter (*Single Horse Properties Ltd v Surrey County Council* [2002] EWCA Civ 367; see also para.15–15).

However, if the termination date has passed and the tenant wants to discontinue he will need to serve a notice of discontinuance and will be responsible for the costs (CPR 38.6). The tenancy will come to an end three months after the date of discontinuance (s.64 of the 1954 Act; see further para.27–02). It is not necessary to serve a notice under s.27(2).

Appeal—new evidence

24-55 In *Mayor and City of London v Davy's of London (Wine Merchants) Ltd* [2004] EWHC 2224 Ch the court ordered a new 14-year lease incorporating a landlord's redevelopment break clause. The tenant appealed against the decision to include the break clause. The landlord appealed against the terms of the break-clause. On the appeal the landlord also applied to adduce further evidence (CPR 52.11) dealing with the proposed sale of the property and the plans for its re-development. It was held that the landlord was permitted to adduce evidence of events that took place after the initial judgment. The court's discretion was exercised in favour of the landlord to do justice to the case.

ADR and negotiation in lease renewal claims

24-56 Alternative methods of dispute resolution are now of course encouraged in all litigation (CPR 3.1); and lease renewal claims are no exception.

Mediation

Introduction

24-57 Mediation is now strongly encouraged by the courts in all areas of litigation. An unreasonable refusal to engage in mediation is likely to lead to an adverse order for costs, and there are very few refusals that are likely to be regarded as reasonable (*PGF II SA v OMFS Company 1 Limited* [2013] EWCA Civ 1288).

Mediation is ideal for lease renewal claims, particularly where a new lease is to be granted. The parties will continue to be in a commercial relationship after the dispute is settled and the less litigious it becomes the better. Settlement by mediation also allows the parties to reach solutions that the court cannot offer. For example, the parties may agree a new contracted out lease. This is often a compromise that suits both parties but could not be ordered by the court without their consent.

Without prejudice and confidential

There are two key "tools" that help mediation to work. The first **24–58** is the "without prejudice" rule. This creates a safe space where everyone can talk openly, knowing that anything that is said at the mediation will stay at the mediation and can't be used at a trial should the mediation not be successful. The second is the mediator's duty of confidentiality to everyone; ie the duty not to disclose the details of any discussions held privately with one party without permission. This allows the mediator to build trust with each side. The more the mediator knows at the earliest possible stage the easier it is for him or her to help the parties to reach a settlement.

The venue

Mediations usually take place in solicitors' offices or in hotels **24–59** with meeting facilities. It is sometimes helpful for the mediation to take place at or near the site of the property in dispute. There are usually three rooms; one for the mediator that is big enough to accommodate all the parties in a joint meeting; and two others, one for each side.

Preparation

Preparation is the key to success but a mediation meeting is **24–60** not like a court hearing. Thus, the sort of preparation that goes into a trial is not necessary. The preparation that should take place is to discuss strategy. In particular the following points should be noted:

- Objectives. What do the clients hope to get out of the mediation? What are their wants and their most important needs?
- What do you consider to be the objectives and needs of the other side?
- What do you consider to be the obstacles to settlement?
- The real drivers behind the dispute—on both sides.
- What have the proceedings have cost so far.
- How much more will it cost if the mediation does not succeed and the case proceeds to trial.
- The position the clients will be in if the case goes to trial and everything goes their way—the best-case scenario.
- The position that they will be in if the case goes to trial and everything goes wrong—the worst-case scenario.
- The clients' strong points—legal, factual and practical.
- The clients' weak points—legal, factual and practical.
- What alternatives the clients have to pursuing the litigation, eg in a lease renewal claim might the clients actually be better off going somewhere else?
- Possible solutions that would be acceptable to the clients and that you think the other side might accept.

Documents

24-61 It is implicit from the above that the sort of documentation that is necessary for a trial is not necessary for a mediation. In far too many mediations large bundles are prepared that are barely looked at!

What the mediator needs is a straight-forward explanation of what the case is about. This might be something similar to a neutral case summary that is used for case management conferences, or if proceedings are already under way it could simply be the statements of case. It is completely unnecessary to provide every letter that has ever been written but copies of any offers that have been made are particularly useful. Depending on the type of case, photographs or plans may be helpful to the mediator.

In many mediations the parties provide "position statements" that they also send to the other side. These are helpful to the extent that they set out what the case is about and are clear and honest in stating what the client wants. Too often however they are over legalisitic and resemble skeleton arguments used in court. It cannot be emphasised too greatly that a mediaiton is not a 'mini-trial'—it is an opportunity to reach a commercial settlement. It is also beneficial for each side to provide the mediator with an honest confidential note setting out the points referred to in the Preparation section above.

The opening session

Mediation is a flexible process and different mediators have **24–62** different styles and practices. Generally speaking, mediations start with the mediator seeing each party separately for the purpose of introducing him or herself. At this stage, some mediators will discuss the process and what will happen during the day. The next step is usually a joint opening session, where each party (whether in person, through their representatives or both) talk about their objectives and concerns.

Clients are sometimes hesitant to engage in meetings with the other side in an open session, even in lease renewal claims, but it is usually a very helpful start to the day. The purpose of the opening session is not to persuade the other side that they have an awful case but to create confidence; to begin to engage in a discussion that will lead to a settlement; to explain what it is the client really wants and to try to find out what the other side really wants. Adversarial behaviour, or focussing on the legal niceties of the dispute, is invariably counter-productive. Some lawyers—particularly barristers—find this difficult to believe! It is however very true and behaviour that is inappropriate to mediation can have a very damaging affect on the process.

Separate meetings

Some joint opening sessions are over quickly. Others can **24–63** involve really helpful discussion and last some time. At some stage however a natural point tends to be reached where it becomes clear that it is appropriate for the parties to go back to their respective rooms, take stock and begin to consider how to proceed further towards settlement. Are there more questions to ask; or information to give? Is it time to start considering making an offer? At this point the mediator will start to go back and forth between the parties.

After further investigation, consideration and discussion with the mediator, the parties will make offers. Sometimes directly, sometimes through the mediator.

Positions, wants and needs

24-64   Throughout the mediation a good mediator will try to get the parties to move from their "positions" and to think about their "interests", to ascertain what it is they want, and more importantly, need. The sooner the parties are forthcoming with that information, as opposed to what a good case they have got, the sooner the mediator can help the parties to reach a settlement. Where appropriate the mediator will play devil's advocate and test the reality of a party's position. Once the mediator knows what it is the parties want and need, he or she can then help them to open up the options for settlement that might meet those needs or at least some of them; to help them to reach a settlement that "they can live with".

The flow of the day

24-65   Most mediations last about a day. There is a flow to the mediation. At some points things seem to be going well, at others everyone seems stuck—often at about 3pm. At this point the mediator may change the dynamics. He or she may get everyone back together again, or perhaps just the clients, or perhaps just the lawyers. There is no fixed procedure. The mediator will do whatever he or she thinks is necessary to bring about a settlement.

Conclusion

24-66   Under the terms of most mediation agreements, settlement only takes place once the terms have been written down and signed by the parties. This is essential to ensure certainty. Most mediation meetings result in agreement.

Where no settlement is reached the meeting may still have been useful. Issues will often have been narrowed and each side will have a better understanding of the other side's needs. Settlement frequently takes place shortly afterwards. The downside of course is that if the agreement is not actually reached at the mediation there is no certainty that it will settle thereafter and costs will continue to mount. It is usually best therefore for the parties to reach agreement on the day if at all possible.

Professional Arbitration on Court Terms

Professional Arbitration on Court Terms ("PACT") is a scheme **24-67**
run jointly by the Law Society and the Royal Institution of
Chartered Surveyors that landlords and tenants can use as an
alternative to court determination in unopposed lease renewal
claims. Instead of relying on a judge, the parties can have the
rent determined by a surveyor, and any other new terms
determined by a surveyor or lawyer, acting either as arbitrator
or independent expert. To give one example (other than rent)
where the scheme could be used is as follows. The parties
cannot agree on the provisions and detailed wording of an
alienation clause. Instead of relying on a judge, who may well
have little landlord and tenant experience, the dispute can be
referred to an experienced conveyancer with the required
expertise. Further details of the scheme can be obtained as
follows: Tel 020 7334 3806; *drs@rics.org* or at the RICS website
http://www.rics.org [Accessed November 24, 2014]–type
PACT into the search function. In practice the scheme is little
used. It is not clear why but the author speculates that it is
because (a) most cases settle anyway and (b) whilst surveyors
(and many solicitors) are familiar with arbitration in rent review
cases, solicitors who deal with lease renewal claims are more
comfortable with the courts.

Part 36 offers

Parties should not forget the importance of making Pt 36 offers **24-68**
in lease renewal claims. Part 36 has been amended in recent
years so that (in particular) in deciding upon the costs
consequences of an offer the court must have consider whether
or not the judgment in favour of a claimant is "more
advantageous" than a defendant's Pt 36 offer; or a judgment
against the defendant is "at least as advantageous" to the
claimant as the proposals contained in a claimant's Pt 36 offer
(CPR 36.14). The use of the word "advantageous" leaves a lot
of scope for dispute about who has effectively won. It is
therefore very important to put a lot of thought into any such
offer that is made. If one party had unreasonably refused to
negotiate or consider an offer, that conduct of itself was a
relevant factor, the fact that the offer had been close (a 'near
miss') but not as much as that awarded was not a sufficient
reason to depart from the general rules about costs
(*Hammersmatch Properties (Welwyn) Ltd v Saint-Gobin
Ceramics & Plastics Ltd* [2013] EWHC 2227 (TCC)).

CHAPTER 25

INTERIM RENT

25-01   If the landlord or the tenant applies for an order for the grant of a new tenancy, or the landlord applies to terminate the current tenancy, the current tenancy continues pursuant to s.24 until (generally) three months after the tenant's application for a new tenancy is finally disposed of (s.64; see para.27-02). The proceedings may take some time to complete and where the market rent is higher than the current rent, the landlord will want to ensure that the rent for the intervening period is increased. Conversely, the tenant will not wish to continue paying a rent that is above the market rent. Section 24A therefore allows either party to apply for an interim rent pending the outcome of the tenant's application for a new tenancy.

However, as will be seen, it will not be possible to determine the amount of the interim rent until after a new tenancy has either been granted or it is certain that there is to be no new tenancy. This means that the rent payable will remain the same in the meantime and that an adjustment will have to be made after the position in relation to a new tenancy is finally resolved.

If there is a "last day rent review" clause in the lease and the landlord operates it, the tenant, if he feels he can achieve a lower rent by doing so, can apply for an interim rent under the provisions in this chapter.

Landlord and Tenant Act 1954 s.24A

25-02   **24A.**–(1) Subject to subsection (2) below, if—

    (a)   the landlord of a tenancy to which this Part of this Act applies has *given notice under section 25* of this Act to terminate the tenancy; or

    (b)   the tenant of such a tenancy has *made a request for a new tenancy* in accordance with section 26 of this Act,

either of them may make an application to the court to determine a rent (an "interim rent") which the tenant is to pay while the tenancy ("the relevant tenancy") continues by virtue of section 24 of this Act and the court *may* order payment of an interim rent in accordance with section 24C or 24D of this Act.

The following particular points should be noted:

- Either the landlord or the tenant can apply for an interim rent.
- An application can be made as soon as a s.25 notice or s.26 request has been served.
- The interim rent is payable from the earliest date for termination that could have been specified in the s.25 notice or s.26 request.
- There are complicated provisions relating to the amount of the interim rent but basically if certain conditions are satisfied the interim rent is the same as the rent that is payable under the new tenancy—although even where the conditions are satisfied, this is subject to qualification in certain cases. If the conditions are not satisfied, a different formula for determining the amount of interim rent is used.

Discretion: The court has a discretion as to whether or not to **25–03** order an interim rent (note the word "may" in s.24A (above)). Under the old law prior to the changes made in 2004, the tenant had to show a good reason why it should not be ordered (*Charles Follett Ltd v Cabtell Investment Ltd* [1987] 2 E.G.L.R. 76 at 91G–K). No doubt that principle will continue to apply now that either the landlord or the tenant can apply.

A tenant who has made a claim for a new tenancy but later changes his mind will not be permitted to defeat the landlord's claim for an interim rent by subsequently denying that the Act applies. The law will not permit a party to approbate and reprobate (*Benedictus v Jalaram Ltd* [1989] 1 E.G.L.R. 251). The claim for interim rent is an independent one, whether or not made in the proceedings for a new tenancy, and continues even if the tenant abandons his claim for a new tenancy (*Coates Bros plc v General Accident Life Assurance Ltd* [1991] 3 All E.R. 929 at 934).

Making the application

Earliest date

The application may be made at any time after the landlord has **25–04** served a s.25 notice or the tenant has served a s.26 request (s.24A(1)). It is not necessary to wait for an application for a new tenancy or termination of the old tenancy to be made to the court.

Latest date

Landlord and Tenant Act 1954 s.24A(2), (3)

25–05   **24A.**–(3) No application shall be entertained under subsection (1) above if it is made more than six months after the termination of the relevant tenancy.

It is not possible to make an application for interim rent more than six months after the termination of the old tenancy (s.24A(3)). This does not mean the expiry date stated in the lease but the end of the continuation tenancy.

> **Example**: Lease with an expiry date of December 10, 2008. On June 2, 2009 L serves a s.25 notice with a termination date of December 10, 2009. T does not apply for a new tenancy and the current tenancy comes to an end on December 10, 2009. The parties have until June 10, 2010 to apply for an interim rent.

> **Example**: Same facts as above but T applies for a new tenancy. The claim is finally disposed of on March 12, 2010. The parties have until September 12, 2010 to apply for an interim rent.

Preventing multiple applications

Landlord and Tenant Act 1954 s.24A(2)

25–06   **24A.**–(2) Neither the tenant nor the landlord may make an application under subsection (1) above if the other has made such an application and has not withdrawn it.

If one party has applied, the other party is not able to apply so long as the first application has not been withdrawn (s.24A(2)). This is to avoid duplicate applications. There is nothing in Pt 56 or PD 56 that states what should happen if both landlord and tenant make an application without the knowledge that the other has done so. No doubt the first in time will proceed; although it hardly matters as the date of the application is not relevant to determining the period for which the interim rent is payable (see below).

Procedure: PD 56

PD 56 paras 3.17 and 3.19

3.17 Where proceedings have already been commenced for the grant of a new tenancy or the termination of an existing tenancy, the claim for interim rent under s.24A of the 1954 Act shall be made in those proceedings by—

25–07

(1) the claim form;
(2) the acknowledgement of service or defence; or
(3) an application on notice under Part 23.

3.19 Where no other proceedings have been commenced for the grant of a new tenancy or termination of an existing tenancy *or where such proceedings have been disposed of*, an application for interim rent under section 24A of the 1954 Act shall be made under the procedure in Part 8 and the claim form shall include details of—

(1) the property to which the claim relates;
(2) the particulars of the relevant tenancy (including date, parties and duration) and the current rent (if not the original rent);
(3) every notice or request given or made under sections 25 or 26 of the 1954 Act;
(4) if the relevant tenancy has terminated, the date and mode of termination; and
(5) if the relevant tenancy has been terminated and the landlord has granted a new tenancy of the property to the tenant—

    (a) particulars of the new tenancy (including date, parties and duration) and the rent; and
    (b) in a case where section 24C(2) of the 1954 Act applies but the claimant seeks a different rent under section 24C(3) of that Act, particulars and matters on which the claimant relies as satisfying section 24C(3).

The references to s.24C are references to the situation where one of the parties argues that the usual figure should not be awarded because one of the qualifications applies; i.e. that there has been a substantial change in market conditions between the date upon which interim rent becomes payable and the date of the grant of the new tenancy; or the terms are very different; or both. (See further below: para.25–13.)

The application for interim rent is an independent application and so will continue even if the tenant's application to renew/the landlord's application to terminate is withdrawn (*Coates Bros plc v General Accident Life Assurance Ltd* [1991] 3 All E.R. 929 at 934).

A tenant who has made a claim for a new tenancy but later changes his mind will not be permitted to defeat a landlord's claim for an interim rent by subsequently denying that the Act applies. The law will not permit a party "to approbate and reprobate" (*Benedictus v Jalaram Ltd* [1989] 1 E.G.L.R. 251; see also *Bell v General Accident Fire & Life Assurance Corp Ltd* [1998] 1 E.G.L.R. 69 CA).

Period in respect of which interim rent is payable

Earliest date

Landlord and Tenant Act 1954 s.24B

25–08

24B.—(1) The interim rent determined on an application under section 24A(1) of this Act shall be payable from the appropriate date.

(2) If an application under section 24A(1) of this Act is made in a case where the landlord has given a notice under section 25 of this Act, the appropriate date is the earliest date of termination that could have been specified in the landlord's notice.

(3) If an application under section 24A(1) of this Act is made in a case where the tenant has made a request for a new tenancy under section 26 of this Act, the appropriate date is the earliest date that could have been specified in the tenant's request as the date from which the new tenancy is to begin.

The interim rent is payable from *the earliest date for termination* of the tenancy *that could have been specified* in the landlord's s.25 notice or the tenant's s.26 request, irrespective of which party applies for the interim rent. This removes any incentive that may exist for a party to delay the proceedings for an interim rent.

The earliest date that can be specified in respect of any particular notice will, in the case of a fixed term, be the termination date stated in the lease (assuming that the notice is served not less than six months beforehand: s.25(2)). In the case of a periodic tenancy, the earliest possible date will usually be six months from service of the s.25 request or the making of the s.26 request (see further ss.25(3) and 26(2)).

> **Example**: Lease with an expiry date of December 10, 2008. L serves a s.25 notice on June 2, 2008 with a termination date of March 2, 2009. The earliest date that

could have been specified in that notice was December 10, 2008, the expiry date in the lease. The interim rent will be backdated to that point in time even though the termination date actually stated was later.

Example: The same lease with an expiry date of December 10, 2008. L serves a s.25 notice on April 3, 2009 with a termination date of December 10, 2009. The interim rent is payable from October 3, 2009, the earliest date that could have been specified in that notice.

Latest date

The interim rent is payable for the period in respect of which the old tenancy continues by virtue of s.24; i.e. it will be payable up until the time when the old tenancy comes to an end by the operation of s.64 (see para.27–02): see the last part of s.24A(1)). If there is a gap between that time and the date of the grant of a new tenancy, there might be a period in which interim rent is not payable. However, if a new tenancy is granted it is likely that agreement will be reached as to payment of rent from the end of the continuation tenancy.

25–09

Example: Lease with an expiry date of March 6, 2009. L serves a Form 1 s.25 notice (i.e. not opposing a new tenancy; see para.14–05) on June 2, 2009 with an expiry date of December 10, 2009. (The earliest date that could have been specified was December 2, 2009.) The parties negotiate but cannot reach agreement by December. They therefore agree an extension of time under s.29B for any application to the court (see Ch.23 para.23–09) to January 10, 2010 and negotiations continue. T overlooks the new expiry date. There is no further extension agreed and neither party applies for an order that there be the grant of a new tenancy prior to that date. The right to apply for a new tenancy is therefore lost on January 10. However, L and T continue to negotiate and terms are soon agreed. On February 3, 2010 L grants T a new tenancy. Technically, the interim rent is payable from December 2, 2009 (the earliest date that could have been specified in the s.25 notice) until January 10, 2010 (the date the current tenancy terminated). However, in agreeing a new lease, the parties are likely to agree that the rent payable under the new tenancy should be payable from January 11, 2010.

Amount of interim rent: new tenancy of whole premises granted and landlord not opposed

Landlord and Tenant Act 1954 s.24C

25-10   **24C.**–(1) This section applies where—

(a)   the landlord gave a notice under *section 25* of this Act at a time when the *tenant was in occupation of the whole* of the property comprised in the relevant tenancy for purposes such as are mentioned in section 23(1) of this Act and stated in the notice that he was *not opposed* to the grant of a new tenancy; or

(b)   the tenant made a request for a new tenancy under *section 26* of this Act at a time when he was in occupation of the *whole* of that property for such purposes and the *landlord did not give notice under subsection (6)* of that section,

and the *landlord grants a new tenancy of the whole* of the property comprised in the relevant tenancy to the tenant (whether as a result of an order for the grant of a new tenancy or otherwise).

(2) Subject to the following provisions of this section, the rent payable under and at the commencement of the new tenancy *shall also be the interim rent.*

(3) Subsection (2) above does not apply where—

(a)   the landlord or the tenant shows to the satisfaction of the court that the interim rent under that subsection *differs substantially* from the relevant rent; or

(b)   the landlord or the tenant shows to the satisfaction of the court that the *terms of the new tenancy differ* from the terms of the relevant tenancy to such an extent that the interim rent under that subsection is substantially different from the rent which (in default of such agreement) the court would have determined under section 34 of this Act to be payable under a tenancy which commenced on the same day as the new tenancy and whose other terms were the same as the relevant tenancy.

(4) In this section "*the relevant rent*" means the rent which (in default of agreement between the landlord and the tenant) the court would have determined under section 34 of this Act to be payable under the new tenancy if the new tenancy had commenced on the appropriate date (within the meaning of section 24B of this Act).

(5) The interim rent in a case where subsection (2) above does not apply by virtue only of subsection (3)(a) above is the relevant rent.

(6) The interim rent in a case where subsection (2) above does not apply by virtue only of subsection (3)(b) above, or by virtue of subsection (3)(a) and (b) above, is the rent which it is *reasonable for the tenant to pay* while the relevant tenancy continues by virtue of section 24 of this Act.

(7) In determining the interim rent under subsection (6) above the court shall have regard—

(a)   to the rent payable under the terms of the relevant tenancy; and

(b)   to the rent payable under any sub-tenancy of part of the property comprised in the relevant tenancy,

but otherwise subsections (1) and (2) of section 34 of this Act shall apply to the determination as they would apply to the determination of a rent under that section if a new tenancy of the whole of the property comprised in the relevant tenancy were granted to the tenant by order of the court and the duration of that new tenancy were the same as the duration of the new tenancy which is actually granted to the tenant.

(8) In this section and section 24D of this Act "the relevant tenancy" has the same meaning as in section 24A of this Act.

Introduction

The provisions relating to the amount of interim rent are somewhat complicated: **25–11**

- There are *two methods of assessment*. The first is set out in this section. If the *three conditions* mentioned below are satisfied, the interim rent will be the same as the rent payable under the new tenancy. If the conditions are not satisfied, the rent is determined in accordance with a different formula that is less favourable to the landlord (see below: para.25–15).
- However, even if the three conditions are satisfied, there are certain circumstances in which the landlord will not get the rent payable under the new tenancy. See *qualifications* below; para.25–13.

The conditions

The three conditions that must be satisfied, before the interim rent will be the same as the new rent, are as follows: **25–12**

- The tenant *occupied the whole* of the property for the purposes of his business at the time that the s.25 notice was given to him; or at the time that he made a request under s.26;
- The landlord stated in the s.25 notice that he *did not oppose* the grant of a new tenancy; or in the case of a s.26 request did not serve a counter-notice under s.26(6) opposing the new tenancy;
- The *landlord grants a new tenancy of the whole* of the property comprised in the tenancy, either by virtue of a court order or "otherwise". (If a new tenancy is ordered but not taken up see para.25–14 below.)

The objective here is to encourage landlords not to oppose renewal, as can be seen from the following explanation offered by the Office of the Deputy Prime Minister at the time that the proposals for reform were proceeding:

> "The reforms also remove any incentive for the landlord to impede renewal. Because it takes account of the rent under the old tenancy and makes an artificial assumption about the period of occupation, the current method of determining interim rent [*i.e. the method before the reforms*] produces a 'cushioning effect'—the rent will be at a discount to the prevailing open market rent for comparable lettings. If the landlord does not oppose renewal and the other qualifying conditions apply . . . the landlord will normally receive the rent for the new tenancy for the period for which interim rent is payable. It will therefore be in the landlord's interest not to oppose renewal unless he or she has strong grounds under s30(1))." (ODPM)

The reason for requiring the order to relate to the whole of the property is that "otherwise the new rent will not be calculated by reference to the premises which the tenant is entitled to enjoy until the current tenancy expires" (Law Commission, 2.69); i.e. the tenancy under the new lease needs to be the same as the tenancy under the old lease otherwise it is not possible to make the rent the same for both. No doubt it might have been possible to make some sort of apportionment but this would have made the provisions even more complicated.

The qualifications

25-13 As stated above, if the conditions are satisfied the interim rent will usually be the same as the rent for the new tenancy. However, the court will vary this amount if:

- The rent payable under the new tenancy differs substantially from the market rent (more accurately, the rent that the court would have determined under s.34; s.24C(4)) at the date in respect of which the interim rent is payable (i.e. the earliest date that could have been specified in a s.25 notice or s.26 request; see para.25-09) (s.24C(3)(a), (4));
- The terms of the new tenancy are so different from the old tenancy that it would make a substantial difference to the

market rent at the date of the grant of the new tenancy
(s.24C(3)(b));
- Both the above apply.

(1) In the first case the rent will be determined according to the
market conditions at the date on which the interim rent became
payable (s.24C(3)(a), (4) and (5)).

(2) In the second case, the interim rent will be that which it is
reasonable for the tenant to pay while the old tenancy
continues. In determining that amount, regard must be had to
the rent payable under the old tenancy; and to the rent payable
under any sub-tenancy of part of the property (s.24C(3)(b), (4)
and (6)). (There could have been no sub-tenant in occupation at
the date of the service of the s.25 notice or s.26 request. If
there had been, the first condition referred to above would not
have been satisfied. However, the tenant may have granted a
sub-tenancy after that date.)

(3) Where both apply (i.e. a change in market conditions and a
change in terms), once again the interim rent is that which it is
reasonable for the tenant to pay (s.24C(6)).

The reason for these modifications were again explained by the
ODPM.

> " . . . in some cases application of the new rules could be
> unfair. If market rents rose significantly between the
> starting date for interim rent and the beginning of the new
> tenancy, the tenant would suffer disadvantage from having
> the higher rent backdated. Conversely, the landlord would
> suffer disadvantage in the event of falling rents. So the
> proposals allow for an adjustment to the rent where there
> is a significant movement in the market conditions over
> the intervening period.
>
> Application of the new rules could also be unfair if the
> occupational terms of the new lease changed significantly.
> For example, if the rent under the new tenancy was
> adjusted upwards to take account of the tenant having
> fewer obligations than under the old tenancy, it would not
> be fair for the tenant to have to pay the full new rent over
> the interim period during which he or she would be having
> to fulfil more onerous obligations. In these cases, the

> courts will have discretion to adjust the interim rent
> appropriately."

New tenancy ordered but not taken up

25-14 If the court makes an order for the grant of a new tenancy and
orders the payment of interim rent in accordance with any part
of the new formula under s.24C but it either subsequently
revokes the order under s.36(2) (revocation of order at request
of tenant within 14 days) or if the landlord and tenant agree not
to act on, the order the court must, if either party applies,
determine a new interim rent using the second method of
assessment discussed below (see s.24D(3); para.25-15). The
wording of the subsection is not absolutely ideal but it seems
clear that it is intended that this is a replacement order for the
previous interim rent order. The reasoning for this provision was
explained by the Law Commission (para.2.69):

> "Also it seems right to recognise that the Act gives the
> tenant a right to apply for the renewal order, once made,
> to be revoked. In such a case, effectively to backdate the
> new rent as interim rent would be wrong, as it would force
> upon the tenant a rent which he could not afford and
> which the Act expressly permits him to escape by vacating
> the property. Accordingly, the actual grant of the tenancy
> is an appropriate additional requirement. It would cover
> two circumstances in which an interim rent at the full
> market figure would be inappropriate. First, if the power to
> require revocation is exercised and, secondly, if the parties
> agree not to act on the order."

Interim rent: conditions not satisfied

Landlord and Tenant Act 1954 s.24(D)

25-15 24D.—(1) The interim rent in a case where section 24C of this Act does
not apply is the rent which it is reasonable for the tenant to pay while the
relevant tenancy continues by virtue of section 24 of this Act.

(2) In determining the interim rent under subsection (1) above the court
shall have regard—

    (a)   to the rent payable under the terms of the relevant tenancy;
and

    (b)   to the rent payable under any sub-tenancy of part of the
property comprised in the relevant tenancy,

but otherwise subsections (1) and (2) of section 34 of this Act shall apply to the determination as they would apply to the determination of a rent under that section if a new tenancy from year to year of the whole of the property comprised in the relevant tenancy were granted to the tenant by order of the court.

(3) If the court—

    (a)   has made an order for the grant of a new tenancy and has ordered payment of interim rent in accordance with section 24C of this Act, but

    (b)   either—

       (i) it subsequently revokes under section 36(2) of this Act the order for the grant of a new tenancy; or

       (ii) the landlord and tenant agree not to act on the order,

the court on the application of the landlord or the tenant shall determine a new interim rent in accordance with subsections (1) and (2) above without a further application under section 24A(1) of this Act.

Where the three conditions set out above do not apply, the amount ordered by way of interim rent is such sum as it is "reasonable for the tenant to pay while the tenancy continues by virtue of s.24". In determining the interim the court has regard to three factors, two of which are as follows:

- the rent payable under the current tenancy; and
- the provisions of s.34(1)(2) as they would apply to a "new tenancy from year to year" for the provisions of s.34.

In practice, these two matters are dealt with in reverse order. The market rent is established on the basis of an annual tenancy and regard is then had to the old rent for the purpose of determining the amount by which the rent should be tempered.

Before turning to the factors to which the court has regard (under sub-section (2)) it is worth emphasising that the governing obligation (under sub-section (1)) is to assess an interim rent "which it is reasonable for the tenant to pay". The approach to be adopted is "broadly equivalent to that used in setting the amount of a quantum meruit . . . requiring reasonable payment to be made for some benefit conferred." (*Humber Oil Terminals Trustee Ltd v Associated British Ports* [2012] EWHC 1336 (Ch), Sales J at paras 154 and 155).

25–16   (1) *The market rent*: this is a valuation exercise to be carried out by the parties' respective experts. Under the old law (i.e. prior to June 2004) it was held that the values to be applied should be those existing when the interim rent begins to run

(*Fawke v Viscount Chelsea* [1980] Q.B. 441 at 452C) and no doubt this is still the case even though the interim rent is payable from an earlier date (para.25–08). In normal times the annual rent is likely to be lower than the rent that the tenant will have to pay under a new fixed term. Almost as a matter of convention, surveyors frequently deduct 10 per cent from the sum that they are suggesting for the new rent under the lease. However, in some periods tenants have been prepared to pay *higher* rents for periodic tenancies than for fixed terms. Thus, the amount suggested for an interim rent could be equal to or higher than the sum being suggested as the rent payable under the lease. In any event, the expert should do a valuation exercise that is appropriate to the area in which the property is situated. He should not simply reduce the figure by 10 per cent because that is "what everyone always does".

25–17   (2) *The old rent*: Having regard to the old rent is undoubtedly *a* purpose of the provision, but I do not think that it is *the* exclusive purpose of it. As stated above the overriding objective is to an order a sum "which it is reasonable for the tenant to pay". "The weight to be given to the current passing rent . . . in assessing the reasonable interim rent and the extent to which it may provide helpful guidance in setting that rent will vary depending on the circumstances of the particular case." The current passing rent does not consitute an upper limit for the interim rent under this provision. (*Humber Oil,* paras 155, 158, 159).

25–18   The third factor is that the court is required to have regard to "the rent payable" under any sub-tenancy of part of the property "comprised in the tenancy" (s.24D(2)(b)). The reason for this was explained by the Law Commission:

> " . . . if part of a property is sublet, what would otherwise be an appropriate interim rent could be seen as unfair in its impact on the intermediate tenant. The circumstances may vary considerably, and we doubt whether it is possible to devise a single firm rule to cover all cases. The matter is, nevertheless, something which should be taken into account. We therefore recommend that, in fixing an interim rent in cases where the full market is not appropriate, the court be directed to have regard to the rent payable under any sub-tenancy of any part of the property" (para.2.71).

The court has power to determine an interim rent that varies from time to time during the period of the tenancy. This has a lot to commend it where proceedings have gone on for some time. In theory, an interim rent should be determined for each year that the tenancy has continued. However, in the past the court has ordered a varied rent only in "extremely rare" circumstances (*Fawke v Viscount Chelsea* [1980] 1 Q.B. at 459—interim rent to increase when the landlord put the property into proper repair).

CHAPTER 26

NEW TENANCY ORDERED

Introduction

Landlord and Tenant Act 1954 s.29(1), (4)

26-01   **29.**–(1) Subject to the provisions of this Act, on an application under section 24(1) of this Act, the court shall make an order for the grant of a new tenancy and accordingly for the termination of the current tenancy immediately before the commencement of the new tenancy.

(4) Subject to the provisions of this Act, where the landlord makes an application under subsection (2) above—

(a)   if he establishes, to the satisfaction of the court, any of the grounds on which he is entitled to make the application in accordance with section 30 of this Act, the court shall make an order for the termination of the current tenancy in accordance with section 64 of this Act without the grant of a new tenancy; and

(b)   if not, it shall make an order for the grant of a new tenancy and accordingly for the termination of the current tenancy immediately before the commencement of the new tenancy.

Where the tenant has applied for a new tenancy, or the landlord has applied to terminate the continuation tenancy, and the landlord has either agreed (in his s.25 notice or s.26 counter-notice) to the grant of a new tenancy, or has failed to satisfy a ground of opposition to a new tenancy, the court must make an order for the grant of a tenancy (s.29(1)(4)).

The terms of the new tenancy are decided in accordance with the provisions of ss.32 to 35 of the 1954 Act. Each of these sections provides for agreement between the parties or a decision by the court in default of such agreement. To be effective, any such agreement must be binding as a matter of ordinary law (*Derby & Co v ITC Pension Trust* [1977] 2 All E.R. 890; *Leslie & Goodwin Investments Ltd v Prudential Assurance Co Ltd* [1987] 2 E.G.L.R. 95—the tenant was not bound by an agreement made subject to contract as to the rent). It must also be in writing (s.69(2)).

Landlord and Tenant Act 1954 s.69(2)

69.–(2) References in this Act to an agreement between the landlord and the tenant (except in section 17 and subsections (1) and (2) of section 38 thereof) shall be construed as references to an agreement in writing between them.

26–02

(See also s.28 of the Act, which provides for agreements.)

When considering the question of rent, the court is required to have regard to the terms of the tenancy (s.34(1)). Thus, where the court is required to determine the new terms the question of rent is always considered last (see para.26–20).

A suggested form of order where the court grants a new lease is set out in Form 23 of this book. Note that in a disputed renewal, it is not possible to specify the precise date upon which the current tenancy will come to an end in accordance with s.64 of the 1954 Act (and the new tenancy will begin) at the date the order is made because of the possibility that there might be an appeal (see para.27–03); unless of course there is an agreement between the parties (s.28; see para.A1–11 and para.26–09).

Form 23

Form A: Order for grant of new tenancy

Upon the Landlord's / Tenant's application for an order for the grant of a new tenancy under s.24(1) of the Landlord and Tenant Act 1954 IT IS ORDERED that:

  (a) The current tenancy of the premises described in the Schedule to this Order shall come to an end in accordance with the provisions of s.64 of the 1954 Act;
  (b) A new tenancy of the premises described in the Schedule to this Order shall be granted by the Landlord to the Tenant to take effect immediately after the termination of the current tenancy for the period, at the rent and on the terms set out in the said Schedule.
  (c) [Costs]

Schedule

Costs are, as always, in the discretion of the court. However, where the parties have always agreed that the tenant should be granted a new tenancy and the dispute has only been over the terms of the new tenancy then, unless the court finds substantially in favour of one party, it will usually make no order as to costs. See further para.26–35.

Execution of new lease

26-03   Where the court makes an order for the grant of a new tenancy, the tenant has a new choice. He may accept the new tenancy or he may ask the court to revoke the order, in which case, no new tenancy is granted (see further para.26-33). Where the tenant decides that he wants to accept the new tenancy ordered, the landlord must execute a lease or tenancy agreement in favour of the tenant on the terms ordered and the tenant must take the lease. If the landlord requires it, the tenant must execute a counterpart of the lease (s.36(1) of the 1954 Act—see para.26-34). The landlord cannot compel the tenant to pay the costs of the new lease (see para.26-17).

Landlord's interest subject to mortgage

26-04   A lease or tenancy granted pursuant to an order of the court under Pt II of the 1954 Act is deemed to be one authorised by s.99 of the Law of Property Act 1925 (i.e. the power conferring on mortgagors in possession power to grant leases). Mortgagees may not therefore take objection to any such lease or tenancy agreement (s.36(4); see para.26-34).

The property to be comprised in the new tenancy: "the holding"

Landlord and Tenant Act 1954 s.32

26-05   **32.**—(1) Subject to the following provisions of this section, an order under section 29 of this Act for the grant of a new tenancy shall be an order for the grant of a new tenancy of the holding; and in the absence of agreement between the landlord and the tenant as to the property which constitutes the holding the court shall in the order designate that property by reference to the circumstances existing at the date of the order.

(1A) Where the court, by virtue of paragraph (b) of section 31A(1) *of* this Act, makes an order under section 29 of this Act for the grant *of* a new tenancy in a case where the tenant is willing to accept a tenancy of part of the holding, the order shall be an order for the grant *of* a new tenancy of that part only.

(2) The foregoing provisions of this section shall not apply in a case where the property comprised in the current tenancy includes other property besides the holding and the landlord requires any new tenancy ordered to be granted under section 29 of this Act to be a tenancy of the whole of the property comprised in the current tenancy; but in any such case—

(a)   any order under the said section 29 for the grant of a new
      tenancy shall be an order for the grant of a new tenancy of the
      whole of the property comprised in the current tenancy, and
(b)   references in the following provisions of this Part of this Act to
      the holding shall be construed as references to the whole of
      that property.

(3) Where the current tenancy includes rights enjoyed by the tenant in
connection with the holding, those rights shall be included in a tenancy
ordered to be granted under section 29 of this Act, except as otherwise
agreed between the landlord and the tenant or, in default of such
agreement, determined by the court.

The basic rules

The extent of the property that is to be comprised in the new   **26-06**
tenancy is determined by s.32 of the 1954 Act. The most
important point to note is that (subject to the matters stated in
(b) below) the court may grant a tenancy only of "the holding"
(s.32(1)).

The holding is defined by s.23(3) as "the property comprised in
the tenancy, there being excluded any part thereof which is
occupied neither by the tenant nor by a person employed by the
tenant and so employed for the purposes of a business by
reason of which the tenancy is one to which Part II of the 1954
Act applies" (para.17–01). If the landlord sublets part of the
property, the part sublet does not form part of his "holding",
although the sub-tenant may well be entitled to rights under Pt
II of the Act (*Graysim Holdings Ltd v P&O Property Holdings Ltd*
[1995] 4 All E.R. 831).

Where the lease is of shop premises with residential
accommodation above and the tenant operates a business from
the shop and sublets the residential accommodation, "the
holding" will consist only of the shop and the court will order
only the shop to be included in the new tenancy. The dwelling
must be returned to the landlord. If there is a regulated tenant
under the Rent Act 1977 in occupation of the dwelling, the
landlord will not be bound by that tenancy and will be able to
recover possession at the expiry of the continuation tenancy:
(*Pittalis v Grant* [1989] 2 All E.R. 622; *Bromley Park Garden
Estates Ltd v George* [1991] 2 E.G.L.R. 95 CA)–see
para.27–07). Generally, the continuation tenancy comes to an
end three months after final disposal of the case: s.64–see
para.27–02. However, a lawfully granted assured sub-tenancy
will continue in existence when the continuation tenancy in

respect of the residential part comes to an end (see para.27–07).

It would seem that so long as the tenant's occupation is real it is irrelevant that his motive in using part of the premises is to ensure that it is included as part of the new lease (*Narcissi v Wolfe* [1960] Ch. 10).

Where the landlord and tenant cannot agree as to the property that constitutes the holding, the court in its order designates that property by reference to the circumstances existing at the date of the *order* (s.32(1)). Thus, a tenant who is able to recover possession of any part of the property that was previously sublet will be entitled to have that part included in the new lease so long as he genuinely occupies it or it is occupied by an employee for the purposes of the tenant's business even though it was not so occupied at, say, the commencement of the proceedings.

Where the landlord has opposed the grant of a new tenancy on ground (f) of s.30(1) (see para.17–10), but the court has held that the landlord can reasonably carry out the work of demolition, reconstruction or construction because the tenant is willing to accept a tenancy of an economically separate part of the holding (s.31A(1)(b); see para.17–13), the court makes an order for the grant of a new tenancy of that part only (s.32(1A); para.26–05).

Qualifications to the basic rules

26–07 The above is subject to two qualifications:

   (1) the parties may agree that more than "the holding" should be included in the new lease (s.32(1)); and
   (2) the landlord may, if he wishes, insist upon the new tenancy including "the whole of the property comprised in the current tenancy" (s.32(2)). See paras 14–19, 24–25 and 24–29 for the requirements to notify the tenant of this wish.

Ancillary rights

26–08 Where the current tenancy includes rights enjoyed by the tenant in connection with the *holding* (see para.26–05 above), the court orders those rights to be included in the new tenancy unless the landlord and tenant agree otherwise or, in default of such agreement, the court determines otherwise (s.32(3)).

The word "rights" in this context includes rights in the nature of easements, where they are additional to other property included in the current tenancy (*Nevill Long and Co (Boards) Ltd v Firmenich and Co* [1983] 2 E.G.L.R. 76–tenant enjoyed under its lease rights of way over adjoining land also owned by the landlord, which gave access to the rear of the demised premises. During the contractual term of the lease, that adjoining land was sold to a third party. A declaration was granted that the rights of way would continue under Part 2 of the 1954 Act after the expiry of the contractual term).

Purely personal rights fall outside the scope of s.32(3) but the court might nonetheless use its powers under s.35(1) (para.26–14) to include them in the lease at least where they were included in a term of the old lease (*No. 1 Albemarle Street, Re* [1959] 2 W.L.R. 171–where the tenant enjoyed a permission under the terms of the old lease to maintain advertising signs on land outside the demise. Held: this was not a right covered by s.32(3) but was a term that could be included using the jurisdiction conferred by s.35(1) when determining "the other terms" of the new tenancy).

However, in *Picture Warehouse Ltd v Cornhill Investments Ltd* [2008] EWHC 45 QB, the tenant had the benefit of a licence (contained in a letter that was therefore not part of the tenancy) from the landlord for its customers and delivery men to park on the forecourt outside the demised premises. On renewing the lease the tenant was unable to obtain a term of the new lease giving it parking rights. It was not a right to which s.32(3) could apply; whatever rights the tenancy had were outside the lease and so outside the section. The section could not be read broadly to include rights not included in the tenancy but which has previously been enjoyed with the tenancy (para.17 of the judgment). and there was no jurisdiction under s.35(1) permitting the court to order the grant of a right over the landlord's land that the tenant had not previously enjoyed. The court did have power under s.35(1) to include in the new tenancy a provision conferring on the tenant a right no greater than that given by the letter. However, in the circumstances of the case it was not appropriate to do so. On the facts of the case it was right, as a matter of the court's discretion, to leave the tenant to rely on the terms of the letter for such rights as the letter gave (para.19 of the judgment).

An option to purchase the reversion, which existed in the old lease, is not a right that may be included in the new lease (*Kirkwood v Johnson* (1979) 38 P. & C.R. 392).

Duration of new tenancy

Introduction

Landlord and Tenant Act 1954 s.33

26-09   **33.** Where on an application under this Part of this Act the court makes an order for the grant of a new tenancy, the new tenancy shall be such tenancy as may be agreed between the landlord and the tenant, or, in default of such an agreement, shall be such a tenancy as may be determined by the court to be reasonable in all the circumstances, being, if it is a tenancy for a term of years certain, a tenancy for a term not exceeding fifteen years, and shall begin on the coming to an end of the current tenancy.

The parties may agree the length of the new tenancy. If they fail to agree, the court will order such tenancy as it considers "to be reasonable in all the circumstances" subject to a maximum term of 15 years (s.33). The court may order the granting of a periodic tenancy. Unless the parties agree on a different date, the new tenancy commences on the coming to an end of the current tenancy, i.e. generally three months after the case is finally disposed of (s.64; para.27-02). In order to achieve certainty, it is wise for the parties to agree (or the court to order) a term to commence on a fixed date (*Warwick & Warwick (Philately) Ltd v Shell (UK) Ltd* (1981) 42 P. & C.R. 136 CA).

In deciding the length of the term to be ordered, the court will in the first instance have regard to the length of the previous tenancy (*Betty's Café Ltd v Phillips Furnishing Stores Ltd* [1959] A.C. 20) but in all cases the court must order what is reasonable in all the circumstances.

For a case in which the tenantasked for a very short term and the landlord argued for the maximum term (which was then 14 years), see *CBS United Kingdom Ltd v London Scottish Properties Ltd* [1985] 2 E.G.L.R. 125 Ch D. The original lease was for a term of 10 years. The tenant wanted a year to permit it to make an orderly departure to new premises. The landlord argued that a term shorter than 14 years would materially diminish the capital value of its interest. The judge found in favour of the tenant.

The new tenancy will itself be subject to the protection afforded by Pt II of the 1954 Act (*National Car Parks Ltd v The Paternoster Consortium Ltd* [1990] 1 E.G.L.R. 99 at 102J).

Future redevelopment by landlord intended

It may be that the landlord is unable to show an intention to demolish or reconstruct the property at the conclusion of the current tenancy (and is therefore unable to object to the grant of a new tenancy pursuant to s.30(1)(f); see para.27–05) but does wish to redevelop the property at some stage in the future. In these circumstances, the court will take into account his intention to redevelop when considering the length of the lease to be ordered and may order the grant of a shorter lease than it would otherwise have done. Alternatively, it may order inclusion in the tenancy of a "redevelopment clause", i.e. a break clause entitling the landlord to determine the lease during its term in the event of his intending to redevelop. (*National Car Parks Ltd v The Paternoster Consortium Ltd* [1990] 1 E.G.L.R. 99.)

26–10

> "There is no dispute as to the relevant law applicable. In cases where a landlord is unable to show that he is immediately in a position to effect a desired reconstruction of the land comprised in the tenancy, if there is a real possibility (as opposed to a probability), that the premises in question will be required for construction during the continuance of the proposed new tenancy, it is right to include in the terms of the new tenancy a break clause which will enable such reconstruction to take place. It is not the policy lying behind Part II of the 1954 Act to permit the rights of the tenant under the new tenancy to stand in the way of reconstruction and redevelopment of commercial property." (*National Car Parks Ltd* at p.101 per Browne-Wilkinson V.C.)

In deciding what length of term to order, the court has to balance two considerations:

(1) that, so far as reasonable, the lease should not prevent the landlord from using the property for the purposes of development; and

(2) that a reasonable degree of security should be provided to the tenant.

These considerations are to some degree in conflict and the function of the court is to strike a reasonable balance between them in all the circumstances of the case (see *Edwards (JH) & Sons Ltd v Central London Commercial Estates Ltd* (1983) 271 E.G. 697, per Fox LJ at p.698; *Becker v Hill Street Properties Ltd* [1990] 2 E.G.L.R. 78 CA—a more recent case in which the main authorities were reviewed).

26-11   By way of example, in *Adams v Green* (1978) 247 E.G. 49 the property was a shop in a line of 12 "rather elderly" shops. The landlord wanted the new lease of the shop to include a break clause to allow reconstruction at a future date in view of the prospects of redevelopment by the landlord or its successor. Seven of the other shops had similar break clauses and the landlord was negotiating similar terms in respect of the remainder. A new lease of 14 years was ordered to include a break clause to operate on two years' notice, to be operable only in the event of subsequent redevelopment.

In *Adams v Green* the Court of Appeal drew attention to the fact that there is some protection for the tenant against improper service of a notice pursuant to a redevelopment clause because, if the landlord does determine the tenancy under the clause, the tenant can apply for a new tenancy under the 1954 Act. The landlord then has to prove the intention to redevelop. (See also *National Car Parks Ltd v The Paternoster Consortium Ltd*, at 102J on this point.) Further, if the landlord obtains possession by a misrepresentation as to his intention, the tenant will be entitled to compensation under s.37A of the Act (see para.27-27).

In *Amika Motors Ltd v Colebrook Holdings Ltd* (1981) 259 E.G. 243 it was going to be feasible to carry out the development with the tenants in occupation but at greater cost and more slowly. The court granted a five-year lease with a landlord's option to determine by giving not less than six months' notice.

(See also the position where the landlord is able to show that he intends to redevelop or occupy within a period of not more than 12 months from the date specified in the s.25 notice or s.26 request: para.27–05.)

Landlord's future intention to occupy

It has been seen that the landlord may not rely upon s.30(1)(g), **26–12** an intention to occupy for own use, if the landlord is caught by the five-year rule (para.17–19). He may, however, be able to argue for a term that will permit him to bring the tenancy to an end once the period of five years has expired (*Wig Creations v Colour Film Services* (1969) 20 P. & C.R. 870 CA).

Terms of new tenancy other than the amount of rent

The terms of the new tenancy other than those relating to **26–13** duration and rent are such as may be agreed between the parties or, in default of agreement, as determined by the court. In determining the terms of the new tenancy, the court will have regard to the terms of the current tenancy and all the relevant circumstances including the effects of the Landlord and Tenant (Covenants) Act 1995 (s.35).

Landlord and Tenant Act 1954 s.35(1), (2)

35.–(1) The terms of a tenancy granted by order of the court under this **26–14** Part of this Act (other than terms as to the duration thereof and as to the rent payable thereunder), including, where different persons own interests which fulfil the conditions specified in section 44(1) of this Act in different parts of it, terms as to the apportionment of the rent, shall be such as may be agreed between the landlord and the tenant or as, in default of such agreement, may be determined by the court; and in determining those terms the court shall have regard to the terms of the current tenancy and to all relevant circumstances.

(2) In subsection (1) of this section the reference to all relevant circumstances includes (without prejudice to the generality of that reference) a reference to the operation of the provisions of the Landlord and Tenant (Covenants) Act 1995.

The court has a wide power under s.35 to change the terms or impose new terms but the burden of persuading the court to alter the existing terms rests on the party proposing the change. That party must show that the change is fair and reasonable in all the circumstances (*O'May v City of London Real Property* [1982] 1 All E.R. 660).

In *O'May* the landlord wished the terms of the tenancy to be changed so as to create a "clear lease", i.e. a lease by which the tenant was to become responsible for the cost of all the outgoings on maintenance, repairs and services to the building. In return, the landlord offered a reduction in the proposed rent but the tenant objected to the arrangement. The House of Lords held that the landlord had failed to show that the proposed change was fair and reasonable.

> " . . . I do not in any way suggest that the court is intended or should in any way attempt to bind the parties to the terms of the current tenancy in any permanent form. But I do believe that the court must begin by considering the terms of the current tenancy, that the burden of persuading the court to impose a change in those terms against the will of either party must rest on the party proposing the change and that the change proposed must, in the circumstances of the case, be fair and reasonable and should take into account, amongst other things, the comparatively weak negotiating position of a sitting tenant requiring renewal, particularly in conditions of scarcity, and the general purpose of the Act which is to protect the business interests of the tenant so far as they are affected by the approaching termination of the current lease, in particular as regards his security of tenure.
>
> . . . There must in my view be a good reason based in the absence of agreement on essential fairness for the court to impose a new term not in the current lease by either party on the other against his will. Any other conclusion would in my view be inconsistent with the terms of the section. But, subject to this the discretion of the court is of the widest possible kind, having regard to the almost infinitely varying circumstances of individual leases, properties, business and parties involved in business tenancies all over the country." (*O'May v City of London Real Property Co Ltd* [1982] 1 All E.R. 660, per Lord Hailsham at 665e, j.)
>
> " . . . [section 35] contains a mandatory guideline or direction to 'have regard to' the terms of the current tenancy and to all relevant circumstances. The words 'have regard to' are elastic: they compel something

between an obligation to reproduce existing terms and an unfettered right to substitute others. They impose an onus upon a party seeking to introduce new, or substituted, or modified terms, to justify the change, with reasons appearing sufficient to the court (see *Gold* v *Brighton Corp* [1956] 1 W.L.R. 1291—on "strong and cogent evidence" per Denning LJ; *Cardshops Ltd* v *Davies* [1971] 1 W.L.R. 591, 596 per Widgery LJ)

If such reasons are shown, then the court, applying the words 'all relevant circumstances', may consider giving effect to them: there is certainly no intention shown to freeze or, in the metaphor used by learned counsel, to 'petrify' the terms of the lease. In some cases, especially where the lease is an old one, many of its terms may be out of date, or unsuitable in relation to the new term to be granted. If so or for other good reasons shown, the court has power to order a modification by changing an existing term or introducing a new one (e.g. a break clause, cf. *Adams* v *Green*). Before doing so it will consider any objections by the tenant, and where there is an insoluble conflict, will decide according to fairness and justice.

. . .

There is no obligation, under section 35 of the Act, to make the new terms conform with market practice, if to do so would be unfair to the tenant. And there is no inherent necessity why the terms on which existing leases are to be renewed should be dictated by those of fresh bargains which tenants may feel themselves obliged to accept. The court has to compare the advantage desired by the landlord with the detriment to be suffered by the tenants and to consider whether any monetary compensation offered against that detriment ought fairly to be imposed upon the tenants in exchange for the acceptance of that detriment. That money is not necessarily fair compensation for a change in existing rights is obvious in itself and is well recognised by the law in relation, for example, to compulsory acquisition and to the granting of damages instead of an injunction." (*O'May*, per Lord Wilberforce)

In *Edwards & Walkden (Norfolk) Ltd v The Mayor & Commonalty & Citizens of the City of London* [2012] EWHC 2527 the court applied the principles in *O'May* but came to a different conclusion on the facts and ordered that there should be a variable service charge inserted into the new leases. (The claims related to stalls, shops and offices in Smithfield Market). One distinguishing factor was that the lease in *O'May* was for a term of 3 years, whereas as the new lease in this case was to be for a term of fifteen years. Sales J at [82]:

> "In my judgment, there are significant differences between this case and the position in *O'May*. Applying the guidance in *O'May* as a whole, I consider that the City has shown that there are good and sufficient reasons good and sufficient reasons to justify a change in the payment structure under the new tenancies back to the original structure of a rent and variable service charge which formed part of the early 1980s leases between the parties."

The largest element of the costs was, in effect, the costs to the tenants of running their businesses and (at [92]) the judge considered that:

> " . . . the tenants are better placed than the [landlord] to manage and control such costs, by being able to adapt their behaviour (and that of their employees) to some degree so as to minimise such costs in a way that the [landlord] cannot readily do. The extent to which there may be scope for the tenants to do this will vary depending on the particular service in issue, but I consider that it is likely that the tenants will generally be more sensitive to the costs of provision of these services (such as cleaning) if they can see clearly year by year how such costs are affected by their actions."

See also para.24–45.

Surety provisions

26–15   The court has jurisdiction under s.35 to include a term requiring the tenant to provide sureties to guarantee observance by the tenant of the terms of the lease (*Cairnplace Ltd v CBL Property Investment Co Ltd* [1984] 1 All E.R. 315). (See also the specific provision in s.41A(6) in relation to partnerships: para.2–27.) See also para.26–19.

Divided reversions

In the rare case where the reversion expectant on the current **26–16** tenancy is divided, an issue arises as to whether or not there should be one new tenancy with different landlords as before or separate tenancies of each part of the building owned by each separate landlord. The amendment to s.35 referring to apportionment of rent clearly implies that there should be one tenancy, with the rent apportioned accordingly.

(For service of s.25 notices where the reversion is divided, see para.14–22 and for service of s.26 requests, see para.15–09.)

Landlord's costs of the new lease

Section 1 of the Costs of Leases Act 1958 provides that "a **26–17** party to a lease shall, unless the parties thereto agree otherwise in writing, be under no obligation to pay the whole or any part of any other party's solicitor's costs of the lease". In *Cairnplace Ltd v CBL Property Investment Co Ltd* [1984] 1 All E.R. 315 it was held that it was an improper exercise of the court's discretion under s.35 of the 1954 Act to deprive the tenant of the protection of s.1 of the 1958 Act and that the court should not therefore include a term in the new tenancy requiring the tenant to pay the landlord costs, *even if* the current tenancy contains such a term.

Rent review clauses: upwards and downwards

Traditionally, rent review clauses in leases have been "upwards **26–18** only", i.e. they have provided that the rent should never fall below the current rent (often referred to as the "passing rent") at each review even if market conditions would otherwise provide for the rent to go down. However, in periods of recession landlords can find it difficult to let their properties and some tenants taking new leases in the open market negotiate rent review clauses that allow the rent to go up or down to the market rent existing at the date of the review. As a result, tenants applying for new tenancies under the 1954 Act have at those periods sought to have similar terms in their new leases.

Although it is s.34 of the 1954 Act that contains an express provision permitting the court to include a rent review clause (s.34(3); see para.26–20), it would seem that in deciding the terms of that clause the court should have regard to the factors set out in s.35 and therefore also the decision in *O'May* (see above). Thus, the fact that the original tenancy had an upwards only rent review clause will put the initial burden on the tenant to satisfy the court that there should be a change. The view of the author is that the most important factor then to be taken into account is the state of the market in the area of the property (as opposed to a more generalised sense of fairness or decisions in other reported cases). If other tenants in the open market are able to negotiate such a term, this should be a powerful factor in determining the issue. See also para.24–45.

Authorised guarantee agreements

26–19   As has been seen in Ch.13, it is now possible for a landlord, on being asked to agree to an assignment of a lease, to require the existing tenant to enter into an authorised guarantee agreement (para.13–21). It is also possible for a landlord, on granting a lease, to make it a condition of consent to an assignment that an authorised guarantee agreement be entered into (para.10–12). Hence, when terms for a new tenancy are being considered, the landlord should argue for a covenant containing a right to refuse consent unless the current tenant enters into an authorised guarantee agreement. However, the term will be such that the landlord will only be able to insist upon the AGA where reasonable (*Wallis Fashion Group Ltd v CGU Life Assurance Ltd* [2000] 2 E.G.L.R. 49, Neuberger J).

Rent payable under the new tenancy

Landlord and Tenant Act 1954 s.34

26–20   **34.**–(1) The rent payable under a tenancy granted by order of the court under this Part of this Act shall be such as may be agreed between the landlord and the tenant or as, in default of such agreement, may be determined by the court to be that at which, having regard to the terms of the tenancy (other than those relating to rent), the holding might reasonably be expected to be let in the open market by a willing lessor, there being disregarded—

   (a)   any effect on rent of the fact that the tenant has or his predecessors in title have been in occupation of the holding,

(b)   any goodwill attached to the holding by reason of the carrying on thereat of the business of the tenant (whether by him or by a predecessor of his in that business),

(c)   any effect on rent of an improvement to which this paragraph applies,

(d)   in the case of a holding comprising licensed premises, any addition to its value attributable to the licence, if it appears to the court that having regard to the terms of the current tenancy and any other relevant circumstances the benefit of the licence belongs to the tenant.

(2) Paragraph (c) of the foregoing subsection applies to any improvement carried out by a person who at the time it was carried out was the tenant, but only if it was carried out otherwise than in pursuance of an obligation to his immediate landlord, and either it was carried out during the current tenancy or the following conditions are satisfied, that is to say—

(a)   that it was completed not more than twenty-one years before the application to the court was made; and

(b)   that the holding or any part of it affected by the improvement has at all times since the completion of the improvement been comprised in tenancies of the description specified in section 23(1) of this Act; and

(c)   that at the termination of each of those tenancies the tenant did not quit.

(2A) If this Part of this Act applies by virtue of section 23(1A) of this Act, the reference in subsection (1)(d) above to the tenant shall be construed as including—

(a)   a company in which the tenant has a controlling interest, or

(b)   where the tenant is a company, a person with a controlling interest in the company.

(3) Where the rent is determined by the court the court may, if it thinks fit, further determine that the terms of the tenancy shall include such provision for varying the rent as may be specified in the determination.

(4) It is hereby declared that the matters which are to be taken into account by the court in determining the rent include any effect on rent of the operation of the provisions of the Landlord and Tenant (Covenants) Act 1995.

The legal principles

The rent payable under the new tenancy is such amount as may be agreed between the landlord and the tenant or in default of agreement as may be determined by the court in accordance with the provisions of s.34 (see para.26-20). Section 34(1) provides that, in determining the rent, regard must be had to the other terms of the tenancy. The court should therefore determine the duration of the new tenancy and the other terms of the lease before considering the amount of rent to be paid

26-21

(*Cardshops Ltd v Davies* [1971] 2 All E.R. 721 CA; see also para.24–44).

The rent payable is an open market rent but the section sets out a number of factors that are to be disregarded when determining that rent. The rent may be a rent that varies depending on the different circumstances that may occur from time to time (*Fawke v Viscount Chelsea* [1979] 3 All E.R. 568 CA). The new tenancy may contain a rent review clause (s.34(3)).

A market can be an open market even though most of the persons occupying premises in that market belonged to a particular profession or engaged in a particular trade. (*Baptist v Masters of the Bench and Trustees of the Honourable Society of Gray's Inn* [1993] 42 E.G. 287, county court—barristers.)

The Act expressly states that, in determining the rent, the court must take into account the effect on rent of the operation of the provisions of the Landlord and Tenant (Covenants) Act 1995.

The only matters to be disregarded when assessing the market rent are those set out in s.34 (*J Murphy & Sons Ltd v Railtrack plc* [2002] EWCA Civ 679).

In *Trans-World Investments Ltd v Anita Dadarwalla* [2007] EWCA Civ 480 it was held that the trial judge should not have disregarded the rent payable under the previous lease. The judge was also wrong to disregard valuation evidence of a neighbouring property as a "rogue figure" on the basis that there was no evidence as to the circumstances in which the rent was calculated. Mummery LJ at para.30:

> "In my judgment, the judge was wrong to disregard the passing rent and the rent of No 106 on the basis stated by him. The rents under the current lease and of the adjoining property at No 106 are relevant valuation evidence of market rent of the Property without the need for the court to require the party relying on those rents to produce positive evidence of the circumstances in which they were determined. Rather it is for the party who challenges the relevance of the passing rent and/or the rent of the adjoining property to adduce evidence of circumstances relied on to show that the rents are *not* relevant factors in

the valuation exercise of determining the open market rent."

As to apportionment of the rent where the reversion is divided, see above, para.26-16.)

(See s.23(1A) where the property is occupied by a company in which the tenant has a controlling interest or where the tenant is a company and the property is occupied by a person with a controlling interest in the company (para.2-21). Where one is concerned with a trust, see s.41(1)(b) at para.2-24; and where one is concerned with a group of companies see s.42(2)(b) at para.2-23.)

Valuation evidence: hearsay

The court determines the open market rental by hearing expert valuation evidence from the parties' valuers. At case management stage an order will be made for a single joint expert or for the exchange of experts' reports and for the giving of such evidence at trial (see para.24-44). The valuer selected should be suitably qualified, such as a fellow of the Royal Institution of Chartered Surveyors, and experienced in dealing with cases similar to the subject property. In a case, where each side has its own expert a direction should be made for the valuers to meet and to agree as much as possible (para.24-44). In particular, they should be able to agree the measurements of the property and the details of the comparables to be relied upon.

26-22

Valuers rely on two main factors when assessing rental values: (1) their general experience and "feel" for a particular case; and (2) evidence of comparable lettings in the area (commonly known as "comparables").

The expert valuer will often be able to give evidence of transactions that he has negotiated personally. However, valuers often also telephone colleagues in the neighbourhood and ask for details of comparable cases that those colleagues have negotiated. Such information is hearsay and it used to be the rule that, in the absence of agreement, the parties could rely only upon comparables that they were able to prove by admissible evidence (*English Exporters (London) Ltd v Eldonwall Ltd* [1973] 1 All E.R. 726). However, s.1 of the Civil Evidence Act 1995 now provides that hearsay evidence, of whatever degree, is admissible. Valuers may therefore give evidence of comparables that they have not personally negotiated. The Act provides for the giving of notice and particulars of the evidence to be relied upon (s.2). In lease renewal cases, exchange of experts' reports containing details of the comparables to be relied upon, with the source of the information, should usually provide sufficient notice. Considerations that are relevant to the weight to be attached to hearsay evidence are set out in s.3 of the Act.

Valuers usually use "transaction sheets" to show the details of comparable properties to be relied upon. These set out the rent and in shorthand form the principal terms of the leases of those properties. The sheets are signed by the agents who dealt with the particular transactions. These transaction sheets are exhibited to the expert's report. The more detail they contain the better because what at first sight might appear to be small variations in lease terms may have a substantial effect on the rent payable. If possible, copies of the relevant leases should be obtained and brought to court. If a valuer is relying on one of his own cases as a comparable he should disclose its existence in his initial report and should bring to court his file relating to that property.

Where a party adduces hearsay evidence of a statement made by a person and does not call that person as a witness, any other party to the proceedings may, with the permission of the court, call that person as a witness and cross-examine him on the statement (s.3). This provision may be of importance in cases where one side produces a comparable that the other side's surveyor says was induced by factors other than ordinary market forces. For example, a tenant may agree to a particularly high rent where he has forgotten to apply to the court for a new lease within the time set by the 1954 Act. If he does not agree the landlord's unreasonable rent he will have to leave the property and suffer severe disruption to his business. Such a comparable is not very good evidence of the market value of the property and the tenant in the proceedings may wish to cross-examine the person who gave the particulars of the comparable on these facts.

Civil Evidence Act 1995 ss.1–4

26–23   1.–(1) In civil proceedings evidence shall not be excluded on the ground that it is hearsay.

(2) In this Act—

    (a)   "hearsay" means a statement made otherwise than by a person while giving oral evidence in the proceedings which is tendered as evidence of the matters stated; and

    (b)   references to hearsay include hearsay of whatever degree.

(3) Nothing in this Act affects the admissibility of evidence admissible apart from this section.

(4) The provisions of sections 2 to 6 (safeguards and supplementary provisions relating to hearsay evidence) do not apply in relation to hearsay evidence admissible apart from this section, notwithstanding that it may also be admissible by virtue of this section.

2.—(1) A party proposing to adduce hearsay evidence in civil proceedings shall, subject to the following provisions of this section, give to the other party or parties to the proceedings—

    (a)   such notice (if any) of that fact, and

    (b)   on request, such particulars of or relating to the evidence,

as is reasonable and practicable in the circumstances for the purpose of enabling him or them to deal with any matters arising from its being hearsay.

(2) Provision may be made by rules of court—

    (a)   specifying classes of proceedings or evidence in relation to which subsection (1) does not apply, and

    (b)   as to the manner in which (including the time within which) the duties imposed by that subsection are to be complied with in the cases where it does apply.

(3) Subsection (1) may also be excluded by agreement of the parties; and compliance with the duty to give notice may in any case be waived by the person to whom notice is required to be given.

(4) A failure to comply with subsection (1), or with rules under subsection (2)(b), does not affect the admissibility of the evidence but may be taken into account by the court—

    (a)   in considering the exercise of its powers with respect to the course of proceedings and costs, and

    (b)   as a matter adversely affecting the weight to be given to the evidence in accordance with section 4.

3. Rules of court may provide that where a party to civil proceedings adduces hearsay evidence of a statement made by a person and does not call that person as a witness, any other party to the proceedings may, with the leave of the court, call that person as a witness and cross-examine him on the statement as if he had been called by the first-mentioned party and as if the hearsay statement were his evidence in chief.

4.—(1) In estimating the weight (if any) to be given to hearsay evidence in civil proceedings the court shall have regard to any circumstances from which any inference can reasonably be drawn as to the reliability or otherwise of the evidence.

(2) Regard may be had, in particular, to the following—

(a)   whether it would have been reasonable and practicable for the party by whom the evidence was adduced to have produced the maker of the original statement as a witness;

(b)   whether the original statement was made contemporaneously with the occurrence or existence of the matters stated;

(c)   whether the evidence involves multiple hearsay;

(d)   whether any person involved had any motive to conceal or misrepresent matters;

(e)   whether the original statement was an edited account, or was made in collaboration with another or for a particular purpose;

(f)   whether the circumstances in which the evidence is adduced as hearsay are such as to suggest an attempt to prevent proper evaluation of its weight.

Evidence of rent reviews

26–24   In addition to evidence of rents negotiated in the open market between parties who have not previously been in a landlord and tenant relationship, valuers will rely upon revised rents, agreed pursuant to rent review clauses in leases of other properties. Such evidence is admissible but is not of the same value as an open market transaction. However, it is not permissible to rely upon a rent review determined by an arbitrator in a rent review arbitration or a new rent determined by a judge in another lease renewal case. The verdict of another tribunal is not admissible evidence because it is a statement of opinion based upon other evidence before it (*Land Securities plc v Westminster City Council* [1993] 4 All E.R. 124 Ch D—an arbitration case but the principle would apply to court hearings; see Hoffmann LJ at 127a):

> "The issue in the arbitration is the rent at which the premises could reasonably have been let in the open market at the rent review date. Evidence of the rents at which comparable properties were actually let in the open market at about the same time is relevant and if properly proved admissible because the fact that someone was willing to pay a certain rent for a property can justify an inference that he or someone else would have been willing to pay a similar rent for a comparable property. A rent which is agreed between the parties at a rent review is admissible on similar grounds although it suffers from the disadvantage that such transactions are not in the open market. The parties are not free to refuse to deal. They bargain under the constraint that if they do not agree, a rent representing an arbitrator's or expert's view of the

reasonable market rent will be imposed upon them. But these matters go to the weight of the evidence rather than its admissibility. It is admissible because it shows what an actual landlord and tenant were willing to agree in a transaction in which real money was to change hands. An arbitration award on the other hand is an arbitrator's opinion, after hearing the evidence before him of the rent at which the premises could reasonably have been let. The letting is hypothetical, not real. It is therefore not direct evidence of what was happening in the market. It is the arbitrator's opinion of what would have happened . . .

Even if [the arbitrator] or someone else were in a position to give admissible evidence of the comparables that support his opinion I think that his award would still be inadmissible on another ground. It would involve a collateral inquiry as to whether [the arbitrator] came to the right decision in his own arbitration. The result of such inquiry would, in my judgment, have insufficient relevance to the issue in the present arbitration to justify undertaking it . . .

. . . This is not in my view a technical decision on outdated rules of evidence. Properly analysed I think that the arbitrator's award has in itself insufficient weight to justify the exploration of otherwise irrelevant issues which its admissibility would require." (*Land Securities*, per Hoffmann LJ at 125f, 128f.)

Valuation principles: ITZA

When assessing the rent in respect of a shop, the valuer will **26–25** also have regard to "zones". Zone A is the front 20 feet of the shop. Zone B is the second 20 feet. Zone C is the next 20 feet. Occasionally, 30 ft zones are used. (Although metric measurements are made they are still converted to imperial for this technique.) The valuer assesses the rent per square foot for Zone A, halves it for Zone B and halves it again for Zone C. For example, if the valuer considers that Zone A should be valued at £20 per square foot, Zone B will be valued at £10 per square foot and Zone C will be valued at £5 per square foot. In a deep shop, there will be a Zone D for the remainder valued at one-eighth of Zone A. This valuation technique reflects the benefit of having space at the front of the shop where it is most visible and therefore most valuable.

If the phrase "ITZA" appears in the valuer's report it means "in terms of Zone A" and refers to the total area of the shop based on the Zone A rent. To determine the total area of the shop "in terms of Zone A" the valuer takes the square footage of the Zone A area; he then takes the square footage of the Zone B area and divides it in half; and then he takes the square footage of the Zone C area and divides it by 4. He adds up the three areas and multiplies the result by the suggested Zone A rent to get a rental for the whole shop.

Example:

Actual area of Zone A: 100 square feet	ITZA 100 sq feet
Actual area of Zone B: 100 square feet	ITZA 50 sq feet
Actual area of Zone C: 200 square feet	ITZA 50 sq feet
	Total ITZA 200 sq feet
Rental for Zone A—£10 per sq foot	x £10 per sq foot
Suggested rent for the premises	£2,000

Other valuation principles

26-26 Other valuation principles that are commonly relied upon when considering rental values are as follows:

(1) The amount of rent is affected by the user clause in the lease. The more restrictive the clause, the lower the rent will be. Conversely, a lease with an open user clause will command a higher rent. A user clause that permits the tenant to put the property to any use to which the landlord has given consent but that precludes the landlord from unreasonably refusing his consent is invariably treated for valuation purposes as an open user clause.

(2) A further factor that affects the amount of the rent is the rent review "pattern" in the lease, that is the number of years between rent reviews. The greater the period between each rent review the higher the rent is likely to be so as to compensate the landlord for having to wait until the next review for an increase.

(3) When the property is a shop, its location is an important factor. The terms "primary", "secondary" and "tertiary" are used when discussing location. A primary location, such as on a busy high street with good transport facilities obviously commands a higher rent than a tertiary location such as an isolated shop in a back street.

Evidence relating to the profitability of the tenant's business is almost invariably irrelevant and the tenant will not be ordered to disclose his accounts (*Humber Oil Terminals Trustee Ltd v Associated British Ports* [2011] EWHC 1184 (Ch)).The court is only likely to admit evidence of the tenant's trading position, as a guide to the open market rent, where there are no comparable properties from which the open market rent can be deduced and the property is such that it has been specially adapted for the business concerned, for example a hotel, filling station, theatre or racecourse (*W J Barton v Long Acre Securities Ltd* [1982] 1 All E.R. 465 CA).

In *Cornwall Coast Country Club v Cardgrange Ltd* [1987] 1 E.G.L.R. 146 the court held that an arbitrator in a rent review case was entitled to take into account the profit earning capacity of a casino in determining the rent. However, only accounts that would have been available to prospective tenants in the hypothetical open market at the valuation date were admissible (see also *Ritz Hotel (London) Ltd v Ritz Casino Ltd* [1989] 46 E.G. 95).

Effect on superior landlords where competent landlord not the freehold owner: Sch.6

It is possible that the new term ordered by the court will extend **26–27** beyond the duration of the tenant's immediate landlord. Schedule 6 therefore provides the court with powers to deal with the position where there are intermediate landlords between the competent landlord and the tenant. They are as follows:

(1) Where the new tenancy will extend beyond the date of the immediate landlord's interest (or that of the immediate landlord and other superior landlords together), the court has power to grant reversionary interests so as to ensure that the combined effects of the grant will result in there being reversionary interests for the period of the new tenancy (para.2).

(2) Any agreement as to the granting, duration or terms of a new tenancy made by competent landlords binds mesne landlords (para.3), subject to the right to compensation of the mesne landlords who do not give their consent (para.4).

(3) Where the competent landlord is himself a tenant, he may not agree a new tenancy with the tenant extending beyond the date of his interest without the consent of all superior landlords (para.5).

Schedule 6 contains other provisions relevant to the situation where the competent landlord is not the freeholder. These have been referred to in the relevant parts of this book.

Landlord and Tenant Act 1954 Sch.6

Definitions

26-28   1. In this Schedule the following expressions have the meanings hereby assigned to them in relation to a tenancy (in this Schedule referred to as "the relevant tenancy"), that is to say:

"the competent landlord" means the person who in relation to the tenancy is for the time being the landlord (as defined by section 44 of this Act) for the purposes of Part II of this Act;

"mesne landlord" means a tenant whose interest is intermediate between the relevant tenancy and the interest of the competent landlord; and

"superior landlord" means a person (whether the owner of the fee simple or a tenant) whose interest is superior to the interest of the competent landlord.

Power of court to order reversionary tenancies

2. Where the period of which in accordance with the provisions of Part II of this Act it is agreed or determined by the court that a new tenancy should be granted thereunder will extend beyond the date on which the interest of the immediate landlord will come to an end, the power of the court under Part II of this Act to order such a grant shall include power to order the grant of a new tenancy until the expiration of that interest and also to order the grant of such a revisionary tenancy or reversionary tenancies as may be required to secure that the combined effects of those grants will be equivalent to the grant of a tenancy for that period; and the provisions of Part II of this Act shall, subject to the necessary modifications, apply in relation to the grant of a tenancy together with one or more reversionary tenancies as they apply in relation to the grant of one new tenancy.

Acts of competent landlord binding on other landlords

3.−(1) Any notice given by the competent landlord under Part II of this Act to terminate the relevant tenancy, and any agreement made between that landlord and the tenant as to the granting, duration, or terms of a future tenancy, being an agreement made for the purposes of the said Part II, shall bind the interest of any mesne landlord notwithstanding that he has not consented to the giving of the notice or was not a party to the agreement.

(2) The competent landlord shall have power for the purposes of Part II of this Act to give effect to any agreement with the tenant for the grant of a new tenancy beginning with the coming to an end of the relevant tenancy, notwithstanding that the competent landlord will not be the immediate landlord at the commencement of the new tenancy, and any instrument made in the exercise of the power conferred by this sub-paragraph shall have effect as if the mesne landlord had been a party thereto.

(3) Nothing in the foregoing provisions of this paragraph shall prejudice the provisions of the next following paragraph.

Provisions as to consent of mesne landlord to acts of competent landlord

4.–(1) If the competent landlord, not being the immediate landlord, gives any such notice or makes any such agreement as is mentioned in sub-paragraph (1) of the last foregoing sub-paragraph without the consent of every mesne landlord, any mesne landlord whose consent has not been given thereto shall be entitled to compensation from the competent landlord for any loss arising in consequence of the giving of the notice or the making of the agreement.

(2) If the competent landlord applies to any mesne landlord for his consent to such a notice or agreement, that consent shall not be unreasonably withheld, but may be given subject to any conditions which may be reasonable (including conditions as to the modification of the proposed notice or agreement or as to the payment of compensation by the competent landlord).

(3) Any question under this paragraph whether consent has been unreasonably withheld or whether any conditions imposed on the giving of consent are unreasonable shall be determined by the court.

Consent of superior landlord required for agreements affecting his interest

5. An agreement between the competent landlord and the tenant made for the purposes of Part II of this Act in a case where—

26–29

    (a)   the competent landlord is himself a tenant, and
    (b)   the agreement would apart from this paragraph operate as respects any period after the coming to an end of the interest of the competent landlord,

shall not have effect unless every superior landlord who will be the immediate landlord of the tenant during any part of that period is a party to the agreement.

Withdrawal by competent landlord of notice given by mesne landlord

6. Where the competent landlord has given a notice under section 25 of this Act to terminate the relevant tenancy and, within two months after the giving of the notice, a superior landlord—

(a)   becomes the competent landlord; and

(b)   gives to the tenant notice in the prescribed form that he withdraws the notice previously given,

the notice under section 25 of this Act shall cease to have effect, but without prejudice to the giving of a further notice under that section by the competent landlord.

Duty to inform superior landlords

7. If the competent landlord's interest in the property comprised in the relevant tenancy is a tenancy which will come or can be brought to an end within sixteen months (or any further time by which it may be continued under section 36(2) or section 64 of this Act) and he gives to the tenant under the relevant tenancy a notice under section 25 of this Act to terminate the tenancy or is given by him a notice under section 26(3) of this Act—

(a)   the competent landlord shall forthwith send a copy of the notice to his immediate landlord; and

(b)   any superior landlord whose interest in property is a tenancy shall forthwith send to his immediate landlord any copy which has been sent to him in pursuance of the preceding sub-paragraph or this sub-paragraph.

Effect on sub-tenants

26–30   Where there is a sub-tenancy in existence that is continuing by virtue of the 1954 Act and the court grants the tenant a new tenancy to the tenant of property that includes that part of the land occupied by the sub-tenant, the new tenancy takes subject to the sub-tenancy (s.65(3)).

Landlord and Tenant Act 1954 s.32(2)

26–31   **32.**—(2) The foregoing provisions of this section shall not apply in a case where the property comprised in the current tenancy includes other property besides the holding and the landlord requires any new tenancy ordered to be granted under section 29 of this Act to be a tenancy of the whole of the property comprised in the current tenancy; but in any such case—

(a)   any order under the said section 29 for the grant of a new tenancy shall be an order for the grant of a new tenancy of the whole of the property comprised in the current tenancy, and

(b)   references in the following provisions of this Part of this Act to the holding shall be construed as references to the whole of that property.

Provisions as to reversions

Landlord and Tenant Act 1954 s.65

65.–(1) Where by virtue of any provision of this Act a tenancy (in this sub-section referred to as "the inferior tenancy") is continued for a period such as to extend to or beyond the end of the term of a superior tenancy, the superior tenancy shall, for the purposes of this Act and of any other enactment and of any rule of law, be deemed so long as it subsists to be an interest in reversion expectant upon the termination of the inferior tenancy and, if there is no intermediate tenancy, to be the interest in reversion immediately expectant upon the termination thereof.

(2) In the case of a tenancy continuing by virtue of any provision of this Act after the coming to an end of the interest in reversion immediately expectant upon the termination thereof, subsection (1) of section 139 of the Law of Property Act 1925 (which relates to the effect of the extinguishment of a reversion) shall apply as if references in the said subsection (1) to the surrender or merger of the reversion included references to the coming to an end of the reversion for any reason other than surrender or merger.

(3) Where by virtue of any provision of this Act a tenancy (in this subsection referred to as "the continuing tenancy") is continued beyond the beginning of a reversionary tenancy which was granted (whether before or after the commencement of this Act) so as to begin on or after the date on which apart from this Act the continuing tenancy would have come to an end, the reversionary tenancy shall have effect as if it had been granted subject to the continuing tenancy.

(4) Where by virtue of any provision of this Act a tenancy (in this subsection referred to as "the new tenancy") is granted for a period beginning on the same date as a reversionary tenancy or for a period such as to extend beyond the beginning of the term of a reversionary tenancy, whether the reversionary tenancy in question was granted before or after the commencement of this Act, the reversionary tenancy shall have effect as if it had been granted subject to the new tenancy.

26–32

Tenant's option not to take the new tenancy

The tenant is not bound to accept the tenancy ordered by the court if he does not wish to do so. The court may have rejected many of the tenant's submissions as to the terms to be included and the new tenancy ordered by the court may not be to his liking. He has 14 days in which to make up his mind. If within that time, he applies to the court for the order to be revoked "the court shall revoke the order" (s.36(2); see below). The parties may also agree not to act upon the order (s.36(1)).

Where the order is revoked, the continuation tenancy (see para.1–02) will generally come to an end three months after the

26–33

"final disposal" of the case (s.64; para.27–02) i.e. three months after the revocation order is made, *unless* the parties agree or the court determines that it should continue beyond that date. If so, the tenancy will continue for such period as is agreed or determined by the court "to be necessary to afford to the landlord a reasonable opportunity for reletting or otherwise disposing of the premises which would have been comprised in the new tenancy" (s.36(2)). During this extended period, the tenancy is not a tenancy to which the Act applies, i.e. it is not necessary to serve a s.25 notice to determine it (s.36(2)).

Any order for costs made in the proceedings is not automatically revoked by reason of the revocation but the court may review the question of costs and make such order as it thinks fit in the light of the new circumstances (s.36(3)).

Landlord and Tenant Act 1954 s.36

26–34   **36.**–(1) Where under this Part of this Act the court makes an order for the grant of a new tenancy, then, unless the order is revoked under the next following subsection or the landlord and the tenant agree not to act upon the order, the landlord shall be bound to execute or make in favour of the tenant, and the tenant shall be bound to accept, a lease or agreement for a tenancy of the holding embodying the terms agreed between the landlord and the tenant or determined by the court in accordance with the foregoing provisions of this Part of this Act; and where the landlord executes or makes such a lease or agreement the tenant shall be bound, if so required by the landlord, to execute a counterpart or duplicate thereof.

(2) If the tenant, within fourteen days after the making of an order under this Part of this Act for the grant of a new tenancy, applies to the court for the revocation of the order the court shall revoke the order; and where the order is so revoked, then, if it is so agreed between the landlord and the tenant or determined by the court, the current tenancy shall continue, beyond the date at which it would have come to an end apart from this subsection, for such period as may be so agreed or determined to be necessary to afford to the landlord a reasonable opportunity for reletting or otherwise disposing of the premises which would have been comprised in the new tenancy; and while the current tenancy continues by virtue of this subsection it shall not be a tenancy to which this Part of this Act applies.

(3) Where an order is revoked under the last foregoing subsection any provision thereof as to payment of costs shall not cease to have effect by reason only of the revocation; but the court may, if it thinks fit, revoke or vary any such provision or, where no costs have been awarded in the proceedings for the revoked order, award such costs.

(4) A lease executed or agreement made under this section, in a case where the interest of the lessor is subject to a mortgage, shall be deemed to be one authorised by section 99 of the Law of Property Act 1925 (which confers certain powers of leasing on mortgagors in possession),

and subsection (13) of that section (which allows those powers to be restricted or excluded by agreement) shall not have effect in relation to such a lease or agreement.

Costs

The general principles set out in the Civil Procedure Rules apply **26–35** to costs in lease renewal claims and one needs to be aware of the extended jurisdiction that the courts now have. In *MBI Inc v Riminex Investments SA* [2002] EWHC 2856 the parties were in dispute over the terms of new lease, which was settled at court after lengthy negotiations. The terms agreed were broadly those proposed by the tenant's surveyor in correspondence beforehand. The judge took the view that the landlord had been holding out for terms that were unreasonable. He therefore ordered the landlord to pay part of the tenant's costs. The landlord's appeal against the order was refused. (See also paras 24–68, 26–02 and 27–28).

CHAPTER 27

REFUSAL TO ORDER A NEW TENANCY

. . . .

Landlord and Tenant Act 1954 ss.29(4) and 31(1)

27-01 **29.**–(4) Subject to the provisions of this Act, where the landlord makes an application under subsection (2) above—

 (a) if he establishes, to the satisfaction of the court, any of the grounds on which he is entitled to make the application in accordance with section 30 of this Act, the court shall make an order for the termination of the current tenancy in accordance with section 64 of this Act without the grant of a new tenancy;

  . . .

31.–(1) If the landlord opposes an application under subsection (1) of section 24 of this Act on grounds on which he is entitled to oppose it in accordance with the last foregoing section and establishes any of those grounds to the satisfaction of the court, the court shall not make an order for the grant of a new tenancy.

Where the landlord establishes one or more of the grounds set out in s.30 of the 1954 Act (see Ch.17), on an application to terminate the continuation tenancy, the court will order its termination (s.29(4)(a)); or on an application for a new tenancy, the court must not order the grant of a new tenancy (s.31(1)).

A suggested form of order where the court makes an order terminating the continuation tenancy or refuses to grant a new tenancy is set out in Form 24 of this book. The first alternative relates to the situation where the landlord has applied to terminate the current tenancy; the second relates to the position where the tenant has applied for a new tenancy. Note that it is not possible to specify the precise date upon which the current tenancy will come to an end in accordance with s.64 of the 1954 Act at the date the order is made because of the possibility that there might be an appeal (see para.27-03).

Form 24

Form B—Order for termination of tenancy/dismissing claim to new tenancy

Upon the Landlord's application for an order for the termination of the Tenant's tenancy under s.29(2) of the Landlord and Tenant Act 1954 IT IS ORDERED that the current tenancy under which the Tenant is a tenant of the premises known as................ is terminated in accordance s.64 of the Landlord and Tenant Act 1954 without the grant of a new tenancy on the following grounds, namely that [*set out the relevant subsection of s.30(1) or any other reason why the order has been made*]

Or

IT IS ORDERED the Tenant's application for a new tenancy under s.24(1) of the Landlord and Tenant Act 1954 be dismissed on the following grounds, namely that [*set out the relevant subsection of s.30(1) or any other reason why the order has been made*] and that the current tenancy under which the Tenant is a tenant of the premises known as................ is terminated in accordance with s.64 of the Landlord and Tenant Act 1954.

Where the court refuses to order the grant of a new tenancy there are four matters to consider:

(1) the date upon which the tenant is to give up possession;
(2) the effect on sub-tenants;
(3) the amount of compensation, if any, payable to the tenant; and
(4) costs.

Termination of the continuation tenancy: s.64

Landlord and Tenant Act 1954 s.64

64.–(1) In any case where—   **27–02**

    (a) a notice to terminate a tenancy has been given under Part I or Part II of this Act or a request for a new tenancy has been made under Part II thereof, and

    (b) an application to the court has been made under the said Part I or under section 24(1) or 29(2) of this Act as the case may be, and

    (c) *apart from this section* the effect of the notice or request would be to terminate the tenancy *before* the expiration of the period of three months beginning with the date on which the application is *finally disposed of,* the effect of the notice or request shall be to terminate the tenancy at the expiration of the said period of *three months* and not at any other time.

(2) The reference in paragraph (c) of subsection (1) of this section to the date on which an application is *finally disposed of* shall be construed as a reference to the *earliest date* by which the proceedings on the application (including any proceedings on or in consequence of an appeal) have been determined and any time for appealing or further *appealing has expired*, except that if the application is withdrawn or any appeal is abandoned the reference shall be construed as a reference to the date of the withdrawal or abandonment.

27-03   The continuation tenancy generally comes to an end three months after the "application is finally disposed of". Thus, if a new tenancy is not ordered, the tenant will have to give up possession to the landlord three months after the conclusion of the case plus time for appealing (s.64). As to time for appealing see CPR 52.4—usually 21 days.

If the tenant fails to leave the landlord will be entitled to seek an order for possession. See Form 25 at para.27–04.

If the tenant appeals against the court's refusal to order a new tenancy, the case is finally disposed of once the appeal has been determined. If the tenant abandons his appeal, the case is finally disposed of when it is abandoned (s.64(2)).

In the unlikely event that the date in the s.25 notice or s.26 request is later than the date upon which the claim is "finally disposed of", that date remains the termination date.

Where the landlord has unsuccessfully relied upon ground (d), (e) or (f) but the court would have been satisfied on any of those grounds within a short period after the date of termination specified in the s.25 notice (or s.26 counter-notice), the court may specify a different date (see para.27–05).

Form 25: Particulars of claim after dismissal of claim for new tenancy

IN THE COUNTY COURT   Case No.

Between:

[*The Former Tenant's immediate Landlord*]

Claimant

-and-

[*The Former Tenant*]

Defendant

PARTICULARS OF CLAIM

1. The Claimant is the [*freehold/leasehold*] owner and is entitled to possession of the business premises known as [*address of premises subject to continuation tenancy*].

2. By a lease dated .... the Claimant let the said premises to the Defendant for a term of .... years expiring on [*adapt if there is a more complicated history*].

3. On .... the Claimant who was both the Defendant's immediate landlord and "the landlord" within the meaning of section 44 of the Landlord and Tenant Act 1954 [*adapt if different*] served a notice on the Defendant pursuant to section 25 of the said Act determining the Defendant's tenancy [*adapt if there is a more complicated history*].

4. On .... the Defendant applied to this court for a new tenancy pursuant to Part II of the 1954 Act [*or*, the Claimant applied to the court for an order for termination of the Defendant's tenancy under s.29(2) of the 1954 Act].

5. On .... 200....... the Claimant successfully resisted the Defendant's claim for a new tenancy [*or*, the court made an order under s.29(4)(a) for the termination of the tenancy in accordance with s.64 without the grant of a new tenancy]. The claim was finally disposed of on .... when the defendant's time for appealing expired.

6. By virtue of section 64 of the 1954 Act the Defendant's tenancy therefore determined on ....

cont

cont

7. Notwithstanding termination of the said tenancy and a request by the Claimant to leave the Defendant has failed to vacate the said premises.

8. A fair and reasonable sum in respect of the Defendant's occupation of the said premises is £.......... per week.

9. Pursuant to section 64 of the County Courts Act 1984 the Claimant claims interest upon such sum as the court may award in respect of mesne profits at such rate and for such period as the court shall think fit.

AND the Claimant claims:

(1) Possession of the said premises;

(2) Mesne profits at the rate of £.......... per week from [*the date upon which the tenancy terminated pursuant to section 64*] until possession be delivered up.

(3) Interest as pleaded.

STATEMENT OF TRUTH

Ground (d), (e) or (f) relied upon but not quite established

Landlord and Tenant Act 1954 s.31(2)

27–05   **31.**—(2) Where the landlord opposes an application under section 24(1) of this Act, or makes an application under section 29(2) of this Act, on one or more of the grounds specified in section *30(1)(d) to (f)* of this Act but *establishes none* of those grounds, *and none of the other grounds* specified in section 30(1) of this Act, to the satisfaction of the court, then if the court *would have been satisfied* on any of the grounds specified in section *30(1)(d) to (f)* of this Act if the date of termination specified in the landlord's notice or, as the case may be, the date specified in the tenant's request for a new tenancy as the date from which the new tenancy is to begin, had been such later date as the court may determine, being a date *not more than one year later* than the date so specified—

     (a)   the court shall make a declaration to that effect, stating of which of the said grounds the court would have been satisfied as aforesaid and specifying the date determined by the court as aforesaid, but shall not make an order for the grant of a new tenancy;

     (b)   if, within fourteen days after the making of the declaration, *the tenant* so requires the court shall make an order substituting the said date for the date specified in the said landlord's notice or tenant's request, and thereupon that notice or request shall have effect accordingly.

Where the landlord relies upon ground (d) suitable alternative accommodation, (e) uneconomic subletting, or (f) reconstruction or redevelopment but fails to establish the ground relied upon, the court must nevertheless *not* make an order for the grant of a tenancy *if* the court would have been satisfied on that ground at some later date not more than a year after the termination date specified in the s.25 notice or s.26 request. Instead, the court makes a declaration to the effect that it would have been satisfied on that date and the tenant is given 14 days to decide whether or not he wishes the date to be substituted in the s.25 notice (or s.26 request) as being the termination date for the current tenancy (s.31(2)).

Effect on sub-tenants

Business sub-tenants

Once a tenancy has come to an end, the general rule is that the **27–06** sub-tenancy disappears along with the head tenancy whether or not it was lawfully granted. Or, as it is often graphically expressed, "the branch falls with the tree" (*Moore Properties (Ilford) Ltd v McKeon* [1976] 1 W.L.R. 1278. However, if the sub-tenant himself has rights under the 1954 Act, the landlord will not be entitled to possession (see para.1–04).

Residential tenants

Section 137 of the Rent Act 1977 gives various sub-tenants of **27–07** residential premises protection against certain landlords (for a full discussion see *Residential Possession Proceedings* 9th edn, Webber and Dovar (*Sweet & Maxwell*) para.8.037). However, s.137 does not apply where the head tenancy is a business tenancy. Thus, where part of the property is residential accommodation (for example a flat above a shop) and the dwelling is occupied by a regulated tenant under the Rent Act 1977, the landlord (i.e. the business tenant's landlord) will not be bound by the regulated tenancy and will be able to recover possession at the expiry of the continuation tenancy (*Pittalis v Grant* [1989] 2 All E.R. 622; *Bromley Park Garden Estates Ltd v George* [1991] 2 E.G.L.R. 95 CA).

However, where the sub-tenant is an *assured* tenant under a *lawful* tenancy, the position is different. By virtue of s.18(1) of the Housing Act 1988 the head landlord becomes the direct landlord of the sub-tenant and the sub-tenancy remains assured. It would seem that the landlord cannot rely upon s.18(2) and para.4 of Sch.1 to the 1988 Act (see below) because the *sub-tenancy* will not be a business tenancy. (To understand the provisions, it is necessary to look at the whole of Sch.1 and note the term "a tenancy under which the interest of the landlord belongs to" in paras 11 and 12 correspond with the words "if the interest which, by virtue of that subsection, would become that of the landlord, is such" in s.18(2). Paragraph 12(1)(a) is set out below by way of example. Thus, it is probably only where the head landlord is the Crown, a local authority or one of the other public bodies listed that s.18(2) operates to allow the landlord to obtain possession.)

Where the sub-tenancy is an assured shorthold, lawfully granted, the head landlord will be able to recover possession at the end of the term by serving a notice under s.21 of the Housing Act 1988 (see *Residential Possession Proceedings*, para.7.013).

Where the assured tenancy was granted in breach of covenant, it will be unlawful and s.18 will not apply to protect the sub-tenant. In those circumstances, the head landlord will be entitled to possession at the end of the head tenant's continuation tenancy.

Housing Act 1988 s.18

27–08   **18.**–(1) If at any time–

(a)   a dwelling-house is for the time being lawfully let on an assured tenancy, and

(b)   the landlord under the assured tenancy is himself a tenant under a superior tenancy; and

(c)   the superior tenancy comes to an end,

then, subject to subsection (2) below, the assured tenancy shall continue in existence as a tenancy held of the person whose interest would, apart from the continuance of the assured tenancy, entitle him to actual possession of the dwelling-house at that time.

(2) Subsection (1) above does not apply to an assured tenancy if the interest which, by virtue of that subsection, *would become that of the landlord*, is such that, by virtue of Schedule 1 to this Act, the tenancy could not be an assured tenancy.

Housing Act 1988 Sch.1 paras 4 and 12(1)(a)

27–09   **4.** A tenancy to which Part II of the Landlord and Tenant Act 1954 applies (business tenancies).

. . .

12.–(1) A tenancy under which the interest of the landlord belongs to—

(a)   a local authority . . .

Compensation for refusal of new tenancy

Landlord and Tenant Act 1954 s.37

37.–(1) Subject to the provisions of this Act, in a case specified in subsection (1A), (1B) or (1C) below (a "compensation case") the tenant shall be entitled on quitting the holding to recover from the landlord by way of compensation an amount determined in accordance with this section.

(1A) The first compensation case is where on the making of an application by the tenant under section 24(1) of this Act the court is precluded (whether by subsection (1) or subsection (2) of section 31 of this Act) from making an order for the grant of a new tenancy by reason of any of the grounds specified in paragraphs (e), (f) and (g) of section 30(1) of this Act (the "compensation grounds") and not of any grounds specified in any other paragraph of section 30(1).

(1B) The second compensation case is where on the making of an application under section 29(2) of this Act the court is precluded (whether by section 29(4)(a) or section 31(2) of this Act) from making an order for the grant of a new tenancy by reason of any of the compensation grounds and not of any other grounds specified in section 30(1) of this Act.

(1C) The third compensation case is where—

(a)   the landlord's notice under section 25 of this Act or, as the case may be, under section 26(6) of this Act, states his opposition to the grant of a new tenancy on any of the compensation grounds and not on any other grounds specified in section 30(1) of this Act; and

(b)   either—

(i) no application is made by the tenant under section 24(1) of this Act or by the landlord under section 29(2) of this Act; or

(ii) such an application is made but is subsequently withdrawn.

(2) Subject to the following provisions of this section, compensation under this section shall be as follows, that is to say—

(a)   where the conditions specified in the next following subsection are satisfied in relation to the whole of the holding it shall be the product of the appropriate multiplier and twice the rateable value of the holding,

(b)   in any other case it shall be the product of the appropriate multiplier and the rateable value of the holding.

(3) The said conditions are—

(a)   that, during the whole of the fourteen years immediately preceding the termination of the current tenancy, premises being or comprised in the holding have been occupied for the

27–10

591

purposes of a business carried on by the occupier or for those
and other purposes;

(b)   that, if during those fourteen years there was a change in the
occupier of the premises, the person who was the occupier
immediately after the change was the successor to the
business carried on by the person who was the occupier
immediately before the change.

27-11   (3A) If the conditions specified in subsection (3) above are satisfied in
relation to part of the holding but not in relation to the other part, the
amount of compensation shall be the aggregate of sums calculated
separately as compensation in respect of each part, and accordingly, for
the purpose of calculating compensation in respect of a part any
reference in this section to the holding shall be construed as a reference
to that part.

(3B) Where section 44(1A) of this Act applies, the compensation shall
be determined separately for each part and compensation determined for
any part shall be recoverable only from the person who is the owner of an
interest in that part which fulfils the conditions specified in section 44(1)
of this Act.

(4) Where the court is precluded from making an order for the grant of
a new tenancy under this Part of this Act in a compensation case, the
court shall on the application of the tenant certify that fact.

(5) For the purposes of subsection (2) of this section the rateable value
of the holding shall be determined as follows:

(a)   where in the valuation list in force at the date on which the
landlord's notice under section 25 or, as the case may be,
subsection (6) of section 26 of this Act is given a value is then
shown as the annual value (as hereinafter defined) of the
holding, the rateable value of the holding shall be taken to be
that value;

(b)   where no such value is so shown with respect to the holding
but such a value or such values is or are so shown with respect
to premises comprised in or comprising the holding or part of
it, the rateable value of the holding shall be taken to be such
value as is found by a proper apportionment or aggregation of
the value or values so shown;

(c)   where the rateable value of the holding cannot be ascertained
in accordance with the foregoing paragraphs of this
subsection, it shall be taken to be the value which, apart from
any exemption from assessment to rates, would on a proper
assessment be the value to be entered in the said valuation list
as the annual value of the holding;

and any dispute arising, whether in proceedings before the court or
otherwise, as to the determination for those purposes of the rateable
value of the holding shall be referred to the Commissioners of Inland
Revenue for decision by the valuation officer.

An appeal shall lie to the Lands Tribunal from any decision of a valuation
officer under this subsection, but subject thereto any such decision shall
be final.

27-12   (5A) If part of the holding is domestic property, as defined in section 66
of the Local Government Finance Act 1988—

(a)   the domestic property shall be disregarded in determining the rateable value of the holding under subsection (5) of this section; and

(b)   if, on the date specified in subsection (5) (a) of this section, the tenant occupied the whole or any part of the domestic property, the amount of compensation to which he is entitled under subsection (1) of this section shall be increased by the addition of a sum equal to his reasonable expenses in removing from the domestic property.

(5B) Any question as to the amount of the sum referred to in paragraph (b) of subsection (5A) of this section shall be determined by agreement between the landlord and the tenant or, in default of agreement, by the court.

(5C) If the whole of the holding is domestic property, as defined in section 66 of the Local Government Finance Act 1988, for the purposes of subsection (2) of this section the rateable value of the holding shall be taken to be an amount equal to the rent at which it is estimated the holding might reasonably be expected to let from year to year if the tenant undertook to pay all usual tenant's rates and taxes and to bear the cost of the repairs and insurance and the other expenses (if any) necessary to maintain the holding in a state to command that rent.

(5D) The following provisions shall have effect as regards a determination of an amount mentioned in subsection (5C) of this section—

(a)   the date by reference to which such a determination is to be made is the date on which the landlord's notice under section 25 or, as the case may be, subsection (6) of section 26 of this Act is given;

(b)   any dispute arising, whether in proceedings before the court or otherwise, as to such a determination shall be referred to the Commissioners of Inland Revenue for decision by a valuation officer;

(c)   an appeal shall lie to the Lands Tribunal from such a decision, but subject to that, such a decision shall be final.

(5E) Any deduction made under paragraph 2A of Schedule 6 to the Local Government Finance Act 1988 (deduction from valuation of hereditaments used for breeding horses etc.) shall be disregarded, to the extent that it relates to the holding, in determining the rateable value of the holding under subsection (5) of this section.

(6) The Commissioners of Inland Revenue may by statutory instrument make rules prescribing the procedure in connection with references under this section.

(7) In this section—

the reference to the termination of the current tenancy is a reference to the date of termination specified in the landlord's notice under section 25 of this Act or, as the case may be, the date specified in the tenant's request for a new tenancy as the date from which the new tenancy is to begin;

the expression "annual value" means rateable value except that where the rateable value differs from the net annual value the said expression means net annual value;

593

the expression "valuation officer" means any officer of the Commissioners of Inland Revenue for the time being authorised by a certificate of the Commissioners to act in relation to a valuation list.

(8) In subsection (2) of this section "the appropriate multiplier" means such multiplier as the Secretary of State may by order made by statutory instrument prescribe and different multipliers may be so prescribed in relation to different cases.

(9) A statutory instrument containing an order under subsection (8) of this section shall be subject to annulment in pursuance of a resolution of either House of Parliament.

Introduction

Compensation grounds

27–13 Where the landlord successfully establishes that the court should not make an order for a new tenancy by reason of one or more of the following three grounds in s.30(1), referred to in the Act as "compensation grounds", the tenant is entitled to compensation pursuant to s.37:

- uneconomic subletting (para.(e)); or
- redevelopment or reconstruction (para.(f)); or
- property required for landlord's use (para.(g)).

Each of these grounds involves a situation where there is no fault on the part of the tenant.

Compensation cases

27–14 The compensation is payable in three different sets of circumstances, each called a "compensation case":

- The first compensation case is where *the tenant makes an application for a new tenancy* and the court is precluded from making an order for the grant of a new tenancy by reason of any of the compensation grounds and not of any of the other grounds of opposition in s.30(1) (s.37(1A)).
- The second compensation case is where *the landlord applies to terminate the tenancy* under the new s.29(2) of the 1954 Act and the court is precluded from making an order for the grant of a new tenancy by reason of any of the compensation grounds and not of any of the other grounds of opposition in s.30(1) (s.37(1B)).
- The third compensation case is where the landlord serves a s.25 notice, or a counter-notice to a s.26 request from the

tenant, and states his opposition on any of the compensation grounds and not on any of the other grounds of opposition in s.30(1); and either the tenant makes *no application for a new tenancy or the landlord does not apply to terminate* under s.29, or one of those applications is made but is subsequently withdrawn (s.37(1C)).

The availability of the third compensation case means that it is not necessary to commence, or to pursue, a pointless application to the court where the tenant accepts that the ground specified applies.

The tenant is also entitled to compensation where the court is precluded from making an order for a new tenancy by reason of s.31(2), i.e. where the court considers that the ground would have been established at a later date within a year of the termination date specified in the s.25 notice or s.26 request (see para.27–05): s.37(1A)).

Relying on other grounds

Note the inclusion of the words and "not on any of the other grounds" in each compensation case. This means that if the landlord does rely upon one of the other "fault" grounds in s.30, in addition to a compensation ground, the tenant will not be able to obtain compensation under s.37 unless and until a trial takes place and the landlord fails to establish the additional ground(s). The tenant may deny that other ground but be prepared to accept that, for example, (g) applies. In these circumstances, the tenant should try to agree terms with the landlord whereby he will be paid the appropriate amount of compensation on or before quitting. If the landlord refuses, it will be necessary to make an application to the court for a new tenancy in order to establish that only a compensation-giving ground applies and to obtain a certificate under s.37(4); see below. In order to do his best to prevent an order for costs being made against him, the tenant should, at an early stage of the proceedings, make it clear to the landlord and to the court that he admits that (e), (f) or (g), as the case may be, applies but that the other ground is denied and that the purpose of the application is to obtain the court's certificate pursuant to s.37(4).

27–15

Landlords, on the other hand, need to think carefully about relying upon a "fault" ground so as to avoid compensation. Is the landlord really going to succeed on that ground? Are the facts good enough? Is the judge likely to use his discretion to refuse renewal or to terminate? The danger is often that the landlord wastes more in costs pursuing the fault ground than in paying s.37 compensation.

Court certificate as to entitlement

Landlord and Tenant Act 1954 s.37(4)

27-16   **37.**—(4) Where the court is precluded from making an order for the grant of a new tenancy under this Part of this Act in a compensation case, the court shall on the application of the tenant certify that fact.

Where the court is precluded from ordering the grant of a new tenancy, the court must, on an application by the tenant, certify that fact (s.37(4)).

The amount payable; the basic sum

Landlord and Tenant Act 1954 s.37(2)

27-17   **37.**—(2) Subject to the following provisions of this section, compensation under this section shall be as follows, that is to say—

(a)   where the conditions specified in the next following subsection are satisfied in relation to the whole of the holding it shall be the product of the appropriate multiplier and twice the rateable value of the holding,

(b)   in any other case it shall be the product of the appropriate multiplier and the rateable value of the holding.

The amount of compensation payable to the tenant is based upon the rateable value of "the holding" as defined in s.23 (see para.17-01). There is a basic rate and an enhanced rate:

● The basic sum payable is the appropriate multiplier multiplied by the rateable value of the holding (s.37(2), (5), (8) of the 1954 Act).
● The enhanced rate is the appropriate multiplier multiplied by twice the rate available (see para.27-20).

The multiplier is set by statutory instrument. The present position is that the multiplier is one, so that the basic sum payable is the rateable value of the holding (Landlord and Tenant Act 1954 (Appropriate Multiplier) Order 1990).

The appropriate multiplier is that which is in force on the date that the tenant actually quits the premises (s.37(1); *Cardshops Ltd v John Lewis Properties Ltd* [1982] 3 All E.R. 746).

Determination of the rateable value

The rateable value is determined in accordance with the provisions in s.37(5), (7) and is generally the sum stated in the valuation list in force at the date of the s.25 notice (or counter-notice to the s.26 request). Any dispute as to the rateable value is referred to the Commissioners for Inland Revenue for decision by a valuation officer (s.37(5)) in accordance with the Landlord and Tenant (Determination of Rateable Value Procedure) Rules 1954. The reference to the Commissioners is made on Form A to those rules. An appeal lies to the Lands Tribunal. No further appeal is permitted (s.37(5)).

27–18

Domestic property included in the holding

Where "the holding" includes domestic property, the domestic part is excluded in determining the rateable value of the holding; but if the tenant occupied the whole or any part of the domestic property on the date the s.25 notice (or the s.26 counter-notice) was served and that notice or counter-notice was given on or after April 1, 1990 the tenant is entitled, in addition to the normal measure of compensation, to a sum equal to the tenant's reasonable expenses in removing from the domestic part (s.37(5A) of the 1954 Act; Sch.7 para.3 of the Local Government and Housing Act 1989). Where the parties cannot agree, the amount of removal expenses they will be determined by the court (s.37(5B)).

27–19

Subsections (5C) and (5D) apply for determining the rateable value where the whole of the property is domestic property as defined by s.66 of the Local Government Finance Act 1988 and the relevant date is on or after April 1, 1990 (Local Government and Housing Act Sch.7 para.3).

Payment of higher sum

Landlord and Tenant Act 1954 s.37(3), (7)

37.–(3) The said conditions are—

    (a)   that, during the whole of the *fourteen* years immediately preceding the *termination of the current tenancy,* premises

27–20

being or comprised in the holding have been occupied for the purposes of a business carried on by the occupier or for those and other purposes;

(b)   that, if during those fourteen years there was a *change in the occupier* of the premises, the person who was the occupier immediately after the change was the successor to the business carried on by the person who was the occupier immediately before the change.

(7) In this section—

the reference to the *termination of the current tenancy* is a reference to the date of termination specified in the landlord's notice under section 25 of this Act or, as the case may be, the date specified in the tenant's request for a new tenancy as the date from which the new tenancy is to begin;

The amount payable is twice the basic sum where, during the whole of the 14 years immediately preceding the *termination of the current tenancy*, premises being or comprised in the holding have been occupied for the purpose of a business carried on by the occupier or for those and other purposes (s.37(3)(a)); and if during those 14 years there was a change in occupier of the premises, the new occupier succeeded also to the business of the predecessor (s.37(3)(b); *Edicron Ltd v William Whitely Ltd* [1984] 1 All E.R. 219).

The relevant date of termination to be taken in calculating the period of occupation for the purpose of deciding whether or not the tenant is entitled to the higher sum is *the date specified in the s.25 notice or the s.26 request as the date of termination of the tenancy* (s.37(7)).

Example: Lease of 14 years, expiring on September 28, 1997. L served a s.25 notice relying on grounds (f) and (g) on February 27, 1997. The termination date specified in the s.25 notice was February 25, 1998. T applied for a new tenancy but later discontinued the application. T vacated a few days before the contractual expiry date. *T's problem*: when he left in September 1997 Part II ceased to apply. The crucial date for determining the amount of compensation was February 25, 1998 (s.37(3)(a)), i.e. the date in the s.25 notice (s.37(7)). At that date, he was clearly not in occupation and so did not satisfy the condition that he had been in occupation "during the whole of the 14 years immediately preceding the termination of the current tenancy" (s.37(3)(a)). *Held:* T was not entitled to double compensation (*Sight & Sound*

Education Ltd v Books etc Ltd [1999] 3 E.G.L.R. 45 High Court).

See also cases referred to in para.2–06.

Different parts

Landlord and Tenant Act 1954 s.37(3A)

37.–(3A) If the conditions specified in subsection (3) above are satisfied in relation to part of the holding but not in relation to the other part, the amount of compensation shall be the aggregate of sums calculated separately as compensation in respect of each part, and accordingly, for the purpose of calculating compensation in respect of a part any reference in this section to the holding shall be construed as a reference to that part.

27–21

Where parts of the premises have been occupied for different lengths of time, compensation will be calculated for each part separately. The higher rate of compensation will apply only to those parts that have been continuously occupied for 14 years. (This change was made to overcome the injustice to the landlord found in the case of *Edicron Ltd v William Whitely Ltd* [1984] 1 All E.R. 219 where it was held that the tenant was entitled to compensation at the higher rate in respect of the whole property even though he had only occupied one floor for over 14 years and the two others for five and a half years: *Law Commission Report 208* para.2.82.)

Different landlords

Landlord and Tenant Act 1954 s.37(3B)

37.–(3B) Where section 44(1A) of this Act applies, the compensation shall be determined separately for each part and compensation determined for any part shall be recoverable only from the person who is the owner of an interest in that part which fulfils the conditions specified in section 44(1) of this Act.

27–22

Landlords are required to operate the procedures under the act collectively (s.44(1A); see para.14–17). However, where the reversion is divided so that different parts of the holding are owned by different landlords, compensation is determined for each part separately. The tenant must claim compensation separately from each relevant landlord.

Date of payment

27-23 The compensation is payable to the tenant "on quitting the holding" (s.37(1)). It is submitted that this is the position even if the tenancy is deemed to continue beyond the date on which the tenant leaves by reason of s.64 of the 1954 Act (see para.27-02) and that the tenant will be entitled to payment of his compensation even if he continues to be liable for rent until the tenancy comes to an end.

Restrictions on agreements excluding or reducing compensation

Landlord and Tenant Act 1954 s.38(2), (3)

27-24   **38.**–(2) Where–

(a) during the whole of the *five years* immediately preceding the date on which the tenant under a tenancy to which this Part of this Act applies is to quit the holding, premises being or comprised in the holding have been occupied for the purposes of a business carried on by the occupier or for those and other purposes, and

(b) if during those five years there was a change in the occupier of the premises, the person who was the occupier immediately after the change was the successor to the business carried on by the person who was the occupier immediately before the change,

any agreement (whether contained in the instrument creating the tenancy or not and whether made before or after the termination of that tenancy) which purports to exclude or reduce compensation under section 37 of this Act shall to that extent be void, so however that this subsection shall not affect any agreement as to the amount of any such compensation which is made after the right to compensation has accrued.

(3) In a case not falling within the last foregoing subsection the right to compensation conferred by section 37 of this Act may be excluded or modified by agreement.

Section 38(2) of the 1954 Act deals with the circumstances in which the parties may not exclude or reduce the tenant's right to compensation on quitting the premises. This right may not be excluded or *reduced* (it may be increased) where the premises have been occupied for the purposes of a business (or for those and other purposes) by the tenant or a predecessor (in the same business) (s.38(2)(b), *Cramas Properties v Connaught Fur Trimmings* [1965] 1 W.L.R. 892 HL) for the whole period of five years ending with the date on which the tenant "is to quit" the holding. In these circumstances, any agreement (whether contained in the lease or not and whenever made), excluding the right to compensation or reducing the sum payable, is void except in so far as the agreement relates to the amount of compensation and is made *after the right to compensation has accrued.* If subs.(2) does not apply, the right to compensation may be excluded or modified by agreement (s.38(3)).

It would seem that the date upon which the tenant "is to quit", **27–25** for the purpose of determining whether or not an agreement may be made excluding or modifying the right to compensation, is the date upon which he is obliged to quit (see *Cardshops v John Lewis Properties* [1982] 3 All E.R. 746 CA) and that this date will vary according to the circumstances of the case so that:

(1) If the landlord has served a s.25 notice and the tenant has failed to serve a counter-notice or has failed to apply to the court for a new tenancy, the date upon which the tenant "is to quit" is the expiry date in the s.25 notice. If on that date the tenant has been in occupation for five years, the provisions excluding compensation will be void.

(2) If the tenant applies to the court for a new tenancy, the date upon which he "is to quit" is a date three months from the date upon which the proceedings are finally disposed of (see s.64; para.27–02). If on that date he has been in occupation for more than five years, the agreement purporting to exclude compensation will be void.

Compare the argument contained in *Woodfall's Law of Landlord and Tenant*, para.22.176, where it is suggested that, although *payable* on quitting the premises, the *right* to compensation, for these purposes, accrues as soon as it becomes clear that on quitting the tenant will be entitled to compensation, e.g. when the landlord relies on ground (g) of s.30(1) and the tenant does not make an application to the court. If the argument is correct, the parties may, in this example, come to an agreement excluding or modifying the right to compensation as soon as the final date for making an application for a new tenancy passes if on that date the five-year period has not expired.

See para.2–06 when one is considering whether or not the tenant has been in sufficient occupation immediately before the quitting of the premises.

Compensation for voluntary improvements whatever the ground: Landlord and Tenant Act 1927

27-26   It should also be noted that a tenant may have a right to claim compensation for improvements he has made to the property, pursuant to Pt I of the Landlord and Tenant Act 1927, whatever the ground for possession relied upon by the landlord. See s.47 of the 1954 Act for time limits for making such an application.

Compensation for possession obtained by misrepresentation

Landlord and Tenant Act 1954 s.37A

27-27   **37A.**–(1) Where *the court*–

(a)   makes an order for the termination of the current tenancy but does not make an order for the grant of a new tenancy, or
(b)   refuses an order for the grant of a new tenancy,

and it is subsequently made to appear to the court that the order was obtained, or the court was induced to refuse the grant, by misrepresentation or the concealment of material facts, the court may order the landlord to pay to the tenant such sum as appears sufficient as compensation for damage or loss sustained by the tenant as the result of the order or refusal.

(2) Where–

(a)   the tenant has quit the holding–
    (i) after *making but withdrawing an application* under section 24(1) of this Act; or
    (ii) *without making* such an application; and
(b)   it is made to appear to the court that he did so by reason of misrepresentation or the concealment of material facts,

the court may order the landlord to pay to the tenant such sum as appears sufficient as compensation for damage or loss sustained by the tenant as the result of quitting the holding.

A landlord who told a tenant in a letter accompanying a s.25 notice that he intended to redevelop (having previously had conversations with him about this) but subsequently changed his mind, without telling the tenant, was liable to the tenant for damages under s.37A. There was a continuing representation, in the letter accompanying the s.25 notice, that had been made false by the change in circumstances. Damages were awarded based on the difference in rent between the assumed market rent for the original premises and the rent for the new premises

(*Inclusive Technology v Williamson* [2009] EWCA Civ 718). Service of the s.25 notice of itself did not of itself amount to a representation. It was the covering letter that made the difference. Carnwarth LJ at paras 18 and 19:

> "I certainly accept that not every case in which a section 30(1)(f) notice is served will give rise to such a continuing obligation on the part of the landlord. However, in this case, the pre-notice exchanges show that the landlord, very fairly, was being entirely open with the tenant as to his plans. The letter of June, which accompanied the notice, as the judge found, was as clear as possible a statement of present intention, and the letter indicated that it was that intention which gave rise to the service of the notice. ... it amounted to a continuing representation, which does bring into play the section. That approach seems to me to be consistent with what I understand to be the purpose of the provision, which is to encourage fair dealing between the parties."

Costs

Where the landlord has relied on a ground other than (f) or (g), **27–28**
the successful party will usually be entitled to his costs.

It is often thought that the court will make no order as to costs where the landlord has successfully relied upon ground (f) or (g) and this used to be the common practice but the practice was disapproved of by Lord Denning in *Decca Navigator Co v Greater London Council* [1974] 1 All E.R. 1178. The court has an unfettered discretion and each case will turn upon its own facts but the usual order will be that costs follow the event. Indeed, since the Civil Procedure Rules, the position has changed dramatically so that costs need to be considered under those rules, including for example the power to make split costs orders where parties have succeeded on different issues, or penalty costs orders where parties have refused to mediate or negotiate reasonably (e.g. see para.26–35).

It might also be appropriate to make an order as to costs, other than that they should follow the event, where the tenant has asked the landlord to disclose details of his evidence relating to his "intention" so that the tenant can make a reasoned decision about whether or not to commence or pursue his application for a new tenancy but the landlord has unreasonably refused to do so.

Offers under Pt 36 may also of course be relevant. See also paras 24–68 and 26–02.

CHAPTER 28

TELECOMMUNICATIONS APPARATUS

. . . .

Seeking the removal of operators of electronic communications apparatus from premises has an additional layer of statutory hurdles to overcome. These hurdles are set out in the Electronic Communications Code ("the Code"), which is contained within Sch.2 to the Telecommunications Act 1984 (as amended by the Communications Act 2003). **28–01**

The Code applies to those operators registered with Ofcom as having powers under the Code. A list of registered operators is available on Ofcom's website; the website is a useful resource for information and forms (although it does not provide a copy of the code (http://stakeholders.ofcom.org.uk/telecoms/policy/electronic-comm-code/ [accessed November 24, 2014]).

There has been much deserved criticism of the Code and as part of the Governments' Policy of *"Making it easier for the communications and telecoms industries to grow, while protecting the interests of citizens"* a review of the Code was undertaken by the Law Commission. The Law Commission's findings were printed on February 27, 2013. Those findings recommended a complete overhaul of the Code. Since then the Department for Culture Media and Sport has been considering the Law Commission's recommendations but as yet no new legislation has been proposed.

This chapter sets out the basic position in relation to electronic communications equipment as it is at the date of publication.

Establishing the Basics

In order to seek the removal of electronic communications apparatus from premises there is a checklist of basic information that needs to be established. **28–02**

The Demised Premises

28-03 If you are dealing with a mast site the demised premises are likely to be obvious; however when dealing with a rooftop site the demised premises may not be quite as obvious. It may not be the roof space itself, but may be an area in the basement or elsewhere in the building where the cabinets are sited.

The telecommunications apparatus

28-04 You also need to establish what telecommunications apparatus there is on the premises, where the apparatus is and to whom it belongs.

The Basis of occupation

28-05 Telecommunications agreements appear in a variety of different forms such as:

- Early Access Agreements;
- Licences;
- Agreements;
- Leases;
- Tenancy at Wills;
- Multi-Site Agreements.

The agreement in each case will need to be examined to establish what property rights each occupier has, that will then determine how those property interests need to be brought to an end.

Who is in Occupation?

28-06 It is important to establish who is in occupation of the Site and the basis of that occupation. Over the years there have been numerous site sharing agreements between the operators and the merger of Orange and T-Mobile to become EE has complicated the situation.

It must be established who is in physical occupation, as what the agreement says might not be what is actually happening on site. Other operators may have been allowed onto the site. Consideration should be given to serving a s.40 notice under the Landlord and Tenant Act 1954 (see Ch.16), although that will not reveal any operators sharing possession.

Once it is been established who is in occupation it is necessary to ascertain whether they are on Ofcom's Register of persons with powers under the Code.

Bringing the tenancy/licence an end

Bringing the tenancy or licence to an end is dealt with in other chapters in this book. The important thing in respect of telecommunications operators is the interaction between the Landlord and Tenant Act 1954 and the Code. There has been on-going debate amongst practitioners as to whether the Landlord and Tenant Act 1954 can apply to tenancies to which the Code applies. This is yet to be determined by the courts and until then landlords should proceed on the basis that it does.   **28–07**

Serving Notice under the Code

In addition to bringing the tenancy to an end, if the Code applies notice will also have to be served under the Code requiring the removal of the equipment.   **28–08**

Most agreements entered into with an operator by an occupier of land will bind owners of superior and inferior interests. Paragraph 2 of the Code sets out the various different scenarios in which a person seeking the removal of the telecommunications apparatus will be bound by the Code even though they did not grant the rights to the operator.

There are two different notices that can be served under the Code when seeking the removal of telecommunications apparatus. The first is a notice to require alteration of apparatus pursuant to para.20 of the Code; and the second is a notice requiring the removal of the apparatus pursuant to para.21 of the Code.

Paragraph 20 Code Notice

"Power to require alteration of apparatus   28–09

20.—(1) Where any electronic communications apparatus is kept installed on, under or over any land for the purposes of the operator's network, any person with an interest in that land or adjacent land may (notwithstanding the terms of any agreement binding that person) by notice given to the operator require the alteration of the apparatus on the ground that the alteration is necessary to enable that person to carry out a proposed improvement of the land in which he has an interest."

The heading to para.20 is fairly misleading as is suggests that notices served under this paragraph are limited to alterations of apparatus on the Site. However, the definition of alteration at para.1(2) of the Code is *"references to the alteration of any apparatus include references to the moving, **removal** or replacement of the apparatus"* [emphasis added].

Points to note:

- The notice can be served by anyone with an interest in the land, which would include the landlord, the freeholder and a purchaser. Notice can also be served by anyone with an interest in any adjacent land.
- The notice requiring removal can be served even though there is a subsisting agreement giving the operator a right to occupy, which means that it can be served at any time during the term of a lease.
- The person serving the notice must show that it is necessary to alter the apparatus to enable them to carry out an improvement to the land in which they have an interest. Improvement is defined at para.20(9) as including development and change of use.
- There is no prescribed form of notice requiring the alteration of apparatus.

The operator will have to comply with the notice unless operator serves a counter-notice within 28 days (para.20(2)).

- The 28-day period for the giving of a counter-notice begins with the giving of the para.20 Notice.
- A counter-notice must be in a form approved by OFCOM (para.24(1)). Model notices are available on OFCOM's website.

If no counter-notice is served then the operator must comply with the notice.

If a counter-notice is given then the operator will only have to comply with the notice if the person serving the notice obtains a court order requiring the operator to comply (para.20(3)).

When considering an application under paragraph 20 the court will have regard to all the circumstances including the principle that no one should unreasonably be denied access to an electronic communications network or electronic communications services. In making an order the court must be satisfied that:

- The alteration sought is necessary; and
- The alteration will not substantially interfere with any service which is or is likely to be provided by the operators' network; and
- The operator has sufficient rights or could be granted those rights to make the alteration sought.

Where an order is made for the removal of apparatus pursuant to para.20 the court may, subject to the applicant's consent, modify the alterations sought. The court will also, unless it otherwise sees fit, require the person seeking the order to reimburse the operator for all expenses incurred as a result of complying with the order. There is no definition of "expenses" within the Code.

Paragraph 21 Code Notice

"Restriction on right to require the removal of apparatus   **28–10**

21.—(1) Where any person is for the time being entitled to require the removal of any of the operator's electronic communications apparatus from any land (whether under any enactment or because that apparatus is kept on, under or over that land otherwise than in pursuance of a right binding that person or for any other reason) that person shall not be entitled to enforce the removal of the apparatus except, subject to sub-paragraph (12) below, in accordance with the following provisions of this paragraph.

(2) The person entitled to require the removal of any of the operator's electronic communications apparatus shall give a notice to the operator requiring the removal of the apparatus."

Paragraph 21 prevents a person *"for the time being entitled to require the removal of . . . apparatus"* from enforcing the removal of the apparatus unless they have served a notice requiring the removal of the apparatus ("a para.21 Code Notice").

The phrase *"for the time being entitled to require the removal of . . . apparatus"* is unclear and potentially conflicts with the provisions of the Landlord and Tenant Act 1954. At what point would a landlord be entitled to require the removal of apparatus? In the case of a contested lease renewal would it be three months after final determination by the court? (See para.27–02). Or would they only be able to require removal at the same time that they are entitled to serve a notice terminating a lease that requires vacant possession? It is also unclear at what point the notice must be served.

There is a clear distinction in the wording used in paras 20 and 21. Paragraph 20 provides a right for notices to be served during the agreement by anyone with an interest in the land or adjacent land; whereas para.21 limits the rights of persons who would otherwise be entitled to vacant possession at the end of the term, by requiring them to serve a Code notice. It is often sensible to serve both para.20 and para.21 Code Notices.

The purpose behind the provisions appears to be to provide the operators with sufficient notice to allow them to serve a counter-notice, propose terms for a new agreement and if necessary, apply to the court for an agreement to be imposed upon the land owner.

There is no prescribed form of notice requiring the removal of apparatus.

Unless the operator serves a counter-notice within 28 days, beginning with the giving of the notice, the person serving the notice will have the right to enforce the removal of the apparatus (para.21(3)).

If the operator fails to serve a notice:

- It will be unable to make an application pursuant to para.5 for an agreement to be imposed on the landowner by the court.
- the landowner can enforce the removal of the apparatus; and
- the landowner has the option of seeking a court order for the right to remove the apparatus themselves.

The counter-notice must be in a form approved by OFCOM (para.24(1)). Model notices are available on OFCOM's website. The counter-notice must do one or both of the following: (para.21(4)):

- State that the person is not entitled to require removal;
- Specify the steps the operator is proposing to take to secure rights against the person serving the notice.

Where a counter-notice is served a court order is required to enforce the removal (para.21(6)). The court will not make an order unless it is satisfied that:

(a) That the operator is not intending to take the steps proposed in its counter-notice or is being unreasonably dilatory in the taking those steps; or
(b) That the taking of those steps has not secured, or will not secure any right to keep the apparatus installed on, under or over the land or, to re-install it if it is removed.

The landowner may also apply to the court;

● For authority to remove the apparatus itself (para.21(7));
● for the operator to pay the landowner's expenses of removing the apparatus (para.21(8)); and
● for authority to sell the apparatus and to retain the whole or part of the proceeds of sale on account of the landowners expenses (para.21(8)).

Service of Code Notices

Notices served under the Code should not be served by post unless they are served by registered post or recorded delivery (para.24(2)). **28–11**

The address for service will be either the address for service provided (para.24(2A)(a)), or where no address has been provided:

● In the case of a body corporate, the registered or principal office;
● In the case of an unincorporated body, the address of the principle office of a partnership, body or association;
● In any other case, the last known address of the person (Communications Act 2003 s.394).

Imposing agreements on land owners

Paragraph 5 provides the operators with the right to apply to a court for an agreement to be imposed upon a landowner to apply the operator to install and maintain telecommunications apparatus on land. **28–12**

"Power to dispense with the need for required agreement

5.–(1) Where the operator requires any person to agree for the purposes of paragraph 2 or 3 above that any right should be conferred on the operator, or that any right should bind that person or any interest in land, the operator may give a notice to that person of the right and of the agreement that he requires.

(2) Where the period of 28 days beginning with the giving of a notice under sub-paragraph (1) above has expired without the giving of the required agreement, the operator may apply to the court for an order conferring the proposed right, or providing for it to bind any person or any interest in land, and (in either case) dispensing with the need for the agreement of the person to whom the notice was given."

The court has to carry out a balancing exercise between the rights of the landowner and the principle that no person should unreasonably be denied access to an electronic communications network or to electronic communications services. The court can only make an order if it is satisfied that any prejudice caused to the landowner:

- Can be adequately compensated in money; or
- Is outweighed by the benefit accruing to the persons whose access to an electronic communications network will be secured by the order (para.5(3)).

If the court does impose an agreement upon a landowner, the court shall include such appropriate terms to ensure the least possible loss and damage to the landowner (para.5(5)). The considerations to be taken into account are dealt with in para.7 of the Code.

Temporary Rights

28-13   Whilst a para.5 application is ongoing, an operator has the right to apply to the court for such necessary temporary rights in respect of the land to allow it to maintain and repair its apparatus whilst the para.5 application is being heard (para.6).

Compensation

28-14   Paragraph 7 of the Code sets out the considerations to be taken into account when determining the payment and compensation terms where the court imposes an agreement on a landowner, being:

- Such fair and reasonable terms which would have been agreed if the agreement had been given willingly;
- Appropriate terms to ensure the person bound by the imposed rights is adequately compensated for any loss and damage sustained by the operator exercising the rights.

There is no guidance as to how wide the payment and compensation terms are. They clearly go beyond mere rent and appear to extend to diminution in value of the landowner's land. What is yet to be decided is whether the compensation would extend to the full development value of the land.

Applications to Court

Seeking the removal of telecommunications apparatus invariably goes hand in hand with possession proceedings and will be pleaded as part of the claim in those proceedings. **28–15**

The type of possession proceedings will depend upon whether the lease is "on the face of it" within the Landlord and Tenant Act 1954, in which case they will be contested renewal proceedings. If the lease was contracted out of the Landlord and Tenant Act 1954 then they will be simple possession proceedings.

There are no courts with special jurisdiction over telecommunications matters and the applications for removal are made to the appropriate county court.

Abandonment of Equipment

Where an operator's apparatus is no longer being used for the operator's network, para.22 of the Code provides that the operator is not entitled to keep that apparatus installed on the land. **28–16**

Part 7

Appendices

APPENDIX 1

LANDLORD AND TENANT ACT 1954 (AS AMENDED IN 2004 SHOWING THE CHANGES)

. . . .

PART II

SECURITY OF TENURE FOR BUSINESS, PROFESSIONAL AND OTHER TENANTS

Tenancies to which Part II applies

23.–(1) Subject to the provisions of this Act, this Part of this Act applies to any tenancy where the property comprised in the tenancy is or includes premises which are occupied by the tenant and are so occupied for the purposes of a business carried on by him or for those and other purposes.

A1–01– A1–02

(1A) Occupation or the carrying on of a business—

(a) by a company in which the tenant has a controlling interest; or

(b) where the tenant is a company, by a person with a controlling interest in the company,

shall be treated for the purposes of this section as equivalent to occupation or, as the case may be, the carrying on of a business by the tenant.

(1B) Accordingly references (however expressed) in this Part of this Act to the business of, or to use, occupation or enjoyment by, the tenant shall be construed as including references to the business of, or to use, occupation or enjoyment by, a company falling within subsection (1A)(a) above or a person falling within subsection (1A)(b) above.

(2) In this Part of this Act the expression "business" includes a trade, profession or employment and includes any activity carried on by a body of persons, whether corporate or unincorporate.

(3) In the following provisions of this Part of this Act the expression "the holding," in relation to a tenancy to which this Part of this Act applies, means the property comprised in the tenancy, there being excluded any part thereof which is occupied neither by the tenant nor by a person employed

by the tenant and so employed for the purposes of a business by reason of which the tenancy is one to which this Part of this Act applies.

(4) Where the tenant is carrying on a business, in all or any part of the property comprised in a tenancy, in breach of a prohibition (however expressed) of use for business purposes which subsists under the terms of the tenancy and extends to the whole of that property, this Part of this Act shall not apply to the tenancy unless the immediate landlord or his predecessor in title has consented to the breach or the immediate landlord has acquiesced therein.

In this subsection the reference to a prohibition of use for business purposes does not include a prohibition of use for the purposes of a specified business, or of use for purposes of any but a specified business, but save as aforesaid includes a prohibition of use for the purposes of some one or more only of the classes of business specified in the definition of that expression in subsection (2) of this section.

Continuation and renewal of tenancies

Continuation of tenancies to which Part II applies and grant of new tenancies

A1–03

24.–(1) A tenancy to which this Part of this Act applies shall not come to an end unless terminated in accordance with the provisions of this Part of this Act; and, subject to the ~~provisions of section twenty-nine of this Act, the tenant under such a tenancy may apply to the court for~~ **following provisions of this Act either the tenant or the landlord under such a tenancy may apply to the court for an order for the grant of** a new tenancy–

(a) if the landlord has given notice under section 25 of this Act to terminate the tenancy, or

(b) if the tenant has made a request for a new tenancy in accordance with section 26 of this Act.

(2) The last foregoing subsection shall not prevent the coming to an end of a tenancy by notice to quit given by the tenant, by surrender or forfeiture, or by the forfeiture of a superior tenancy unless–

(a) in the case of a notice to quit, the notice was given before the tenant had been in occupation in right of the tenancy for one month; ~~or~~

(b) ~~in the case of an instrument of surrender, the instrument was executed before, or was executed in pursuance of an agreement made before, the tenant had been in occupation in right of the tenancy for one month.~~

(2A) Neither the tenant nor the landlord may make an application under subsection (1) above if the other has made such an application and the application has been served.

(2B) Neither the tenant nor the landlord may make such an application if the landlord has made an application under section 29(2) of this Act and the application has been served.

(2C) The landlord may not withdraw an application under subsection (1) above unless the tenant consents to its withdrawal.

(3) Notwithstanding anything in subsection (1) of this section—

(a) where a tenancy to which this Part of this Act applies ceases to be such a tenancy, it shall not come to an end by reason only of the cesser, but if it was granted for a term of years certain and has been continued by subsection (1) of this section then (without prejudice to the termination thereof in accordance with any terms of the tenancy) it may be terminated by not less than three nor more than six months' notice in writing given by the landlord to the tenant;

(b) where, at a time when a tenancy is not one to which this Part of this Act applies, the landlord gives notice to quit, the operation of the notice shall not be affected by reason that the tenancy becomes one to which this Part of this Act applies after the giving of the notice.

~~24A.—(1) The landlord of a tenancy to which this Part of this Act applies may,—~~

~~(a) if he has given notice under section 25 of this Act to terminate the tenancy; or~~

~~(b) if the tenant has made a request for a new tenancy in accordance with section 26 of this Act;~~

~~apply to the court to determine a rent which it would be reasonable for the tenant to pay while the tenancy continues by virtue of section 24 of this Act, and the court may determine a rent accordingly.~~

~~(2) A rent determined in proceedings under this section shall be deemed to be the rent payable under the tenancy from the date on which the proceedings were commenced or the date specified in the landlord's notice or the tenant's request, whichever is the later.~~

~~(3) In determining a rent under this section the court shall have regard to the rent payable under the terms of the tenancy, but otherwise subsections (1) and (2) of section 34 of this Act shall apply to the determination as they would apply to the determination of a rent under that section if a new tenancy from year to year of the whole of the property comprised in the tenancy were granted to the tenant by order of the court.~~

Applications for determination of interim rent while tenancy continues

24A.—(1) Subject to subsection (2) below, if—   A1–04

(a) the landlord of a tenancy to which this Part of this Act applies has given notice under section 25 of this Act to terminate the tenancy; or

(b) the tenant of such a tenancy has made a request for a new tenancy in accordance with section 26 of this Act,

either of them may make an application to the court to determine a rent (an "interim rent") which the tenant is to pay while the tenancy ("the relevant tenancy") continues by virtue of section 24 of this Act and the court may order payment of an interim rent in accordance with section 24C or 24D of this Act.

(2) Neither the tenant nor the landlord may make an application under subsection (1) above if the other has made such an application and has not withdrawn it.

(3) No application shall be entertained under subsection (1) above if it is made more than six months after the termination of the relevant tenancy.

Date from which interim rent is payable

A1-05   24B.—(1) The interim rent determined on an application under section 24A(1) of this Act shall be payable from the appropriate date.

(2) If an application under section 24A(1) of this Act is made in a case where the landlord has given a notice under section 25 of this Act, the appropriate date is the earliest date of termination that could have been specified in the landlord's notice.

(3) If an application under section 24A(1) of this Act is made in a case where the tenant has made a request for a new tenancy under section 26 of this Act, the appropriate date is the earliest date that could have been specified in the tenant's request as the date from which the new tenancy is to begin.

Amount of interim rent where new tenancy of whole premises granted and landlord not opposed

A1-06   24C.—(1) This section applies where—

(a)   the landlord gave a notice under section 25 of this Act at a time when the tenant was in occupation of the whole of the property comprised in the relevant tenancy for purposes such as are mentioned in section 23(1) of this Act and stated in the notice that he was not opposed to the grant of a new tenancy; or

(b)   the tenant made a request for a new tenancy under section 26 of this Act at a time when he was in occupation of the whole of that property for such purposes and the landlord did not give notice under subsection (6) of that section,

and the landlord grants a new tenancy of the whole of the property comprised in the relevant tenancy to the tenant (whether as a result of an order for the grant of a new tenancy or otherwise).

(2) Subject to the following provisions of this section, the rent payable under and at the commencement of the new tenancy shall also be the interim rent.

(3) Subsection (2) above does not apply where—

(a)   the landlord or the tenant shows to the satisfaction of the court that the interim rent under that subsection differs substantially from the relevant rent; or

(b)   the landlord or the tenant shows to the satisfaction of the court that the terms of the new tenancy differ from the terms of the relevant tenancy to such an extent that the interim rent under that subsection is substantially different from the rent which (in default of such agreement) the court would have determined under section 34 of this Act to be payable under a tenancy which commenced on the same day as the new tenancy and whose other terms were the same as the relevant tenancy.

(4) In this section "the relevant rent" means the rent which (in default of agreement between the landlord and the tenant) the court would have determined under section 34 of this Act to be payable under the new tenancy if the new tenancy had commenced on the appropriate date (within the meaning of section 24B of this Act).

(5) The interim rent in a case where subsection (2) above does not apply by virtue only of subsection (3)(a) above is the relevant rent.

(6) The interim rent in a case where subsection (2) above does not apply by virtue only of subsection (3)(b) above, or by virtue of subsection (3)(a) and (b) above, is the rent which it is reasonable for the tenant to pay while the relevant tenancy continues by virtue of section 24 of this Act.

(7) In determining the interim rent under subsection (6) above the court shall have regard—

(a) to the rent payable under the terms of the relevant tenancy; and

(b) to the rent payable under any sub-tenancy of part of the property comprised in the relevant tenancy,

but otherwise subsections (1) and (2) of section 34 of this Act shall apply to the determination as they would apply to the determination of a rent under that section if a new tenancy of the whole of the property comprised in the relevant tenancy were granted to the tenant by order of the court and the duration of that new tenancy were the same as the duration of the new tenancy which is actually granted to the tenant.

(8) In this section and section 24D of this Act "the relevant tenancy" has the same meaning as in section 24A of this Act.

Amount of interim rent in any other case

24D.–(1) The interim rent in a case where section 24C of this Act does not apply is the rent which it is reasonable for the tenant to pay while the relevant tenancy continues by virtue of section 24 of this Act. **A1–07**

(2) In determining the interim rent under subsection (1) above the court shall have regard—

(a) to the rent payable under the terms of the relevant tenancy; and

(b) to the rent payable under any sub-tenancy of part of the property comprised in the relevant tenancy,

but otherwise subsections (1) and (2) of section 34 of this Act shall apply to the determination as they would apply to the determination of a rent under that section if a new tenancy from year to year of the whole of the property comprised in the relevant tenancy were granted to the tenant by order of the court.

(3) If the court—

(a) has made an order for the grant of a new tenancy and has ordered payment of interim rent in accordance with section 24C of this Act, but

(b) either—

> **(i) it subsequently revokes under section 36(2) of this Act the order for the grant of a new tenancy; or**
>
> **(ii) the landlord and tenant agree not to act on the order,**

the court on the application of the landlord or the tenant shall determine a new interim rent in accordance with subsections (1) and (2) above without a further application under section 24A(1) of this Act.

Termination of tenancy by the landlord

A1–08 25.–(1) The landlord may terminate a tenancy to which this Part of this Act applies by a notice given to the tenant in the prescribed form specifying the date at which the tenancy is to come to an end (hereinafter referred to as "the date of termination"):

Provided that this subsection has effect subject to **the provisions of section 29B(4) of this Act and** Part IV of this Act as to the interim continuation of tenancies pending the disposal of applications to the court.

(2) Subject to the provisions of the next following subsection, a notice under this section shall not have effect unless it is given not more than twelve nor less than six months before the date of termination specified therein.

(3) In the case of a tenancy which apart from this Act could have been brought to an end by notice to quit given by the landlord—

(a) the date of termination specified in a notice under this section shall not be earlier than the earliest date on which apart from this Part of this Act the tenancy could have been brought to an end by notice to quit given by the landlord on the date of the giving of the notice under this section; and

(b) where apart from this Part of this Act more than six months' notice to quit would have been required to bring the tenancy to an end, the last foregoing subsection shall have effect with the substitution for twelve months of a period six months longer than the length of notice to quit which would have been required as aforesaid.

(4) In the case of any other tenancy, a notice under this section shall not specify a date of termination earlier than the date on which apart from this Part of this Act the tenancy would have come to an end by effluxion of time.

(5) A notice under this section shall not have effect unless it requires the tenant, within two months after the giving of the notice, to notify the landlord in writing whether or not, at the date of termination, the tenant will be willing to give up possession of the property comprised in the tenancy.

~~(6) A notice under this section shall not have effect unless it states whether the landlord would oppose an application to the court under this Part of this Act for the grant of a new tenancy and, if so, also states on which of the grounds mentioned in section 30 of this Act he would do so.~~

(6) A notice under this section shall not have effect unless it states whether the landlord is opposed to the grant of a new tenancy to the tenant.

(7) A notice under this section which states that the landlord is opposed to the grant of a new tenancy to the tenant shall not have effect unless it also specifies one or more of the grounds specified in section 30(1) of this Act as the ground or grounds for his opposition.

(8) A notice under this section which states that the landlord is not opposed to the grant of a new tenancy to the tenant shall not have effect unless it sets out the landlord's proposals as to—

(a) **the property to be comprised in the new tenancy (being either the whole or part of the property comprised in the current tenancy);**

(b) **the rent to be payable under the new tenancy; and**

(c) **the other terms of the new tenancy.**

Tenant's request for a new tenancy

26.—(1) A tenant's request for a new tenancy may be made where the ~~tenancy under which he holds for the time being (hereinafter referred to as "the current tenancy")~~ **current tenancy** is a tenancy granted for a term of years certain exceeding one year, whether or not continued by section 24 of this Act, or granted for a term of years certain and thereafter from year to year.

A1–09

(2) A tenant's request for a new tenancy shall be for a tenancy beginning with such date, not more than twelve nor less than six months after the making of the request, as may be specified therein;

Provided that the said date shall not be earlier than the date on which apart from this Act the current tenancy would come to an end by effluxion of time or could be brought to an end by notice to quit given by the tenant.

(3) A tenant's request for a new tenancy shall not have effect unless it is made by notice in the prescribed form given to the landlord and sets out the tenant's proposals as to the property to be comprised in the new tenancy (being either the whole or part of the property comprised in the current tenancy), as to the rent to be payable under the new tenancy and as to the other terms of the new tenancy.

(4) A tenant's request for a new tenancy shall not be made if the landlord has already given notice under the last foregoing section to terminate the current tenancy, or if the tenant has already given notice to quit or notice under the next following section; and no such notice shall be given by the landlord or the tenant after the making by the tenant of a request for a new tenancy.

(5) Where the tenant makes a request for a new tenancy in accordance with the foregoing provisions of this section, the current tenancy shall, subject to the provisions of ~~subsection (2) of section thirty-six~~ **sections 29B(4) and 36(2)** of this Act and the provisions of Part IV of this Act as to

the interim continuation of tenancies, terminate immediately before the date specified in the request for the beginning of the new tenancy.

(6) Within two months of the making of a tenant's request for a new tenancy the landlord may give notice to the tenant that he will oppose an application to the court for the grant of a new tenancy, and any such notice shall state on which of the grounds mentioned in section 30 of this Act the landlord will oppose the application.

Termination by tenant of tenancy for fixed term

A1–10 **27.**–(1) Where the tenant under a tenancy to which this Part of this Act applies, being a tenancy granted for a term of years certain, gives to the immediate landlord, not later than three months before the date on which apart from this Act the tenancy would come to an end by effluxion of time, a notice in writing that the tenant does not desire the tenancy to be continued, section 24 of this Act shall not have effect in relation to the tenancy, unless the notice is given before the tenant has been in occupation in right of the tenancy for one month.

(1A) Section 24 of this Act shall not have effect in relation to a tenancy for a term of years certain where the tenant is not in occupation of the property comprised in the tenancy at the time when, apart from this Act, the tenancy would come to an end by effluxion of time.

(2) A tenancy granted for a term of years certain which is continuing by virtue of section 24 of this Act **shall not come to an end by reason only of the tenant ceasing to occupy the property comprised in the tenancy but** may be brought to an end on any quarter day by not less than three months' notice in writing given by the tenant to the immediate landlord, whether the notice is given after the date on which apart from this Act the tenancy would have come to an end or before that date, but not before the tenant has been in occupation in right of the tenancy for one month.

(3) Where a tenancy is terminated under subsection (2) above, any rent payable in respect of a period which begins before, and ends after, the tenancy is terminated shall be apportioned, and any rent paid by the tenant in excess of the amount apportioned to the period before termination shall be recoverable by him.

Renewal of tenancies by agreement

A1–11 **28.** Where the landlord and tenant agree for the grant to the tenant of a future tenancy of the holding, or of the holding with other land, on terms and from a date specified in the agreement, the current tenancy shall continue until that date but no longer, and shall not be a tenancy to which this Part of this Act applies.

~~Application to court for new tenancies~~

~~Order by court for grant of a new tenancy~~

~~**29.**–(1) Subject to the provisions of this Act, on an application under subsection (1) of section 24 of this Act for a new tenancy the court shall~~

~~make an order for the grant of a tenancy comprising such property, at such rent and on such other terms, as are hereinafter provided.~~

~~(2) Where such an application is made in consequence of a notice given by the landlord under section 25 of this Act, it shall not be entertained unless the tenant has duly notified the landlord that he will not be willing at the date of termination to give up possession of the property comprised in the tenancy.~~

~~(3) No application under subsection (1) of section 24 of this Act shall be entertained unless it is made not less than two nor more than four months after the giving of the landlord's notice under section 25 of this Act or, as the case may be, after the making of the tenant's request for a new tenancy.~~

Applications to court

Order by court for grant of new tenancy or termination of current tenancy

29.—(1) Subject to the provisions of this Act, on an application under section 24(1) of this Act, the court shall make an order for the grant of a new tenancy and accordingly for the termination of the current tenancy immediately before the commencement of the new tenancy.

A1–12

(2) Subject to the following provisions of this Act, a landlord may apply to the court for an order for the termination of a tenancy to which this Part of this Act applies without the grant of a new tenancy—

(a) if he has given notice under section 25 of this Act that he is opposed to the grant of a new tenancy to the tenant; or

(b) if the tenant has made a request for a new tenancy in accordance with section 26 of this Act and the landlord has given notice under subsection (6) of that section.

(3) The landlord may not make an application under subsection (2) above if either the tenant or the landlord has made an application under section 24(1) of this Act.

(4) Subject to the provisions of this Act, where the landlord makes an application under subsection (2) above—

(a) if he establishes, to the satisfaction of the court, any of the grounds on which he is entitled to make the application in accordance with section 30 of this Act, the court shall make an order for the termination of the current tenancy in accordance with section 64 of this Act without the grant of a new tenancy; and

(b) if not, it shall make an order for the grant of a new tenancy and accordingly for the termination of the current tenancy immediately before the commencement of the new tenancy.

(5) The court shall dismiss an application by the landlord under section 24(1) of this Act if the tenant informs the court that he does not want a new tenancy.

(6) The landlord may not withdraw an application under subsection (2) above unless the tenant consents to its withdrawal.

Time limits for applications to court

A1-13 29A.—(1) Subject to section 29B of this Act, the court shall not entertain an application—

(a) by the tenant or the landlord under section 24(1) of this Act; or

(b) by the landlord under section 29(2) of this Act,

if it is made after the end of the statutory period.

(2) In this section and section 29B of this Act "the statutory period" means a period ending—

(a) where the landlord gave a notice under section 25 of this Act, on the date specified in his notice; and

(b) where the tenant made a request for a new tenancy under section 26 of this Act, immediately before the date specified in his request.

(3) Where the tenant has made a request for a new tenancy under section 26 of this Act, the court shall not entertain an application under section 24(1) of this Act which is made before the end of the period of two months beginning with the date of the making of the request, unless the application is made after the landlord has given a notice under section 26(6) of this Act.

Agreements extending time limits

A1-14 29B.—(1) After the landlord has given a notice under section 25 of this Act, or the tenant has made a request under section 26 of this Act, but before the end of the statutory period, the landlord and tenant may agree that an application such as is mentioned in section 29A(1) of this Act may be made before the end of a period specified in the agreement which will expire after the end of the statutory period.

(2) The landlord and tenant may from time to time by agreement further extend the period for making such an application, but any such agreement must be made before the end of the period specified in the current agreement.

(3) Where an agreement is made under this section, the court may entertain an application such as is mentioned in section 29A(1) of this Act if it is made before the end of the period specified in the agreement.

(4) Where an agreement is made under this section, or two or more agreements are made under this section, the landlord's notice under section 25 of this Act or tenant's request under section 26 of this Act shall be treated as terminating the tenancy at the end of the period specified in the agreement or, as the case may be, at the end of the period specified in the last of those agreements.

Opposition by landlord to application for new tenancy

30.–(1) The grounds on which a landlord may oppose an application under ~~subsection (1) of section twenty-four of this Act~~ **section 24(1) of this Act, or make an application under section 29(2) of this Act,** are such of the following grounds as may be stated in the landlord's notice under section 25 of this Act or, as the case may be, under subsection (6) of section 26 thereof, that is to say:

A1–15

(a) where under the current tenancy the tenant has any obligations as respects the repair and maintenance of the holding, that the tenant ought not to be granted a new tenancy in view of the state of repair of the holding, being a state resulting from the tenant's failure to comply with the said obligations;

(b) that the tenant ought not to be granted a new tenancy in view of his persistent delay in paying rent which has become due;

(c) that the tenant ought not to be granted a new tenancy in view of other substantial breaches by him of his obligations under the current tenancy, or for any other reason connected with the tenant's use or management of the holding;

(d) that the landlord has offered and is willing to provide or secure the provision of alternative accommodation for the tenant, that the terms on which the alternative accommodation is available are reasonable having regard to the terms of the current tenancy and to all other relevant circumstances, and that the accommodation and the time at which it will be available are suitable for the tenant's requirements (including the requirement to preserve goodwill) having regard to the nature and class of his business and to the situation and extent of, and facilities afforded by, the holding;

(e) where the current tenancy was created by the sub-letting of part only of the property comprised in a superior tenancy and the landlord is the owner of an interest in reversion expectant on the termination of that superior tenancy, that the aggregate of the rents reasonably obtainable on separate lettings of the holding and the remainder of that property would be substantially less than the rent reasonably obtainable on a letting of that property as a whole, that on the termination of the current tenancy the landlord requires possession of the holding for the purpose of letting or otherwise disposing of the said property as a whole, and that in view thereof the tenant ought not to be granted a new tenancy;

(f) that on the termination of the current tenancy the landlord intends to demolish or reconstruct the premises comprised in the holding or a substantial part of those premises or to carry out substantial work of construction on the holding or part thereof and that he could not reasonably do so without obtaining possession of the holding;

(g) subject as hereinafter provided, that on the termination of the current tenancy the landlord intends to occupy the holding for the purposes, or partly for the purposes, of a business to be carried on by him therein, or as his residence.

(1A) Where the landlord has a controlling interest in a company, the reference in subsection (1)(g) above to the landlord shall be construed as a reference to the landlord or that company.

(1B) Subject to subsection (2A) below, where the landlord is a company and a person has a controlling interest in the company, the reference in subsection (1)(g) above to the landlord shall be construed as a reference to the landlord or that person.

(2) The landlord shall not be entitled to oppose an application **under section 24(1) of this Act, or make an application under section 29(2) of this Act,** on the ground specified in paragraph (g) of the last foregoing subsection if the interest of the landlord, or an interest which has merged in that interest and but for the merger would be the interest of the landlord, was purchased or created after the beginning of the period of five years which ends with the termination of the current tenancy, and at all times since the purchase or creation thereof the holding has been comprised in a tenancy or successive tenancies of the description specified in subsection (1) of section 23 of this Act.

(2A) Subsection (1B) above shall not apply if the controlling interest was acquired after the beginning of the period of five years which ends with the termination of the current tenancy, and at all times since the acquisition of the controlling interest the holding has been comprised in a tenancy or successive tenancies of the description specified in section 23(1) of this Act.

(3) Where the landlord has a controlling interest in a company any business to be carried on by the company shall be treated for the purposes of subsection (1) (g) of this section as a business to be carried on by him.

For the purposes of this subsection, a person has a controlling interest in a company if and only if either—

(a) he is a member of it and able, without the consent of any other person, to appoint or remove the holders of at least a majority of the directorships; or

(b) he holds more than one-half of its equity share capital, there being disregarded any shares held by him in a fiduciary capacity or as nominee for another person;

and in this subsection "company" and "share" have the meanings assigned to them by section 455(1) of the Companies Act 1948 and "equity share capital" the meaning assigned to it by section 154(5) of that Act.

Dismissal of application for new tenancy where landlord successfully opposes

A1-16
31.—(1) If the landlord opposes an application under subsection (1) of section 24 of this Act on grounds on which he is entitled to oppose it in accordance with the last foregoing section and establishes any of those grounds to the satisfaction of the court, the court shall not make an order for the grant of a new tenancy.

(2) **Where the landlord opposes an application under section 24(1) of this Act, or makes an application under section 29(2) of this Act, on one or more of the grounds specified in section 30(1)(d) to (f) of this**

Act but establishes none of those grounds, and none of the other grounds specified in section 30(1) of this Act, to the satisfaction of the court, then if the court would have been satisfied on any of the grounds specified in section 30(1)(d) to (f) of this Act ~~Where in a case not falling within the last foregoing subsection the landlord opposes an application under the said subsection (1) on one or more of the grounds, specified in paragraphs, (d), (e), and (f) of subsection (1) of the last foregoing subsection but establishes none of those grounds to the satisfaction of the court, then if the court would have been satisfied of any of these grounds~~ if the date of termination specified in the landlord's notice or, as the case may be, the date specified in the tenant's request for a new tenancy as the date from which the new tenancy is to begin, had been such later date as the court may determine, being a date not more than one year later than the date so specified—

(a)   the court shall make a declaration to that effect, stating of which of the said grounds the court would have been satisfied as aforesaid and specifying the date determined by the court as aforesaid, but shall not make an order for the grant of a new tenancy;

(b)   if, within fourteen days after the making of the declaration, the tenant so requires the court shall make an order substituting the said date for the date specified in the said landlord's notice or tenant's request, and thereupon that notice or request shall have effect accordingly.

Grant of new tenancy in some cases where section 30(1)(f) applies

31A.—(1) Where the landlord opposes an application under section 24(1) of this Act on the ground specified in paragraph (f) of section 30(1) of this Act, **or makes an application under section 29(2) of this Act on that ground**, the court shall not hold that the landlord could not reasonably carry out the demolition, reconstruction or work of construction intended without obtaining possession of the holding if—

A1–17

(a)   the tenant agrees to the inclusion in the terms of the new tenancy of terms giving the landlord access and other facilities for carrying out the work intended and, given that access and those facilities, the landlord could reasonably carry out the work without obtaining possession of the holding and without interfering to a substantial extent or for a substantial time with the use of the holding for the purposes of the business carried on by the tenant; or

(b)   the tenant is willing to accept a tenancy of an economically separable part of the holding and either paragraph (a) of this section is satisfied with respect to that part or possession of the remainder of the holding would be reasonably sufficient to enable the landlord to carry out the intended work.

(2) For the purposes of subsection (1) (b) of this section a part of a holding shall be deemed to be an economically separate part if, and only if, the aggregate of the rents which, after the completion' of the intended work, would be reasonably obtainable on separate lettings of that part and the remainder of the premises affected by or resulting from the work would not

be substantially less than the rent which would then be reasonably obtainable on a letting of those premises as a whole.

Property to be comprised in new tenancy

A1-18   **32.**–(1) Subject to the following provisions of this section, an order under section 29 of this Act for the grant of a new tenancy shall be an order for the grant of a new tenancy of the holding; and in the absence of agreement between the landlord and the tenant as to the property which constitutes the holding the court shall in the order designate that property by reference to the circumstances existing at the date of the order.

(1A) Where the court, by virtue of paragraph (b) of section 31A(1) *of* this Act, makes an order under section 29 of this Act for the grant *of* a new tenancy in a case where the tenant is willing to accept a tenancy of part of the holding, the order shall be an order for the grant *of* a new tenancy of that part only.

(2) The foregoing provisions of this section shall not apply in a case where the property comprised in the current tenancy includes other property besides the holding and the landlord requires any new tenancy ordered to be granted under section 29 of this Act to be a tenancy of the whole of the property comprised in the current tenancy; but in any such case—

(a)   any order under the said section 29 for the grant of a new tenancy shall be an order for the grant of a new tenancy of the whole of the property comprised in the current tenancy, and

(b)   references in the following provisions of this Part of this Act to the holding shall be construed as references to the whole of that property.

(3) Where the current tenancy includes rights enjoyed by the tenant in connection with the holding, those rights shall be included in a tenancy ordered to be granted under section 29 of this Act, except as otherwise agreed between the landlord and the tenant or, in default of such agreement, determined by the court.

Duration of new tenancy

A1-19   **33.** Where on an application under this Part of this Act the court makes an order for the grant of a new tenancy, the new tenancy shall be such tenancy as may be agreed between the landlord and the tenant, or, in default of such an agreement, shall be such a tenancy as may be determined by the court to be reasonable in all the circumstances, being, if it is a tenancy for a term of years certain, a tenancy for a term not exceeding ~~fourteen~~ **fifteen** years, and shall begin on the coming to an end of the current tenancy.

Rent under new tenancy

A1-20   **34.**–(1) The rent payable under a tenancy granted by order of the court under this Part of this Act shall be such as may be agreed between the landlord and the tenant or as, in default of such agreement, may be determined by the court to be that at which, having regard to the terms of the tenancy (other than those relating to rent), the holding might reasonably be expected to be let in the open market by a willing lessor, there being disregarded—

(a) any effect on rent of the fact that the tenant has or his predecessors in title have been in occupation of the holding,

(b) any goodwill attached to the holding by reason of the carrying on thereat of the business of the tenant (whether by him or by a predecessor of his in that business),

(c) any effect on rent of an improvement to which this paragraph applies,

(d) in the case of a holding comprising licensed premises, any addition to its value attributable to the licence, if it appears to the court that having regard to the terms of the current tenancy and any other relevant circumstances the benefit of the licence belongs to the tenant.

(2) Paragraph (c) of the foregoing subsection applies to any improvement carried out by a person who at the time it was carried out was the tenant, but only if it was carried out otherwise than in pursuance of an obligation to his immediate landlord, and either it was carried out during the current tenancy or the following conditions are satisfied, that is to say—

(a) that it was completed not more than twenty-one years before the application ~~for the new tenancy~~ **to the court** was made; and

(b) that the holding or any part of it affected by the improvement has at all times since the completion of the improvement been comprised in tenancies of the description specified in section 23(1) of this Act; and

(c) that at the termination of each of those tenancies the tenant did not quit.

(2A) If this Part of this Act applies by virtue of section 23(1A) of this Act, the reference in subsection (1)(d) above to the tenant shall be construed as including—

(a) a company in which the tenant has a controlling interest, or

(b) where the tenant is a company, a person with a controlling interest in the company.

(3) Where the rent is determined by the court the court may, if it thinks fit, further determine that the terms of the tenancy shall include such provision for varying the rent as may be specified in the determination.

(4) It is hereby declared that the matters which are to be taken into account by the court in determining the rent include any effect on rent of the operation of the provisions of the Landlord and Tenant (Covenants) Act 1995.

Other terms of new tenancy

35.—(1) The terms of a tenancy granted by order of the court under this Part of this Act (other than terms as to the duration thereof and as to the rent payable thereunder), **including, where different persons own interests**

A1–21

which fulfil the conditions specified in section 44(1) of this Act in different parts of it, terms as to the apportionment of the rent, shall be such as may be agreed between the landlord and the tenant or as, in default of such agreement, may be determined by the court; and in determining those terms the court shall have regard to the terms of the current tenancy and to all relevant circumstances.

(2) In subsection (1) of this section the reference to all relevant circumstances includes (without prejudice to the generality of that reference) a reference to the operation of the provisions of the Landlord and Tenant (Covenants) Act 1995.

Carrying out of order for new tenancy

A1-22
36.–(1) Where under this Part of this Act the court makes an order for the grant of a new tenancy, then, unless the order is revoked under the next following subsection or the landlord and the tenant agree not to act upon the order, the landlord shall be bound to execute or make in favour of the tenant, and the tenant shall be bound to accept, a lease or agreement for a tenancy of the holding embodying the terms agreed between the landlord and the tenant or determined by the court in accordance with the foregoing provisions of this Part of this Act; and where the landlord executes or makes such a lease or agreement the tenant shall be bound, if so required by the landlord, to execute a counterpart or duplicate thereof.

(2) If the tenant, within fourteen days after the making of an order under this Part of this Act for the grant of a new tenancy, applies to the court for the revocation of the order the court shall revoke the order; and where the order is so revoked, then, if it is so agreed between the landlord and the tenant or determined by the court, the current tenancy shall continue, beyond the date at which it would have come to an end apart from this subsection, for such period as may be so agreed or determined to be necessary to afford to the landlord a reasonable opportunity for reletting or otherwise disposing of the premises which would have been comprised in the new tenancy; and while the current tenancy continues by virtue of this subsection it shall not be a tenancy to which this Part of this Act applies.

(3) Where an order is revoked under the last foregoing subsection any provision thereof as to payment of costs shall not cease to have effect by reason only of the revocation; but the court may, if it thinks fit, revoke or vary any such provision or, where no costs have been awarded in the proceedings for the revoked order, award such costs.

(4) A lease executed or agreement made under this section, in a case where the interest of the lessor is subject to a mortgage, shall be deemed to be one authorised by section 99 of the Law of Property Act 1925 (which confers certain powers of leasing on mortgagors in possession), and subsection (13) of that section (which allows those powers to be restricted or excluded by agreement) shall not have effect in relation to such a lease or agreement.

Compensation where order for new tenancy precluded on certain grounds

~~**37.**–(1) Where on the making of an application under section 24 of this Act the court is precluded (whether by subsection (1) or subsection (2) of~~

~~section 31 of this Act) from making an order for the grant of a new tenancy by reason of any of the grounds specified in paragraphs (e), (f) and (g) of subsection (1) of section 30 of this Act and not of any grounds specified in any other paragraph of that subsection, or where no other ground is specified in the landlord's notice under section 25 of this Act or, as the case may be, under section 26(6) thereof, than those specified in the said paragraphs (e), (f) and (g) and either no application under the said section 24 is made or such an application is withdrawn, then, subject to the provisions of this Act, the tenant shall be entitled on quitting the holding to recover from the landlord by way of compensation an amount determined in accordance with the following provisions of this section.~~

37.—(1) Subject to the provisions of this Act, in a case specified in subsection (1A), (1B) or (1C) below (a "compensation case") the tenant shall be entitled on quitting the holding to recover from the landlord by way of compensation an amount determined in accordance with this section.

A1–23

(1A) The first compensation case is where on the making of an application by the tenant under section 24(1) of this Act the court is precluded (whether by subsection (1) or subsection (2) of section 31 of this Act) from making an order for the grant of a new tenancy by reason of any of the grounds specified in paragraphs (e), (f) and (g) of section 30(1) of this Act (the "compensation grounds") and not of any grounds specified in any other paragraph of section 30(1).

(1B) The second compensation case is where on the making of an application under section 29(2) of this Act the court is precluded (whether by section 29(4)(a) or section 31(2) of this Act) from making an order for the grant of a new tenancy by reason of any of the compensation grounds and not of any other grounds specified in section 30(1) of this Act.

(1C) The third compensation case is where—

(a) the landlord's notice under section 25 of this Act or, as the case may be, under section 26(6) of this Act, states his opposition to the grant of a new tenancy on any of the compensation grounds and not on any other grounds specified in section 30(1) of this Act; and

(b) either—

(i) no application is made by the tenant under section 24(1) of this Act or by the landlord under section 29(2) of this Act; or

(ii) such an application is made but is subsequently withdrawn.

(2) Subject to ~~subsections (5A) to (5E) of this section the said amount~~ **the following provisions of this section, compensation under this section** shall be as follows, that is to say—

(a) where the conditions specified in the next following subsection are satisfied **in relation to the whole of the holding** it shall be the product of the appropriate multiplier and twice the rateable value of the holding,

(b) in any other case it shall be the product of the appropriate multiplier and the rateable value of the holding.

(3) The said conditions are—

(a) that, during the whole of the fourteen years immediately preceding the termination of the current tenancy, premises being or comprised in the holding have been occupied for the purposes of a business carried on by the occupier or for those and other purposes;

(b) that, if during those fourteen years there was a change in the occupier of the premises, the person who was the occupier immediately after the change was the successor to the business carried on by the person who was the occupier immediately before the change.

(3A) If the conditions specified in subsection (3) above are satisfied in relation to part of the holding but not in relation to the other part, the amount of compensation shall be the aggregate of sums calculated separately as compensation in respect of each part, and accordingly, for the purpose of calculating compensation in respect of a part any reference in this section to the holding shall be construed as a reference to that part.

(3B) Where section 44(1A) of this Act applies, the compensation shall be determined separately for each part and compensation determined for any part shall be recoverable only from the person who is the owner of an interest in that part which fulfils the conditions specified in section 44(1) of this Act.

(4) Where the court is precluded from making an order for the grant of a new tenancy under this Part of this Act in ~~the circumstances mentioned in subsection (1) of this section~~ **a compensation case**, the court shall on the application of the tenant certify that fact.

(5) For the purposes of subsection (2) of this section the rateable value of the holding shall be determined as follows—

(a) where in the valuation list in force at the date on which the landlord's notice under section 25 or, as the case may be, subsection (6) of section 26 of this Act is given a value is then shown as the annual value (as hereinafter defined) of the holding, the rateable value of the holding shall be taken to be that value;

(b) where no such value is so shown with respect to the holding but such a value or such values is or are so shown with respect to premises comprised in or comprising the holding or part of it, the rateable value of the holding shall be taken to be such value as is found by a proper apportionment or aggregation of the value or values so shown;

(c) where the rateable value of the holding cannot be ascertained in accordance with the foregoing paragraphs of this subsection, it shall be taken to be the value which, apart from any exemption from assessment to rates, would on a proper assessment be the value to be entered in the said valuation list as the annual value of the holding;

and any dispute arising, whether in proceedings before the court or otherwise, as to the determination for those purposes of the rateable value of the holding shall be referred to the Commissioners of Inland Revenue for decision by the valuation officer.

An appeal shall lie to the Lands Tribunal from any decision of a valuation officer under this subsection, but subject thereto any such decision shall be final.

(5A) If part of the holding is domestic property, as defined in section 66 of the Local Government Finance Act 1988—

(a) the domestic property shall be disregarded in determining the rateable value of the holding under subsection (5) of this section; and

(b) if, on the date specified in subsection (5) (a) of this section, the tenant occupied the whole or any part of the domestic property, the amount of compensation to which he is entitled under subsection (1) of this section shall be increased by the addition of a sum equal to his reasonable expenses in removing from the domestic property.

(5B) Any question as to the amount of the sum referred to in paragraph (b) of subsection (5A) of this section shall be determined by agreement between the landlord and the tenant or, in default of agreement, by the court.

(5C) If the whole of the holding is domestic property, as defined in section 66 of the Local Government Finance Act 1988, for the purposes of subsection (2) of this section the rateable value of the holding shall be taken to be an amount equal to the rent at which it is estimated the holding might reasonably be expected to let from year to year if the tenant undertook to pay all usual tenant's rates and taxes and to bear the cost of the repairs and insurance and the other expenses (if any) necessary to maintain the holding in a state to command that rent.

(5D) The following provisions shall have effect as regards a determination of an amount mentioned in subsection (5C) of this section—

(a) the date by reference to which such a determination is to be made is the date on which the landlord's notice under section 25 or, as the case may be, subsection (6) of section 26 of this Act is given;

(b) any dispute arising, whether in proceedings before the court or otherwise, as to such a determination shall be referred to the Commissioners of Inland Revenue for decision by a valuation officer;

(c) an appeal shall lie to the Lands Tribunal from such a decision, but subject to that, such a decision shall be final.

(5E) Any deduction made under paragraph 2A of Schedule 6 to the Local Government Finance Act 1988 (deduction from valuation of hereditaments used for breeding horses etc.) shall be disregarded, to the extent that it relates to the holding, in determining the rateable value of the holding under subsection (5) of this section.

(6) The Commissioners of Inland Revenue may by statutory instrument make rules prescribing the procedure in connection with references under this section.

(7) In this section—

the reference to the termination of the current tenancy is a reference to the date of termination specified in the landlord's notice under section 25 of this Act or, as the case may be, the date specified in the tenant's request for a new tenancy as the date from which the new tenancy is to begin;

the expression "annual value" means rateable value except that where the rateable value differs from the net annual value the said expression means net annual value;

the expression "valuation officer" means any officer of the Commissioners of Inland Revenue for the time being authorised by a certificate of the Commissioners to act in relation to a valuation list.

(8) In subsection (2) of this section "the appropriate multiplier" means such multiplier as the Secretary of State may by order made by statutory instrument prescribe and different multipliers may be so prescribed in relation to different cases.

(9) A statutory instrument containing an order under subsection (8) of this section shall be subject to annulment in pursuance of a resolution of either House of Parliament.

Compensation for possession obtained by misrepresentation

A1–24   **37A.–(1) Where the court—**

(a) makes an order for the termination of the current tenancy but does not make an order for the grant of a new tenancy, or

(b) refuses an order for the grant of a new tenancy,

and it is subsequently made to appear to the court that the order was obtained, or the court was induced to refuse the grant, by misrepresentation or the concealment of material facts, the court may order the landlord to pay to the tenant such sum as appears sufficient as compensation for damage or loss sustained by the tenant as the result of the order or refusal.
(2) Where—

(a) the tenant has quit the holding—

   (i) after making but withdrawing an application under section 24(1) of this Act; or
   (ii) without making such an application; and

(b) it is made to appear to the court that he did so by reason of misrepresentation or the concealment of material facts,

the court may order the landlord to pay to the tenant such sum as appears sufficient as compensation for damage or loss sustained by the tenant as the result of quitting the holding.

Restriction on agreements excluding provisions of Part II

A1–25   **38.–(1)** Any agreement relating to a tenancy to which this Part of this Act applies (whether contained in the instrument creating the tenancy or not) shall be void (except as provided by ~~subsection (4) of this section~~ **section 38A of this Act**) in so far as it purports to preclude the tenant from making an application or request under this Part of this Act or provides for the termination or the surrender of the tenancy in the event of his making such an application or request or for the imposition of any penalty or disability on the tenant in that event.

(2) Where—

(a) during the whole of the five years immediately preceding the date on which the tenant under a tenancy to which this Part of this Act applies is to quit the holding, premises being or comprised in the holding have been occupied for the purposes of a business carried on by the occupier or for those and other purposes, and

(b) if during those five years there was a change in the occupier of the premises, the person who was the occupier immediately after the change was the successor to the business carried on by the person who was the occupier immediately before the change,

any agreement (whether contained in the instrument creating the tenancy or not and whether made before or after the termination of that tenancy) which purports to exclude or reduce compensation under ~~the last foregoing section~~ **section 37 of this Act** shall to that extent be void, so however that this subsection shall not affect any agreement as to the amount of any such compensation which is made after the right to compensation has accrued.

(3) In a case not falling within the last foregoing subsection the right to compensation conferred by ~~the last foregoing section~~ **section 37 of this Act** may be excluded or modified by agreement.

~~(4) The court may—~~

~~(a) on the joint application of the persons who will be the landlord and the tenant in relation to a tenancy to be granted for a term of years certain which will be a tenancy to which this Part of this Act applies, authorise an agreement excluding in relation to that tenancy the provisions of sections 24 to 28 of this Act; and~~

~~(b) on the joint application of the persons who are the landlord and the tenant in relation to a tenancy to which this Part of this Act applies, authorise an agreement for the surrender of the tenancy on such date or in such circumstances as may be specified in the agreement and on such terms (if any) as may be so specified;~~

~~if the agreement is contained in or endorsed on the instrument creating the tenancy or such other instrument as the court may specify; and an agreement contained in or endorsed on an instrument in pursuance of an authorisation given under this subsection shall be valid notwithstanding anything in the preceding provisions of this section.~~

Agreements to exclude provisions of Part II

38A.—(1) The persons who will be the landlord and the tenant in relation to a tenancy to be granted for a term of years certain which will be a tenancy to which this Part of this Act applies may agree that the provisions of sections 24 to 28 of this Act shall be excluded in relation to that tenancy.

A1–26

(2) The persons who are the landlord and the tenant in relation to a tenancy to which this Part of this Act applies may agree that the tenancy shall be surrendered on such date or in such circumstances as may be specified in the agreement and on such terms (if any) as may be so specified.

(3) An agreement under subsection (1) above shall be void unless—

(a) the landlord has served on the tenant a notice in the form, or substantially in the form, set out in Schedule 1 to the Regulatory Reform (Business Tenancies) (England and Wales) Order 2003 ("the 2003 Order"); and

(b) the requirements specified in Schedule 2 to that Order are met.

(4) An agreement under subsection (2) above shall be void unless—

(a) the landlord has served on the tenant a notice in the form, or substantially in the form, set out in Schedule 3 to the 2003 Order; and

(b) the requirements specified in Schedule 4 to that Order are met.

General and supplementary provisions

Saving for compulsory acquisitions

A1-27   **39.**–(1) [Repealed]

(2) If the amount of the compensation which would have been payable under section 37 of this Act if the tenancy had come to an end in circumstances giving rise to compensation under that section and the date at which the acquiring authority obtained possession had been the termination of the current tenancy exceeds the amount of the compensation payable under section 121 of the Lands Clauses Consolidation Act 1845, or section 20 of the Compulsory Purchase Act 1965, in the case of a tenancy to which this Part of this Act applies, that compensation shall be increased by the amount of the excess.

(3) Nothing in section 24 of this Act shall affect the operation of the said section 121.

Duty of tenants and landlords of business premises to give information to each other

40.—(1) Where any person having an interest in any business premises, being an interest in reversion expectant (whether immediately or not) on a tenancy of those premises, serves on the tenant a notice in the prescribed form requiring him to do so, it shall be the duty of the tenant to notify that person in writing within one month of the service of the notice—

(a) whether he occupies the premises or any part thereof wholly or partly for the purposes of a business carried on him, and

(b) whether his tenancy has effect subject to any sub-tenancy on which his tenancy is immediately expectant and, if so, what premises are comprised in the sub-tenancy, for what term it has effect (or, if it is terminable by notice, by what notice it can be terminated), what is the rent payable thereunder, who is the sub-tenant, and (to the best of his knowledge and belief) whether the sub-tenant is in occupation of the premises or of part of the premises comprised in the sub-tenancy and, if not, what is the sub-tenant's address.

(2) Where the tenant of any business premises, being a tenant under such a tenancy as is mentioned in subsection (1) of section 26 of this Act, service on any persons mentioned in tire next following subsection a notice in the prescribed form requiring him to do so, it shall be the duty of that person to notify the tenant in writing within one month after the service of the notice—

(a) whether he is the owner of the fee simple in respect of those premises or any part thereof or the mortgagee in possession of such an owner and, if not,

(b) (to the best of his knowledge and belief) the name and address of the person who is his or, as the case may be, his mortgagor's immediate landlord in respect of those premises or of the part in respect of which he or his mortgagor is not the owner in fee simple, for what term his or his mortgagor's tenancy thereof has effect and what is the earliest date (if any) at which that tenancy is terminable by notice to quit given by the landlord.

(3) The persons referred to in the last foregoing subsection are, in relation to the tenant of any business premises—

(a) any person having an interest in the premises, being an interest in reversion expectant (whether immediately or not) on the tenant's, and

(b) any person being a mortgagee in possession in respect of such an interest in reversion as is mentioned in paragraph (a) of this subsection;

and the information which any such person as is mentioned in paragraph (a) of this subsection is required to give under the last foregoing subsection shall include information whether there is a mortgagee in possession of his interest in the premises and, if so, what is the name and address of the mortgagee.

(4) The foregoing provisions of this section shall not apply to a notice served by or on the tenant more than two years before the date on which apart from this Act his tenancy would come to an end by effluxion of time or could be brought to an end by notice to quit given by the landlord.

(5) In this section

the expression "business premises" means premises used wholly or partly for the purposes of a business;
the expression "mortgagee in possession" includes a receiver appointed by the mortgagee or by the court who is in receipt of the rents and profits, and the expression "his mortgagor" shall be construed accordingly;

~~the expression "sub-tenant" includes a person retaining possession of any premises by virtue of the Rent Act 1977 after the coming to an end of a sub-tenancy, and the expression "sub-tenancy" includes a right so to retain possession.~~

A1-28   **40.**—(1) Where a person who is an owner of an interest in reversion expectant (whether immediately or not) on a tenancy of any business premises has served on the tenant a notice in the prescribed form requiring him to do so, it shall be the duty of the tenant to give the appropriate person in writing the information specified in subsection (2) below.
    (2) That information is—

(a) whether the tenant occupies the premises or any part of them wholly or partly for the purposes of a business carried on by him;

(b) whether his tenancy has effect subject to any sub-tenancy on which his tenancy is immediately expectant and, if so—

  (i) what premises are comprised in the sub-tenancy;
  (ii) for what term it has effect (or, if it is terminable by notice, by what notice it can be terminated);
  (iii) what is the rent payable under it;
  (iv) who is the sub-tenant;
  (v) (to the best of his knowledge and belief) whether the sub-tenant is in occupation of the premises or of part of the premises comprised in the sub-tenancy and, if not, what is the sub-tenant's address;
  (vi) whether an agreement is in force excluding in relation to the sub-tenancy the provisions of sections 24 to 28 of this Act; and
  (vii) whether a notice has been given under section 25 or 26(6) of this Act, or a request has been made under section 26 of this Act, in relation to the sub-tenancy and, if so, details of the notice or request; and

(c) (to the best of his knowledge and belief) the name and address of any other person who owns an interest in reversion in any part of the premises.

    (3) Where the tenant of any business premises who is a tenant under such a tenancy as is mentioned in section 26(1) of this Act has served on a reversioner or a reversioner's mortgagee in possession a notice in the prescribed form requiring him to do so, it shall be the duty of the person on whom the notice is served to give the appropriate person in writing the information specified in subsection (4) below.
    (4) That information is—

(a) whether he is the owner of the fee simple in respect of the premises or any part of them or the mortgagee in possession of such an owner,

(b) if he is not, then (to the best of his knowledge and belief)—

    (i) the name and address of the person who is his or, as the case may be, his mortgagor's immediate landlord in respect of those premises or of the part in respect of which he or his mortgagor is not the owner in fee simple;

    (ii) for what term his or his mortgagor's tenancy has effect and what is the earliest date (if any) at which that tenancy is terminable by notice to quit given by the landlord; and

    (iii) whether a notice has been given under section 25 or 26(6) of this Act, or a request has been made under section 26 of this Act, in relation to the tenancy and, if so, details of the notice or request;

(c) (to the best of his knowledge and belief) the name and address of any other person who owns an interest in reversion in any part of the premises; and

(d) if he is a reversioner, whether there is a mortgagee in possession of his interest in the premises and, if so, (to the best of his knowledge and belief) what is the name and address of the mortgagee.

    (5) A duty imposed on a person by this section is a duty—

(a) to give the information concerned within the period of one month beginning with the date of service of the notice; and

(b) if within the period of six months beginning with the date of service of the notice that person becomes aware that any information which has been given in pursuance of the notice is not, or is no longer, correct, to give the appropriate person correct information within the period of one month beginning with the date on which he becomes aware.

    (6) This section shall not apply to a notice served by or on the tenant more than two years before the date on which apart from this Act his tenancy would come to an end by effluxion of time or could be brought to an end by notice to quit given by the landlord.

    (7) Except as provided by section 40A of this Act, the appropriate person for the purposes of this section and section 40A(1) of this Act is the person who served the notice under subsection (1) or (3) above.

    (8) In this section—

"business premises" means premises used wholly or partly for the purposes of a business;

"mortgagee in possession" includes a receiver appointed by the mortgagee or by the court who is in receipt of the rents and profits, and "his mortgagor" shall be construed accordingly;

"reversioner" means any person having an interest in the premises, being an interest in reversion expectant (whether immediately or not) on the tenancy;

"reversioner's mortgagee in possession" means any person being a mortgagee in possession in respect of such an interest; and

"sub-tenant" includes a person retaining possession of any premises by virtue of the Rent (Agriculture) Act 1976 or the Rent Act 1977 after the coming to an end of a sub-tenancy, and "sub-tenancy" includes a right so to retain possession.".

Duties in transfer cases

A1-29 40A.–(1) If a person on whom a notice under section 40(1) or (3) of this Act has been served has transferred his interest in the premises or any part of them to some other person and gives the appropriate person notice in writing—

(a) of the transfer of his interest; and

(b) of the name and address of the person to whom he transferred it,

on giving the notice he ceases in relation to the premises or (as the case may be) to that part to be under any duty imposed by section 40 of this Act.
　　(2) If—

(a) the person who served the notice under section 40(1) or (3) of this Act ("the transferor") has transferred his interest in the premises to some other person ("the transferee"); and

(b) the transferor or the transferee has given the person required to give the information notice in writing—

　　(i) of the transfer; and
　　(ii) of the transferee's name and address,

the appropriate person for the purposes of section 40 of this Act and subsection (1) above is the transferee.
　　(3) If—

(a) a transfer such as is mentioned in paragraph (a) of subsection (2) above has taken place; but

(b) neither the transferor nor the transferee has given a notice such as is mentioned in paragraph (b) of that subsection,

any duty imposed by section 40 of this Act may be performed by giving the information either to the transferor or to the transferee.

Proceedings for breach of duties to give information

A1-30 40B. A claim that a person has broken any duty imposed by section 40 of this Act may be made the subject of civil proceedings for breach of statutory duty; and in any such proceedings a court may order that person to comply with that duty and may make an award of damages.

Trusts

A1-31 41.–(1) Where a tenancy is held on trust, occupation by all or any of the beneficiaries under the trust, and the carrying on of a business by all or any of the beneficiaries, shall be treated for the purposes of section 23 of this Act as equivalent to occupation or the carrying on of a business by the tenant; and in relation to a tenancy to which this Part of this Act applies by virtue of the foregoing provisions of this subsection—

(a) references (however expressed) in this Part of this Act and in the Ninth Schedule to this Act to the business of, or to carrying on of business, use, occupation or enjoyment by, the tenant shall be construed as including references to the business of, or to carrying on of business, use, occupation or enjoyment by, the beneficiaries or beneficiary;

(b) the reference in paragraph (d) of subsection (1) of section 34 of this Act to the tenant shall be construed as including the beneficiaries or beneficiary; and

(c) a change in the persons of the trustees shall not be treated as a change in the person of the tenant.

(2) Where the landlord's interest is held on trust the references in paragraph (g) of subsection (1) of section 30 of this Act to the landlord shall be construed as including references to the beneficiaries under the trust or any of them; but, except in the case of a trust arising under a will or on the intestacy of any person, the reference in subsection (2) of that section to the creation of the interest therein mentioned shall be construed as including the creation of the trust.

Partnerships

41A.—(1) The following provisions of this section shall apply where—   **A1–32**

(a) a tenancy is held jointly by two or more persons (in this section referred to as the joint tenants); and

(b) the property comprised in the tenancy is or includes premises occupied for the purposes of a business; and

(c) the business (or some other business) was at some time during the existence of the tenancy carried on in partnership by all the persons who were then the joint tenants or by those and other persons and the joint tenants' interest in the premises was then partnership property; and

(d) the business is carried on (whether alone or in partnership with other persons) by one or some only of the joint tenants and no part of the property comprised in the tenancy is occupied, in right of the tenancy, for the purposes of a business carried on (whether alone or in partnership with other persons) by the other or others.

(2) In the following provisions of this section those of the joint tenants who for the time being carry on the business are referred to as the business tenants and the others as the other joint tenants.

(3) Any notice given by the business tenants which, had it been given by all the joint tenants, would have been—

(a) a tenant's request for a new tenancy made in accordance with section 26 of this Act; or

(b) a notice under subsection (1) or subsection (2) of section 27 of this Act shall be treated as such if it states that it is given by virtue of this section and sets out the facts by virtue of which the persons giving it are the business tenants;

and references in those sections and in section 24A of this Act to the tenant shall be construed accordingly.

(4) A notice given by the landlord to the business tenants which, had it been given to all the joint tenants, would have been a notice under section 25 of this Act shall be treated as such a notice, and references in that section to the tenant shall be construed accordingly.

(5) An application under section 24(1) of this Act for a new tenancy may, instead of being made by all the joint tenants, be made by the business tenants alone; and where it is so made—

(a) this Part of this Act shall have effect, in relation to it, as if the references therein to the tenant included references to the business tenants alone; and

(b) the business tenants shall be liable, to the exclusion of the other joint tenants, for the payment of rent and the discharge of any other obligation under the current tenancy for any rental period beginning after the date specified in the landlord's notice under section 25 of this Act or, as the case my be, beginning on or after the date specified in their request for a new tenancy.

(6) Where the court makes an order under ~~section 29(1) of this Act for the grant of a new tenancy on an application made by the business tenants it may order the grant to be made to them or to them jointly~~ **section 29 of this Act for the grant of a new tenancy it may order the grant to be made to the business tenants or to them jointly** with the persons carrying on the business in partnership with them, and may order the grant to be made subject to the satisfaction, within a time specified by the order, of such conditions as to guarantors, sureties or otherwise as appear to the court equitable, having regard to the omission of the other joint tenants from the persons who will be the tenants under the new tenancy.

(7) The business tenants shall be entitled to recover any amount payable by way of compensation under section 37 or section 59 of this Act.

Groups of companies

A1-33 **42.**—(1) For the purposes of this section two bodies corporate shall be taken to be members of a group if and only if one is a subsidiary of the other or both are subsidiaries of the third body corporate **or the same person has a controlling interest in both**.

~~In this subsection "subsidiary" has the same meaning given by section 736 of the Companies Act 1985.~~

(2) Where a tenancy is held by a member of a group, occupation by another member of the group, and the carrying on of a business by another member of the group, shall be treated for the purposes of section 23 of this Act as equivalent to occupation or the carrying on of a business by the member of the group holding the tenancy; and in relation to a tenancy to which this Part of this Act applies by virtue of the foregoing provisions of this subsection—

(a) references (however expressed) in this Part of this Act and in the Ninth Schedule to this Act to the business of or to use occupation or enjoyment by the tenant shall be construed as including references to the business of or to use occupation or enjoyment by the said other member;

(b) the reference in paragraph (d) of subsection (1) of section 34 of this Act to the tenant shall be construed as including the said other member; and

(c) an assignment of the tenancy from one member of the group to another shall not be treated as a change in the person of the tenant.

(3) Where the landlord's interest is held by a member of a group—

(a) the reference in paragraph (g) of subsection (1) of section 30 of this Act to intended occupation by the landlord for the purposes of a business to be carried on by him shall be construed as including intended occupation by any member of the group for the purposes of a business to be carried on by that member; and

(b) the reference in subsection (2) of that section to the purchase or creation of any interest shall be construed as a reference to a purchaser from or creation by a person other than a member of the group.

Tenancies excluded from Part II

43.—(1) This Part of this Act does not apply— **A1–34**

(a) to a tenancy of an agricultural holding which is a tenancy in relation to which the Agricultural Holdings Act 1986 applies or a tenancy which would be a tenancy of an agricultural holding in relation to which that Act applied if subsection (3) of section 2 of that Act did not have effect or, in a case where approval was given under subsection (1) of that section, if that approval had not been given;

    (aa) to a farm business tenancy;

(b) to a tenancy created by a mining lease; or

(c) [Repealed]

(d) [Repealed]

(2) This Part of this Act does not apply to a tenancy granted by reason that the tenant was the holder of an office, appointment or employment from the grantor thereof and continuing only so long as the tenant holds the office, appointment or employment, or terminable by the grantor on the tenant's ceasing to hold it, or coming to an end at a time fixed by reference to the time at which the tenant ceases to hold it:

Provided that this subsection shall not have effect in relation to a tenancy granted after the commencement of this Act unless the tenancy was granted by an instrument in writing which expressed the purpose for which the tenancy was granted.

(3) This Part of this Act does not apply to a tenancy granted for a term certain not exceeding six months unless—

(a) the tenancy contains provision for renewing the term or for extending it beyond six months from its beginning; or

(b) the tenant has been in occupation for a period which, together with any period during which any predecessor in the carrying on of the business carried on by the tenant was in occupation, exceeds twelve months.

Jurisdiction of county court to make declaration

A1–35   **43A.** Where the rateable value of the holding is such that the jurisdiction conferred on the court by any other provision of this Part of this Act is, by virtue of section 63 of this Act, exercisable by the county court, the county court shall have jurisdiction (but without prejudice to the jurisdiction of the High Court) to make any declaration as to any matter arising under this Part of this Act, whether or not any other relief is sought in the proceedings.

Meaning of 'the landlord,' in Part II, and provisions as to mesne landlords, etc.

A1–36   **44.**–(1) Subject to the next following subsection **subsections (1A) and (2) below**, in this Part of this Act the expression "the landlord" in relation to a tenancy (in this section referred to as "the relevant tenancy"), means the person (whether or not he is the immediate landlord) who is the owner of that interest in the property comprised in the relevant tenancy which for the time being fulfils the following conditions, that is to say–

(a) that it is an interest in reversion expectant (whether immediately or not) on the termination of the relevant tenancy, and

(b) that it is either the fee simple or a tenancy which will not come to an end within fourteen months by effluxion of time and, if it is such a tenancy, that no notice has been given by virtue of which it will come to an end within fourteen months or any further time by which it may be continued under section 36(2) or section 64 of this Act, and is not itself in reversion expectant (whether immediately or not) on an interest which fulfils those conditions.

(1A) The reference in subsection (1) above to a person who is the owner of an interest such as is mentioned in that subsection is to be construed, where different persons own such interests in different parts of the property, as a reference to all those persons collectively.

(2) References in this Part of this Act to a notice to quit given by the landlord are references to a notice to quit given by the immediate landlord.

(3) The provisions of the Sixth Schedule to this Act shall have effect for the application of this Part of this Act to cases where the immediate landlord of the tenant is not the owner of the fee simple in respect of the holding.

A1–37   **45.** [Repealed]

Interpretation of Part II

46.—(1) In this Part of this Act:— 　　　　　　　　　　**A1–38**

"business" has the meaning assigned to it by subsection (2) of section 23 of this Act;

~~"current tenancy" has the meaning assigned to it by subsection (1) of section 26 of this Act;~~ **"current tenancy" means the tenancy under which the tenant holds for the time being;**

"date of termination" has the meaning assigned to it by subsection (1) of section 25 of this Act;

subject to the provisions of section 32 of this Act, "the holding" has the meaning assigned to it by subsection (3) of section 23 of this Act;

"interim rent" has the meaning given by section 24A(1) of this Act;

"mining lease" has the same meaning as in the Landlord and Tenant Act 1927.

(2) For the purposes of this Part of this Act, a person has a controlling interest in a company if, had he been a company, the other company would have been its subsidiary; and in this Part—

"company" has the meaning given by section 735 of the Companies Act 1985; and

"subsidiary" has the meaning given by section 736 of that Act.

PART IV

MISCELLANEOUS AND SUPPLEMENTARY

~~Compensation for possession obtained by misrepresentation~~

~~**55.**—(1) Where under Part I of this Act an order is made for possession of the property comprised in a tenancy, or under Part II of this Act the court refuses an order for the grant of a new tenancy, and it is subsequently made to appear to the court that the order was obtained, or the court induced to refuse the grant, by misrepresentation or the concealment of material facts, the court may order the landlord to pay to the tenant such sum as appears sufficient as compensation for damage or loss sustained by the tenant as the result of the order or refusal.~~

~~(2) In this section the expression "the landlord" means the person applying for possession or opposing an application for the grant of a new tenancy and the expression "the tenant" means the person against whom the order for possession was made or to whom the grant of a new tenancy was refused.~~

Application to Crown

56.—(1) Subject to the provisions of this and the four next following 　**A1–39** sections, Part II of this Act shall apply where there is an interest belonging to Her Majesty in right of the Crown or the Duchy of Lancaster or belonging to the Duchy of Cornwall, or belonging to a Government department or held on behalf of Her Majesty for the purposes of a Government department, in like manner as if that interest were an interest not so belonging or held.

(2) The provisions of the Eighth Schedule to this Act shall have effect as respects the application of Part II of this Act to cases where the interest of the landlord belongs to Her Majesty in right of the Crown or the Duchy of Lancaster or to the Duchy of Cornwall.

(3) Where a tenancy is held by or on behalf of a Government department and the property comprised therein is or includes premises occupied for any purposes of a Government department, the tenancy shall be one to which Part II of this Act applies; and for the purposes of any provision of the said Part II or the Ninth Schedule to this Act which is applicable only if either or both of the following conditions are satisfied, that is to say—

(a) that any premises have during any period been occupied for the purposes of the tenant's business;

(b) that on any change of occupier of any premises the new occupier succeeded to the business of the former occupier,

the said conditions shall be deemed to be satisfied respectively, in relation to such a tenancy, if during that period or, as the case may be, immediately before and immediately after the change, the premises were occupied for the purposes of a Government department.

(4) The last foregoing subsection shall apply in relation to any premises provided by a Government department without any rent being payable to the department therefor as if the premises were occupied for the purposes of a Government department.

(5) The provisions of Parts III and IV of this Act, amending any other enactment which binds the Crown or applies to land belonging to Her Majesty in right of the Crown or the Duchy of Lancaster, or land belonging to the Duchy of Cornwall, or to land belonging to any Government department, shall bind the Crown or apply to such land.

(6) Sections 53 and 54 of this Act shall apply where the interest of the landlord, or any other interest in the land in question, belongs to Her Majesty in right of the Crown or the Duchy of Lancaster or to the Duchy of Cornwall, or belongs to a Government department or is held on behalf of Her Majesty for the purposes of a Government department, in like manner as if that interest were an interest not so belonging or held.

(7) Part I of this Act shall apply where—

(a) there is an interest belonging to Her Majesty in right of the Crown and that interest is under the management of the Crown Estate Commissioners;

or

(b) there is an interest belonging to Her Majesty in right of the Duchy of Lancaster or belonging to the Duchy of Cornwall;

as if it were an interest not so belonging.

Modification on grounds of public interest of rights under Part II

57.–(1) Where the interest of the landlord or any superior landlord in the **A1–40** property comprised in any tenancy belongs to or is held for the purposes of a Government department or is held by a local authority, statutory undertakers or a development corporation, the Minister or Board in charge of any Government department may certify that it is requisite for the purposes of the first-mentioned department, or, as the case may be, of the authority, undertakers or corporation, that the use or occupation of the property or a part thereof shall be changed by a specified date.

(2) A certificate under the last foregoing subsection shall not be given unless the owner of the interest belonging or held as mentioned in the last foregoing subsection has given to the tenant a notice stating–

(a) that the question of the giving of such a certificate is under consideration by the Minister or Board specified in the notice, and

(b) that if within twenty-one days of the giving of the notice the tenant makes to that Minister or Board representations in writing with respect to that question, they will be considered before the question is determined, and if the tenant makes any such representations within the said twenty-one days the Minister or Board shall consider them before determining whether to give the certificate.

(3) Where a certificate has been given under subsection (1) of this section in relation to any tenancy, then–

(a) if a notice given under subsection (1) of section 25 of this Act specifies as the date of termination a date not earlier than the date specified in the certificate and contains a copy of the certificate ~~subsections (5) and~~ **subsection** (6) of that section shall not apply to the notice and no application for a new tenancy shall be made by the tenant under **subsection (1) of** section 24 of this Act;

(b) if such a notice specifies an earlier date as the date of termination and contains a copy of the certificate, then if the court makes an order under Part II of this Act for the grant of a new tenancy the new tenancy shall be for a term expiring not later than the date specified in the certificate and shall not be a tenancy to which Part II of this Act applies.

(4) Where a tenant makes a request for a new tenancy under section 26 of this Act, and the interest of the landlord or any superior landlord in the property comprised in the current tenancy belongs or is held as mentioned in subsection (1) of this section, the following provisions shall have effect–

(a) if a certificate has been given under the said subsection (1) in relation to the current tenancy, and within two months after the making of the request the landlord gives notice to the tenant that the certificate has been given and the notice contains a copy of the certificate, then–

(i) if the date specified in the certificate is not later than that specified in the tenant's request for a new tenancy, the tenant shall not make an application under section 24 of this Act for the grant of a new tenancy;

  (ii) if, in any other case, the court makes an order under Part II of this Act for the grant of a new tenancy the new tenancy shall be for a term expiring not later than the date specified in the certificate and shall not be a tenant to which Part II of this Act applies;

(b) if no such certificate has been given but notice under subsection (2) of this section has been given before the making of the request or within two months thereafter, the request shall not have effect, without prejudice however, to the making of a new request when the Minister or Board has determined whether to give a certificate.

(5) Where application is made to the court under Part II of this Act for the grant of a new tenancy and the landlord's interest in the property comprised in the tenancy belongs or is held as mentioned in subsection (1) of this section, the Minister or Board in charge of any Government department may certify that it is necessary in the public interest that if the landlord makes an application in that behalf the court shall determine as a term of the new tenancy that is shall be terminable by six months' notice to quit given by the landlord.

Subsection (2) of this section shall apply in relation to a certificate under this subsection, and if notice under the said subsection (2) has been given to the tenant—

(a) the court shall not determine the application for the grant of a new tenancy until the Minister or Board has determined whether to give a certificate,

(b) if a certificate is given, the court shall on the application of the landlord determine as a term of the new tenancy that it shall be terminable as aforesaid, and section 25 of this Act shall apply accordingly.

(6) The foregoing provisions of this section shall apply to an interest held by a Health Authority or Special Health Authority as they apply to an interest held by a local authority but with the substitution, for the reference to the purposes of the authority, of a reference to the purposes of the National Health Service Act 1977.

(7) Where the interest of the landlord or any superior landlord in the property comprised in any tenancy belongs to the National Trust the Minister of Works may certify that it is requisite, for the purpose of securing that the property will as from a specified date be used or occupied in a manner better suited to the nature thereof, that the use or occupation of the property should be changed; and subsections (2) to (4) of this section shall apply in relation to certificates under this subsection, and to cases where the interest of the landlord or any superior landlord belongs to the National Trust, as those subsections apply in relation to certificates under subsection (1) of this section and to cases where the interest of the landlord or any superior landlord belongs or is held as mentioned in that subsection.

(8) In this and the next following section the expression "Government department" does not include the Commissioners of Crown Lands and the expression "landlord" has the same meaning as in Part II of this Act; and in the last foregoing subsection the expression "National Trust" means the National Trust for Places of Historic Interest or Natural Beauty.

Termination on special grounds of tenancies to which Part II applies

58.—(1) Where the landlord's interest in the property comprised in any tenancy belongs or is held for the purposes of a Government department, and the Minister or Board in charge of any Government department certifies that for reasons of national security it is necessary that the use or occupation of the property should be discontinued or changed, then— **A1–41**

(a) if the landlord gives a notice under subsection (1) of section 25 of this Act containing a copy of the certificate, subsections (5) and **subsection (6)** of that section shall not apply to the notice and no application for a new tenancy shall be made by the tenant under **subsection (1) of** section 24 of this Act;

(b) if (whether before or after the giving of the certificate) the tenant makes a request for a new tenancy under section 26 of this Act, and within two months after the making the request the landlord gives notice to the tenant that the certificate has been given and the notice contains a copy of the certificate—

   (i) the tenant shall not make an application under section 24 of this Act for the grant of a new tenancy, and

   (ii) if the notice specifies as the date on which the tenancy is to terminate a date earlier than that specified in the tenant's request as the date on which the new tenancy is to begin but neither earlier than six months from the giving of the notice nor earlier than the earliest date at which apart from this Act the tenancy would come to an end or could be brought to an end, the tenancy shall terminate on the date specified in the notice instead of that specified in the request.

(2) Where the landlord's interest in the property comprised in any tenancy belongs to or is held for the purposes of a Government department, nothing in this Act shall invalidate an agreement to the effect—

(a) that on the giving of such a certificate as is mentioned in the last foregoing subsection the tenancy may be terminated by notice to quit given by the landlord of such length as may be specified in the agreement, if the notice contains a copy of the certificate; and

(b) that after the giving of such a notice containing such a copy the tenancy shall not be one to which Part II of this Act applies.

(3) Where the landlord's interest in the property comprised in any tenancy is held by statutory undertakers, nothing in this Act shall invalidate an agreement to the effect—

(a) that where the Minister or Board in charge of a Government department certifies that possession of the property comprised in the tenancy or a part thereof is urgently required for carrying out repairs (whether on that property or elsewhere) which are needed for the proper operation of the landlord's undertaking, the tenancy may be terminated by notice to quit given by the landlord of such length as may be specified in the agreement, if the notice contains a copy of the certificate; and

(b) that after the giving of such a notice containing such a copy, the tenancy shall not be one to which Part II of this Act applies.

(4) Where the court makes an order under Part II of this Act for the grant of a new tenancy and the Minister or Board in charge of any Government department certifies that the public interest requires the tenancy to be subject to such a term as is mentioned in paragraph (a) or (b) of this subsection, as the case may be, then—

(a) if the landlord's interest in the property comprised in the tenancy belongs to or is held for the purposes of a Government department, the court shall on the application of the landlord determine as a term of the new tenancy that such an agreement as is mentioned in subsection (2) of this section and specifying such length of notice as is mentioned in the certificate shall be embodied in the new tenancy;

(b) if the landlord's interest in that property is held by statutory undertakers, the court shall on the application of the landlord determine as a term of the new tenancy that such an agreement as is mentioned in subsection (3) of this section and specifying such length of notice as is mentioned in the certificate shall be embodied in the new tenancy.

Compensation for exercise of powers under sections 57 and 58

A1–42   **59.**–(1) Where by virtue of any certificate given for the purposes of either of the two last foregoing sections or, subject to subsection (1A) below, section 60A below the tenant is precluded from obtaining an order for the grant of a new tenancy, or of a new tenancy for a term expiring later than a specified date, the tenant shall be entitled on quitting the premises to recover from the owner of the interest by virtue of which the certificate was given an amount by way of compensation, and subsections (2), (3) **to (3B)** and (5) to (7) of section 37 of this Act shall with the necessary modifications apply for the purposes of ascertaining the amount.

(1A) No compensation shall be recoverable under subsection (1) above where the certificate was given under section 60A below and either—

(a) the premises vested in the Welsh Development Agency under section 7 (property of Welsh Industrial Estates Corporation) or 8 (land held under Local Employment Act 1972) of the Welsh Development Agency Act 1975, or

(b) the tenant was not tenant of the premises when the said Agency acquired the interest by virtue of which the certificate was given.

(2) Subsections (2) and (3) of section 38 of this Act shall apply to compensation under this section as they apply to compensation under section 37 of this Act.

Special provisions as to premises in development or intermediate areas

60.–(1) Where the property comprised in a tenancy consists of premises of which the Secretary of State or the Urban Regeneration Agency is the landlord, being premises situated in a locality which is either—   **A1–43**

(a)   a development area; or

(b)   an intermediate area;

and the Secretary of State certifies that it is necessary or expedient for achieving the purpose mentioned in section 2(1) of the Local Employment Act 1972 that the use or occupation of the property should be changed, paragraphs (a) and (b) of subsection (1) of section 58 of this Act shall apply as they apply where such a certificate is given as is mentioned in that subsection.

(2) Where the court makes an order under Part II of this Act for the grant of a new tenancy of any such premises as aforesaid, and the Secretary of State certifies that it is necessary or expedient as aforesaid that the tenancy should be subject to a term, specified in the certificate, prohibiting or restricting the tenant from assigning the tenancy or sub-letting, charging or parting with possession of the premises or any part thereof or changing the use of the premises or any part thereof, the court shall determine that the terms of the tenancy shall include the terms specified in the certificate.

(3) In this section "development area" and "intermediate area" mean an area for the time being specified as a development area or, as the case may be, as an intermediate area by an order made, or having effect as if made, under section 1 of the Industrial Development Act 1982.

Welsh Development Agency premises

60A.–(1) Where property comprised in a tenancy consists of premises of which the Welsh Development Agency is the landlord, and the Secretary of State certifies that it is necessary or expedient, for the purpose of providing employment appropriate to the needs of the area in which the premises are situated, that the use or occupation of the property should be changed, paragraphs (a) and (b) of section 58(l) above shall apply as they apply where such a certificate is given as is mentioned in that sub-section.   **A1–44**

(2) Where the court makes an order under Part II of this Act for the grant of a new tenancy of any such premises as aforesaid, and the Secretary of State certifies that it is necessary or expedient as aforesaid that the tenancy should be subject to a term, specified in the certificate, prohibiting or restricting the tenant from assigning the tenancy or subletting, charging or parting with possession of the premises or any part of the premises or changing the use of the premises or any part of the premises, the court shall determine that the terms of the tenancy shall include the terms specified in the certificate.

60B to 62 [Repealed]

Jurisdiction of court for purposes of Parts I and II and of Part I of Landlord and Tenant Act 1927

A1-45   **63.**—(1) Any jurisdiction conferred on the court by any provision of Part I of this Act shall be exercised by the county court.

(2) Any jurisdiction conferred on the court by any provision of Part II of this Act or conferred on the tribunal by Part I of the Landlord and Tenant Act 1927, shall, subject to the provisions of this section, be exercised, by the High Court or a county court.

(3) [Repealed]

(4) The following provisions shall have effect as respects transfer of proceedings from or to the High Court or the county court, that is to say—

(a)   where an application is made to the one but by virtue of an Order under section 1 of the Courts and Legal Services Act 1990, cannot be entertained except by the other, the application shall not be treated as improperly made but any proceedings thereon shall be transferred to the other court;

(b)   any proceedings under the provisions of Part II of this Act or of Part I of the Landlord and Tenant Act 1927, which are pending before one of those courts may by order of that court made on the application of any person interested be transferred to the other court, if it appears to the court making the order that it is desirable that the proceedings and any proceedings before the other court should both be entertained by the other court.

(5) In any proceedings where in accordance with the foregoing provisions of this section the county court exercises jurisdiction the powers of the judge of summoning one or more assessors under subsection (1) of section 63 (1) of the County Courts Act 1984, may be exercised notwithstanding that no application is made in that behalf by any party to the proceedings.

(6) Where in any such proceedings an assessor is summoned by a judge under the said subsection (1)—

(a)   he may, if so directed by the judge, inspect the land to which the proceedings relate without the judge and report to the judge in writing thereon;

(b)   the judge may on consideration of the report and any observations of the parties thereon give such judgment or make such order in the proceedings as may be just;

(c)   the remuneration of the assessor shall be at such rate as may be determined by the Lord Chancellor with the approval of the Treasury and shall be defrayed out of moneys provided by Parliament.

(7) In this section the expression "the holding"—

(a)   in relation to proceedings under Part II of this Act, has the meaning assigned to it by subsection (3) of section 23 of this Act,

(b)   in relation to proceedings under Part I of the Landlord and Tenant Act 1927, has the same meaning as in the said Part I.

(9) Nothing in this section shall prejudice the operation of section 41 of the County Courts Act 1984 (which relates to the removal into the High Court of proceedings commenced in a county court).

(10) In accordance with the foregoing provisions of this section, for section 21 of the Landlord and Tenant Act 1927, there shall be substituted the following section—

> "The tribunal
>
> 21. The tribunal for the purposes of Part I of this Act shall be the court exercising jurisdiction in accordance with the provisions of section 63 of the Landlord and Tenant Act 1954".

64.—(1) In any case where—   **A1–46**

(a) a notice to terminate a tenancy has been given under Part I or Part II of this Act or a request for a new tenancy has been made under Part II thereof, and

(b) an application to the court has been made under the said Part I or ~~the said Part II~~, **under section 24(1) or 29(2) of this Act** as the case may be, and

(c) apart from this section the effect of the notice or request would be to terminate the tenancy before the expiration of the period of three months beginning with the date on which the application is finally disposed of,

the effect of the notice or request shall be to terminate the tenancy at the expiration of the said period of three months and not at any other time.

(2) The reference in paragraph (c) of subsection (1) of this section to the date on which an application is finally disposed of shall be construed as a reference to the earliest date by which the proceedings on the application (including any proceedings on or in consequence of an appeal) have been determined and any time for appealing or further appealing has expired, except that if the application is withdrawn or any appeal is abandoned the reference shall be construed as a reference to the date of the withdrawal or abandonment.

Provisions as to reversions

65.—(1) Where by virtue of any provision of this Act a tenancy (in this   **A1–47**
sub-section referred to as "the inferior tenancy") is continued for a period such as to extend to or beyond the end of the term of a superior tenancy, the superior tenancy shall, for the purposes of this Act and of any other enactment and of any rule of law, be deemed so long as it subsists to be an interest in reversion expectant upon the termination of the inferior tenancy and, if there is no intermediate tenancy, to be the interest in reversion immediately expectant upon the termination thereof.

(2) In the case of a tenancy continuing by virtue of any provision of this Act after the coming to an end of the interest in reversion immediately expectant upon the termination thereof, subsection (1) of section 139 of the Law of Property Act 1925 (which relates to the effect of the extinguishment of a reversion) shall apply as if references in the said subsection (1) to the

surrender or merger of the reversion included references to the coming to an end of the reversion for any reason other than surrender or merger.

(3) Where by virtue of any provision of this Act a tenancy (in this subsection referred to as "the continuing tenancy") is continued beyond the beginning of a reversionary tenancy which was granted (whether before or after the commencement of this Act) so as to begin on or after the date on which apart from this Act the continuing tenancy would have come to an end, the reversionary tenancy shall have effect as if it had been granted subject to the continuing tenancy.

(4) Where by virtue of any provision of this Act a tenancy (in this subsection referred to as "the new tenancy") is granted for a period beginning on the same date as a reversionary tenancy or for a period such as to extend beyond the beginning of the term of a reversionary tenancy, whether the reversionary tenancy in question was granted before or after the commencement of this Act, the reversionary tenancy shall have effect as if it had been granted subject to the new tenancy.

Provisions as to notices

A1-48   **66.**–(1) Any form of notice required by this Act to be prescribed shall be prescribed by regulations made by the Secretary of State by statutory instrument.

(2) Where the form of a notice to be served on persons of any description is to be prescribed for any of the purposes of this Act, the form to be prescribed shall include such an explanation of the relevant provisions of this Act as appears to the Secretary of State requisite for informing persons of that description of their rights and obligations under those provisions.

(3) Different forms of notice may be prescribed for the purposes of the operation of any provision of this Act in relation to different cases.

(4) Section 23 of the Landlord and Tenant Act 1927 (which relates to the service of notices) shall apply for the purposes of this Act.

(5) Any statutory instrument under this section shall be subject to annulment in pursuance of a resolution of either House of Parliament.

Provisions as to mortgagees in possession

A1-49   **67.** Anything authorised or required by the provisions of this Act, other than subsection (2) or (3) of section 40, to be done at any time by, to or with the landlord, or a landlord of a specified description, shall, if at that time the interest of the landlord in question is subject to a mortgage and the mortgagee is in possession or a receiver appointed by the mortgagee or by the courts is in receipt of the rents and profits, be deemed to be authorised or required to be done by, to or with the mortgagee instead of that landlord.

A1-50   **68.** [Not reproduced here]

Interpretation

A1-51   **69.**–(1) In this Act, the following expressions have the meanings hereby assigned to them respectively, that is to say–

"agricultural holding" has the same meaning as in the Agricultural Holdings Act 1986;

"development corporation" has the same meaning as in the New Towns Act 1946;

"farm business tenancy" has the same meaning as in the Agricultural Tenancies Act 1995;

"local authority" means any local authority within the meaning of the Town and Country Planning Act 1990, any National Park Authority, the Broads Authority or joint authority established by Part 4 of the Local Government Act 1985;

"mortgage" includes a charge or lien and "mortgagor" and "mortgagee" shall be construed accordingly;

"notice to quit" means a notice to terminate a tenancy (whether a periodical tenancy or a tenancy for a term of years certain) given in accordance with the provisions (whether express or implied) of that tenancy;

"repairs" includes any work of maintenance, decoration or restoration, and references to repairing, to keeping or yielding up in repair and to state of repair shall be construed accordingly;

"statutory undertakers" has the same meaning as in the Town and Country Planning Act 1990;

"tenancy" means a tenancy created either immediately or derivatively out of the freehold, whether by a lease or underlease, by an agreement for a lease or underlease or by a tenancy agreement or in pursuance of any enactment (including this Act), but does not include a mortgage term or any interest arising in favour of a mortgagor by his attorning tenant to his mortgagee, and references to the granting of a tenancy and to demised property shall be construed accordingly;

"terms", in relation to a tenancy, includes conditions.

(2) References in this Act to an agreement between the landlord and the tenant (except in section 17 and subsections (1) and (2) of section 38 thereof) shall be construed as references to an agreement in writing between them.

(3) Reference in this Act to an action for any relief shall be construed as including references to a claim for that relief by way of counterclaim in any proceedings.

Short title and citation, commencement and extent

70.–(1) This Act may be cited as the Landlord and Tenant Act, 1954, and the Landlord and Tenant Act, 1927, and this Act may be cited together as the Landlord and Tenant Acts, 1927 and 1954. **A1–52**

(2) This Act shall come into operation on the first day of October, nineteen hundred and fifty-four.

(3) This Act shall not extend to Scotland or to Northern Ireland.

SCHEDULE 1 TO THE LANDLORD AND TENANT ACT 1954 PART 2 (NOTICES) REGULATIONS 2004 (SI 2004/1005)

. . . .

PRESCRIBED FORMS, AND PURPOSES FOR WHICH THEY ARE TO BE USED

A2-01

(1)	(2)
Form number	Purpose for which to be used
1	Ending a tenancy to which Part 2 of the Act applies, where the landlord is not opposed to the grant of a new tenancy (notice under section 25 of the Act).
2	Ending a tenancy to which Part 2 of the Act applies, where: (a) the landlord is opposed to the grant of a new tenancy (notice under section 25 of the Act); and (b) the tenant is not entitled under the 1967 Act to buy the freehold or an extended lease.
3	Tenant's request for a new tenancy of premises where Part 2 of the Act applies (notice under section 26 of the Act).
4	Landlord's notice activating tenant's duty under section 40(1) of the Act to give information as to his or her occupation of the premises and as to any sub-tenancies.
5	Tenant's notice activating duty under section 40(3) of the Act of reversioner or reversioner's mortgagee in possession to give information about his or her interest in the premises.

cont

cont

6   Withdrawal of notice given under section 25 of the Act ending a tenancy to which Part 2 of the Act applies (notice under section 44 of, and paragraph 6 of Schedule 6 to, the Act).

7   Ending a tenancy to which Part 2 of the Act applies, where the landlord is opposed to the grant of a new tenancy but where the tenant may be entitled under the 1967 Act to buy the freehold or an extended lease (notice under section 25 of the Act and paragraph 10 of Schedule 3 to the 1967 Act).

8   Ending a tenancy to which Part 2 of the Act applies, where:

(a) the notice under section 25 of the Act contains a copy of a certificate given under section 57 of the Act that the use or occupation of the property or part of it is to be changed by a specified date;

(b) the date of termination of the tenancy specified in the notice is not earlier than the date specified in the certificate; and

(c) the tenant is not entitled under the 1967 Act to buy the freehold or an extended lease.

9   Ending a tenancy to which Part 2 of the Act applies, where:

(a) the notice under section 25 of the Act contains a copy of a certificate under section 57 of the Act that the use or occupation of the property or part of it is to be changed at a future date;

(b) the date of termination of the tenancy specified in the notice is earlier than the date specified in the certificate;

(c) the landlord opposes the grant of a new tenancy; and

(d) the tenant is not entitled under the 1967 Act to buy the freehold or an extended lease.

10   Ending a tenancy to which Part 2 of the Act applies, where:

(a) the notice under section 25 of the Act contains a copy of a certificate given under section 57 of the Act that the use or occupation of the property or part of it is to be changed at a future date;

(b) the date of termination of the tenancy specified in the notice is earlier than the date specified in the certificate;

(c) the landlord does not oppose the grant of a new tenancy; and

cont

cont

(d) the tenant is not entitled under the 1967 Act to buy the freehold or an extended lease.

11 Ending a tenancy to which Part 2 of the Act applies, where the notice under section 25 of the Act contains a copy of a certificate given under section 58 of the Act that for reasons of national security it is necessary that the use or occupation of the property should be discontinued or changed.

12 Ending a tenancy to which Part 2 of the Act applies, where—

(a) the notice under section 25 of the Act contains a copy of a certificate given under section 58 of the Act (as applied by section 60 of the Act) that it is necessary or expedient for achieving the purpose mentioned in section 2(1) of the Local Employment Act 1972 that the use or occupation of the property should be changed; and

(b) the tenant is not entitled under the 1967 Act to buy the freehold or an extended lease.

13 Ending a tenancy to which Part 2 of the Act applies, where:

(a) the notice under section 25 of the Act contains a copy of a certificate given under section 57 of the Act that the use or occupation of the property or part of it is to be changed by a specified date; and

(b) the date of termination of the tenancy specified in the notice is not earlier than the date specified in the certificate; and

(c) the tenant may be entitled under the 1967 Act to buy the freehold or an extended lease.

14 Ending a tenancy to which Part 2 of the Act applies, where:

(a) the notice under section 25 of the Act contains a copy of a certificate given under section 57 of the Act that the use or occupation of the property or part of it is to be changed at a future date;

(b) the date of termination of the tenancy specified in the notice is earlier than the date specified in the certificate; and

(c) the tenant may be entitled under the 1967 Act to buy the freehold or an extended lease the landlord opposes the grant of a new tenancy.

cont

cont

15   Ending a tenancy to which Part 2 of the Act applies, where:

(a) the notice under section 25 of the Act contains a copy of a certificate given under section 58 of the Act (as applied by section 60 of the Act) that it is necessary or expedient for achieving the purpose mentioned in section 2(1) of the Local Employment Act 1972 that the use or occupation of the property should be changed; and

(b) the tenant may be entitled under the 1967 Act to buy the freehold or an extended lease the landlord opposes the grant of a new tenancy.

16   Ending a tenancy of Welsh Development Agency premises where:

(a) the notice under section 25 of the Act contains a copy of a certificate given under section 58 of the Act (as applied by section 60A of the Act) that it is necessary or expedient, for the purposes of providing employment appropriate to the needs of the area in which the premises are situated, that the use or occupation of the property should be changed; and

(b) the tenant is not entitled under the 1967 Act to buy the freehold or an extended lease.

17   Ending a tenancy of Welsh Development Agency premises where:

(a) the notice under section 25 of the Act contains a copy of a certificate given under section 58 of the Act (as applied by section 60A of the Act) that it is necessary or expedient, for the purposes of providing employment appropriate to the needs of the area in which the premises are situated, that the use or occupation of the property should be changed; and

(b) the tenant may be entitled under the 1967 Act to buy the freehold or an extended lease.

APPENDIX 3

ARTICLE 29 OF THE REGULATORY REFORM (BUSINESS TENANCIES) (ENGLAND AND WALES) ORDER 2003

. . . .

Transitional provisions

A3-01 **29.**–(1) Where, before this Order came into force—

(a) the landlord gave the tenant notice under section 25 of the Act; or

(b) the tenant made a request for a new tenancy in accordance with section 26 of the Act,

nothing in this Order has effect in relation to the notice or request or anything done in consequence of it.

    (2) Nothing in this Order has effect in relation—

(a) to an agreement—

    (i) for the surrender of a tenancy which was made before this Order came into force and which fell within section 24(2)(b) of the Act; or

    (ii) which was authorised by the court under section 38(4) of the Act before this Order came into force; or

(b) to a notice under section 27(2) of the Act which was given by the tenant to the immediate landlord before this Order came into force.

    (3) Any provision in a tenancy which requires an order under section 38(4) of the Act to be obtained in respect of any subtenancy shall, so far as is necessary after the coming into force of this Order, be construed as if it required the procedure mentioned in section 38A of the Act to be followed, and any related requirement shall be construed accordingly.

    (4) If a person has, before the coming into force of this Order, entered into an agreement to take a tenancy, any provision in that agreement which requires an order under section 38(4) of the Act to be obtained in respect of the tenancy shall continue to be effective, notwithstanding the repeal of

that provision by Article 21(2) of this Order, and the court shall retain jurisdiction to make such an order.

(5) Article 20 above does not have effect where the tenant quit the holding before this Order came into force.

(6) Nothing in Articles 23 and 24 above applies to a notice under section 40 of the Act served before this Order came into force.

APPENDIX 4

THE TELECOMMUNICATIONS CODE
(Telecommunications Act 1984 Sch 2)

. . . .

Interpretation of code

A4–01 1.–(1) In this code, except in so far as the context otherwise requires—

"agriculture" and "agricultural"—

    (a) in England and Wales, have the same meanings as in the Highways Act 1980;

    (b) in Scotland, have the same meanings as in the Town and Country Planning (Scotland) Act 1972; and

    (c) in Northern Ireland, have the same meanings as in the Agriculture Act (Northern Ireland) 1949;

"alter", "alteration" and "altered" shall be construed in accordance with sub-paragraph (2) below;

"bridleway" and "footpath"—

    (a) in England and Wales, have the same meanings as in the Highways Act 1980;

    (b) in Scotland, have the same meanings as in Part III of the Countryside (Scotland) Act 1967; and

    (c) in Northern Ireland, mean a way over which the public have, by virtue of the Access to the Countryside (Northern Ireland) Order 1983, a right of way on horseback and on foot, respectively;

"conduit" includes a tunnel, subway, tube or pipe;

"conduit system" means a system of conduits provided so as to be available for use by providers of electronic communications networks for the purposes of the provision by them of their networks;

"the court" means, without prejudice to any right of appeal conferred by virtue of paragraph 25 below or otherwise—

    (a) in relation to England and Wales and Northern Ireland, the county court: and

    (b) in relation to Scotland, the sheriff;

"electronic communications apparatus" means—

(a) any apparatus (within the meaning of the Communications Act 2003) which is designed or adapted for use in connection with the provision of an electronic communications network;

(b) any apparatus (within the meaning of that Act) that is designed or adapted for a use which consists of or includes the sending or receiving of communications or other signals that are transmitted by means of an electronic communications network;

(c) any line;

(d) any conduit, structure, pole or other thing in, on, by or from which any electronic communications apparatus is or may be installed, supported, carried or suspended;
and references to the installation of electronic communications apparatus are to be construed accordingly;

"electronic communications network" has the same meaning as in the Communications Act 2003, and references to the provision of such a network are to be construed in accordance with the provisions of that Act;

"electronic communications service" has the same meaning as in the Communications Act 2003, and references to the provision of such a service are to be construed in accordance with the provisions of that Act;

"emergency works", in relation to the operator or a relevant undertaker for the purposes of paragraph 23 below, means works the execution of which at the time it is proposed to execute them is requisite in order to put an end to, or prevent, the arising of circumstances then existing or imminent which are likely to cause—

(a) danger to persons or property,

(b) the interruption of any service provided by the operator's network or, as the case may be, interference with the exercise of any functions conferred or imposed on the undertaker by or under any enactment; or

(c) substantial loss to the operator or, as the case may be, the undertaker,

and such other works as in all the circumstances it is reasonable to execute with those works; "line" means any wire, cable, tube, pipe or similar thing (including its casing or coating) which is designed or adapted for use in connection with the provision of any electronic communications network or electronic communications service;
[. . .]

"the operator" means—

(a) where the code is applied in any person's case by a direction under section 106 of the Communications Act 2003, that person; and

(b) where it applies by virtue of section 106(3)(b) of that Act, the Secretary of State or (as the case may be) the Northern Ireland department in question;

"the operator's network" means—

(a) in relation to an operator falling within paragraph (a) of the definition of 'operator', so much of any electronic communications network or conduit system provided by that operator as is not excluded from the application of the code under section 106(5) of the Communications Act 2003; and

(b) in relation to an operator falling within paragraph (b) of that definition, the electronic communications network which the Secretary of State or the Northern Ireland department is providing or proposing to provide;

"public road" means a public road within the meaning of Part IV of the New Roads and Street Works Act 1991 other than one which is a footpath or a bridleway that crosses, and forms part of, any agricultural land or any land which is being brought into use for agriculture;

"railway" includes a light railway;

"road" has the same meaning as in Part IV of the New Roads and Street Works Act 1991;

"signal" has the same meaning as in section 32 of the Communications Act 2003;

"the statutory purposes" means the purposes of the provision of the operator's network;

[. . .]

"structure" does not include a building.

(a)–(b) [. . .]

(2) In this code, references to the alteration of any apparatus include references to the moving, removal or replacement of the apparatus.

(3) In relation to any land which, otherwise than in connection with a road on that land, is divided horizontally into different parcels, the references in this code to a place over or under the land shall have effect in relation to each parcel as not including references to any place in a different parcel.

(3A) References in this code to the provision of a conduit system include references to establishing or maintaining such a system.

(4) [. . .]

(5) [. . .]

Agreement required to confer right to execute works etc.

A4–02   **2.**–(1) The agreement in writing of the occupier for the time being of any land shall be required for conferring on the operator a right for the statutory purposes—

(a) to execute any works on that land for or in connection with the installation, maintenance, adjustment, repair or alteration of electronic communications apparatus; or

(b) to keep electronic communications apparatus installed on, under or over that land;

or

(c) to enter that land to inspect any apparatus kept installed (whether on, under or over that land or elsewhere) for the purposes of the operator's network.

(2) A person who is the owner of the freehold estate in any land or is a lessee of any land shall not be bound by a right conferred in accordance with sub-paragraph (1) above by the occupier of that land unless—

(a) he conferred the right himself as occupier of the land; or

(b) he has agreed in writing to be bound by the right; or

(c) he is for the time being treated by virtue of sub-paragraph (3) below as having so agreed; or

(d) he is bound by the right by virtue of sub-paragraph (4) below.

(3) If a right falling within sub-paragraph (1) above has been conferred by the occupier of any land for purposes connected with the provision, to the occupier from time to time of that land, of any electronic communications services and—

(a) the person conferring the right is also the owner of the freehold estate in that land or is a lessee of the land under a lease for a term of a year or more, or

(b) in a case not falling within paragraph (a) above, a person owning the freehold estate in the land or a lessee of the land under a lease for a term of a year or more has agreed in writing that his interest in the land should be bound by the right,

then, subject to paragraph 4 below, that right shall (as well as binding the person who conferred it) have effect, at any time when the person who conferred it or a person bound by it under sub-paragraph (2)(b) or (4) of this paragraph is the occupier of the land, as if every person for the time being owning an interest in that land had agreed in writing to the right being conferred for the said purposes and, subject to its being exercised solely for those purposes, to be bound by it.

(4) In any case where a person owning an interest in land agrees in writing (whether when agreeing to the right as occupier or for the purposes of sub-paragraph (3)(b) above or otherwise) that his interest should be bound by a right falling within sub-paragraph (1) above, that right shall (except in so far as the contrary intention appears) bind the owner from time to time of that interest and also—

(a) the owner from time to time of any other interest in the land, being an interest created after the right is conferred and not having priority over the interest to which the agreement relates; and

(b) any other person who is at any time in occupation of the land and whose right to occupation of the land derives (by contract or otherwise) from a person who at the time the right to occupation was granted was bound by virtue of this sub-paragraph.

(5) A right falling within sub-paragraph (1) above shall not be exercisable except in accordance with the terms (whether as to payment or otherwise)

subject to which it is conferred; and, accordingly, every person for the time being bound by such a right shall have the benefit of those terms.

(6) A variation of a right falling within sub-paragraph (1) above or of the terms on which such a right is exercisable shall be capable of binding persons who are not parties to the variation in the same way as, under sub-paragraphs (2), (3) and (4) above, such a right is capable of binding persons who are not parties to the conferring of the right.

(7) It is hereby declared that a right falling within sub-paragraph (1) above is not subject to the provisions of any enactment requiring the registration of interests in, charges on or other obligations affecting land.

(8) In this paragraph and paragraphs 3 and 4 below—

(a) references to the occupier of any land shall have effect—

  (i) in relation to any footpath, bridleway or restricted byway that crosses and forms part of any agricultural land or any land which is being brought into use for agriculture, as references to the occupier of that land;

  (ii) in relation to any street or, in Scotland, road (not being such a footpath, bridleway or restricted byway), as references—

  in England and Wales or Northern Ireland, to the street managers within the meaning of Part III of the New Roads and Street Works Act 1991 (which for this purpose shall be deemed to extend to Northern Ireland), and

  in Scotland, to the road managers within the meaning of Part IV of that Act; and

  (iii) in relation to any land (not being a street or, in Scotland, road) which is unoccupied, as references to the person (if any) who for the time being exercises powers of management or control over the land or, if there is no such person, to every person whose interest in the land would be prejudicially affected by the exercise of the right in question;

(b) "lease" includes any leasehold tenancy (whether in the nature of a head lease, sub-lease or underlease) and any agreement to grant such a tenancy but not a mortgage by demise or sub-demise and "lessee" shall be construed accordingly; and

(c) references to the owner of a freehold estate shall, in relation to land in Scotland, have effect as references to the person—

  (i) who is infeft proprietor of the land; or

  (ii) who has right to the land but whose title thereto is not complete; or

  (iii) in the case of land subject to a heritable security constituted by *ex facie* absolute disposition, who is the debtor in the security, except where the creditor is in possession of the land,

  other than a person having a right as a superior only.

(9) Subject to paragraphs 9(2) and 11(2) below, this paragraph shall not require any person to give his agreement to the exercise of any right conferred by any of paragraphs 9 to 12 below.

Power to dispense with the need for required agreement

5.—(1) Where the operator requires any person to agree for the purposes of paragraph 2 or 3 above that any right should be conferred on the operator, or that any right should bind that person or any interest in land, the operator may give a notice to that person of the right and of the agreement that he requires.

A4–03

(2) Where the period of 28 days beginning with the giving of a notice under sub-paragraph (1) above has expired without the giving of the required agreement, the operator may apply to the court for an order conferring the proposed right or providing for it to bind any person or any interest in land, and (in either case) dispensing with the need for the agreement of the person to whom the notice was given.

(3) The court shall make an order under this paragraph if, but only if, it is satisfied that any prejudice caused by the order—

(a) is capable of being adequately compensated for by money; or

(b) is outweighed by the benefit accruing from the order to the persons whose access to an electronic communications network or to electronic communications services will be secured by the order;

and in determining the extent of the prejudice, and the weight of that benefit, the court shall have regard to all the circumstances and to the principle that no person should unreasonably be denied access to an electronic communications network or to electronic communications services.

(4) An order under this paragraph made in respect of a proposed right may, in conferring that right or providing for it to bind any person or any interest in land and in dispensing with the need for any person's agreement, direct that the right shall have effect with such modifications, be exercisable on such terms and be subject to such conditions as may be specified in the order.

(5) The terms and conditions specified by virtue of sub-paragraph (4) above in an order under this paragraph, shall include such terms and conditions as appear to the court appropriate for ensuring that the least possible loss and damage is caused by the exercise of the right in respect of which the order is made to persons who occupy, own interests in or are from time to time on the land in question.

(6) For the purposes of proceedings under this paragraph in a county court in England and Wales or Northern Ireland, section 63(1) of the County Courts Act 1984 and Article 33(1) of the County Courts (Northern Ireland) Order 1980 (assessors) shall have effect as if the words "on the application of any party" were omitted; and where an assessor is summoned, or, in Northern Ireland, appointed, by virtue of this sub-paragraph—

(a) he may, if so directed by the judge, inspect the land to which the proceedings relate without the judge and report on the land to the judge in writing; and

(b) the judge may take the report into account in determining whether to make an order under this paragraph and what order to make.

In relation to any time before 1st August 1984, the reference in this sub-paragraph to section 63(1) of the County Courts Act 1984 shall have effect as a reference to section 91(1) of the County Courts Act 1959.

(7) Where an order under this paragraph, for the purpose of conferring any right or making provision for a right to bind any person or any interest in land, dispenses with the need for the agreement of any person, the order shall have the same effect and incidents as the agreement of the person the need for whose agreement is dispensed with and accordingly (without prejudice to the foregoing) shall be capable of variation or release by a subsequent agreement.

Acquisition of rights in respect of apparatus already installed

A4-04   **6.**—(1) The following provisions of this paragraph apply where the operator gives notice under paragraph 5(1) above to any person and—

(a)   that notice requires that person's agreement in respect of a right which is to be exercisable (in whole or in part) in relation to electronic communications apparatus already kept installed on, under or over the land in question, and

(b)   that person is entitled to require the removal of that apparatus but, by virtue of paragraph 21 below, is not entitled to enforce its removal.

(2) The court may, on the application of the operator, confer on the operator such temporary rights as appear to the court reasonably necessary for securing that, pending the determination of any proceedings under paragraph 5 above or paragraph 21 below, the service provided by the operator's network is maintained and the apparatus properly adjusted and kept in repair.

(3) In any case where it is shown that a person with an interest in the land was entitled to require the removal of the apparatus immediately after it was installed, the court shall, in determining for the purposes of paragraph 5 above whether the apparatus should continue to be kept installed on, under or over the land, disregard the fact that the apparatus has already been installed there.

Court to fix financial terms where agreement dispensed with

A4-05   **7.**—(1) The terms and conditions specified by virtue of sub-paragraph (4) of paragraph 5 above in an order under that paragraph dispensing with the need for a person's agreement, shall include—

(a)   such terms with respect to the payment of consideration in respect of the giving of the agreement, or the exercise of the rights to which the order relates, as it appears to the court would have been fair and reasonable if the agreement had been given willingly and subject to the other provisions of the order; and

(b)   such terms as appear to the court appropriate for ensuring that that person and persons from time to time bound by virtue of paragraph 2(4) above by the rights to which the order relates are adequately compensated (whether by the payment of such consideration or otherwise) for any loss or damage sustained by them in consequence of the exercise of those rights.

(2) In determining what terms should be specified in an order under paragraph 5 above for requiring an amount to be paid to any person in respect of—

(a) the provisions of that order conferring any right or providing for any right to bind any person or any interest in land, or

(b) the exercise of any right to which the order relates,
the court shall take into account the prejudicial effect (if any) of the order or, as the case may be, of the exercise of the right on that person's enjoyment of, or on any interest of his in, land other than the land in relation to which the right is conferred.

(3) In determining what terms should be specified in an order under paragraph 5 above for requiring an amount to be paid to any person, the court shall, in a case where the order is made in consequence of an application made in connection with proceedings under paragraph 21 below, take into account, to such extent as it thinks fit, any period during which that person—

(a) was entitled to require the removal of any electronic communications apparatus from the land in question, but

(b) by virtue of paragraph 21 below, was not entitled to enforce its removal;

but where the court takes any such period into account, it may also take into account any compensation paid under paragraph 4(4) above.

(4) The terms specified by virtue of sub-paragraph (1) above in an order under paragraph 5 above may provide—

(a) for the making of payments from time to time to such persons as may be determined under those terms; and

(b) for questions arising in consequence of those terms (whether as to the amount of any loss or damage caused by the exercise of a right or otherwise) to be referred to arbitration or to be determined in such other manner as may be specified in the order.

(5) The court may, if it thinks fit—

(a) where the amount of any sum required to be paid by virtue of terms specified in an order under paragraph 5 above has been determined, require the whole or any part of any such sum to be paid into court;

(b) pending the determination of the amount of any such sum, order the payment into court of such amount on account as the court thinks fit.

(6) Where terms specified in an order under paragraph 5 above require the payment of any sum to a person who cannot be found or ascertained, that sum shall be paid into court.

Power to require alteration of apparatus

A4-06   **20.**—(1) Where any electronic communications apparatus is kept installed on, under or over any land for the purposes of the operator's network , any person with an interest in that land or adjacent land may (notwithstanding the terms of any agreement binding that person) by notice given to the operator require the alteration of the apparatus on the ground that the alteration is necessary to enable that person to carry out a proposed improvement of the land in which he has an interest.

(2) Where a notice is given under sub-paragraph (1) above by any person to the operator, the operator shall comply with it unless he gives a counter-notice under this sub-paragraph within the period of 28 days beginning with the giving of the notice.

(3) Where a counter-notice is given under sub-paragraph (2) above to any person, the operator shall make the required alteration only if the court on an application by that person makes an order requiring the alteration to be made.

(4) The court shall make an order under this paragraph for an alteration to be made only if, having regard to all the circumstances and the principle that no person should unreasonably be denied access to an electronic communications network or to electronic communications services, it is satisfied—

(a)   that the alteration is necessary as mentioned in sub-paragraph (1) above; and

(b)   that the alteration will not substantially interfere with any service which is or is likely to be provided using the operator's network.

(5) The court shall not make an order under this paragraph for the alteration of any apparatus unless it is satisfied either—

(a)   that the operator has all such rights as it appears to the court appropriate that he should have for the purpose of making the alteration, or

(b)   that—

  (i)   he would have all those rights if the court, on an application under paragraph 5 above, dispensed with the need for the agreement of any person, and

  (ii)   it would be appropriate for the court, on such an application, to dispense with the need for that agreement;

and, accordingly, for the purposes of dispensing with the need for the agreement of any person to the alteration of any apparatus, the court shall have the same powers as it would have if an application had been duly made under paragraph 5 above for an order dispensing with the need for that person's agreement.

(6) For the purposes of sub-paragraph (5) above, the court shall have power on an application under this paragraph to give the applicant directions for bringing the application to the notice of such other interested persons as it thinks fit.

(7) An order under this paragraph may provide for the alteration to be carried out with such modifications, on such terms and subject to such

conditions as the court thinks fit, but the court shall not include any such modifications, terms or conditions in its order without the consent of the applicant, and if such consent is not given may refuse to make an order under this paragraph.

(8) An order made under this paragraph on the application of any person shall, unless the court otherwise thinks fit, require that person to reimburse the operator in respect of any expenses which the operator incurs in or in connection with the execution of any works in compliance with the order.

(9) In sub-paragraph (1) above "improvement" includes development and change of use.

Restriction on right to require the removal of apparatus

21.–(1) Where any person is for the time being entitled to require the removal of any of the operator's electronic communications apparatus from any land (whether under any enactment or because that apparatus is kept on, under or over that land otherwise than in pursuance of a right binding that person or for any other reason) that person shall not be entitled to enforce the removal of the apparatus except, subject to sub-paragraph (12) below, in accordance with the following provisions of this paragraph. **A4–07**

(2) The person entitled to require the removal of any of the operator's electronic communications apparatus shall give a notice to the operator requiring the removal of the apparatus.

(3) Where a person gives a notice under sub-paragraph (2) above and the operator does not give that person a counter-notice within the period of 28 days beginning with the giving of the notice, that person shall be entitled to enforce the removal of the apparatus.

(4) A counter-notice given under sub-paragraph (3) above to any person by the operator shall do one or both of the following, that is to say—

(a) state that that person is not entitled to require the removal of the apparatus;

(b) specify the steps which the operator proposes to take for the purpose of securing a right as against that person to keep the apparatus on the land.

(5) Those steps may include any steps which the operator could take for the purpose of enabling him, if the apparatus is removed, to re-install the apparatus; and the fact that by reason of the following provisions of this paragraph any proposed re-installation is only hypothetical shall not prevent the operator from taking those steps or any court or person from exercising any function in consequence of those steps having been taken.

(6) Where a counter-notice is given under sub-paragraph (3) above to any person, that person may only enforce the removal of the apparatus in pursuance of an order of the court; and, where the counter-notice specifies steps which the operator is proposing to take to secure a right to keep the apparatus on the land, the court shall not make such an order unless it is satisfied—

(a) that the operator is not intending to take those steps or is being unreasonably dilatory in the taking of those steps; or

(b) that the taking of those steps has not secured, or will not secure, for the operator as against that person any right to keep the apparatus installed on, under or over the land or, as the case may be, to re-install it if it is removed.

(7) Where any person is entitled to enforce the removal of any apparatus under this paragraph (whether by virtue of sub-paragraph (3) above or an order of the court under sub-paragraph (6) above), that person may, without prejudice to any method available to him apart from this sub-paragraph for enforcing the removal of that apparatus, apply to the court for authority to remove it himself; and, on such an application, the court may, if it thinks fit, give that authority.

(8) Where any apparatus is removed by any person under an authority given by the court under sub-paragraph (7) above, any expenses incurred by him in or in connection with the removal of the apparatus shall be recoverable by him from the operator in any court of competent jurisdiction; and in so giving an authority to any person the court may also authorise him, in accordance with the directions of the court, to sell any apparatus removed under the authority and to retain the whole or a part of the proceeds of sale on account of those expenses.

(9) Any electronic communications apparatus kept installed on, under or over any land shall (except for the purposes of this paragraph and without prejudice to paragraphs 6(3) and 7(3) above) be deemed, as against any person who was at any time entitled to require the removal of the apparatus, but by virtue of this paragraph not entitled to enforce its removal, to have been lawfully so kept at that time.

(10) Where this paragraph applies (whether in pursuance of an enactment amended by Schedule 4 to this Act or otherwise) in relation to electronic communications apparatus the alteration of which some person ("the relevant person") is entitled to require in consequence of the stopping up, closure, change or diversion of any street or the extinguishment or alteration of any public right of way—

(a) the removal of the apparatus shall constitute compliance with a requirement to make any other alteration;

(b) a counter-notice under sub-paragraph (3) above may state (in addition to, or instead of, any of the matters mentioned in sub-paragraph (4) above) that the operator requires the relevant person to reimburse him in respect of any expenses which he incurs in or in connection with the making of any alteration in compliance with the requirements of the relevant person;

(c) an order made under this paragraph on an application by the relevant person in respect of a counter-notice containing such a statement shall, unless the court otherwise thinks fit, require the relevant person to reimburse the operator in respect of any expenses which he so incurs; and

(d) sub-paragraph (8) above shall not apply.

(11) References in this paragraph to the operator's electronic communications apparatus include references to electronic communications apparatus which (whether or not vested in the operator) is being, is to be or has been used for the purposes of the operator's network.

(12) A person shall not, under this paragraph, be entitled to enforce the removal of any apparatus on the ground only that he is entitled to give a notice under paragraph 11, 14, 17 or 20 above; and this paragraph is without prejudice to paragraph 23 below and to the power to enforce an order of the court under the said paragraph 11, 14, 17 or 20.

21.—(1) Where any person is for the time being entitled to require the removal of any of the operator's electronic communications apparatus from any land (whether under any enactment or because that apparatus is kept on, under or over that land otherwise than in pursuance of a right binding that person or for any other reason) that person shall not be entitled to enforce the removal of the apparatus except, subject to sub-paragraph (12) below, in accordance with the following provisions of this paragraph.

A4–08

(2) The person entitled to require the removal of any of the operator's electronic communications apparatus shall give a notice to the operator requiring the removal of the apparatus.

(3) Where a person gives a notice under sub-paragraph (2) above and the operator does not give that person a counter-notice within the period of 28 days beginning with the giving of the notice, that person shall be entitled to enforce the removal of the apparatus.

(4) A counter-notice given under sub-paragraph (3) above to any person by the operator shall do one or both of the following, that is to say—

(a) state that that person is not entitled to require the removal of the apparatus;

(b) specify the steps which the operator proposes to take for the purpose of securing a right as against that person to keep the apparatus on the land.

(5) Those steps may include any steps which the operator could take for the purpose of enabling him, if the apparatus is removed, to re-install the apparatus; and the fact that by reason of the following provisions of this paragraph any proposed re-installation is only hypothetical shall not prevent the operator from taking those steps or any court or person from exercising any function in consequence of those steps having been taken.

(6) Where a counter-notice is given under sub-paragraph (3) above to any person, that person may only enforce the removal of the apparatus in pursuance of an order of the court; and, where the counter-notice specifies steps which the operator is proposing to take to secure a right to keep the apparatus on the land, the court shall not make such an order unless it is satisfied—

(a) that the operator is not intending to take those steps or is being unreasonably dilatory in the taking of those steps; or

(b) that the taking of those steps has not secured, or will not secure, for the operator as against that person any right to keep the apparatus installed on, under or over the land or, as the case may be, to re-install it if it is removed.

(7) Where any person is entitled to enforce the removal of any apparatus under this paragraph (whether by virtue of sub-paragraph (3) above or an order of the court under sub-paragraph (6) above), that person may, without prejudice to any method available to him apart from this sub-paragraph for

enforcing the removal of that apparatus, apply to the court for authority to remove it himself; and, on such an application, the court may, if it thinks fit, give that authority.

(8) Where any apparatus is removed by any person under an authority given by the court under sub-paragraph (7) above, any expenses incurred by him in or in connection with the removal of the apparatus shall be recoverable by him from the operator in any court of competent jurisdiction; and in so giving an authority to any person the court may also authorise him, in accordance with the directions of the court, to sell any apparatus removed under the authority and to retain the whole or a part of the proceeds of sale on account of those expenses.

(9) Any electronic communications apparatus kept installed on, under or over any land shall (except for the purposes of this paragraph and without prejudice to paragraphs 6(3) and 7(3) above) be deemed, as against any person who was at any time entitled to require the removal of the apparatus, but by virtue of this paragraph not entitled to enforce its removal, to have been lawfully so kept at that time.

(10) Where this paragraph applies (whether in pursuance of an enactment amended by Schedule 4 to this Act or otherwise) in relation to electronic communications apparatus the alteration of which some person ("the relevant person") is entitled to require in consequence of the stopping up, closure, change or diversion of any road or the extinguishment or alteration of any public right of way—

(a) the removal of the apparatus shall constitute compliance with a requirement to make any other alteration;

(b) a counter-notice under sub-paragraph (3) above may state (in addition to, or instead of, any of the matters mentioned in sub-paragraph (4) above) that the operator requires the relevant person to reimburse him in respect of any expenses which he incurs in or in connection with the making of any alteration in compliance with the requirements of the relevant person;

(c) an order made under this paragraph on an application by the relevant person in respect of a counter-notice containing such a statement shall, unless the court otherwise thinks fit, require the relevant person to reimburse the operator in respect of any expenses which he so incurs; and

(d) sub-paragraph (8) above shall not apply.

(11) References in this paragraph to the operator's electronic communications apparatus include references to electronic communications apparatus which (whether or not vested in the operator) is being, is to be or has been used for the purposes of the operator's network.

(12) A person shall not, under this paragraph, be entitled to enforce the removal of any apparatus on the ground only that he is entitled to give a notice under paragraph 11, 14, 17 or 20 above; and this paragraph is without prejudice to paragraph 23 below and to the power to enforce an order of the court under the said paragraph 11, 14, 17 or 20.

Abandonment of apparatus

22. Without prejudice to the preceding provisions of this code, where the operator has a right conferred by or in accordance with this code for the statutory purposes to keep electronic communications apparatus installed on, under or over any land, he is not entitled to keep that apparatus so installed if, at a time when the apparatus is not, or is no longer, used for the purposes of the operator's network, there is no reasonable likelihood that it will be so used.

A4–09

Notices under code

24.–(1) Any notice required to be given by the operator to any person for the purposes of any provision of this code must be in a form approved by OFCOM as adequate for indicating to that person the effect of the notice and of so much of this code as is relevant to the notice and to the steps that may be taken by that person under this code in respect of that notice.

A4–10

(2) A notice required to be given to any person for the purposes of any provision of this code is not to be sent to him by post unless it is sent by a registered post service or by recorded delivery.

(2A) For the purposes, in the case of such a notice, of section 394 of the Communications Act 2003 and the application of section 7 of the Interpretation Act 1978 in relation to that section, the proper address of a person is—

(a) if the person to whom the notice is to be given has furnished the person giving the notice with an address for service under this code, that address; and

(b) only if he has not, the address given by that section of the Act of 2003.

(5) If it is not practicable, for the purposes of giving any notice under this code, after reasonable inquiries to ascertain the name and address—

(a) of the person who is for the purposes of any provision of this code the occupier of any land, or

(b) of the owner of any interest in any land,

a notice may be given under this code by addressing it to a person by the description of "occupier" of the land (describing it) or, as the case may be, "owner" of the interest (describing both the interest and the land) and by delivering it to some person on the land or, if there is no person on the land to whom it can be delivered, by affixing it, or a copy of it, to some conspicuous object on the land.

(6) In any proceedings under this code a certificate issued by OFCOM and stating that a particular form of notice has been approved by them as mentioned in sub-paragraph (1) above shall be conclusive evidence of the matter certified.

Index